THE LAX FAMILY EDITION

T'ZURBA צורבא
M'RABANAN מרבנן
לעילוי נשמת מאיר (מיש) אלימלך ז"ל

צורבא מרבנן

TZURBA M'RABANAN

SELWYN & ROS SMITH AND FAMILY

מנהיגות תורנית

MANHIGUT TORANIT

IN PARTNERSHIP WITH
ERETZ HEMDAH AND WORLD MIZRACHI

MIZRACHI

ארץ חמדה

ERETZ HEMDAH
Institute for Advanced Jewish Studies
Jerusalem

Tzurba M'Rabanan English Series
The Lax Family Edition
Volume 24
First English Edition, 2026

ISBN: 978-1-972200-20-9

Tzurba M'Rabanan English Series
54 King George Street, PO Box 7720
Jerusalem, 9107602, Israel
www.mizrachi.org

Distributed by the World Tzurba Institute, New York, NY

Written and compiled by Rav Benzion Algazi
Translation and Authors of the Footnotes: Rav Joel Kenigsberg, Rav Yonatan Kohn, Rav Eli Ozarowski, and Rav Daniel Westbrook

Essays by *Selwyn & Ros Smith and Family – Manhigut Toranit* participants and graduates:
Rav Maor Azar, Rav Meir Ben David, Rav Avichai Goodman, Rav Barak Katz, Rav David Ohr, Rav Lavi Peles, Rav Eitan Yanai

Director: Rav Doron Podlashuk
General Editor: Rav Eli Ozarowski

Design and Typesetting: Daniel Safran

With thanks to Sefaria for some of the English translations, including those from the William Davidson digital edition of the Koren Noé Talmud, with commentary by Rabbi Adin Even-Israel Steinsaltz.

Feedback is welcome: office@tzurbaolami.com

www.tzurbaolami.com
@tzurbamrabanan

THE LAX FAMILY EDITION

צורבא מרבנן

TZURBA M'RABANAN

A concise learning method from the Talmudic source through modern-day halachic application

THE ZICHRON YOSEF VOLUME

Volume 24

Orach Chaim: Toiletries and Medicine on Pesach, Mechirat Chametz, Kitniyot, Erev Pesach, Mourning Customs of Sefirat Ha'Omer, Shavuot, Zeicher L'Churban

THE LAX FAMILY EDITION
IS DEDICATED
IN LOVING MEMORY
OF OUR DEAR SONS AND BROTHERS

Jonathan Theodore Lax z"l
Ethan James Lax z"l

לעילוי נשמת

יונתן טוביה בן מרדכי ז״ל
איתן אליעזר בן מרדכי ז״ל

ת.נ.צ.ב.ה.

MARSHA AND MICHAEL LAX
AMANDA AND AKIVA BLUMENTHAL
REBECCA AND RAMI LAIFER

זכרון יוסף

THIS VOLUME IS DEDICATED
IN LOVING MEMORY OF OUR GRANDFATHERS
WHO MODELED A LIFE OF DEDICATION
TO TORAH LEARNING

Jozef Adler z"l

יוסף בן ישראל ז"ל

נפטר כ"ד אדר תשכ"ד

MARCH 8, 1964

Joseph Hirshman z"l

יוסף בן שלמה ז"ל

נפטר בהושענא רבה כ"א תשרי תשס"ה

OCTOBER 6, 2004

TZURBA M'RABANAN PATRONS

INAUGURAL EDITION
The Goodvach and Belleli Families Volume

YOREH DE'AH

VOLUME 1
The Kupferberg and Ucko Families Volume

VOLUME 2
The Chasen and Finn Families Volume

VOLUME 3
The Feinblum and Monderer Families Volume

VOLUME 4
The Dr. Agatstein Chabura of Los Angeles Volume

VOLUME 5
The Lax Family Volume

VOLUME 6
The Ellis Family Volume

VOLUME 7
The Grauer Family Volume

ORACH CHAIM

VOLUME 8
The Billet Family Volume

VOLUME 9
The Bronner, Feinblum and Monderer Families Volume

VOLUME 10
The Moreinu HaRav Hershel Schachter Volume

VOLUME 11
The Cohen and Goldenberg Families Volume

VOLUME 12
The Rabbi Menachem M. Schneerson *zt"l* Volume

VOLUME 13
The Dr. Harold and Magda Katz Volume

TZURBA M'RABANAN PATRONS

ORACH CHAIM

VOLUME 14
The Lamm Family of Melbourne Volume

VOLUME 15
The Parker Family Volume

VOLUME 16
The Weisz Family Volume

VOLUME 17
The Perez Family Volume

VOLUME 18
The Yakir Hexter *z"l* and David Schwartz *z"l* Volume

VOLUME 19
The Aron Family Volume

VOLUME 20
The Niazoff Family Volume

VOLUME 21
The Mirvis Family Volume

VOLUME 22
The Dr. Harold and Magda Katz Volume

VOLUME 23
The Lesser Family Volume

VOLUME 24
The Zichron Yosef Volume

UPCOMING VOLUMES

ORACH CHAIM
VOLUME 25

EVEN HA'EZER
VOLUME 26 • VOLUME 27

CHOSHEN MISHPAT
VOLUME 28 • VOLUME 29 • VOLUME 30 • VOLUME 31

CONTENTS

7. Halachot of Zeicher L'churban

Nisan 5786
March 2026

Dear Reader,

On behalf of Manhigut Toranit, Mizrachi World Movement and the Tzurba M'Rabanan Institute, we are honored to present the Zichron Yosef volume 24 of the *Tzurba M'Rabanan* English Series, which deals with *chagim* and *moadim*. These form a critical part of the Jewish calendar and it behooves every Jew to learn these halachot.

Tzurba M'Rabanan, initiated in Hebrew by one of the Jewish world's leading scholars, Rav Benzion Algazi *shlit"a*, is an incredible learning program which takes its participants through the major halachic areas of *Shulchan Aruch*. Its unique ability to be an in-depth learning program, while at the same time being accessible and relevant, has seen it take communities around Israel by storm, with over 20,000 participants. We have joined forces with Tzurba to bring this unique series of *talmud Torah* to thousands of learners across the English-speaking world.

We thank the family who sponsored this volume in honor of their grandfathers Jozef Adler *z"l* and Joseph Hirshman *z"l*. May the learning of this volume be a merit for them, their descendants, and the entire family.

An enormous debt of gratitude is due to Michael and Marsha Lax of Toronto, Canada, for sponsoring the entire series of this English edition, enabling both the sustainability and, *im yirtzeh Hashem*, the great expansion of this unique program. May all the Torah studied serve as a great *zechut* in memory of Jonathan *z"l* and Ethan *z"l*, and a source of comfort to the Lax family.

Yashar koach to Rav Eli Ozarowski and the other members of the translating team for their sterling work in translating, adapting, and editing the entire *Tzurba M'Rabanan* series, and to the members of Manhigut Toranit for the outstanding essays. Mizrachi has the privilege of being a partner with Eretz Hemdah in the ground-breaking Manhigut Toranit program. Special thanks to Daniel Safran for the design, to Rav Sam Millunchick, Rav Joel Kenigsberg, and to the entire board for their unwavering support.

May this program be an ongoing fulfillment of the verse, כִּי מִצִּיּוֹן תֵּצֵא תוֹרָה וּדְבַר ה' מִירוּשָׁלָםִ, in connecting communities around the world through the Torah of Eretz Yisrael.

Rav Doron Perez
Executive Chairman
Mizrachi World Movement

Rav Danny Mirvis
CEO
Mizrachi World Movement

Rav Doron Podlashuk
Director
The Selwyn & Ros Smith and Family
Manhigut Toranit Program

Rav Benzion Moshe Algazi
Head
The Tzurba M'Rabanan Institute

APPROBATION

RABBI HERSHEL SCHACHTER

ROSH YESHIVA, RIETS

Rabbi Hershel Schachter
24 Bennett Avenue
New York, New York 10033
(212) 795-0630

הרב צבי שכטר
ראש ישיבה וראש כולל
ישיבת רבינו יצחק אלחנן

מכתב ברכה

זכיתי וזכיתי לראות הכרך שנפתחו
מעיינות החכמה בקשר להרחבת התורה
ברבים ע"י ידידי-יקירי מוהר"ר בנציון
אליספור שליט"א, מייסד מפעל הצורבא מרבנן
ומגיע למארגני העולמי לכוללים אלף
יישר כח גדול על שהרחיבו את
הפעולה - לתרגם את הצורבא מרבנן
לשונות, ולפי קבלת רז"ל עה"פ גם כי
יתנו בגוים - עתה אקבצם, אין ישראל
נגאלים אלא בזכות לימוד המשניות,
זה ברמב"ם לימוד התושבע"פ, וע"י לימוד
התורה בע"פ תתקדש הארץ - ומלאה
הארץ דעה את ד', ובפרט ללומדה
שהתורה היא חכמתו של הקב"ה, והוא
וחכמתו אחד!

בברכה,
צבי שכטר
אדר תשפ"ג

APPROBATION

RABBI YA'AKOV ARIEL

FORMER CHIEF RABBI, RAMAT-GAN

11 Tamuz 5768
July 14, 2007

Tzurba M'Rabanan is well known in Israel and around the world as an excellent program for teaching practical halacha. Thousands of students can attest to the fact that their study in the program was enriching and enjoyable and added another level to their spiritual persona.

We hereby recommend that all lovers of Torah join the circle of students dedicating time for Torah study through the program. The unique combination of in-depth study and practical halachic rulings focusing on relevant topics ensures productive and fascinating study. The learning takes place using well-constructed booklets that encourage successful study.

May Rabbi Benzion Algazi be blessed, for it is his dynamic personality that spearheads the institute with great success. We wish him continued blessing in increasing and glorifying Torah.

With Torah blessings,

Rabbi Ya'akov Ariel
[Former] Chief Rabbi, Ramat-Gan

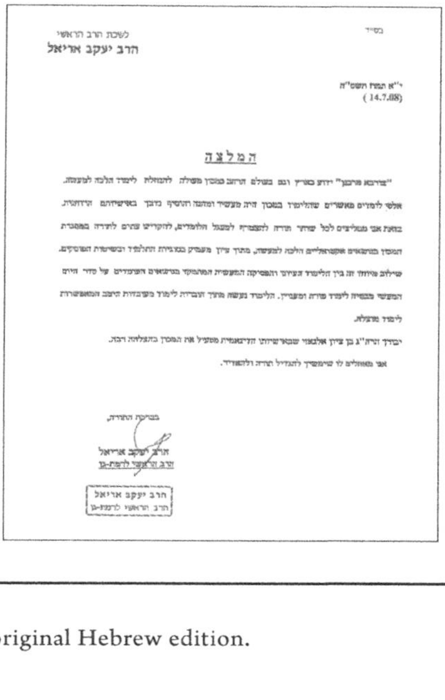
בס"ד

לשכת הרב הראשי
הרב יעקב אריאל

י"א תמוז תשס"ח
(14.7.08)

המלצה

"צורבא מרבנן" ידוע בארץ וגם בעולם הרחב כמכון מעולה להנחלת לימוד הלכה למעשה.
[illegible]

יבורך הרה"ג בן ציון אלגאזי שבאישיותו הדינאמית מוביל את המכון בהצלחה רבה.

אנו מאחלים לו שימשיך להגדיל תורה ולהאדיר.

בברכת התורה,

הרב יעקב אריאל
הרב הראשי לרמת-גן

הרב יעקב אריאל
הרב הראשי לרמת-גן

This approbation was written for the original Hebrew edition.

APPROBATION

RABBI MORDECHAI ELIYAHU זצ"ל

FORMER SEPHARDIC CHIEF RABBI OF ISRAEL
AND RISHON LETZION

2 Adar 5766

I hereby recommend and support the Tzurba M'Rabanan Institute, which aims to increase and glorify Torah, and to train the generation in studying practical halacha from all sections of the *Shulchan Aruch*, for we have learned that great is the study that leads to action.

I encourage and strengthen this great initiative which is transforming Jewish homes. So many come to learn and then apply the halacha they have learned in a special way that wins over the listeners and is spiritually uplifting.

I am also happy that you have accepted my advice to teach women and children practical halacha, and you are still aiming for more.

May it be God's will that many more join the study because this is the basic obligation of Torah study – "One who studies halachot every day is promised the World to Come."

May you continue onwards to increase and glorify Torah and may your springs of wisdom flow far and wide; may you be blessed with the very best and may God be with you in all your endeavors. Amen.

With blessings,

Rabbi Mordechai Eliyahu
Former Sephardic Chief Rabbi of Israel
and Rishon Letzion

ב"ה

MORDECHAI ELIAHU
FORMER CHIEF RABBI OF ISRAEL & RISHON LEZION

מרדכי אליהו
הראשון לציון והרב הראשי לישראל לשעבר

בס"ד, ב' אדר תשס"ו
5-9614.06

לכבוד
הרה"ג בן-ציון אלגזי שליט"א
ראש מכון צורבא מרבנן

השלום והברכה

באתי בזאת להמליץ ולעמוד לימין מכון "צורבא מרבנן" אשר שם לו למטרה להגדיל תורה ולהאדירה, ולהכשיר את הדור ללימוד הלכה למעשה בכל חלקי השו"ע שהרי נמנו וגמרו גדול תלמוד שמביא לידי מעשה.

הריני בא לעודד ולחזק מהלך גדול זה שהופך בתים בישראל. רבים הם המגיעים ללמוד ובכך מיישמים את ההלכה הנלמדת באופן מיוחד הכובשת את השומעים וגורמת להתעלות רוחנית.

שמחתי לשמוע שקבלתם את עצתי ללמד גם נשים וילדים הלכה למעשה, ועוד ידכם נטויה.

יתן ה' שיצטרפו רבים ללימוד כי זוהי חובת תלמוד תורה הבסיסית "כל השונה הלכות בכל יום מובטח לו שהוא בן העולם הבא".

יהי"ר שתמשיך הלאה להגדיל תורה ולהאדירה, ויפוצו מעיינותיך חוצה, ותתברך בכל מילי דמיטב, ויהי ה' עמך בכל אשר אתה עושה, אכי"ר.

בברכה,

מרדכי אליהו
הראשון לציון הרב הראשי לישראל לשעבר

This approbation was written for the original Hebrew edition.

1

Halachot of Toiletries and Medicine on Pesach

הלכות מוצרי טיפוח ותרופות בפסח

Bal Yeira'eh and Bal Yimatzei

Inedible Chametz

Soaps and Creams

Toothpaste

Medicines

Machshava

DEDICATED IN MEMORY OF

BIRANIT (KOHN) COHEN Z"L

בירנית טובה בת אפרים מרדכי הכהן ז״ל

A source of kindness and integrity, Biranit was a beloved pillar of Jewish communal life in Chicago and Dallas. Among her substantial contributions to the Jewish community, Biranit was the longtime Project Coordinator of the Chicago Rabbinical Council's Pesach Guide.

For quick reference, some long website URLs have been shortened.
For the complete list of referenced websites visit www.tzurbaolami.com.

ת	**Tanach**
ח	**Talmud (Chazal)**
ר	***Rishonim***
א	***Acharonim***
פ	**Contemporary Halachic Sources**

In this volume of *Tzurba M'Rabanan*, our primary focus will be the halachot of Pesach. While many of the foundational laws of Pesach have already been covered in earlier volumes – such as the halachot of *bedikat chametz*, *bitul chametz*, and *bi'ur chametz* (volume 5, *shiur* 9), as well as the halachot of the *Seder* (volume 1, *shiurim* 9–10), there remain many important and highly practical areas that warrant further study. Accordingly, this volume will address additional halachot that arise regularly and demand careful attention, including the halachot of cosmetics and medicines, *kitniyot*, *mechirat chametz*, and a range of halachot that apply specifically on Erev Pesach.

In this first *shiur*, we will examine the halachic status of *chametz* that has become unfit for consumption, with particular emphasis on its application to cosmetics and medicines. Must inedible *chametz* be removed from one's possession on Pesach, or does it lose its halachic status as *chametz* altogether? And if products known to contain inedible *chametz* may be retained, may they also be used on Pesach, such that creams may be applied to the body and toothpaste may be used in the mouth?

These questions, which arise frequently in practice, will serve as the foundation for our discussion in this *shiur*. However, we first must preface this with an explanation of the prohibitions of *bal yeira'eh* and *bal yimatzei*, the prohibitions against owning and finding *chametz* on Pesach.

Bal Yeira'eh and Bal Yimatzei

The Torah in ***Sefer Shemot*** commands us to be sure that no *chametz* will be in our possession on Pesach. This prohibition against owning *chametz* on Pesach is linked to the prohibition of eating *chametz* on Pesach, which carries the severe punishment of *karet*, being cut off from the Jewish People.[1]

1. שמות | יב:יט

שִׁבְעַת יָמִים שְׂאֹר לֹא יִמָּצֵא בְּבָתֵּיכֶם כִּי כָּל־אֹכֵל מַחְמֶצֶת וְנִכְרְתָה הַנֶּפֶשׁ הַהִוא מֵעֲדַת יִשְׂרָאֵל בַּגֵּר וּבְאֶזְרַח הָאָרֶץ׃

ת Shemot 12:19

Seven days sourdough shall not be found in your houses, as if anyone eats any leaven, that soul will be cut off from the congregation of Israel, whether it is of the convert or of a citizen of the land.

2. שמות | יג:ז

מַצּוֹת יֵאָכֵל אֵת שִׁבְעַת הַיָּמִים וְלֹא־יֵרָאֶה לְךָ חָמֵץ וְלֹא־יֵרָאֶה לְךָ שְׂאֹר בְּכָל־גְּבֻלֶךָ׃

ת Shemot 13:7

Matzot should be eaten during the seven days. No *chametz* shall be seen with you, neither shall there be sourdough seen with you, in all your borders.

The **Gemara (*Masechet Pesachim*)** discusses the nature of these prohibitions and concludes that they apply only to one's own *chametz* or to *chametz* of a gentile for which a Jew has accepted responsibility. However, they apply to any *chametz* that one owns, irrespective of where it is found.

---

1. This punishment is not clearly defined, but it could involve dying young or without children, and/or losing one's portion in the World to Come. Merely possessing *chametz* on Pesach, although biblically prohibited, does not carry this punishment.

3. מסכת פסחים ה:

תנו רבנן: שבעת ימים שאר לא ימצא בבתיכם מה תלמוד לומר? והלא כבר נאמר לא יראה לך שאר ולא יראה לך חמץ בכל גבלך. לפי שנאמר לא יראה לך שאר – שלך אי אתה רואה, אבל אתה רואה של אחרים ושל גבוה. יכול יטמין ויקבל פקדונות מן הנכרי – תלמוד לומר לא ימצא...

אין לי אלא שבבתיכם, בבורות בשיחין ובמערות מנין? תלמוד לומר: בכל גבלך...

אמר מר: יכול יטמין ויקבל פקדונות מן הנכרים – תלמוד לומר לא ימצא. הא אמרת רישא: שלך – אי אתה רואה, אבל אתה רואה של אחרים ושל גבוה!

לא קשיא; הא – דקביל עליה אחריות, הא – דלא קביל עליה אחריות. כי הא דאמר להו רבא לבני מחוזא: בעירו חמירא דבני חילא מבתייכו, כיון דאילו מיגנב ואילו מיתביד – ברשותייכו קאי ובעיתו לשלומי – כדילכון דמי, ואסור.

ח Masechet Pesachim 5b

The Sages taught in a *baraita*: **"Seven days sourdough shall not be found in your houses"**. To **what** purpose does **the verse state** this prohibition? **Wasn't it already stated:** "**No *chametz* shall be seen with you, neither shall there be leavened bread seen with you, in all your borders**"? The *baraita* answers: **Because it is stated: "No *chametz* shall be seen with you,"** which teaches that **your** own *chametz* **you** may **not see, but you may see** *chametz* that belongs **to others,** i.e., gentiles, **and** *chametz* consecrated **to God.** In light of this halacha, I **might** have thought that **one** may **conceal** *chametz* in one's home or **accept deposits** of *chametz* **from a gentile.** Therefore, **the verse states: "Shall not be found,"** meaning that one may not retain any type of *chametz* in one's house at all…

The *baraita* further states that from the verse: "It shall not be found in your houses," **I have** derived **nothing other** than the fact that this prohibition applies to *chametz* **that is** actually **in your houses. From where** is it derived that this halacha applies even to *chametz* **in pits, ditches, and caves? The verse states: In all your borders,** i.e., anywhere that belongs to you…

The Gemara continues its analysis of the *baraita*. **The Master said:** I **might** have thought that **one** may **conceal** *chametz* in one's home or **accept deposits** of *chametz* **from the gentiles.** Therefore, **the verse states: It shall not be found.** The Gemara asks: **But didn't you say in the first clause** of the *baraita*: **Your** own *chametz* **you may not see, but you may see** *chametz* that belongs **to others and** *chametz* consecrated **to God,** indicating that it is permitted to have *chametz* in one's house if it belongs to a gentile?

The Gemara answers: This is **not difficult;** in **this** case it is prohibited, **as he accepted upon himself responsibility** to pay for the *chametz* if it is destroyed. Therefore, it is considered as though the *chametz* belonged to him. In **that** case it is permitted, **as he did not accept upon himself responsibility,** and therefore the *chametz* remains the full-fledged property of the gentile. That ruling **is like that which Rava said to the residents of Mechoza: Remove the *chametz* that belongs to the members of the** gentile **army from your houses.** Gentile soldiers would bring flour with them and force the people in the city to prepare bread on their behalf. Rava explained the rationale for his ruling: **Since if** the flour **were stolen or if it were lost, it stands in your possession and you** would be **required to pay** for it, its legal status **is as** if it were **yours, and it is prohibited** to keep it during Pesach.

The **Rambam** codifies these principles as halacha.

4. רמב"ם | הל' חמץ ומצה ד:ב–ג

ב. הא למדת שחמץ של ישראל אם הניחו ברשותו אפילו טמון ואפילו בעיר אחרת ואפילו מופקד ביד גוים הרי זה עובר משום לא יראה ולא ימצא, וחמץ של הקדש או של גוי שהיה אצל ישראל אפילו היה עמו בבית הרי זה מותר מפני שאינו שלו...

ג. גוי שהפקיד חמצו אצל ישראל אם קבל עליו ישראל אחריות... הרי זה חייב לבערו הואיל וקבל עליו אחריות נעשה כשלו, ואם לא קבל עליו אחריות מותר לקיימו אצלו ומותר לאכול ממנו אחר הפסח שברשות הגוי הוא.

ד Rambam, Hilchot Chametz Umatza 4:2–3

2. [From the above] one can learn that [regarding] *chametz* belonging to a Jew, if he left it in his own jurisdiction, even if it is hidden, even if it is in another city, and even if it is deposited with a gentile, he violates *"lo yeira'eh"* and *"lo yimatzei."* Consecrated *chametz* or *chametz* of a gentile that was with a Jew, even if it was with him in his home, is permitted, as the *chametz* is not his...

3. If a gentile deposited his *chametz* with a Jew, if the Jew accepts responsibility for it... he is obligated to destroy it. Since he accepted responsibility for it, it is considered as though it were his. If he did not accept responsibility for it, keeping it with him is permitted and eating from it after Pesach is permitted, as it is in the gentile's jurisdiction.

Further details appear in the ***Shulchan Aruch*** (O.C. 440:1).

In the next few sections, we will analyze whether the prohibition against owning *chametz* applies to foods or other products that are not normally eaten by humans.

FURTHER IYUN

For further *iyun* on the permissibility of owning items that contain a small amount of *chametz* on Pesach, see page 60.

INEDIBLE CHAMETZ

The **Gemara (*Masechet Pesachim*)** quotes a *baraita* in which the *tanna'im* dispute the halachic status of moldy bread that is unfit for human consumption but would be eaten by a dog. According to the *Tanna Kamma*, it is still considered food, and accordingly, it is susceptible to *tumah* (ritual impurity). Rabbi Natan disagrees, maintaining that it is not considered food and is thus not susceptible to *tumah*.

5. מסכת פסחים מה:

תנו רבנן: הפת שעיפשה ונפסלה מלאכול לאדם, והכלב יכול לאוכלה – מטמאה טומאת אוכלין בכביצה, ונשרפת עם הטמאה בפסח. משום רבי נתן אמרו: אינה מטמאה.

ח Masechet Pesachim 45b

The Sages taught: With regard to **bread that grew moldy and was rendered inedible for consumption by a person, but a dog can eat it,** it **can become impure** with the **ritual impurity of foods in** the measure **of an egg-bulk** in size, as animal food is still considered food. If the moldy bread was ritually pure *teruma*, **it** may **be burned with ritually impure** *teruma* **on** Erev **Pesach.** The prohibition against actively rendering *teruma* impure applies only to food that is fit for human consumption. **They said in the name of Rabbi Natan: It cannot become ritually impure.**

The halacha is in accordance with the *Tanna Kamma*. The **Rif** understands that the moldy bread must therefore be burned before Pesach since it is still considered edible *chametz* and is included in the prohibition of owning *chametz* on Pesach. But he infers from the Gemara that if it becomes unfit even for a dog to eat, one would not need to burn it.

6. רי"ף | פסחים יג:-יד. (בדפי הרי"ף)

...הא אם נפסלה מלאכול לכלב אינה צריכה שריפה.

ר Rif, Pesachim 13b–14a (Pagination of the Rif)

...This implies that if it became unfit for a dog to eat it, it does not require burning.

The **Ran** explains that although food that is not fit for human consumption is not usually considered significant, regarding *chametz*, we are more stringent since even moldy *chametz* can be used to cause dough to ferment. The Torah explicitly prohibits *se'or* (*Shemot* 12:15, 19), a type of hardened *chametz*, for this reason.

7. ר"ן על הרי"ף | פסחים יג:-יד.

וכי תימא אמאי צריכה ביעור והא נבלה שאינה ראויה לגר לא שמה נבלה... יש לומר דהכא שאני מפני שראויה לחמע בה כמה עיסות אחרות... דהא שאור לא חזי לאכילה ואפילו הכי אסריה רחמנא מהאי טעמא.

ר Ran on the Rif, Pesachim 13b–14a

In case you ask: Why does [inedible *chametz*] require removal, surely a carcass that is not fit for a *ger* [*toshav*] is not considered a carcass![2]... One can answer that here it is different, since [moldy bread] is fit to ferment several other doughs... As *se'or* is not fit to eat, but the Torah nevertheless prohibits it for this reason.

2. The Torah prohibits eating *neveila*, the meat of an animal that was not ritually slaughtered in accordance with halacha. The Torah also says that one should give this meat to a *ger toshav*, a gentile who has committed to observe the seven Noachide

The **Ritva** quotes the **Ra'ah**, who maintains that there is no obligation to burn moldy bread even if a dog would eat it. The *baraita* only permits burning the bread together with ritually impure food, but does not obligate doing so. However, the Ritva himself concurs with the Rif.

8. חידושים מהריטב"א | פסחים מה:

כתב הרי"ט ז"ל, מדברי רב אלפסי נראה דחייב לבער אפילו נפסלה מאכילת אדם... ולדידיה מתניתא תרתי אשמעינן, שהוא חייב לבער ושהוא מותר לטמאה. אבל יש אומר דלא אתי לאשמעינן אלא דין טומאה, אבל אינו חייב לבער מכיון שנפסלה מאכילת אדם... זו היא שיטת הרא"ה ז"ל. אבל הרי"ט ז"ל כתב דדברי רבינו אלפסי נראה יותר.

ר Chiddushim MehaRitva,[3] Pesachim 45b

The Ritva writes, "It appears from the comments of Rav Alfasi [the Rif] that one is obligated to destroy [moldy bread] even if it has become unfit for human consumption..." According to him, the *baraita* teaches us two halachot, that one is obligated to destroy and that it is permitted to make it ritually impure. But some say that it only comes to teach us the halacha of ritual impurity, but one is not obligated to destroy it since it has become unfit for human consumption... This is the view of the Ra'ah. But the Ritva writes that the comments of Rav Alfasi appear more correct.

The ***Shulchan Aruch*** rules in accordance with the Rif that moldy bread may only be kept in one's possession if it has become unfit for a dog.

9. שולחן ערוך | או"ח תמב:ב

הפת עצמה שעיפשה ונפסלה מלאכול הכלב... אינו חייב לבער.

א Shulchan Aruch, Orach Chaim 442:2

Bread itself which has become moldy and unfit for consumption by a dog... need not be destroyed.

The clear implication is that *chametz* that a dog would eat must be destroyed before Pesach, even if it is not fit for human consumption.

Earlier in the same chapter, the **Mishna (*Masechet Pesachim*)** addresses other substances that do not fully consist of *chametz* or are not consumed. The Mishna lists various types of *chametz* and *chametz* mixtures which are biblically prohibited on Pesach[4] but for which the severe punishment of *karet* does not apply if one consumes them.

10. משנה | פסחים ג:א

ואלו עוברין בפסח: כותח הבבלי, ושכר המדי, וחומץ האדומי,

ח Mishna, Pesachim 3:1

For possessing **the following, one transgresses** [*overin*] the prohibitions of: It shall not be seen, and: It shall not be found, **on Pesach,** although not all of them are considered food: **Babylonian *kutach*,** a dip with a sharp flavor that contains flour; **Median beer; Edomite vinegar;**

---

laws. The Gemara (*Avoda Zara* 68a) derives from this that only *neveila* that is fit for a *ger toshav* to eat is prohibited.

3. Although the Ritva's commentary on *Masechet Pesachim* has not been found, this *sefer* of undetermined authorship consists mostly of a collection of quotes from the Ritva's commentary. See the introduction to the Mossad HaRav Kook edition of the Ritva to *Masechet Pesachim*.
4. We will see further below that some commentaries interpret the biblical prohibition here to be only against eating such *chametz*, whereas the prohibition against owning such *chametz* is rabbinic in nature, or there may not even be such a prohibition.

וזיתום המצרי, וזומן של צבעים, ועמילן של טבחים, וקולן של סופרים.

רבי אליעזר אומר: אף תכשיטי נשים.

זה הכלל: כל שהוא ממין דגן – הרי זה עובר בפסח. הרי אלו באזהרה, ואין בהן משום כרת.

Egyptian *zitom*, a type of beer; **dyers' broth** [*zoman*]; **bakers' well-worked dough; and *kolan of soferim*.**[5]

Rabbi Eliezer says: The same prohibition **also** applies to **women's adornments,** i.e., cosmetics, that contain *chametz*.

This is the principle: If one possesses **any** substance **that is** derived **from a type of grain** that became leavened, although it is not actually bread, **one transgresses** the prohibitions of: It shall not be seen, and: It shall not be found, **on Pesach. These** substances are included **in the warning,** i.e., the biblical prohibition of possessing *chametz*, **but there is no element of *karet*** if one eats them.

The **Gemara (*Masechet Pesachim*)** on this Mishna addresses the status of another type of *chametz* that is not normally edible, known as *chametz nuksheh* (pure, hardened *chametz*, which is inedible).[6] The Gemara wishes to infer that such items are biblically prohibited on Pesach.

11. מסכת פסחים מג.

ח Masechet Pesachim 43a

מאן תנא דחמץ דגן גמור על ידי תערובות, ונוקשה בעיניה בלאו? – אמר רב יהודה אמר רב: רבי מאיר היא...

The Gemara asks: **Who is the *tanna*** of the Mishna **who** maintains that both **full-fledged, leavened grain bread in a mixture,**[7] **and hardened** leaven [*nuksheh*], **in its pure,** unadulterated form, which is not suitable for consumption, are both included **in a biblical prohibition?** The Gemara answers that **Rav Yehuda said** that **Rav said: It is** the opinion of **Rabbi Meir**...[8]

Rashi explains that cosmetics are an example of *chametz nuksheh* and are not subject to the punishment of *karet* because they are inedible.

12. רש"י | פסחים מג.

ר Rashi, Pesachim 43a

מאן תנא – ...ותכשיטי נשים – בעיניה הוא, אבל נוקשה הוא, דאינו ראוי לאכילה.

Who is the *tanna* – ...Women's cosmetics are pure [*chametz*], but are *nuksheh*, as they are not fit for [human] consumption.

So far, we have understood the Mishna cited above as stating that one violates [*overin*] the biblical prohibition against possessing *chametz* if one owns any of the items listed, even though according to Rashi, some of these items are inedible. This interpretation of the Mishna follows Rashi and the Rambam

5. The Gemara (42b) cites two possible interpretations of this phrase. It either refers to shoemakers' glue (made from flour) or a depilatory paste used by women.
6. The meaning of the term *chametz nuksheh* is discussed in more detail by the *Magen Avraham*, quoted in source 17 below.
7. We will discuss mixtures containing *chametz* further on.
8. The Gemara concludes that Rabbi Eliezer disputes this and maintains that hardened *chametz* is not biblically prohibited. Tosafot (42a, s.v. Rabbi Eliezer) question how this can be the case, as Rabbi Eliezer is cited in the Mishna as prohibiting *chametz* cosmetics, and he appears to agree that all the other substances listed in the Mishna are also biblically prohibited. Tosafot therefore conclude that either in the Mishna or in the Gemara, there must be a printing error, and one of these *tanna'im* is Rabbi Elazar and not Rabbi Eliezer.

in his commentary on the Mishna and is consistent with the opinions of the Rif, Ran, and *Shulchan Aruch* we learned earlier that only food that has become unfit for a dog may be kept in one's possession during Pesach. However, **Tosafot** cite two alternative explanations. The first is given by **Riva**, who agrees with Rashi that one must not possess *chametz nuksheh* on Pesach, but renders the word *overin* differently. It means that these items must be destroyed before Pesach.

The second is given by **Rabbeinu Tam**, who argues, in contrast to Rashi and Riva, that there is no biblical prohibition against owning these items on Pesach. The word *overin* means only that they must be removed from the table, i.e., there is a biblical prohibition to eat them on Pesach.[9]

13. תוספות | פסחים מב.

ואלו עוברין בפסח – פירש הקונטרס לעבור עליהן בבל יראה ובבל ימצא **וגם ריב"א מדקדק מלשון עוברים דמשמע עוברין מן העולם.**

ואין נראה לרבינו תם דמשמע דכל הנך מרבינן מכל מחמצת לא תאכלו ואפילו באכילה לא הוה מיחייב אי לאו דרבייא קרא ומהיכי תיתי בל יראה ובל ימצא.

ונראה לרבינו תם דאלו עוברין פירושו האוכלין ועוברין היינו מעל השולחן דלאו בני מיכל נינהו אבל בל יראה ליכא.

Tosafot, Pesachim 42a

For the following, *overin* on Pesach – Rashi explains that [*overin* means that] for [possessing] these substances, one transgresses [the prohibitions of:] "It shall not be seen," and: "It shall not be found." **Riva also infers that the term *overin* means that they must be removed from the world.**

But this does not seem correct to Rabbeinu Tam, as [the Gemara] implies that all these items are included [in the prohibition] based on [the word "anything" in the verse], "You shall not eat anything leavened," and that one would not even have been liable for eating [these items] if this verse has not included them. So why should we think that "It shall not be seen" and "It shall not be found" apply?

Rather, it seems to Rabbeinu Tam that "For the following, *overin*" refers to the foods, and "*overin*" means [must be removed] from the table, as they must not be eaten. But "It shall not be seen" does not apply.

The **Ran** agrees with Rabbeinu Tam that there is no biblical prohibition against owning *chametz nuksheh* on Pesach. Nevertheless, he writes that owning such items is rabbinically prohibited, even according to the view that eating them on Pesach is only rabbinically prohibited. Accordingly, he interprets the Mishna to mean that *chametz nuksheh* must be destroyed, similar to the Riva, but he understands this requirement to be a rabbinic one.

14. ר"ן | פסחים יג. (בדפי הרי"ף)

נראה דאלו עוברין אלו מתבערין קאמר, **אף על גב דמאורייתא לא קאי עלייהו בבל יראה ובל ימצא מדרבנן מיהא צריכין ביעור**, ולא מיבעיא לתנא דמתניתין

Ran, Pesachim 13a (Pagination of the Rif)

It appears that "these [items] *overin*" means that they must be destroyed. **Although on a biblical level, the prohibitions of "It shall not be seen" and "It shall not be found" do not apply to them, nevertheless, they require removal on a rabbinic level.** This is not only according to the *tanna* of our Mishna,

9. According to Rabbeinu Tam, the biblical prohibition alluded to in the Mishna and in the Gemara (43a) with respect to these items is that of eating them, not owning them.

דסבירא ליה דהרי אלו כולן באזהרה, אלא אפילו למאן דאמר נוקשה בעיניה בלא כלום, כיון דאיסורא דרבנן מיהא איכא צריך ביעור.

who holds that all of these fall under the biblical prohibition [against eating *chametz*], but even according to the view that [one who eats] pure [*chametz*] *nuksheh* is not liable to any [punishment], since there is at least a rabbinic prohibition, it requires removal.[10]

In contrast, the ***Tur*** writes that according to the *Chachamim* (cited later in source 22), who dispute the *tanna* of the Mishna and maintain that even eating *chametz nuksheh* is not prohibited biblically, one may keep *chametz nuksheh* on Pesach.

15. טור | או"ח תמב

Tur, Orach Chaim 442

ולרבנן אפילו לאו אין בהן אלא איסורא בעלמא ולדבריהן מותר להשהותן.

According to the *Chachamim*, there is not even a [biblical] negative commandment against these items, merely a [rabbinic] prohibition. According to them, keeping these items [on Pesach] is permitted.

Although the ***Shulchan Aruch*** does not rule explicitly regarding this dispute, he does say that if one owned *chametz nuksheh* on Pesach, one may benefit from it after Pesach.[11]

16. שולחן ערוך | או"ח תמז:יב

Shulchan Aruch, Orach Chaim 447:12

חמץ נוקשה, אפילו בעיניה אינו אסור בהנאה אחר הפסח.

Chametz nuksheh, even if in its original form, is not prohibited to benefit from after Pesach.

The ***Magen Avraham*** concludes that the position of the *Shulchan Aruch* is in accordance with the Ran, that owning *chametz nuksheh* on Pesach is rabbinically prohibited. Were owning *chametz nuksheh* on Pesach to be a violation of a biblical prohibition, it would have also been prohibited to benefit from it after Pesach.[12] However, the necessity to state this halacha implies that owning *chametz nuksheh* on Pesach is rabbinically prohibited.

The *Magen Avraham* here also offers a more precise definition of *chametz nuksheh*. He explains that it refers either to dough that has not fully leavened or to *chametz* that was never fully fit for human consumption. This is different than owning *chametz* that was at one point edible, which is biblically prohibited on Pesach unless it became unfit for a dog, as we saw in source 6.

---

10. Tosafot (*Pesachim* 2a, s.v. *ohr*) also write explicitly that even according to Rabbeinu Tam, Chazal obligated one to remove even *chametz nuksheh* before Pesach.

11. Bona fide *chametz* that was owned by a Jew on Pesach is prohibited to benefit from even after Pesach, as will be discussed in *shiur* 3.

12. The *Magen Avraham* understands that even eating *chametz nuksheh* is not prohibited after Pesach, but the *Shulchan Aruch* does not mention eating, since *chametz nuksheh* is not usually eaten. However, the *Mishna Berura* (442:107) observes that most *Acharonim* prohibit eating *chametz nuksheh* after Pesach and only permit deriving other benefit from it. This is also explicit in the Responsa of the Rivash (*siman* 3), the source for this ruling of the *Shulchan Aruch*.

17. מגן אברהם | או"ח תמב:א

ודעת השולחן ערוך כדעת התוספות שהרי פסק בסוף סימן תמ"ז דחמץ נוקשה וכו' לא עבר עליו בבל יראה מן התורה...

וחמץ נוקשה היינו שאינו חמץ גמור כמו אותן שהסופרים מדבקין בו ניירותיהם שעושין מקמח ומים או עיסה שהכסיפו פניה שלא נעשה חמץ גמור ורש"י ור"ן פירשו חמץ רע שאינו ראוי לאכילה וכן כתב הסמ"ג, **וצריך לומר דמעולם לא היה ראוי לאכילה דאם היה חמץ גמור ראוי לאכילה אסורה עד שיפסל מלאכול לכלב** כמו שכתוב סעיף ב וצריך לומר דעל כל פנים ראוי לאכילה קצת דהא כתב הר"ן דגזרינן דלמא אתי למיכל מיניה.

א Magen Avraham, Orach Chaim 442:1

The view of the *Shulchan Aruch* is in accordance with Tosafot, as he rules at the end of *siman* 447 that [for keeping] *chametz nuksheh* one does not violate the biblical prohibition of "It shall not be seen"...

Chametz nuksheh is *chametz* that is not fully-leavened, such as that which scribes use to glue their papers, which they make from flour and water, or dough whose surface has darkened, that has not become fully leavened. But Rashi and the Ran explain [that *chametz nuksheh* is] "bad *chametz*," that is not fit to eat, and the *Semag* writes similarly. **One must explain that it was never fit to eat, as if it was [originally] fully-leavened *chametz* that was fit to eat, it would be [biblically] prohibited until it becomes unfit for a dog to eat**, as is written in *se'if* 2. [But] one must say that it is at least somewhat edible, as the Ran writes that we decree lest one come to eat from it.[13]

The ***Mishna Berura* (442:2)** also rules in accordance with the *Magen Avraham*. Thus, *chametz* that is not usually fit for human consumption but a dog would eat must be destroyed before Pesach, either on a biblical level (if it was once fit for human consumption) or on a rabbinic level (if it never was).

Eating *Chametz* That Is Not Fit for a Dog

Although obviously one would not usually want to eat *chametz* that even a dog wouldn't eat, it is important to determine whether doing so is also prohibited by halacha. For one reason, as we will later see, applying such substances to one's skin may have the same status as eating. Furthermore, in rare circumstances, consuming such substances may be beneficial for health reasons.

The **Gemara (*Masechet Pesachim*)** states that it is permitted to derive benefit from *chametz* that became charred prior to the time that *chametz* became prohibited.

18. מסכת פסחים כא:

דאמר רבא: חרכו קודם זמנו – מותר בהנאה, אפילו לאחר זמנו.

ח Masechet Pesachim 21b

Rava said: If one **charred** *chametz* **before its time,** i.e., before it became prohibited, **it is permitted to** derive **benefit from it even after its time,** since it no longer has the legal status of *chametz*.

The **Rosh** quotes a view that even eating such *chametz* is permitted. However, he rejects this view as unreasonable, and cites Rav Yehuda Bartzeloni who concurs that this is prohibited.

13. The implication is that if the *chametz* is totally inedible for humans in all circumstances, one need not destroy it before Pesach.

19. רא"ש | פסחים ב:א

יש שרוצים לומר לאו דוקא הנאה דהוא הדין נמי אכילה דעפרא בעלמא הוא. ולא מסתבר דאף על פי דבטלה דעת האוכל אצל כל אדם **מכל מקום כיון דאיהו קאכיל ליה אסור**. וכן כתב הרב הברצלוני ז"ל וזה לשונו: והני מילי דמותר בהנאה לאחר זמנו אבל באכילה לא.

ר Rosh, Pesachim 2:1

Some want to say that [this leniency] applies not only to benefit, but the same applies also regarding eating, since [charred *chametz*] is [equivalent to] mere earth. But this is not reasonable, as although the mindset of one who eats it is negated by all other people [who would not eat it], **nevertheless, since he eats it, it is prohibited.**[14] Rav Bartzeloni also writes similarly: "This means only that benefiting from [charred *chametz*] is permitted after its time, but eating it is not [permitted]."

In contrast, the **Ran** writes that eating this *chametz* is permitted, provided that it became charred before the time when *chametz* becomes prohibited. He explains that the Gemara did not specify this leniency because it is not usually relevant, as people do not eat food that has spoiled to this extent.

20. ר"ן | פסחים ה: (בדפי הרי"ף)

ודאמרינן מותר בהנאתו בדין הוא דאפילו באכילה נמי שרי כיון שיצא מתורת פת קודם שיחול בו איסור חמץ אלא לפי שאין דרך אכילה בלחם חרוך נקט לישנא דמותר בהנאתו דאפילו אכיל ליה לאו אכילה היא אלא דמיתהני מיניה ודוקא שחרכו קודם זמנו אבל לאחר זמנו לא פקע אסוריה עד דשריף ליה לגמרי.

ר Ran, Pesachim 5b (Pagination of the Rif)

That which we say that it is permitted to derive benefit from [charred *chametz*], in fact even eating it is permitted, since it lost its status as bread before the prohibition against *chametz* took effect. But since it is not usual to eat charred bread, the Gemara uses the language that it is permitted to derive benefit from it, as even if one eats it, this is not [defined as] eating, rather as benefiting from it. This is only if one charred it before the time [that *chametz* becomes prohibited], but [if one charred it] after this time, its prohibition does not dissipate until one burns it entirely.

The ***Turei Zahav* (*Taz*)** rules stringently in accordance with the Rosh, but clarifies that even according to this view, the prohibition against eating charred *chametz* is only rabbinic.

21. טורי זהב (ט"ז) | או"ח תמב:ח

מותר לקיימו – אבל באכילה אסור אף על גב דאינו ראוי לאכילה מכל מקום איהו אחשביה ליה לאכילה כך כתב הרא"ש. ונראה לדידיה דודאי אין חיוב דאורייתא בזה דהא ביום כיפור כי אכל אכילה שאינה ראויה פטור.

א Turei Zahav (Taz), Orach Chaim 442:8

Keeping [charred *chametz*] is permitted – But eating it is prohibited. Although it is not fit to eat, nevertheless, he conveys the significance of food to it [by eating it] – so writes the Rosh. It appears that [even] according to him, there is certainly no Torah liability for this, as on Yom Kippur, one who eats [food] that is unfit is exempt [from bringing a sin-offering].

---

14. As the act of eating this otherwise unfit food reinstates its *chametz* status subjectively for the person who eats it.

The ***Mishna Berura* (442:43)** and most *poskim* also rule in accordance with the position of the *Taz.*[15] We will see later in the *shiur* how this applies to practical cases such as taking medication.

Mixtures Containing Inedible *Chametz*

The Mishna quoted in source 10 listed mixtures containing *chametz* together with *chametz nuksheh*. Consuming either is biblically prohibited on Pesach, but it is not subject to the severe punishment of *karet*. The **Gemara (*Masechet Pesachim*)** quoted in source 11 says that this Mishna represents the view of Rabbi Meir. The continuation of this Gemara quotes a *baraita* in which Rabbi Eliezer also agrees that mixtures containing *chametz* are biblically prohibited on Pesach, but the *Chachamim* disagree.

22. מסכת פסחים מג.

דתניא: על חמץ דגן גמור – ענוש כרת, על עירובו – בלאו, דברי רבי אליעזר. וחכמים אומרים: על חמץ דגן גמור – ענוש כרת, על עירובו – בלא כלום.

ח Masechet Pesachim 43a

...**It was taught** in a *baraita*: **For** eating **full-fledged, leavened grain bread** one is **punishable** by ***karet*,** whereas **for** eating **a mixture** that contains *chametz* one is punished merely **for** violating **a prohibition.** This is **the statement of Rabbi Eliezer. But the *Chachamim* say: For** eating **full-fledged, leavened grain bread** one is **punishable by *karet*;** however, **for** eating *chametz* in **its mixture** one is **not** punished **at all.**[16]

The **Rif** writes that although according to the *Chachamim*, one does not receive lashes for eating a mixture containing *chametz*, it is nevertheless prohibited.

23. רי"ף | פסחים יג.-יג: (בדפי הרי"ף)

אף על גב דאמור רבנן על עירובו בלא כלום מילקא הוא דלא לקי אבל איסורא איכא.

ד Rif, Pesachim 13a–13b (Pagination of the Rif)

Although the *Chachamim* say that for [eating *chametz*] in its mixture one is not punished at all, this means only that one does not receive lashes. However, there is a prohibition involved.

---

15. The *Pri Chadash* (442:9) infers that this is also the position of the *Shulchan Aruch*. However, the *Pri Chadash* himself rules that *chametz* that is unfit for a dog is equivalent to earth and may be eaten.

16. Further on, the Gemara (*Pesachim* 44a) clarifies that even according to the *Chachamim*, eating a mixture containing a *k'zayit* of *chametz* within the volume of "half a loaf" ("*kedei achilat peras*") is biblically prohibited. The *Rishonim* dispute whether the volume of the standard loaf referred to is the volume of six or eight eggs, and accordingly whether half of this is the volume of three or four eggs. The percentage of a *k'zayit* of *chametz* within half a loaf varies depending on the exact calculation used in halacha for the volume of an olive and an egg, which is subject to dispute and may have changed over the generations. For a synopsis of opinions, see volume 15, *shiur* 1, sources 50–53. In short, some assume an olive's volume to be approximately 7.5 cc (the volume of an olive today), while others calculate it as 19 cc, and a third approach, more widely accepted today, estimates it at approximately 28 cc. An egg's volume is usually estimated as between 50–60 cc (see *Peninei Halakha, Berachot* 10:5, n. 6). Accordingly, a *k'zayit* of *chametz* within half a loaf could range between a percentage of approximately 5% to 20%. As noted, the measurements of a *k'zayit* given by different *poskim* vary significantly, as some believe that the volume of both olives and eggs have changed significantly over the generations.

The **Rambam** rules that the biblical prohibition against owning *chametz* on Pesach also applies to mixtures containing *chametz*. However, he adds that if the mixture is not fit for (human) consumption, one may keep it in one's possession on Pesach, but one may not eat it.

ר Rambam, Hilchot Chametz Umatza 4:8, 12

24. רמב"ם | הל' חמץ ומצה ד:ח, יב

8. [One who possesses] a mixture containing *chametz* violates the prohibitions of "It shall not be seen" and "It shall not be found." [This includes,] for example, pickle-brine, Babylonian *kotach*, and Median beer, which are made from flour, and all other similar substances which are eaten.[17] However, a substance which contains a mixture of *chametz*, but is not fit to be eaten, may be kept on Pesach…

12. A substance with which *chametz* has become mixed but is not human food at all, or it is not considered food by most people, e.g., *tiriac*[18] and the like, although one may keep it [during Pesach], eating it is prohibited until after Pesach. Although it contains only the smallest amount of *chametz*, eating it is prohibited.

ח. תערובת חמץ עוברין עליה משום בל יראה ובל ימצא, כגון המוריס וכותח הבבלי ושכר המדי שעושין אותו מן הקמח, וכל כיוצא באלו מדברים הנאכלים, אבל דבר שיש בו תערובת חמץ ואינו ראוי לאכילה הרי זה מותר לקיימו בפסח...

יב. דבר שנתערב בו חמץ ואינו מאכל אדם כלל, או שאינו מאכל כל אדם כגון התריאק וכיוצא בו אף על פי שמותר לקיימו אסור לאכלו עד אחר הפסח, ואף על פי שאין בו מן החמץ אלא כל שהוא הרי זה אסור לאכלו.

The ***Shulchan Aruch*** (O.C. 442:1, 4) rules similarly.[19]

17. The *Tur* (O.C. 442) understands that the Rambam rules in accordance with Rabbi Eliezer, presumably because the Mishna follows his view in this regard. The Rambam in his commentary on the Mishna (*Pesachim* 3:1) also appears to accept the ruling of the Mishna, that eating a mixture containing *chametz* is subject to lashes on a biblical level. The *Beit Yosef* discusses this at length, and concludes that according to this view, the dispute between Rabbi Eliezer and the *Chachamim* is limited to a case of a mixture that contains a *k'zayit* of *chametz* within the volume of three eggs (see above, n. 15), but in which the mixture itself is usually eaten together with other food. When eaten together with other food, there will not be a *k'zayit* of *chametz* within a total volume of three eggs. The Rambam rules that eating in this manner, or even possessing a *chametz* mixture of this nature, is biblically prohibited. If, however, the mixture itself does not contain a *k'zayit* of *chametz* within the volume of three eggs, eating it in the normal way is only rabbinically prohibited and one may keep it on Pesach. For further discussion concerning the Rambam's position about owning these types of *chametz*, see *Magid Mishneh* and *Kesef Mishneh* here. See also *Mishna Berura* (442:1), who summarizes the dispute concerning whether the prohibition against owning *chametz* applies to a *k'zayit* of *chametz* in total in a mixture or only to a mixture with a *k'zayit* in *kedei achilat peras* [see previous note] but does not rule definitively in favor of either opinion. This issue has relevance for those who refrain from selling actual *chametz* – the definition of "actual *chametz*" is often assumed to follow this parameter. Thus, a food product with less than a *k'zayit* of *chametz* in total may be sold even by those who do not sell actual *chametz*. See also *shiur* 2, sources 53 and n. 69.

18. Rabbeinu Mano'ach writes (*Sefer HaMenucha, Chametz Umatza* 4:10) that this is an effective medicine containing meat of a viper, an egg of a specific wild animal known to doctors, dry, ground *chametz* kneaded with honey, and other ingredients.

19. The Rema does not dispute this ruling in principle, but points out that according to some *Rishonim*, if the *chametz* was nullified before Pesach by becoming mixed with a volume of at least sixty times as much non-*chametz*, it remains permitted even on Pesach.

INEDIBLE *CHAMETZ* AND MIXTURES CONTAINING *CHAMETZ*

	On Its Own	In a Mixture
Edible *Chametz*	Must be destroyed before Pesach One who eats it on Pesach is subject to *karet*	Must be destroyed before Pesach One who eats it on Pesach is not subject to *karet* **(Rambam, *Shulchan Aruch*)**
***Chametz* unfit for humans but fit for a dog**	Must be destroyed before Pesach One who eats it on Pesach is not subject to *karet*	May be kept on Pesach **(Rambam, *Shulchan Aruch*)** Eating it on Pesach is prohibited **(Rambam, *Shulchan Aruch*)**
Chametz Nuksheh	Keeping it on Pesach violates a biblical prohibition **(Rashi, Rambam, Riva)**, a rabbinical prohibition **(Ran, *Magen Avraham*, *Mishna Berura*)** or is permitted **(*Tur* according to one opinion)** One who eats it on Pesach is not subject to *karet*	May be kept on Pesach **(Rambam, *Shulchan Aruch*)** Eating it on Pesach is prohibited **(Rambam, *Shulchan Aruch*)**
***Chametz* unfit for a dog**	May be kept on Pesach Eating it on Pesach is prohibited **(Rosh)** on a rabbinical level **(*Taz*, *Mishna Berura*)** or permitted **(Ran)**	May be kept on Pesach Eating it on Pesach is prohibited **(Rosh)** on a rabbinical level **(*Taz*, *Mishna Berura*)** or permitted **(Ran)**

Soaps and Creams

One of the questions that arises regularly concerning inedible *chametz* and mixtures of *chametz* on Pesach is whether creams must be free of *chametz* in order to be used or even kept in the home. Since creams that are applied to the skin would not usually be eaten even by a dog, it would seem that based on what we learned above, keeping and applying these creams should be permitted on Pesach even if they contain *chametz*.

However, there is one potential issue with this. The **Mishna (*Masechet Shabbat*)** cites a verse in *Tehillim* as an allusion indicating that applying oil to one's body is prohibited on Yom Kippur, as it is similar to drinking.

25. משנה | שבת ט:ד

מנין לסיכה שהיא כשתיה ביום הכפורים? אף על פי שאין ראיה לדבר, זכר לדבר, שנאמר: (תהילים קט:ח) ותבא כמים בקרבו וכשמן בעצמותיו.

ח Mishna, Shabbat 9:4

From where is it derived **that smearing** oil on one's body **is like drinking** and is similarly prohibited **on Yom Kippur? Although there is no proof for this, there is an allusion to it, as it is stated: "It comes into his inward parts like water and like oil into his bones"** (*Tehillim* 109:18). The verse appears to equate smearing oil on one's body with drinking water.

If applying oil to the body is tantamount to drinking, might applying *chametz* creams to the body be prohibited, just as eating or drinking *chametz* is prohibited?[20] A similar question exists all year round regarding the use of soap made from non-kosher items, as in the past, it was common for soap to be made from *cheilev* (non-kosher animal fat). **Tosafot** write that one may use this soap, as smearing is only like drinking in relation to specific prohibitions.

26. תוספות | יומא עז.

דתנן מניין לסיכה שהיא כשתייה... – ומותר אדם לסוך בחלב דלא אשכחן דאתסר סיכה כשתיה אלא ביום הכיפורים ובתרומה ובאיסורי הנאה...

ו Tosafot, Yoma 77a

As we learned in a Mishna, "From where is it derived that smearing is like drinking..." – One is permitted to smear oneself with *cheilev*, as we only find that smearing is prohibited like drinking regarding Yom Kippur, *teruma* and substances that are prohibited to benefit from...

According to Tosafot, although *chametz* is included in the category of substances that are prohibited in benefit, nevertheless, it would appear that smearing oneself with *chametz* that is not fit for a dog is permitted and is not equivalent to drinking it. Therefore, it is permitted on Pesach, just as deriving other benefit from such *chametz* is permitted.

In contrast, the ***Beit Yosef*** quotes the ***Orchot Chaim***, who writes that smearing oneself with *cheilev* is certainly prohibited. Presumably, he would say the same about using products containing *chametz*, even if it would not be eaten by a dog.

20. Even if the *chametz* is not fit for a dog, we have seen above that according to most authorities, consuming such *chametz* is prohibited.

27. בית יוסף | יו"ד קיז

כתוב בארחות חיים שיש מי שמתיר מכאן לעשות סחורה בחלב חזיר... אבל לסוך בו בשרו ודאי אסור משום דבכלל שתיה הוא.

ו Beit Yosef, Yoreh De'ah 117

The *Orchot Chaim* writes that based on [the ruling of the Rambam in *Hilchot Ma'achalot Assurot* 8:16][21] there are those who permit doing business with *cheilev* of a pig... But smearing one's flesh with it is certainly prohibited, as this is categorized as drinking.

The ***Taz*** writes that we do not accept this stringency of the *Orchot Chaim* as halacha, as Tosafot and other *Rishonim* disagree. However, he quotes the ***Issur V'heter Ha'aroch*** who writes that one may only smear oneself with *cheilev* in order to ease pain, not just for pleasure. Nonetheless, one need not prevent non-Jewish babysitters from smearing *cheilev* on the bodies of Jewish babies. The *Taz* concurs with this ruling.

28. ט"ז (טורי זהב) | יו"ד קיז:ד

כתב בית יוסף בשם ארחות חיים דאסור לסוך בשרו בחלב חזיר דסיכה בכלל שתייה היא ונראה דלא קיימא לן כן דבהדיא כתב התוספות פרק בתרא דיומא (עז.) דמותר לאדם לסוך בחלב דלא אשכחן סיכה כשתיה אלא ביום כיפור ואיסורי הנאה משום דאיכא אסמכתא אבל חלב דהיתירא הנאה מותר... וכן כתב בית יוסף סימן קכ"ג בשם רשב"א בתשובה שמותר לסוך בחלב חזיר אפילו שלא במקום סכנה.

אלא שבאיסור והיתר הארוך סוף כלל ל"ט ראיתי שכתב דאין היתר סיכה בחלב או בחזיר אלא היכא דאיכא צערא אבל אדם בריא משום תענוג לא ועל כן אין לסוך תינוק בחלב חזיר שאין זה אלא לתענוג אבל מניחין עובד כוכבים לסוכן ולהאכילן שאין אמור להזהיר גדולים על הקטנים אלא לסוך אותם בידים עד כאן לשונו וכן עיקר.

א Taz, Yoreh De'ah 117:4

The *Beit Yosef* writes in the name of the *Orchot Chaim* that smearing one's flesh with pig's milk is prohibited, as smearing is categorized as drinking. But it appears that this is not the halacha, as the Tosafot write explicitly in the last chapter of *Yoma* (77a) that a person is permitted to smear himself with *cheilev*, as we only find that smearing is like drinking regarding Yom Kippur and substances that are prohibited to benefit from, where there is an *asmachta* [hint to this effect from a verse], but [smearing] *cheilev*, from which benefiting from is permitted, is certainly allowed... Similarly, the *Beit Yosef* writes in the name of the Rashba in a responsum that it is permitted to smear *cheilev* of a pig even when not in a situation of danger.

However, I saw that the *Issur V'heter Ha'aroch* writes that smearing *cheilev* or pig [products] is permitted only where there is pain, but for a healthy person, for pleasure, it is not permitted. Therefore, one should not smear an infant with *cheilev* of a pig, as that is only for pleasure. But one may allow a gentile to smear them and feed them, since we are not required to warn adults regarding minors [having *cheilev* smeared], only that we may not smear them with our own hands. This ruling [of the *Issur V'heter Ha'aroch*] is correct.

The ***Shach*** writes that the rationale for the stringency of the *Issur V'heter Ha'aroch* is unclear. Nevertheless, the practice is to avoid using soap made from *cheilev*, and he writes that this practice is proper.

---

21. The Rambam there writes that doing business with any prohibited food is prohibited, with the exception of *cheilev*. According to the lenient view quoted by the *Orchot Chaim*, just like doing business with *cheilev* of a kosher animal is permitted, so too doing business with *cheilev* of a pig is also permitted, despite the prohibition of eating the meat of a non-kosher animal.

א Nekudot HaKesef, Yoreh De'ah 117:1

…His words are unclear… The *Issur V'heter Ha'aroch* rules that [smearing *cheilev*] is prohibited, and writes that when Tosafot… write in the name of Rabbeinu Tam that this is permitted, perhaps this is also only in a situation of pain, for one who has skin eruptions. But this is not correct, as the simple meaning of the words of Rabbeinu Tam is that this is permitted in all cases… Nevertheless, I have seen that some are stringent not to wash in soap made from *cheilev*, and this is proper.

29. נקודות הכסף | יו"ד קיז:א

...לא נתבררו דבריו... ובאיסור והיתר הארוך שם פסק לאסור, וכתב דהתוספות... שכתבו בשם רבינו תם דשרי, שמא היינו גם כן דוקא במקום צער למי שיש לו חטטין. ולא נהירא, דפשט דברי רבינו תם שם משמע דבכל ענין שרי... ומכל מקום ראיתי יש מחמירין שלא לרחוץ בזיי"ף העשויה מחלב, ונכון הוא.

However, the ***Aruch HaShulchan*** understands that even these stringencies only apply to soap that was somewhat edible. Modern soap is repulsive to eat, even for a dog, and may be used even if it contains *cheilev*.

א Aruch HaShulchan, Yoreh De'ah 117:29

Some wish to prohibit rubbing soap… because smearing is equivalent to drinking, and some permit this… However, with our soap, which is repulsive and is not even fit for a dog, nothing renders food more unfit than it, so it is obvious that no concern exists even for healthy people.[22] Accordingly, the widespread practice throughout all Jewish communities is to rub with soap in the bathhouse, and no one speaks out to protest.

30. ערוך השולחן | יו"ד קיז:כט

יש רוצים לאסור לסוך בבורית... מטעם סיכה כשתיה ויש מתירין... אמנם בבורית שלנו שהוא מסריח ואף לכלב אינו ראוי ואין לך לפגם יותר מזה פשיטא שאין בזה חשש אפילו לבריאים וכן המנהג פשוט בכל תפוצות ישראל לסוך בבורית במרחץ ואין פוצה פה ומצפצף.

The ***Bi'ur Halacha*** also observes that common practice is to be lenient in this regard. However, he does not distinguish between modern soap and the soap used in previous generations, and writes that where possible, it is proper to use soap that does not contain *cheilev*.

א Bi'ur Halacha, Orach Chaim 326:10

With other *cheilev* – …The universal practice is to wash using our soap, that is made from *cheilev*, and only some punctilious individuals are careful about this. But if it is common to be able to obtain soap that is not made from *cheilev*, it is certainly proper to be concerned for the view of those who rule stringently in this regard.

31. ביאור הלכה | או"ח שכו:י

בשאר חלב וכו' – ...מנהג העולם לרחוץ בבורית שלנו הנעשים מחלב ורק איזה מדקדקים זהירין בזה. ואם מצוי להשיג בורית שנעשים שלא מחלב בודאי נכון לחוש לדעת המחמירין בזה.

Rav Ovadia Yosef[23] writes that the *Bi'ur Halacha* did not consider any distinction between earlier soaps and modern soaps. However, since today's soaps are clearly inedible, Rav Ovadia rules that anyone may use soap that contains *cheilev*, pig fat or the like.[24]

---

22. See *Pri Chadash* (Y.D. 117) and Chazon Ish (*Demai* 4:13) who also discuss this approach.
23. Responsa *Yechaveh Da'at* 4:43.
24. For further discussion on this subject, see https://oukosher.org/blog/consumer-kosher/whats-the-truth-aboutkosher-soap. According to this article, Rav Hershel Schachter favors the reasoning of Rav Ovadia Yosef.

For Pesach, some *kashrut* authorities do compile approved lists of soaps and creams, as they are concerned that products containing alcohol or other ingredients produced from *chametz* may be problematic. **Rav Yirmiyah Cohen**, *av beit din* in Paris, explains that since unlike with *cheilev*, benefiting from *chametz* is prohibited even without eating it, using these products may be problematic even according to Tosafot. Since these products are made for washing with rather than for eating, they may be prohibited even if not fit for a dog to eat.[25]

32. שו"ת והרים הכהן | ד:כב-כג

...ונראה לעניות דעתי דגם אלכוהול זה הנעשה לערב בו מיני הבשמים ותמרוקים הרי הוא כשאור. וממילא אינו נעשה לאכילה, ואין בו שום גריעותא באיסורו, אם הוא נפסד מאכילת כלב...

ולכן אם הוא לוקח אלכוהול של חמץ ומשתמש בו לסיכה על בשרו וכדומה, ודאי הוא בזה כמו אכילה ושייך בהנאה זו אחשביה, גם אם אינו ראוי לאכילת כלב. ולא שאני רוצה להחליט ולאמר דסיכה בכלל שתיה בזה. דהיא סוגיא שלימה, האם אנו אוסרים סבון של חלב – בצירי – לסיכה, והרי חלב אינו איסורי הנאה. מה שאין כן בערלה וחמץ שהם איסורי הנאה הרי יש בכלל שימושו כדבר שסך בו משום אחשביה...

Responsa V'heirim HaKohen 4:22–23

...In my humble opinion, it appears that this alcohol, which is produced to mix with types of scents and cosmetics, is also like *se'or* [sourdough, forbidden by the Torah even when it is not edible itself]. It follows that it is not produced for food, and its prohibition is not at all lessened if it becomes unfit for a dog to eat...[26]

Therefore, if one takes *chametz* alchohol and uses it for rubbing on one's flesh or the like, this is certainly like eating, and it is appropriate to say that by [deriving] this benefit, one considers it important, even if it is not fit for a dog to eat. This is not because I mean to rule decisively that smearing is included in drinking in this regard. As this is a lengthy discussion, whether we prohibit rubbing soap made from *cheilev* (with a *tzeirei*). But benefiting from *cheilev* [without eating it] is not prohibited, unlike with *orla* and *chametz*, which are prohibited to benefit from. Accordingly, using them as a substance that one smears oneself with conveys importance upon them...

However, many other *poskim* maintain that using *chametz* for purposes other than eating does **not** confer halachic importance upon it, and therefore rule that one need not be particular about the soaps and creams used on Pesach. **Rav Ben Zion Abba Shaul** explains that, in the case of something unfit for the consumption of a dog, the principle of "assigning importance (*achshevei*)" applies only according to rabbinic law, and it is likewise only according to rabbinic law that smearing is likened to drinking. Consequently, where both of these factors are at play, there is no basis for adopting a stringent ruling.

---

25. Rav Moshe Sternbuch and Rav Yosef Shalom Eliashiv take a similar stringent approach.
26. Although he does not say so explicitly, the implication of this rationale seems to be that even keeping these products in one's possession is prohibited on Pesach.

33. שו"ת אור לציון | חלק ג, פרק ח, הערה ו

...מלבד שאף בסבון הנעשה מחלב נראה עיקר שאין בו איסור, ומשום שאין לומר סיכה כשתיה אלא בדבר הראוי לאכילה ולא בדבר פגום... אף שהסכימו הפוסקים לחוש לחידושו של הרא"ש שלענין אכילה אמרינן מדאכליה אחשביה, ואף זה אין זה אלא מדרבנן כמבואר בט"ז בסימן תמ"ב סעיף קטן ח'.

אם כן לענין סיכה, שכל דין סיכה כשתיה הוא מדרבנן... לא נוסיף לומר מדסך ביה אחשביה, אלא כל שנפסל מאכילת כלב קודם זמנו, מותר ליהנות ממנו בכל צורה, ואף דרך סיכה. ועל כן **אין צריך להחמיר ולחזור אחר סבונים וחומרי ניקוי, בשמים, ותמרוקים שאינם ראויים אף לאכילת כלב שיהו דוקא כשרים לפסח.**

Responsa Ohr L'tziyon, Vol. 3, Ch. 8, n. 6

...Apart from the fact that it appears correct that there is not even a prohibition against soap made from *cheilev*, because one can only say that smearing is like drinking regarding something that it is fit for consumption, not regarding something that has been rendered unfit... although the *poskim* agree that one should have concern for the novel principle of the Rosh, that regarding eating, if a person eats something, he conveys importance to it, this itself is only on a rabbinic level, as is explained by the *Taz*.

Accordingly, regarding smearing, where the entire halacha that smearing is equivalent to drinking is rabbinic... we do not add to this, to say that if one smears oneself with a substance, he conveys importance to it. Rather, anything that is unfit for a dog to eat before the time [of the prohibition of *chametz* takes effect], it is permitted to benefit from it in any manner, even through smearing. Therefore, **one need not be stringent and search for soaps and cleaning agents, perfumes and cosmetics that are not even fit for a dog to eat, that they should be specifically kosher for Pesach.**

Similarly, **Rav Moshe Feinstein**,[27] **Rav Nissim Karelitz**,[28] and **Rav Asher Weiss**[29] all rule that no *hechsher* is required for soaps and creams for Pesach. This is also the position of most Kashrut agencies in the United States, such as the **OU, Chicago Rabbinical Council (CRC)**, and **Star-K.**[30]

Rav Eliezer Melamed observes that since the majority of soaps and creams do not contain *chametz*, even those who wish to be stringent in this regard only need do so regarding soaps and creams that are known to contain *chametz*. If one is not sure, one may assume that a particular soap or cream does not contain *chametz*.[31]

---

27. Responsa *Igrot Moshe*, O.C. 3:62.
28. *Chut Shani, Pesach*, O.C. 442:10.
29. *Haggada shel Pesach, Minchat Asher, siman* 24.
30. See, e.g., https://oukosher.org/passover/guidelines/non-food-items/non-food-items, www.star-k.org/articles/articles/seasonal/4614/pesach-cosmetics-and-personal-care; and https://consumer.crckosher.org/pesach-faqs/oats-in-soap. It should be noted that some people are personally stricter to use dishwashing soap that is kosher for Pesach since it comes in contact with dishes on which food is placed.
31. *Peninei Halakha, Pesach* 8:9, n. 11.

Toothpaste

We have seen above that most *poskim* permit the use of all soaps and creams on Pesach, since eating them is repugnant, even for a dog. Is the same true for toothpaste, mouthwash and the like, which are not repugnant, and are used orally?[32] Although one does not normally consume these products intentionally, one might easily swallow small amounts.

The first question that must be investigated is a factual question – would a dog eat toothpaste? The answer is not as obvious as it may seem. **Rav Yosef Dov Soloveitchik** is often quoted as ruling that toothpaste need not have a *hechsher* for Pesach, as a dog would not eat it. The following amusing incident is related by **Rav Chaim Jachter** and others.

34. Rav Chaim Jachter, "Cosmetics and Toiletries for Pesach"[33]

A charming anecdote that occurred in Rav Yosef Dov Soloveitchik's Shiur at Yeshiva University in the 1970's (reported by Rav Yosef Adler and many others) is often cited in support of the common practice to be lenient. The Rav stated in Shiur that toothpaste is not Ra'ui Liachilat Kelev (unfit for canine consumption) and thus one is permitted to consume it on Pesach even if it contains Chametz. The next day in Shiur a student raised his hand and explained that he conducted an "experiment" the night before. He related that he placed toothpaste in his dog's feeding bowl to see if his dog would eat it – and indeed, the dog ate the toothpaste!! Rav Soloveitchik simply responded, "Your dog is crazy." This story illustrates the ruling that we cited last week from Rav Soloveitchik that the standards of edibility are not determined by aberrant behavior.

The difficulty in making this judgement is also illustrated by Rav Jachter in the same source.

35. Ibid.

I recall that in 1986 I told Rav Yehuda Amital that Rav Soloveitchik stated that toothpaste was not Ra'ui Liachilat Kelev. Rav Amital responded that he disagreed as he recalled that in the Russian labor camps during World War Two, people would put toothpaste on their bread to give it some taste. Rav Amital's response illustrates the difficulty (and subjectivity) involved in assessing what is considered Ra'ui Liachilat Kelev.

RABBI JOSEPH BAER HALEVI SOLOVEITCHIK – "THE RAV" (1903–1993)

Rav Joseph Baer (Yosef Dov) HaLevi Soloveitchik was the oldest child of Rav Moshe and Pesha (Feinstein) Soloveitchik, born in Pruzhana (today's Belarus) in 1903. His father taught him Gemara and the Rambam in the analytic "Brisker method" of his grandfather, Rav Chaim Soloveitchik. He also studied academics, earning a doctorate in philosophy from the University of Berlin. In 1931, already known as an outstanding *talmid chacham*, he married Tonya Lewit. In 1932, the family left for the United States, and Rav Soloveitchik became the chief rabbi of 11 synagogues in greater Boston.

Rav Soloveitchik was engaged in communal life, founding the Maimonides School (1937) and improving kashrut and protecting the *shochatim* (slaughterers). In 1941, Rav Soloveitchik was appointed to succeed his late father at the Rabbi Isaac Elchanan

32. *Poskim* also discuss whether toothpaste requires kashrut certification for the rest of the year. This was discussed previously in volume 6, *shiur* 6, sources 15–22.

33. The complete article can be viewed online at www.koltorah.org/halachah/cosmetics-and-toiletries-for-pesach-part-three-by-rabbi-chaim-jachter.

Theological Seminary (RIETS), part of the school which would later become Yeshiva University. He continued to split time between Boston and New York until 1985.

On a national and international scale, "the Rav," as he is known in many circles in the Diaspora, was revered as an authority with contemporary sensibilities. Although he did not publish responsa or works of practical halacha, he ruled on matters of communal interest, particularly in his roles with the Rabbinical Council of America and Mizrachi. In addition, his Gemara *shiurim*, public lectures in Boston and New York, and assorted philosophical writings influenced generations and cemented him as a figure of unique authority in American and world Jewry. Since his passing in 1993, students and relatives have published many of his teachings, on Torah, Gemara, halachic practice, and Jewish philosophy.

Nonetheless, today it is usually assumed that toothpaste would not be eaten by a dog. The question remains, however, since we put toothpaste in our mouths, and even swallow small amounts unintentionally, does this convey importance to the toothpaste, meaning that it would require a *hechsher*? It may be possible to derive an answer to this from a ruling of the ***Terumat HaDeshen*** regarding ink containing beer. He writes that even if one sometimes holds the quill with one's mouth and may inadvertently taste some of the ink, this does not convey importance to the ink, and one need not be concerned about writing with this ink on Pesach.

ו Responsa Terumat HaDeshen Siman 129

Question:[34] Ink that is cooked with barley beer, and among the ingredients of the ink are, e.g., ground gallnuts and vitriol, which we call *glitzen shtein*, is writing with it permitted on Pesach or not?

Answer: It appears that writing with it is permitted... It seems that ink cooked with the above ingredients, which are more bitter than wormwood and aloe, certainly becomes unfit for a dog's consumption before Pesach...

Although Tosafot (*Avoda Zara* 33a)... write in the name of Ri that one may not write with ink cooked with *yayin nesech*,[35] according to the opinion that benefiting from regular wine [of gentiles] is prohibited; and even [according to] Rabbeinu Tam, who rules that benefiting from regular wine [of gentiles] is permitted, it proper to be stringent, as sometimes one puts the quill in one's mouth while there is still ink on it, and it is made from wine of gentiles... **one can say that we need not be stringent in our case [regarding Pesach, and not non-kosher wine].**

As it appears that that which the above Geonim prohibited eating *chametz* that was charred before its time [i.e., before Pesach], is because since one considers it [important]

36. שו"ת תרומת הדשן | סימן קכט

שאלה: דיו שהוא מבושל בשכר שעורים, ובסממני הדיו כגון טחינת עפצים ויטראו"ל שאנו קורין גליצ"ן שטיי"ן, שרי לכתוב בו בפסח או לאו?

תשובה: יראה דשרי לכתוב בו... ונראה דדיו המבושל בסממנים דלעיל, שהן מרים יותר מראש ולענה ודאי נפסל משתיית כלב קודם הפסח...

ואף על גב דכתבו תוספות (עבודה זרה לג. ד"ה האי)... בשם ר"י דדיו המבושל ביין נסך, למאן דפסק דסתם יינות אסור בהנאה, לא שרי לכתוב באותו דיו. ואפילו רבינו תם דפסק סתם יינות מותר בהנאה, נכון להחמיר משום דלפעמים נותן הקולמוס בפיו בעוד שיש עליו דיו, והוא נעשה מיין של נכרים עד כאן... **ויש לומר דלא צריכינן להחמיר בנידון דידן.**

דנראה דהא דאסרי גאונים דלעיל חמץ שחרכו קודם זמנו באכילה, היינו משום דכיון דמחשבינן

34. It should be noted that although the *Terumat HaDeshen* is written in question-and-answer form, unlike most other halachic responsa, both the questions and the answers were compiled by the author himself as an educational tool.

35. This term literally means wine that was poured as a libation for idolatry, but here is used to refer to any wine made by gentiles. Such wine is forbidden for drinking, but opinions differ regarding deriving other benefit from this wine.

ובעי למיכליה לא איפסיל לדידיה מאכילת אדם, וכל שכן מאכילת כלב... אבל **במה שנותן הקולמוס בפיו כדי להחזיקה, ואגב זה טועם מן הדיו בלא כוונה לא מחשבינן בהא מידי.**

and wishes to eat it, for him it is not unfit for a person to eat, and certainly not unfit for a dog... But **when one puts the quill in his mouth to hold it and incidentally tastes some of the ink unintentionally, one does not consider it [important] at all.**

The ***Shulchan Aruch*** (O.C. 442:10) rules accordingly. Based on this ruling, **Rav Ben Zion Abba Shaul** writes that one may use any toothpaste on Pesach, even if it contains ingredients derived from *chametz*. The same applies to lipstick.

37. שו"ת אור לציון | חלק ג, פרק ח, הערה ו

ואף משחת שיניים שפסולה מאכילת כלב מותר להשתמש בה בפסח. ואין לחוש שמא יבלע ממנה. שכיון שלא מכוין לאכילה, לא שייך למימר מדאכליה אחשביה. וכן מבואר בדברי התרומת הדשן...

והוא הדין לענין אודם שנפסל מאכילת כלב, ונותנים אותו על השפתיים, שאין לחוש בו משום חמץ בפסח, שאף שלפעמים נבלע עם האוכל, כיון שאין מכוונים לאכילה שרי, וכמו שנתבאר, ואין צריך לחזר שיהא כשר לפסח דוקא.

Responsa Ohr L'tziyon, Vol. 3, Ch. 8, n. 6

Toothpaste that is unfit for a dog to eat is permitted for use on Pesach, and one need not be concerned that one may swallow some of it. As since one does not intend to eat it, it is not appropriate to say that by eating it, one conveys importance to it. This is also clear from the comments of the *Terumat HaDeshen*...

The same applies to lipstick that is unfit for a dog to eat, that is placed on the lips. One need not be concerned about it due to *chametz* on Pesach, as although sometimes it gets swallowed together with food, since one does not intend to eat it, it is permitted, as has been explained. There is no need to make an effort that it should be kosher for Pesach.

As mentioned earlier, Rav Yosef Dov Soloveitchik also takes that approach. Others, such as **Rav Eliezer Melamed**, rule that if the toothpaste has a pleasant taste, it is not similar to ink and one should only use it on Pesach if it is certified as kosher for Pesach.

38. פניני הלכה | פסח ח:ט

משחת שיניים שיש לה טעם טוב אסורה בלא הכשר לפסח כשאר מוצרי מזון.

Peninei Halakha, Pesach 8:9

Toothpastes must be certified kosher for Pesah because they are flavored and thus like any other food product.

Rav Shimon Eider writes that although toothpaste may technically be permitted, one should try to use brands that are kosher for Pesach since it is not difficult to obtain.

39. Halachos of Pesach, p. 27

Although it may be considered as נפסל מאכילת כלב, many Poskim hold that since toothpaste approved for use during Pesach is available, one should not use any containing alcohol or other chometz.[36]

36. In n. 108, Rav Eider writes that he heard this orally from both Rav Moshe Feinstein and Rav Aharon Kotler. The CRC and Star-K take the same position (https://consumer.crckosher.org/otcmeds/toothpaste and www.star-k.org/articles/articles/seasonal/4614/pesach-cosmetics-and-personal-care). The OU writes that *poskim* disagree about toothpaste (https://oukosher.org/passover/guidelines/non-food-items/toothpaste-mouthwash-and-lipsticks).

Medicines

Background

The question of whether medicine must be kosher for Pesach has also become a major one in the modern era. Some medicines contain ingredients derived from *chametz,* and contemporary *poskim* have had to clarify how those who need such medicines should conduct themselves on Pesach. Unlike toothpaste, medicines are intentionally swallowed, and therefore the rationale quoted above for permitting toothpaste may not apply to medicines.

However, the **Gemara (*Masechet Pesachim*)** discusses whether prohibited substances may be used for medicinal purposes. According to one answer of the Gemara, it is permitted to benefit from prohibited items in an unusual manner, even if one's life is not in danger.[37]

ח Masechet Pesachim 25b

40. מסכת פסחים כה:

מר בר רב אשי אשכחיה לרבינא דשייף לה לברתיה בגוהרקי דערלה, אמר ליה: אימור דאמור רבנן בשעת הסכנה, שלא בשעת הסכנה מי אמור?

אמר ליה: האי אישתא צמירתא נמי כשעת הסכנה דמיא. איכא דאמרי, אמר ליה: מידי דרך הנאה קא עבידנא?

The Gemara relates: **Mar bar Rav Ashi found Ravina rubbing his daughter with unripe** olives [*guharkei*] **of *orla*** for medicinal purposes.[38] Mar bar Rav Ashi **said to him: Say** that **the Sages said** that one may derive benefit from such a prohibited item **at a time of danger;** however, **who says** that one is permitted to do so **when** it is **not a time of danger?**

Ravina **said to him: A high fever is also deemed a time of danger,** and one may derive benefit from a prohibited item in such a situation. **Some say** that Ravina **said to him** as follows: **Am I deriving benefit in a usual manner?** The usual way to derive benefit from these olives is to use them after they have become ripe, so that their oil can be drawn out. Since Ravina was not deriving benefit in the usual manner, he was permitted to do so, although his daughter's life was not in danger.

The ***Shulchan Aruch*** rules in accordance with this leniency.

א Shulchan Aruch, Yoreh De'ah 155:3

41. שולחן ערוך | יו"ד קנה:ג

בשאר איסורים מתרפאים במקום סכנה, אפילו דרך הנאתן. ושלא במקום סכנה, כדרך הנאתן אסור; שלא כדרך הנאתן, מותר,

One may use other prohibited items [or actions] for healing [other than murder, *arayot* relationships and idolatry] in a case of danger [to human life], even in their usual manner. In a case where there is no danger, using them in their usual manner of benefit is prohibited. Using them in an unusual manner is permitted,

37. It a person's life is in danger, it goes without saying that any medicine needed to cure him is permitted. Our discussion relates only to someone whose life is not in danger but is sick to some degree.

38. Like *chametz* on Pesach, deriving any benefit from *orla* is usually prohibited.

חוץ מכלאי הכרם ובשר בחלב שאסורים אפילו שלא כדרך הנאתן אלא במקום סכנה.

apart from cross-bred produce in a vineyard and meat together with milk, which are prohibited even in an unusual manner,[39] other than in a case of danger.

Pills

On the basis of the Gemara and *Shulchan Aruch* cited above, contemporary *poskim* analyze whether swallowing medicines containing *chametz* is considered a "usual" or "unusual" manner of benefit. This question pertains to both swallowing *chametz* in tablets as well as medicine in liquid form that is mixed with other substances that are not usually eaten. In addition, in light of the sources discussed earlier in the *shiur*, *poskim* address whether medicine is considered to be an "edible" or "inedible" substance, and if the latter, whether its status should be more lenient than other regular food.

The ***Chazon Ish*** writes that as long as the ingredients derived from *chametz* are not the active ingredients and the medicine is not fit to eat (other than as medicine), no prohibition applies and one may take it on Pesach. Although one intentionally swallows it, doing so only conveys importance to the active ingredients, not to ingredients which one has no specific interest in consuming.

42. חזון איש | או"ח קטז:ח

טבלאות רפואה שמעורב בהן קמח... ואם הן מעורבין בדברים שאינן ראויין לאכילת אדם אין בהן משום חמץ כדין נפסל מאכילת אדם, כיון דאי אפשר להפריד הקמח וגם אינו ראוי לחמע בו ומותר לבולען בפסח לרפואה.

ואף למאי דמשמע מהאחרונים ז"ל דלאכול לכתחלה אסור אפילו חמץ שנפסל מאכילת כלב... מכל מקום על ידי תערובות שאר דברים מותר **דלא שייך כאן אחשביה דדעתו על הסמים.**

ואם לא נפסלו לאכילת אדם אסורין באכילה וחייבין לבער.

Chazon Ish, Orach Chaim 116:8

Medical pills that contain flour... if they are mixed with ingredients that are not fit for human consumption, [the prohibition against] *chametz* does not apply to them, in accordance with the halacha of food rendered unfit for human consumption, since it is impossible to separate the flour, and it is also not suitable for fermenting,[40] it is permitted to swallow them on Pesach for medical purposes.

Although according to what is implied by the *Acharonim* that *ab initio*, even *chametz* that has become unfit for a dog to eat is prohibited to eat... nevertheless, when mixed with other ingredients it is permitted. **As [the principle that eating] conveys importance to it does not apply here, as his intention is directed toward the medicinal ingredients.**

But if [the medicine] has not been rendered unfit for human consumption, consuming it is prohibited, and one must destroy it.

Rav Moshe Feinstein goes further and permits taking medicines containing *chametz* on Pesach even if the active ingredients are *chametz*.[41] He explains that consuming substances only for medicinal purposes does not convey importance to them.

39. The reason for these exceptions is because the Torah expresses these prohibitions without referring specifically to eating.
40. Based on the explanation of the Ran in source 20, the *Chazon Ish* maintains that *chametz* that is not fit for human consumption but is fit for a dog to eat is prohibited only if it can be used to ferment other dough.
41. See also Rav Asher Weiss, Haggada shel Pesach, *siman* 22, who assumes that the *Chazon Ish* also agrees with Rav Moshe Feinstein regarding this point, and only mentioned the fact that *chametz* is a non-active ingredient as an extra reason for leniency.

43. שו"ת אגרות משה | או"ח ב:צב

ובדבר הרפואה שאתה צריך ליקח... ובעצם אף בלא סכנה אין חשש דכבר נבטל קודם הפסח משם אוכל, **ואחשביה לא שייך בדבר שלוקח לרפואה** דאף דברים מרים ומאוסים נוטלין לרפואה. **ולכן אין לך מה לחשוש ותקח הרפואה כפי שאמר לך הרופא והשם יתברך יתן שיהיה זה לרפואה.**

Responsa Igrot Moshe, Orach Chaim 2:92

Regarding the medicine that you need to take... In actuality, even without danger [to life] there is no concern, as it already lost the status of food before Pesach, and [**the principle that eating**] **conveys importance to it does not apply to something that one takes as medicine**, as even bitter and repulsive substances are taken as medicine. **Therefore, you have nothing to be concerned about, and you should take the medicine as the doctor told you.** May Hashem grant that it should serve as a cure.

Rav Shlomo Zalman Auerbach questions whether it is true that one does not attach importance to the non-active ingredients of medicines, as they are necessary to facilitate taking the medicine. However, he concludes that this is not considered the usual manner of consuming *chametz* if the medicine is indeed considered unfit for eating. On the other hand, some medicines may be considered fit for eating, even if they are not usually consumed due to our delicate nature.

44. שו"ת מנחת שלמה | א:יז

לכאורה יש לדון כיון דנקטינן שגם בליעה ללא שום לעיסה חשיב כדרך אכילה, אם כן בנידון דידן שעושין בתחלה את העיסה שהיא חמץ נוקשה אך ורק לדבק בה את התרופה וגם להחליק ולהמתיק בכך קצת את המרירות להקל על החולים להכניס את הגלולה לתוך הפה ולבלוע, וכיון שכן אפשר דהרי זה חשיב כחמץ שעומד למאכל עבור חולים מפני שהם צריכים לכך בגלל התרופה שמעורבת בה, ופשוט הדבר שהמערב תרופה מותרת שהיא מרה תוך יין מתוק של ערלה דודאי אסור אף לחולה שאין בו סכנה, וגם כאן הבולע מחשיב מאד את החמץ מפני שעל ידי זה הוא יכול לבלוע התרופה וגם החמץ נראה לעינים יותר מהתרופה עצמה...

אך אף על פי כן נראה דדוקא באוכל גמור שרגילים ללעוס ולאכול רק אז אמרינן שגם בליעה חשיב כדרך אכילה, מה שאין כן **בדבר דלא חזי כלל לאכילה ועומד רק לבלוע וגם רק לחולים כמו גלולות דנידון דידן, שפיר חשיב לכולי עלמא שלא כדרך אכילה ושרי לחולה שאין בו סכנה**, שהרי גם מלוגמא

Responsa Minchat Shlomo 1:17

At first glance, there is room to consider that since we hold that even swallowing without any chewing is considered a normal manner of eating, then in our case, where they initially make the dough into *chametz nuksheh* only for the purpose of binding the medicine and also to smooth and slightly sweeten its bitterness, to make it easier for the ill to put the pill into their mouth and to swallow, perhaps this is considered *chametz* that is food for the sick, as they need it because of the medicine mixed into it. It is obvious that if one mixes a permitted but bitter medicine into sweet wine of *orla*, it would certainly be prohibited even for a sick person whose life is not in danger. Here too, the one who swallows the medicine conveys significant importance to the *chametz* because through it, he is able to swallow the medicine, and the *chametz* is more visible than the medicine itself...

Nevertheless, it appears that only with respect to real food, which people ordinarily chew and eat, do we say that swallowing also constitutes normal eating. This is not the case **with something that is not fit for eating at all and is intended only to be swallowed, and only by sick people, such as the pills in our case, it is indeed considered not the normal manner of eating according to all views and is permitted for a sick person whose life is not in danger.** As even concerning dressings and

ורטיה על מכתו לאחר שכבר נעשו הרי הם עומדים לכך ואפילו הכי שרי...

יש הרבה תרופות דאף שסם התרופה מר מעט מכל מקום אפשר דלא חשיב כאינו ראוי למאכל אדם מפני זה שאנחנו מפונקים... ולכן **אפשר שצריכים לבדוק היטב כל סוג לדעת אם זה חשיב כעירב בו דברים מרים הפוסלים מאכילת אדם.**

plasters [made from ingredients that are prohibited to benefit from], once they have been prepared, they are designated for such use, but they are nevertheless permitted [since the original ingredients are not usually used for this purpose]…

There are many medicines where although the medicinal substance is slightly bitter, nevertheless, it is possible that they may not be considered unfit for human consumption just because we are so pampered… Therefore, **it may be necessary to examine each type carefully in order to determine whether it is considered to have been mixed with bitter ingredients that disqualify it from human consumption.**

Who May Rely on Leniencies for Medicine

In the continuation of the same *teshuva* cited in the previous source, Rav Auerbach is unsure as to whether this leniency applies to anyone with even a minor ailment, or only to one who has an illness that significantly limits his ability to function normally (*choleh she'ein bo sakana*).[42]

45. שם

לא ברור אצלי מהו הגדר של חולה לענין נידון דידן שהרי מצינן דאסרי רבנן רפואה בשבת ולא התירו אלא לחולה שאין בו סכנה שנפל למשכב או כאיב לי טובא אבל לא עבור כאב ראש רגיל או כדור שינה וכדומה, ואם כן **אפשר שגם בנידון דידן לא שרי אלא בחולים כאלה**, אך גם אפשר דשאני שבת שעיקר איסור רפואה הוא עבור חולה ולכן אמרינן שרק בכי האי גוונא הוא דשרי, מה שאין כן בינדון דידן הרי יש גם שכתבו בדעת התוספות שמותר אפילו לבריא, ואם כן **אפשר דבכל ענין של חולי קצת שרי וצריך עיון.**

Ibid.

It is not clear to me what the definition of "ill" is in this regard. As we find that the Sages prohibited medical treatment on Shabbat and permitted it only for one who is bedridden but not in danger, or one who is in significant pain, but not for an ordinary headache or for a sleeping pill and the like. If so, **perhaps in our case, too, it would be permitted only for those who are sick to this degree.** However, it is also possible that Shabbat is different, as the main prohibition against medical treatment is for one who is ill, and therefore we say that treatment is only permitted in such a case [of significant illness]. But in our case, some write that according to Tosafot [using prohibited substances in an unusual manner for medicine] is permitted even for a healthy person.[43] Accordingly, **it is possible that this is permitted for any slight illness. This requires [further] analysis.**

Rav Ovadia Yosef rules that only a *choleh she'ein bo sakana* may take medicine containing *chametz*, not one who has a minor ailment. He adds that today most medicines do not contain *chametz*, and although they often contain *kitniyot*, one certainly should not be stringent in this regard. One who is dangerously

42. According to the *Chazon Ish* and Rav Moshe Feinstein in sources 42–43, it appears that there is no distinction, and consuming *chametz* in this form is permitted even for one who is healthy.

43. This conclusion can be inferred from several places, such as Tosafot, *Pesachim* 26a, s.v. *shani*; 29b, s.v. *ein*; and *Kiddushin* 56b, s.v. *hamekadesh*. See *Mishneh L'melech*, *Yesodei HaTorah* 5:8.

ill who requires medicine containing *chametz* should buy it before Pesach and intend not to acquire the *chametz*. If it tastes good, it should be taken together with something bitter-tasting if possible.

46. חזון עובדיה | פסח, מצרכי מזון הכשרים לפסח יח

טבליות וכדורי הרגעה, נגד מיחושי ראש וכאב שיניים, מותר להשתמש בהם בפסח, אפילו יש בהם תערובת חמץ (עמילן של חיטה), כל שטעמם פגום וכבר נפסלו מאכילת הכלב קודם הפסח, ובולעים אותם כמות שהם. ואם נזקק לתרופות בפסח עצמו, מותר לקנות מבית מרקחת של גוי תרופות שיש בהם חמץ ונפסלו מאכילת הכלב. **וכל זה בחולה שחלה כל גופו, ואף על פי שאין בו סכנה, אבל אם הוא מיחוש בעלמא, אין להתיר.**

וטבליות שמוצצים אותם וטעמם טוב אסור למצוץ מהם בפסח לרפואת דלקת-גרון וכיוצא בזה, אלא אם כן נתברר שנעשו בעמילן של תירס או תפוחי אדמה. ומה טוב לבקש מהרופא בעת רישום התרופות שירשום לו תרופות שאינן מכילות חשש חמץ כתחליף לאלה שיש בהן חשש תערובת חמץ.

ובזמנינו רוב התרופות עשויות ללא חמץ כלל, אלא עשויות עם עמילן הנעשה מקטניות, (ואפילו המיעוט שמעורב בהם חמץ, החמץ נפסל מאכילת כלב לפני הפסח), **הילכך בודאי יש להתיר לחולה שאין בו סכנה לקחתם בפסח**, וחלילה לחולה כזה להחמיר על עצמו ולהפסיק לקחת הכדורים הנחוצים לו על פי הוראת רופא מומחה במשך הפסח, ובפרט במקום שיש חשש הכי קטן שהוא יגיע על ידי זה למצב אפילו של ספק סכנה.

חולה שיש בו סכנה ויודע שיצטרך להשתמש בפסח בתרופה שיש בה חמץ, יש לו לקנות התרופה קודם לפסח, ויכוין בפירוש שאינו רוצה לזכות בחמץ שבתרופה, ויניח אותה במקום מוצנע, וכשיצטרך יקח ממנה בכל פעם כפי הצורך. ואם התרופה טעימה לחיך, טוב שיתן בתוכה דבר מר, שתהיה שלא כדרך הנאתה, ובעודה בכפו יבלענה.

Chazon Ovadia, Pesach, Mitzrachei Mazon HaKesherim L'Pesach 18

It is permitted to use pills or painkillers for headaches and toothaches on Pesach, even if they contain *chametz* (wheat starch), as long as their taste is spoiled and they were rendered unfit for a dog to eat before Pesach, and one swallows them as they are. If one [starts to] require medication during Pesach itself, it is permitted to purchase medications that contain *chametz* which has been rendered unfit for a dog to eat from a non-Jewish pharmacy. **All of this applies to a person who is sick throughout his body, even if [his life] is not in danger. But if it is only a minor ailment, one should not permit this.**

Sucking pills that taste good to treat a sore throat or the like are prohibited on Pesach unless it has been verified that they are produced from corn starch or potato starch. It is proper to ask the doctor when prescribing medication to prescribe medication that does not contain anything that may be *chametz* as an alternative to those that do.

In our times, most medications are made entirely without *chametz*, but rather with starch produced from *kitniyot* (and even regarding the minority that contain *chametz*, that *chametz* is rendered unfit for a dog's consumption before Pesach). **Therefore, it is certainly permitted for a sick person whose life is not in danger to take such medication on Pesach** and such a patient should not, God forbid, be stringent upon himself and stop taking medication he requires according to the instruction of a qualified doctor during Pesach, especially where there is even the slightest concern that this may bring him into a situation of possible danger.

A dangerously ill patient who knows that he will need to use a medicine on Pesach that contains *chametz* should buy the medicine before Pesach and explicitly intend not to acquire ownership of the *chametz* within it. He should store it in a concealed place and when needed, he should take from it each time as required. If the medicine is tasty, it is proper to mix something bitter into it so that it is not benefited from in its standard manner, and he should swallow it immediately [lit. while it is still in his hand].

Rav Eliezer Melamed writes that most *poskim* permit taking medicines that contain denatured *chametz*, even for minor ailments, or simply as a preventative measure.

47. פניני הלכה | פסח ח:ז

יש מדקדקים שמשתדלים לא לבלוע אפילו תרופות מרות שיש בהן תערובת חמץ, מפני שחוששים לדעת אותם פוסקים בודדים הסוברים שהואיל והתרופה חשובה לנו, אין היא נחשבת פסולה מאכילת כלב, ואסור מדברי חכמים לבולעה. ויש שהתירו לבלוע תרופות מרות שמעורב בהן חמץ לחולים שנאלצים לשכב במיטתם או שכל גופם כואב, אבל החמירו למי שסובל מכאבים ומיחושים קלים, שלא יטול תרופה זו. **ודעת רוב הפוסקים, שמותר ליטול תרופה מרה שיש בה חמץ לצורך כל חולה, ואפילו לצורך הפגת כאבים קלים או מניעת מחלות או חיזוק הגוף.**

Peninei Halakha, Pesach 8:7

Some meticulously observant people try to avoid even bitter medicines that contain Hametz. They show concern for the opinion of the few poskim who maintain that medicine is not considered unfit for a dog's consumption since we deem it significant, and it is thus rabbinically prohibited. Other poskim permit swallowing bitter medicines that contain Hametz starch for one who is bedridden or whose entire body is in pain, but rule stringently for one suffering from mild aches and pains. **But the view of most poskim is that bitter medicines containing Hametz starch may be taken by any ill person and even only to reduce mild pain, as a prophylactic, or to fortify the body.**

Liquid and Chewable Medicines

Concerning chewable or liquid medications that have a more pleasant taste, many *poskim*[44] consider this to have the same status as regular food, and those that may have *chametz* are problematic in most cases (other than potential danger to life). As we saw in source 46, Rav Ovadia clearly states that one may not consume such medicine without determining that it does not contain *chametz*. **Rav Shimon Eider** summarizes the issue in the following excerpt:

48. "Halachos of Pesach," p. 24

Liquid medicines are usually a more serious problem. Many liquid medicines contain grain alcohol in high percentages. Grain alcohol may be חמץ גמור (actual chametz). Liquid medicines may also contain chametz in the flavoring. This is especially true for cough medicines. Where one knows before Pesach that a liquid medicine will be required, a Rav should be consulted for advice how to mix it – in order to use it during Pesach.[45]

---

44. Responsa *Ohr L'tzion* 3:8:2; *Ashrei Ha'Ish*, O.C. 58:11; *Shemirat Shabbat K'hilchata* 40:87; and *Chut Shani, Pesach*, p. 95.

45. When necessary, some authorities suggest consuming the medicine inside an empty medicine cap (available at pharmacies) or other options designed to reduce the the severity of the action by not consuming it in the normal manner. It should be noted that some *poskim* consider the possibility that even many liquid medicines are not considered to have the halachic status of regular food since no one would ever ingest them normally if not medically necessary. Therefore, in their opinion, when necessary, those types of medicine would be permitted on Pesach. See, e.g., www.crcweb.org/Sappirim/Sappirim%20 14%20%28Oct%202008%29.pdf.

The **OU** offers a series of guidelines concerning medicine on Pesach and specifies a number of important details concerning liquid and chewable medicine. They also offer an important warning that a person should never discontinue a medication prescribed by a doctor, even on Pesach, without first consulting the doctor and one's rabbi.

49. OU Guidelines for Medication[46]

Guidelines for Medication

1. You should exercise extreme caution and consult with your doctor and rabbi before making a decision not to take a medicine.

2. Known and tested medications in the form of creams, non-chewable pills and injections may be owned, used and consumed on Passover, even if they contain *chametz* or *kitniyot,* since they are inedible. This covers most medicines used by adults.[47] However, if an equally effective *chametz*-free alternative is available or procurable, this should be used instead.[48]

- It is permissible to grind pills and mix the powder into food items so that a child can take medicine on Passover. However, a doctor must be consulted to make sure that the child is getting the correct dosage and that the potency of the pill is not compromised by altering its consistency.

3. Liquid medicines, chewable pills and pills coated with a flavored glaze are considered palatable and may contain *chametz.* Also gelcaps may present a problem because they may contain non-kosher edible gelatin. Therefore:

- If possible, they should be replaced, under the direction of a doctor, with a non-chewable, uncoated pill.
- If substitution is not possible and the person is in a state of *sakana* or *safek sakana* (any possible danger to human life), the medication may be owned and consumed. The same applies if the condition is not yet a *safek sakana* but may deteriorate to that point. A rabbi should be consulted as to whether it is preferable to purchase the medicine before or during Passover, and as to how to dispose of the medicine once the danger passes.
- If substitution is not possible and a doctor determines that there is no possibility of *sakana* if the person does not take the medicine, a rabbi should be consulted. He may be able to determine that the medicine does not contain *chametz* and/or *kitniyot,* or he may decide that the medicine may be consumed due to the seriousness of the patient's condition.

4. In many cases, medicinal items which contain *kitniyot* are permitted for people who are ill. Questions on this issue should be directed to your rabbi...

8. Products should be purchased before Passover and be maintained segregated from Kosher for Passover foods.

---

46. The full list of guidelines are available at https://oukosher.org/passover/medicine-guidelines.

47. With regard to vitamins, Rav Yisroel Belsky rules that in general, they should not be used without certification (except perhaps in cases when prescribed by a doctor). However, Rav Hershel Schachter rules that vitamins also may be taken when needed without certification (see https://res.cloudinary.com/ouwp/images/v1675094278/Kosher/kosher/Daf-12-2/Daf-12-2.pdf?_i=AA). The same dispute may apply as well to vitamins on Pesach. Today, there are often *chametz*-free vitamin substitutes that can be obtained, and one should try to use these if possible.

48. See Responsa *Tzitz Eliezer* (10:25:20) and *Minchat Asher, Haggada shel Pesach* (*siman* 22), who suggest this as well.

There are many guides today, both in the United States and Israel, that provide lists of medications permitted on Pesach. These allow individuals to avoid pills that may contain *chametz* by seeking alternatives, as recommended by numerous *poskim* and also help ensure that liquid or chewable medicines are suitable for use on Pesach.[49]

Medicines on Pesach often create tension between two important values: fidelity to the laws of *chametz* and the need to care properly for one's health. Contemporary halacha recognizes this complexity and provides multiple legitimate pathways – leniencies regarding inedible ingredients, distinctions between pills and liquids, and room for rabbinic guidance in individual cases. As a result, most people who genuinely require medication can, with proper consultation, find a halachically acceptable solution without compromising their wellbeing.

49. In North America, notable lists include the *Star-K Pesach Guide*, which features a section titled "Passover Medicines and Cosmetics" by Rav Gershon Bess; Rabbi Avrohom Blumencrantz, *Halachic Digest for Pesach*; the Chicago Rabbinical Council (CRC) Medicine and Cosmetics List; and the Kashruth Council of Canada (COR) list of *chametz*-free medications, available at https://cor.ca/passover/chametz-free-medications. In Israel, these include lists compiled by Clalit Health Services and the Edah Charedit, both available on the Kosharot website: www.kosharot.co.il/index2.php?id=44166&lang=HEB. For historical context, see also the Star-K article available at www.star-k.org/articles/articles/seasonal/369/history-of-passover-medicine-lists on a medicine list published in Germany in the 1920s, which was structured similarly to modern lists.

Machshava

Preparing for Pesach often involves long hours of cleaning. The process can feel exhausting, tedious, and at times overwhelming. Chazal, however, offer a perspective that gives this effort deeper meaning. The Gemara in ***Masechet Berachot*** teaches that the *yetzer hara* (the evil inclination) is referred to as *se'or,* the yeast which causes dough to rise and become *chametz.*

ח Masechet Berachot 17a

And after Rabbi Alexandri prayed, he would say the following: Master of the Universe, it is revealed and known before You that our will is to perform Your will, and what prevents us? On the one hand, **the yeast in the dough,** the evil inclination that is within every person; **and the subjugation to the kingdoms** on the other. **May it be Your will that You will deliver us from their hands,** of both the evil inclination and the foreign kingdoms, so that **we may return to perform the edicts of Your will with a perfect heart.**

48. מסכת ברכות יז.

ור' אלכסנדרי בתר דמצלי אמר הכי: רבון העולמים גלוי וידוע לפניך שרצוננו לעשות רצונך, ומי מעכב? שאור שבעיסה ושעבוד מלכיות. יהי רצון מלפניך שתצילנו מידם ונשוב לעשות חוקי רצונך בלבב שלם.

Why is the *yetzer hara* compared to *se'or,* which causes dough to rise and become *chametz*? The **Maharsha** explains that this comparison highlights the way *chametz* expands beyond its original state, much like the human tendency toward excess.

א Maharsha, Chidushei Agadot, Berachot 17a

The evil inclination entices a person to go to extremes even within what is technically permitted, such as acting with arrogance or indulging excessively in desire. Therefore, it is compared to the yeast in dough, which causes the dough to rise and become greater than it originally was.

49. מהרש"א | חידושי אגדות, ברכות יז.

והנה היצר הרע מסית שילך האדם בקצה האחד במותר לו כגון להתגאות ולהתנהג במותר התאוה וע"כ מדמה ליה לשאור שבעיסה שמגביה את העיסה ועושה אותה יותר מכמות שהיתה.

Chametz thus becomes a powerful symbol of arrogance and inflated self-importance. Just as leaven causes dough to rise, the *yetzer hara* causes a person to become "puffed up," distancing him from humility and proper perspective. This symbolism leads to a powerful insight regarding our preparations for Pesach. The **Radbaz** writes that the search for *chametz* can also be understood as a call for inner spiritual searching.

50. שו"ת רדב"ז | ג:תקמו

ועל כן אני סומך על מה שאמרו רבותינו ז"ל במדרשות כי חמץ בפסח רמז ליצר הרע והוא "שאור שבעיסה". ולכן כולו גרש יגרש אותו האדם מעליו ויחפש עליו בכל מחבואות מחשבותיו ואפילו כל שהוא לא בטיל.

א Responsa of the Radbaz 3:546

Therefore, I rely upon that which the Rabbis taught in their *midrashim* that *chametz* symbolizes the "evil inclination," the "yeast in the dough." Therefore, a person should utterly banish it from his midst and search for it everywhere it hides in his consciousness, as even the smallest amount is not nullified.

Just as we carefully search our homes for even the smallest crumb of *chametz*, we are called to search within ourselves as well for traces of arrogance, impatience, and other negative traits that may have accumulated throughout the year. The physical act of cleaning can thus become a form of spiritual *avodat Hashem*.

Rav David Brofsky develops another dimension of this idea. If *chametz* represents the *yetzer hara*, what is the connection between removing *chametz* and celebrating our freedom on Pesach? He explains that as we celebrate our freedom, we must keep our focus on Hashem and adopt a life of simplicity.

51. הרב דוד ברובסקי | "מבוא להלכות פסח ואיסור חמץ"

מהו הקשר בין יצר הרע – כפי שהוא מיוצג על ידי החמץ – ובין חג הפסח, שמנציח את גאולתנו משעבוד מצרים?

ניתן להציע כי יחד עם היציאה מהעבדות הפיזית של מצרים אנו דוחים את "סיר הבשר" (שמות טז, ג) המצרי, במובן החומרי שלו, ומקבלים במקום זאת כעבדי ה' חיים של פשטות. חיינו הינם 'תֵּאוֹצֶנְטְרִים'; הקב"ה הוא המרכזי ולא רצונותינו ותשוקותינו. מסיבה זו איננו אוכלים חמץ אלא מצה הקרויה 'לחם עוני' – לחם פשוט של אדם עני.

Rav David Brofsky, "Introduction to Chametz and the Laws of Pesach"[50]

What is the relevance of the evil inclination, as represented by *chametz*, to *Pesach*, the festival that commemorates our redemption from the bonds of Egyptian slavery?

Some suggest that upon attaining freedom from the physical slavery of Egypt, we reject the "fleshpots of Egypt" (*Shemot* 16:3). We reject the emphasis on physicality, and embrace, as servants of the Lord, a life of simplicity. Our lives are now "theocentric;" God is at the center, and not our own will and desires. We eat, therefore, not *chametz*, but *matza*, "*lechem oni*," the simple, poor-man's bread.

With this perspective, Pesach cleaning takes on greater meaning. As we remove *chametz* from our homes, we can reflect on the parallel process of removing "spiritual *chametz*" from within ourselves. Each act of sweeping, scrubbing, and searching becomes an opportunity to refine our character and renew our commitment to *avodat Hashem*. In this way, the physical act of cleaning becomes part of the broader process of preparing ourselves for the freedom that Pesach represents.

---

50 This article is available in both Hebrew and English on the Torat Har Etzion website at www.etzion.org.il/en/halakha/orach-chaim/holidays/laws-pesach-introduction-chametz-and-laws-pesach.

Summary of the Halachot of Toiletries and Medicine on Pesach

Bal Yeira'eh and Bal Yimatzei

1. ***Shemot*** – We must not be in possession of, or own, *chametz* during Pesach. One who eats *chametz* on Pesach is liable to *karet.*
2. **Gemara (*Masechet Pesachim*)** – These prohibitions only apply to one's own *chametz* or to *chametz* of a gentile which a Jew has accepted responsibility for. They apply irrespective of where the *chametz* is found.

Inedible Chametz

1. **Gemara (*Masechet Pesachim*)**
   a. ***Tanna Kamma*** – Moldy bread that is unfit for human consumption but would be eaten by a dog is considered food and is susceptible to *tumah.*
   b. **Rabbi Natan** – It is not considered food and is not susceptible to *tumah.*
2. **Rif, Ritva, *Shulchan Aruch*** – The moldy bread must be burned before Pesach, in accordance with the *Tanna Kamma,* but if it becomes unfit for a dog to eat, one would not need to burn it.
3. **Ran** – Although food that is not fit for human consumption is not usually significant, regarding *chametz* we are more stringent, as the Torah explicitly prohibits *se'or,* which is not fit for human consumption, since it can cause dough to ferment.
4. **Ra'ah** – There is no obligation to burn moldy bread even if a dog would eat it. The *baraita* does not obligate burning the bread together with ritually impure food.
5. **Gemara (*Masechet Pesachim*)** – According to the Mishna, *chametz nuksheh* (hardened *chametz*) is biblically prohibited on Pesach.
6. **Rashi, Rambam, Riva** – Cosmetics are an example of *chametz nuksheh* and are not subject to the punishment of *karet* because they are inedible. But one violates the biblical prohibition against possessing *chametz* if one owns such items.
7. **Rabbeinu Tam** – There is no biblical prohibition against owning *chametz nuksheh* on Pesach. It must only be removed from the table, i.e., not eaten.
8. **Ran** – Owning *chametz nuksheh* on Pesach is rabbinically prohibited, even according to the view that eating it on Pesach is only rabbinically prohibited.

9. ***Tur*** – According to the view that eating *chametz nuksheh* is only rabbinically prohibited, one may keep it on Pesach.
10. ***Shulchan Aruch*** – If one owned *chametz nuksheh* on Pesach, one may benefit from it after Pesach.
11. ***Magen Avraham, Mishna Berura*** – The ruling of the *Shulchan Aruch* is in accordance with the Ran, that owning *chametz nuksheh* on Pesach is rabbinically prohibited. *Chametz nuksheh* refers either to dough that has not fully leavened or to *chametz* that was never fully fit for human consumption. Owning *chametz* that was at one point edible is biblically prohibited on Pesach unless it became unfit for a dog.

- **Eating *Chametz* That Is Not Fit for a Dog**

1. **Gemara (*Masechet Pesachim*)** – It is permitted to derive benefit from *chametz* that became charred prior to the time that *chametz* became prohibited.
2. **Rosh** – Some say that even eating such *chametz* is permitted, but this is unreasonable. Rav Yehuda Bartzeloni concurs that this is prohibited.
3. **Ran** – Eating this *chametz* is permitted if it became charred before the time that *chametz* becomes prohibited.
4. ***Taz, Mishna Berura*** – The halacha is in accordance with the Rosh, but even according to this view, the prohibition against eating charred *chametz* is only rabbinic.

- **Mixtures Containing Inedible *Chametz***

1. **Gemara (*Masechet Pesachim*)**
   a. **Rabbi Meir, Rabbi Eliezer** – Mixtures containing *chametz* are biblically prohibited on Pesach.
   b. ***Chachamim*** – They are not prohibited on a biblical level.
2. **Rif** – According to the *Chachamim*, although one does not receive lashes for eating a mixture containing *chametz*, it is nevertheless prohibited.
3. **Rambam, *Shulchan Aruch*** – The biblical prohibition against owning *chametz* applies to mixtures containing *chametz*. If the mixture is not fit for (human) consumption, one may keep it but not eat it on Pesach.

Soaps and Creams

1. **Mishna (*Masechet Shabbat*)** – A verse in *Tehillim* alludes to the fact that applying oil to one's body is similar to drinking and therefore prohibited on Yom Kippur.
2. **Tosafot** – One may use soap made from non-kosher items, as smearing is only like drinking in relation to specific prohibitions.

3. ***Orchot Chaim*** – Smearing oneself with *cheilev* is prohibited.
4. ***Taz*** – We do not accept this stringency of the *Orchot Chaim* as halacha. However, the *Issur V'heter Ha'aroch* writes correctly that one may only smear oneself with *cheilev* in order to ease pain, not just for pleasure. Nonetheless, one need not prevent non-Jewish babysitters from smearing *cheilev* on the bodies of Jewish babies.
5. ***Shach*** – The rationale for this stringency is unclear. Nevertheless, the practice is to avoid using soap made from *cheilev*, and this is proper.
6. ***Aruch HaShulchan*** – Modern soap is repulsive even for a dog and may be used even if it contains *cheilev*.
7. ***Bi'ur Halacha*** – Common practice is to be lenient in this regard. But where possible, it is proper to use soap that does not contain *cheilev*.
8. **Rav Ovadia Yosef** – Anyone may use soap that contains *cheilev*, pig fat or the like.
9. **Rav Yirmiyah Cohen** – Since benefiting from *chametz* is prohibited even without eating it, using soaps and creams containing *chametz* may be problematic according to all views. Since they are made for washing, they may be prohibited even if not fit for a dog to eat.
10. **Rav Ben Zion Abba Shaul** – Using something otherwise unfit for a dog only conveys importance to it on a rabbinic level, and smearing oneself is only equivalent to drinking on a rabbinic level. Therefore, there is no need to rule stringently in this regard.
11. **Rav Moshe Feinstein, Rav Nissim Karelitz, Rav Asher Weiss** – No *hechsher* is required for soaps and creams for Pesach.
12. ***Peninei Halakha*** – Since the majority of soaps and creams do not contain *chametz*, if one is not sure, one may assume that a particular soap or cream does not contain *chametz*.

Toothpaste

1. **Rav Chaim Jachter** – Rav Soloveitchik stated that toothpaste is not fit for a dog to eat. Rav Yehuda Amital disagreed, as in the Russian labor camps during World War Two, people would put toothpaste on their bread to give it taste.
2. ***Terumat HaDeshen, Shulchan Aruch*** – One may write with ink containing beer, even if one sometimes holds the quill with one's mouth and may inadvertently taste some ink.
3. **Rav Ben Zion Abba Shaul** – One may use any toothpaste or lipstick on Pesach, even if it contains ingredients derived from *chametz*.

4. ***Peninei Halakha*** – If the toothpaste has a pleasant taste, one should only use it on Pesach if it is certified as kosher for Pesach.
5. **Rav Shimon Eider** – One should try to obtain brands that are kosher for Pesach, since this is not difficult.

Medicines

1. **Gemara (*Masechet Pesachim*), *Shulchan Aruch*** – It is permitted to benefit from prohibited items for medicinal purposes in an unusual manner.
2. ***Chazon Ish*** – If the ingredients derived from *chametz* are not the active ingredients, and the medicine is not fit to eat, one may take it on Pesach. Swallowing it only conveys importance to the active ingredients.
3. **Rav Moshe Feinstein** – One may take medicines containing *chametz* on Pesach even if the active ingredients are *chametz*, as consuming substances only for medicinal purposes does not convey importance to them.
4. **Rav Shlomo Zalman Auerbach** – Even the non-active ingredients of medicines are necessary to facilitate taking the medicine. However, if the medicine is not fit to eat, this is not considered the usual manner of consuming *chametz* and is permitted for medicinal purposes. But some medicines may be considered fit to eat, even if they are not usually consumed due to our delicate nature.
5. **Rav Shlomo Zalman Auerbach** – It is unclear if the leniency applies to anyone with even a minor ailment, or only to a *choleh she'ein bo sakana*.
6. **Rav Ovadia Yosef** – Only a *choleh she'ein bo sakana* may take medicine containing *chametz*, not one who has a minor ailment. Today most medicines do not contain *chametz*, and although they often contain *kitniyot*, one should not be stringent about this. One who is dangerously ill and requires medicine containing *chametz* should buy it before Pesach and intend not to acquire the *chametz*. If it tastes good, it should be taken together with something bitter-tasting, if possible.
7. ***Peninei Halakha*** – Most *poskim* permit taking medicines that contain denatured *chametz*, even for minor ailments or as a preventative measure.

Further Iyun

The Prohibition of Bal Yeira'eh and Bal Yimatzei in Mixtures of Chametz

Rav Barak Katz (Participant, Manhigut Toranit)

Sometimes, questions arise before Pesach regarding the permissibility of owning products that may contain small amounts of *chametz*. For example, must small bottles of perfume (5–10 ml) or medicines that contain a *chametz*-based ingredient be destroyed or sold before Pesach? More broadly, what is the halachic status of mixtures containing *chametz*? Must they be removed from one's possession before Pesach, or does the prohibition apply only to pure *chametz*?

For the purpose of clarifying the halachic principles, we will temporarily set aside an important practical factor: many such substances are not fit for consumption (*eino ra'ui le'achila*). Ignoring that consideration allows us to focus on the underlying question: does the prohibition of possessing *chametz* (*bal yeira'eh ubal yimatzei*) apply to mixtures that contain *chametz*? To answer this question, we must first examine the biblical source of the prohibition of possessing *chametz*.

The Biblical Source of *Bal Yeira'eh* and *Bal Yimatzei*

The Torah in several verses prohibits not only the consumption of *chametz* during Pesach, but also its presence in a Jew's possession. In *Shemot* 12:15, the Torah commands that leaven be removed from one's homes: "Seven days you shall eat matzah; however, on the first day you shall eliminate leaven from your houses..." Similarly, *Shemot* 12:19–20 states that leaven may not be found in Jewish homes during Pesach, and *Shemot* 13:7 adds that *chametz* may not even be seen within one's boundaries.

From these verses the Sages derive two distinct prohibitions: *Bal yeira'eh* – *chametz* may not be seen in one's possession (if one owns or takes responsibility for it), and *bal yimatzei* – *chametz* may not be found in one's possession. The central question of our discussion is whether these prohibitions apply only to pure *chametz*, or whether they extend as well to mixtures that contain *chametz*.

The Prohibition of Eating *Chametz* in a Mixture

The **Mishna** in *Masechet Pesachim*[1] lists several substances that are prohibited during Pesach because they contain *chametz* as an ingredient:

> These are items that one transgresses with on Pesach: Babylonian *kutach*, Median beer, Edomite vinegar, Egyptian zitom, dyers' broth, cooks' starch, and scribes' paste. Rabbi Eliezer adds women's cosmetics. The general rule is: anything containing a grain component is subject to the prohibition on Pesach. These

1. 42a.

are included in a prohibition (*lav*), but not subject to the penalty of *kareit*.

The Mishna establishes that mixtures containing *chametz* are indeed prohibited during Pesach. However, it does not clarify which prohibition applies. The **Gemara**[2] explains that the Torah includes mixtures under the prohibition of eating *chametz* through the verse: "Any leavened substance you shall not eat."[3] However, the punishment differs: Only eating pure *chametz* incurs the penalty of *kareit*, while eating a mixture containing *chametz* violates a biblical prohibition [*lav*] but does not incur *kareit*. The question that remains is whether, in addition to being forbidden for consumption, the prohibition of owning *chametz* [*bal yeira'eh ubal yimatzei*] applies to these mixtures as well.

Does the Prohibition of *Bal Yeira'eh Ubal Yimatzei* Apply to *Chametz* Mixtures?

The View of Rashi

Rashi understands that the Mishna's phrase "these are items that one transgresses with on Pesach" refers not merely to a prohibition of eating them, but to the prohibition of possessing them during Pesach. In his commentary to *Pesachim*,[4] Rashi explains that these mixtures are items for which one violates the prohibitions of *bal yeira'eh* and *bal yimatzei.*

Rabbeinu David raises a difficulty with Rashi's interpretation. The Gemara derives the prohibition of eating *chametz* mixtures from the verse "Any leavened substance you shall not eat." This verse extends the prohibition of **consumption** to mixtures, but it does not explicitly extend the prohibition of *bal yeira'eh* and *bal yimatzei* to them. If so, why should one violate these prohibitions by merely possessing such mixtures?

Rabbeinu David resolves this difficulty by distinguishing between different types of mixtures. In the cases listed by the Mishna, such as Babylonian *kutach* and Median beer, the mixture contains actual *chametz* that remains present in significant form within the mixture. Since the *chametz* has not been nullified based on the regular rules of *bitul* (nullification, discussed below), the mixture still contains genuine *chametz*. Therefore, the prohibition of *bal yeira'eh* and *bal yimatzei* applies. However, this applies only when the mixture contains at least an olive-sized quantity (*k'zayit*) of *chametz* within it. If a mixture contains less than this amount, the prohibition of *bal yeira'eh* would not apply.

Accordingly, Rashi's position can be summarized as follows: The prohibition of *bal yeira'eh and bal yimatzei* applies to mixtures containing *chametz* only when the mixture includes a *k'zayit* of *chametz* that has not been halachically nullified. If the *chametz* is present in a smaller amount or has become nullified according to the ordinary rules of nullification, such as majority (*rov*) in a mixture of the same type (*min b'mino*) or a ratio of sixty in a mixture of different types (*b'she eino mino*), then the prohibition of *bal yeira'eh* does not apply, and the mixture may remain in one's possession during Pesach.

The View of Ri (and Razah)

The Mishna at the beginning of *Pesachim* states:

2. *Pesachim* 43a.
3. *Shemot* 12:20.
4. 42a.

"On the night of the fourteenth one searches for *chametz* by the light of a candle".[5] **Rashi** explains that the purpose of this search is to prevent one from violating the prohibitions of *bal yeira'eh* and *bal yimatzei.*

However, **Ri** challenges this explanation.[6] If the concern were only the prohibition of possessing *chametz,* then a formal search would not be necessary. One could simply perform *bitul chametz,* nullifying the *chametz* in one's possession, and thereby avoid the biblical prohibition altogether. Indeed, the Gemara itself states that from a biblical perspective, *bitul* alone is sufficient.

Ri therefore concludes that the institution of *bedikat chametz* must have a different purpose. The Sages required a search for *chametz* out of concern that one might accidentally come to eat *chametz* during Pesach if it remains in one's possession. By removing it from the home, this risk is eliminated.

This understanding leads to an important conceptual implication. According to Ri, the obligation to remove *chametz* from one's home is not limited to situations where the prohibition of *bal yeira'eh* and *bal yimatzei* applies. Rather, any substance that is prohibited to eat on Pesach must be removed so that one does not mistakenly consume it. Therefore, in Ri's view, even if no formal prohibition of *bal yeira'eh* and *bal yimatzei* applies, a mixture containing less than a *k'zayit* of *chametz* would still need to be removed, since the concern is for accidental consumption. For Rashi, on the other hand, the prohibition of ownership would only apply where there is a *k'zayit* of actual *chametz.*

A further practical difference emerges in the laws of *chametz she'avar alav hapesach, chametz* remaining in a Jew's possession during Pesach. If the prohibition involves only the concern of accidental consumption and not a violation of *bal yeira'eh,* then keeping such a mixture during Pesach would not render it prohibited afterward. Since no biblical prohibition of possession was violated, the mixture would be permitted after Pesach.

The View of Rabbeinu Tam

Rabbeinu Tam raises a similar challenge to Rashi based on the wording of the Mishna.[7] The Mishna concludes its discussion of *chametz* mixtures by stating that they are included in a prohibition but do not incur the punishment of *kareit.* This wording suggests a comparison with the prohibition of eating *chametz,* where pure *chametz* incurs *kareit,* while mixtures do not. If the Mishna were referring to the prohibition of *bal yeira'eh,* this formulation would be difficult. The prohibition of possessing *chametz* never carries the penalty of *kareit,* even in the case of pure *chametz.* The contrast drawn by the Mishna therefore indicates that its discussion concerns the prohibition of eating, not possession.

Rabbeinu Tam therefore interprets the Mishna differently. The phrase "these are items that one transgresses (*ovrim*) with on Pesach" does not mean that one violates *bal yeira'eh* by keeping them. Rather, it means that these substances must be removed from the table, i.e., one should ensure they are not present in a way that could lead to eating them. Accordingly, Rabbeinu Tam maintains that *chametz* mixtures are not subject to the prohibition of *bal yeira'eh* and *bal yimatzei.* They may remain in one's possession during Pesach, provided they are kept away so that one will not accidentally eat them.

5. *Pesachim* 2a.
6. Tosafot Rabbeinu Peretz 2a, s.v. *bodkin hachametz.*
7. *Pesachim* 42a.

However, Rabbeinu Tam adds an important qualification. If the *chametz* content of the mixture is sufficiently concentrated, specifically, if the mixture contains a *k'zayit* of *chametz* within the amount normally consumed within the time of *kedei achilat pras*, then the mixture attains the status of actual *chametz*. In such a case, the prohibition of *bal yeira'eh* would indeed apply. This leads to a key distinction between the approaches of Rashi and Rabbeinu Tam.

According to Rashi, the prohibition of *bal yeira'eh* applies whenever the mixture contains a total *k'zayit* of *chametz*, even if it is dispersed within a much larger mixture. According to Rabbeinu Tam, this is insufficient. The mixture is considered *chametz* for purposes of *bal yera'eh* only if the *chametz* is present in a concentration of *k'zayit* within *kedei achilat pras*. Consequently, mixtures containing a smaller concentration of *chametz* would not require removal according to Rabbeinu Tam, whereas they might still fall under the prohibition according to Rashi.

The View of the Rambam

The Rambam addresses the laws of *chametz* mixtures in two separate contexts: the prohibition of eating *chametz* and the prohibition of possessing *chametz*. In *Hilchot Chametz Umatza*,[8] the **Rambam** rules that one incurs lashes for eating a *chametz* mixture only when the mixture contains a *k'zayit* of *chametz* within the amount normally eaten in the time of *kedei achilat pras*. In such a case, the Torah prohibition applies. If the mixture contains less than this concentration, the mixture remains forbidden to eat, but the prohibition is rabbinic, and the punishment is only *makkat mardut* (rabbinic lashes). However, in a later passage,[9] the Rambam appears to rule more broadly regarding possession:

> A mixture containing *chametz* is subject to the prohibition of *bal yeira'eh and bal yimatzei*, such as *moryas*, Babylonian *kutach*, Median beer, and similar substances made with flour. However, a substance containing *chametz* that is not fit for consumption may be kept during Pesach.

At first glance, this formulation suggests that any mixture containing *chametz* is subject to the prohibition of *bal yeira'eh and bal yimatzei*, without the limitation mentioned earlier regarding the quantity of *chametz* required. This apparent inconsistency prompted discussion among later commentators.

Two Interpretations of the Rambam

The ***Kesef Mishneh*** explains that the Rambam intentionally distinguishes between the laws of eating and the laws of possession. With regard to eating, the Torah requires that the prohibited quantity be consumed within the time frame of *kedei achilat pras*. If the *chametz* in the mixture is too diluted, eating it is halachically comparable to consuming small amounts over an extended period, which does not incur lashes.

The prohibition of *bal yera'eh*, however, functions differently. It concerns the presence of *chametz* in one's possession, not the act of consumption. Since the mixture as a whole contains a total *k'zayit* of *chametz*, the *chametz* is considered present in its entirety at once. Therefore, even if the *chametz* is dispersed within a larger mixture and does not reach the threshold of *k'zayit* within *kedei achilat pras*, the prohibition of *bal yeira'eh* would still apply. According to this interpretation, the Rambam's view closely resembles that of Rashi: the prohibition of possessing *chametz* applies whenever the mixture contains a total

8. 1:8.
9. *Hilchot Chametz Umatza* 4:8.

k'zayit of *chametz*, even if it is diluted.

The ***Maggid Mishneh***, however, understands the Rambam differently. In his view, the Rambam does not intend to introduce a new standard for possession. Rather, when the Rambam lists examples such as Babylonian *kutach* and Median beer, he is referring to the same type of mixtures discussed earlier – those that contain a *k'zayit* of *chametz* within *kedei achilat pras*. According to this interpretation, the Rambam maintains a single consistent standard for both eating and possession. Only a mixture containing *chametz* in this significant concentration is treated as *chametz* with respect to the prohibition of *bal yeira'eh and bal yimatzei*.

Thus, the Rambam's position can be understood in two ways: According to the *Kesef Mishneh*, the Rambam follows a position similar to Rashi, requiring only a total *k'zayit* of *chametz* in the mixture for the prohibition of possession to apply. According to the *Maggid Mishneh*, the Rambam aligns with Rabbeinu Tam, requiring a concentration of *k'zayit* within *kedei achilat pras*.

The Ruling of the *Shulchan Aruch* and *Mishna Berura*

The ***Shulchan Aruch*** rules in accordance with his view of the Rambam in the *Kesef Mishneh* and adopts the Rambam's language. He writes: "A mixture containing *chametz* is subject to the prohibitions of *bal yeira'eh* and *bal yimatzei*, such as *moryas*, Babylonian *kutach*, Median beer, and similar edible substances."

The ***Mishna Berura***[10] explains that the *Shulchan Aruch* is referring specifically to the prohibition of possessing *chametz*, and he clarifies the parameters of this ruling. According to his interpretation, one violates *bal yeira'eh and bal yimatzei* only if the mixture contains a total *k'zayit* of *chametz*. Even if the *chametz* is diluted and does not reach the concentration of *k'zayit* within *kedei achilat pras*, the prohibition of possession still applies so long as the mixture contains a *k'zayit* overall. However, if the mixture contains less than a *k'zayit* of *chametz* in total, the prohibition of *bal yeira'eh* does not apply, and it may remain in one's possession during Pesach.

Nevertheless, the *Mishna Berura* adds important qualifications. A mixture containing a *k'zayit* violates *bal yeira'eh* and *bal yimatzi* only if the *chametz* is not nullified within the mixture, such as when *chametz* of one type becomes mixed with a different type (*min b'she'eino mino*) – in this case, it is not nullified by a simple majority according to many authorities. In contrast, a mixture that is halachically nullified is not subject to the prohibition of possession, even if it contains more than a *k'zayit*. For example, in mixtures that involve substances of the same type (*min b'mino*), such as flour from *chametz* grain mixed with flour that is not *chametz*, the *chametz* may be nullified by a majority according to biblical law. In such a case the mixture could technically remain in one's possession according to Torah law. Nevertheless, the Sages prohibited leaving it in one's home during Pesach lest one come to eat from it, and therefore it must still be removed before Pesach. But the *Mishna Berura* notes that if one did leave such a mixture in one's possession throughout Pesach, it does not become prohibited after Pesach as *chametz she'avar alav hapesach*, because no biblical prohibition of *bal yeira'eh* was violated.

Conclusion

From the discussion above, it emerges that the

---

10. O.C. 442:1.

prohibition of *bal yeira'eh ubal yimatzei* does not apply to every instance in which *chametz* is present within a mixture. According to the ruling of the *Shulchan Aruch*, as explained by the *Mishna Berura*, the determining factor is the total quantity of *chametz* contained within the mixture. The prohibition of possessing *chametz* applies, but only if the mixture contains a *k'zayit* of *chametz*. When the total amount of *chametz* is less, one does not violate *bal yeira'eh ubal yimatzei*, and the mixture may remain in one's possession during Pesach.

At the same time, the Sages sometimes required the removal of certain mixtures because of the concern that one might accidentally eat them during Pesach. However, where the *chametz* content is extremely small and does not reach a *k'zayit* in the entire mixture, this concern is generally not treated as requiring destruction.

Returning to the practical question raised at the beginning: small items such as perfume bottles or medicines that contain a *chametz* component do not require destruction or sale for Pesach if the total amount of *chametz* contained within them is less than a *k'zayit*. In such cases, the prohibition of *bal yeira'eh ubal yimatzei* does not apply, and they may remain in one's possession during Pesach.

Why Is There No Prohibition of *Chatzi Shiur* for *Bal Yeira'eh*?

A final question arises. In most areas of halacha, even less than the minimum quantity (*chatzi shiur*) of a forbidden substance is prohibited by Torah law. Why, then, does the prohibition of *bal yeira'eh and bal yimatzei* not apply even to smaller amounts of *chametz*?

The ***Chacham Tzvi***[11] addresses this question. He notes that although eating less than the minimum quantity of forbidden food is normally prohibited, the same principle does not apply to the prohibition of possessing *chametz*. He suggests that the reason may be that the concept of *chatzi shiur* is derived from verses relating specifically to prohibitions of eating. Alternatively, even if the principle applies more broadly, it applies primarily when a person actively performs an act that gives significance to the prohibited substance. In the case of *chametz* possession, however, the individual performs no action – he merely leaves the *chametz* in his home. Since no act demonstrates that he attributes significance to the small quantity, the concept of *chatzi shiur* does not apply.

The ***Sha'agat Aryeh***[12] offers a related explanation. The Talmud explains that the prohibition of *chatzi shiur* in eating is based on the idea that the partial amount could combine with additional quantities to form a full measure (*chazi le'itztarufei*). When someone eats a small amount of forbidden food, it could potentially combine with further consumption within the relevant time frame, eventually constituting the full prohibited measure.

This reasoning does not apply to the prohibition of possessing *chametz*. If someone possesses less than a *k'zayit* of *chametz* and later acquires more, the prohibition applies only from the moment the full measure is present onward. The earlier period, when he possessed less than the required quantity, does not retroactively become prohibited. Since the earlier possession can never combine retroactively into a full violation, the principle of *chatzi shiur* does not apply.

11. Responsa *Chacham Tzvi* 86.
12. Responsa §81.

2

Halachot of Mechirat Chametz and Chametz She'avar Alav HaPesach

הלכות מכירת חמץ וחמץ שעבר עליו הפסח

Selling Chametz Before Pesach

Selling With the Intention to Repurchase

The Act of Acquisition (Kinyan)

Chametz She'avar Alav HaPesach

For quick reference, some long website URLs have been shortened.
For the complete list of referenced websites visit www.tzurbaolami.com.

ת	**Tanach**
ח	**Talmud (Chazal)**
ר	***Rishonim***
א	***Acharonim***
פ	**Contemporary Halachic Sources**

In volume 5, *shiur* 9, we explored the obligations surrounding *chametz* before Pesach: The biblical requirement to nullify it (*bitul chametz*), as well as the rabbinic obligations to search for and destroy it (*bedikat chametz* and *bi'ur chametz*).[1] We also examined the prohibition against owning *chametz* on Pesach itself in *shiur* 1 of this volume. In this *shiur*, we turn to a practical and widely relevant question: Does the halacha permit selling [*mechira*] some or all of one's *chametz* instead of burning it or otherwise disposing of it? If selling is allowed, may one also repurchase it again after Pesach? And how does the *mechirat chametz* widely practiced in our day work?[2] We will also consider the status of *chametz* that remained in one's possession until after Pesach, known as *chametz she'avar alav hapesach*.

Selling Chametz Before Pesach

The notion that one may sell one's *chametz* already appears in the **Mishna (*Masechet Pesachim*)**, which permits selling *chametz* to a non-Jew on Erev Pesach during the first part of the day when eating *chametz* is still permitted.

1. משנה | פסחים ב:א

כל שעה שמותר לאכול – מאכיל לבהמה לחיה ולעופות, ומוכר לנכרי, ומותר בהנאתו.

ח Mishna, Pesachim 2:1

For the **entire time that it is permitted to eat** *chametz,* **one** may also **feed** it **to** his **domesticated animals, to non-domesticated animals, and to birds; one** may **sell** it **to a gentile; and it is permitted to derive benefit from it.**[3]

The **Gemara** questions why it was necessary to write that selling *chametz* to a gentile is permitted, and answers that this is because according to Beit Shammai, this is in fact prohibited unless one knows that the gentile will finish consuming the *chametz* before Pesach. However, the halacha follows Beit Hillel, who permit selling *chametz* to a gentile.

---

1. Of course, these mitzvot apply only to one who possesses *chametz*. The *Minchat Chinuch* (Mitzva 9, no. 1) understands that according to some *Rishonim*, on a biblical level, it would have been proper for one who does not possess any *chametz* to obtain some *chametz* in order to fulfill the mitzva. However, he concedes that on a rabbinic level this is not possible, as the Sages instituted that one must remove all *chametz* from one's possession at least an hour before the biblical mitzva takes effect.
2. For English resources online discussing the contemporary selling of *chametz*, see, e.g., https://oukosher.org/blog/kosher-professionals/mechiras-chametz; https://outorah.org/p/33326; https://halachipedia.com/index.php?title=Selling_Chametz; www.yutorah.org/lectures/lecture.cfm/714420; www.torahmusings.com/2012/04/cyber-selling-chametz-2; https://rabbimanning.com/wp-content/uploads/2020/04/Chametz-After-Pesach.pdf; and www.koltorah.org/halachah/mechirat-chametz-the-source-of-the-deal-by-rabbi-chaim-jachter.
3. The Gemara observes that according to Rabbi Yehuda, on a rabbinic level, one may only eat *chametz* during the first four hours of the day of Erev Pesach, whereas one may feed it to animals, sell it to a gentile or benefit from it in other ways until the end of the fifth hour (as we shall see, the halacha is in accordance with this view). The Mishna follows dissenting views among the *Tanna'im*.

ח Masechet Pesachim 21a

2. מסכת פסחים כא.

ומוכרו לנכרי. פשיטא! – לאפוקי מהאי תנא דתניא, בית שמאי אומרים: לא ימכור אדם חמצו לנכרי, אלא אם כן יודע בו שיכלה קודם פסח. ובית הלל אומרים: כל שעה שמותר לאכול – מותר למכור.

It was stated in the Mishna that whenever it is permitted to eat *chametz*, one may also **sell it to a gentile.** The Gemara asks: Isn't that **obvious,** as the Mishna already taught that one may benefit from it? The Gemara answers: This is stated **to exclude** the opinion **of this *tanna*, as it was taught** in a *baraita* that **Beit Shammai say: A person** may **not sell his *chametz* to a gentile unless he knows that** the *chametz* **will be consumed before Pesach.** According to Beit Shammai, a person retains some responsibility for his *chametz* even when it is no longer in his possession. **Beit Hillel say:** For the **entire time that it is permitted** for a Jew **to eat** *chametz*, **it is** also **permitted for him to sell it** to a gentile. The Jew ceases to be responsible for *chametz* sold to a gentile from the moment it is sold.

Rashi explains that according to Beit Shammai, one is obligated on a biblical level to destroy any *chametz* that is in one's possession, and it is not sufficient to remove it from one's possession.

ו Rashi, Pesachim 21a

3. רש"י | פסחים כא.

קודם – שיבוא הפסח, דקסברי: מצוה עליו לבערו מן העולם, ולא שיהא קיים.

Before – Pesach arrives, as they maintain that one is commanded to remove it from the world, not that it should remain.[4]

In contrast, **Rabbeinu David** writes that if one sells his *chametz* to a gentile, he certainly does not transgress any biblical prohibition. Beit Shammai prohibit doing so on a rabbinic level, out of concern that people may only sell their *chametz* in a fictitious manner.

ו Rabbeinu David, Pesachim 21a

4. רבינו דוד | פסחים כא.

...שדבר ברור שמן הדין כל שקנאו הגוי שעה אחת קודם הפסח לא קרינא ביה לא יראה לך, אלא דבית שמאי גזרי למכירה של הערמה.

...As it is clear that according to the letter of the law, whenever the gentile acquires [the *chametz*] one moment before Pesach, [the prohibition of] "it shall not be seen by you" does not apply to it. Rather, Beit Shammai decreed [against this out of concern] for *ha'arama* [pretense] of a sale.[5]

RABBEINU DAVID BONAFED (c. 1240–?)

Rabbeinu David ben Reuven Bonafed was a 13th century Gemara commentator and *posek* in Northeast Spain, in the region of Gerona and Barcelona. Rabbeinu David often quotes interpretations from his teacher, the Ramban, and the Ran also refers to Rabbeinu David as the Ramban's student. Unfortunately, his commentaries to most tractates have not survived to present day. Among those which are extant are commentaries to *Masechet Pesachim* and to *Masechet Sanhedrin*, and both of these have been republished within the past generation. The Ran quotes him extensively in his own commentaries on these tractates.

---

4. In the continuation on 21b, Rashi explains that this applies to any *chametz* that is in one's possession in the thirty days before Pesach.

5. A third explanation, provided by Tosafot Rabbeinu Peretz and the Maharam Chalava, is that Beit Shammai prohibit selling *chametz* to a gentile before Pesach out of concern that others will suspect that the person merely gave the *chametz* to the gentile to watch over during Pesach.

According to Beit Hillel and the Mishna, one may sell *chametz* to a gentile even if it will not be consumed before Pesach. This is sufficient to fulfill one's obligation to remove *chametz*, and we are not concerned that people may only pretend to sell their *chametz*.

In accordance with the standard rule, the ***Shulchan Aruch*** rules in accordance with Beit Hillel.

5. שולחן ערוך | או"ח תמג:א

חמץ משש שעות ולמעלה ביום י"ד, אסור בהנאה... ואסרוהו חכמים שתי שעות קודם דהיינו מתחלת שעה חמישית, ומיהו כל שעה חמישית מותר בהנאה ורשאי למוכרו לאינו יהודי, אפילו הרבה ביחד שודאי לא יאכלנו קודם פסח.

א Shulchan Aruch, Orach Chaim 443:1

From six hours into the fourteenth day [of Nisan], benefitting from *chametz* is [biblically] prohibited... The Sages prohibited [eating] it two hours beforehand, i.e., from the beginning of the fifth hour. However, throughout the fifth hour, benefitting from it is permitted, and one may sell it to a gentile, even large amounts together, such that he will certainly not consume it before Pesach.

Selling With the Intention to Repurchase

We have seen so far that according to the halacha, one may sell *chametz* to a gentile before Pesach rather than destroy it physically. However, the sources we have seen only discuss permanent sales. May one also sell *chametz* before Pesach if one intends to buy it back after Pesach?

The ***Tosefta* (*Masechet Pesachim*)** permits selling or giving *chametz* to a gentile before Pesach and rebuying it after Pesach, provided that the original gift (or sale) is bona fide.

ח Tosefta, Pesachim, 2:6–7[6]

6. If a Jew and a gentile were travelling by boat, and the Jew has *chametz* in his possession, he may sell it to the gentile or give it to him as a gift and rebuy it after Pesach, provided that he gives it to him as a bona fide gift.

7. A Jew may say to a gentile, "Rather than you buying a *maneh*'s [a hundred *dinar*'s] worth, buy two hundred [*dinar*'s] worth, in case I will need to come and buy it from you after Pesach."

6. תוספתא | פסחים ב:ו-ז

ו. ישראל וגוי שהיו באין בספינה וחמץ ביד ישראל הרי זה מוכרו לנכרי ונותנו במתנה וחוזר ולוקח ממנו לאחר הפסח ובלבד שיתנו לו במתנה גמורה.

ז.רשאי ישראל שיאמר לנכרי עד שאתה לוקח במנה קח במאתים שמא אצטרך ואבוא ואקח ממך אחר הפסח.

However, **Rav Amram Gaon** writes that one may only do this as a one-off, not every year.

ו Responsa Ge'onei Mizrach U'ma'arav, Siman 110

This is what Rav Amram says: "The halacha is that a Jew who sold his *chametz* to a gentile, or gave it to him as a bone fide gift, if the gentile took [lit. pulled] it and there was no *ha'arama* involved, and **the Jew does not regularly do so in other years, rather it was an isolated occurrence**, the Jew is permitted to repurchase [the *chametz*] from the gentile after Pesach. What is the reason [for this]? Since the gentile purchases it, he acquires it.

7. תשובות גאוני מזרח ומערב | סימן קי

והכי אמר רבי עמרם: והלכתא ישראל שמכר לגוי חמצו או שנתן לו במתנה גמורה אם משך אותו גוי ואין בו הערמה **ואינו רגיל ישראל לעשות כן בשאר שנים אלא מאורע הוא** ומותר ישראל לחזור וליקח ממנו אחר הפסח מן הגוי. מאי טעמא? כיון דקנייה גוי קני להו.

The **Rambam** makes no such stipulation that selling *chametz* must be a one-time occurrence, but he does stress that the original sale must be unconditional. One who makes the sale of his *chametz* subject to a condition violates the prohibition against owning *chametz* on Pesach.

6. The reference is to the edition of the Tosefta in the standard printed edition of the Gemara. In the Lieberman edition of the Tosefta, this quote is found in *Pesachim* 2:12–13.

8. רמב"ם | הל' חמץ ומצה ד:ו–ז

ו. ישראל וגוי שהיו באין בספינה והיה חמץ ביד ישראל והגיעה שעה חמישית הרי זה מוכרו לגוי או נותנו לו במתנה וחוזר ולוקחו ממנו אחר הפסח, ובלבד שיתננו לו מתנה גמורה.

ז. אומר הוא ישראל לגוי עד שאתה לוקח במנה בוא וקח במאתים, עד שאתה לוקח מגוי בוא וקח מישראל שמא אצטרך ואקח ממך אחר הפסח, **אבל לא ימכור לו ולא יתן לו על תנאי, ואם עשה כן הרי זה עובר על בל יראה ובל ימצא.**

Rambam, Hilchot Chametz Umatza 4:6–7

6. If a Jew and a gentile were travelling by boat, and the Jew had *chametz* in his possession, when the fifth hour [on Erev Pesach] arrives, he may sell it to the gentile or give it to him as a gift and rebuy it after Pesach, provided that he gives it to him as a bona fide gift.

7. A Jew may say to a gentile, "Rather than you buying a *maneh*'s [a hundred *dinar*'s] worth, come and buy two hundred [*dinar*'s] worth," [or], "Rather than buy from a gentile, come and buy from a Jew, in case I will need to buy it from you after Pesach." **However, he may not sell or give *chametz* to him conditionally. If he does so, he transgresses [the prohibitions of] "it shall not be seen" and "it shall not be found."**[7]

Hagahot Maimoniot also infer from the *Tosefta* in source 6 that one may not give the *chametz* to a gentile with a stipulation that the gentile must return the *chametz* after Pesach. Although a gift with such a stipulation is usually considered valid, they suggest that Chazal were more stringent here due to the stringent nature of Pesach.

9. הגהות מיימוניות | שבת ו:ב

...ועל אותה ברייתא הייתי תמיה דפסקינן בפרק קמא דקידושין בכולהו קנו הכי נמי אמאי לא יתן לנכרי במתנה על מנת להחזיר ושמא משום חומרא דפסח.

Hagahot Maimoniot, Shabbat 6:2

...I was astonished about that *baraita* [in the *Tosefta*], as in the first chapter of *Kiddushin* (6b) we rule that [a gift conditional on return] is effective in all cases. Here too, why shouldn't one give [*chametz*] to the gentile on condition that he returns it? Perhaps this is due to the severity of Pesach.

From these comments of the *Hagahot Maimoniot*, it is clear that no biblical prohibition is violated if one gives his *chametz* to a gentile, even if he stipulates that the *chametz* must be returned. At first glance, this seems to contradict the ruling of the Rambam, that one who sells or gives *chametz* conditionally violates the prohibition against owning *chametz* on Pesach.

However, in truth there is no contradiction, as the Rambam and *Hagahot Maimoniot* are discussing two different types of conditions. The Rambam discusses a condition which prevents the sale taking effect until it is fulfilled.[8] *Hagahot Maimoniot* discuss a condition which allows the sale to take effect immediately, provided that it is ultimately fulfilled.[9]

---

7. This is true even if the condition is ultimately fulfilled and the sale takes effect, as shall be explained in the following footnote.

8. The standard conditional transaction is usually expressed by the word אם ("if," e.g., "If the descendants of Gad and Reuven fight with their brethren to conquer Eretz Yisrael, they will receive the inheritance they requested on the east of the Jordan.") Such a transaction completes only once the condition is fulfilled (see Rambam, *Ishut* 6:15).

9. A sale conditional on return clearly can never be made using the word אם, as the sale would only take effect once the item is returned. Rather, this condition is made using the phrase על מנת ("on condition"). The Gemara (*Kiddushin* 60b) concludes that all agree that the use of this language is equivalent to specifying that the transaction will take effect immediately,

The ***Shulchan Aruch*** (O.C. 448:4) also rules in accordance with the Rambam. However, the ***Mishna Berura*** clarifies that if one specifies that the sale will take effect immediately, provided that the condition is ultimately fulfilled, no biblical prohibition is violated.

10. משנה ברורה | או"ח תמח:כד

על תנאי – מיירי שאמר בלשון אם, דהיינו אם תעשה דבר פלוני בתוך הפסח או לאחר הפסח החמץ נתון לך או מכור לך, דכל זמן שלא נתקיים התנאי עדיין אין החמץ מכור ונתון, ולפיכך עובר בבל יראה.

אבל אם אמר לו הריני נותן לך מעכשיו על מנת שתעשה דבר פלוני שייך החמץ לגוי תיכף אם יתקיים התנאי לבסוף ואינו אסור רק משום חומרא דחמץ...

א Mishna Berura, Orach Chaim 448:24

On condition – this refers to a case where one used the term "if," i.e., "If you perform such-and-such an act during Pesach/after Pesach, the *chametz* is given to you/sold to you." So long as the condition has not been fulfilled, the *chametz* is not sold or given, and therefore one violates [the prohibition of] "it shall not be seen."

But if he said to him, "I hereby give it to you from now, on condition that you perform such-and-such an act," the *chametz* belongs to the gentile immediately, if the condition is ultimately fulfilled. [Doing so] is only prohibited due to stringency regarding *chametz*[10]...

Nevertheless, the *Acharonim* agree that one should not make even this type of stipulation in case the condition is not fulfilled, thus invalidating the sale.[11] Some do permit limiting the ability of the gentile to sell the *chametz* to others, as long as this is not made a condition of the sale.

11. שם

ודע עוד דהסכימו אחרונים דהוא הדין שאסור לומר לגוי אני מוכר לך החמץ על מנת שתחזיקנו לעצמך ולא תמכור לאדם אחר חוץ ממני דכיון דבלשון תנאי הוא כשיעבור הגוי וימכרנו לאדם אחר תבטל המכירה למפרע ונמצא שלא היה החמץ קנוי לגוי מעולם וחיישינן שמא ימכרנו ויעבור הישראל על בל יראה.

אבל אם אמר לו הריני מוכר לך מכירה גמורה לחלוטין וזכות זה שיירתי לי בו שאם תרצה למוכרו לא תמכרנו לשום אדם חוץ ממני

א Ibid.

Know further that the *Acharonim* agree that it is also prohibited to say to a gentile, "I am selling you the *chametz* on condition that you keep it for yourself and do not sell it to anyone other than me," as since he uses conditional language, if the gentile violates [the condition] and sells it to someone else, the sale is voided retroactively. It then turns out that the *chametz* was never acquired by the gentile at all, and we are concerned that he might sell it and the Jew would thereby transgress "it shall not be seen."

But if he said to him, "I am selling it to you in an absolute bona fide sale, but I have retained for myself the right that if you wish to sell it, you shall not sell it to anyone other than me,"

---

subject to the condition subsequently being fulfilled. Only if the condition is not fulfilled, the transaction is null and void retroactively.

10. As explained by *Hagahot Maimoniot* above.

11. In truth, there is much debate among the *Rishonim* regarding when one is obligated to be stringent based on the possibility that a condition is not fulfilled. Regarding such a concern following a conditional divorce, the *Shulchan Aruch* (*Even HaEzer* 143:2) rules that the divorced woman may remarry if the condition is within her control to keep, and she can fulfill the condition simply by being passive. Regarding our case of *chametz*, the *Hagahot Maimoniot* quoted above implies that one need only be stringent due to the severity of Pesach; see, however, *Bi'ur Halacha* 448:3, s.v. *lo mehani*, who questions this.

יש אומרים דזה מותר אפילו לכתחלה דאפילו אם יעבור הגוי וימכור לא תבטל המכירה בשביל זה כיון דלא אמר בלשון תנאי רק שמכירת הגוי תהיה בטלה.

some say that this is permitted even *lechatchila*.[12] As even if the gentile violates [this limitation] and sells it, the [original] sale is not voided because of this, since he did not use conditional language. Only the gentile's [subsequent] sale would be void.

Thus, provided that one makes no conditions on the sale, the *Shulchan Aruch* and the *Mishna Berura* clearly permit selling *chametz* to a gentile before Pesach, even if this is done every year. However, the ***Shulchan Aruch*** does imply that there is a significant limitation on this leniency. One should only sell *chametz* that is outside of one's home.[13]

12. שולחן ערוך | או"ח תמח:ג

...ואם מכרו או נתנו לאינו יהודי **שמחוץ לבית** קודם הפסח, אף על פי שהישראל מכירו לאינו יהודי ויודע בו שלא יגע בו כלל אלא ישמרנו לו עד לאחר הפסח ויחזור ויתננו לו, מותר...

א Shulchan Aruch, Orach Chaim 448:3

...If one sold or gave [*chametz*] to a gentile **outside of the house** before Pesach, even though the Jew knows the gentile and knows he will not touch it at all, rather, he will keep it for him until after Pesach and will give it back to him, it is permitted...

The ***Mishna Berura*** quotes a dispute among the *Acharonim* as to how to understand the requirement for the *chametz* to be outside one's home. The ***Chok Ya'akov*** writes that this is merely a technical means of effecting the transaction – the gentile acquires the *chametz* by taking it from the Jew's home, but may subsequently return it to the Jew's home for safekeeping before Pesach.

13. משנה ברורה | או"ח תמח:יב

שמחוץ לבית – כתבו האחרונים שאין קפידא בגוי גופא אם הוא דר בביתו או לא אלא עיקר הקפידא שיוציא הגוי החמץ מבית ישראל...

ומה שהצריכו הכא להוציא החמץ מרשותו אף על פי שמכרו כבר והוא אצלו פקדון בעלמא ובלא אחריות... **כתב בחוק יעקב... ולא הצריכו הכא להוציא מרשותו אלא כדי שיקנה הגוי החמץ במשיכה** ואין הכי נמי אם כבר הוציא הגוי החמץ וקנהו במשיכה לביתו או לסימטא כדין

א Mishna Berura, Orach Chaim 448:12

Outside the house – The *Acharonim* write that regarding the gentile himself, whether he lives in the Jew's house or not it is not critical. Rather, the essential requirement is that the gentile remove the *chametz* from the Jew's house...

That which they required one to remove the *chametz* from his jurisdiction, even though he has already sold it and it is merely deposited with him, without responsibility [for it]... **The *Chok Ya'akov* writes... they only required one to remove [the *chametz*] from his jurisdiction so that the gentile should acquire the *chametz* through *meshicha* [pulling].**[14] Accordingly, if the gentile already removed the *chametz* and acquired it by pulling it to his own house or to an alleyway, in accordance with halacha,

---

12. This is based on the *Shulchan Aruch HaRav*. In the *Sha'ar HaTziun* (448:64), the *Mishna Berura* questions this, as by placing this limitation on the sale, the Jew retains some control over the *chametz* during Pesach.
13. The source for this limitation is a responsum of the *Terumat HaDeshen* (*siman* 120).
14. This is one method of transferal of ownership. *Meshicha* can only be used to acquire an item in one's own jurisdiction, or in a neutral jurisdiction that is not a public thoroughfare. Further on, we shall explain in detail the various methods used to transfer ownership (known as *kinyanim*) to a gentile for the purposes of *mechirat chametz*.

מותר לו אחר כך להכניס החמץ לביתו של ישראל ודי במחיצה עשרה בלבד.

it is subsequently permitted to bring the *chametz* [back] into the Jew's house, and a partition ten-*tefachim* high [in front of the *chametz*] suffices.

Others argue that this is not permitted, as if the Jew keeps the *chametz* in his home, the sale appears fictitious. There is also a concern that the Jew may eat it during Pesach.

14. שם

אבל כמה אחרונים כתבו... כיון דעיקר החמץ יודע הגוי שהוא של ישראל ולא יגע בו אף על פי שקנהו, מחזי כחמצו של ישראל אם היה בביתו, וגם איכא למיחש שמא יבא לאכלו דכיון דדידיה הוי מעיקרא לא בדיל מינה. ולסברא זו, **אפילו אם יחד לו בביתו זוית בפני עצמה או שעשה מחיצה עשרה נמי לא מהני...**

א Ibid.

But several *Acharonim* write... since the gentile knows that the *chametz* originally belonged to the Jew, and he will not touch it even though he acquired it, it appears like the *chametz* of the Jew if it is in his house. There is also a concern that one may come to eat it, as since it was his originally, he does not distance himself from it. According to this rationale, **even if one designates a separate corner in his house for it, or he makes a partition ten *tefachim* high, this does not help...**

However, removing all the *chametz* from one's home[15] is often not practical. The *Acharonim* therefore suggest that one who has a large amount of *chametz* should sell the room in which the *chametz* is stored to the gentile, together with the *chametz*, and provide him access to this room. In this way, since the *chametz* is in a room owned by the gentile, it is equivalent to being outside the Jew's house.

15. שם

וכתבו האחרונים דאם יש לו חמץ הרבה ואי אפשר לו להוציאו מביתו, ימכור לו גם החדר והוי כמו שמכר לו חוץ לביתו... וצריך למסור לו המפתח מחדר שמונח בו החמץ כדי שיוכל לכנוס בשעה שירצה וליטול את חמצו שנמכר או ניתן לו, או שעל כל פנים יאמר לו הישראל: בכל עת שתרצה תוכל ליקח המפתח מחדרך וליכנס בו ליטול את חמצך, ואיסור גמור הוא להניח שום חותם או מסגר על החדר או על החמץ כדי שלא יוכל הנכרי ליטול את החמץ דמוכח מזה דכל המכירה לא היה רק הערמה בעלמא...

א Ibid.

The *Acharonim* write that if one possesses a large quantity of *chametz* and it is impossible for him to remove it from his house, he should also sell the room to the gentile, and this is tantamount to selling to him outside his house... One must give the gentile the key to the room in which the *chametz* is left, so that he is able to enter whenever he wishes and take his *chametz* that was sold or given to him. Or at least, the Jew should say to him: "Any time you wish, you may take the key to your room and enter it to take your *chametz*." Placing any seal or lock on the room or on the *chametz* so that the gentile cannot take the *chametz* is absolutely prohibited. As this proves that the entire sale was only a *ha'arama*...

Although the *Mishna Berura* writes that one should sell the room to the gentile together with the *chametz*, the generally accepted practice is to rent the space where the *chametz* is placed to the gentile rather than to sell it to him.[16] The ***Piskei Teshuvot*** explains the pros and cons of renting rather than selling and

---

15. It should be noted that all references to *chametz* in one's home also include any *chametz* owned elsewhere, such as at work. This, too, must be sold or disposed of.

16. *Poskim* discuss whether one may enter the space rented or sold to the gentile on Pesach in order to take out a non-*chametz*

how the accepted practice seeks to address all halachic concerns.

16. פסקי תשובות | או"ח תמח:כג

ונחלקו גדולי הפוסקים מה עדיף, אם למכור לנכרי את החדר או להשכיר לו, **יש שסברו שמכירה עדיף**, שאם ישכיר לו... דינו כחמץ של נכרי שקיבל עליו אחריות בבית היהודי שחייב עליו בבל יראה ובל ימצא, **ויש שסברו ששכירות עדיף ממכירה**, כי במכירת חדר אחד בבית או חלק חדרים ועליות ומרתפים וכדומה הרי זה הערמה הניכרת כי אין מי שקונה חדרים וקרקעות בצורה כזאת, רק בשביל חמץ וכלי חמץ שיש שם, ובהשכרה יש יותר גמירות דעת לשכור עקב החמץ וכלי החמץ שיש שם.

ולמעשה נתפשט המנהג ברוב המקומות להשכיר לנכרי ולא למכור, חדא, משום שבשכירות די בקנין כסף לחוד כדי להקנותו לנכרי, ואין צריך שטר, כך שאם יהיה איזה פקפוק על השטר לא יהיה פקפוק על עצם המכירה, ועוד למי שדר בשכירות אצל אחר, אינו יכול למכור הבית ללא רשות רק להשכיר, ובארץ ישראל מתעורר עוד חשש אם נמכור חדר לנכרי משום שאסור למכור בית לנכרי בארץ ישראל.

ועקב החשש הנ"ל של אלו הסוברים שצריך דווקא מכירה, יש שדקדקו לכתוב ולהוסיף בשטר מכירה "שהנכרי פוטר את היהודי מרצונו הטוב מכל מיני אחריות ואפילו פשיעה באופן שחל גם על פי דינא דמלכותא".

Piskei Teshuvot, Orach Chaim 448:23

The great *poskim* disagree as to which is preferable: selling the room to the gentile or renting it to him. **Some hold that selling is preferable**, as if one rents it to him… it has the status of a gentile's *chametz* for which the Jew has accepted responsibility while it is in the Jew's house, for which one is liable for violating "it shall not be seen" and "it shall not be found."[17] **Others hold that renting is preferable to selling**, because selling one room in a house, or parts of rooms, attics, cellars, and the like, is a recognizable *ha'arama*, as no one buys rooms or land in such a manner, other than for the sake of *chametz* and *chametz* utensils that are there. When renting, there is more serious intent to rent, due to the *chametz* and *chametz* utensils located there.

In practice, the widespread custom in most places has become to rent to the gentile and not to sell. First, because for rental, payment of money alone suffices to transfer ownership to the gentile, and no deed is required, so that if there should be any flaw in the document, there will be no doubt regarding the validity of the transaction itself. Additionally, one who lives in a rented [property] cannot sell the house without permission, he may only rent it. In Eretz Yisrael, an additional concern arises if one sells a room to a gentile, as selling a house to a gentile in Eretz Yisrael is prohibited.[18]

Because of the above concern raised by those who hold that a sale is specifically required, some are particular to add to the bill of sale "that the gentile, of his own free will, exempts the Jew from all forms of liability, even [due to] negligence, in a manner that is effective also according to the law of the land."[19]

---

item that is needed over the course of the festival. Some forbid this (Rav Mordechai Eliyahu, Responsa *Ma'amar Mordechai* 1:19), others permit in cases of great need (Rav Shlomo Zalman Auerbach, *Halichot Shlomo* 6:18), while a third opinion suggests adding a stipulation of some sort explicitly in the contract that the gentile agrees, which is indeed often used in the contracts today (Responsa *Shivat Tzion* 10; Rav Asher Weiss, *Mishpat HaMechira*, p. 662). See *Piskei Teshuvot* 448:14; *Mechirat Chametz K'hilchato* 2:26; and *Oholei Halacha*, p. 60, n. 20 (the entire volume of *Oholei Halacha* is available online at www.toraland.org.il/books/שבת-ומועדים/הלכות-פסח). One should certainly try to avoid the issue by removing anything one might need from that area before Pesach.

17. See *Shulchan Aruch*, O.C. 440:1 and commentaries.
18. See *Avoda Zara* 19b and *Shulchan Aruch*, Y.D. 151:8, as well as the *Tzurba M'Rabanan* volume on Shemita, *shiur* 4, where this was discussed in the context of the *heter mechira* (selling portions of the Land of Israel to avoid violating Shemita prohibitions by Jews working the land).
19. In this manner, the gentile thereby absolves the Jew of any responsibility, effectively creating the same conditions as a sale.

Opposition to *Mechirat Chametz*

Despite all the warnings given by Chazal and the *poskim* that the sale of *chametz* must be genuine, some *poskim* maintain that the sale as it is practiced today is indeed a *ha'arama*. The ***Bechor Shor*** explains that such a sale would not usually be valid, but since one also nullifies all the *chametz* in one's possession (*bitul chametz*), after this verbal nullification, the obligation to search out and destroy one's *chametz* is only rabbinic.[20] The *ha'arama* of a sale suffices to fulfill this rabbinic obligation.

17. בכור שור | פסחים כא.

...מכירת חמץ הנהוג הלא מוכחא מילתא דהערמה טובא שזה הקונה לאו גברא דאורחיה מעולם לקנות כך וזה אין דרכו למכור כך ועל הרוב הקונה הוא עני וקונה בכמה מאות חמץ כנהוג עתה שאין מוכרים בדבר מועט ושאר הוכחות טובא.

אלא נראה לי כיון דהאיסור מדרבנן הוא דמדאורייתא בביטול בעלמא סגי וכל אחד מבטל חמצו בלב שלם... ולא נשאר כי אם איסור דרבנן שצריך לבערו מן העולם הם אמרו והם אמרו להתיר מכירה זו.

א Bechor Shor, Pesachim 21a

...Is it not clear that the customary sale of *chametz* is a great *ha'arama*? As the buyer is not a person who usually ever purchases in such a manner, and this one [the seller] does not usually sell in such a manner; in most cases the buyer is a poor person who purchases *chametz* worth many hundreds, as is customary nowadays, as we do not sell for a small amount. There are also many other [similar] indications.

Rather, it appears to me that since the prohibition is rabbinic, as on a Torah level mere nullification suffices, and everyone nullifies his *chametz* with complete sincerity... only a rabbinic prohibition remains that requires its removal from the world. They [Chazal] declared [the prohibition] and [therefore] they [had the authority to] declare that this sale is permitted.[21]

The ***Sho'el Umeishiv*** concurs and writes that since the sale is only a *ha'arama* in order to avoid the rabbinic obligation to destroy the *chametz*, one cannot appoint a *shaliach* (agent) to sell one's *chametz* (which is the standard method of selling *chametz* today).

18. שו"ת שואל ומשיב | מהדורה תניינא ב:עז

...וצריך לומר דעיקר הוא הביטול רק שמדרבנן צריך ביעור ועל כן הוא מוכרו ובאמת לא סמכינן על מכירה דהמכירה היא רק הערמה בלבד רק שבדרבנן מועיל הערמה...

ולפי זה נראה לפי עניות דעתי ברור דלכך

א Responsa Sho'el Umeishiv, Mahadura Tinyana 2:77

...One must say that the main [obligation] is the nullification, just that on a rabbinic level removal is required, and therefore one sells it. But in truth, we do not rely on the sale, as the sale is merely a *ha'arama*, but regarding rabbinic matters *ha'arama* is effective...

Accordingly, in my humble opinion it appears clear that for

20. This is explicit in the Gemara (*Pesachim* 4b).

21. Others disagree with the *Bechor Shor* on this point, pointing out that the *chametz* sold is not included in the nullification (*Shulchan Aruch HaRav*, O.C. 448). The stringency of avoiding selling actual *chametz* may result from combining together the opinion of the *Bechor Shor* with this opinion. It should also be noted as well that *poskim* disagree about whether the sale of *chametz* should be before or after the nullification, since *chametz* that has been nullified cannot be sold, but conversely, if all of one's *chametz* has been sold, there is no *chametz* left in one's possession concerning which the nullification will take effect. See *Piskei Teshuvot* (448:7) and *Oholei Halacha*, p. 66, n. 47 concerning this issue.

לא מהני על ידי שליח דעד כאן לא מרבינן שליחות רק כשזה רוצה שיהיה שלוחו ומוסר לו כחו אמרינן דשליח של אדם כמותו. אבל כאן באמת הוא אינו רוצה למכור וזה אינו רוצה לקנות דהיא רק הערמה בלבד, ואיך שייך שמועיל שליחות בדבר שהוא בעצמו עושה רק להערמה בעלמא ואין לו כח כלל למכור כי הוא באמת מבטל החמץ, והמכירה אינו רק להערמה שלא יצטרך לבערו, ובכהאי גוונא לא נתרבה שליחות כלל וזה ברור כשמש...

this reason [the sale] does not work through an agent. As we only derive [the principle of] agency in cases where one wants the agent to act on his behalf and empowers him [to do so]. Then we say that a person's agent is like himself. But here, in truth, he does not wish to sell, and [the buyer] does not wish to buy, as it is only a *ha'arama*. How, then, could agency be effective in a matter which he himself performs only as a *ha'arama,* and he has no ability to sell at all, since in truth he nullifies the *chametz,* and the sale is only a *ha'arama* so that he need not remove it? In such a case, we do not derive the [principle] of agency, and this is as clear as the sun...

The **Gra** is quoted as objecting to any sale of *chametz* with the intention of buying it back, to the extent that he would not permit buying *chametz* after Pesach from a Jew who sold it in this manner.

19. מעשה רב | קפ–קפא

קפ. שלא למכור שום דבר חמץ כי אם מכירה עולמית.

קפא. אחר הפסח אין ליקח מן השוק מה שאופין מקמח של ישראל ומשמרים ויין שרף ושכר של ישראל כי המכירה גרוע.

א Ma'aseh Rav 180–181

180. One should not sell any *chametz* item, other than by a permanent sale.

181. After Pesach, one should not buy in the market that which is baked from flour of Jews, nor sourdough, whisky, or beer of a Jew, as the sale is deficient.

However, the vast majority of *poskim* permit selling *chametz* rather than destroying it before Pesach, even when intending to buy it back immediately after Pesach. The ***Chatam Sofer*** explains that the sale is valid even on a biblical level and criticizes those who speak against it.

20. שו"ת חתם סופר | א:קיג

דהערמת מכירה זו היא היתר גמור מן התורה בלי שום פקפוק שהוא מוכר מכירה גמורה באחד מהקנינים שהגוי קונה, אף על פי ששניהם יודעים שרוצים בחזרת החמץ לאחר הפסח, מכל מקום השתא מכור הוא ויכול הלוקח למכרו ולאוכלו להקדישו להאבידו מבלי מוחה, אלא שהוא אוהבו ואינו עושה כן ומשמרו עד לאחר הפסח וחוזר ומכרו לישראל... ואפילו בפירוש יכול לומר להגוי אם נשאר החמץ בידך עד אחר הפסח ותרצה למוכרו אז קרוב לודאי שאקחנו ממך במקח השוה...

ועל פי זה נהגו בכל תפוצות ישראל למכור החמץ לנכרי המכירו ומחזירו אחר הפסח...

א Responsa Chatam Sofer 1:113

The "*ha'arama*" of this sale is absolutely permitted on a biblical level, without any reservation, as one sells it as a bona fide sale through one of the acts of sale by which a gentile acquires. Although both parties know that they desire the return of the *chametz* after Pesach, nevertheless, now it is sold, and the purchaser is able to sell it, eat it, consecrate it, or destroy it without protest, except that he is his friend and does not do so, and keeps it until after Pesach and sells it back to the Jew... One may even say to the gentile explicitly: "If the *chametz* remains in your possession until after Pesach and you wish to sell it, it is almost certain that I will buy it from you for its fair value"...

Accordingly, it has become the practice throughout all Jewish communities to sell *chametz* to a gentile who knows him and returns it after Pesach...

The sale is bona fide, and anyone who casts doubt upon it is worthy of rebuke.

המכירה גמורה היא וכל המפקפק ראוי לגערה.

The ***Peninei Halakha*** summarizes how the sale of *chametz* developed, why it is a genuine sale and not just a *ha'arama*, and why it is preferable for it to be performed by a rav.

Peninei Halakha, Pesach 6:2

About 400 years ago, many Jews living in Europe began to support themselves through the production and sale of whiskey. This was because the barons, the landowners, would often contract Jews to manage their affairs, and it was common for them to lease their distilleries and inns to Jews in exchange for a fixed price and/or a percentage of sales. This whiskey, which was made from barley and wheat, is considered *Chametz gamur*. To prevent the great financial loss that would come each year with its disposal before Pesach, it became necessary to sell it to a gentile before Pesach and buy it back again immediately thereafter, in order to continue selling the whiskey as usual.

Over time, rabbinic leaders noticed that the sale was sometimes carried out improperly, leading to serious problems. If the sale is improper, the *chametz* remains in the possession of the Jew, and with every hour that passes he violates *bal yeira'eh* and *bal yimatzei*. Additionally, it is forbidden to derive benefit from such *chametz* after Pesach, and it must all be completely destroyed. **Therefore, rabbinic authorities began to oversee the sale of *chametz*, in order to ensure its proper sale.** Seeing that the sale was being carried out in an orderly manner, other Jews began to participate in the transaction, in order to save their own *chametz* from being lost. This is how *mekhirat chametz* began to spread and become increasingly common.

However, a number of prominent rabbis claimed that *mekhirat chametz* was not a real sale, but merely a fiction. In the first place, it is clear that after Pesach the *chametz* will return to the Jew. Moreover, no sales tax is paid to the government on this sale.[22] Thirdly, in a normal sale the buyer pays for all of the *chametz* and physically takes it into his possession, but here the gentile neither pays the full price, nor takes the *chametz* with him.

21. פניני הלכה | פסח ו:ב

לפני כארבע מאות שנה החלו יהודים רבים באירופה להתפרנס מייצור יין שרף (יי"ש) ומכירתו. וזאת משום שהרוזנים אדוני הארץ נהגו לתת ליהודים לנהל את עסקיהם, והיו רגילים להחכיר להם את עסקי היי"ש תמורת דמי חכירה ואחוזים מהמכירות. יי"ש זה, שנעשה משעורים וחיטים, נחשב לחמץ גמור. כדי שלא להפסיד הון עתק בכל שנה באיבוד היי"ש לפני הפסח, היה הכרח למוכרו לפני הפסח לגוי, ואחר הפסח לשוב לקנותו מידו, כדי להמשיך במכירתו לכל דורש.

במשך הזמן ראו גדולי ישראל שלפעמים קורה שהמכירה נעשית שלא כדין, ואזי החמץ נשאר ברשותו של היהודי, ועליו לאבדו מן העולם, ובכל שעה ושעה שיתעכב הוא עובר עליו באיסור תורה של 'בל יראה' ו'בל ימצא'. וגם לאחר הפסח יהיה אסור בהנאה ויצטרך לאבדו. **לפיכך נהגו רבני ישראל לנהל בעצמם את מכירת החמץ, כדי לוודא שהחמץ ימכר כדין.** וכיוון שהמכירה נעשתה מסודרת, יהודים נוספים נצטרפו למכירה כדי להציל את החמץ שברשותם מאיבוד, וכך החלה מכירת החמץ להיות רווחת יותר ויותר.

אלא שכמה מגדולי ישראל טענו כנגד מכירת החמץ, שאין היא מכירה אמיתית אלא הערמה, שהרי ברור שאחר הפסח החמץ יחזור לידי היהודי. ועוד, שאין משלמים על מכירה זו מס למלכות כדרך שמשלמים על כל מכירה. ועוד, שבכל מכירה רגילה הקונה משלם עבור כל החמץ ולוקחו לרשותו, ואילו כאן הגוי אינו משלם סכום מלא עבור היי"ש ואינו לוקחו לרשותו.

22. This approach contends that the sale must be legally valid according to secular law as well. But some *poskim* maintain that it need not be legally binding according to secular law as long as it is halachically valid, since the entire purpose of the sale is only a religious one (Responsa *Divrei Chaim* 2:37; see *Piskei Teshuvot* 448:22).

אולם דעת הפוסקים, רובם ככולם, שיש לסמוך על מכירת החמץ, מפני שיש לה תוקף ככל מכירה, ועל פי החוק והדין יכול הגוי אחר הפסח שלא למכור את החמץ בחזרה ליהודי, נמצא שהמכירה מוחלטת ואין בה הערמה. כלומר המכירה אינה מכירה פיקטיבית אלא מכירה משפטית (פורמלית)...

Nevertheless, the opinion of the vast majority of *poskim* is that *mekhirat chametz* may be relied upon and is as valid as any sale. By law, the gentile can refuse to sell the *chametz* back to the Jew after Pesach. It is a real, binding sale, not a fiction…[23]

In practice, the sale is accepted by most *poskim* today as entirely valid, and all *chametz* included in the sale is viewed as belonging to a gentile over Pesach. Nevertheless, a number of *poskim* recommend not selling actual *chametz* [*chametz gamur*] as part of the sale due to the multiple issues raised with the sale as practiced today. For example, **Rav Hershel Schachter** reports that **Rav Yosef Dov Soloveitchik** suggested to avoid selling actual *chametz.*[24]

22. נפש הרב | עמ' קעז

רבנו היה תמיד מעורר בכל שנה גם לתלמידיו שבישיבה וגם להבעלי הבתים שבמוריה שלא יסמכו על מכירת חמץ לחמץ דגן גמור בעין, אלא רק לתערובת חמץ, דלדעת ר"ת ליכא בל יראה דאורייתא אתערובת חמץ, ויש לסמך עליו לענין זה – להתיר הערמה בדרבנן. אבל בחמץ בעין, שבודאי יש בו בל יראה דאורייתא, אין לסמוך על ההערמה, וכדעת הבכור שור...

Nefesh HaRav, p. 177

Our teacher would consistently remind every year – both his students in the yeshiva and the *ba'alei batim* at Moriah – not to rely on a sale of *chametz* when the *chametz* is actual, fully recognizable *chametz,* but only [on a sale] involving mixtures containing *chametz*. According to Rabbeinu Tam, there is no Torah-level prohibition against owning a mixture containing *chametz,* and one may rely on this in order to permit a *ha'arama* regarding a rabbinic [prohibition]. By contrast, with actual *chametz,* where the Torah prohibition against owning *chametz* certainly applies,[25] one may not rely on a *ha'arama* – as explained by the *Bechor Shor*…

Other contemporary sources also report this custom among those who wish to be stringent.[26] For example, the ***Piskei Teshuvot*** notes:

23. See also Rav Shlomo Yosef Zevin, "*HaMo'adim B'halacha,*" vol. 2, ch. 4, who also outlines the history behind the development of the sale. He suggests four different periods: (1) A simple, concrete permanent sale; (2) Actual sale in which the *chametz* was transferred to the gentile but was understood that the *chametz* would be repurchased after Pesach; (3) Individual sale in which the *chametz* was not removed from the home of the Jew; (4) Current form of a general sale performed by the rabbi.

24. For a list of which products are considered actual *chametz* and which are not, see www.kashrut.com/articles/PeddlePurge; www.star-k.org/images/passover_book-abridged.pdf (p. 61); and www.kosharot.co.il/index2.php?id=51171&lang=HEB (Hebrew).

25. It appears that Rav Soloveitchik does not accept the claim of the *Bechor Shor* that since one also performs *bitul chametz,* no biblical prohibition is involved. See n. 21 above.

26. See also, e.g., *Kaf HaChaim* 448:45; *Masoret Moshe,* vol. 2, p. 147; *Hilchot Chagim* (Rav Mordechai Eliyahu) 3:42; *Minchat Asher, Pesach,* p. 9; *Oholei Halacha, Pesach,* p. 63; and Rav Shimon Eider, "Halachos of Pesach," p. 123.

23. פסקי תשובות | או"ח תמח:י

...אמנם עקב כל החששות הנ"ל נוהגים בעלי תורה ויראי שמים שאין משאירים בביתם חמץ בעין ומוכרים לנכרי רק כלי החמץ וחמץ נוקשה וע"י תערובת כתרופות וכיוצא בזה...

Piskei Teshuvot, Orach Chaim 448:10

...Nevertheless, due to all of the aforementioned concerns,[27] Torah scholars and God-fearing individuals do not leave actual *chametz* in their homes. They sell to a gentile only the vessels containing *chametz, chametz nuksheh,* and *chametz* included in mixtures,[28] such as in medicines or similar cases...

27. Among the concerns mentioned are many of those discussed above, such as the fact that the *chametz* remains in the home of the Jew, the fact that selling *chametz* was originally designed primarily for cases of significant loss, the fact that it will be repurchased after Pesach and is not viewed as a serious sale, and that the key to the room with the *chametz* is not given to the gentile.
28. The subject of *chametz nuksheh* (hard, inedible *chametz*) and *chametz* in mixtures, including medicine, was discussed in detail in *shiur* 2.

The Act of Acquisition (Kinyan)

One of the most difficult aspects of selling *chametz* to a gentile is ensuring that the *chametz* is transferred to the gentile through a valid, formal *kinyan* (transaction). Although there are many potential options, all of them are subject to dispute, and some are also impractical.

Meshicha (Pulling) or Payment?

The **Gemara (*Masechet Avoda Zara*)** quotes the view of Ameimar, that *meshicha* (pulling) is an effective *kinyan* for a gentile. Rav Ashi disputes this.

24. מסכת עבודה זרה עא.

אמר אמימר: משיכה בגוי קונה; תדע, דהני פרסאי משדרי פרדשני להדדי ולא הדרי בהו. רב אשי אמר, לעולם אימא לך: משיכה בגוי אינה קונה, והאי דלא הדרי בהו, דרמות רוחא הוא דנקיטא להו.

ח Masechet Avoda Zara 71a

Ameimar says: The legal act of **acquiring** an object **by pulling** it applies **to a gentile. Know** that it is so, **as those Persians send gifts to one another and do not retract them,** which shows that they acquire one from another by pulling the object alone, even without paying for it.[29] **Rav Ashi says: Actually, I will say to you** that **pulling** an object **does not acquire** it **in** a transaction involving **a gentile, and** the fact **that they do not retract their** gifts is not due to the halachot of acquisition but **because they are taken over by haughtiness,** and they consider it shameful to retract a gift.

The Gemara concludes that one can prove from a ruling of Rabbi Yochanan that *meshicha* is indeed an effective *kinyan* for a gentile, in accordance with Ameimar.

25. מסכת עבודה זרה עא:-עב.

אמר ליה רבינא לרב אשי: תא שמע, דאמר רבי חייא בר אבא אמר רבי יוחנן: בן נח נהרג על פחות משוה פרוטה, ולא ניתן להישבון... [עב.] בא חבירו ונטלה ממנו –

ח Masechet Avoda Zara 71b–72a

Ravina said to Rav Ashi: Come and **hear** another proof against your opinion, **as Rabbi Chiya bar Abba says** that **Rabbi Yochanan says: A descendant of Noach,** i.e., a gentile, **is executed** by the court **for** theft of even **less than the value of one *peruta*; but** if he stole less than the value of one *peruta* from a Jew, **it is not subject to restitution,** i.e., he is not obligated to return it, as the Jew presumably waived the debt… [72a] If **another** descendant of Noach **came and took** the stolen item **from him,**

29. This passage could be understood to mean that since the Persians follow this practice, it becomes, *de facto*, a halachically valid method of acquisition as well. Another interpretation is given by Tosafot, who suggest that this is not an actual proof to Ameimar's position, which, in truth, is derived from the Torah. Rather, the point is that this long-standing practice of the Persians not to retract may stem initially from a Torah rule that pulling effects acquisition for a gentile.

נהרג עליה. בשלמא רישא – משום דצעריה לישראל, אלא סיפא – מאי עביד?

אלא שמע מינה: משיכה בגוי קונה, שמע מינה.

he is also **executed for it. Granted,** with regard to **the first clause** it can be explained that although there is no obligation to return the item, the gentile is executed **because he caused the Jew distress; but** with regard to **the latter clause, what did he do?** He did not cause the Jew distress, and if pulling an item does not acquire it in a transaction involving a gentile, he did not commit a legally significant act by stealing the item, as it remains in the possession of the owner.

Rather, should one not **conclude from it** that one **pulling** an item **acquires** it **in** a transaction performed by **a gentile?** Accordingly, the actions of both the first and second gentiles are legally significant acts of theft, for which they are liable to be executed. The Gemara affirms: **Conclude from it** that this is so.

The **Gemara (*Masechet Bechorot*)** quotes the view of Reish Lakish, that a gentile can acquire an animal from a Jew by paying money for it, without pulling the animal. The Gemara also provides the Scriptural derivation for this ruling, and that a Jew acquires from his fellow Jew by pulling.

26. מסכת בכורות יג.

ח Masechet Bechorot 13a

אמר רבי יצחק בר נחמני אמר ריש לקיש משום רבי אושעיא... וגוי שנתן מעות לישראל בבהמתו בדיניהם, אף על פי שלא משך – קנה, ופטור מן הבכורה... אמר אביי: בדיניהם שפסקה להם תורה, וכי תמכרו ממכר לעמיתך, לעמיתך – במשיכה, הא לגוי – בכסף...

Rabbi Yitzchak bar Nachmani says that **Reish Lakish said in the name of Rabbi Oshaya**... In the case of **a gentile who gave money to a Jew to** buy the Jew's **animal** from him **according to their laws, even though** the gentile **did not pull** the animal, **he has acquired** it, **and** the Jew **is** therefore **exempt from** giving the animal's **firstborn** offspring to a priest... **Abaye said:** That which it states, that a gentile purchases an animal with money **according to their laws,** means: With the acts of acquisition **that the Torah prescribed** to gentiles, the manner in which they acquire items from Jews, i.e., with money, as it is stated: **"If you sell a sale item to your counterpart"** (*Vayikra* 25:14), from which it may be inferred: **To your counterpart,** i.e., a Jew, property **is** acquired **by pulling,**[30] but property **from the hand of a gentile** is acquired **with money**...

The Gemara then quotes the view of Ameimar, that a gentile acquires by pulling, and notes that this may indicate that he subscribes to the position of Rabbi Yochanan, that on a biblical level, a Jew acquires from his fellow Jew by paying money.[31]

27. מסכת בכורות יג:

ח Masechet Bechorot 13b

אמרי: ולאמימר דאמר משיכה בגוי קונה, הניחא אי סבר לה כרבי יוחנן דאמר דבר תורה מעות קונות משיכה לא,

The Sages **said: And according to** the opinion of **Ameimar, who says** that **pulling effects acquisition in** the case of **a gentile, this works out well if he holds in accordance with** the opinion of **Rabbi Yochanan, who says: By Torah law, money effects acquisition,** but **pulling** does **not.**

30. This is derived from the next phrase in the *pasuk*, "or a purchase from the hand of your counterpart," implying that the method of purchase involves delivering the item from one hand to another, i.e., pulling (Rashi).

31. All agree that practically speaking, a Jew acquires movable items from his fellow Jew by pulling and not by paying money. However, according to Rabbi Yochanan, this is not Torah law but a rabbinic institution (*Bava Metzia* 47b).

אהני לעמיתך, לעמיתך – בכסף, לעובד כוכבים במשיכה.

אלא אי סבר לה כריש לקיש דאמר משיכה מפורשת מן התורה, לעמיתך – במשיכה, ולגוי – במשיכה, לעמיתך למה לי?...

If Ameimar accepts Rabbi Yochanan's opinion, then it can be derived from the phrase **"of your counterpart"** that transactions **with your counterpart,** i.e., a Jew, are effected **through** payment of **money,** whereas transactions **with a gentile** are effected **by pulling.**

But if Ameimar **holds in accordance with** the opinion of **Reish Lakish, who says:** The act of acquisition of **pulling is explicit in the Torah,** then the halacha is that transactions **with your counterpart** are effected **by pulling, and** transactions **with a gentile** are also effected **by pulling.** Accordingly, **why do I** need the phrase **"of your counterpart"?...**

Elsewhere, **Rashi** implies that the halacha is in accordance with Reish Lakish, that a Jew acquires from a Jew by pulling an item, whereas a gentile acquires by payment.

28. רש"י | קידושין יד:

הואיל וכל קנינו – של גוי בכסף שלא נאמרה בו משיכה במטלטלין אלא בישראל כתיב מיד עמיתך עד שימשוך מיד ליד...

Rashi, Kiddushin 14b

Since all the acquisition – Of a gentile is through money, as pulling movable items is not mentioned [as a means of acquisition] regarding a gentile. Only regarding a Jew, it is written: "From the hand of your counterpart," [implying that the transaction is not complete] until one pulls from hand to hand...

Tosafot quote **Rabbeinu Tam**, who rules in accordance with Ameimar and Rabbi Yochanan that a gentile acquires through *meshicha*. One who wishes to take both Rashi's and Rabbeinu Tam's rulings into account must ensure that the gentile both pays and performs *meshicha*.

29. תוספות | עבודה זרה עא.

רב אשי אמר משיכה בגוי אינו קונה – ...**פירש רבינו תם** דאף על גב דרב אשי בתרא הוה לית הלכתא כוותיה בהאי אלא **קיימא לן כאמימר דאמר משיכה בגוי קונה** דסבירא ליה כרבי יוחנן כדפרישית והלכה כרבי יוחנן לגבי רבי שמעון בן לקיש... אם כן המקנה בהמה לגוי כדי לפוטרה מן הבכורה צריך שימשכנה הגוי ובכך סגי בלא כסף.

Tosafot, Avoda Zara 71a

Rav Ashi says: Pulling does not acquire in [a transaction involving] a gentile – Rabbeinu Tam explains that although Rav Ashi [lived] later [than Ameimar], the halacha does not follow him in this matter.[32] Rather, **we establish the halacha in accordance with Ameimar, who says that pulling effects acquisition for a gentile**, as he holds in accordance with Rabbi Yochanan, as I have explained. The halacha follows Rabbi Yochanan against Rabbi Shimon ben Lakish...Accordingly, one who transfers ownership of an animal to a gentile in order to exempt it from the laws of *bechora* [firstborn sanctity][33] must have the gentile perform *meshicha*, and that is sufficient without payment.

32. Rav Ashi was a younger contemporary of Ameimar. This would usually mean that the halacha is in accordance with his view, since he had the final authority to rule. This is especially true regarding Rav Ashi, who compiled the Gemara together with Ravina.

33. A firstborn [*bechor*] calf, goat or sheep owned by a Jew is automatically sanctified as a *korban* and must be given to a kohen. Today, since we are unable to offer sacrifices, we ensure that the mother is at least partially owned by a gentile before it

מיהו רש"י פירש דמשיכה אינה קונה בגוי אלא כסף דאין הלכה כרבי יוחנן אלא כרבי שמעון בן לקיש... **והרוצה לחוש לדברי רש"י ורבינו תם המקנה בהמה לגוי לפוטרה מן הבכורה צריך שיתן הגוי כסף וגם משיכת הגוי** בסימטא או לרשותו של גוי שהוא שלו...

However, Rashi explains that *meshicha* does not acquire for a gentile, rather money [does], as the halacha is not in accordance with Rabbi Yochanan but with Rabbi Shimon ben Lakish... **One who wishes to be concerned for the rulings of both Rashi and Rabbeinu Tam, when transferring an animal to a gentile to exempt it from *bechora*, must have the gentile give money and also perform *meshicha*,** either in an alleyway or into the gentile's own domain which belongs to him.

The **Rema** rules in a responsum that although *lechatchila*, one should have both *kinyanim* performed, *bedi'eved*, the gentile performing *meshicha* is sufficient, as most *Rishonim* concur with Rabbeinu Tam that a gentile acquires in this manner.

30. שו"ת הרמ"א | סימן פז

...דקיימא לן כרבינו תם דסבירא ליה דגבי גוי אינו קונה רק משיכה וכמו שכתבו התוספות והרא"ש והמרדכי פרק הזהב וכן דעת הפוסקים דמעות בישראל קונה, ואם כן לגוי קונה במשיכה... ואם כן המקנה בהמה לגוי כדי לפוטרה מן הבכורה צריך שימשכנה הגוי ובכך סגי בלא כסף.

ואף על גב דכתבו שם... והרוצה לחוש לדברי רש"י ולדברי ר"ת... צריך שיתן הגוי כסף וגם משיכה וכו', וכן כתב הרא"ש ריש בכורות, היינו דוקא לכתחילה...

א Responsa of the Rema, Siman 87

...**We establish the halacha in accordance with Rabbeinu Tam, who maintains that regarding a gentile, he acquires only by *meshicha*,** as Tosafot, the Rosh, and the Mordechai write. It is also the view of the *poskim* that regarding a Jew, money acquires, and accordingly regarding a gentile, *meshicha* acquires... Accordingly, one who transfers an animal to a gentile in order to exempt it from *bechora* must have the gentile perform *meshicha*, and that suffices without payment.

Although they write there... that one who wishes to be concerned for the rulings of both Rashi and Rabbeinu Tam... must have the gentile give money and also perform *meshicha*, etc., and the Rosh writes similarly at the beginning of *Bechorot*, this applies only *lechatchila*...

The ***Siftei Kohen* (*Shach*)** argues that one must perform both *kinyanim*, and that if one does not do so, even *bedi'eved* one must be concerned that the gentile may not have acquired.

31. שפתי כהן (ש"ך) | יו"ד שכ:ח

...ולצאת ידי ספק צריך לעשות קנין דמשיכה ומעות. ומשמע דאפילו דיעבד אם לא עשה אלא קנין אחד משיכה או מעות לא נפטר מבכורה...

א Siftei Kohen (Shach), Yoreh De'ah 320:8

...In order to avoid any doubt, one must perform the *kinyan* of *meshicha* and also of money. It is implied that even *bedi'eved*, if one performed only one *kinyan*, *meshicha* or money, [the animal] is not exempt from *bechora*...

According to both the Rema and the *Shach*, one cannot rely on the gentile paying for the *chametz* alone to complete the transaction, as this is only effective according to the minority of *Rishonim*. This creates

---

gives birth to its firstborn, to avoid sanctity taking effect. The halachot of transfer of ownership of the animal for this purpose are identical to those governing transfer of ownership of *chametz* to a gentile.

a difficulty when selling *chametz*, as it is usually impractical for the gentile to perform *meshicha* on all the *chametz* that he must acquire. Accordingly, the standard practice is for the gentile to pay a nominal amount in order to satisfy Rashi's position,[34] and we also perform other *kinyanim* in order to satisfy the majority view that this is not sufficient. As we shall see, the effectiveness of each of these alternative *kinyanim* is disputed.

Chalifin

A common *kinyan* first described in *Megillat Rut* (4:7) is *chalifin*, whereby the buyer gives the seller an item[35] and thereby acquires the item being sold. In *Megillat Rut*, this item is a shoe; nowadays, a handkerchief, pen, or the like is commonly used. The item is usually returned to the buyer after the sale is completed. This *kinyan* is convenient and can be used to acquire either land or movable items. But is it effective between a Jew and a gentile? **Tosafot** quote **Rabbeinu Tam**, who maintains that this *kinyan* may indeed be used to transfer ownership to a gentile.

32. תוספות | קידושין ג.

...שמע מינה דשאר דברים נקנין בחליפין לגוי וכן היה רגיל רבינו תם לשלוח הרשאה ביד גוי והיה מקנה בחליפין.

ו Tosafot, Kiddushin 3a

...One can infer from here that other items can be transferred to a gentile through *chalifin*.[36] Similarly, Rabbeinu Tam would regularly grant power of attorney to a gentile, and would transfer [authority to him] through *chalifin*.

However, the ***Shach*** writes that he is hesitant to rely on this practice of Rabbeinu Tam, as the Gemara and other *poskim* never mention that *chalifin* can be effective for a gentile.

33. ש"ך | חושן משפט (חו"מ) קכג:ל

...**לבי מהסס בעיקר הדין שסובר רבינו תם דחליפים מועיל לגוי** דלא אישתמיט בשום מקום בש"ס דגוי קונה בחליפים וכן בפוסקים לא אישתמיט חד מנייהו שהזכיר דין זה במקומות שהזכירו דיני קנין לגוי... וכן גבי חמץ האריכו הפוסקים וכל האחרונים לעשות בהיתר להקנות לו היכא דלא אפשר במשיכה

א Shach, Choshen Mishpat 123:30

...**My heart is hesitant regarding the basic halacha held by Rabbeinu Tam, that *chalifin* is effective for a gentile.** As it cannot be found anywhere in the Gemara that a gentile acquires by *chalifin*; and likewise, among the *poskim*, not one of them mentions this halacha in the places where they mention the halchot of acquisition for a gentile... Similarly, regarding *chametz*, the *poskim* and all the *Acharonim* write at length to formulate a permitted method to transfer ownership to [a gentile] when *meshicha* is not possible,

---

34. Since the gentile only pays a small portion of the value of the *chametz* at the time of the sale, he becomes obligated to pay the rest of the value of the *chametz*, but that is only determined by appraisers after Pesach. In the standard case, after Pesach the gentile agrees to sell back the *chametz*, the debt is therefore forgiven, and the deposit paid is returned to the gentile.

35. The Gemara (*Bava Metzia* 47a) cites a debate as to which party gives the other an item, but the halacha follows the opinion that the buyer gives the seller an item.

36. Tosafot here cite the Gemara (*Kidushin* 8a) that a Jew may not be purchased through *chalifin* when sold as a slave to a gentile, and infer that *chalifin* may be used for other purchases involving a gentile.

ואם איתא לקנינהו ניהליה בחליפים...

and if it were true [that *chalifin* is effective], one should simply transfer it to him by *chalifin*...[37]

Agav Karka

Another potential method of selling *chametz* is to sell or rent land to the gentile and include the *chametz* in the *kinyan* used for the land (which could be payment or giving the gentile a bill of sale or rental, either of which are more convenient than *meshicha*). This is known as *kinyan agav karka* (or just *kinyan agav*), acquiring together with land.

The ***Nachalat Shiva*** quotes a responsum of **Rav Shmuel Kaidanover** regarding *mechirat chametz*. He concludes that due to practical and halachic difficulties involved with using other methods, the ideal way to sell *chametz* is through *kinyan agav*.

34. נחלת שבעה | תשובה ל

ומצאתי ברבינו ירוחם חלק אדם וחוה (כ:ב) שכתב וזה לשונו: ולצאת ידי שניהם יקבל מהגוי מעות בשביל אוזן הבהמה פרוטה וימשוך הבהמה, או יקנה להגוי המקום שהבהמה עומדת שם ויקנה לו אגביו אוזן הבהמה עם העובר עד כאן לשונו.

ואמרתי טבא חדא פלפלא וכו' דלכולהו אית להו פירכא ולדידיה לית ליה פירכא כלל, דמבואר שלא מדין חצר קני ליה אלא מתורת מטלטלין אגב קרקע...

ולפי זה **גם במכירת חמץ יש לנו להזהר למכור להגוי החדר שהחמץ בתוכו וליקח פרוטה, ואקני חדר וחמץ אגביה** ולא שנותן בתורת חצר, וקלסו רבותי את דברי. וכך אני מורה לבא בפסח לשאול אותי. ומקום הניחו לי רבותי האחרונים להתגדר בו ודו"ק.

א Nachalat Shiva, Responsum 30

I found that Rabbeinu Yerucham writes as follows: "In order to satisfy both views, one should receive payment from the gentile for the ear of the animal, a *peruta*, and [have the gentile] pull the animal; or he should transfer to the gentile the place where the animal stands, and transfer to him the ear of the [mother] animal together with [*agav*] the fetus."

I said: One [sharp] pepper is better [than a basketful of pumpkins][38]... as there are difficulties with all the other [methods], but with [the method of Rabbeinu Yerucham] there is no difficulty at all. As it is clear that he does not acquire based on the halacha of *chatzer* [a courtyard acquiring items placed in it on behalf of its owner],[39] but rather based on the halacha of movable items acquired together with land...

Accordingly, **regarding the sale of *chametz* as well, we should take care to sell the gentile the room in which the *chametz* is located, receive a *peruta*, and transfer the room and the *chametz* together with it**, not transfer it based on the halacha of *chatzer*. My teachers praised my words, and I instruct those who come to ask me [before] Pesach accordingly. My teachers, the *Acharonim*, left room for me to establish myself in this matter; consider this.

37. See also *Ketzot HaChoshen* 195:1, who writes at length to support the position of Rabbeinu Tam that a gentile can acquire through *chalifin* and to resolve all the difficulties raised by the *Shach*.

38. A quote from *Megilla* 7a.

39. This would be another potential method of selling *chametz* to a gentile. This method is also disputed, but we have not discussed this at length here as it is usually impractical to ask the gentile to bring the *chametz* to his own domain.

However, the ***Ketzot HaChoshen*** comments that contrary to the statement of Rav Kaidanover, there is a potential problem with using *kinyan agav* to sell to a gentile. As since *kinyan agav* is merely a rabbinic institution according to some, it is possible that this institution was only made for Jews and not for gentiles.

35. קצות החושן | חו"מ קצד:ג

...אמנם מה שכתב הרב הנזכר דלכולהו אית להו פירכא ולדידיה לית ליה פירכא, **כד דייקת גם בתורת אגב יש לגמגם** לפי מה שכתבו תוספות והרא"ש פרק קמא דבבא קמא דף י"ב דקנין אגב אינו אלא מדרבנן וקרא דויתן להם ערים בצורות (דברי הימים ב כא, ג) אינו אלא אסמכתא...

ואפילו לפי מה שכתב הבית יוסף באבן העזר שם (סימן כח) דכיון שתקנו חכמים שיהיה קונה הוה ליה קידושי תורה, אכתי יש לחוש לדעת העיר שושן (סו, כה) והסמ"ע (סו, א) דלמאן דאמר מכירת שטרות דרבנן גוי אינו קונה בתקנתא דרבנן... ואם כן **בקנין אגב קרקע דאינו אלא מדרבנן אפשר דגוי אינו קונה.**

א Ketzot HaChoshen, Choshen Mishpat 194:3

...However, regarding what the aforementioned rav [Rav Kaidanover] wrote, that there are difficulties with all the other [methods], but with [the method of Rabbeinu Yerucham] there is no difficulty at all, **if you analyze, there is also room for hesitation regarding [using] the halacha of *agav*.** As according to that which Tosafot and the Rosh write in the first chapter of *Bava Kamma* (12a), *kinyan agav* is only rabbinic, and the verse [quoted as the source for this *kinyan*], "He gave them fortified cities" (*Divrei HaYamim* 2, 21:3) is merely an *asmachta* [hint]...

Even according to that which the *Beit Yosef* writes in *Even HaEzer* that since the Sages instituted that it acquires, [betrothal performed using an item acquired in this manner] is a valid betrothal on a Torah level, one must still be concerned for the view of the *Ir Shushan* and the *Sema*, that according to the view that the sale of [promissory] documents is rabbinic, a gentile cannot acquire based on this rabbinic institution[40]... Therefore, **it is possible that a gentile cannot acquire through *kinyan agav karka*, which is only rabbinic.**[41]

Udita

The **Gemara (*Masechet Bava Batra*)** relates that a *ger* named Issur had a biological son named Rav Mari, who was conceived before he converted and would not inherit him. Before he died, Issur wanted to give his money to Rav Mari, but there was a difficulty in finding an appropriate *kinyan*. Eventually, a suggestion was made that Issur should simply admit that his property already belonged to Rav Mari. Issur followed this recommendation, although Rava felt that this was inappropriate.

---

40. According to the *Beit Yosef*, once Chazal instituted that a *kinyan* is effective, this becomes valid even on a biblical level. This is either because Chazal had the power to transfer ownership (*hefker beit din*) or because the Torah itself recognizes any *kinyan* that becomes accepted. However, others dispute this, and the *Ketzot* is concerned that their view may be correct.

41. See however *Milu'ei Choshen*, n. 32א, who claims that even the *Ketzot HaChoshen* only objects to using *kinyan agav* when selling part of an animal to a gentile to avoid the sanctity of *bechora* taking effect. In this case, it is possible that Chazal never instituted that this *kinyan* should be effective for the benefit of the gentile. However, regarding the sale of *chametz*, since *chametz* becomes valueless during Pesach, the sale only benefits the Jew. In this case, the *Ketzot HaChoshen* agrees that *kinyan agav* is effective. Support for this can be found in the comments of the *Ketzot HaChosen* regarding *udita*, where he understands it to be another rabbinic *kinyan*, but recommends using for selling *chametz*, as we shall see shortly.

36. מסכת בבא בתרא קמט.

דאיסור גיורא הוה ליה תריסר אלפי זוזי בי רבא. רב מרי בריה, הורתו שלא בקדושה ולידתו בקדושה הואי, ובי רב הוה.

אמר רבא: היכי ניקנינהו רב מרי להני זוזי? אי בירושה – לאו בר ירושה הוא; אי במתנה – מתנת שכיב מרע כירושה שויוה רבנן, כל היכא דאיתיה בירושה איתיה במתנה, כל היכא דליתיה בירושה ליתיה במתנה.

אי במשיכה – ליתנהו גביה; אי בחליפין – אין מטבע נקנה בחליפין; אי אגב קרקע – לית ליה ארעא; אי במעמד שלשתן – אי שלח לי לא אזילנא.

מתקיף לה רב איקא בריה דרב אמי: אמאי? ולודי איסור דהלין זוזי דרב מרי נינהו, וליקנינהו באודיתא! אדהכי נפק אודיתא מבי איסור. איקפד רבא, אמר: קא מגמרי טענתא לאינשי ומפסדי לי.

ח Masechet Bava Batra 149a

Issur the convert had twelve thousand dinars deposited in **the house of Rava. Rav Mari,** Issur's **son, whose conception was not in** the **sanctity** of the Jewish People, i.e., he was conceived before his father converted, **but his birth was in** the **sanctity** of the Jewish People, i.e., he was born after his father converted, **was** in **a study hall** elsewhere when his father was on his deathbed.

Rava reasoned that he would acquire possession of the deposit for himself, as he **said: How can Rav Mari acquire these dinars? If** he attempts to acquire the money **as inheritance, he is not fit to inherit** from Issur. Since he was conceived before his father converted, he is therefore not halachically considered his son. **If** he attempts to acquire it **as a gift, the Sages equated** the halachic status of the **gift of a person on his deathbed with** that of **inheritance.** Therefore, **anywhere that** the property **can be** acquired **as inheritance, it can** also **be** acquired **as** such **a gift,** and **anywhere that** the property **cannot be** acquired **as inheritance, it cannot be** acquired **as a gift.**

If he attempts to acquire the dinars **by pulling** them, which is a formal act of acquisition, he will not be able to do this, as the dinars **are not with him. If** he attempts to acquire them **by** means of symbolic **exchange,** a pro forma act of acquisition effecting the transfer of ownership of an article, **money cannot be acquired by** means of symbolic **exchange. If** he attempts to acquire them **by means of** the acquisition of **land,** Issur **does not have** any **land. If** he attempts to acquire them by means of verbal instruction made by his father **in the presence of** all **three** parties, i.e., the giver, the recipient, and the bailee, **if he sends for me,** the bailee, **I shall not go,** as without the presence of the bailee he cannot transfer ownership of the money.

Rav Ika, son of Rav Ami, objected to this: Why is Rav Mari unable to acquire the money? **But** why not **let Issur admit that these dinars are** owned **by Rav Mari, and he shall transfer** ownership of **them** to Rav Mari **by admission? In the meantime,** a document of **admission** stating that the dinars belonged to Rav Mari **emerged from Issur's house. Rava became angry,** and **said: They are teaching people** legal **claims and causing me loss.**[42]

The *Rishonim* dispute how the admission of Issur enabled Rav Mari to "acquire" the money. There are three main views:[43]

---

42. Rava's objection was likely due to the fact that he did not accept that the admission was a legitimate form of *kinyan*, but viewed it merely as a deceptive method of causing people to believe that Rav Mari already owned the money, although this was false. This would support the view of Rashbam quoted shortly. See also Meiri, who explains that Rava wanted to give Rav Mari the money himself, as an act of kindness or piety.

43. There appears to be a contradiction within the Gemara itself as to what the admission achieves. Rav Ikka says that through the admission, Rav Mari will **acquire** the money. However, Rava's objection is that the idea of Rav Ikka is merely a **claim**. The *Rishonim* appear to dispute which of these terms is more accurate.

1. Just as any admission by a litigant (*hoda'at ba'al din*) that money he holds does not belong to him is believed, the same is true in this case. Thus, although no *kinyan* was possible, Rav Mari was now assumed to be the original owner of the money. (**Rashbam**).
2. Chazal instituted that a person on his deathbed is able to transfer ownership of his property by means of an "admission" (*udita*) that the property belongs to the recipient (first explanation of **Tosafot; Ri Migash**).
3. Anyone can transfer ownership through admission, whether healthy or sick (second explanation of **Tosafot**).[44]

Only according to the third view, it may be possible to transfer ownership of *chametz* to a gentile by means of admission. The ***Turei Zahav*** assumes that the first view is correct, and accordingly, he writes that admission is not a valid *kinyan* when one wishes to avoid prohibitions. He therefore rejects a similar suggestion made by his father-in-law, the ***Bayit Chadash*** (***Bach***), that a Jew could lend money to another Jew, "admit" that the money in fact belongs to a gentile, and thereby charge interest on the loan.

37. טורי זהב (ט"ז) | יו"ד קסח:יד

...ומורי וחמי ז"ל כתב דאפשר ליישב דהכי קאמר **שיהיה זוכה בו בדרך שיזכה בו הגוי כגון באודיתא שמודה שהוא של גוי** כההיא דפרק מי שמת בעובדא דאיסור גיורא כו'.

ולא נהירא לי דההיא אודיתא דאיסור גיורא שהודה שהממון אינו שלו אינו ענין לכאן כלל דודאי לגבי ממון אמרינן שאדם נאמן לחובתו והודאת בעל דין כמאה עדים דמי אף על פי שאנו יודעים שהוא משקר... אבל **זהו ודאי אינו שיועיל לאפקועי איסורא בשביל שקר שלו** דהגע עצמך אם ילוה ישראל מחבירו ויתן לו רבית ויאמר לו הנני מודה שמעות אלו הם של גוי אם יעלה על הדעת שעל ידי זה יהיה מותר למלוה ליקח הרבית אלא שאין סברא כלל בזה להתיר האיסור בשביל השקר שהוא מפורסם.

א Turei Zahav (Taz), Yoreh De'ah 168:14

My teacher and father-in-law [**the** ***Bach***] **writes that it is possible** to resolve that this is what [the Mordechai] means, **that the gentile would acquire it in a manner through which a gentile can acquire, such as through** ***udita*****, that** [**the Jew**] **admits that it belongs to the gentile**, like the case of Issur the *ger* in chapter *Mi Shemet*, etc.

But this does not appear correct to me, as the case of the *udita* of Issur the *ger*, where he admitted that the money was not his, is not relevant here at all. As certainly, regarding monetary matters, we say that a person is believed when it is to his own detriment, and a litigant's admission is like a hundred witnesses, even if we know that he is lying... However, **it is certainly not the case that his lie would help to remove a prohibition.** Consider for yourself: if a Jew were to borrow from his fellow and pay him interest, and then say to him, "I hereby admit that this money belongs to a gentile," could it enter your mind that by this means it would become permissible for the lender to take interest? Rather, there is absolutely no rationale to permit a prohibition because of a known lie.

The ***Ketzot HaChoshen*** argues that the majority of *Rishonim* accept the third view, that admission is itself a *kinyan*, and not only for a person on his deathbed. He calls this *kinyan udita* and writes that it may be used to transfer ownership of *chametz* to a gentile.

---

44. Tosafot conclude that their first explanation is more correct.

א Ketzot HaChoshen, Choshen Mishpat 194:3

When I directed my attention to this matter, I found *kinyan udita*, i.e., that one should write, "My signature shall testify concerning me, etc., how I sold all the *chametz* to so-and-so in an effective manner." Since he admits that he sold it in an effective manner, the gentile acquires it through this admission (*udita*). As **admission constitutes a *kinyan*, even though both parties know that it is not true... The comments of the *Bach*, that even regarding prohibitions, an admission is valid, appear correct**.

It is true that the *Rishonim* already disagreed concerning *kinyan udita*, whether it is effective for a healthy person or only for someone on his deathbed. However, the *Shach* already ruled that that which those who dissent write, that the case of Issur the *ger* speaks specifically of one on his deathbed and not of a healthy person, is incorrect, and all the *poskim* dispute that view.[45]

38. קצות החושן | חו"מ קצד:ג

וכאשר שמתי אל לבי בזה מצאתי קנין אודיתא דהיינו שיכתוב חתימת ידי תעיד עלי כו' איך שמכרתי את כל החמץ לפלוני באופן המועיל, וכיון שמודה שמכר באופן המועיל קנה הגוי באודיתא זו ומשום **דאודיתא הוי קנין אף על פי ששניהן יודעין שאינו כן... ונראין דברי הב"ח דאפילו באיסורין מהני הודאה...**

והן אמת דכבר נחלקו רבוותא בקנין אודיתא אם מהני בבריא או אינו אלא בשכיב מרע, אלא שכבר הכריע בש"ך סימן ס' (סעיף קטן ל"ב) דמה שכתבו החולקין דהך דאיסור גיורא איירי דוקא בשכיב מרע ולא בבריא ליתיה וכל הפוסקים חולקין בזה.

The ***Mishna Berura*** summarizes some of the *kinyanim* that can potentially be used to sell *chametz* to a gentile and the disputes regarding them. He concludes that ideally, one should indeed both receive payment and have the gentile perform *meshicha*, but where this is not possible, other methods can be used. *Bedi'eved*, even if the gentile only paid for the *chametz* and did not perform any other *kinyan*, the *chametz* is nevertheless permitted after Pesach.

א Mishna Berura, Orach Chaim 448:17, 19

17. **He should sell it to him** – There are differing views among the *poskim* regarding by which *kinyanim* a gentile can acquire. There are those who say that the *kinyan* for a gentile is only through payment. Some say that a gentile acquires only by pulling (*meshichah*) into his domain or by lifting an item that can be lifted.[46]

Some write further that the other *kinyanim* also apply to a gentile, such as acquiring movable items together with (*agav*) land, acquisition by courtyard (*chatzer*), and *kinyan chalifin*, i.e., *kinyan* using a kerchief (but one must take care to ensure

39. משנה ברורה | או"ח תמח:יז, יט

יז. **או שימכרנו לו** – ובאיזה קנינים קונה הגוי יש בזה דעות בין הפוסקים יש מי שאומר דקנינו של גוי הוא בכסף דוקא ויש אומרים שאין הגוי קונה אלא במשיכה לרשותו או בהגבהה דבר שאפשר להגביה.

ויש שכתבו עוד דגם שארי קנינים נוהגין בגוי כגון קניית מטלטלין אגב קרקע וקנין חצר וקנין חליפין דהיינו קנין סודר (אלא דצריך ליזהר בזה

---

45. See, however, *Tur* and *Shulchan Aruch*, C.M. 250:3, who appear to assume that only a person on his deathbed can transfer ownership in this manner. See also Rema, C.M. 207:15, who does rule that a false admission can facilitate a *kinyan* (although see *Sema* 207:42 who explains that this admission merely removes the problem of *asmachta* and does not necessarily achieve the *kinyan* alone).

46. Items that can be lifted must be lifted in order to acquire them; *meshicha* is ineffective for such items (*Bava Batra* 86a).

שיהא הסודר של גוי ולא סגי שעדי הקנין יתנו סודרם כמו בישראל דזה אינו אלא מטעם זכיה שמזכין להמקנה וגבי גוי אין דין זכיה) ויש מפקפקים בקנינים אלו ואומרים דלא מצינו קנינים אלו רק בישראל.

ולענין דינא לכתחלה בודאי צריך להקנות בקנין גמור ומוסכם לכולי עלמא דהיינו בכסף ובמשיכה ביחד מאחר שנוגע באיסור דאורייתא דבל יראה ועל כל פנים במשיכה בלבד דיוצא בזה גם כן על כל פנים לרוב הפוסקים.

אבל בדיעבד אף אם לא מכר אלא בכסף בלבד או שמכר באחד משארי קנינים שהזכרנו ועבר עליו הפסח מותר דמאחר דחמץ לאחר הפסח אינו אסור אלא מקנסא דרבנן ועוד כיון דחמץ לאחר זמן איסורו בלאו הכי אינו ברשותו אלא שעשה הכתוב כאלו היה ברשותו לעבור עליו בקנין כל דהו סגי דעל כל פנים מגלי דעתיה דלא ניחא ליה ואפקיה מרשותו.

יט. ...**כתבו האחרונים דאף על גב דלכתחלה יש למכור בכסף ובמשיכה מכל מקום אם החמץ מרובה ואי אפשר למשוך החמץ כולו וכן אם אין החמץ כאן שיכול הגוי למושכו אלא הוא בעיר אחרת או בדרך יש לו להקנותו לנכרי בשאר קנינים** כגון:

- על ידי רושם שנהגו בקצת מקומות שהלוקח רושם על דבר הנקנה כדי שיהיה לו סימן ידוע ועל ידי זה קנוי לו הרבה;
- או על ידי תקיעת כף דהיינו שמכין כפיהם זה על זה;
- או על ידי נתינת פרוטה במקומות שנהגו שכשהלוקח נותן פרוטה למוכר נגמר המקח;
- או במקום שנהגו שמסירת המפתח הוי גמר המקח...
- וכן כל כיוצא בו כל מקום ומקום כפי מנהג הסוחרים.

that the kerchief belongs to the gentile, and it is not sufficient for the witnesses to provide their own kerchief, as is valid with a Jew, as this works only because of *zechiya* [the witnesses act on behalf of the seller], and with a gentile there is no halacha of *zechiya*). Some question [the use of] these *kinyanim* [for *mechirat chametz*] and say that we only find these *kinyanim* regarding a Jew.

Regarding practical halacha, *lechatchila* one must certainly perform a *kinyan* that is fully and unanimously accepted, i.e., through payment and *meshicha* together, since the matter involves a biblical prohibition of "*bal yeira'eh*." Or at least, one should use *meshicha* alone, as this also fulfills the requirement, at least according to most *poskim*.

But *bedi'eved*, even if one sold [the *chametz*] through payment alone, or if he sold it through one of the other *kinyanim* mentioned above, and Pesach passed, [the *chametz*] is permitted. As since *chametz* that was owned during Pesach is prohibited only because of a rabbinic penalty, and further, since *chametz* after the time of prohibition arrives is, in any case, not [considered to be] in one's possession, but the Torah considers it "as though" it is in his possession only regarding violating the prohibition, any *kinyan* is sufficient, since one at least reveals that in his mind he does not want it and he [attempts to] remove it from his possession.

19. ...**The *Acharonim* write that even though, *lechatchila*, one should sell through payment and *meshicha*, nevertheless, if there is a large quantity of *chametz* and it is not possible to pull all the *chametz*, or if the *chametz* is not present for the gentile to be able to pull it, but is in another city or en route, one may transfer ownership to the gentile through other *kinyanim***, such as:

- by marking it, as is customary in some places, where the buyer marks the item being acquired so that it has a known identifying mark, and through this [even] a large quantity becomes acquired by him;
- by handshake, i.e., by striking their hands together;
- by giving a coin, in places where it is customary that when the buyer gives a coin to the seller, the transaction is complete;
- in places where handing over the key [to the room in which an item is stored] constitutes completion of the sale...
- or any similar method, in each place according to its custom.

These are considered *kinyanim* according to Torah law, and one may legitimately transfer ownership of *chametz* through such *kinyanim*. Alternatively, one may sell the *chametz* by means of [*kinyan*] *agav*…

חשיב הדבר כקנין על פי דין תורה ושפיר יש להקנות גם החמץ בקנין כזה. או יש למכור החמץ על ידי אגב...

Today, *rabbanim* who are responsible for selling *chametz* of a community typically do so using all or many of these *kinyanim*, to ensure that at least one of the *kinyanim* used is valid. This is noted by **Rav Shmuel Stern** in his work ***Mechirat Chametz K'hilchato***.[47]

Mechirat Chametz K'hilchato 20:2, 4

40. מכירת חמץ כהלכתו כ:ב, ד

2. One should also explain to the buyer clearly the various methods of *kinyan* that will be used to effect the acquisition of the *chametz* and the rented areas, including *kesef* (payment), *shtar* (document), *chatzer* (acquisition through one's domain), *agav karka* (with land), *chalifin* (symbolic exchange), and *situmta* (commercial practice).

4. It should be emphasized to the buyer that all of the *kinyanim* being performed are not intended so that the acquisition should take effect only through all of them together; rather, each *kinyan* on its own is sufficient to complete the transaction, and none of the acts of acquisition is meant to negate the others.

ב. כן יסביר לו היטב את דרכי הקניינים השונים, שישתמשו בהם לשם הקנאת החמץ והמקומות המושכרים, כסף, שטר, חצר, אגב קרקע, חליפין, וסיטומתא.

ד. יש להדגיש לקונה, שכל הקניינים הנעשים, אינם נעשים בכדי שחלות הקנין, יהא על ידי כולם, אלא שכל אחד בפני עצמו יהא ראוי לגמור את הקנין, ושלא יבטל מעשה קנין אחד את השני.

47. For a sample text of the *mechirat chametz* in English, see https://rabbis.org/resource/shtar-mechirat-chametz-english.

WHICH *KINYANIM* CAN BE USED FOR *MECHIRAT CHAMETZ*?

	Meshicha (pulling)	Payment	*Chalifin*	*Agav Karka*	*Udita*
Ameimar, Rabbi Yochanan, Ravina	Effective	Not effective	–	–	–
Reish Lakish, Rav Ashi	Not effective	Effective	–	–	–
Rashi	Not effective	Effective	–	–	–
Rabbeinu Tam	Effective	Not effective	Effective	–	–
Tur, Shulchan Aruch	–	–	–	–	Not effective (implication)
Rema	Effective	Not effective	–	–	Effective (implication)
Shach	May not be effective alone	May not be effective alone	Not effective	–	–
Taz	–	–	–	–	Not effective
Rav Shmuel Kaidanover	May not be effective alone	May not be effective alone	–	Effective	–
Ketzot HaChoshen	May not be effective alone	May not be effective alone	Effective	May not be effective alone	Effective
Mishna Berura	May not be effective alone, but this is the best method	May not be effective alone, but works *bedi'eved*	May not be effective, but works *bedi'eved*	May not be effective, but works *bedi'eved*	May not be effective, but works *bedi'eved*

Appointing an Agent to Sell *Chametz*

We have seen in source 21 that the standard practice today is for each individual to appoint a rav as his agent to sell his *chametz* to a gentile before Pesach.[48] This typically involves signing an authorization document that defines the terms of that agency. **Rav Eliezer Melamed** emphasizes that this process must be understood and treated as a genuine sale: while many of its details are ideal rather than essential, the central requirement is that the seller recognize that ownership of the *chametz* truly transfers to the non-Jew and that he would be obligated to allow the non-Jew to take possession if he so wished.

41. Peninei Halakha, Pesach 8:7

Every Jew, before selling *chametz*, should read the authorization contract he will be signing, so that he understands that he is empowering the rabbi to sell his *chametz*, and that the sale is absolute. But even if instead of reading the contract one simply relied on the rabbi, the sale is valid, for, if the gentile comes during Pesach to take the *chametz*, and the rabbi tells the Jew that the *chametz* indeed belongs to the gentile, and that he must give it to the gentile, he will do so.

The seller should write his name and address in clear script on the contract of sale so that the gentile buyer knows who he is and where he lives. Thus, the gentile buyer will be able, if he wants, to collect his *chametz*.

Le-khathila, it is proper to give the gentile the key to the place where the *chametz* is located so that he can enter and take his *chametz*. In practice, though, it is sufficient to give the gentile the seller's phone number so that if the gentile wants, he can call to come and take his *chametz*. This is the most important principle: all sellers must know that after the sale, the *chametz* indeed belongs to the gentile, and the seller must allow him to enter the house and take his *chametz*.

***Le-khathila*, the seller should indicate the various types of *chametz*, and even list their prices, on the contract the rabbi gives him to sign**, and some people are

41. פניני הלכה | פסח ח:ז

ראוי שכל יהודי שעומד למכור את חמצו יקרא את שטר ההרשאה שעליו הוא חותם, כדי שיבין שהוא ממנה את הרבנות למכור את חמצו וידע שהמכירה מוחלטת. אמנם גם אם לא קרא וסמך על הרב, מכירתו כשרה, שכן אם בפסח יבוא הגוי לקחת את החמץ והרב יאמר לו שאכן החמץ שייך לגוי ועליו לתת לגוי את חמצו – יתן, נמצא שהמכירה כשרה.

יש לכתוב בשטר המכירה את שם המוכר ואת כתובתו בכתב קריא, כדי שידע הקונה הגוי מי המוכר והיכן הוא גר, וכך אם ירצה הגוי, יוכל לקחת את חמצו.

בעבר, לכתחילה נתנו לגוי את המפתח של המקום שבו מונח החמץ. אולם כיום מסתפקים בכך שמציינים את מספר הטלפון של מוכר החמץ, כדי שאם הגוי ירצה, יוכל להתקשר אליו כדי לקחת את חמצו. וזה היסוד החשוב ביותר, שידעו כל המוכרים, שאחר המכירה אכן החמץ שייך לגוי וצריך לאפשר לו להיכנס לבית ולקחת את חמצו.

לכתחילה היה ראוי לציין בשטר את כל מיני החמץ הנמכרים, ואף לציין את מחירם, והיו

48. *Poskim* discuss how one should sell *chametz* if he plans to be in a different time zone for Pesach than his *chametz*, such as if he travels to Israel while his *chametz* is in the United States, or the reverse case. Most *poskim* conclude that one must follow the time zone in which the owner is located on Erev Pesach (e.g., Responsa *Eretz Tzvi* 83; Responsa *Minchat Yitzchak* 7:25; Responsa *Igrot Moshe*, O.C. 4:94), but recommend being stringent in both directions to accommodate the other opinion (Responsa *Oneg Yom Tov*) as well that the time zone of the *chametz* itself is significant. Accordingly one who travels from the U.S. to Israel for Pesach should make sure his *chametz* is sold by the latest time to sell *chametz* in Israel (many *rabbanim* perform two sales to address this issue, with one being on the day before Erev Pesach), and that the *chametz* is not repurchased until after Pesach is over in the U.S. The same rules would be true in reverse for one who travels from Israel to the U.S. for Pesach. See *Mechirat Chametz K'hilchato* 3:14.

שדקדקו בזה. אולם למעשה קשה מאוד לבצע זאת, ולכן **נוהגים לכתוב שכל החמץ של המוכר כלול במכירה, והמחיר הוא לפי המקובל בשוק וכפי שיקבעו אותו שמאים.**

נכון לכתוב בשטר המכירה היכן בדיוק יהיה החמץ מונח. כגון: "בארון המטבח העליון משמאל", או "בחדר הימני בארגז שיסומן לכך". אפשר גם לציין מספר מקומות. **בדיעבד גם בלא זה המכירה כשרה, אבל צריך לרכז את החמץ במקום מיוחד ולסמנו.** וכל מה שמכניסים לאותו מקום שנקבע למכירה עד כשעתיים לפני זמן איסור הנאה מחמץ נכלל במכירה. לכתחילה משכירים לגוי את המקום שעליו החמץ עומד, כדי שעל ידי כך החמץ יהיה מונח ברשותו של הגוי והמכירה תראה ככל המכירות שבהם הקונה מעביר את קניינו לרשותו.

אפשר למכור את החמץ על ידי שליח שיכתוב את כל הפרטים הנדרשים ויחתום על השטר במקום בעל החמץ. ניתן למכור את החמץ בטלפון או באינטרנט. ואף שבאופן זה אין המוכר מבצע פעולת קניין שבה הוא ממנה את הרב לשליחו למכירת החמץ, העיקר הוא הקניין שנעשה בעת שהרבנות מוכרת את החמץ לגוי, וקניין זה חל עבור כל המבקשים מהרבנות למכור את חמצם. במטבחים של מוסדות ציבור ימכור המנהל או מישהו מטעמו את החמץ.

אין למכור את החמץ הבלוע ודבוק בכלים, שכמה וכמה דינים נקבעו כדי להבהיר לכל שמדובר במכירה אמיתית, וכאשר כותבים שמוכרים את החמץ הבלוע ודבוק בכלים המכירה נראית כחוכא ואיטלולא, שאין לחמץ

meticulous about this. In practice, though, this is very difficult to carry out. Therefore, **the custom is to write that all *chametz* in one's possession is included in the sale, and that the price is in accordance with the accepted market price, as determined by appraisers.**

It is proper to write in the contract where exactly the *chametz* is located, for example: "In the upper left kitchen cupboard," or "in the room on the right, in the box so marked." Several places may be listed.[49] ***Be-di'avad*, even without this, the sale is still valid, though all *chametz* should be gathered to one place and labeled.** Everything gathered to the place determined for the sale by two hours before the onset of the prohibition against deriving benefit from *chametz* is included in the sale. *Le-khathila,* the place where the *chametz* is kept is also rented to the gentile, so that the *chametz* is in the gentile's possession and the sale resembles any other sale in which the buyer transfers the purchase into his possession.

One may sell *chametz* through a proxy who writes all relevant details and signs on the owner's behalf. One may also sell *chametz* over the phone, by fax, or via the Internet. Even though it is proper for the seller to sign and perform a *kinyan* (act that formalizes a transaction) to reinforce the sale, *be-di'avad* it does not prevent the sale from taking effect, as the most important thing is the *kinyan* performed when the rabbi sells the *chametz* to the gentile, and this *kinyan* is effective for everyone who asked the rabbi to sell their *chametz*.[50] In kitchens that belong to public institutions, the manager or his representative sells the *chametz.*

One should not sell the *chametz* that is stuck to and absorbed into *kelim*. Quite a few laws relating to *mekhirat chametz* were introduced in order to make it clear to all that it is an actual sale, but if one writes that he is selling the *chametz* absorbed in or stuck to his *kelim,* the sale will appear to be lacking seriousness, since this has no

49. *Poskim* dispute whether one who goes away for Pesach may sell the entire house together with all *chametz* inside and thereby be exempted from cleaning and searching for *chametz*. To accommodate both opinions, it is often recommended to clean at least one room for Pesach and sell the rest of the house so that one can fulfill the mitzva of disposing of *chametz* in the ideal manner. See *Peninei Halakha, Pesach* 4:11; *Piskei Teshuvot* 436:2; and www.etzion.org.il/en/halakha/orach-chaim/holidays/bedikat-and-biur-chametz.

50. In many communities today, authorizing the rabbi to sell one's *chametz* by completing an online form has become the standard practice. This reflects contemporary commercial norms, in which people routinely conduct serious and legally binding transactions through electronic means. Accordingly, authorizing *mechirat chametz* in this manner does not detract from the validity or seriousness of the sale.

value and nobody is interested in buying it.[51] Therefore, one should not indicate this in the sale contract. **Selling the *kelim* themselves to a gentile is not worthwhile**, since after Pesach one would be required to immerse the *kelim* in a *mikveh* [like any eating implement bought from a gentile].[52]

זה שום שווי, ואין בעולם גוי שמעוניין לקנות אותו. **גם אין למכור את הכלים עצמם לגוי**, כי לאחר הפסח יצטרכו לטבול אותם במקווה לפני השימוש.

Owning Stocks in Companies That Own *Chametz*

Many halachic questions arise regarding ownership of stocks. According to civil law, a limited company is an independent entity that owns its own property. The stockholders have certain rights, but do not own the property of the company themselves. However, the *Acharonim* debate whether the rights of the stockholders amount to ownership according to halacha.[53] This question has ramifications for questions relating to many topics, such as lending with interest, businesses that operate on Shabbat, and the subject of this *shiur* – owning *chametz* on Pesach.

Rav Yitzchak Yaakov Weiss writes at length to prove that according to halacha, ownership with limited rights is considered ownership, and therefore stockholders who have some degree of decision-making power are considered partial owners of the property of the company. However, stockholders who only have the rights to a percentage of the company's profits are considered merely to be creditors of the company, and do not own any of its property.

Responsa Minchat Yitzchak 3:1

...In a limited company, there still remain many matters pertaining to ownership in which the stockholders have, at the very least, a limited say... But all of this applies to a limited company [created by] private individuals who have formed a partnership, with equal rights for each member of the group. This is not the case, however... with stocks of the type known as Class A shares, whose holders have no voting rights in the affairs of the company.[54] With respect to these, it is correct to say that they are akin to loan contracts, which stipulate that the holder receives a percentage of the profit and likewise bears a share of the loss...

42. שו"ת מנחת יצחק | ג:א

...בחברת מניות, נשארו עוד הרבה עניינים השייכים לבעלות, שיש להם על כל פנים חוות דעת מוגבלת... אבל כל זה בחברת מניות שהשתתפו ביניהם אנשים פרטיים, בשיוי זכויות לכל אחד מבני החבורה, מה שאין כן... במניות ממין שקוראין מניות א', שאין לבעליהן זכות הצבעה בעניני החברה, באלו שפיר יש לומר שהמה כמו שטרי מלוה, על תנאי שיקח חלק מהריוח לפי אחוז, וכן להפסד...

51. See n. 6, where Rav Melamed explains that in his opinion, it is unnecessary to destroy *chametz* less than the size of a *k'zayit*, so any *chametz* that remains in one's dishes is meaningless. He adds that to comply with those who hold that *chametz* less than a *k'zayit* must be destroyed, one should make sure to clean out one's dishes well or wash them with soap or detergent to remove any residue or absorbed flavor.

52. This is the opinion of many *poskim*, including Responsa *Chatam Sofer*, O.C. 109 and *Orchot Rabbeinu, Pesach* 16. Some write or imply that *tevila* is unnecessary in such cases, where the utensils were never actually transferred to the domain of the gentile (*Aruch HaShulchan*, Y.D. 108:52; see also *Ben Ish Chai*, First Year, *Tzav* 9; *Mechirat Chametz K'hilchato* 7:16).

53. See, for example, Responsa Maharam Shick, Y.D. 158, who discusses a bank formed as an early version of a limited company, by a group of Jews and gentiles. He permits borrowing with interest from this bank, based on the fact that the owners were not full owners of the bank, among other factors. See also Responsa Maharshag, Y.D. 3, who disputes this logic but finds other reasons to permit borrowing.

54. Although this is often the case, the law does not actually define A or B shares, and their specific rights are determined by the company's articles of association.

והיוצא מכל הנ"ל, דאין שום ראיה לומר דבעלות מוגבלת לא הוי בעלות, ואדרבה יש סברות להיפוך, ושוב חוזר הדבר לסיני, **דיש להם לבעלי מניות דין בעלות, והמה כשותפים דעלמא**, וכעת אקבע בזה עוד מסמרות בראיות מדברי הש"ס ופוסקים, דדין בעלות לבעלות מוגבלת...

The conclusion that emerges from all of the above is that there is no proof whatsoever to say that limited ownership is not considered ownership. On the contrary, there are reasons to say the opposite. Thus, the matter returns to first principles, and **stockholders do have the halachic status of owners, and they are like ordinary partners.** Now I shall further strengthen this conclusion through proofs from the words of the Gemara and the *poskim*, that limited ownership confers the halacha of ownership...

Accordingly, Rav Weiss concludes that one who owns stocks in a company that owns *chametz* must include these stocks in his sale of *chametz*. This is sufficient for halachic purposes, and one need not sell the stocks in a legally binding manner.

43. שם

...**קודם פסח, אין עצה אחרת, רק שימכור הישראל המניות קודם פסח לנכרי, כמו שמוכרים שאר חמץ**, ואף שהעיר כבוד תורתו, דמכיון שהבעלות של המניות, צריכה רישום על שם הקונה אותם... ובלעדה אין למכירה כזו שום תוקף חוקי... מכל מקום נראה דיש בזה כדי סמיכה, לסמוך על גדולי האחרונים, שכבר דנו בכיוצא בזה... אנו אזלינן לענין איסור חמץ בתר דינינו בין להחמיר בין להקל, ואמרינן דסמכא דעת הקונה על דינינו... אף אם אינו מועיל בדיניהם... ואף שאין הדבר מוסכם לכל הפוסקים, מכל מקום בענין שלנו שאי אפשר בענין אחר, יש לסמוך על זה.

Ibid.

...**Before Pesach, there is no other solution except that the Jew sell the stocks to a gentile before Pesach, just as one sells other *chametz*.** Although his honor has noted that since ownership of stocks requires registration in the name of the purchaser... and without this such a sale has no legal validity... nevertheless, it appears that there is sufficient basis here to rely upon the great *Acharonim*, who have already discussed similar cases... With respect to the prohibition against *chametz*, we follow our halachot, whether stringent or lenient, and we say that the purchaser relies upon our halachot... even if [the transaction] is not effective according to their law... Although this matter is not agreed upon by all *poskim*, nevertheless, in our case, where it is impossible to find another solution, one may rely on this approach.

Rav Moshe Feinstein discusses a similar question regarding owning stocks in companies that operate on Shabbat. While he agrees in principle that limited ownership is considered ownership, he writes that this is only problematic for one who owns a percentage of stocks in a company that is significant enough for the directors to care about his view. Most stockholders, even if they technically have a vote over issues such as electing a president, are not considered owners, as their vote is insignificant. In reality, they only have a right to a share of the profits and are not owners of the company or its property. It follows that they also need not sell their stocks before Pesach.

44. שו"ת אגרות משה | אבן העזר (אה"ע) א:ז

ובדבר ליקח שערס מקאמפאניעס שעושין מלאכה ומסחר בשבת הא חזינן שנתפשט להיתר והטעם פשוט **שאין להחשיב את הקונים**

Responsa Igrot Moshe, Even HaEzer 1:7

Regarding buying shares in companies that perform *melacha* and business on Shabbat, we see that the practice has spread to permit it. The reason is simple, as **the shareholders, who own**

only a portion of the business, should not be regarded [as owners of the business], since they have no say in [the operation of] the business, not even proportionally to their share as owners. This is unlike a partnership, where one does have a say as an owner. The shareholder also does not want to be an owner of the business, nor to acquire any part of the business; **rather, he is merely as one who acquires [a share of] the profit and loss of the business, according to the amount he has purchased...**

That which, according to the terms of sale, the shareholder has a vote in the election of a president, this is merely empty words, as in practice [the controlling interest] retains more than a majority, such that it is not possible for [other shareholders] to have a say. The shareholders also do not want to express an opinion in this regard, since it is not their intention to acquire that right.

Therefore, in my humble opinion, there is no need to be concerned about what the owners of the companies do, as they are not attributable to the shareholders. Even if there are Jews among the [significant] owners, [a shareholder] is not considered to be assisting transgressors, as the business would operate even if one did not purchase shares from them, as there is no shortage of those who would buy the shares, and the purchaser buys only for his own benefit. **Therefore, there is no prohibition against [buying shares], as is the practice of many people, including God-fearing individuals, who purchase shares. However, purchasing a large enough quantity of shares for one's opinion to be taken into account is certainly prohibited.**

שערס שהוא רק משהו מהמסחר שאין להם שום דעה בהמסחר אף לענין חלקם לבעלים שלא דומה לשותפות במקצת שיש לו דעה כבעלים, וגם אין הקונה שערס רוצה להיות בעלים בהמסחר ואינו רוצה לקנות כלום בהמסחר **אלא הוא רק כקונה ריוח והפסד שיהיה בהמסחר לפי סך כך וכך שקנה...**

ומה שלפי תנאי המכירה יש לבעל השערס דעה לבחירת פרעזידענט הוא רק פטומי מילי בעלמא כי למעשה משאירין לעצמן יותר מהרוב שלא שייך שיאמרו דעה וגם הקונים אין רוצים לומר דעה בזה כי אין כוונתם לקנות זה.

ולכן לעניות דעתי אין לחוש למה שעושים הבעלים דהקאמפאניעס שאינו נוגע להם. ואף אם יש גם יהודים בהבעלים אין להחשיב מסייע לעוברי עברה שהמסחר יעשו גם כשלא יקנה שערס מהם כי לא חסר מי שיקנה שערס והקונה קונה רק לטובת עצמו **ולכן אין בזה שום איסור וכמו שנוהגין הרבה בני אדם ואף יראי חטא לקנות. אבל ודאי לקנות מדה מרובה כל כך עד שיתחשבו בדעתו יש לאסור.**

Rav Eliezer Melamed also writes that although some are stringent in this regard, one who has an investment account or a private pension fund that invests in stocks need not be concerned about ownership of *chametz* through this investment, since he does not have a say in the running of the businesses involved.[55,56]

FURTHER IYUN

For further *iyun* on owning stocks in companies with *chametz* on Pesach, see page 112.

55. *Peninei Halakha, Pesach* 3:3. A third opinion concerning the status of corporations is taken by Rav Shlomo Dichovsky (*Piskei Dinim Rabbaniyim* 10) and Rav Asher Weiss (Responsa *Minchat Asher* 1:104–105). They argue that a corporation has a new and independent halachic status, and none of the shareholders or others involved in the company are ever considered the halachic owners. It would seem that according to this approach, no shareholders or others involved in the corporation would be required to sell their portions before Pesach. For further discussion of this approach, see https://olamot.net/shiurim/חברה-בעמ-על-פי-ההלכה. and www.koltorah.org/halachah/halachic-status-of-a-corporation-part-three-a-bold-ruling-of-rav-asher-weiss-by-rabbi-chaim-jachter.

56. For further discussion in English concerning this subject, see Rav Asher Meir, "Owning Stock in a Company that Possesses Chametz During Pesach," available at www.ou.org/holidays/owning-stock-company-possesses-chametz-pesach; and Rav George Lintz, "May a Jew Purchase Stock in McDonalds," Journal of Halacha and Contemporary Society, Fall 1992.

Chametz She'avar Alav HaPesach

We have discussed thus far the proper methods for selling one's *chametz* before Pesach. An important question remains: what is the status of *chametz* that was not destroyed or sold before Pesach, or that was discovered during Pesach and not disposed of?[57,58] May such *chametz* be used or benefited from after Pesach?

To answer this question, let us turn to the **Mishna** in ***Masechet Pesachim***, which teaches that benefitting from such *chametz* is prohibited after Pesach.

45. משנה | פסחים ב:ב

חמץ של נכרי שעבר עליו הפסח – מותר בהנאה, ושל ישראל אסור בהנאה שנאמר וְלֹא יֵרָאֶה לְךָ שְׂאֹר.

ח Mishna, Pesachim 2:2

It is permitted for a Jew **to** derive **benefit from *chametz* of a gentile over which Pesach has elapsed,** i.e., *chametz* that remains after the conclusion of Pesach. However, **it is prohibited to** derive **benefit from** *chametz* **of a Jew** over which Pesach **to** derive **benefit from** *chametz* **of a Jew** over which Pesach has elapsed, **as it is stated:** "No *chametz* shall be seen with you, **neither shall there be *se'or* seen with you,** in all your borders" (*Shemot* 13:7). One who owned *chametz* over Pesach has violated this prohibition and is therefore penalized.[59]

The **Gemara (*Masechet Pesachim*)** quotes a *baraita* in which the *Tanna'im* dispute this prohibition. Rabbi Yehuda indeed maintains that one who benefits from the *chametz* after Pesach violates a biblical prohibition, but Rabbi Shimon disputes this. Rabbi Yosei HaGelili argues that even during Pesach, there is no biblical prohibition against benefitting from *chametz*.

46. מסכת פסחים כח.-כח:

דתניא: חמץ בין לפני זמנו בין לאחר זמנו – עובר עליו בלאו, תוך זמנו – עובר עליו בלאו וכרת, דברי רבי יהודה.

רבי שמעון אומר: חמץ לפני זמנו ולאחר זמנו – אינו עובר עליו בלא כלום, תוך זמנו – עובר עליו בכרת ובלאו...

ח Masechet Pesachim 28a–28b

It was taught in a *baraita*: One who eats or derives benefit from ***chametz*, whether before its time,** starting at midday on Erev Pesach, **or after its time,** i.e., *chametz* over which Pesach has elapsed, **transgresses a negative mitzva. During its time,** on Pesach itself, one who eats *chametz* **transgresses a negative mitzva and** is liable to receive ***karet*.** This is **the statement of Rabbi Yehuda.**

Rabbi Shimon says: One who eats or derives benefit from ***chametz*,** both **before its time and after its time, does not transgress any** prohibition. **During its time one** is liable to receive ***karet*** for eating **and transgresses a negative mitzva** for deriving benefit from *chametz*…

---

57. The question of what to do if one discovers *chametz* in one's possession on Pesach was addressed in volume 5, *shiur* 9, sources 58–62.

58. If a package arrives on Pesach containing *chametz*, one should refuse to accept it or to take ownership of it. In such a case, even if the package remains in one's property, he is not considered to own it and thus does not violate the prohibition of *bal yeira'eh* (see *Shulchan Aruch*, O.C. 448:2, *Mishna Berura* there, and "Halachos of Pesach," p. 103).

59. See the next few sources, which discuss whether this penalty is of a biblical nature or rabbinic.

רבי יוסי הגלילי אומר: תמה על עצמך, היאך חמץ אסור בהנאה כל שבעה?...

Rabbi Yosei HaGelili says: Be astounded with yourself. How can it be prohibited to derive **benefit from *chametz* for all seven** days? In other words, he disagrees with the premise that it is prohibited to derive benefit from *chametz* even during the seven days of Pesach…

Further on in the **Gemara,** Rava claims that even according to Rabbi Shimon, the Sages imposed a penalty for violating the biblical prohibition against owning *chametz* on Pesach, and prohibited benefitting from such *chametz* after Pesach.

47. מסכת פסחים כט. / Masechet Pesachim 29a

רבא אמר: לעולם רבי שמעון היא, ורבי שמעון קנסא קניס הואיל ועבר עליה בבל יראה ובבל ימצא.

Rava said: Actually, our Mishna **is** in accordance with the opinion of **Rabbi Shimon.** However, this is difficult, as Rabbi Shimon states that it is permitted for a Jew to derive benefit from *chametz* that had been owned by another Jew during Pesach, while our Mishna explicitly states that this is forbidden. This can be resolved by explaining that **Rabbi Shimon** argues that it is permitted only according to Torah law. However, one who intentionally commits such a transgression **incurs a penalty. Since he transgressed** the prohibition **it shall not be seen and** the prohibition **it shall not be found,** the Sages decreed that it is forbidden for him to derive benefit from this *chametz.*

Further on in the Gemara, the *Amora'im* dispute whether to rule in accordance with Rabbi Yehuda or Rabbi Shimon. Rava concludes that the halacha is in accordance with Rabbi Shimon, and that although the *chametz* is rabbinically prohibited after Pesach, a mixture containing such *chametz* is permitted.

48. מסכת פסחים ל. / Masechet Pesachim 30a

אמר רבא: הלכתא, חמץ... שלא בזמנו, בין במינו בין שלא במינו – מותר, כרבי שמעון.

ומי אמר רבא הכי? והאמר רבא: רבי שמעון קנסא קניס, הואיל ועבר עליו בבל יראה ובל ימצא! – הני מילי – בעיניה, אבל על ידי תערובת – לא.

Rava said: The halacha is that with regard to the prohibition against eating a mixture of ***chametz*… not during its time** of prohibition, but rather after the conclusion of Pesach, regardless of whether the *chametz* was mixed **with its own type or with another type, it is permitted.**[60] This is **in accordance with** the opinion of **Rabbi Shimon,** who states that *chametz* owned by a Jew during Passover is permitted after Passover.

The Gemara asks: **Did Rava** actually **say this,** that according to Rabbi Shimon, *chametz* owned by a Jew on Pesach is permitted after Passover? **But didn't Rava** himself **say** that **Rabbi Shimon imposed a penalty** forbidding one from deriving benefit from *chametz* owned by a Jew during Passover, **since he transgressed** the prohibition **it shall not be seen and** the prohibition **it shall not be seen and** the prohibition **it shall not be found?** The Gemara resolves this challenge: **This** penalty **applies** only to *chametz* that is **in its pure** unadulterated form, **but** with regard to **a mixture, no,** one does not impose a penalty, even though the *chametz* is still extant.

---

60. Rashi explains that the mixture is permitted even if the *chametz* gives it flavor. and the *Beit Yosef* (O.C. 447) infers that this is also the position of the Rambam (*Chametz Umatza* 1:5). However, the *Tur* writes that the mixture is only permitted if the volume of non-*chametz* ingredients is sixty times greater than the volume of *chametz,* and this is also the ruling of the *Shulchan Aruch* (O.C. 447:11).

The **Rambam** also rules in accordance with Rabbi Shimon regarding *chametz* after Pesach,[61] and clarifies that the penalty that prohibits benefitting from the *chametz* after Pesach applies even if one kept the *chametz* inadvertently.

49. רמב"ם | הל' חמץ ומצה א:ד

חמץ שעבר עליו הפסח אסור בהנייה לעולם, ודבר זה קנס הוא מדברי סופרים מפני שעבר על בל יראה ובל ימצא אסרוהו, ואפילו הניחו בשגגה או באונס, כדי שלא יניח אדם חמץ ברשותו בפסח כדי שיהנה בו אחר הפסח.

ר Rambam, Hilchot Chametz Umatza 1:4

Benefitting from *chametz* which was possessed over Pesach is prohibited forever. This [prohibition] is a penalty instituted by the Sages. Since the person transgressed the prohibitions against *chametz* being seen and being found [in his possession], they prohibited it, even if he left the *chametz* [in his possession] inadvertently or was forced to do so, so that one not leave *chametz* in his possession during Pesach in order to benefit from it after Pesach.

The ***Shulchan Aruch*** rules in accordance with the Rambam.

50. שולחן ערוך | או"ח תמח:ג

חמץ של ישראל שעבר עליו הפסח אסור בהנאה אפי' הניחו שוגג או אנוס...

א Shulchan Aruch, Orach Chaim 448:3

It is forbidden to benefit from *chametz*[62] that belonged to a Jew over Pesach, even if he left it [in his possession] inadvertently or was forced to do so...[63]

As we have seen above, *chametz* that was sold to a gentile is permitted after Pesach. However, **Rav Eliezer Melamed** writes that when buying *chametz* from Jewish owned stores after Pesach, one should take care to ensure that the *chametz* was sold in a proper manner.

---

61. Regarding *chametz* on Erev Pesach, the Rambam rules that this is prohibited on a biblical level in accordance with Rabbi Yehuda (*Chametz Umatza* 1:8). This topic is discussed in *shiur* 4.

62. The definition of *chametz* in this regard may follow the definition used for the prohibition of owning *chametz* on Pesach (on which this halacha is based), i.e., there must be at least a *k'zayit* of *chametz* present within the entire package of food (according to some, it must be a *k'zayit* within the amount of *kedei achilat peras*, the amount of 3 or 4 *k'beitza*), as noted in *Mishna Berura* 442:1. See, however, source 53 below, citing Rav Schachter, and n. 56.

63. In cases of uncertainty, where it is unclear whether the *chametz* was in the possession of a Jew or gentile over Pesach, the *Mishna Berura* (448:9, 449:5) cites differing opinions as to whether we follow the rule of *safeik derabanan l'kula* (rabbinic uncertainties are decided leniently) or whether the *chametz* is forbidden to eat, as we are more strict about a penalty of this nature than other rabbinic halachot. See also Rav Asher Weiss (https://minchasasher.com/he/shiur/פרשה-שיעורים/חמץ-שעבר-עליו-הפסח-תשעה), who is inclined to rule leniently if it is not easily determinable whether the *chametz* was owned by a Jew over Pesach. See also the continuation of that *shiur*, where Rav Asher Weiss responds to a question from Rav Hershel Schachter concerning a Jewish factory where gentile workers engaged in packaging *chametz* on Pesach that had been sold to a gentile, and whether that thereby forbade the *chametz*.

51. פניני הלכה | פסח ו:ו

יש נוהגים להחמיר שלא לאכול מחמץ שנמכר, מפני שלדעת המחמירים המכירה אינה כדין, וממילא דינו כדין חמץ שעבר עליו הפסח שאסור באכילה והנאה.

אבל למעשה אין צריך לחוש לזה, מפני שאיסור חמץ שעבר עליו הפסח מדברי חכמים, ובכל ספק בדברי חכמים הלכה כמיקל. וקל וחומר שכך ההלכה בדין שרק מעט מן הפוסקים מפקפקים בו ואילו דעת רובם המכריע של הפוסקים להתיר. ויש מהגדולים שהיו מקפידים לאכול אחר הפסח מחמץ שנמכר, כדי להראות בזה שהמכירה נעשתה כדת וכדין.

הקונה בחנות אחר הפסח צריך לבדוק אם יש למוכר תעודה שמכר את חמצו כדין, כדי שלא לקנות חמץ שעבר עליו הפסח. ואם המוכר אינו שומר מצוות יש לדקדק בזה יותר, מפני שאם לא הבין את משמעות המכירה והמשיך למכור בחנותו חמץ בפסח, לדעת מקצת הפוסקים המכירה בטלה, וממילא כל החמץ שבחנותו אסור באכילה והנאה. במקרה כזה, נכון לחוש לדעת המחמירים ולהמתין עד שתגיע לחנות סחורה שיוצרה אחר הפסח. אבל אם התברר שבעל החנות מכר את חמצו כדין, ונזהר שלא יתקרבו בפסח אל החמץ המכור, מותר מיד לאחר הפסח לקנות אצלו חמץ.

Peninei Halakha, Pesach 6:6

Some people are strict and do not eat *chametz* that was sold because, according to the stringent *poskim*,[64] such a sale is not legitimate, and so this *chametz* has the status of *chametz she-avar alav ha-Pesach*, which one may neither eat nor derive benefit from.

In practice, however, one need not be concerned about this stringency, because the prohibition of *chametz she-avar alav ha-Pesach* is rabbinic, and whenever there is uncertainty about a rabbinic law, halakha follows the lenient opinion. This is certainly true where only a small number of *poskim* are strict, while the overwhelming majority permit. Indeed, there were great rabbis who, after Pesach, would make a point of eating *chametz* that had been sold through *mekhirat chametz*, to demonstrate that the sale was in keeping with halakha.

When shopping for food after Pesach, one must make sure that the seller has a certificate verifying that he sold his *chametz* in keeping with the halakha so that one does not buy *chametz she-avar alav ha-Pesach*. Even more caution is needed if the seller is not religious, because if he did not understand the significance of the sale and continued to sell *chametz* in his store during Pesach, a few *poskim* maintain that the sale was not legitimate, and that it is forbidden to eat or derive benefit from any *chametz* in his store.[65] In this case, it is proper to follow the stringent *poskim* and wait for goods produced after Pesach to arrive. If, however, it becomes clear that the seller performed *mekhirat chametz* in keeping with the halakha and was careful not to let anybody go near the *chametz* that was sold one may buy *chametz* from him immediately after Pesach.

In some places, especially in the Diaspora, there are Jewish-owned stores and supermarkets that do not sell their *chametz*, or stores supplied by a Jewish distributor that has not sold *chametz*. It would therefore

64. Such as, for example, the Gra in source 19 above.

65. See *Piskei Teshuvot* 448:20 for a full list of authorities who address this question. The stringent opinions maintain that the entire basis for the validity of the sale is the premise that the seller does not want the *chametz* in his possession over Pesach. Accordingly, one who does business with and uses the sold *chametz* on Pesach clearly demonstrates that the sale is invalid. The lenient opinions contend that even if the seller uses or sells some of the *chametz*, the sale itself is still valid since it was performed properly with all of the methods of acquisition normally used for a sale, and his actions merely constitute theft from the gentile who owns the *chametz*. It should be noted that although the rest of the *chametz* that was sold is still permitted after Pesach, even the lenient opinions agree that the actual *chametz* used or sold on Pesach by the seller is forbidden after Pesach.

be prohibited to purchase *chametz* from such a store. The **OU** discusses some of the practical details of this and until what date the *chametz* can be assumed to have been owned by a Jew on Pesach.

52. Rav Gavriel Price, Chametz After Pesach: What, When, and Why [66]

Many *va'adim*, or local rabbinical councils, provide a list to their constituents of local establishments that are recommended and those that are best avoided. Here are some of the considerations they make:

When a store is Jewish-owned, and the owner never engaged in a sale, at what point can we reasonably assume that the *chametz* now on the shelves appeared after Pesach and was never in the hands of the Jewish store-owner? The answer, in part, is that it depends on the product and its shelf-life. Bread has a shorter shelf-life than granola and will be restocked more frequently. By determining how often the fresh bread is restocked — simply speaking to a stock clerk may be a good start — we can determine whether the bread, or the granola for that matter, was restocked after Pesach.

Making an item-per-item evaluation at a supermarket, however, is not particularly practical. At one point, then, can we assume that any *chametz* on a store's shelves is from after Pesach?

Rav Yaakov Luban, senior rabbinic coordinator at the OU and distinguished rav of Ohr Torah of Edison, NJ since 1983, discussed this question with Rav Belsky zt"l many times. Although the prohibition against *chametz she'avar alav haPesach* is rabbinic, and there is generally a principle that, in case of a doubt, we may be lenient, it is not simple to apply that principle in a case where we know for sure that at one time all of the *chametz* in a given establishment was prohibited. "...It is unreasonable to allow the purchase of *chametz* at all times when we know that, at some instance, the *chametz* is prohibited." In other words, until we are confident that the majority of the products in the store are not *chametz she'avar alav haPesach*, we must avoid purchasing *chametz* items from such a store.

A further consideration: supermarkets do not always receive their products directly from manufacturers. For many items, supermarkets depend on food distributors... The average amount of time that a grocery distributor holds product is 37.3 days. One of the major grocery distributors in the United States is a Jewish-owned company that continues buying and selling inventory during Pesach.

Based on these considerations, many rabbanim therefore suggest waiting until after Lag B'Omer before purchasing *chametz* from supermarkets that are either Jewish-owned or rely on Jewish distributors.

The **OU** also cites **Rav Hershel Schachter**, who notes that Kellogg's Corn Flakes[67] owned by a Jew may be forbidden after Pesach as well.

53. OU Halacha Yomis [68]

Corn flakes products typically contain malt flavor (*chametz*) present at about two to three percent of the product, which means the malt flavor is not *batel b'shishim* (less than one sixtieth of the product). Shulchan Aruch (Orach Chaim 447: 11) rules that if a food containing *chametz* that is not *batel b'shishim*

66. The full article is available at https://oukosher.org/passover/articles/chametz-after-pesach-what-when-and-why.

67. Kellogg's Corn Flakes is under OU certification and is one of the main types of corn flakes referred to in this source (confirmed by rabbinic representatives at OU Kosher).

68. This source can be viewed online at https://oukosher.org/halacha-yomis/may-i-purchase-corn-flakes-or-rice-crispy-cereals-after-pesach-from-a-jewish-owned-store-that-did-not-sell-its-chametz-on-pesach.

was owned by a Jew on *Pesach*, it is prohibited to derive benefit from it after *Pesach*. It would seem, therefore, that corn flakes should not be permitted. There is a discussion as to whether this ruling of Shulchan Aruch applies even if there is less than a *kezayis* of *chametz* in the entire product.[69] In a standard sized box of corn flakes, one can assume that there is less than a *kezayis* of malt flavor. The conclusion of Biur Halacha (447: end) is that this matter remains unresolved.

Therefore, Rav Hershel Schachter, *shlita*, advised against purchasing these corn flakes. Furthermore, he questioned whether the qualification of requiring a *kezayis* of *chametz* would help in a supermarket, when multiple boxes sit side by side and there is clearly more than a *kezayis* altogether. However, if there is a doubt as to whether the corn flakes were actually in the possession of a Jewish owner on *Pesach*, then Rav Schachter said that the corn flakes may be purchased and consumed.

---

69. See *shiur* 1, n. 16–17, where we discussed whether the prohibition of *bal yeira'eh* applies to *chametz* that is less than a *k'zayit* in total volume. According to the *Shulchan Aruch* and many *poskim* (see, e.g., *Mishna Berura* 442:1), it does not, even if the amount of *chametz* in the product is not *batel b'shishim*. Nevertheless, the *Bi'ur Halacha* (447:11) referred to by Rav Schachter notes that some *poskim* maintain that *bal yeira'eh* does apply to a mixture containing less than a *k'zayit* of *chametz*; therefore, one may still not eat such a product after Pesach if it was in the possession of a Jew over Pesach. It should be noted that in a standard box of Kellogg's Corn Flakes (18 oz, or about 510 grams), the amount of *chametz* would be approximately 17 grams, which is less than the standard measurements used for *k'zayit* by many contemporary *poskim*.

Summary of the Halachot of Mechirat Chametz and Chametz She'avar Alav HaPesach

Selling Chametz Before Pesach

1. **Mishna (*Masechet Pesachim*)** – Selling *chametz* to a non-Jew is permitted during the first part of the day of Erev Pesach, when eating *chametz* is still permitted.
2. **Gemara (*Masechet Pesachim*)** – It was necessary for the Mishna to specify the allowance of selling *chametz* to a gentile because Beit Shammai prohibit this unless one knows that the gentile will finish consuming the *chametz* before Pesach.
3. **Rashi** – According to Beit Shammai, one is obligated to remove *chametz* from the world. It is not sufficient to remove it from one's possession.
4. **Rabbeinu David** – Beit Shammai only prohibit selling *chametz* to a gentile on a rabbinic level, out of concern that people may only sell it in a fictitious manner.
5. ***Shulchan Aruch*** – One may sell *chametz* to a gentile even if it will not be consumed before Pesach, in accordance with Beit Hillel.

Selling With the Intention to Repurchase

1. ***Tosefta* (*Masechet Pesachim*)** – One may sell or give *chametz* to a gentile before Pesach and rebuy it after Pesach, provided that the original gift (or sale) is bona fide.
2. **Rav Amram Gaon** – One may only do this on a one-time basis, not every year.
3. **Rambam, *Shulchan Aruch*** – The original sale must be unconditional. One who makes the sale subject to a condition violates the prohibition against owning *chametz* on Pesach.
4. ***Hagahot Maimoniot*** – The *Tosefta* implies that one may not stipulate that the gentile must return the *chametz* after Pesach. Chazal were stringent here due to the stringent nature of Pesach.
5. ***Mishna Berura*** – If one specifies that the sale will take effect immediately, provided that the condition is ultimately fulfilled, no biblical prohibition is violated. But one should not make even this type of stipulation, in case the condition is not fulfilled. Some permit limiting the ability of the gentile to sell the *chametz* to others, if this is not made a condition of the sale.
6. ***Shulchan Aruch*** – One should only sell *chametz* that is outside of one's home.

a. ***Chok Ya'akov*** – The reason for the *Shulchan Aruch*'s ruling is that the gentile acquires the *chametz* by taking it from the Jew's home. He may subsequently return it to the Jew's home before Pesach.

b. ***Mishna Berura*** – Others prohibit a Jew keeping the *chametz* in his home, as then the sale appears fictitious. He also may end up eating it during Pesach. The *Acharonim* suggest that one who has a large amount of *chametz* should sell the room in which the *chametz* is stored to the gentile, together with the *chametz*, and provide him access to this room. This is equivalent to the *chametz* being outside the Jew's house.

7. ***Piskei Teshuvot*** – The *poskim* disagree as to whether selling or renting the room is preferable. The widespread custom has become to rent, as with rental payment suffices to transfer ownership to the gentile (no deed is required), one who lives in a rented property cannot sell it, and in Eretz Yisrael, selling a house to a gentile is prohibited.

- **Opposition to *Mechirat Chametz***

1. ***Bechor Shor*** – The sale of *chametz* is a *ha'arama*, but since one also nullifies all the *chametz* in one's possession, the *ha'arama* of a sale suffices to fulfill the rabbinic obligation to search out and destroy one's *chametz* is only rabbinic.
2. ***Sho'el Umeishiv*** – Since the sale is only a *ha'arama* to avoid the rabbinic obligation to destroy the *chametz*, one cannot appoint a *shaliach* to sell *chametz*.
3. ***Ma'aseh Rav*** – The Gra objected to any sale of *chametz* with the intention of buying it back, and would not permit buying *chametz* after Pesach from a Jew who sold it in this manner.
4. ***Chatam Sofer*** – The sale is valid even on a biblical level, and one should not speak against it.
5. ***Peninei Halakha*** – The sale is genuine and not just a *ha'arama*. It is preferable for it to be performed by a rav to ensure that it is done correctly.
6. **Rav Hershel Schachter** – Rav Soloveitchik suggested avoiding selling actual *chametz*.
7. ***Piskei Teshuvot*** – Torah scholars and God-fearing individuals do not leave actual *chametz* in their homes.

The Act of Acquisition (Kinyan)

- ***Meshicha* (Pulling) or Payment?**

1. **Gemara (*Masechet Avoda Zara*)**

   a. **Ameimar** – *Meshicha* (pulling) is an effective *kinyan* for a gentile.

   b. **Rav Ashi** – *Meshicha* is not effective for a gentile.

   c. **Rabbi Yochanan** – The Gemara derives from his ruling that *meshicha* is an effective *kinyan* for a gentile.

2. **Gemara (*Masechet Bechorot*)**
   a. **Reish Lakish** – A gentile can acquire an animal from a Jew by paying money for it, without pulling the animal, contrary to the view of Ameimar.
3. **Rashi** – The halacha is in accordance with Reish Lakish, that a gentile acquires by payment.
4. **Rabbeinu Tam** – The halacha is in accordance with Ameimar and Rabbi Yochanan that a gentile acquires through *meshicha*.
5. **Tosafot** – One who wishes to take both Rashi's and Rabbeinu Tam's rulings into account must ensure that the gentile both pays and performs *meshicha*.
6. **Rema (Responsum)** – *Lechatchila*, one should have both *kinyanim* performed, but *bedi'eved*, the gentile performing *meshicha* is sufficient, as most *Rishonim* concur with Rabbeinu Tam.
7. ***Shach*** – One must perform both *kinyanim*. If one does not do so, even *bedi'eved* one must be concerned that the gentile may not have acquired.

- ***Chalifin***

1. **Rabbeinu Tam** – *Chalifin* may be used to transfer ownership to a gentile.
2. ***Shach*** – This is not straightforward, as the Gemara and other *poskim* never mention that *chalifin* can be effective for a gentile.

- ***Agav Karka***

1. **Rav Shmuel Kaidanover** – Due to practical and halachic difficulties involved with using other methods, the ideal way to sell *chametz* is through *kinyan agav*.
2. ***Ketzot HaChoshen*** – Using *kinyan agav* to sell to a gentile is potentially problematic, as according to some, it is merely a rabbinic institution, and it is possible that this institution was not made for gentiles.

- ***Udita***

1. **Gemara (*Masechet Bava Batra*)** – A *ger* named Issur falsely admitted that his property belonged to his biological son, Rav Mari, so that he would inherit him. Rava felt that this was inappropriate.
2. **Rashbam** – Although no *kinyan* was possible, Rav Mari was now assumed to be the original owner of the money based on Issur's admission.
3. **Tosafot (First Explanation), Ri Migash** – Chazal instituted that a person on his deathbed is able to transfer ownership of his property by means of an "admission" (*udita*) that the property belongs to the recipient.

4. **Tosafot** – Anyone can transfer ownership through admission, whether healthy or sick.
5. ***Bach*** – A Jew can lend money to another Jew, "admit" that the money in fact belongs to a gentile, and thereby charge interest on the loan.
6. ***Taz*** – Admission is not a valid *kinyan* when one wishes to avoid prohibitions.
7. ***Ketzot HaChoshen*** – The majority of *Rishonim* maintain that admission is itself a *kinyan*, and not only for a person on his deathbed. This *kinyan udita* may be used to transfer ownership of *chametz* to a gentile.
8. ***Mishna Berura*** – Ideally, one should both receive payment and have the gentile perform *meshicha*. Where this is not possible, other methods can be used. *Bedi'eved*, even if the gentile only paid for the *chametz* and did not perform any other *kinyan*, the *chametz* is permitted after Pesach.
9. ***Mechirat Chametz K'hilchato*** – *Rabbanim* who are responsible for selling *chametz* of a community typically do so using all or many of the various *kinyanim*.

• Appointing an Agent to Sell *Chametz*

1. ***Peninei Halakha*** – One should ideally understand the authorization document for *mechirat chametz* well. The document should make it clear that the sale is a genuine sale.

• Owning Stocks in Companies That Own *Chametz*

1. ***Minchat Yitzchak*** – Ownership with limited rights is considered ownership, and therefore stockholders who have some degree of decision-making power are considered partial owners of the property of the company. They therefore must include these stocks in their *mechirat chametz*.
2. **Rav Moshe Feinstein** – Even stockholders who have a vote over some issues are not considered owners, unless their share is significant enough to have a real effect on the business.
3. ***Peninei Halakha*** – One who has an investment in stocks need not be concerned about ownership of *chametz* through this investment if he does not have a say in the running of the businesses involved.

Chametz She'avar Alav HaPesach

1. **Mishna (*Masechet Pesachim*)** – Benefitting from *chametz* that was owned by a Jew during Pesach is prohibited after Pesach.
2. **Gemara (*Masechet Pesachim*)**
   a. **Rabbi Yehuda** – One who benefits from the *chametz* after Pesach violates a biblical prohibition.

   b. **Rabbi Shimon** – There is no biblical prohibition.
      i. **Rava** – Even according to Rabbi Shimon, benefitting from the *chametz* is prohibited rabbinically, as a penalty. The halacha is in accordance with Rabbi Shimon, and therefore a mixture containing such *chametz* is permitted after Pesach.
   c. **Rabbi Yosei HaGelili** – Even during Pesach, there is no biblical prohibition against benefitting from *chametz*.
3. **Rambam, *Shulchan Aruch*** – The halacha is in accordance with Rabbi Shimon. The penalty applies even if one kept the *chametz* inadvertently.
4. ***Peninei Halakha*** – When buying *chametz* after Pesach, one should take care to ensure that the *chametz* was sold in a proper manner.
5. **Rav Gavriel Price** – One should wait until after Lag B'Omer to purchase *chametz* from a Jewish-owned store or distributor that did not sell *chametz* for Pesach.
6. **Rav Hershel Schachter** – Kellogg's Corn Flakes that was owned by a Jewish supermarket over Pesach should not be purchased.

Further Iyun

The Sale of Chametz Stocks

Rav Lavi Peles (Participant, Manhigut Toranit)

Modern economic life sometimes presents a profound challenge to classical halachic definitions. A Jew today may hold shares in multinational corporations, pension funds, and investment portfolios – often without direct awareness of the specific assets involved. This raises a fundamental question: If a company owns and trades *chametz,* does holding that stock render the shareholder halachically defined as an owner of that *chametz,* thereby violating the Torah's prohibition against owning *chametz* on Pesach?

At first glance, this seems unlikely. Stocks are abstract financial instruments, not physical goods stored in one's home. Yet halacha does not define ownership solely in terms of physical possession. Rather, ownership can exist in more subtle legal and economic forms, raising the possibility that financial investments may carry halachic consequences.

In this essay, we will trace the halachic development of this question: whether stock ownership of companies that own *chametz* constitutes ownership of *chametz,* whether such ownership violates the prohibitions of *bal yeira'eh* and *bal yimatzei,* and what practical steps, if any, are required before Pesach. At its core, the issue turns on how halacha defines ownership in the context of modern corporate structures.

The Prohibition of *Chametz* Ownership

The Torah establishes two distinct prohibitions regarding *chametz* during Pesach:

> "For seven days, no leaven shall be found in your houses"[1]
>
> "No *chametz* shall be seen by you, nor shall leaven be seen by you in all your borders"[2]

These verses prohibit not only the consumption of *chametz,* but its very presence within a Jew's domain. The **Ramban** explains that the Torah prohibition applies specifically to *chametz* that is considered within one's possession (*reshut*). *Chametz* belonging to a gentile and located in his domain without Jewish responsibility for it does not violate the biblical prohibition – even if it continues to exist elsewhere in the world.

However, Chazal expanded the scope of this obligation. They required a Jew not only to avoid possessing *chametz* physically, but to ensure that no *chametz* remains under his legal responsibility or ownership in any form. As the Ramban notes, this expansion reflects the Torah's broader formulation, "in all your borders," which includes not merely physical proximity, but legal ownership.

This principle is codified in the ***Shulchan***

1. *Shemot* 12:19.
2. *Shemot* 13:7.

Aruch,[3] who rules that if a Jew assumes legal responsibility for *chametz* – even if it physically belongs to a gentile – he is obligated to destroy/remove it from his possession before Pesach. The ***Mishna Berura***[4] clarifies that halachic ownership is defined not only by possession, but by responsibility and liability. Even partial responsibility may create sufficient ownership to trigger the prohibition. For example, one who accepts liability as a *shomer* for another's *chametz* may be required to remove it before Pesach, even though he does not own it outright.

The halachic conclusion is clear: ownership of *chametz* is defined not only by physical control, but by legal and financial responsibility. This definition becomes critical when considering modern financial instruments such as stocks.

What Is a Stock?

Before addressing the halachic question, we must clarify the economic reality. A stock represents a fractional share in a company. In exchange for capital invested, the shareholder receives certain rights: the right to profit (dividends), participation in shareholder meetings, voting rights (in some cases), and a claim to residual assets if the company is liquidated.

Importantly, the value of a stock is not tied to any specific asset owned by the company. Rather, it reflects the market's assessment of the company's overall value. Stocks are traded freely on public exchanges, often changing hands multiple times in a single day.

Today, many individuals hold stocks indirectly – through pension funds, mutual funds, or investment portfolios managed by financial institutions. In such cases, the investor may not even know which specific companies are included in the fund. This reality raises a critical question: when I hold shares in a company, am I halachically considered an owner of the company's assets – including its *chametz*?

Does a Shareholder Have Halachic Ownership?

Contemporary authorities analyze this issue through two broader halachic lenses. First, what is the halachic status of a corporation itself? Is it a partnership, a new legal entity, or something else? Second, and more relevant to our discussion, what is the halachic status of the shareholder? Is he considered a partner and owner, or merely a financial creditor?

Three primary approaches emerge in the responsa literature.

Approach I: The Shareholder Is Not an Owner

Maharam Schick[5] maintains that a shareholder is not halachically considered an owner of the company's assets. When an individual purchases shares, he does not thereby acquire a proportional portion of the company's factory, inventory, or merchandise. Rather, he acquires a financial interest – a right to share in the company's profits and losses.

He therefore compares shareholding to a loan arrangement: the shareholder contributes capital to the enterprise, but the company's assets are not directly his. The shareholder holds a monetary claim within the corporate framework, not ownership of its physical property.

3. O.C. 440:1.
4. 440:7.
5. *Yoreh De'ah* 158.

According to this model, even if the company possesses *chametz* over Pesach, the shareholder would not violate *bal yeira'eh* or *bal yimatzei*, since those prohibitions apply only to *chametz* that one owns, not to assets in which one merely holds a financial stake.

Approach II: The Shareholder Is an Owner, Though Not in the Classical Sense

Rav Shimon Greenfield[6] sharply disputes this model. He argues that corporate assets must belong to someone; if not to the shareholders, then to whom?

He therefore maintains that shareholders are genuine partners in the company. Admittedly, their ownership is structured and limited by corporate bylaws – they cannot independently sell assets or manage daily operations. However, these limitations do not undermine ownership; they merely regulate how it is exercised.

Under this approach, the shareholder does not own a specific sack of flour or a particular machine. Rather, he owns a proportional share in the enterprise as a whole – including its assets. Consequently, if the company possesses *chametz*, the shareholder would appear to have halachic ownership in that *chametz*.

Approach III: Halachically Limited Ownership

The third approach seeks a middle path. The **Rav Yitzchak Yaakov Weiss**[7] argues that limited ownership does not automatically cease to be ownership. Even if shareholders lack direct managerial control, they retain a proprietary interest that may carry halachic consequences.

However, he distinguishes between meaningful ownership and ownership so diluted that it lacks halachic substance. Where shareholders have no voting rights, no practical influence, and no control over corporate decisions – as is common in modern public corporations – their ownership may be too attenuated to constitute halachic possession.

Rav Moshe Feinstein[8] develops this further. Even if shareholders technically possess voting rights, if those rights are practically meaningless, because controlling interests remain elsewhere, this does not create halachically significant ownership. Only when one holds a sufficiently large share to influence management would ownership become halachically substantive.

Similarly, **Rav Yitzchak Aharon Halevi**[9] rules that where shareholders have no authority to destroy or sell the company's *chametz*, and corporate management operates independently, they do not violate *bal yeira'eh*. He adds an additional consideration: in many companies, the majority of shares are held by non-Jews, further weakening any claim of Jewish ownership over specific *chametz* assets.

Rav Shlomo Kluger[10] likewise writes that ordinary shareholders possess only a right to profit or loss, not direct control over the company's transactions. Therefore, he does not require them to sell such holdings before Pesach.

Thus far we have seen that the halachic debate turns on a fundamental question: Is stock

6. Responsa Maharshag, Y.D. 3. Rav Greenfield was a student of the Maharam Schick.
7. 3:1:12 and 7:26.
8. Responsa *Igrot Moshe, Even Ha'Ezer* 1:7.
9. Responsa *Mahari'a HaLevi* 2:124.
10. Responsa *Ha'Elef Lecha Shlomo*, O.C. 238.

ownership considered genuine partnership in corporate assets, or merely a financial instrument detached from concrete ownership? If it is considered full ownership, the prohibition of *chametz* would apply. If it is merely a financial claim, no violation occurs. If it is limited ownership, the question becomes one of degree: at what point does economic participation translate into halachic possession?

This conceptual framework now allows us to address an additional dimension: even if technical ownership does not exist, does investment itself constitute assisting in a transgression?

Does Investment Constitute Assisting in a Transgression?

Even if one adopts the more lenient view that a shareholder does not halachically own the company's *chametz*, another question arises. By investing in a company that violates halacha, is the shareholder guilty of *mesayei'a l'davar aveira*, assisting in a transgression?

The Torah states: "You shall not place a stumbling block before the blind".[11] Chazal understand this not only literally, but as a prohibition against enabling another person to sin. ***Sefer HaMitzvot HaKatzar***[12] explains that this includes assisting or strengthening someone in the commission of a transgression.

At first glance, then, even if a shareholder lacks direct ownership of *chametz*, his financial participation strengthens the company. If the company is Jewish-owned and continues to operate in violation of halacha, whether through *chametz* on Pesach, *ribbit* (interest), or Shabbat desecration, shouldn't investment constitute assistance?

Rav Moshe Feinstein[13] addresses this concern. He writes that purchasing shares in such a company does not constitute prohibited assistance, because the company's operations do not depend on any particular shareholder. The commerce will proceed regardless; there is no shortage of potential investors. The individual shareholder is acting for personal financial benefit, not to enable transgression.

In halachic terms, this resembles a case where the transgressor could easily perform the act without one's involvement (known as "*chad avrei d'nahara*," one side of the river). In such circumstances, the prohibition of *lifnei iver* does not apply in its biblical form, and many authorities do not extend the rabbinic prohibition of *mesayei'a* either.

Accordingly, Rav Feinstein notes that even scrupulous individuals commonly invest in publicly traded companies without concern for this issue.

Including Shares in the Sale of *Chametz*

According to those authorities who regard a shareholder as possessing halachic ownership in a company's assets, a practical question arises: how should such shares be addressed before Pesach? Must the shareholder sell the shares through the standard mechanisms required in financial markets – which often involve formal registration and regulatory procedures – or is it

11. *Vayikra* 19:14.
12. Negative Commandment 76.
13. Responsa *Igrot Moshe*, E.H. 1:7.

sufficient to include them in the standard *shtar mechirat chametz*?

Rav Shlomo Ishon[14] writes that shares may be included in the regular *chametz* sale, provided this is stated explicitly. Although civil law generally requires formal registration to transfer ownership of shares, the sale document may stipulate that the shares are sold together with the *chametz*, and that the seller undertakes to complete any required registration if necessary.

In other words, from a halachic standpoint, the shares can be transferred through the standard mechanisms of *mechirat chametz*, so long as the intent is clearly articulated. No separate commercial transaction is required. This solution reflects a broader principle in *mechirat chametz*: the sale need not follow conventional commercial norms, but must meet halachic standards of valid transfer and intent.

Shares that Were Not Sold Before Pesach

If one accepts the stringent view that a shareholder is halachically considered an owner of the company's *chametz*, a serious question follows: What if the shares were not sold before Pesach?

The ***Shulchan Aruch***[15] rules that *chametz* which remained in a Jew's possession over Pesach is forbidden even after the festival, known as "*chametz she'avar alav haPesach*," a rabbinic penalty imposed even if the *chametz* was nullified before Pesach.

At first glance, this would suggest that unsold shares in a company holding *chametz* should likewise become prohibited after Pesach. However, several considerations may mitigate this conclusion.

1. *Chametz* Beyond One's Reach

The ***Mishna Berura***[16] discusses a case in which a person was traveling and unable to sell or physically destroy his *chametz*. If he declared it ownerless (*hefker*) before Pesach, some authorities rule that he may reacquire it afterward, particularly in a case of significant financial loss. Since he had no practical ability to dispose of it in the usual way, Chazal did not impose the penalty.

Applying this reasoning to shares: although shares can generally be traded remotely, a shareholder does not have direct control over the company's inventory and cannot personally destroy or remove its *chametz*. If he performed *bittul chametz* using the standard formula, thereby fulfilling the biblical requirement and rendering the *chametz* ownerless, there is room to argue that the rabbinic penalty should not automatically apply.

2. Mixed Ownership

A second possible basis for leniency emerges from another ruling of the ***Shulchan Aruch***[17] regarding *chametz* found after Pesach in a setting where ownership is uncertain or mixed. The ***Mishna Berura***[18] explains that where it is unclear whether the *chametz* belonged to a Jew or a non-Jew, some authorities permit it, especially where the matter concerns a rabbinic prohibition.

In the case of publicly traded companies, shares are typically held by a mixture of Jewish and non-Jewish shareholders. One could therefore argue that the *chametz* cannot be definitively

---

14. Cited by *Machon HaTorah V'Ha'Aretz*, within the discussion of selling shares before Pesach.
15. O.C. 448:5.
16. 448:25.
17. O.C. 449:1.
18. 449:5.

attributed to Jewish ownership during Pesach. Some authorities invoke this factor as additional support for leniency.

Conclusion

The question of *chametz* stocks illustrates the interaction between eternal halachic principles and modern economic structures. What appears at first glance to be a purely financial instrument may, upon analysis, raise fundamental questions of ownership, responsibility, and participation.

We have seen that the issue hinges on how one defines shareholding: Is it merely a financial claim? Is it genuine ownership, though limited in form? Or is it ownership whose halachic weight depends on the shareholder's actual ability to influence the company's conduct?

Even where ownership is not established, the related concern of assisting in transgression must be evaluated within its proper halachic parameters. And even according to stringent opinions, practical solutions exist within the established framework of *mechirat chametz*.

This discussion reminds us that halacha does not retreat before complexity. Rather, it penetrates it – carefully distinguishing between formal ownership and economic participation, between legal control and theoretical interest. In doing so, it ensures that the mitzvot of Pesach remain fully applicable even in a world of corporations and capital markets.

May we merit to fulfill the mitzvot of Pesach with clarity and integrity, sanctifying even the most intricate areas of our economic lives in accordance with the Torah.

ERETZ HEMDAH
Institute for Advanced Jewish Studies
Jerusalem

Kinshasa, Zaire

קינשסה, זאיר

ניסן תשנ״א

לז. ״מכירת חמץ״ על-ידי יהודי המפעיל את מאפייתו (חמץ) גם בימי הפסח

שאלה:
האם יש עניין בכך שהיהודי ימכור את חמצו, אף על פי שידוע, שוודאי יאפה חמץ וימכרנו בפסח, כדי שלא יעבור על איסור כרת, אלא על איסור גזל בלבד? ויצוין שמדובר במאפיה שאין בה שותף נכרי.

תשובה:
אין בפתרון המוצע שום תועלת, ואדרבה, הוא עושה את עניין המכירה פלסתר, ובעצם מכירה זו אינה מכירה כלל, ועל כן אין לעשות זאת בשום אופן. מי שמחזיק מאפיה של חמץ בפסח, עובר על איסורים חמורים, ויש להניאו מזה ככל האפשר.
(הבהרה לשואל: יצויין שלרוב השיטות אסור גזל עכו״ם מן התורה[1] ובאיסור בל יראה ובל ימצא ובהנאה מחמץ אין כרת[2], ויש כרת רק באכילה).

---

[1] עיין ב״ים של שלמה״ (ב״ק פרק עשירי) בדעת הרמב״ם, בש״ך (שו״ע חושן משפט סי׳ שמח ס״ק ב) וב״נתיבות המשפט״ (שם ס״ק א), וכן ב״חלקת מחוקק״ ו״בית שמואל״ (שו״ע אבן העזר סי׳ כח, א) ועוד. ויש לציין שנוסף על איסור גזל יש בזה גם איסור חילול השם, עיין ב״משך חכמה״ (שמות כא יד בעניין איסור לא תרצח בגוי).

[2] פסחים כא ע״ב תוס׳ ד״ה כל מקום.

ERETZ HEMDAH
Institute for Advanced Jewish Studies
Jerusalem

קינשסה, זאיר Kinshasa, Zaire

ניסן תשנ״א

לח. ״מכירת חמץ״ על-ידי בעל מאפיה השותף עם גוי

שאלה:
יהודי שיש לו מאפיה יחד עם גוי, כיצד יעשה מכירת חמץ? מצד הרווחים וכדומה?

תשובה:
במצב של קהילתכם, על השותפים לעשות חלוקה מחדש של המאפיה ותכולתה למשך השבועיים הקרובים. היהודי צריך להציע לשותפו הגוי ליטול את כל חלקו (של היהודי) במאפיה למשך חג הפסח, והיהודי יקבל את כל המאפיה לזמן מקביל לאחר הפסח. במשך החג אסור ליהודי להיות מעורב בנעשה במאפיה ואסור לו לעשות חישובים של רווח והפסד בהשוואה לתקופה שהמאפיה תהיה כולה בבעלותו שלו[1].

[1] שו״ע (אורח חיים סי׳ תנ, ג).

3

Halachot of Kitniyot on Pesach

הלכות קטניות בפסח

The Halachic Definition of Grain

The Custom to Avoid Eating Kitniyot

Which Foods are Considered Kitniyot?

Mixtures Containing Kitniyot

For quick reference, some long website URLs have been shortened.
For the complete list of referenced websites visit www.tzurbaolami.com.

ת	**Tanach**
ח	**Talmud (Chazal)**
ר	***Rishonim***
א	***Acharonim***
פ	**Contemporary Halachic Sources**

In the previous *shiurim*, we studied some of the halachot of owning *chametz* on Pesach, specifically as they relate to non-food items such as cosmetics and to the sale of *chametz* before Pesach. In this *shiur*, we will discuss the status of *kitniyot* and the custom to avoid their consumption on Pesach. The term *kitniyot* is usually translated as "legumes," but potentially includes any food that grows from the ground and shares certain characteristics with grain. We will examine the origins and rationale of this custom, who it applies to, which foods are included in the category of *kitniyot*, and a range of contemporary applications.

The Halachic Definition of Grain

The **Gemara (*Masechet Pesachim*)** explains in two places that rice and millet cannot become *chametz*, and as a result, one also cannot make them into matza for the purposes of fulfilling the obligation to eat matza on the first night of Pesach. The *tanna* Rabbi Yochanan ben Nuri disagrees and maintains that rice is considered grain, although his position is not accepted as halacha.

1. מסכת פסחים לה.

משנה: אלו דברים שאדם יוצא בהן ידי חובתו בפסח: בחטים, בשעורים, בכוסמין, ובשיפון, ובשיבולת שועל...

גמרא: תנא: כוסמין מין חיטין, שיבולת שועל ושיפון – מין שעורין. כוסמין – גולבא, שיפון – דישרא, שיבולת שועל – שבילי תעלא. הני – אין, אורז ודוחן – לא.

מנהני מילי? אמר רבי שמעון בן לקיש, וכן תנא דבי רבי ישמעאל, וכן תנא דבי רבי אליעזר בן יעקב: אמר קרא: "לא תאכל עליו חמץ שבעת ימים תאכל עליו מצות", דברים

ח Masechet Pesachim 35a

MISHNA: These are the types of grain **with which a person fulfills his obligation** to eat matza **on the** first night of **Pesach: With wheat, with barley, with spelt** [***kusmin***], **with rye** [***shifon***], **and with oats** [***shibbolet shu'al***][1]...

GEMARA: One of the Sages **taught** in the *Tosefta*: **Spelt** is **a type of wheat,** while **oats** [***shibbolet shu'al***] **and rye** [***shifon***] are **a type of barley.** The Gemara translates the lesser-known species into the vernacular Aramaic: **Spelt** is called ***gulba***; **rye** is ***dishra***; and **oats** are ***shevilei ta'ala***. The Gemara infers: **These** species, **yes,** they may be used for *matza*; however, **rice** [***orez***] **and millet** [***dochan***], **no,** they may not be used.

From where are these matters, that matza cannot be prepared from rice or millet, **derived? Rabbi Shimon ben Lakish said, and likewise** a Sage **of the school of Rabbi Yishmael taught, and likewise** a Sage **of the school of Rabbi Eliezer ben Ya'akov taught** that **the verse states: "You shall eat no leavened bread with it; seven days you shall eat with it matza,** the bread of affliction" (*Devarim* 16:3). This verse indicates that only with **substances**

1. Although we have used the traditional translation of the Hebrew term *shibbolet shu'al*, oats, this translation is somewhat disputed among scholars today, as oats are very different than the other four species of grain and certainly do not appear to be a type of barley, as the Gemara describes *shibbolet shu'al*. Furthermore, they were not grown in Eretz Yisrael during the Mishnaic period. See, for example, www.toraland.org.il/מאמרים/הארץ-ומצוותיה/תכניות-לימוד/משנה-וארץ/משנה-וארץ-/שיבולת-שועל-חלק-א. This question has significant halachic ramifications regarding the correct *beracha* on oat products, as well as whether those who are unable to eat gluten can fulfill their obligation on Pesach by eating matza made from oats.

דברים הבאים לידי חימוץ – אדם יוצא בהן ידי חובתו במצה, יצאו אלו שאין באין לידי חימוץ אלא לידי סירחון.

מתניתין דלא כרבי יוחנן בן נורי, דאמר: אורז מין דגן הוא, וחייבין על חימוצו כרת. דתניא: רבי יוחנן בן נורי אוסר באורז ודוחן, מפני שקרוב להחמיץ.

substances which will come to a state of **leavening, a person fulfills his obligation to** eat **matza with them,** provided he prevents them from becoming leavened. This **excludes these** foods, i.e., rice, millet, and similar grains, **which,** even if flour is prepared from them and water is added to their flour, **do not come to** a state of **leavening but to** a state of **decay** [*sirachon*].[2]

The Gemara notes: **The Mishna is not in accordance with** the opinion of **Rabbi Yochanan ben Nuri, who said: Rice is** a full-fledged **type of grain, and one is liable** to receive ***karet*** **for** eating it in **its leavened** state, like other types of grain. **As it was taught** in a *baraita*: **Rabbi Yochanan ben Nuri prohibits** eating cooked **rice and millet** on Pesach, **due to** the fact **that they are close to being leavened.**

2. מסכת פסחים קיד.

ח Masechet Pesachim 114b

מאי שני תבשילין? אמר רב הונא: סילקא וארוזא. רבא הוה מיהדר אסילקא וארוזא, הואיל ונפיק מפומיה דרב הונא.

אמר רב אשי: שמע מינה דרב הונא: לית דחייש להא דרבי יוחנן בן נורי. דתניא, רבי יוחנן בן נורי אומר: אורז מין דגן הוא, וחייבין על חימוצו כרת, ואדם יוצא בו ידי חובתו בפסח.

The Gemara asks: **What** are these **two cooked foods** mentioned in the Mishna, that would be brought before the leader of the Seder? **Rav Huna said: Beets and rice.** The Gemara relates that **Rava would seek beets and rice** for his meal on Pesach night, **since** this ruling **came from Rav Huna's mouth.** Although Rava realized that Rav Huna was merely citing examples and did not mean that one must eat those specific foods, he wanted to fulfill the statement of his teacher precisely.

Rav Ashi said: Learn incidentally another halacha **from** this statement **of Rav Huna,** that there is **no** one **who is concerned about that** statement **of Rabbi Yochanan ben Nuri. As it was taught in** a *baraita*: **Rabbi Yochanan ben Nuri says: Rice is a type of grain** in all regards; **and one is liable** to receive ***karet*** **for** eating it in **its leavened** state on Pesach; **and one fulfills his obligation with it on Pesach,** if it was properly baked into *matza*. It can be inferred from Rav Huna's suggestion to use cooked rice that rice cannot become leavened.

All *Rishonim*, including the **Rambam** (*Chametz Umatza* 5:1), rule in accordance with the opinion that rice is not considered a grain and therefore cannot become *chametz*. Therefore, in theory, there should be no problem with consuming rice and legumes on Pesach.

2. The Gemara and commentators do not explain the difference between leavening and decay. Dr. B.P. Munk writes (*Techumin*, vol. 1, p. 97) that each of these is a different way of breaking down the grain. Leavening is a three-stage process caused by the enzymes beta-amylase, alma-amylase and oxidase respectively. Decay is caused by a fourth enzyme, proteinase. Beta-amylase is not present in *kitniyot*, making leavening impossible.

The Custom to Avoid Eating Kitniyot

Although as we have seen, eating *kitniyot* is permitted on Pesach according to the Gemara, a custom developed in Ashkenazic communities beginning around the twelfth century to refrain from eating them. **Rabbeinu Peretz**, writing in ***Hagahot Semak***, quotes a dispute regarding the appropriateness of this practice, but concludes that it is indeed proper to avoid *kitniyot* since they could be confused with the five species of grain.

3. הגהות סמ"ק | רכב:יב

ועל הקטניות כגון פויי"ש ופול"י ורי"ש ועדשים וכיוצא בהם רבותינו נוהגים בהם איסור שלא לאוכלם בפסח כלל... וגדולים נוהגים בהם היתר, ומורי רבינו יחיאל היה נוהג לאכול בפסח פול הלבן שקורין פויי"ש וגם היה אומר כן בשם גדולים, ומביא ראיה דאפילו באורז דחשיב ליה רבי יוחנן בן נורי מין דגן לגבי חימוץ, קאמר תלמודא לית דחש לה להא דרבי יוחנן.

מיהו קשה הדבר מאד להתיר דבר שנוהגין בו העולם איסור מימי חכמים הקדמונים דמסתמא לא נהגו בו איסור מחמת חימוץ עצמו דלא טעו בדבר שהתינוקות של בית רבן שלמדו ההלכה יודעין דאיכא בהדיא בפסחים דאין בא לידי חימוץ כי אם מחמשת המינין.

ולכך נראה לקיים המנהג ולאסור כל קטנית בפסח, ולא מחמת חימוץ עצמו כי טעות הוא לומר כן אלא מטעם גזירה הוא דכיון דקטנית מעשה קדרה הוא, ודגן נמי מעשה קדרה הוא כדייסא אי הוי שרינן קטנית אולי אתי לאיחלופי ולהתיר דייסא, כיון דאידי ואידי מעשה קדרה הוא.

וגם מידי דמידגן הוא כמו חמשת המינים, כדאיתא בפרק השוכר את הפועלים דקרי לקטנית מידי דמידגן וגם יש מקומות

ו Hagahot Semak 222:12

Regarding *kitniyot*, such as white beans, broad beans, rice, lentils, and the like, our rabbis are accustomed to treat them as prohibited, not eating them on Pesach at all... But some great authorities permit them. My teacher, Rabbeinu Yechiel, was accustomed to eating white beans called *fuyi"sh* on Pesach, and he would also say in the name of other great authorities [that they are permitted]. He would cite a proof: Even regarding rice, which Rabbi Yochanan ben Nuri considers a type of grain for the purposes of *chametz*, the Gemara says that no one is concerned with Rabbi Yochanan's opinion.

However, it is very difficult to permit something that the masses have treated as prohibited since the days of the early authorities. As presumably, they did not prohibit it because of actual leavening, as they would not have erred in something that even schoolchildren who learned the halacha know, that it is explicitly stated in *Masechet Pesachim* that only the five species of grain can become *chametz*.

Therefore, it appears correct to maintain the custom and to prohibit all *kitniyot* on Pesach. Not because of actual leavening, as it would be a mistake to say that, but as a decree. As since *kitniyot* are cooked in a pot, and grain is also cooked in a pot, such as [when making] porridge, if we were to permit *kitniyot*, people might confuse the two and permit porridge, since both are cooked in a pot.

Furthermore, [*kitniyot*] are foods that are piled like the five species [of grain], as is stated (*Bava Metzia* 87a), that *kitniyot* are referred to as "foods that are piled up" [*midi d'midgan*].[3] There are also places

3. This does not appear in our text of the Gemara there, but it does appear in *Nedarim* 55a. The idea appears to be that both grain and *kitniyot* are piled up when stored.

שרגילים לעשות מהם פת כמו מחמשת המינים ולכך אתי לאיחלופי לאותן שאינן בני תורה ולא דמי למיני ירקות כגון כרוב וכרשין וכיוצא בהן דהנהו לא דמי כלל לדגן ולא אתי לאיחלופי.

ומנהג הגון הוא ליזהר מכל קטנית כדפרישית, ואפילו מחרדל משום דהוי מידי דמידגן, אף על גב דתלמודא שרי אורז זהו דוקא בימיהם שהיו כולם בקיאים בהלכות איסור והיתר, אבל עכשיו בדורות אחרונות ודאי יש לגזור כדפרישית.

where people commonly make bread from *kitniyot* just like they do from the five species of grain. Therefore, those who are not well-versed in Torah law may confuse them. [In this regard, *kitniyot*] are not comparable to vegetables such as cabbage, leeks, and the like, as those are completely unlike grain and one will not confuse them.

[Therefore], it is an appropriate custom to avoid all *kitniyot* on Pesach, as I have explained. One should even avoid mustard, because it is a food that is piled up. Although the Gemara permits rice, that was only in their days, when all were knowledgeable in the laws of permitted and forbidden foods. But now, in later generations, it is certainly appropriate to enact a decree, as I have explained.

Thus, according to Rabbeinu Peretz, the reason for the custom was that people may confuse *kitniyot* and grain since both are used to make bread and both are baked into dishes, and may thereby mistakenly come to prepare and eat *chametz* on Pesach.

The **Ritva**, who lived in Spain, where there was no communal custom to prohibit *kitniyot*, writes that one must take the necessary precautions to avoid any *chametz* that is mixed with them. He adds that even in his locale, many pious individuals avoid *kitniyot* out of concern that *chametz* may be mixed with them.

4. חדושים מהריטב"א | פסחים לה.

ומכל מקום צריך להזהר מאד שהרי נמצא עם האורז ממין הכוסמין תמיד ואם נשאר שם אפילו גרגיר אחד נמצא שנאסר הכל בבשולו במשהו, ולכן **צריך לבדוק אותו פעם אחר פעם בעיון גדול**, דהא לאו אחזוקי איסורא הוא כיון דמילתא דשכיחא טובא, **והרבה מן החסידים נמנעו מלאכול מהם בפסח מבושלים מפני ערבובים שעולה עמהם.**

ר Chiddushim MehaRitva,[4] Pesachim 35a

Nevertheless [although rice is not *chametz*], one must be very careful. As spelt is regularly found together with rice, and if even a single grain remains, the entire mixture becomes prohibited when it is cooked, because of the smallest amount [of *chametz*]. Therefore, **it must be checked repeatedly with great scrutiny**, as this is not considered "presuming a prohibition" [without sufficient basis], since this issue is very common. **Many of the pious individuals refrain from eating cooked rice on Pesach because of the mixtures that become mixed with it.**

Rabbeinu Manoach suggests a novel reason for this custom. He writes that we avoid *kitniyot* as these foods are not conducive to rejoicing on the festival.

4. Although the Ritva's commentary on *Masechet Pesachim* has not been found, this *sefer* of undetermined authorship consists mostly of a collection of quotes from the Ritva's commentary. It has been published by Mossad HaRav Kook as part of their set of the commentary of the Ritva.

5. ספר המנוחה | חמץ ומצה ה:א

וכתוב בספר המנהגות: ונהגו כל העולם שלא לאכול זרעונים בפסח מפני שהן מחמיצין ועל כן נקראין חימצי, עד כאן. ולא מסתבר לומר שיהיה המנהג תלוי באיסור כלל שאין בשום קטניות בעולם שום חימוץ **אלא מפני שאין דרך לאכול קטניות במועד שהרי כתוב ושמחת בחגך ואין שמחה באכילת תבשיל קטנית.**

ר Sefer HaMenucha, Chametz Umatza 5:1

It is written in *Sefer HaMinhagot*: "The universal custom is not to eat legumes on Pesach because they become *chametz*, and therefore they are called *chimtzi*." But it is not reasonable to say that the custom is based on a prohibition at all, as there is no legume in the world that undergoes leavening. **Rather, it is not customary to eat *kitniyot* during the festival, as it is written, "You shall rejoice on your festival," and there is no joy [experienced] in eating a dish of *kitniyot*.**

In contrast, the ***Tur*** writes that refraining from *eating kitniyot* is an excessive stringency.

6. טור | או"ח תנג

ויש אוסרין לאכול אורז וכל מיני קטניות בתבשיל לפי שמיני חטין מתערבין בהן וחומרא יתירא היא זו ולא נהגו כן.

ר Tur, Orach Chaim 453

Some prohibit eating rice and all types of *kitniyot* in a cooked dish, as types of wheat get mixed with them. But this is an excessive stringency and is not practiced.

Similarly, the ***Beit Yosef*** writes that only the Ashkenazim avoid eating *kitniyot* on Pesach.

7. בית יוסף | או"ח תנג

ולית דחש לדברים הללו זולתי האשכנזים.

ר Beit Yosef, Orach Chaim 453

None are concerned about these matters, other than the Ashkenazim.[5]

From the comments of Rabbeinu Peretz and the *Tur* above, it appears that during their time (13th–14th centuries), the practice to avoid eating *kitniyot* was not even adhered to by all Ashkenazic communities. However, the **Rema** writes that in his time, this was the practice of all Ashkenazim, and that one must not deviate from this practice.

8. שולחן ערוך | או"ח תנג:א

אלו דברים שיוצאים בהם ידי חובת מצה... אבל לא באורז ושאר מיני קטניות.

וגם אינם באים לידי חימוץ ומותר לעשות מהם תבשיל.

הגה: ויש אוסרים. והמנהג באשכנז להחמיר, ואין לשנות.

א Shulchan Aruch, Orach Chaim 453:1

These are the [types of grain] with which a person fulfills his obligation to eat matza... but not with rice or other types of *kitniyot*.

These foods also do not become *chametz*, and making them into a cooked dish is permitted.

Rema: Some prohibit this. The custom in Ashkenaz is to be stringent, and one should not deviate from this.

---

5. While precise numbers are not available, it is likely that at the time of the *Beit Yosef* (16th century), Ashkenazim represented less than 30% of the world's Jews. See www.bjpa.org/content/upload/bjpa/dell/DellaPergola%20Some%20Fundamentals.pdf.

Rav Yaakov Emden cites his father, the ***Chacham Tzvi***, who wished to end this stringent practice. He argues that as well as having no halachic basis, the restriction necessitates an increased consumption of matza, which results in laxity regarding *chametz* and also is financially difficult for many. Rav Yaakov Emden agrees with his father and writes that he would be happy to join with other Ashkenazic rabbis to rescind the decree.

9. מור וקציעה | או"ח תנג

...ובשעת הדחק ודאי יש להתיר גם כל הקטניות באכילה, שהרי אפילו רבינו בעל הטור שהיה אשכנזי, ובימיו כבר התחיל מנהג חומרא זו, לא השגיח בה וכתב וחומרא יתרה היא ולא נהגו בה. מכלל שלא קבלוה אבותינו האשכנזים ז"ל בימיו ולא נתפשטה ביניהם וכמה פוסקים חושבים אותה לשטות ומנהג טעות, שאין צריך אפילו חרטה והתרה...

ומעידני על אבא מורי הגאון זצ"ל, כמה צער נצטער אותו צדיק על זאת, כל חג המצות היה מתרעם ואומר אי איישר חילי אבטליניה למנהג גרוע הלז שהיא חומרא דאתיא לידי קולא ונפק מנה חורבא ומכשול באיסור חמץ גמור, כי מתוך שאין מיני קטניות מצויים להמון לאכול ולשבוע, צריכין לאפות לחם מצה הרבה, בפרטות העניים ומי שבני ביתו מרובים ולא יספיקו להם תבשילים הרבה לשבר רעבונם, מוכרחים על כרחם להספיק להם מצה די לחמם לביתם וחיים לנערותם. מתוך כך אינם נזהרים בעסה כראוי וכחובה, עושים אותה גדולה הרבה ושוהים עליה מאד. קרוב הדבר שנכשלים באיסור כרת רחמנא לצלן.

גם המצות עומדים להם ביוקר ואין יד כל אדם משגת לעשותם די הצורך לבני ביתו, ולא ימצא להם אפילו די שבעם אף בלחם חמץ כל השנה, וקטניות נמצאים בזול בלי טורח ובהתר, ואתו לאמנועי משמחת יום טוב, בסבת חומרא שאין לה טעם וריח, לכן אשרי שיאחז צדיק דרכו, יתן אוכל למכביר ונפץ את עלולי החומרות הזרות אל הסלע...

א Mor U'ketzia, Orach Chaim 453

...At a time of need, one should certainly permit eating all kinds of *kitniyot*. As even our teacher, the author of the *Tur*, who was an Ashkenazi, and in whose days this stringent custom had already begun, did not give it credence, and wrote, "This is an excessive stringency, and is not practiced." This implies that our Ashkenazi ancestors did not accept it in his time, and it did not become widespread among them. Several halachic authorities also consider it nonsense and a misguided custom, such that it does not even require regret or [formal] permission [by three people, as is usually required for one who wishes to abandon a meritorious practice]...

I bear witness about my father, my teacher, the Gaon, how much anguish that righteous man suffered over this. Every Pesach he would lament and say: "If I had the power, I would abolish this bad custom, which is a stringency that leads to leniency, and it has led to ruin and stumbling in the prohibition of actual *chametz*." As since types of *kitniyot* are not available for the multitudes to eat and be satisfied, they must bake a great deal of matza. Especially the poor and those with large households, since they are unable to provide many cooked foods to satisfy their hunger, they are compelled to provide enough matza to feed their families. As a result, they are not careful with the dough as is proper and required; they make it very large and delay excessively over it. It is almost inevitable that they stumble into a prohibition [punishable by] *karet* [excision], God forbid.

Additionally, matzot are expensive, and not everyone can afford to make enough for their household. Some cannot even afford enough *chametz* bread to satisfy themselves during the year. [In contrast], *kitniyot* are available cheaply, without effort, and permissibly. [Avoiding them] can lead to refraining from rejoicing on Yom Tov, because of a stringency that has no real basis. Therefore, happy is the righteous person who will follow the proper path, providing ample food and smashing strange new stringencies against the rock...[6]

6. Paraphrasing *Tehillim* 137:9.

...על כן אני אומר בטח, המבטל מנהג זה של מניעת אכילת קטניות יהי חלקי עמו! הלואי יסכימו עמדי גדולי הדור במחוז הלז. הנני הנני להיות נטפל לדבר מצוה זו, וכל ימי הייתי עומד ומצפה מתי יבוא לידי ואפרסם דעת אבא מורי הגאון להפקיע חבל חומרות כאלו שאין רוב הצבור יכולין לעמוד בהן. לקיים "ותגזר אומר ויקם," ואקבענה בדפוס ואעשנה כיון להביאה לידי מעשה לתקוע בה מסמרות, לקבעה הלכה לדורות, לזכות את הרבים ולהסיר מכשול מדרך עמינו, בודאי למצוה רבה יחשב.

...**Therefore, I say with certainty: one who abolishes this custom of refraining from eating *kitniyot*, may my lot be with him!** If only the great authorities of this generation in this region would agree with me. I am more than ready to involve myself in this mitzva, and all my life I have hoped for and awaited the time when I would get the opportunity to publicize the view of my father, the Gaon, to release the bond of such stringencies that the majority of the public cannot uphold. To fulfill [the verse in *Iyov* 22:28]: "You shall decree a matter, and it shall be established." I would print it and fix the practice firmly, to make it a permanent halachic ruling for generations, to bring merit to the public and remove obstacles from the path of our people. This would certainly be considered a great mitzva.[7]

However, this position of the *Chacham Tzvi* and his son Rav Yaakov Emden was not accepted by any of the Ashkenazic communities in Europe, who continued to adhere to this stringent practice. The ***Aruch HaShulchan*** even attacks the credentials of those who wished to abolish the custom to refrain from eating *kitniyot* on Pesach.

10. ערוך השולחן | או"ח תנג:ד

ודע דאף דמדינא מותר לאכול אורז וכל מיני קטניות בפסח, מכל מקום הנהיגו רבותינו ואבותינו זה הרבה מאות מן השנים וקבלו עליהם באיסור לבלי לאכול אורז ומיני קטניות בפסח... **ואיסור זה כיון שקבלו אבותינו משום גדר, מדין תורה אסור לנו לבטל, והמפקפקים והמקילים בזה מעידין על עצמן שאין בהם יראת שמים ויראת חטא ואין בקיאין בדרכי התורה.**

א Aruch HaShulchan, Orach Chaim 453:4

You should know that although based on [pure] halacha, eating rice and all types of *kitniyot* is permitted on Pesach, nevertheless, for many hundreds of years our rabbis and ancestors initiated a custom, and accepted a prohibition on themselves, not to eat rice and types of *kitniyot* on Pesach... **Once our ancestors accepted this prohibition as a fence, abolishing it is prohibited based on Torah law. Those who cast doubt or act leniently in this regard testify about themselves that they do not have any fear of Heaven or fear of sin, and are not experts in the ways of the Torah.**

Nevertheless, the ***Mishna Berura*** writes that if circumstances are pressing, such that one has no other food, one may eat *kitniyot*, provided that precautions are taken to avoid actual *chametz*.

11. משנה ברורה | או"ח תנג:ז

ואין לשנות – ...ומכל מקום בשעת הדחק שאין לאדם מה לאכול מותר לבשל כל המינים חוץ מחמשת מיני דגן.

א Mishna Berura, Orach Chaim 453:7

One should not deviate – ...Nevertheless, in pressing circumstances where a person has nothing to eat, cooking all types [of food] other than the five species of grain is permitted.

7. Rav Michael Avraham offers a contemporary argument against maintaining the custom of *kitniyot*. He argues that since no formal decree was ever made against eating *kitniyot*, and people only avoided eating them due to real concerns of *chametz*, today when, in his opinion, no such concern exists, there is no basis for this stringency. However, nearly all rabbinic authorities today do not accept this argument in practice, as customs accepted so widely are given great weight in halacha. Moreover, concern still often does exist today that kernels of grain may be mistakenly mixed in with *kitniyot* during production (see, e.g., www.yeshiva.org.il/ask/103636 and https://etzion.org.il/en/halakha/orach-chaim/holidays/kitniyot).

ומכל מקום גם בכגון זה יקדים קטניות לאורז ודוחן ורעצקע שהם דומין יותר לחמישה מינים ושייך בהו טפי למיגזר (ופשוט דהוא הדין לחולה אף שאין בו סכנה דמותר לבשל לו אם צריך לזה) אלא דצריך לבדוק ולברור יפה יפה בדקדוק היטב שלא ימצאו בם גרעינים מחמשת מיני דגן.

וכתב החתם סופר בתשובה סימן קכ"ב דאפילו במקום שיש להתיר, מכל מקום יחלטנו לכתחלה ברותחין דכל מה דאפשר לתקן מתקנינן, וכן כתב החיי אדם.

Nevertheless, even in such a case, one should rather [eat] legumes over rice, millet, and buckwheat, since those are more similar to the five species and there is greater reason to make a decree regarding them. (It is obvious that the same applies to a sick person, even if he is not in danger; cooking for him is permitted if he needs it.) However, one must check and sort them very meticulously to ensure that no kernels of the five species of grain are found in them.

The *Chatam Sofer* writes in a responsum that even in circumstances where one can permit [*kitniyot*], nevertheless one should first boil them in boiling water [to prevent leavening], as we take all possible precautions. The *Chayei Adam* writes similarly.

Sephardim and *Kitniyot*

Although in most Sephardic communities, there is no custom to avoid *kitniyot*, there are some exceptions, especially among Moroccan communities. The ***Ben Ish Chai*** writes that in his city (Baghdad), many avoided eating rice, due to the difficulty in checking that no *chametz* was mixed with it.

12. בן איש חי | שנה ראשונה, פרשת צו מא

פה עירנו יש הרבה בעלי בתים נוהגים שלא לאכול אורז בפסח, מפני כי האורז ימצא בו תערובת חיטין ושעורים, וצריך לבדקו תחלה פעמיים ושלש וחוששין שמא ישגו בבדיקה וישאר באורז חיטה ושעורה ויכשלו בו, לכך בדלין ממנו, ויש נוהגים לאכול אחר בדיקה.

א Ben Ish Chai, First Year, Parshat Tzav 41

Here in our city, many lay individuals are accustomed not to eat rice on Pesach, as wheat and barley can be found in rice, and one must first check it two or three times. People are concerned that they may err when checking, and wheat or barley may remain in the rice, and they will inadvertently transgress because of it. Therefore, they refrain from eating it. Some are accustomed to eat it after checking.

However, **Rav Ovadia Yosef** understands that this custom is not as binding as the Ashkenazic custom to avoid *kitniyot*. Accordingly, a Sephardi who has a need to do so may obtain permission from three people to annul his personal stringent practice (known as *hatarat nedarim*). In addition, one who was raised in a Sephardic home in which this stringency was followed is not obligated to continue it once he moves out of his parents' home.

13. חזון עובדיה | פסח, מצרכי מזון הכשרים לפסח ב

...וגם יש מהספרדים מהשרידים אשר ה' קורא, שנהגו להמנע מאכילת אורז בלבד בפסח,

ב Chazon Ovadia, Pesach, Food That Is Kosher for Pesach 2

...There are also some Sephardim, from the remaining few whom Hashem has called,[8] who are accustomed to refrain

8. Paraphrasing *Yoel* 3:5.

out of concern that they may not be able to check it properly. Sephardim who have adopted this stringent custom regarding rice and *kitniyot*, if they wish to annul their custom (due to some reason such as illness, or the like), it is possible to permit them to do so through *hatara*. One who practiced a prohibition regarding rice because he was dependent on his parents, who practiced this prohibition, and now he has married and is independent, may act leniently without any *hatara* from a halachic authority.

מחשש פן לא יוכלו לבודקו יפה. והספרדים שנהגו להחמיר באורז וקטניות אם ירצו לבטל מנהגם (מחמת איזו סיבה של חולי, וכיוצא בזה) אפשר להקל להם על ידי התרה. ומי שנהג איסור באורז, בגלל היותו סמוך על שלחן הוריו, שנהגו בו איסור, וכיום נשא אשה ועומד ברשות עצמו, רשאי לנהוג היתר בלי שום התרת חכם.

Conflicting Customs in Marriage

In earlier periods, most Jewish communities maintained uniform local customs. Regarding issues such as *kitniyot* on Pesach, individuals generally followed the custom of the place in which they lived. If one moved from one place to another, whether due to marriage or any other reason, one would typically adopt the custom of the new community. This principle appears in the **Mishna (*Masechet Pesachim*)** in relation to the custom not to work on Erev Pesach.

ח Mishna, Pesachim 4:1

In **a place where** the people were **accustomed to perform *melacha* on Erev Pesach until midday, one** may **do** so. In **a place where** the people were **accustomed not to perform** *melacha*, **one** may **not do** so. The performance of *melacha* on Erev Pesach until midday is not prohibited by law, but is dependent on local custom.

14. משנה | פסחים ד:א

מקום שנהגו לעשות מלאכה בערבי פסחים עד חצות עושין מקום שנהגו שלא לעשות אין עושין.

In his responsa **(*Tashbetz*)**, the **Rashbatz** addresses a situation where differing customs were followed by different communities within the same city, which was more unusual in earlier times. He writes that this is acceptable, and that under these circumstances, if a man from one community marries a woman from another community, the wife must adopt the customs of her husband's community.

ו Responsa Tashbetz 3:179

In places where there are communities that differ in their enactments, such that they are like two *batei din* in one city, some ruling like Beit Shammai and some ruling like Beit Hillel, where there is no prohibition of "*lo titgodedu*" – do not form separate factions, as stated in the first chapter of *Yevamot* (14a),[9] **if a man from one community marries a woman from another community, there is no doubt that the wife becomes included**

15. שו"ת תשב"ץ | ג:קעט

במקומות שיש קהלות חלוקות בתקנותיהם שהם כמו שני בתי דינין בעיר אחת פלג מורין כבית שמאי ופלג מורין כבית הלל דלית ביה משום לא תתגודדו לא תעשו אגודות אגודות כדאיתא בפרק קמא דיבמות (יד.). **ונשא איש מאנשי קהלה אחת אשה מאנשי קהלה אחרת אין ספק שהאשה היא נכללת**

9. It should be noted that although this appears to be the conclusion of the Gemara, the Rambam rules that maintaining two *batei din* in one city does violate this prohibition, as it leads to great disputes (*Hilchot Avoda Zara* 12:14). However, common

עם בעלה בכל חיובו דאשתו כגופו בכל הדברים ונפטרת מקהלת בית אביה. ודבר זה מלתא דפשיטא היא ואין בו ספק שלא יהיו שנים מסובין על שולחן אחד חלוקין בעסותיהן האסור לזה מותר לזה...

והשאלה אינה אלא **אם נתאלמנה האשה** אם היא חוזרת לבית אביה כאשר היתה קודם שנשאת, או תשאר עם בית בעלה כאשר היתה קודם שנתאלמנה. **ונראה שאם יש לה זרע ממנו תשאר עם זרעה בכלל חיוביהם ותקנותיהם. ואם אין לה זרע ממנו תשוב לבית אביה.** ודבר זה נלמד מן התורה ומדברי חז"ל...

with her husband in all his obligations. As a man's wife is like himself in all matters, and she is released from the community of her father's household. This matter is obvious and beyond doubt, as two people seated at one table [permanently, i.e., living in the same house] cannot use separate dough, i.e., what is prohibited to one cannot be permitted to the other...

The only question is, **if the wife becomes widowed**, does she return to her father's community, as she was before she was married, or does she remain with her husband's community as she was before she was widowed? **It seems that if she has children from him, she remains together with her children, under their obligations and enactments. But if she has no children from him, she returns to her father's household.** This matter is learned from the Torah and from the words of the Sages...

Today, it is increasingly common not only for there to be different communities within a city, but also for different customs to exist within the same community. Many maintain that even under these circumstances, a wife must take on her husband's customs. For example, **Rav Moshe Feinstein** rules that a wife must follow her husband's customs, whether they are more lenient or stricter. Even if they are more lenient, no *hatara* is required. Thus, if an Ashkenazi woman marries a Sephardic man, she would be permitted to eat *kitniyot* on Pesach, in accordance with her husband's custom, while if a Sephardic woman marries an Ashkenazi man, she would be required to refrain from eating *kitniyot*.

16. שו"ת אגרות משה | או"ח א:קנח

...לגבי האשה שניסת לבעל שמנהגיו אחרים ממנהגי בית אביה כיצאה ממקום בית אביה ובאה למקום בעלה **שצריכה להתנהג במנהגי בעלה בין לקולא בין לחומרא** בין בדברים שאין נוגעים לאיסורים בין בדברים הנוגעים לאיסורים. **ואין צריך התרת נדרים**. ואם היה צריך לא היה מועיל להרבה שיטות...

Responsa Igrot Moshe, Orach Chaim 1:158

...Regarding a woman who marries a husband whose customs are different than the customs of her father's household, she is equivalent to one who leaves the place of her father's house and comes to the place of her husband, and **she must practice the customs of her husband, whether they are lenient or strict**, whether regarding matters unrelated to prohibitions or whether regarding matters that relate to prohibitions. **There is no need for *hatarat nedarim***, and were there to be a need, it would not work according to many views...

Rav Ovadia Yosef concurs that an Ashkenazi woman who marries a Sephardic man may eat *kitniyot*, but he writes that nevertheless, she should ideally obtain *hatara*.

---

practice today is in accordance with the *Tashbetz* here and others, who do not accept this ruling of the Rambam.

17. חזון עובדיה | פסח, מצרכי מזון הכשרים לפסח ג

...ואם ברצונה לבטל מנהג הוריה, ולנהוג משעת נישואיה כמנהג בעלה, על צד היותר טוב, נכון שתעשה התרה כדי שתוכל לאכול בבית בעלה אורז וקטניות כמנהג הספרדים.

Chazon Ovadia, Pesach, Food That Is Kosher for Pesach 3

...If she wishes to discontinue the practice of her parents and act in accordance with her husband's custom from the time of her marriage, optimally it is proper for her to perform *hatara* in order to be able to eat rice and *kitniyot* in her husband's house, in accordance with the custom of the Sephardim.[10]

By contrast, **Rav Nachum Rabinovitch** writes that although one must not treat customs lightly, compromises are sometimes required in order to avoid dispute.[11] Therefore, one should look for ways to adapt personal customs to the current reality, and one can be more lenient regarding which custom to follow.

18. שו"ת שיח נחום | פח

...יש להיזהר מאוד לא לזלזל במנהגים, אפילו מנהגים של מה בכך, כי להרבה אנשים זהו הקשר היחידי שיש להם עם המסורת. אבל בציבור של קיבוץ גלויות, וכל שכן באיש ואשתו, אם כל אחד יקפיד על המנהג שלו דווקא – אין לך גורם פירוד יותר מזה. נמצא שכל התועלת של המנהגים מתבטלת והנזק מרובה, כי המחלוקת הורסת כל חלקה טובה. לפיכך צריך לנהוג בחכמה יְתֵרה להבטיח שלא יבואו לזלזל במנהג הקודם, ומצד שני להתאימו בצורה נוחה ומועילה לתנאים המשתנים...

אמנם **יש רבנים המקפידים יותר על שמירת המנהגים העדתיים, והם בדרך כלל עומדים על כך שמנהג הבעל יקבע בכל דבר. לפי עניות דעתי, יש מקום להקל בדבר זה**, כיון שאנו חיים בתקופה של קיבוץ גלויות ויצירת קהילות חדשות, ועדיין לא גובשו מנהגי המקום, ולפיכך ניתן לקבוע מנהגים מחדש. וכל מנהגי ישראל מכל העדות – יש להם על מה שיסמוכו.

Responsa Siach Nachum 88

...One must be very careful not to treat customs lightly, even trivial customs, as for many people they are the only connection they have to the tradition. But in a society composed of an ingathering of exiles [from different parts of the world], and all the more so between husband and wife, if each person insists specifically on his or her own custom, there is no greater cause of division than this. Thus, the entire benefit of the customs is negated, and the damage is great, as discord destroys every good thing. Therefore, one must act with great wisdom to ensure that the previous custom is not treated lightly, but on the other hand, adapt it in a comfortable and constructive manner to changing circumstances...

Nevertheless, **there are rabbis who are stricter about preserving customs of *eidot* [former communities from different parts of the world], and they generally insist that the husband's custom should determine everything. In my humble opinion, there is room to be lenient in this matter**, because we are living in a period of ingathering of exiles and the formation of new communities, and the local customs have not yet solidified. Therefore, it is possible to establish new customs. All Jewish customs from all *eidot* have legitimate sources upon which they may rely.

---

10. For further discussion of the subject of whether wives should adopt the customs of their husbands, see Responsa *Benei Banim* 3:29 (available at www.sefaria.org.il/Responsa_Benei_Banim%2C_Volume_III. 29. 8?lang=he&with=all&lang2=he); *Piskei Teshuvot* 468:11; Rav Chaim Jachter, *Gray Matter*, vol. 3, pp. 128–135 (and at www.sefaria.org.il/Gray_Matter_III%2C_Family_Matters%2C_Divergent_Family_Customs_between_Husband_and_Wife); *Kol Nidrei*, ch. 77; and *Techumin*, vol. 15, p. 301.
11. It should be noted that some *poskim*, such as Rav Shlomo Zalman Auerbach, permit a wife to continue following a former custom in cases where she wishes to continue it if her husband consents (*Yom Tov Sheini K'hilchato*, p. 188).

When Does the Custom Take Effect?

Despite the fact that avoiding *kitniyot* on Pesach is merely a custom, **Rav Shmuel Wosner** observes that the custom begins from the same time that *chametz* is prohibited on Erev Pesach.

19. שו"ת שבט הלוי | ג:לא

ומה שכתב כבודו בענין אכילת קטניות בערב פסח אם המנהג רק בפסח או גם בערב פסח, אין להאריך בזה כיון דכתב החק יעקב סימן תע"א סעיף קטן ב דגם בערב פסח אסור ומביאו גם הגאון מהרש"ם בדעת תורה סימן תנ"ג.

Responsa Shevet HaLevi 3:31

That which his honor writes regarding eating *kitniyot* on Erev Pesach, whether the custom is only on Pesach or also on Erev Pesach, there is no need to write at length about this, since the *Chok Ya'akov* writes that this is also prohibited on Erev Pesach [from the same time as *chametz* is forbidden]. The Maharsham also quotes this in *Da'at Torah*.

FURTHER IYUN

For further *iyun* on the nature of *minhag* in general and its impact on *kitniyot* in particular, see page 154.

Which Foods are Considered Kitniyot?

We saw above in source 3 that Rabbeinu Peretz lists beans, rice, and lentils as examples of *kitniyot*. He explains that *kitniyot* are similar to grain in that they are piled up,[12] and for this reason, mustard is also included. However, vegetables such as cabbage and leeks are not included, as they are nothing like grain. In this section, we will examine the criteria used by the various *poskim* to determine which other species are included and apply those principles to modern foods to determine what is considered *kitniyot*.

The ***Turei Zahav* (*Taz*)** discusses whether various types of food are considered *kitniyot* and also understands that the determining factor is the similarity to grain. He appears to conclude that foods that are either shaped like grain or grow in a similar manner to other *kitniyot*, such as mustard, are considered *kitniyot*. Other foods are not considered *kitniyot*, even if grain commonly gets mixed with them.[13]

20. טורי זהב (ט"ז) | או"ח תנג:א

ועני"ס ואליינד"ר צריך בדיקה רבה שלא יהיה בהם אחד מחמשת מינים. וקצת שקורין קימ"ל שמעתי מחלקין דאותו שקורין קרא"ם קימ"ל מביאין אותו ממדינות אחרות אסור בפסח שגרעיניו דומין לדגן אבל אותו הנקרא פעל"ד קימ"ל מותר בפסח לפי שאין צורתו כדגן.

ובסימן תס"ד כתב רמ"א שחרדל אין אוכלין בפסח ואיני יודע למה ישתנה מעניס. ונראה הטעם לפי שגידול החרדל הוא בשרביטין דומה לגידול קטניות על כן הוי בכלל איסור קטניות.

א Turei Zahav (Taz), Orach Chaim 453:1

Anise and coriander require thorough checking to ensure that none of the five species of grain are mixed in [but if not, they are not prohibited under *kitniyot*]. Regarding *ketsach*, which is called *kimmel* [caraway], I have heard that we distinguish [between types]. The type called *krom kimmel*, which is imported from other countries, is forbidden on Pesach, because its seeds resemble grain. But the type called *feld kimmel* is permitted on Pesach, because its shape is not like that of grain.[14]

In *siman* 464, the Rema writes that we do not eat mustard on Pesach, but I do not know why it should be different from anise. It seems that the reason is that mustard grows in pods, similar to the way *kitniyot* grow, and therefore it is included in the prohibition against *kitniyot*.

The ***Mishna Berura*** writes that corn is also considered *kitniyot*.

---

12. Although he also mentions that in some places, bread is made from them, this reason is clearly not the defining factor. This can be shown from the fact that bread is not made from mustard and some other types of *kitniyot*, and by contrast, bread can be made from almonds, but almonds are not classified as *kitniyot*.
13. The *Chayei Adam* suggested that potatoes should also be considered *kitniyot* since it is also used to make flour, like grain. Thus, the concern that one may confuse one type of flour for the other applies. However, the overwhelming majority of authorities did not accept this opinion, and today, it is assumed that it is entirely permitted to eat potatoes on Pesach.
14. By contrast, the *Magen Avraham* (453:3) implies that all types of caraway are not *kitniyot*, although he writes that it is proper to refrain from eating them during Pesach due to the difficulty of ensuring no grain is mixed with them.

א Mishna Berura, Orach Chaim 453:4

Or other types of *kitniyot* – *Tetraki,* which in our region is called *grika* [buckwheat], and *kakeruzi,* which in our region is called *tirkishe veyts* ["Turkish wheat," i.e., corn/maize], are also considered types of *kitniyot* (*Acharonim*).

21. משנה ברורה | או"ח תנג:ד

ושאר מיני קטניות – וטטרקי שקורין אצלנו (גריקע) וקאקערוזי שקורין אצלנו (טירקישע ווייץ) ג"כ מיני קטניות הן (אחרונים).

The reason that corn is included as *kitniyot*, even though it is a New World food that was not available in Europe at the time that the *kitniyot* custom began to take hold, is presumably since it also has similar characteristics to legumes.

The ***Avnei Nezer*** extrapolates from the comments of the *Taz* quoted above that rapeseed is also considered *kitniyot*, since it too grows in pods.

א Responsa Avnei Nezer, Orach Chaim 533

Now the *Taz* writes that the reason that it is customary to prohibit mustard, despite it not being a species of legume, is because it grows in pods, like legumes. The same applies to rapeseed, which grows in pods.

22. שו"ת אבני נזר | או"ח תקלג

הנה הט"ז (תנג:א) כתב טעם שנהגו איסור בחרדל אף שאינו מין קטניות רק משום שגדל בשרביטין כמו הקטניות. והכי נמי ברעפס שגדל בשרביטין.

It appears from this ruling of the *Avnei Nezer* that although there was no clear custom to avoid consuming rapeseed on Pesach, since it fits into the definition of *kitniyot* due to the way in which it grows, it is prohibited.[15]

However, **Rav Moshe Feinstein** takes a different approach. He writes that the prohibition applies only to foods regarding which there is a clear custom to avoid. Accordingly, he rules that peanuts are permitted during Pesach for those who have no custom to avoid them, despite their similarity to other *kitniyot.*

פ Responsa Igrot Moshe, Orach Chaim 3:63

Now regarding the matter of peanuts, about which I wrote that in many places they were eaten on Pesach, the esteemed Torah [scholar who asked the question] was astonished why this was the case. As he heard that in some places, they both make flour from them and they are sown in fields like other *kitniyot*. However, the esteemed Torah [scholar] should know that **it is not at all [correct to think that] all foods from which flour is made are prohibited based on this custom.** As there is nothing from which flour is made from more than potatoes, not only in this country but also in [Jewish] areas in Europe, and also in earlier generations, yet no one ever thought to prohibit them.[16]

23. שו"ת אגרות משה | או"ח ג:סג

הנה בדבר הפינאט שכתבתי שבהרבה מקומות אכלו אותם בפסח וכבוד תורתו הרמה תמה בטעם הדבר משום ששמע שעושין ממנו באיזה מקום גם קמח וגם שמע שנזרעין בשדות כשאר קטניות, אבל ידע כבוד תורתו הרמה **שאין זה ענין כלל, שכל הדברים העושין מהם קמח נאסרו ממנהג זה,** דאין לך דבר העושין ממנו קמח כתפוחי אדמה לא רק במדינה זו אלא גם ביוראפ במקומותינו וגם בדורות הקודמים ומעולם לא חשו לאסור זה.

15. We will see further on that rapeseed oil, known today as canola, may be permitted on Pesach for other reasons.

16. In actual fact, Rav Yaakov Emden writes in a responsum that there were those who wished to prohibit eating potatoes on Pesach, but he was successful in defeating this attempt (*She'eilat Ya'avetz* 2:147).

וכן הטעם שמיני חטים מתערבין בהם שכתב הטור נמי אינו כלל שכל המינים שיש לחוש למיני חטים ושעורים שיתערבו נהגו לאסור, דהא עניס וקימעל שמתערבין בהן מיני חטים ושעורים... ומכל מקום לא אסרום כמפורש ברמ"א, וחרדל כתב הרמ"א בסימן תס"ד שנוהגין לאסור דהוי כמיני קטניות אף שאין בו הטעמים.

Similarly, the reason that the Tur wrote, that strains of wheat might get mixed with [*kitniyot*], is also not [a basis] to be concerned that there may be a custom to prohibit all species in which wheat and barley grains could become mixed. As wheat and barley can become mixed with anise and cumin... and nevertheless, they were not prohibited, as the Rema states explicitly. [Conversely], the Rema writes in *siman* 464, that mustard is equivalent to other species of *kitniyot*, even though the reasons [to prohibit] do not apply to it.

ולכן אין לנו בדבר אלא מה שמפורש שנהגו לאסור וכן מה שידוע ומפורסם... כיון שלא תיקנו בקבוץ חכמים לאכול דברים שיש חשש שיתערב בהן מיני דגן ודברים שעושין מהם קמח, אלא שהנהיגו שלא לאכול איזה מינים לא נאסרו אלא המינים שהנהיגו ולא שאר מינים שלא הנהיגו מפני שלא היו מצויין אז...

Therefore, regarding this matter, we only [prohibit] that which is explicitly stated to have been the custom to prohibit, or that which is known and widely accepted [to be prohibited]... Since it was not instituted by a formal rabbinic gathering [against] eating items that might be mixed with species of grain and items from which flour is made; rather, they directed not to eat certain foods, only those foods regarding which the custom was established were prohibited, not other foods regarding which no directive was given, since they were uncommon at that time...[17]

ולכן גם הפינאטס לא אסרו בהרבה מקומות עוד מכל שכן. ובמקום שליכא מנהג אין לאסור כי בדברים כאלו אין להחמיר כדאיתא בחק יעקב. ולאלו שיש להם מנהג ביחוד שלא לאכול פינאט אסור גם בפינאט אבל מספק אין לאסור. ולכן שייך שיתן הכשר שלא נתערב שם חמץ ויאכלו אלו שלא נהגו בזה איסור. וכן ראיתי שנותנים הכשר על פינאט אולי מהאי טעמא.

Therefore, they also certainly did not prohibit peanuts in many places. In a place where there is no established custom, one should not prohibit them, as in such matters one should not add stringencies, as the *Chok Yaakov* states. For those who have a specific custom not to eat peanuts, peanuts are also prohibited, but one should not prohibit them out of doubt. Therefore, it is appropriate to certify that no *chametz* is mixed with them, and those who have no custom to prohibit them may eat them. Indeed, I have seen that kashrut certification is given on peanuts, perhaps for this reason.

Rav Tzvi Pesach Frank also writes that peanuts should not be included within *kitniyot*, but he uses different reasoning. He concludes that in any case, the custom is not to eat peanuts on Pesach.

24. מקראי קודש | ב:ס

Mikraei Kodesh 2:60

...ולענין אם אוכלים אותם בפסח, אף שש לעיין אם הם נכללו בגזירת קטניות דבאסור קטניות בפסח יש שני טעמים:

...With regard to whether one may eat them on Pesach: although it is necessary to examine whether they are included in the decree of *kitniyot* – for the prohibition of *kitniyot* on Pesach has two reasons:

17. Rav Moshe Feinstein does not explain why he would agree that corn is to be considered *kitniyot* despite not having been extant in Europe in the time when the custom began to take hold. Perhaps he would say that when corn did arrive in Europe, Jews generally refrained from using it on Pesach, and once they treated it as *kitniyot*, it became forbidden to use as part of the custom. Alternatively, perhaps even Rav Moshe agrees that species that are clearly included in the criteria for *kitniyot* would be included, but peanuts, which do not behave fully like legumes, are not if the practice to avoid them is not fully widespread.

1. **Concern for confusion** (*chiluf*), lest one come to confuse them with the five species of grain, since *kitniyot* are prepared as cooked dishes (*ma'aseh kedeirah*), and grain is likewise prepared as cooked dishes; moreover, they are things that grow from the ground like the five species, and in some places it is customary to make bread from them, as from the five species…

2. **Concern for admixture**, because it is difficult to separate them from grain that becomes mixed with them…

Now, according to the first reason, namely concern for confusion, one could argue that pistachios should not be included in the prohibition of *kitniyot*, for although they grow from the ground in pods like *kitniyot*, nevertheless they are not piled: their produce is not gathered on a threshing floor like grain, but rather left in their pods, and they are neither prepared as cooked dishes nor baked into bread…

Likewise, the second reason, concern for admixture, does not apply when one eats them whole, one by one… **Nevertheless, we do not have the practice of eating them on Pesach."**

א' **משום חילוף**, דאתי לאחלופי בחמשת מיני דגן מכיון דקטניות מעשה קדרה הוא ודגן נמי מעשה קדרה הוא וגם מידי דמידגן הוא כמו חמשת המינים וגם יש מקומות שרגילין לעשות מהם פת כמו מחמשת המינים...

ב' **משום תערובת** שקשה לבררן מהתבואה המעורבת בהן...

והנה לפי הטעם משום חילוף יש לדון דפיסטוקעס לא יהיו בכלל איסור קטניות דאמנם הם גדלים באדמה בשרביטים כקטניות מ"מ אינו מידגן דאין אוספים הפירות בגורן כדגן אלא מניחים אותם בשרביטין שלהן וכן אין עושין ממנו מעשה קדרה ולא אופין ממנו פת...

גם הטעם משום תערובת לא שייך כשהוא אוכלם שלמים אחד אחד... **עם כל זה אין אנו נוהגין לאוכלם בפסח.**

Today, in the overwhelming majority of Ashkenazic communities, the custom has spread not to eat peanuts on Pesach. Thus, Rav Feinstein would likely rule today that most Ashkenazim should treat peanuts as *kitniyot*. However, **Rav Dov Lior** applies the same logic to permit consuming soy and quinoa products on Pesach. As these foods were not known at the time the custom to avoid *kitniyot* developed, they were not included in the custom and should be permitted as long as no specific custom to refrain from eating them exists.[18] Nevertheless, similar to Rav Frank's ruling about peanuts, the widespread custom today in the Diaspora, and a large number of Ashkenazi communities in Israel, is to treat soy and soybeans as *kitniyot*, and this is the approach of major U.S. Kashrut organizations.[19]

Quinoa is another New World food that became popular even more recently than the other foods mentioned so far. Is quinoa considered *kitniyot*? Some, such as **Rav Asher Weiss, Rav Yosef Shalom Eliashiv,** and **Rav Yisroel Belsky,**[20] suggest that quinoa should be considered *kitniyot* since it does have certain characteristics of rice and other legumes: Its appearance is similar to grain, it is sometimes used like grain, and it grows in fields near grain.[21] Many of the Mehadrin Kashrut organizations in Israel also treat quinoa as *kitniyot*.

---

18. See www.yeshiva.org.il/midrash/7392. He also permits eating peas or green beans when they are in their pods, as they are then considered vegetables and not *kitniyot*. Others rule stringently regarding all of these products. See, for example, *Peninei Halakha, Pesach* 9:4.

19. See https://oukosher.org/passover/guidelines/food-items/kitniyot-list, www.ok.org/consumers/passover/pesach-oils, and www.star-k.org/articles/wp-content/uploads/2016/08/KCSmall_Kitniyos.pdf.

20. See www.yutorah.org/lectures/791649.

21. See *Kovetz Eitz Chaim* (Bobov), 27 and https://minchasasher.com/shiur/vayikra-vayikra-shiurim/kitniyot-pesach-5778.

However, others, such as **Rav Dovid Feinstein,**[22] **Rav Yaakov Ariel,**[23] and **Rav Hershel Schachter,**[24] have argued that based on Rav Moshe's logic, quinoa should not be included in *kitniyot* since it was not available in Europe at the time. This was also the position adopted by the **Star-K.**[25]

Although the OU originally did not issue a decision concerning the issue, after extensive research, in 2013, the OU approved quinoa for use on Pesach even for Ashkenazim, with proper supervision that it is *chametz*-free.

ט 25. OU Kosher, "Quinoa"[26]

Due to conflicting reports regarding growing conditions and final usage of this new world, gluten-free pseudo-cereal plant, OU Kosher was hesitant to conclusively declare it Kosher for Passover and *non-kitniyot*...

Following extensive research and on-site investigation of cross-contamination issues by OU Kosher personnel at all quinoa growing areas... as well as the collection, washing and milling stations of quinoa, OU Kosher is pleased to announce that, for the first time, it is recommending quinoa for Passover, when processed with special OU Passover supervision and bearing the OU-P symbol.[27,28]

Kitniyot That Are Kept Dry

We learned above in source 1 that only foods from the five species of grain can become *chametz*, and only when they come in contact with water. If one ensures that the five grains do not come into contact with water, or if they are baked before they become *chametz* (i.e., matza), even the five species of grain are permitted to eat.[29] Many *poskim* rule that similarly, one may eat *kitniyot* on Pesach if one ensures that they do not come into contact with water. Thus, the ***Chayei Adam*** writes that one may bake *kitniyot* into a matza-like food and eat it on Pesach.

26. חיי אדם | קכז:א

מותר לטחון ולאפותה כעין מצות ולאכלה.

א Chayei Adam 127:1

It is permitted to grind and bake [*kitniyot*] into a matza-like food and to eat it.[30]

---

22. See *Kovetz Eitz Chaim* (Bobov), 27.
23. See *Oholei Halacha, Pesach*, p. 88.
24. See www.yutorah.org/lectures/791649.
25. See www.star-k.org/articles/articles/seasonal/13692/quinoa.
26. See the full article at https://oukosher.org/passover/guidelines/food-items/quinoa.
27. See also https://oukosher.org/passover/articles/quinoa-passover, where some of the reasons for the decision are given, such as that quinoa was traditionally not used in the same manner as other grains, plus that it is grown and stored separately from other grains.
28. For further discussion in English on the subject of quinoa, see https://ohr.edu/holidays/pesach/laws_and_customs/5390, www.torahmusings.com/2014/04/the-use-of-quinoa-on-pesach, and www.koltorah.org/halachah/the-great-ou-quinoa-policy-by-rabbi-chaim-jachter.
29. The halachot of guarding grain to prevent it from becoming *chametz* are complex and beyond the scope of this *shiur*.
30. Interestingly, a certain company in Israel that manufactures rice cakes uses a process in which no water ever comes in contact with the rice kernels. Although the kashrut certification on the product states that is kosher for Pesach only for those who consume *kitniyot* [*l'ochlei kitniyot bilvad*], some *poskim*, such as Rav Elyakim Levanon (rabbi of the Shomron regional

However, the ***Sho'el U'meishiv*** argues that the custom is to avoid eating even baked *kitniyot*. Furthermore, baked *kitniyot* are even more likely to be confused with *chametz*, and they could also be confused with matza and lead people to think that one could use them to fulfill the mitzva of eating matza on the first night of Pesach.

27. שו"ת שואל ומשיב | מהדורא קמא, א:קעה

והנה גאון אחד כתב בספרו להתיר לאפות מיני קטניות דהיינו רעצקי וקאקריזע אבל אינו כדאי והגון לזה שיתיר דבר שאבותינו ואבות אבותינו נהגו איסור ואדרבא במה שאופים יותר יש לחוש לאחלופי וגם שמא יצא בו ידי חובת מצה.

א Responsa Sho'el U'meishiv, Mahadura Kamma 1:175

Now one Gaon in his *sefer* permitted baking types of *kitniyot*, namely lentils and buckwheat. But it is inappropriate and unbecoming of him to permit something that our fathers and grandfathers had a custom to prohibit, and on the contrary, regarding that which is baked, there is a greater concern of confusion [with *chametz*]. One might also [attempt to] use it to fulfill the obligation to eat matza.

Kitniyot Oil

Unlike *chametz*, it is permitted to derive benefit from *kitniyot*, as the custom is only to avoid eating them. Accordingly, the **Rema** writes that one may use *kitniyot* oil as fuel.

28. רמ"א | או"ח תנג:א

...מותר להדליק בשמנים הנעשים מהם...

א Rema, Orach Chaim 453:1

...Lighting a fire using oils made from [*kitniyot*] is permitted...

The clear implication is that the custom to avoid eating *kitniyot* also includes avoiding consumption of oil made from *kitniyot*.[31] Accordingly, sesame oil was traditionally not used during Pesach by Ashkenazim.[32] However, based on the reasoning of *Acharonim* such as the *Chayei Adam* quoted in source 26, **Rav Avraham Yitzchak HaKohen Kook** approves the use of sesame oil during Pesach if produced without

council), have ruled that even Ashkenazim may eat these rice cakes on Pesach based on this ruling of the *Chayei Adam*; see www.kosharot.co.il/index2.php?id=413768&lang=HEB and https://rabbimanning.com/wp-content/uploads/2019/04/Mixed-Marriages-and-Kitniyot-Conundrums.pdf. Those, of course, who follow the *Sho'el Umeshiv* and the stricter ruling about sesame oil (discussed below), would forbid this product for Ashkenazim. In addition, Rav Yonatan Don Yechiya notes that Rav Kook permitted only sesame oil, but not sesame itself, and consequently, he permits such products only in cases of significant need. See https://asif.co.il/wpfb-file/מנהג-הקטניות-בימינו, also published in his work "*L'yamim Tovim*" (published by Tzomet Sefarim).

31. However, Rav Yitzchak Elchanan Spektor argues that if one checked the *kitniyot* to ensure that no wheat was mixed in and then produced whisky or oil from these *kitniyot*, such that any *chametz* would be nullified before Pesach, one may consume these products on Pesach (Responsa *Be'er Yitzchak* 11. See also *Marcheshet* 1:3, who permits such oil and even considers permitting all *kitniyot* oil, before ultimately lacking the conviction to do so). However, this leniency is not accepted by most *poskim*.

32. Sesame itself is assumed to be included in the custom to not eat *kitniyot*, perhaps based on its classification as *kitniyot* by the Rambam (*Hilchot Kilayim* 1:8).

any contact with water. He explains further that the oil is permitted even if it subsequently comes into contact with water, since the custom to be stringent regarding *kitniyot* does not apply to this situation.[33]

29. שו"ת אורח משפט | או"ח קיא

ואין כאן שום מנהג כלל, כי דרך העשייה של שמן שומשמין היה כך עד כה: שהיו הנכרים לותתין אותם במי מלח ואחר כך היו סוחטים מהם את שמנם, **אבל אותו השמן שנסחט על ידי המכונה החדשה בלא שום לחלוחית של מים, כי אם משומשמין יבשים, איזה סרך מנהג יש בזה**, מאחר שהוא דבר שלא היה מעולם.

וכן בתרומת הדשן כפל ושלש כמה פעמים, שהוא מדבר רק במיני קטניות לתותין... ובספר חיי אדם... דקדק גם כן כפי לשון הראשונים וכפל כמה פעמים, שכל האיסור הוא רק לבשל מיני קטניות או לשרות במים, אבל לטחון אותם ולאפות מהם מצה מותר.... והוא הדין ודאי שבכי האי גוונא מותר היוצא מהם, שלא יחמירו ביוצא מהם יותר מהם עצמם...

וזה פשוט הוא, שאפילו אם יתערב אחר כך זה השמן בתבשיל אין שום חשש איסור, שלא אסרו אלא את היוצא מן הקטניות שכבר נלתת, ונאסר כיוצא בו אם היה מין דגן. רק לרווחא דמילתא, אין בענין זה שום חשש אפילו כל דהו, מפני שדרך הוא לטגן את השמן שומשמין לפני תשמישו, וכשמטגנים אותו אין בו עדיין שום תערובות מים ואחר כך נעשה מבושל שאינו מחמיץ.

Responsa Orach Mishpat, Orach Chaim 111

There is no custom [to prohibit such oil] at all, as until now the method of producing sesame oil was that the non-Jews would moisten the [sesame seeds] with salt water, and afterwards they would press the oil from them. But **what trace of a custom could there be [to prohibit] the oil that is extracted by the new machine, without any moisture from water, only from dry sesame seeds**, since this never existed before?

Moreover, the *Terumat HaDeshen* repeated several times that he was speaking only about types of *kitniyot* that are moistened... The *sefer Chayei Adam*... also inferred this from the wording of the *Rishonim* and repeated several times that the prohibition applies only to cooking *kitniyot* or soaking them in water, but grinding them and baking matza from them is permitted... Certainly, the same applies in our case, that what is extracted from [*kitniyot*] should not be treated more strictly than [*kitniyot*] themselves...

It is obvious that even if this oil is later mixed into a cooked dish, there is no concern of this being prohibited. As they prohibited only that which is produced from *kitniyot* that had already been moistened, and would have been prohibited if it were a species of grain. Only [to put the minds of those who are still concerned] at rest, [one can add that] in this case there is not even the slightest cause for concern, as the common practice is to fry sesame oil before using it, and when it is fried it no longer contains any trace of water mixture. Subsequently, it becomes cooked, such that it cannot ferment.

This leniency was the subject of fierce debate at the time the responsum was written (1909), but today it is less relevant, as no precautions are taken to prevent commonly used oils from coming into contact with water. However, **Rav Eliezer Melamed** writes that soybean oil may be used on Pesach even today,

33. In contrast, the *Avnei Nezer*, in the continuation of the responsum quoted in source 22, permits using rapeseed oil only if one first cooks it without water, preferably before Pesach. In a responsum (373) written four years later, he retracts this leniency entirely and writes in accordance with the *Sho'el U'meishiv*, that *kitniyot* oil is prohibited for consumption even if it never comes into contact with water.

since it is produced without water. He adds, like Rav Lior cited above, that other soy products may also be permitted, since soy was not available at the time the custom to avoid *kitniyot* developed.

Peninei Halakha, Pesach 6:9, n. 6

Soybean oil is produced without moistening the soybeans, so according to Rav Kook and most *poskim* it is not forbidden... Furthermore, it is questionable whether soybeans were even included in the prohibition of *kitniyot*, since they did not arrive in Europe until about 100 years ago...

30. פניני הלכה | פסח ו:ט, הערה ו

שמן סויה מופק בלא שמרטיבים את הסויה, נמצא שלדעת רוב הפוסקים ומרן הרב קוק, אין בו איסור... ועוד, שספק אם הוא בכלל האיסור, שרק לפני כמאה שנה הגיעה הסויה לאירופה...

Nevertheless, the prevalent custom in the Diaspora and among the Mehadrin Kashrut certifications in Israel is generally not to certify soybean oil for Pesach for those who do not consume *kitniyot*.

A similar contemporary question can be raised concerning canola oil. In addition, many manufactured products in Israel are labelled "*l'ochlei liftit*" ("for those who eat rapeseed"), as they contain either canola oil or its derivative, lecithin. May those who avoid *kitniyot* on Pesach consume such products?

Canola oil is produced from rapeseed, which, as we saw in source 22, the *Avnei Nezer* writes is considered *kitniyot*. However, many of the leniencies explained above apply to canola oil as well, as it is a product which did not exist at the time the custom to avoid *kitniyot* developed.[34] In addition, another potential reason to be lenient is raised by the questioner in the following responsum written by the **Maharsham**. Since only the oil is edible, not the rapeseed itself, it is possible that the custom to avoid eating *kitniyot* does not apply to this oil.

Responsa of the Maharsham 1:183

...As only substances that are used as dips for food or for cooking are included in the decree against *kitniyot*, since they could be mixed [with grain]. But rapeseed is not [itself] used for any food or dip, only for its oil, [so] according to all views it is not included in the decree, and is permitted for consumption...[35]

31. שו"ת מהרש"ם | א:קפג

...דדוקא בדבר שעושין ממנו טיבול לאכילה או מעשה קדרה הוא בכלל גזירת קטניות דאתי לאחלופי, אבל מין הראפס אינו עומד לשום מאכל ולא לשום טיבול רק לצורך השמן לכולי עלמא אינו בכלל הגזירה ומותר באכילה...

In practice, in Eretz Yisrael, customs differ, and even many Ashkenazim in Eretz Yisrael do use canola oil on Pesach, as summarized in an article by the **Kosharot** organization.

---

34. See also www.kosharot.co.il/index2.php?id=411911 for a discussion of water contact in the production of canola oil.

35. The questioner himself appears to acknowledge that this reason alone is not sufficient to permit canola oil, as the Rema implies that sesame oil and hemp oil are only permitted for use as fuel and not for food, despite sesame and hemp not themselves being used as food (presumably this was the case at the time). However, this factor is nevertheless to be taken into account as another reason for leniency.

Rav Tzvi ben Reuven, "For Those Who Consume Rapeseed – Practical Halacha: What is the Status of Canola?"[36]

A. **According to the Ashkenazic custom** of refraining from *kitniyot*, we find several approaches regarding canola oil. Some permit canola oil entirely, on the grounds that it was never included in the decree of *kitniyot*, leaving only the issue of crop rotation to be addressed. Others permit it only when it appears in a mixture. Still others define canola as full-fledged *kitniyot*. Each person should follow the ruling of their rabbinic authority.

B. **According to the Sephardic custom,** which does not accept the prohibition of *kitniyot*, attention must nevertheless be paid to the issue of crop rotation (as noted above even by those who permit canola oil). One should therefore purchase products bearing kosher supervision that addresses this concern through one of the methods described above.

There are several approaches used by different kosher certification agencies to deal with the issue of crop rotation in the production of canola oil…[37]

Based on information I received from Rabbi Chagai Bar Giora of the Chief Rabbinate of Israel, the Rabbinate's policy is to state that canola oil or related products contain rapeseed or lecithin, rather than to label them as "for those who eat *kitniyot*." This is done in order to avoid entering into the halachic dispute and to leave the decision to the consumer, since some authorities maintain that the decree of *kitniyot* never applied to rapeseed at all, as it is not consumed on its own, as noted above.

32. הרב צבי בן ראובן | לאוכלי לפתית' – הלכה למעשה | מה דין הקנולה?

א. **לשיטת האשכנזים** הנוהגים באיסור קטניות, אנחנו רואים שיש שהתירו לגמרי את שמן הקנולה משום שלא נכלל בגזרת הקטניות, ונותר לטפל רק בנקודה של מחזור הזרעים; יש שמתירים אותו רק בתערובת; ויש שהגדירו אותו כקטנית לכל דבר, וכל אחד ינהג כרבותיו.

ב. **לשיטת הספרדים** שלא נוהגים את איסור הקטניות, צריכים בכל זאת לשים לב לבעיית מחזור הזרעים (כנ"ל במתירים את שמן הקנולה) ולקנות מכשרויות שפותרות בעיה זו באחת מהדרכים דלעיל.

ישנן כמה שיטות לטיפול בנושא מחזור הזרעים בכשרויות השונות של שמן הקנולה...

ממידע שקיבלתי מהרב חגי בר גיורא מהרבנות הראשית לישראל, נוהלי הרבנות הם לכתוב ששמן הקנולה או מוצרים כאלה ואחרים מכילים לפתית או לציטין, ולא לכתוב 'לאוכלי קטניות', כדי לא להיכנס למחלוקות בעניין ולהשאיר את ההחלטה לצרכן, שהרי יש סוברים שהגזרה כלל לא חלה על הלפתית, שאינה נאכלת בפני עצמה, כמו שנכתב לעיל.

However, in America, the OU and other Ashkenazi Kashrut organizations do not permit canola oil for Pesach, and the Mehadrin Ashkenazi Kashrut certifications in Israel generally are strict as well.[38] This approach is summarized by the **Chicago Rabbinical Council (CRC)** in the following excerpt:

---

36. The complete article is available at www.kosharot.co.il/index2.php?id=411911&lang=HEB.

37. In the continuation of the article, the author adds that some *kashrut* authorities are concerned that due to crop rotation, rapeseed may be intermingled with wheat or other grains. Those who are lenient rely either on mechanical separation of the rapeseed, or on the assumption that any remaining grain does not meaningfully contribute to the oil and is nullified during the high-heat processing stages prior to Pesach.

38. See https://outorah.org/p/45005. However, the OU does permit the use of cottonseed oil (see https://oukosher.org/passover/articles/kitniyot-custom and https://bit.ly/tz24s3f38). A possible source for this distinction may be a responsum of the *Divrei Yatziv* (O.C. 196), who does not consider cottonseed to be a species of *kitniyot* at all. Some have also claimed that

33. Chicago Rabbinical Council, "Canola and Safflower Oils"

Q. Why is it that Canola oil is kitnios, but safflower oil is not?

A. Many food items potentially qualify as kitnios, but we accept the rulings of Chok Yaakov 453:9 and Iggeros Moshe (OC 3:63) that only those items used for food and considered kitnios in previous generations (when the minhag was established) are forbidden, but others are not. We do not have record of safflower oil being used for food purposes at the time of the minhag starting or subsequent generations, and therefore assume it is permitted...

On the other hand, canola oil has quite a history of being used and treated as kitnios, as follows: Rapeseed oil was (and is still) used in Europe for hundreds of years, was likely even used when the minhag was first beginning, and in a well-known teshuvah of the Maharsham 1:183 regarding oil of kitnios he assumes that raps, the German word for rapeseed, is kitnios. Thus, we see that rapeseed was treated as kitnios even in earlier times...

In the 1970s, Canadian researchers bred a form of rapeseed that had low levels of erucic acid, and that oil was approved for use in the United States in the 1980s... they named the new breed "canola"... "CANadian OiL"... Thus, canola oil is really a form of rapeseed oil... and since rapeseed is kitnios, the canola version is also forbidden on Pesach.

In the UK and Western Europe, sunflower oil is more commonly used for cooking. In halachic terms, sunflower oil is similar to canola oil and raises many of the same questions. Most communities in these countries do permit its use on Pesach,[39] although most authorities in Israel and the US consider sunflower seeds and sunflower oil to be *kitniyot*.[40,41]

THE *KITNIYOT* STATUS OF DIFFERENT FOODS

Certain *Kitniyot*	*Kitniyot* According to Some *Poskim*	Not *Kitniyot*
Beans, rice, lentils, mustard	**Rapeseed (and canola oil), peanuts, soy, quinoa, sunflower seeds and oil, caraway that resembles grain**	**Potatoes, cabbage, leeks, caraway that does not resemble grain**

rapeseed oil has in fact been used for food for centuries, and may have been used even when the custom to avoid *kitniyot* developed.

39. See, for example, https://kosher.org.uk/assets/uploads/2025/07/sunflower_oil_article.pdf.pdf.

40. See, for example, *Peninei Halakha, Pesach* 9:4, who writes that sunflower seeds are *kitniyot*, although in 9:6 he writes that canola oil is permitted. The reason for this distinction is presumably the fact that sunflower seeds are themselves edible, unlike rapeseed.

41. For a list of what is considered *kitniyot* by the OU, see https://oukosher.org/passover/guidelines/food-items/kitniyot-list. For a more comprehensive list of opinions concerning products that may be considered *kitniyot*, see www.kosharot.co.il/index2.php?id=411940&lang=HEB#_ftn55.

Mixtures Containing Kitniyot

Although the prevalent custom in Ashkenazic communities today is to avoid eating *kitniyot*, the **Rema** writes that if *kitniyot* fell into a dish, the dish certainly does not become prohibited. In addition, one may keep *kitniyot* at home and use them as fuel.

א Rema, Orach Chaim 453:1

The custom in Ashkenaz is to be stringent [regarding *kitniyot*], and one should not deviate from this. However, it is obvious that *bedi'eved*, if [*kitniyot*] fell into a dish, they do not make the dish prohibited. Likewise, lighting a fire using oils made from [*kitniyot*] is permitted.[42] Similarly, keeping types of *kitniyot* in the house is permitted.

34. רמ"א | או"ח תנג:א

והמנהג באשכנז להחמיר, ואין לשנות. מיהו פשוט דאין אוסרים בדיעבד אם נפלו תוך התבשיל. וכן מותר להדליק בשמנים הנעשים מהם, ואינן אוסרים אם נפלו לתוך התבשיל. וכן מותר להשהות מיני קטניות בבית.

The ***Mishna Berura*** explains that the custom to avoid *kitniyot* is limited to the *kitniyot* themselves and not to other foods that get mixed with *kitniyot*. However, one must remove any recognizable pieces of *kitniyot* before eating. If the majority of the mixture is *kitniyot*, one also may not eat it.

א Mishna Berura, Orach Chaim 453:8–9

8. **If [*kitniyot*] fell, etc.** – As there is no custom to be stringent in this regard. Nevertheless, one must throw out those grains [of *kitniyot*] that one finds, unless they are not recognizable.

9. **Into a dish** – This refers to a situation where there is at least a majority of permitted food, as otherwise this is not considered a mixture at all, and this would be equivalent to eating a dish from *kitniyot* themselves.

35. משנה ברורה | או"ח תנג:ח–ט

ח. **אם נפלו וכו'** – דבהא לא נהגו להחמיר ומכל מקום אותן גרגרין שמוצאין צריך לזורקן אם לא שאינו ניכר.

ט. **תוך התבשיל** – ומיירי שיש על כל פנים רוב בהיתר דאם לא כן לא מיקרי תערובות כלל והוי כאוכל תבשיל מקטניות עצמה.

The ***Pri Chadash*** implies that one may even intentionally mix *kitniyot* with other food in order to eat them, as is the case with *challa* in *chutz la'aretz*.[43]

א Pri Chadash, Orach Chaim 453:1

...[*Kitniyot*] are no more severe than *challa* in *chutz la'aretz*, which one may nullify [by mixing] into a majority [of other food] and eat

36. פרי חדש | או"ח תנג:א

...דלא עדיף מחלת חוץ לארץ (יורה דעה שכג:א) שמבטלה ברוב ואוכלה.

---

42. This line was already quoted above in source 28.

43. The mitzva to separate *challa* applies in the Diaspora on a rabbinic level, as opposed to in Eretz Yisrael, where, in principle, the mitzva is biblical (though today, it may be rabbinic). As a result, one may be more lenient with *challa* separated in the Diaspora and intentionally mix it with other dough to nullify it. See also volume 6, *shiur* 5.

This leniency of the *Pri Chadash* is not generally accepted by most *poskim*. However, *poskim* discuss whether the halacha differs concerning the purchase of food products in the store that contain small amounts of *kitniyot* and are labeled as kosher for Pesach only for those who consume *kitniyot* (an especially common scenario in Eretz Yisrael). The ***Peninei Halakha*** writes that even one who does not eat *kitniyot* may eat confectionery that contains *kitniyot*, even if the confectionery is labelled "for those who eat *kitniyot* only." As since the *kitniyot* was mixed with the other ingredients before Pesach, they are nullified by the other ingredients.

37. פניני הלכה | פסח ט:ו

שוקולדים וממתקים שיש בהם מיני קטניות שבטלים ברוב, אף שכתוב עליהם כשר לפסח לאוכלי קטניות בלבד, מצד הדין גם מי שנמנע ממאכלי קטניות רשאי לאוכלם, מפני שנתערבו לפני הפסח, ובטלו ברוב. בנוסף לכך, מדובר בדרך כלל בשמנים המופקים מקטניות, ודעת כמה מגדולי הפוסקים שמנהג איסור קטניות לא חל על שמני קטניות. אמנם כיוון שיש מחמירים בזה, גופי הכשרות כותבים עליהם שהם כשרים לאוכלי קטניות בלבד.

Peninei Halakha, Pesach 9:6

Chocolate and candy that contain *kitniyot* that are *batel be-rov*, even if they are labeled "Kosher for Pesah only for those who eat *kitniyot*," may technically be eaten even by those who do not eat *kitniyot*, because the *kitniyot* in these products are added before Pesah and are *batel be-rov*. In addition, these products generally contain *kitniyot* oils, which, according to several leading *poskim*, are not included in the custom to prohibit *kitniyot*. In practice, however, since many people are stringent in this respect, kosher certification agencies label them as kosher for Pesah only for those who eat *kitniyot*.

The ***Oholei Halacha*** cites differing opinions concerning this question. It cites **Rav Yaakov Ariel** as stating, similar to the *Peninei Halakha*, that one may follow the more lenient opinion. Nevertheless, Rav Ariel adds that "*Yisrael kedoshim hem*" ("the Jewish People are holy") and many follow the stringent opinion in practice.

38. אהלי הלכה | פסח, עמ' 92

מוצרי מזון תעשייתיים שעירבו בהם מעט קטניות, כגון שעירבו בהם שמן קטניות, יש סוברים שאסור ליוצאי אשכנז לאוכלם בפסח. ואף שתערובת קטניות שאין הקטניות ניכרות בה מותרת באכילה, תערובת זו אסורה, כיוון שכלל בידינו, שאסור לבטל איסור לכתחילה, כלומר אסור לערב בכוונה דבר איסור כדי שהוא יתבטל. לכן אסור לבעלי המפעל לערב קטניות במוצר שמיועד ליוצאי אשכנז, על דעת שהן תתבטלנה.

ויש חולקים וסוברים שמוצרים אלו מותרים באכילה ליוצאי אשכנז, ואין בעֵרוּב הקטניות מפעל בעיה של ביטול איסור לכתחילה,

Oholei Halacha, Pesach, p. 92

Industrial food products into which a small amount of *kitniyot* has been mixed, such as products containing *kitniyot* oil, are, according to some authorities, prohibited for Ashkenazim to consume on Pesach. Although a mixture in which the *kitniyot* are not discernible is generally permitted, this case is forbidden because of the principle that one may not intentionally nullify a prohibition (*ein mevatlin issur le-chatchila*), meaning that it is prohibited to deliberately mix a forbidden substance with the intent that it be nullified. Therefore, it is prohibited for a manufacturer to add *kitniyot* to a product intended for Ashkenazic consumers on the assumption that the *kitniyot* will be nullified.

Others disagree and maintain that such products are permitted for Ashkenazim to consume, and that the industrial admixture of *kitniyot* does not constitute prohibited intentional nullification.

כיון שיש סוברים שאיסור שיסודו במנהג מותר לבטל לכתחילה, ואף שיש חולקים על כך, אפשר לומר שהתערובת נעשתה עבור יוצאי ספרד, שרשאים לאכול קטניות בפסח, ואף שעיקר ההלכה כדעה זו, ישראל קדושים ונוהגים להימנע מאכילת מוצרי מזון תעשייתיים שעירבו בהם מעט קטניות.

This is based on the view that a prohibition rooted in custom may be intentionally nullified, and although there are authorities who dispute this, it can also be argued that the mixture was produced for Sephardic consumers, who are permitted to eat *kitniyot* on Pesach. Nevertheless, even though the primary halachic ruling follows this lenient position, the Jewish People are meticulous in practice and customarily refrain from consuming industrial food products into which small amounts of *kitniyot* have been mixed.[44]

A similar issue arises for Ashkenazim eating in the home of Sephardim on Pesach. Even if they do not consume foods consisting of *kitniyot* directly,[45] may they eat foods that were cooked with dishes that had been used previously for *kitniyot*? **Rav Ovadia Yosef** rules based on some of the sources we have seen that Ashkenazim who do not eat *kitniyot* on Pesach may eat non-*kitniyot* food in a Sephardi home, even if the utensils were used for *kitniyot* within the past 24 hours. As non-*kitniyot* food cooked using utensils previously used for *kitniyot* is no worse than a mixture of *kitniyot* and a majority of non-*kitniyot*, it should be permitted.

39. שו"ת יחוה דעת | ה:לב

הדבר ברור שאין פליטת הכלים שבישלו בהם אורז וקטניות אוסרת התבשיל לבני אשכנז שנוהגים להחמיר באורז וקטניות, ואפילו אם הכלים בני יומן יש להתיר, שבודאי יש רוב היתר כנגד פליטת הכלים.

Responsa Yechaveh Da'at 5:32

It is clear that that which is extracted from utensils in which rice or [other] *kitniyot* were cooked does not cause the dish to become prohibited for Ashkenazim who are accustomed to be stringent regarding rice and [other] *kitniyot*. Even if the utensils were used the same day [for *kitniyot*], one can permit this, as there is certainly a majority of permitted food relative to that which is extracted from the utensils.[46]

The ***Kaf HaChaim*** writes that those who do not eat *kitniyot* may only use utensils in which *kitniyot* were cooked more than twenty-four hours previously.[47] However, he adds that one who eats in a home where

---

44. This issue is relevant for many products sold in Eretz Yisrael today that contain a minority of *kitniyot*. Nevertheless, one who follows the lenient position must be knowledgeable enough and careful to avoid products that contain a majority of *kitniyot*, such as mayonnaise, mustard, or corn cereal.

45. In this case, it is more accepted that a Sephardi host may not prepare food that contains a minority of *kitniyot* for Ashkenazi guests due to the principle of *bitul issur lechatchila* – it is generally forbidden to nullify a prohibited item by adding in permitted items to a mixture, such as by causing a food product with a non-kosher ingredient to become *batel b'shishim* (nullified in a ratio of 1:60) by adding in more kosher ingredients (see *Shulchan Aruch*, Y.D. 99:6). The same is true here when preparing food containing small amounts of *kitniyot* (or a larger quantity than one would eat oneself) specifically for an Ashkenazi.

46. In the continuation, he cites a ruling of the Rema (Y.D. 64:9) regarding a type of fat which most *Rishonim* rule is *cheilev* and is biblically prohibited, yet the custom in the Rhineland was to eat this *cheilev* based on the ruling of the Ra'avia. The Rema rules that although one should not eat this fat, one need not avoid using the utensils of the inhabitants of the Rhineland, since they have a right to follow their own custom. Based on this ruling of the Rema, one may eat in the home of a person who follows a lenient view even when there is a possibility of a biblical prohibition, provided one does not eat the questionable food itself.

47. It seems from the continuation of the *Kaf HaChaim* that the reason for this approach stems from the principle of *bitul issur lechatchila* discussed above (n. 46). According to the *Kaf HaChaim* and those who follow this approach, the same was

kitniyot are eaten need not ask whether the utensils were used for *kitniyot* in the past twenty-four hours, and may assume that they were not.

א Kaf HaChaim, Orach Chaim 453:27

...Regarding utensils in which types of *kitniyot* were cooked, for those who have the custom to prohibit types of *kitniyot*, these utensils are permitted after twenty-four hours... Even one from a city where the custom is to prohibit *kitniyot* who is a guest in a city where the custom is to permit them may eat from their utensils and need not ask if they cooked *kitniyot* in the same pot that day...

40. כף החיים | או"ח תנג:כז

...ולענין כלים שנתבשלו בהם מיני קטניות לנוהגין איסור במיני קטניות, אחר מעת לעת מותרים... דאפילו אחד מעיר שנוהגין איסור בקטניות, מתארח בעיר אחרת שנוהגים בהם היתר, יכול לאכול בכליהם, ואין צריך לשאול אם בישלו באותה קדרה קטניות באותו יום...

However, **Rav Nissim Karelitz** writes that those who do not eat *kitniyot* but prepare food for those who do, such as young children or those who must eat *kitniyot* for medical reasons, have the custom to use separate utensils to prepare this food.

Chut Shani, Pesach 12:13

...The custom is to set aside special utensils for those who are permitted to eat *kitniyot* on Pesach.[48]

41. חוט שני | פסח יב:יג

...והמנהג לייחד כלים מיוחדים לאלו שמותר להם לאכול קטניות בפסח.

The Custom to Avoid *Sheruya* ("*Gebrochts*")

We will conclude the *shiur* by briefly mentioning that there is another less widespread custom on Pesach of those who refrain from eating "*sheruya*," also known as "*gebrochts*." This refers to eating any type of cooked matza or cooked matza meal, due to concern that even after having been baked, the matza can still rise when being cooked.

The ***Mishna Berura*** mentions this custom, though he notes that such a practice is not necessary to observe according to the letter of the law.

א Mishna Berura, Orach Chaim 458:4

...Note that by the letter of the law, it is permitted to bake matza on Pesach. But the meticulous are accustomed to baking everything before Pesach, so that if trace amounts of *chametz* becomes mixed into the [*matza* dough], it would be nullified. By contrast, on Pesach, it becomes forbidden even with trace amounts.

42. משנה ברורה | או"ח תנח:ד

...ודע דמצד הדין מותר לאפות מצה בפסח אך המדקדקים נוהגים לאפות הכל קודם פסח שאם יתערב משהו חמץ בתוכם יתבטל מה שאין כן בפסח איסורו במשהו.

applied to the custom of *kitniyot* as well, that using vessels that had been used for *kitniyot* within twenty-four hours for a non-*kitniyot* dish is considered *bitul issur lechatchila*.

48. This approach is based on a ruling of the Maharam Schick, O.C. 24. For further discussion on the subject of those who do not consume *kitniyot* eating foods prepared with *kitniyot* dishes, see Rav Chaim Jachter, *Gray Matter*, vol. 1, p. 245 (available online at www.koltorah.org/halachah/the-minhag-of-kitniyot-part-ii-by-rabbi-howard-jachter), and https://rabbimanning.com/wp-content/uploads/2019/04/Mixed-Marriages-and-Kitniyot-Conundrums.pdf.

ופשוט דכשנאפה קודם פסח אפילו היה בו משהו חמץ בהקמח כבר נתערב ונתבטל ומותר אחר כך לבשל המצות בפסח דאין חימוץ אחר אפיה.

ויש אנשי מעשה שמחמירין על עצמן ואין שורין ואין מבשלין מצות בפסח מחשש שמא נשאר מעט קמח בתוך המצות מבפנים שלא נילוש יפה ועל ידי השריה יתחמץ. ועיין בשע"ת סימן ת"ס דמצד הדין אין לחוש לזה דאחזוקי איסורא לא מחזקינן ובפרט בימינו שנוהגין לעשות רקיקין דקים. ומכל מקום מי שנוהג בחומרא זו אין מזניחין אותו ועיין שם שהאריך בזה.

And it is obvious that when it is baked prior to Pesach, even if there was trace *chametz* in the flour, it is already mixed and null. It is permitted to cook it thereafter on Pesach, because there is no leavening after baking [has been completed].

There are some men of piety who conduct themselves with stringency and refrain from soaking or cooking their matza on Pesach, out of concern that perhaps a bit of flour which has not been kneaded remains within the matza, on the inside, and through soaking it will become leavened. See *Sha'arei Teshuva* that by the letter of the law one need not be concerned about this, because we do not simply assume that [people are doing something] forbidden [when the terms are unknown], especially in our days, when we are accustomed to making thin, flat crunchy matza. Nonetheless, if someone is accustomed to observing this stringency, we do not cast it aside. See his lengthy discussion there.

Most who practice this stringency today are from the Chasidic community. Many contemporary *poskim* write that one whose family avoids eating *sheruya* should continue to practice it in most situations.[49]

49 See *Piskei Teshuvot* 458:6 and *Halichot Shlomo* 4:19. *Poskim* disagree whether one may perform *hatarat nedarim* to abolish this *minhag* (see Responsa *Igrot Moshe*, O.C. 3:64; *Ashrei Ha'ish* 3:60:20).

Summary of the Halachot of Kitniyot on Pesach

The Halachic Definition of Grain

1. **Gemara (*Masechet Pesachim*)**
   a. ***Tanna Kamma*** – Rice and millet cannot become *chametz,* so one also cannot use them for matza on the first night of Pesach.
   b. **Rabbi Yochanan ben Nuri** – Rice is considered grain, but his position is not accepted as halacha.

The Custom to Avoid Eating Kitniyot

1. ***Hagahot Semak*** – It is proper to avoid *kitniyot,* since they could be confused with grain.
2. **Ritva** – One must take precautions to avoid *chametz* that is mixed with *kitniyot.* Many pious individuals avoid *kitniyot,* as *chametz* may be mixed with them.
3. **Rabbeinu Manoach** – We avoid *kitniyot* as these foods are not conducive to rejoicing on the festival.
4. ***Tur*** – This is an excessive stringency.
5. ***Beit Yosef*** – Only the Ashkenazim avoid eating *kitniyot* on Pesach.
6. **Rema** – Ashkenazim must not deviate from this practice.
7. **Rav Yaakov Emden** – The *Chacham Tzvi* wished to end this stringent practice, which has no halachic basis, results in laxity regarding *chametz,* and is also financially difficult. He would have been happy to join with other rabbis to rescind the decree.
8. ***Aruch HaShulchan*** – Those who wish to abolish the custom to refrain from eating *kitniyot* on Pesach do not have fear of Heaven or sin and are not Torah experts.
9. ***Mishna Berura*** – If one has no other food, one may eat *kitniyot,* provided that precautions are taken to avoid actual *chametz.*

- **Sephardim and *Kitniyot***

1. ***Ben Ish Chai*** – In Baghdad, many avoid eating rice due to the difficulty in checking it for *chametz* mixed with it.
2. **Rav Ovadia Yosef** – A Sephardi may obtain *hatara* to annul his personal stringent practice. One who was raised to follow this stringency need not continue it once he moves out of his parents' home.

Conflicting Customs in Marriage

1. **Mishna (*Masechet Pesachim*)** – One must follow the custom of the place one lives regarding work on the morning of Erev Pesach.
2. ***Tashbetz*** – Where differing customs are followed by different communities in a city, a wife must adopt the customs of her husband's community.
3. **Rav Moshe Feinstein** – A wife must follow her husband's customs, whether they are more lenient or stricter. Even if they are more lenient, no *hatara* is required.
4. **Rav Ovadia Yosef** – Nevertheless, one should ideally obtain *hatara*.
5. **Rav Nachum Rabinovitch** – Today, although one must not treat customs lightly, compromises are required and one can be more lenient regarding which custom to follow.

When Does the Custom Take Effect?

1. **Rav Shmuel Wosner** – The custom to avoid *kitniyot* starts from the time that we stop eating *chametz* on Erev Pesach.

Which Foods are Considered Kitniyot?

1. ***Hagahot Semak*** – Beans, rice, and lentils are *kitniyot*. *Kitniyot* are similar to grain as they are piled up, so mustard is also *kitniyot*. Cabbage and leeks are not *kitniyot*, as they are nothing like grain.
2. ***Taz*** – Foods that are shaped like grain, or grow in a similar manner to other *kitniyot*, such as mustard, are *kitniyot*. Other foods are not *kitniyot*, even if grain commonly gets mixed with them.
3. ***Mishna Berura*** – Corn is considered *kitniyot*.
4. ***Avnei Nezer*** – Rapeseed is also *kitniyot*, since it too grows in pods.
5. **Rav Moshe Feinstein** – Only foods regarding which there is a clear custom to avoid are prohibited. Accordingly, peanuts are permitted.
6. **Rav Tzvi Pesach Frank** – Although they are not *kitniyot*, our custom is to refrain from eating peanuts on Pesach.
7. **Rav Dov Lior** – Soy and quinoa products are permitted, as they were not known of at the time the custom to avoid *kitniyot* developed.
8. **Rav Asher Weiss, Rav Eliashiv, Rav Belsky** – Quinoa should be included in the category of *kitniyot*.
9. **Rav Dovid Feinstein, Rav Yaakov Ariel, Rav Hershel Schachter, Star-K, OU** – Where there is no concern for *chametz*, it is permitted to use quinoa on Pesach.

- ***Kitniyot* That Are Kept Dry**

1. ***Chayei Adam*** – One may bake *kitniyot* into a matza-like food and eat it on Pesach.
2. ***Sho'el U'meishiv*** – The custom is to avoid even baked *kitniyot*. They also are more likely to be confused with *chametz* or matza.

- ***Kitniyot* Oil**

1. **Rema** – One may use *kitniyot* oil as fuel.
2. **Rav Avraham Yitzchak HaKohen Kook** – Sesame oil produced without contact with water may be used, even if it subsequently comes into contact with water.
3. ***Peninei Halakha*** – Soybean oil may be used on Pesach even today, since it is produced without water. All soy products may also be permitted, since soy was not available at the time the custom to avoid *kitniyot* developed.
4. **Maharsham** – Canola oil may be permitted for the reasons above, and also since only the oil is edible and not the rapeseed itself.
5. **Kosharot** – Customs differ as to whether Ashkenazim in Israel may use canola oil or rapeseed on Pesach.
6. **Chicago Rabbinical Council** – The custom among Ashkenazim in the Diaspora is to treat canola oil as *kitniyot*, since it comes from rapeseed, which was already considered as *kitniyot* by some *Acharonim*.

Mixtures Containing Kitniyot

1. **Rema** – If *kitniyot* fell into a dish, the dish certainly does not become prohibited. One may keep *kitniyot* at home and use them as fuel.
2. ***Mishna Berura*** – The custom to avoid *kitniyot* does not include other foods that get mixed with *kitniyot*. However, one must remove any recognizable grains of *kitniyot*. If the majority of a mixture is *kitniyot*, one may not eat it.
3. ***Pri Chadash*** – One may intentionally mix *kitniyot* with other food in order to eat them, as with *challa* in *chutz la'aretz*.
4. **Other *Poskim*** – One may not intentionally mix *kitniyot* with other food in order to eat them.
5. ***Peninei Halakha*** – Even one who does not eat *kitniyot* may eat confectionery that contains *kitniyot*, as they are nullified by the other ingredients.
6. **Rav Yaakov Ariel** – Although mixtures of small amounts of *kitniyot* are technically not classified as *kitniyot*, it is customary to refrain from eating them.
7. **Rav Ovadia Yosef** – Ashkenazim may eat non-*kitniyot* food in a Sephardi home, even if the utensils were used for *kitniyot* within the past 24 hours.

8. ***Kaf HaChaim*** – Those who do not eat *kitniyot* may use utensils in which *kitniyot* have been cooked after 24 hours. A guest need not ask whether the utensils were used for *kitniyot*.

9. **Rav Nissim Karelitz** – Those who do not eat *kitniyot* but prepare food for those who do have the custom to use separate utensils to prepare this food.

- **The Custom to Avoid *Sheruya* (“*Gebrochts*”)**

1. ***Mishna Berura*** – Some refrain from eating matza that comes in contact with water on Pesach (known as “*sheruya*” or “*gebrochts*”) due to concern that it will rise, but this is not necessary according to the letter of the law.

Further Iyun

The Nature of Minhag and the Mechanism of Halachic Obligation

Rav David Ohr (Participant, Manhigut Toranit)

SELWYN & ROS SMITH AND FAMILY
MANHIGUT TORANIT
IN PARTNERSHIP WITH ERETZ HEMDAH AND WORLD MIZRACHI

At first glance, the halachic system appears to rest on two primary foundations: the commandments of the Torah (*de'oraita*) and the enactments of the Sages (*derabanan*). Yet anyone who traces the lived reality of Jewish practice quickly encounters a third layer of remarkable force: ***minhag***.

Minhag is often misunderstood as custom, folklore, or cultural preference. In halachic reality, however, it possesses genuine legal power. A practice adopted voluntarily by a community can evolve into a binding obligation that persists across generations. How does this transformation occur? What grants a communal practice the authority to obligate future generations who never consciously accepted it?

This essay examines how *minhag* emerges, why it binds the descendants of the original community that accepted it, and what halachic mechanism allows a voluntary practice to become a lasting legal commitment.

I. The Case of *Kitniyot*: From Permission to Prohibition

One of the clearest illustrations of the binding power of *minhag* appears in the well-known Ashkenazic practice of refraining from eating *kitniyot* on Pesach. The ***Shulchan Aruch***[1] states unequivocally that legumes such as rice, millet, and lentils do not undergo the process of *chimutz* and are therefore technically permissible on Pesach. Nevertheless, the **Rema** records that the Ashkenazic custom is to refrain from consuming them and that this practice should not be changed.

Why does this custom carry such force? The Rema does not claim that *kitniyot* are halachically equivalent to chametz. Instead, he relies on a principle articulated by the ***Tur***[2]: when a community knowingly adopts a restriction of a religious nature on something that is technically permitted, their conduct assumes the status of a ***neder***.

A *neder* is not merely a verbal declaration. It is a halachic instrument that changes the status of an object for the person who undertakes it. When a community collectively accepts a practice of restraint, that practice acquires the binding force of a vow. *Minhag*, therefore, is not simply a different interpretation of the law. Rather, it represents a conscious decision by a community to establish an additional safeguard around the Torah. Once accepted, that decision becomes a halachic commitment.

II. *Bnei Bayshan* and the Intergenerational Covenant

The central challenge in understanding the binding nature of *minhag* is the question of continuity:

1. O.C. 453.
2. Y.D. 214.

Why should a vow adopted by previous generations obligate their descendants? A foundational source addressing this question appears in the Gemara in ***Masechet Pesachim***,[3] in the story of the *Bnei Bayshan*.

The residents of that city had adopted a custom not to engage in commerce on Friday afternoon in order to devote themselves to preparations for Shabbat. Their descendants later found themselves in difficult financial circumstances and approached **Rabbi Yochanan** seeking permission to abandon the practice. Their argument was straightforward: their ancestors had enjoyed economic stability and could afford such stringency, whereas they could not.

Rabbi Yochanan rejected their request with a striking response: "Your fathers already accepted this practice upon themselves." He based this ruling on the verse in ***Mishlei***[4] "Hear, my son, the instruction of your father, and do not forsake the teaching of your mother." Through this interpretation, Rabbi Yochanan frames *minhag* as "*Torat Imecha*" – the living tradition transmitted within the home and community. The binding force of the practice does not stem solely from the practical logic that originally motivated it, but from the fact that previous generations consciously adopted it as part of their religious life.

Once accepted, the practice becomes embedded in the identity of the community itself. Descendants inherit not merely the specific practice, but the spiritual framework created by their predecessors. In this sense, *minhag* forms a kind of intergenerational covenant. What began as a voluntary act of piety becomes part of the inherited religious landscape within which later generations live.

III. The Mechanism of Transmission: Inheritance or Communal Acceptance?

How exactly does a *minhag* pass from one generation to the next? The *poskim* offer two different models to explain this phenomenon.

1. The Inheritance Model – The *Chatam Sofer*

The ***Chatam Sofer***[5] analyzes the issue through the framework of *nedarim* – specifically the case of *nezirut*. In his view, when a community adopts a stringency upon itself, it is comparable to a vow whose effects extend to future generations. To illustrate this idea, he points to the case of *nezirut shimshon* (lifelong acceptance to become a *nazir*, like Shimshon was). Just as if a father declares that his son who is a fetus will be a *nazir shimshon*, the son cannot release himself from the conditions associated with that status, so too descendants cannot simply annul the commitments undertaken by their ancestors.

According to this model, *minhag* functions almost like an inheritance. The original vow was accepted by the previous generation, but its binding force remains even after they are no longer present to express regret or seek annulment. The obligation therefore passes from father to son as a continuing personal commitment. In this framework, the authority of the *minhag* derives primarily from the original act of acceptance.

---

3. 50b.
4. *Mishlei* 1:8.
5. Responsa *Chatam Sofer*, O.C. 122.

2. The Communal Model – The Rivash and the Ramban

The **Rivash**[6] and **Ramban**[7] offer a broader perspective. In their view, the power of *minhag* lies not merely in individual acceptance but in the authority of the community to legislate norms for itself and its descendants. They compare this process to the covenant at Har Sinai. Just as the acceptance of the Torah bound not only those present but also future generations, so too, a communal acceptance of a practice can extend to those who will later belong to that community.

Accordingly, the ***Shulchan Aruch***[8] rules that a person who moves into a particular city becomes obligated in its established customs. *Minhag*, in this sense, operates as a communal ordinance that defines the religious life of the place. Under this model, the binding force of *minhag* is not inherited privately, but arises from belonging to the community that accepted it.

IV. *Neder* and *Shevua*: The Conceptual Framework

To understand the halachic depth of *minhag*, we must examine a fundamental conceptual distinction discussed by the **Ramban**[9]: the difference between *neder* and *shevua*. The Torah often mentions these two categories together, such as: "When a man makes a vow (*neder*) or swears an oath (*shevua*)."[10] Nevertheless, they represent two very different halachic mechanisms.

Neder – A Prohibition on the Object (*Cheftza*)

A *neder* operates upon the object itself. When a person declares, "This loaf is forbidden to me," the prohibition attaches to the loaf. The object then becomes halachically prohibited for that person. Because the prohibition rests on the object, a *neder* can even apply to matters connected to mitzvot. For example, if a person vows that he may not benefit from a *sukka*, the vow can take effect despite the existence of the mitzva, because the *neder* transforms the status of the object. The *neder* therefore changes the halachic reality of the object itself.

Shevua – An Obligation on the Person (*Gavra*)

A *shevua*, by contrast, focuses on the person. Instead of prohibiting an object, it obligates or restrains the individual. The person declares: "I swear that I will not eat." Because the oath operates on the individual rather than the object, it cannot override an existing mitzva obligation. A person is already "sworn" at Sinai to fulfill the commandments; therefore, an oath cannot nullify them. In halachic terminology, the difference is clear: *neder* operates on the *cheftza* (the object) and *shevua* operates on the *gavra* (the person). This distinction helps illuminate the nature of *minhag*.

The distinction between the Rivash and the *Shulchan Aruch* can be understood precisely through this conceptual framework. The Rivash and the Ramban view a *minhag* as resembling a *shevua* – that is, a personal commitment (*gavra*) undertaken in order to strengthen one's observance of a mitzva or to adopt an additional measure of restraint. According to this understanding, the obligation rests primarily on the individuals who accepted the practice.

---

6. Responsa of the Rivash 399.
7. *Milchamot Hashem, Pesachim.*
8. Y.D. 214.
9. Commentary to *Bamidbar* 30.
10. *Bamidbar* 30:3.

By contrast, the *Shulchan Aruch* understands *minhag* as functioning more like a *neder*, which operates upon the object (*cheftza*). When a community accepts a restriction, such as refraining from eating *kitniyot* on Pesach, the acceptance effectively renders it as a prohibited object for that community.

When the prohibition rests upon the object, its force extends more naturally across generations. The prohibition is no longer merely a personal commitment of the original generation; rather, the halachic status of the object has changed for members of that community, and this altered reality continues to bind their descendants.

V. Is There a Way Out? Annulment of *Minhagim*

Despite the strong binding force of *minhag*, halacha does not view it as entirely irreversible. The **Rosh** rules that when a community adopts a practice as a form of additional restraint or safeguarding, that practice assumes the halachic status of a *neder*. As with other vows, it may therefore be annulled by a qualified halachic authority through the process of *hatarat nedarim*, based on the identification of *petach* (a new consideration) and *charata* (regret). Accordingly, a person who finds himself unable to continue observing a family or communal custom may approach a halachic authority and seek release from the obligation.

However, the ***Beit Yosef***[11] cautions that such annulments should not be granted lightly. In communities where people are not firmly grounded in Torah learning, there is concern that if they see customs being easily annulled, they may come to treat even clear halachic obligations with similar leniency. For this reason, the annulment of *minhagim* requires careful judgment. A halachic authority must weigh not only the technical validity of the request, but also the broader educational and communal consequences of permitting the change.

Conclusion

Minhag represents a form of communal self-legislation. What begins as a voluntary act of piety – a desire to add a safeguard or an extra layer of devotion – can develop into a binding halachic commitment. Through mechanisms such as *neder* or *shevua*, that commitment acquires legal force and is transmitted to future generations as an inherited obligation, whether through familial continuity or communal belonging.

The conceptual distinction between *neder* and *shevua* helps illuminate the deeper nature of *minhag*. *Minhag* is not merely a habit or cultural practice; it can function as a genuine halachic transformation. When a community accepts a practice as a *neder*, the very status of the act changes for those who belong to that community.

Ultimately, *minhag* serves as a bridge between formal halachic law and the lived religious experience of generations of Jews. Through *minhag*, communities express their desire to deepen their commitment to the Torah, adding layers of sanctity to the commandments themselves. In this way, *minhag* embodies the ongoing partnership between the eternal structure of halacha and the spiritual aspirations of the Jewish People.

11. Y.D. 214.

ERETZ HEMDAH
Institute for Advanced Jewish Studies
Jerusalem

נז. שמן-קטניות בשעת הדחק בפסח

מונטווידאו, אורוגואי (Montevideo, Uruguay), תמוז תשנ״ד

שאלה

בערב פסח עמדתי בפני בעיה הקשורה לנושא שמן קטניות. ידוע לי שבצה״ל ובמקומות אחרים מתבססים על פסקים המקילים בדבר. (דווקא בשמן או חומרים שאין בהם קטניות בעין).

באיזה מקרים מתירים שמן קטניות?

מי הם הפוסקים המתירים ומדוע?

תשובה

רמ״א אסר לאכול שמן-קטניות בפסח[1], ועל אף זאת יש מקום להקל לגבי שמן שנעשה מקטניות בלא מגע מים בתהליך יצורו, שמותר לאוכלו בפסח[2]. ואף שמן שבתהליך יצורו שורין את הקטניות במים, יש מקום להתיר - על-ידי שיבררו את הקטניות היטב ויחלטו אותן ברותחים קודם עשיית השמן[3]. ושמנים אלה מותר לאכול בפסח אפילו בתוך תבשיל שיש בו מים[4]. גם למחמירים בשמן-קטניות יש יותר מקום להתיר אכילת שמן-סויה בפסח[5].

1 באו״ח (סי תנג סעיף א) התיר רמ״א להדליק בפסח נרות בשמן-קטניות, שלא נאסרו קטניות בפסח אלא באכילה, ולא בהנאה והשהיה. ומקורו ב״תרומת הדשן״ (סי׳ קיג) שכתב: ״ונראה ג״כ דמותר להנות באותו התבואה (קטניות) בפסח, כגון ע״י הדלקה משמן זרע ושומשומין וזרע קנבוס, אע״פ שרגילים שלותתים אותם זרעונים במים קודם שעושים מהם שמנים, ואע״כ קרוב לוודאי שנתחמצן, אפ״ה שרי, דאיסורי הנאה נמי אינם אלא בלאו כמו השהיה״. ואף-על-פי שסיים ב״תרומת הדשן״ שם: ״אך כמדומה שהעולם נהגו איסור להדליק בשמנים שנעשו ממיני קטניות בפסח״, אחז הרמ״א שעיקר דעתו להתיר להדליק בשמן-קטניות בפסח. ומדלא התיר ב״תרומת הדשן״ וברמ״א אלא להדליק בשמן-קטניות, משמע שאסרו באכילה. ועיין ב״אבני נזר״ (או״ח סי׳ שעג) וב״מנחת אליעזר״ (ח״א) ובשו״ת ״מלמד להועיל״ (סי׳ פז) שפסקנו ששמן-קטניות אסור באכילה בפסח.

2 בטעם איסור קטניות בפסח כתב רבנו פרץ בהגהותיו לסמ״ק (מצוה רכב הגה יב) משום שקטניות מעשה קדירה הן, ודגן נמי מעשה קדירה הוא, ומשניהם רגילים לעשות פת ושניהם מידי דמדגן, וגזרינן שלא יבואו להחליף ביניהם ולאכול דגן בפסח.
ובטור (או״ח סי׳ תנג) כתב שיש אוסרים לאכול אורז וקטניות בפסח בתבשיל, לפי שמיני חיטים מתערבין בהם.
וב״מרחשת״ (סי׳ ג) כתב שלטעם הטור לא נאסרו קטניות אלא כשבא לבשל מהן כמו שהן בעין בפסח, שבזה יש חשש שמא לא ברנן יפה עד שלא נשתייר אלא אחד מאלף, שחמץ בפסח אסור במשהו. אך אם ברנן קודם הפסח וטחנן לקמח או עשה מהן שמן, מותר לאוכלן בפסח, דלא גרעו מחמשת מיני דגן שבררם וטחנם קודם הפסח, שמותר לאוכלם בפסח אע״פ שיש שם חיטים שצמחו, משום שבררם קודם הפסח עד שהיה ששים בתבואה כנגד החיטים שנטחנו קודם הפסח, הוי לח בלח ונתבטלו קודם הפסח ושוב אינו חוזר וניעור. והוא הדין בקטניות שהואיל ובררן יפה קודם הפסח, אפילו אם נשתייר בהן מעט מחמשת המינים המחמיצים, כבר נתבטלו בששים קודם הפסח ומותרים באכילה.
ואף לטעם שכתב רבנו פרץ דהקטניות עצמן אסורות אפילו אין בהן חמץ כלל, גזירה אטו חמשת מיני דגן, יש לומר שאין גזירתן קשה מחמשת מיני דגן. וכשם שבדגן עצמו, אם נזהרים בו מלבוא לידי חימוץ, הרי מותר לאוכלו בפסח, כן קטניות, אם נזהרים שלא להרטיבן ושלא יבואו לידי חימוץ, ודאי הן מותרות באכילה בפסח, דלא יהא הטפל חמור מן העיקר. וז״ל המרחשת ״ולפ״ז בנדון שאלתנו, אם היה אפשר לעשות את השמנים לכובשם ולעוצרם בבית הבד שלהם בזהירות הנוהגת בדגן לפסח שלא יבוא במים, הא ודאי מותר שהשמנים עצמם אינם מחמיצים, דקי״ל דמי פירות אינם מחמיצים. ובודאי באופן כזה היה מותר לעשות מהן שמנים לפסח בלי שום פקפוק וחשש כללי״. ומסיבה זו פרסם בשנת התרס״ט הגראי״ה קוק הכשר לשמן-שומשומין לפסח, וזה לשונו ב״אורח משפט״ (סי׳ קיא): ״שאין גזירת קטניות חמורה מגוף מיני דגן... וחלילה לנו לשיווי מילי דרבנן כי חוכא ולומר שהקטניות אסורים הם אפילו לא הובאו במים כלל, (בעוד) שמיני דגן גופא מותרים באפן זה בלא פקפוק״.
וכן כתב בשו״ע הגר״ז (או״ח סי׳ תנג סעיף ה): ״ואפילו במיני קטניות לא נהגו אלא איסור אכילה אם נפלו עליהם מים, בעניין שבכיוצא בזה בה׳ מיני דגן אסור מעיקר הדין. אבל מותר להנות מהם בפסח״.
ועיין ב״משנה ברורה״ (שם ס״ק י) ובדברי הראי״ה קוק (שם) שלא אסר רמ״א באכילה והתיר בהנאה אלא בשמן שנלתת במים. אבל שמן-קטניות שלא נלתת במים, אף רמ״א ו״תרומת הדשן״ לא אסרו. וכן מדוקדק מלשון ״תרומת הדשן״ הנ״ל שכתב: ״אע״פ שרגילים שלותתים אותם זרעונים במים קודם שעושים מהם שמן״, הא בלאו הכי מותר אפילו באכילה, וכן כתב שו״ת ״שרידי אש״ (ח״ב סי׳ לז אות ב).

3 ״מרחשת״ (סי׳ ג) שאפילו דגן ע״י חליטה שוב אינו מחמיץ. ואף שהגאונים אסרו את החליטה מטעם דאנן לא בקיאינן בחליטה, ויש לחוש שמא לא סליק דיקולא דמיא מכל הצדדים ולא נחלטה יפה, זה דווקא בה׳ מיני דגן. אבל במיני קטניות שבעיקרן לא נאסרו אלא משום גזירה, ואין איסורן אלא מכוח מנהג, שפיר יש להתיר בחליטה, דאף אם נשארו מעט קטניות שלא נחלטו, הרי הם בטלים. וז״ל: ״ולפי זה יש תקנה לעשות את השמנים ממיני קטניות ע״י שיחלטו מקודם ברותחים, ושוב לא אתיין לידי חימוץ״.

4 ואין לחוש בזה לגזירת קטניות, שהרי אין השמן דומה לדגן שיבואו להחליפו. וכמו כן אין לחוש שיבואו להחליפו בשמן אסור, שהרי השמנים שונים במראיהם ובסימונם. ובמקום שיצא השמן מתוך הקטניות בהיתר, ונשתנה גופיה ונעשה לשמן, אין לומר שנהגו בזה לאסור, שלא נהגו לאסור אלא היוצא מקטניות שכבר הושרו במים ונאסר כיוצא בו אם היה מין דגן, אבל ביוצא מקטניות שלא הושרו במים, אין מנהג לאסור כלל ומותר לאוכלו אפילו בתבשיל (״אורח משפט״ סי׳ קי-קיד).
ולרווחא דמילתא הוסיף שם דשמן-שומשומין הנדון, בדרך עשייתו מטגנים אותו בלא שום תערובת מים, ואח״כ נעשה מבושל שאינו מחמיץ. אך גם בלאו הכי יש להתיר.
(וע״ע בשו״ת ״שרידי אש״ המוזכר בסוף הע׳ 2).

5 שהרי בזמן שנגזרה גזירת קטניות, עדיין לא הוכר צמח הסויה בארצותינו, ואם כן יש לומר שמין זה לא כלול כלל בגזירה זו - בשם הרה״ג דוב ליאור, רב העיר קרית ארבע - חברון (הובא ב״תחומין״ כרך יג עמ׳ 178). וכן כתב ב״אגרות משה״ (או״ח ח״ג סי׳ סג) שאין לאסור אלא מה שמפורש שנהגו לאסור.

ERETZ HEMDAH
Institute for Advanced Jewish Studies
Jerusalem

פראג, צ'כיה

Prague, Czech Republic

ניסן, ה'תשנ"ו

נא. תערובת קטניות בפסח

שאלה

כיצד יש לנהוג בקהילה אשכנזית בנושא תערובת קטניות בפסח, בדיעבד?
האם קניה בחנות במקום שיש חשש תערובת מקרי "דיעבד"? כיצד לנהוג במקום שלא ידוע אחוז הקטניות, ואי אפשר לברר זאת?

תשובה

מותר לקנות ולאכול בפסח מאכלים שיש בהם תערובת קטניות, בתנאי שרוב המאכל אינו קטניות[1] ובפרט יש להתיר במקום שנתערבו לפני פסח[2], או במוצרים שמכילים רק שמן קטניות[3] או מינים שיש לגביהם ספק, אם הם בכלל גזירת קטניות, כגון אגוזי-אדמה וסויה[4].

ואולם בפסח אין להכין תבשיל כזה לכתחילה, ויש מתירים לבטל את הקטניות לפני פסח[5].

וכאשר בא לפניך תבשיל בפסח, אשר אי-אפשר לברר את כמות הקטניות שבו, מותר להרבות עליו בתבשיל אחר, כך שהקטניות יהיו בוודאי מיעוט[6].

---

[1] א. כתב ב"תרומת הדשן" (סו"ס קיג): "אפס, נראה אם נמצא גרגיר של מיני קטניות בקדירה או בתבשיל, לא מחמירינן כלל לאסור התבשיל אפילו באכילה, דגזירה דאיסור משהו ליתא אלא בתבואה דה' מינים". וכן פסק רמ"א בשו"ע אורח חיים (סי' תנג סע' א): "מיהו פשוט דאין אוסרים בדיעבד אם נפלו [קטניות] תוך התבשיל". ואף-על-פי שמדברי "תרומת הדשן" משמע שלא התיר אלא במשהו, אבל אם ששים נגדו - אסור, מדברי רמ"א משמע שהתיר אפילו אין ס' כנגד הקטניות. וב"חק יעקב" (שם ס"ק ו) כתב שמדברי אחרונים משמע כרמ"א, שאפילו אין ששים כנגד הקטניות, מותר, וסיים שם: "ועיקר נ"ל כדעת האחרונים כיון שבלא"ה הוא חומרא והרחקה בעלמא... מ"מ רוב (של היתר) על כל פנים בעינן, ואם לא כן, לא מקרי תערובת כלל, דהוי כאוכל התבשיל מקטניות עצמן". וכן פסק ב"משנה ברורה" (סי' תנג ס"ק ח-ט) שכתב שם: "ומכל מקום, אותם גרגירים שמוצאים, צריך לזורקן, אם לא שאינו ניכר". ובשו"ת "באר יצחק" (סי' יא) כתב שדי שההיתר מרובה מן האיסור במשהו, כדי להתיר התערובת.
בטעם היתר תערובת קטניות כתבו אחרונים שהוא, שעל תערובת קטניות לא גזרו כלל. ועיין שו"ת "באר יצחק" (סי' יא) שדקדק כן בדברי ה"חק יעקב", וכן כתב בספר "חוקת הפסח" (סי' תנג סעיף ג).

ב. ב"פרי חדש" (שו"ע או"ח סי' תנג סוף סע' א) כתב: "מה שאמר [הרמ"א] ואינן אסורים אם נפלו לתוך התבשיל, מסתברא דכיון דאיכא רוב היתר, מבטלי, דלא עדיף מחלת חו"ל שמבטלה ברוב ואוכלה". משמע שלדעתו מותר לבטל קטניות לכתחילה ולאוכלן בפסח. וכן כתב בשו"ת "זרע אמת" (ח"ג או"ח סי' מח והובא ב"יחוה דעת" ח"ה סי' לב),. וכן דעת שו"ת "באר יצחק" (סי' יא הנ"ל) וזה לשונו: "משא"כ קטניות דבנ"ד דמערבין אותו מקודם הפסח, דאז מותר לבטלו ברוב כיון דשם היתר עליו מקודם הפסח, לכן ליתא בזה לאסור (משום) דאין מבטלין איסור לכתחילה, בפרט דאינו רק תקנת הגאונים, וקילא זו מן חלת חו"ל דמבטלי לכתחילה ברוב אף דהוי גזירה הקדומה, וכל שכן זה. וכיון דמבואר בחק יעקב (סי' תנג) דבתערובות רוב לא גזרו בקטניות אם כן הוא הדין בערבו במתכוין, ולהעמיד בטעם גמור גם כן מותר". אמנם לא התיר שם אלא לבטל קודם הפסח. וב"כף החיים" מובא בדעת הרמ"א שמותר לבטל רק בדיעבד, אבל לא לכתחילה.

ג. כתב הט"ז (יו"ד סי' קח ס"ק ד) ש"מותר לקנות מן העכו"ם דברים המבושלים בכליהם, שאין בהם משום בישול עכו"ם דסתם כליהם אינם בני יומם. ואע"פ שנותן טעם לפגם אסור לכתחילה, מכל מקום לא חשבינן לקניה לכתחילה". אם כן קנייה נחשבת דיעבד, ובדיעבד נותן טעם לפגם מותר. ויש לומר שהוא הדין בנדון דידן, דקנייה נחשבת דיעבד, ולפי זה מותר אפוא אף לדעת רמ"א לקנות מוצרים שיש בהם תערובת קטניות.

ד. רבים מן הראשונים סוברים שאיסור שאין לו עיקר מן התורה מותר לבטלו לכתחילה (עיין "אנציקלופדיה תלמודית" ערך: אין מבטלין איסורין לכתחילה, ציון 50).

ה. בשו"ת "יחוה דעת" (חלק ה סי' לב) דן המחבר בשאלה, האם לאשכנזים הנוהגים איסור בקטניות, מותר לאכול בכלים של ספרדים שנתבשלו בהם קטניות בפסח, והעלה להתיר, והסתמך על דברי רמ"א הנ"ל שהתיר בדיעבד תערובת קטניות כשהרוב היתר, "ולפי זה הדבר ברור שאין פליטת הכלים שבישלו בהם אורז וקטניות אוסר את התבשיל לבני אשכנז שנוהגים להחמיר באורז ובקטניות. ואפילו אם הכלים בני יומם יש להתיר שבודאי יש רוב היתר כנגד פליטת הכלים". והוא הדין בנדון דידן שמאכל, שיש בו תערובת קטניות לפסח, אין לאוסרו לאשכנזים, ואין כאן משום מבטל קטניות לכתחילה לפי שעושה כן בהיתר, לצורך אלה הנוהגים היתר בקטניות, כמו שהותרה פליטת הכלים לפי שבושלו בהם קטניות בהיתר. וכן כתב ב"יחוה דעת" (שם עמ' קנב). ו. נמצא דבנדון דידן הצטרפו כמה טעמים להתיר: (א) לא גזרו כלל על תערובת קטניות; (ב) לדעת ה"פרי חדש" ו"באר יצחק" מותר לבטל קטניות לכתחילה; (ג) איסור שאין לו עיקר מן התורה מותר לבטלו לכתחילה, לדעת הרבה ראשונים; (ד) מאחר שנתערבו המאכלים בהיתר - לצורך הנוהגים היתר בקטניות, אין לאסור - לדעת רמ"א המתיר במקום שהתערבו בדיעבד.

[2] ראה שו"ת "באר יצחק" (סי' יא) שהתיר לבטל קטניות קודם הפסח. ואף יש דעות באחרונים (סי' תמז סעיף ד) שאפילו חמץ גמור מותר לבטל קודם הפסח, וקל וחומר שמותר לבטל קטניות קודם הפסח שכן איסורם שאינו אלא חומרא. ואפילו החולקים על ה"פרי חדש" יש לומר שיודו, שקודם הפסח מותר לבטל קטניות לכתחילה.

[3] נחלקו אחרונים בשאלה, אם גם שמן-קטניות אסור בגזירת קטניות או לאו. עיין "מרחשת" (סי' ג) ו"אורח משפט" למרן הראי"ה קוק (סי' קח-קיא). ונהי דיש מחמירים בשמן-קטניות עצמו, בתערובת ודאי שאין להחמיר.

[4] כנ"ל הערה 3, שאין להחמיר בתערובת קטניות במקום שיש מתירים לאכול את הקטניות עצמן. ועיין "תחומין" (כרך ג עמ' 166) שדן בעניין זה וב"מנחת יצחק" (ח"ו סי' עב) שם משמע שהוא אוסר לבטל לכתחילה, כדי למכור ולאכול בפסח.

[5] כנ"ל הערה 1 כרמ"א שאסר לבטל קטניות לכתחילה. ואולם בשו"ת "באר יצחק" (סי' יא) התיר לבטל קטניות לכתחילה קודם הפסח.

[6] על-פי עצת הראשל"צ הרב עובדיה יוסף, בעל-פה.

4

Halachot of Erev Pesach

הלכות ערב פסח

Fast of the Firstborn

Matza on Erev Pesach

The Holiday of Erev Pesach

Eating on Erev Pesach Afternoon

When Erev Pesach Coincides with Shabbat

Removing Ma'aserot

For quick reference, some long website URLs have been shortened.
For the complete list of referenced websites visit www.tzurbaolami.com.

ת	**Tanach**
ח	**Talmud (Chazal)**
ר	***Rishonim***
א	***Acharonim***
פ	**Contemporary Halachic Sources**

Erev Pesach is one of, if not the, busiest day of the year. As we transition into Pesach, there are many halachot of which one must be aware relating to the disposal of *chametz*, the fast of the firstborn, the use of matza before the Seder, and commemorating the *korban Pesach* (even while we cannot currently offer it). In this *shiur*, we will address some of the important halachot that arise on this very special day.[1]

Fast of the Firstborn

The dramatic birth of *Bnei Yisrael* as a nation coincides with the moment that the once-enslaved people burst forth from Egypt, on the heels of the devastating plague of the firstborn. The immediate connection of these events is described in ***Shemot***.

1. שמות | יב:כט-לא, נא

כט. וַיְהִי בַּחֲצִי הַלַּיְלָה וַה' הִכָּה כָל בְּכוֹר בְּאֶרֶץ מִצְרַיִם מִבְּכֹר פַּרְעֹה הַיֹּשֵׁב עַל כִּסְאוֹ עַד בְּכוֹר הַשְּׁבִי אֲשֶׁר בְּבֵית הַבּוֹר וְכֹל בְּכוֹר בְּהֵמָה:

ל. וַיָּקָם פַּרְעֹה לַיְלָה הוּא וְכָל עֲבָדָיו וְכָל מִצְרַיִם וַתְּהִי צְעָקָה גְדֹלָה בְּמִצְרָיִם כִּי אֵין בַּיִת אֲשֶׁר אֵין שָׁם מֵת:

לא. וַיִּקְרָא לְמֹשֶׁה וּלְאַהֲרֹן לַיְלָה וַיֹּאמֶר קוּמוּ צְּאוּ מִתּוֹךְ עַמִּי גַּם אַתֶּם גַּם בְּנֵי יִשְׂרָאֵל וּלְכוּ עִבְדוּ אֶת ה' כְּדַבֶּרְכֶם:

נא. וַיְהִי בְּעֶצֶם הַיּוֹם הַזֶּה הוֹצִיא ה' אֶת בְּנֵי יִשְׂרָאֵל מֵאֶרֶץ מִצְרַיִם עַל צִבְאֹתָם:

ת Shemot 12:29–31, 51

29. It came to pass at midnight, and the Lord smote every firstborn in the land of Egypt, from the firstborn of Pharaoh who sits on his throne to the firstborn of the captive who is in the dungeon, and every firstborn animal.

30. And Pharaoh arose at night, he and all his servants and all the Egyptians, and there was a great outcry in Egypt, for there was no house in which no one was dead.

31. So he called for Moses and Aaron at night, and he said, "Get up and get out from among my people, both you, as well as the children of Israel, and go, worship the Lord as you have spoken."

51. It came to pass on that very day, that the Lord took the children of Israel out of the land of Egypt with their legions.

While among the Egyptians, "there was no house in which no one was dead," the firstborns of Israel were spared. Thus, in recognition of their protection from the plague, Jewish firstborns had the practice to observe a fast on the (near-) anniversary of the plague, the 14th of Nisan (Erev Pesach).[2] This practice is first mentioned explicitly in a *baraita* in ***Masechet Soferim***.[3]

1. The halachot related to *bi'ur chametz* and *bitul chametz*, which are also performed on Erev Pesach, were discussed previously in volume 5, *shiur* 9. Although not discussed directly there or in this *shiur*, it is important to note the times relevant to *chametz* on Erev Pesach: *Chametz* is forbidden by rabbinic law for consumption at the end of the fourth halachic daylight hour, it is forbidden to benefit from on a rabbinic level at the end of the fifth halachic hour, and it is forbidden to eat or benefit from biblically at the end of the sixth hour, i.e., halachic midday. These times are usually publicized in community mailings and websites displaying halachic times, such as www.myzmanim.com.
2. *Mishna Berura* 470:1. Noting that it is unusual to commemorate a miracle though fasting, the *Piskei Teshuvot* (470:1) writes that some explain that the fast commemorates the prayers or fasts undertaken by the firstborns of *Bnei Yisrael* after Moshe warned Pharaoh that the plague was imminent (see also Eliyahu Kitov, *The Book of Our Heritage*, vol. 2, p. 548).
3. See also the *Yerushalmi* (*Pesachim* 10:1), which states that Rabbi [Yehuda HaNasi] ate neither leaven nor matza on Erev Pesach because he was a firstborn, which could be an even earlier precedent to the fact. However, others in the *Yerushalmi* are quoted as having eaten on Erev Pesach.

ח Masechet Soferim 21:1

2. מסכת סופרים | כא:א

There is no fasting until the month of Nisan has passed,[4] except for the firstborn, who fast on Erev Pesach…

ואין מתענין עד שיעבור ניסן, אלא הבכורות שמתענין בערב הפסח...

In the ***Shulchan Aruch,*** Rav Yosef Karo writes that the fast applies to all firstborns, perhaps even women. However, the **Rema** writes that it is not customary for firstborn women to fast.

א Shulchan Aruch, Orach Chaim 470:1

3. שולחן ערוך | או"ח תע:א

The firstborn fast on Erev Pesach, both those who are firstborn to their fathers and those who are firstborn to their mothers. And some say **that a firstborn female also fasts.** (Rema: **But this is not the custom.**)

הבכורות מתענין בערב פסח בין בכור מאב בין בכור מאם. ויש מי שאומר **שאפילו נקבה בכורה מתענה (ואין המנהג כן)**.

The ***Mishna Berura*** explains the respective arguments for women participating, or not participating, in the fast of the firstborns. On the one hand, firstborn Jewish women were saved; on the other hand, the other mitzvot associated with firstborns do not apply to women.[5]

א Mishna Berura, Orach Chaim 470:3–4

4. משנה ברורה | או"ח תע:ג-ד

3. **A firstborn female also** – As the plague of the firstborn befell them [Egyptian women] also.

4. **This is not the custom** – The Torah did not apply the "sanctity of firstborns" to females in any matter.

ג. **שאפילו נקבה בכורה** – שמכת בכורות היתה גם עליהן.

ד. **ואין המנהג כן** – שהתורה לא נתנה קדושת בכורות לנקבה לשום דבר.

Because the custom to fast relates to the acknowledgment that the firstborns of *Bnei Yisrael*, including children, were spared, the concept of the fast applies to children as much as it applies to adults. However, as the halacha generally requires fasting only of those who have reached majority (twelve years for young women and thirteen years for young men), the **Rema** writes that a parent should fast in place of the firstborn child.[6]

Although the custom for the firstborn to fast is very old and has been observed in communities around the world, the *poskim* mention that many firstborns participate in a *seudat mitzva* (a celebratory "feast" to mark a milestone or mitzva), superseding the obligation to fast.[7] Thus, the ***Mishna Berura*** mentions

---

4. The month of Nisan is distinguished in the halacha as having an elevated status. This expresses itself most notably in the omission of *Tachanun* after the *Amida* and the significant restrictions on fasting throughout the month (*Shulchan Aruch*, O.C. 429:1). For explanations for Nisan's distinction, see *Aruch HaShulchan*, O.C. 429:1–2 and *Mishna Berura* 429:7.
5. The sons born first to their fathers receive a double inheritance; the sons born first to their mothers must be redeemed from the *Kohen* when they are infants (subject to many conditions). See also *Aruch HaShulchan*, O.C. 470:3.
6. The Rema writes that if the child's father is not a firstborn, then the father should fast on behalf of the child. But if the father is also a firstborn and the father has his own obligation to fast, then the mother should fast on behalf of the child (*Shulchan Aruch*, O.C. 470:2). However, the *Mishna Berura* qualifies this practice. Today, the *Peninei Halakha* rules that the child's fast falls upon the father even if he himself is also a firstborn (*Peninei Halakha, Pesach* 13:4; see there and *Piskei Teshuvot* 470:2 for more details surrounding those who need not fast).
7. It should be noted that participating in a *siyum* does not serve to exempt from one of the minor fasts. Nevertheless, it has been accepted today to be more lenient regarding this fast specifically because it originates only from *minhag* and not as an

that in many places, it is customary to arrange a *siyum* (formal completion) of a tractate of the Gemara or an order of the Mishna on Erev Pesach, so that the firstborns will not be required to fast.

א Mishna Berura, Orach Chaim 470:10

5. משנה ברורה | או"ח תע:י

In some places, the firstborns have the practice to be lenient and eat at a *seudat mitzva*. This is also the practice today in a number of places in our country, to be lenient and **to eat even at the *seuda* of the completion of a tractate.** And even [when] the firstborns themselves did not learn the tractate, nonetheless, **since for the one concluding [the learning], it is considered a *seudat mitzva*, the [firstborns] may join his meal.**

ויש מקומות שנהגו הבכורים להקל ולאכול בסעודת מצוה וכן נוהגין כהיום בכמה מקומות במדינתנו **להקל ולאכול אף בסעודת סיום מסכת**, ואף שהבכורים בעצמן לא למדו את המסכת, מכל מקום **כיון שאצל המסיים הוא סעודת מצוה מצטרפים לסעודתו.**

This practice is common among Sephardic communities as well. In his contemporary work ***Be'erot Yitzchak*, Rav Yitzchak Arama**[8] acknowledges that, as fasting can negatively impact upon a person's ability to perform the mitzvot of the Pesach Seder, it is widely practiced to terminate the fast through participating in a *siyum* or another *seudat mitzva*. Once someone has done so, the fast need not be completed or made up at a later time.

Be'erot Yitzchak, p. 129

6. בארות יצחק | עמ' 129

In these generations, when weakness has descended into the world and the fast disturbs the proper orchestration of the Seder, **people are accustomed to being lenient and stop the fast by actively participating in the *siyum* of a tractate.** One should attempt to understand the material which has been studied [rather than study it quickly without understanding simply to make a *siyum*]. Similarly, [one may participate in another type of] *seudat mitzva*. Ideally, one should eat a *k'zayit* ofgrain-based foods or drink [the measure of] a *revi'it* [of wine or grape juice].[9] (But some are lenient with even less.)[10]

בדורות אלו שירדה חולשה לעולם והתענית גורמת להפרעת עריכת הסדר כמצותו, **נהגו להקל להפסיק את התענית על ידי השתתפות בפועל בסיום מסכת** וישתדל להבין את הנלמד וכן בסעודת מצוה ולכתחילה צריך לאכול כזית מזונות ולשתות רביעית (ויש מקלים אפילו בפחות).

FURTHER IYUN

For further *iyun* on the mitzva of *tashbitu* (destroying *chametz*) on Erev Pesach, see page 211.

---

obligation. In addition, some understand that this leniency is also a function of the difficulty in our generation in fasting on Erev Pesach before the Seder, as noted in source 6 below.

8. Not to be confused with a Medieval Torah commentator by the same name, this is the former rabbi of Netzer Hazani in Gush Katif. After Rav Arama (1962–2002) was killed in a terrorist attack, his writings were collected and published in the work *Be'erot Yitzchak*.

9. Practically, this is sometimes difficult on Erev Pesach, when most people do not have any more *chametz* remaining (or the venue of the *siyum* is already *chametz*-free) and as we will see below, many *poskim* do not allow the consumption of products containing matza meal on Erev Pesach.

10. For further discussion of the details of a *siyum* for the firstborn on Erev Pesach, such as whether one must eat at the *siyum* or may eat at home later, whether one may eat if one misses the actual *siyum* and arrives only in time for the food, whether one must eat *mezonot* foods, and what works of Torah study qualify for this formal *siyum*, see *Piskei Teshuvot* (470:6–11) and Rav Moshe Harari, *Mikraei Kodesh*, Pesach (1:30–39).

Matza on Erev Pesach

Aside from the specific prohibition to eat *chametz* for much of the day on Erev Pesach, Chazal describe other practices and regulations restricting eating on Erev Pesach. These light limitations serve the purpose of creating an appetite for the matza which is eaten in fulfillment of a mitzva on the first night of Pesach.[11] On the basis of the ***Yerushalmi,*** the **Rambam** rules that it is forbidden to eat matza on Erev Pesach.[12]

7. רמב"ם | הל' חמץ ומצה ו:יב

אסרו חכמים לאכול מצה בערב הפסח כדי שיהיה הכר לאכילתה בערב, ומי שאכל מצה בערב הפסח מכין אותו מכת מרדות...

ו Rambam, Hilchot Chametz Umatza 6:12

The Sages forbade a person from eating matza on Erev Pesach, in order for there to be a distinction [between partaking of it as food and eating it] on the evening [of the fifteen as a mitzva].[13] Whoever eats matza on Pesach eve is given "stripes for rebellious conduct"...

The **Rema** rules in accordance with the Rambam, noting that this does not apply to small children who have no understanding of the Exodus.

8. רמ"א | או"ח תעא:ב

אבל מצה שיוצאין בה בלילה, אסורים לאכול כל יום ארבעה עשר. וקטן שאינו יודע מה שמספרין בלילה מיציאת מצרים, מותר להאכילו.

א Rema, Orach Chaim 471:2

Regarding matza with which one fulfills the obligation at night, this may not be eaten over the whole day of the 14th [of Nisan]. In the case of a child who does not understand what we recount at night concerning the Exodus from Egypt, it is permitted to feed him [matza on the day of the 14th].

Although the *poskim* emphasize that the formal prohibition applies only on Erev Pesach itself, they note that some people have the custom to refrain from eating matza as early as Rosh Chodesh Nisan, or for others, even 30 days before Pesach (which is Purim).[14] This is stated clearly by the ***Peninei Halakha.***

---

11. According to the *baraita* from *Masechet Soferim* cited above, aside from the firstborns, there were others who were accustomed to fasting the whole day Erev Pesach for the express purpose of creating an appetite for the *matza.* Although this practice was not broadly adopted, it does reflect the wider sensitivity to coming to the Seder with a degree of hunger. Other reflections of this goal are explored more fully below.
12. *Yerushalmi (Masechet Pesachim)* 10:1. The Gemara likens eating matza on the eve of the *Seder* to being with one's betrothed wife before the wedding, stating that the latter is subject to lashes *miderabanan.* The Rambam here understands that the lashes also apply to one who eats matza on Erev Pesach.
13. Here, the Rambam writes that the halacha creates a space between optional matza and obligatory matza. In this way, Erev Pesach resembles Erev Rosh Hashana, and the day separates between customary *shofar* blasts during Elul and the obligatory *shofar* blasts of Rosh Hashana. Later, the Rambam also mentions the motivation to retain an appetite for the obligatory matza of the Pesach Seder.
14. Some *Rishonim* held that the formal prohibition begins only at midday on Erev Pesach, but most *poskim* have understood that it begins at daybreak. The *Ben Ish Chai* (*Tzav*, 26) rules that matza is formally forbidden beginning already on the night of

9. פניני הלכה | פסח יג:ו

האיסור מתחיל מעלות השחר. ויש שהחמירו על עצמם שלא לאכול מצה כבר מראש חודש ניסן, ויש שנהגו להימנע מאכילת מצה שלושים יום לפני הפסח. אבל מצד הדין רק ביום י"ד בניסן צריכים להימנע מאכילת מצה.

Peninei Halakha, Pesach 13:6

The prohibition begins at dawn on the 14th of Nisan, though some choose to be stringent and refrain from eating matza from the beginning of Nisan. Others refrain from eating matza thirty days before Pesah. However, the letter of the law only requires one to refrain from eating matza on the 14th of Nisan.

We have seen that the Rema specifies that it is forbidden on Erev Pesach to eat specifically "matza with which one fulfills the obligation at night." What is the status of foods made with matza components, i.e., foods made from matza meal (baked matza ground into flour-like granules), soaked matza, and the like? The **Rema** writes that if matza has been prepared properly but then processed and used as a base for other foods, such food may not be eaten on Erev Pesach.

10. רמ"א | או"ח תעא:ב

...מצה שנאפה כתקנה ואחר כך נתפררה ונילושה ביין ושמן, אינה נקראת מצה עשירה ואסורה לאכלה בערב פסח.

Rema, Orach Chaim 471:2

...Regarding matza which was properly baked and thereafter crumbled and mixed with wine or oil, it is not called "*matza ashira* (rich matza)" and is thus forbidden to be eaten on Erev Pesach.[15]

According to this, it would appear that it is forbidden to eat cakes, cookies, and rolls, etc. baked from matza-ground flour or matza meal.[16] However, the ***Peninei Halakha*** writes that not every matza-based baked product may be included in the Rema's stringency. If the matza has been ground up so finely and mixed with other ingredients so that all appearances of the matza are erased, then it may be that the baked products no longer have the status of matza, though some rule more stringently.

11. פניני הלכה | פסח יג:ו

איסור אכילת מצה בערב פסח חל גם על שברי מצה קטנים שנילושו ביין או בשמן. ואף אם יאפו את התערובת הזו, כל זמן שצורת המצה נשארה על השברים, הרי שברכתם 'המוציא', ואסור לאוכלם בערב פסח. אבל אם השברים שנילושו ונאפו איבדו

Peninei Halakha, Pesach 13:6

The prohibition against eating matza on Erev Pesah includes even small pieces of matza that have been kneaded with wine or oil. Even if such a mixture is baked, as long as the pieces are identifiable as matza, the blessing before eating them is "ha-motzi" and it is forbidden to eat them on Erev Pesah. However, if after being kneaded and baked the pieces are no longer

---

the 14th. This practice is also cited by Rav Mordechai Eliyahu (*Ma'amar Mordechai, Mo'adim* 8:5). Some understand the *Magen Avraham* (471:6) this way as well.

15. On *matza ashira*, see below.

16. According to this position, it would seem that matza-derivative foods have the same status as matza. Thus, for those who refrain from eating matza even 15 or 30 days before Erev Pesach, it may be appropriate to also refrain from eating whatever has the status of matza-derivative foods. On the other hand, one could argue that since matza is forbidden only according to the letter of the law on Erev Pesach itself, and the rest of the time is merely a custom, it might not be necessary to apply the custom to matza-derivatives as well.

identifiable as matza, their berakha is "mezonot" and they may be eaten on Erev Pesah (implied in Rema 461:2 and MB ad loc. 19–20).[17]

Some poskim are more stringent, maintaining that even if the matza is crumbled like matza meal, kneaded with oil or wine, and baked into cake or cookies so that they are no longer identifiable as matza, it is forbidden to eat them. This is because one who eats enough of them to constitute a meal ("kevi'at se'uda") still must recite the berakha of "ha-motzi." Thus, it is apparent that they have not yet lost the status of matza, and consequently the prohibition applies to pastries made of matza meal (Gra, Rav Kook, and Hazon Ish).

איבדו את צורת המצה שלהם, ברכתם 'מזונות', ומותר לאוכלם בערב פסח (כך נראה מדברי הרמ"א תעא, ב, ומ"ב יט–כ).

ויש מחמירים בזה, ולדעתם אפילו אם פוררו את המצה לפירורים קטנים כקמח מצה, ולשו אותם בשמן או בדברי מתיקה ואפו מהם עוגה או עוגיות ולא נותרה להם צורת מצה – אסור לאוכלם. משום שעדיין ברכת 'המוציא' שייכת להם, שאם יאכלו מהם כשיעור קביעת סעודה יברכו עליהם 'המוציא', נמצא שעדיין לא פג מהם שם מצה, וממילא איסור אכילת מצה בערב פסח חל גם על מאפים המבוססים על קמח מצה (הגר"א, הרב קוק, חזו"ע).

There is at least one other matza-derived product that may be permitted to eat on Erev Pesach. Several ***Acharonim***, such as the ***Aruch HaShulchan***, write that the Rema's stringent ruling applies only if the matza or matza-flour batter is baked. But if one takes proper matza or matza flour batter and cooks it, it may be eaten on Erev Pesach because the cooking eliminates the identity of the matza.

א Aruch HaShulchan, Orach Chaim 471:5

Know that in the case of matza baked properly and thereafter crumbled and mixed with wine, oil, or honey, and not cooked, it is not called *matza ashira*; and it is forbidden to eat it on Erev Pesach… **But if it was cooked, it is permitted to eat** [it], but not baking without a liquid.

12. ערוך השולחן | או"ח תעא:ה

ודע דמצה שנאפית כתקונה ואחר כך נתפררה ונלושה ביין ושמן ודבש ולא נתבשלה אינה קרויה מצה עשירה ואסור לאוכלה בערב פסח... **אבל נתבשלה מותר לאכול** ולא באפייה בלא משקה.

Thus, even if foods baked from crumbled matza remain subject to the ban on eating matza on Erev Pesach, this does not include matza cooked or boiled in liquid. Accordingly, it is permitted to eat matza balls on Erev Pesach.[18] In addition, today there are many baked products sold that are made out of potato starch, and all agree that these may be consumed all day on Erev Pesach.[19]

17. See also *Halichot Shlomo* (8:4) and *Shemirat Shabbat K'hilchata* (ch. 56, n. 50), who suggest that the *Mishna Berura* and *Sha'ar HaTziun* (16) imply this because of their mention that the matza must still have the appearance of matza to be prohibited. However, see *Piskei Teshuvot* (471:3) who claims that cookies or cakes made with matza meal still have the appearance of matza even according to the Rema and *Mishna Berura* and are therefore prohibited all of Erev Pesach.

18. See also *Mishna Berura* 471:20; *Peninei Halakha, Pesach* 13:6, n. 7. It should be noted that some Sephardic *poskim* forbid eating cooked matza (see *Ben Ish Chai*, First Year, *Tzav* 26; see also Rav Mordechai Eliyahu, *Hilchot Chagim* 8:2, who rules that it if it still has the appearance of matza, it is forbidden).

19. It should also be noted that although Chazal caution against eating *mezonot* products in the late afternoon on Erev Pesach to ensure one has an appetite for the matza, it is not necessary to starve. Many people today are often ravenous by the time they actually reach the stage of eating matza in the Seder, following the first part of the Seder and Magid, which can take several hours. For such individuals, it is worthwhile to consider eating a light meal, such as soup and fish, eggs, or the like,

Matza Ashira

At the very beginning of *Magid* (the narrative portion of the *Seder Pesach*), we directly identify the matza as *lechem oni*, translated and interpreted alternatively as "the bread of affliction," "poor bread," or "the poor man's bread." The identity of matza as fitting one or more of these roles is a central theme in several statements of Chazal and thematic essays by later thinkers.[20] The term itself is taken from a verse in ***Devarim***.

13. דברים | טז:ג

לֹא תֹאכַל עָלָיו חָמֵץ שִׁבְעַת יָמִים תֹּאכַל עָלָיו **מַצּוֹת לֶחֶם עֹנִי** כִּי בְחִפָּזוֹן יָצָאתָ מֵאֶרֶץ מִצְרַיִם לְמַעַן תִּזְכֹּר אֶת יוֹם צֵאתְךָ מֵאֶרֶץ מִצְרַיִם כֹּל יְמֵי חַיֶּיךָ:

ת Devarim 16:3

You shall not eat leaven with it; for seven days you shall eat with it ***matzot, lechem oni,*** for in haste you went out of the land of Egypt, so that you shall remember the day when you went out of the land of Egypt all the days of your life.

The **Gemara (*Masechet Pesachim*)** assumes that matza qualifies as "poor bread" only when it is made from literally the barest and simplest of ingredients, i.e., water and flour. Accordingly, the Gemara states that if flour is kneaded with other liquids, this does not yield "poor bread" but rather *matza ashira*, "rich" matza, which is not true matza and cannot be used for the mitzva of eating matza.

14. מסכת פסחים לה.-לה:

אמר רבה בר בר חנה אמר ריש לקיש: עיסה שנילושה ביין ושמן ודבש אין חייבין על חימוצה כרת. יתיב רב פפא ורב הונא בריה דרב יהושע קמיה דרב אידי בר אבין ויתיב רב אידי בר אבין וקא מנמנם, א"ל רב הונא בריה דרב יהושע לרב פפא: מאי טעמא דריש לקיש?

א"ל, דאמר קרא, "לא תאכל עליו חמץ [וגו']", דברים שאדם יוצא בהן ידי חובתו במצה חייבין על חימוצו כרת, והא

ת Masechet Pesachim 35a–35b

Rabba bar bar Chana said that **Reish Lakish said:** With regard to **dough that was kneaded with wine, oil, or honey, one is not liable** to receive ***karet*** **for** eating it in **its "leavened"** state, since these liquids will not cause the dough to be leavened, according to the halacha. **Rav Pappa and Rav Huna, son of Rav Yehoshua, were sitting before Rav Idi bar Avin, and Rav Idi bar Avin was sitting and dozing** as his students conversed. **Rav Huna, son of Rav Yehoshua, said to Rav Pappa: What is the reason of Reish Lakish,** who maintains that one is not liable to receive *karet* for this type of leavening?

Rav Pappa **said to him: The verse states: "You shall not eat leaven with it;** for seven days you shall eat with it matzot, *lechem oni*, etc." In light of the juxtaposition of leavened bread and *matza*, Reish Lakish compares these two types of bread: With regard to those **substances** through **which a person fulfills his obligation to** eat ***matza*****, one is liable** to receive ***karet*** **for** eating them in their **leavened** state. **And** with regard

---

towards the end of the afternoon to ensure they can enjoy the first part of the Seder properly and still have an appetite for the matza when it is eaten.

20. See the many references to this verse in the Gemara cited by *Torah Temima* (*Devarim* 16:3).

הואיל ואין אדם יוצא בה ידי חובתו דהויא ליה מצה עשירה אין חייבין על חימוצה כרת...

איתער בהו רב אידי בר אבין, אמר להו: דרדקי היינו טעמא דריש לקיש, משום דהוו להו מי פירות [לה:] ומי פירות אין מחמיצין.

to **this** dough, which was kneaded with wine, oil, or honey, **since a person does not fulfill his obligation** to eat *matza* **with it,** as **it is** called **rich,** i.e., enhanced, ***matza,*** **one is not liable** to receive ***karet*** **for** eating it in **its leavened** state on Passover. *Matza* is called the bread of affliction, or the poor man's bread, a description that does not apply to dough prepared with wine, oil, or honey…

At this point **Rav Idi bar Avin woke up,** due to their discussion, and **said to them: Children, this is the reasoning of Reish Lakish:** One is not liable to receive *karet* for eating dough kneaded with oil or honey, **because** oil and honey **are** considered **fruit juices,** [35b] **and fruit juice does not** cause dough to be **leavened.** Therefore, dough prepared with these liquids is not considered full-fledged leavened bread.

However, the Gemara later (36a) cites a dispute among the *Tanna'im* in which it is clear that there is a danger of dough becoming leavened when it has been kneaded with these same liquids. The *Rishonim* debate how these details should be understood. There, Rashi comments that this demonstrates that although such dough is not true, proper *chametz,* it is nonetheless included in the category of *chametz nuksheh,* which is forbidden only secondarily.[21] Most other *Rishonim* agree that the issue is one of *chametz nuksheh,* but in their view, this would be only if the flour was mixed with **both water and other liquids.** But if **no water** was involved, the dough would not be *chametz* at all (and, correspondingly, it could never become *chametz*).

Thus, the *Rishonim* debate the halacha regarding two issues surrounding *matza ashira*: (1) What if flour is mixed with a combination of **water and other liquids**? Is the resulting dough also something which cannot be used for proper matza (and likewise, can never become true *chametz*)? (2) When something is categorized as *matza ashira,* is this something which one may readily eat on Pesach? The assorted opinions are summarized by the ***Tur.***

15. טור | או"ח תסב

מי פירות אין מחמיצין. ורבו בזה הדיעות. לרש"י אין חייבין על חימוצה כרת, אבל חמץ נוקשה הוי, ואפילו במי פירות לבדן אסור ללוש. ולרב אלפס אפילו במי פירות עם מים מותר ללוש מליל ראשון ואילך. ויש אוסרים ללוש במי פירות עם המים אף מליל ראשון ואילך...

ו Tur, Orach Chaim 462

Fruit juice does not cause leavening. But there are many opinions on this matter. According to Rashi, its "leaven" is not subject to *karet,* but it qualifies as *chametz nuksheh,* and it is forbidden to knead even in fruit juice alone.[22] According to the Rif, it is permitted to knead even with water and fruit juice, from the first night and on. And some forbid kneading with fruit juice together with water even from the first night and on…

21. On *chametz nuksheh,* see *shiur* 1 in this volume.
22. Someone who eats a full measure of leavened *chametz* on Pesach is subject to the divine punishment of *karet* (excision), whose exact nature is debated by the commentators. Rashi's reference to *chametz nuksheh* indicates that this leavened product is not classified as proper *chametz* and is thus not subject to the severe terms of eating normal *chametz,* i.e., *karet.* And yet it is nonetheless forbidden (*mide'oraita*) to eat *chametz nuksheh* of this kind.

ור"י פירש דמי פירות בלא מים אין מחמיצין כלל, ומותר ללוש בהן מליל ראשון ואילך, אבל בליל ראשון ושני אין יוצאין בהם ידי חובת מצה, דהוה ליה מצה עשירה.

ומי ביצים היה מסתפק רש"י אם מחמיצין, ורבינו תם היה מתיר, ולזה הסכים אדוני אבי הרא"ש ז"ל.

ומי פירות עם מים, הוי חמץ נוקשה ואין בו כרת, אבל ממהר להחמיץ יותר משאר עיסה, הלכך אין ללוש בהם, ואם לש בהם פסק בהלכות גדולות כר"ג דאמר ישרף מיד, והרי"ץ גיאת ז"ל פסק כחכמים דאמרי יאפה מיד, ולזה הסכים אדוני אבי הרא"ש ז"ל.

וכל משקין הוו בכלל מי פירות...

The Ri explains that fruit juice without water does not cause leavening at all, and it is permitted to knead with it from the first night and on. However, on the first and second nights, people cannot fulfill their obligation [to eat] matza with it, as it is *matza ashira*.

Regarding the liquid of an egg, Rashi was uncertain if this causes leavening. But Rabbeinu Tam permitted, and my father and master the Rosh agreed.

Regarding fruit juice with water, [the dough] is *chametz nuksheh* and it is not subject to *karet*. However, it leavens more quickly than other dough, and thus one should not knead with it.[23] But if one did knead with it, the *Halachot Gedolot* (*Behag*) ruled in accordance with Rabban Gamliel, who said it must be incinerated immediately. But the Ritz Giat ruled in accordance with the Rabbis, who said that it must be baked immediately [and may then be eaten], and my father and master the Rosh agreed with this.

And all liquids fall into the category of "fruit juice"...

The ***Shulchan Aruch*** rules that *matza* made from fruit juice and other liquids may be readily eaten on Pesach, but it is not fit for the mitzva of matza. The **Rema** notes that Ashkenazim are not accustomed to use it on Pesach, except for those whose health requires it.

16. שולחן ערוך | או"ח תסב:א-ד

א. מי פירות בלא מים אין מחמיצין כלל. ומותר לאכול בפסח מצה שנלושה במי פירות אפילו שהתה כל היום, אבל אין יוצא בה ידי חובתו מפני שהיא מצה עשירה וקרא כתיב לחם עוני (דברים טז, ג).

ב. מי פירות עם מים ממהרים להחמיץ יותר משאר עיסה הילכך אין ללוש בהם; ואם לש בהם, יאפה מיד.

ג. מותר ללוש ביין אף על פי שאי אפשר לו בלא טיפת מים שנופלת בשעת הבציר... הואיל וכבר נתבטלו המים ביין קודם שלשו העיסה.

ד. מי בצים ושאר משקים, כולם הוו בכלל מי פירות.

א Shulchan Aruch, Orach Chaim 462:1–4

1. Fruit juice without water does not cause leavening at all. And it is permitted to eat matza kneaded from fruit juice, even if it sat all day [and was not hastily baked within 18 minutes]. But one cannot fulfill his obligation [to eat matza] with it, because it is "rich matza," and the verse states, "poor bread."

2. Fruit juice with water hastens leavening more than other dough, and thus one should not knead with it. But if one did knead with it, it should be baked immediately.

3. It is permitted to knead with wine, even though it is impossible that no drop of water fell into it during the harvest... since the water is already negated by the wine before the dough is kneaded.

4. Regarding liquid from an egg, and other liquids, they are included in fruit juice.

---

23. This is the same opinion as the third opinion mentioned in the first paragraph above, according to which kneading water and fruit juice is forbidden because the resulting dough may be *chametz nuksheh*.

הגה: ובמדינות אלו אין נוהגין ללוש במי פירות... ואין לשנות אם לא בשעת הדחק לצרכי חולה או זקן הצריך לזה.

Rema: In these countries, we are not accustomed to kneading with fruit juice... And one must not deviate, except for extenuating circumstances, for the needs of someone who is ill or elderly, who needs it.

Accordingly, the *Shulchan Aruch* readily endorses using *matza ashira* without hesitation on Pesach. But in Ashkenazic practice, although it is not assumed to be proper *chametz*, *matza ashira* is not used due to the concern that it might be categorized as *chametz nuksheh*, except by those who have heightened need for it since it is more easily eaten.[24]

Similarly, the ***Shulchan Aruch*** permits eating *matza ashira* until the late afternoon on Erev Pesach. And the **Rema** underscores that the prohibition to eat matza on Erev Pesach does not apply to *matza ashira*, since it may not be used for the mitzva of matza at the Seder.

17. שולחן ערוך | או"ח תעא:ב

א Shulchan Aruch, Orach Chaim 471:2

וקודם שעה עשירית מותר לאכול מצה עשירה.

הגה: אבל מצה שיוצאין בה בלילה אסורים לאכול כל יום ארבעה עשר.

Before the tenth hour [of the day on Erev Pesach], it is permitted to eat *matza ashira.*

Rema: But matza with which one fulfills the mitzva at night is forbidden to eat the entire day of the fourteenth.

The Rema does not directly address the status of *matza ashira* on Erev Pesach here. However, as noted above, he comments that *matza ashira* is avoided wholesale in Ashkenazic communities, with only minimal exceptions. Thus, we are left wondering; if indeed, fundamentally, *matza ashira* is not considered true *chametz*, would it be permitted for Ashkenazim on Erev Pesach? As recorded by **Tosafot,** Rabbeinu Tam was accustomed to eating *matza ashira* on Erev Pesach (until the late afternoon, as explained below),[25] but that was long before the Rema. The ***Aruch HaShulchan*** holds[26] that there is no specific need to refrain from eating *matza ashira* on Erev Pesach. However, according to many contemporary *poskim*, the Ashkenazic custom to refrain from eating *matza ashira* is in full force from the time that *chametz* becomes forbidden on Erev Pesach.[27]

It should also be noted that even some Sephardic *poskim*, such as **Rav Mordechai Eliyahu,** recommend against using *matza ashira* on Pesach, because it is difficult to entirely prevent the addition of water during production.[28] Furthermore, Rav Eliyahu forbids entirely the use of certain commercially produced cookies in Israel using wine and other chemicals, which in his opinion, have the halachic status of water. If so, the products may indeed be true *chametz*. However, in the view of **Rav Ovadia Yosef,** even commercially produced cookies such as these remain permitted on Pesach according to the *Shulchan Aruch*.[29]

---

24. See *Aruch HaShulchan, Orach Chaim* 462:4–5.
25. Tosafot, *Pesachim* 99b.
26. *Aruch HaShulchan*, O.C. 444:5, 471:3.
27. Responsa *Igrot Moshe*, O.C. 1:155. See also *Peninei Halakha, Pesach* 13:7; and Rav Dov Lior (www.yeshiva.org.il/ask/26141). For a different, although speculative, view, see https://daf-yomi.com/DYItemDetails.aspx?itemId=55769.
28. *Hilchot Chagim* 4:14.
29. See *Peninei Halakha, Pesach* 8:1, n. 1 and *Oholei Halacha*, p. 70. For further discussion of the controversy regarding the cookies in Israel produced with wine, see www.kosharot.co.il/index2.php?id=44542&lang=HEB and www.kosharot.co.il/index2.php?id=44583&lang=HEB.

Finally, it should be emphasized that part and parcel of the classification of alternative-ingredient doughs as *matza ashira* is an acknowledgment that not only is such matza never *chametz*, but it **cannot be used for the mitzva of eating matza,** either. This is true according to both Ashkenazim and Sephardim, in accordance with the clear rulings of the Gemara.

Baking Matza on Erev Pesach

In ancient times, many had the custom to bake matza for their Pesach Seder only after midday on Erev Pesach, the proper time for the *korban Pesach*, because the Torah mentions the *korban Pesach* together with the eating of matza (*Devarim* 16:2–3). Therefore, the matza should be prepared only after the time at which the *korban Pesach* may be offered. Thus, the ***Shulchan Aruch*** also writes that it is the standard practice to bake matza for the *Seder* only in the afternoon of Erev Pesach.

18. שולחן ערוך | או"ח תנח:א

נוהגים שלא ללוש מצת מצוה בערב פסח עד אחר שש שעות שהוא זמן הקרבת קרבן פסח.

א Shulchan Aruch, Orach Chaim 458:1

We are accustomed on Erev Pesach not to knead the matza for the mitzva until after six [daytime] hours [have passed], which is the time of the offering of the *korban Pesach*.

However, the *poskim* accepted that matza baked before Erev Pesach is also valid for the *Seder*. This is because:

1. The *pesukim* referenced above relate to the eating of the matza rather than the baking.
2. As explained by the ***Mishna Berura,*** even if matza is baked when there is still *chametz* in the house, people can be trusted to bake the matza in a leaven-sterile way.

19. משנה ברורה | או"ח תנח:א, ג–ד

א. **נוהגים וכו'** – משמע דאינו אלא מנהג והמנהג נסמך משום דאיתקש אכילת מצה לקרבן פסח דכתיב וזבחת פסח לה' אלהיך וגו' שבעת ימים תאכל עליו מצות וגו' ואמרינן כמו ששחיטת הפסח היה אחר שש כן עשיית מצות של מצוה אחר שש שעות.

אבל מעצם הדין הוכיחו הפוסקים דאין לחוש לזה דעיקר היקש נאמר לענין אכילת מצה בלילה הראשונה שיהא זהיר לאכול קודם חצות כמו הפסח שהוא נאכל עד חצות

א Mishna Berura, Orach Chaim 458:1, 3–4

1. **We are accustomed, etc.** – This implies that it is only a custom, and the custom is based on a halachic connection between [consecutive verses concerning] eating matza and the *korban Pesach*, as it is written, "You shall slaughter the Passover sacrifice to the Lord, your God… for seven days you shall eat with it matzot…" (*Devarim* 16:2–3). And we say that just as the slaughtering of the *Pesach* was after six [i.e. midday], so too the making of the matza of the mitzva is after six hours.

But regarding the strict halacha, the *poskim* demonstrated that one need not be concerned for this. The primary connection was stated regarding eating matza on the first night, i.e., that one should be careful to eat before midnight, just like the *Pesach*, which must be eaten before midnight,

וכמבואר לקמן בסימן תע"ז **אבל לא לענין עשיית המצה** ועל כן בדיעבד אם אפה המצה קודם שש ואפילו חודש או שני חדשים קודם פסח ועשאן לשם מצה כשר.

ג. **עד אחר וכו' –** ...והנה רוב ישראל אין נוהגין ליזהר אפילו במצת מצוה ללוש בערב פסח כי אם איזה מהם וחפשתי באחרונים ומצאתי בבגדי ישע טעם להליץ בעד המנהג מפני שיש כמה דעות שאפילו בערב פסח במשהו כאשר מבואר לעיל בסימן תנ"ב וזה קשה ליזהר שלא ימצאו אף משהו חמץ בהחטים שלא יהיו מצומחים ועל כן אופין מקודם כדי שיתבטל החמץ. ובמאמר מרדכי מצאתי שכתב וזה לשונו האידנא מקילין הרבה בדבר מפני הדוחק זולת קצת שנזהרין בזה ללוש ולאפות אחר שש המצות שיוצאין בהם בשני הלילות וכן ראוי לעשות.

as explained later, **but not regarding making the matza.**[30] Therefore, *bedi'eved*, if one baked the matza before [midday], and even one or two months before Pesach, and one made them for the sake of [the mitzva of] matza, it is valid.

3. **Until after, etc.** – ...Most Jews are not accustomed to being careful even to knead the matza of the mitzva on Erev Pesach, except for a few of them. And I looked among the *Acharonim* and found in the *Bigdei Yesha* a reason to defend the practice. For according to several opinions, even on Erev Pesach [a mixture of] trace amounts [of *chametz* would render food forbidden], as explained above, and it is difficult to be cautious that there will be no *chametz* whatsoever among the wheat that has not previously blossomed.[31] Therefore, we bake earlier so that [any trace amounts of] *chametz* would be null. And I found in *Ma'amar Mordechai* that he wrote, "Now, we are very lenient in this matter, because of the difficulty, except few who are careful about this, to knead and bake the matzas with which they fulfill [the mitzva] on the two nights only after [midday]. And it is proper to do so."

Today, most people refrain from baking matza on Erev Pesach, due to the considerable effort and logistical challenges in doing such a delicate and demanding task during some of the busiest hours of the entire year, in addition to the considerations mentioned by the *Mishna Berura* (see *Peninei Halakha, Pesach* 13:8).

---

30. There is a dispute whether the *korban Pesach* must be eaten before midnight or before dawn, and the latest time to eat matza is equivalent to that of *korban Pesach*. Many *poskim* maintain that ideally, the time of midnight should be followed. See *Masechet Pesachim* 120b, *Shulchan Aruch*, O.C. 477:1 and *Bi'ur Halacha*, and *Tzurba M'Rabanan*, volume 1, *shiur* 10, sources 35–38.

31. Regarding wheat kernels which have blossomed, they are assumed to be true *chametz*, and flour ground from them may not be used in Pesach foods. Unlike in many other areas of the laws of *kashrut*, in which small quantities of unkosher food would be considered null when constituting less than 1/60 of a mixture (and when they have been only inadvertently added to the whole mixture), even trace amounts of *chametz* render mixtures forbidden on Pesach. This is true when the *chametz* falls into the mixture on Pesach itself, but if it is mixed in well before Pesach, then trace amounts would be considered null. The question here is whether Erev Pesach has the status of Pesach itself, in which case matza baked on Erev Pesach with trace amounts of blossomed wheat or other *chametz* is forbidden; or if Erev Pesach is considered "prior to Pesach," in which case matza baked with trace amounts of *chametz* would be permitted for eating on Pesach.

The Holiday of Erev Pesach

Although the Yom Tov of Pesach begins only with the onset of the 15th of Nisan, the Torah conspicuously enumerates the previous day – the 14th of Nisan – in its list of the major festivals of the year in ***Sefer Vayikra.***

20. ויקרא | כג:ד–ז

ד. אֵלֶּה מוֹעֲדֵי ה' מִקְרָאֵי קֹדֶשׁ אֲשֶׁר תִּקְרְאוּ אֹתָם בְּמוֹעֲדָם:

ה. בַּחֹדֶשׁ הָרִאשׁוֹן בְּאַרְבָּעָה עָשָׂר לַחֹדֶשׁ בֵּין הָעַרְבָּיִם פֶּסַח לַה':

ו. וּבַחֲמִשָּׁה עָשָׂר יוֹם לַחֹדֶשׁ הַזֶּה חַג הַמַּצּוֹת לַה' שִׁבְעַת יָמִים מַצּוֹת תֹּאכֵלוּ:

ז. בַּיּוֹם הָרִאשׁוֹן מִקְרָא קֹדֶשׁ יִהְיֶה לָכֶם כָּל מְלֶאכֶת עֲבֹדָה לֹא תַעֲשׂוּ:

ת **Vayikra 23:4–7**

4. These are the Lord's appointed [holy days], holy occasions, which you shall designate in their appointed time.

5. In the first month, on the fourteenth of the month, in the afternoon, [you shall sacrifice] the Passover offering to the Lord.

6. And on the fifteenth day of that month is the Festival of Matzot to the Lord; you shall eat unleavened cakes for a seven-day period.

7. On the first day, there shall be a holy occasion for you; you shall not perform any work of labor.

From one perspective, it is only natural for the Torah to mention the *korban Pesach* before introducing the Yom Tov itself, because the *Seder Pesach* is built around the fullest experience of eating the sacrifice and understanding its significance. The offering is slaughtered and prepared on the afternoon of the fourteenth, and it is eaten only at night. It is for this reason that the phrase "on the fourteenth… the Passover" is understood to mean: on the fourteenth **you shall sacrifice** the Passover. Read in this way, the fourteenth derives its significance from being the day the offering **is sacrificed.**[32]

Yet the verse does not say this directly. In its simple meaning, it is saying: the fourteenth **is** the Passover. Accordingly, the fourteenth is termed the proper "Pesach," and the holiday beginning on the fifteenth is referred to here as "the Festival of Matzot."[33] While these days are fundamentally connected, and all agree that the Pesach is eaten on the fifteenth, nonetheless, the text here suggests that the fourteenth itself also has the characteristic of a festival.

Given this background, we can better understand the ruling of the **Gemara (*Masechet Pesachim*)** that *melacha* was forbidden after midday on Erev Pesach, as this is the time for offering the *korban Pesach*.

32. Rashi, *Vayikra* 23:5.

33. Chizkuni, *Vayikra* 23:5. See www.torahweb.org/torah/2004/moadim/rros_Pesach.html and www.etzion.org.il/en/tanakh/torah/sefer-shemot/parashat-bo/bo-Pesach-and-chag-hamatzot.

21. מסכת פסחים נ:

מאי איריא ערבי פסחים? אפילו ערבי שבתות וערבי ימים טובים נמי! דתניא: העושה מלאכה בערבי שבתות וימים טובים, מן המנחה ולמעלה – אינו רואה סימן ברכה לעולם.

התם מן המנחה ולמעלה הוא דאסור, סמוך למנחה – לא. הכא – מחצות. אי נמי: התם – סימן ברכה הוא דלא חזי, אבל שמותי – לא משמתינן ליה. – הכא שמותי נמי משמתינן ליה.

ח Masechet Pesachim 50b

The Mishna (*Pesachim* 4:1) notes that in some places, there was a custom to refrain from performing *melacha* on the morning of Erev Pesach. The Gemara asks: **Why** discuss this prohibition **particularly** with regard to **Passover eves? It** is prohibited to perform labor **even** on **Shabbat eves and Festival eves as well, as it was taught** in a *baraita*: **One who performs labor on Shabbat eves and Festival eves from *mincha*** time **onward never sees a sign of blessing** from this work.

The Gemara answers that there is a difference between the two situations: **There,** in the case of Shabbat and Festivals, performing labor **is prohibited from *mincha*** time **onward;** it is **not** prohibited **adjacent to *mincha*** time, i.e., just before it. **Here,** in the case of Passover eve, it is prohibited **from midday. Alternatively, there,** on Shabbat eve and Festival eve, it is **a sign of blessing that he does not see; however,** the Sages **do not excommunicate him** for performing labor. **Here,** in the case of Passover eve, the Sages **also excommunicate him** for performing labor, as it is explicitly prohibited.[34]

Accordingly, the commentators and *poskim* understood that it is forbidden to perform *melacha* on Erev Pesach after midday. However, this does not mean *melacha* on Erev Pesach is defined by the same standards as those which apply on Shabbat, or even Yom Tov. As explained by the **Rambam,** the status of *melacha* on the afternoon of Erev Pesach is comparable to that of *Chol HaMo'ed.*[35]

22. רמב"ם | הל' יום טוב ח:יח

לפיכך יום ארבעה עשר בניסן אסור בעשיית מלאכה מדברי סופרים כמו חולו של מועד, והוא קל מחולו של מועד, ואינו אסור אלא מחצי היום ולמעלה שהוא זמן השחיטה, אבל מהנץ החמה עד חצי היום תלוי במנהג.

ר Rambam, Hilchot Yom Tov 8:18

Therefore, the performance of labor on the fourteenth of Nisan is forbidden by rabbinic decree, as on *Chol HaMo'ed*,[36] and it [this day] is more lenient than *Chol HaMo'ed*. What's more, it is forbidden to perform labor only from midday onward, for this is the time when the sacrifice is offered, but from sunrise until midday, [the permissibility of labor] depends upon local custom.

On the basis of this ruling, the ***Shulchan Aruch*** also rules that it is forbidden to perform *melacha* after midday on Erev Pesach.

---

34. The subject of performing *melacha* on Friday afternoon was discussed in volume 16, *shiur* 1. As discussed there, opinions differ as to whether the restrictions on *melacha* begin at *chatzot* or at *plag hamincha*. Those two opinions stem from the two approaches suggested in the Gemara cited here.
35. For this reason, any food preparation is entirely permitted, like *Chol HaMo'ed*.
36. The prohibition of *melacha* on *Chol HaMo'ed* was discussed in volume 23, *shiur* 5, where multiple opinions were brought as to whether it is biblical or rabbinic in nature, or somewhere in between. The Rambam here clearly holds that it is entirely rabbinic.

23. שולחן ערוך | או"ח תסח:א-ג

א. העושה מלאכה בערב פסח מחצות ולמעלה, היו משמתין אותו. ואפילו לעשות בחנם אסור...

ב. במה דברים אמורים, כשעושה מלאכה להשתכר, (או בחנם והוא מלאכה גמורה לתפור בגדים ממש), אבל מתקן הוא כליו ליום טוב; וכן מי שכותב ספרים לעצמו דרך לימודו, מותר.

ג. קודם חצות, מקום שנהגו לעשות מלאכה, עושין. מקום שנהגו שלא לעשות, אין עושין.

הגה: ולדידן מקום שנהגו שלא לעשות; ודוקא מלאכות גמורות, אבל שאר מלאכות אפילו מנהג ליכא.

א Shulchan Aruch, Orach Chaim 468:1–3

1. If someone would perform *melacha* on Erev Pesach after midday, they would excommunicate him. Even doing so without pay is forbidden…

2. Under what circumstances is this stated? When one is performing the labor to be paid (or for free, if it is true labor [such as] sewing new garments). However, one may repair his items for Yom Tov. Similarly, regarding one who writes personal notebooks over the course of his learning, this is permitted.

3. Prior to midday, in a place where they are accustomed to perform labor, people may do so. In a place where they are accustomed not to perform labor, people may not do so.

Rema: Regarding our communities, it is a place where they are accustomed not to perform labor. And this is specifically regarding complete labor, but regarding other labors, there is not even a custom [to refrain].[37]

In clarifying which labors are forbidden on Erev Pesach, the Rema writes that it is permitted to perform small repairs or adjustments, but not *melacha gemura* ("true" or "complete" labor). Thus, it is permitted to repair an old garment, but it is forbidden to sew a new garment. The ***Mishna Berura*** further explains the parameters of forbidden labor and work done for pay.

24. משנה ברורה | או"ח תסח:ו-ז, ט

ו. **מלאכה להשתכר** - ובזה אפילו אינו מלאכה גמורה אסור ואפילו אם הוא לצורך יום טוב. כתבו האחרונים דפועל שאין לו מה יאכל מותר לעשות מלאכה להשתכר.

ז. **והוא מלאכה גמורה** - ובזה אסור אפילו לצורך יום טוב. וכיבוס כליו הוא בכלל מלאכה גמורה ואסור. ולכובסת עכו"ם מותר בכל גווני ליתן אחר חצות. כתבו האחרונים **דכל מה שמותר לעשות בחולו של מועד** כגון דבר האבד או שעושה מעשה הדיוט ולא מעשה אומן ויש בו צורך המועד וכיוצא בזה

א Mishna Berura, Orach Chaim 468:6–7, 9

6. **Labor to be paid** – In this case, even if it is not true labor, it is forbidden, even if it is needed for Yom Tov. The *Acharonim* write in the case of a laborer who does not have anything to eat, it is permitted to work in order to be paid.

7. **If it is true labor** – In this case, it is forbidden even if it is needed for Yom Tov. Laundering one's clothing is included in true labor and is forbidden. But it is permitted in all cases for a gentile launderer [even] after midday. The *Acharonim* wrote that regarding **whatever is permitted to do on *Chol HaMo'ed*** – such as matters of [substantial loss] or if one does an act in an unskilled way, as opposed to skilled labor, when there is need for the festival, etc.,

---

37. Although the Rema writes that the custom in his area was not to engage in true *melacha* in the morning of Erev Pesach, the *Mishna Berura* (12) writes that many communities do not practice such a custom and engage in *melacha* normally. Today, the nearly universal custom is to be lenient in this regard (see *Aruch HaShulchan*, O.C. 468:5; *Halichot Shlomo* 8:5; *Oholei Halacha*, Pesach, p. 188).

משאר דברים המותרים בחולו של מועד כל שכן **שמותרים בערב פסח אחר חצות.**

aside from the other things which are permitted on *Chol HaMo'ed* – all the more so, they **are permitted on Erev Pesach after midday.**[38]

ח. **מתקן הוא כליו ליו"ט** – ...וכתבו האחרונים דאפילו מעשה אומן מותר בזה.

8. **One may repair his items for Yom Tov** – The *Acharonim* write that even the work of a craftsman is permitted for this.

ט. **לעצמו דרך לימודו** – דכיון שדרך לימודו ולעצמו הוא כותב אינה נראית כמלאכה גמורה שבודאי אינו מתכוין לכתיבה גמורה והגונה והוי כתיקון בעלמא שהתירו לצורך המועד. ולאחרים אפילו בחנם אסור בזה.

9. **Personal notebooks over the course of his learning** – Since it is over the course of his learning, and he is writing for himself, it does not have the appearance of true labor, for he certainly does not intend for it to be true and proper writing. Thus, it is like mere "repair," which they permitted for the needs of the *Mo'ed*. But for others, even for free, it is forbidden in this manner.

Thus, according to the *Mishna Berura*, it is forbidden to perform any type of *melacha* after midday (unless one has no money to purchase food), and it is forbidden to perform true *melacha* even when done for free (except for in cases such as a loss or unskilled *melacha*).

The ***Mishna Berura*** also writes that after midday, one must stop performing even *melacha* that one began before that time.

25. משנה ברורה | או"ח תסח:לב

עושין עד חצות – ומכיון שהגיע חצות מחוייב להפסיק באמצע מלאכה.

א Mishna Berura, Orach Chaim 468:32

Performed until midday – Once midday comes, one is required to cease [these three crafts] in the middle of the labor.

Contemporary Sephardic *poskim* agree with the *Mishna Berura*'s rulings. **Rav Mordechai Eliyahu** writes that the status of *melacha* after midday on Erev Pesach is much like that of *Chol HaMo'ed*. Nonetheless, although certain labor is permitted, and it is likewise permitted to make purchases and sales during this time,[39] it is proper to be stringent regarding these in the last quarter of the daylight hours.

26. מאמר מרדכי | מועדים וימים ח:יא–יב

יא. **מלאכות מותרות** – מחצות היום ואילך אסור בעשיית מלאכה. ומותר לעשות רק מה שמותר לעשות בחול המועד, כגון: דבר האבד, או מלאכה שאינה מעשה אומן ויש בה צורך הפסח, וכן פועל עני שאין לו מה לאכול, יכול לעבוד אחר חצות. וכן מותר למכור

פ Ma'amar Mordechai, Mo'adim V'yamim 8:11–12

11. **Permitted work** – From midday and on, performing labor is forbidden. And it is permitted to perform only what is permitted to perform on *Chol HaMo'ed*, namely: matters of loss, or work which is not skilled labor and is necessary for Pesach; and a poor laborer who has nothing to eat may work after midday. It is similarly permitted to sell

38. The parameters and guidelines for which *melacha* is permitted and forbidden on *Chol HaMo'ed* was discussed in volume 23, *shiurim* 5–6. In essence, *melacha* for *Chol HaMo'ed* is generally defined as activities that are time consuming and not quick and easily done. For this reason, most home improvement activities would be forbidden on *Chol HaMo'ed* and Erev Pesach, while striking a match or turning on a light are usually permitted when needed.

39. See volume 16, *shiur* 1, where it is explained that commerce is not treated as complete *melacha.*

ולקנות אחר חצות. וטוב להחמיר גם בדברים אלו סמוך לכניסת החג משעת מנחה קטנה ולמעלה.

יב. מותר לצחצח נעלים בערב פסח אחר חצות. מותר לגהץ או לתקן בגד שנקרע קצת לצורך החג.

and purchase after midday. But it is good to be stringent in these matters also close to the onset of the Yom Tov, from the time of *mincha ketana* (after nine daylight "hours") and beyond.

12. It is permitted to polish shoes on Erev Pesach after midday. It is permitted to iron or to repair a garment which has been lightly torn, for the needs of the Yom Tov.

Personal Grooming

Certain acts of personal grooming, including haircutting, shaving, and trimming nails, are also subject to restrictions after midday on Erev Pesach. In one respect, these acts qualify as *melacha*, and they are restricted for that reason. However, as was discussed with regard to *Chol HaMo'ed*, there is an additional consideration; to prevent people from neglecting to groom themselves before Yom Tov, Chazal forbade these grooming activities on *Chol HaMo'ed*. Similarly, haircutting and shaving are among those *melachot* which are permitted only before midday on Erev Pesach, as summarized by the ***Shulchan Aruch.***[40]

27. שולחן ערוך | או"ח תסח:ה

שלשה אומניות בלבד הם שמתחילים בהם במקום שנהגו לעשות ועושין עד חצות ואלו הם, החייטים והספרים והכובסים...

הגה: ויש מקילין לומר ששלשה אומניות הנזכרים מתחילין ועושין עד חצות אפילו במקום שנהגו שלא לעשות...

א Shulchan Aruch, Orach Chaim 468:5

Only three crafts may be started where the people are accustomed to perform [*melacha*], and they may be done until midday. The following [may perform their crafts]: tailors, barbers, and launderers…

Rema: Some are lenient to say that the three enumerated crafts may be started and performed until midday even in a place where they are accustomed not to perform [*melacha*]…

The ***Mishna Berura*** explains the leniencies for personal grooming and caring for one's clothing.

28. משנה ברורה | או"ח תסח:כו

ואלו הן החייטים וכו' – רצונו לומר אם הן לצורך יום טוב ולא הקילו אלא באלו מפני שהעם צריכים להם הרבה.

א Mishna Berura, Orach Chaim 468:26

The following: tailors, etc. – This means [these are permitted] if they are necessary for the festival. [Chazal] permitted only these because the people have great need for them.

The ***Aruch HaShulchan*** and other *Acharonim* agree with the *Mishna Berura* that a person may not cut hair after midday on Erev Pesach, but some note that it is permitted to have a haircut from a non-Jew at that time.

40. In extenuating circumstances, some people are permitted to shave and cut hair on *Chol HaMo'ed*, and the same leniency applies after midday on Erev Pesach (*Mishna Berura* 468:7).

MELACHA ON EREV PESACH

	"True" *Melacha*	"Light" *Melacha* Necessary for Yom Tov, Commerce	Labor for Wages	Laundry	Shaving and Haircuts
Before midday	Permitted, in accordance with local custom **(Mishna, Rambam, *Shulchan Aruch*)**				
After midday	Forbidden **(Mishna, Rambam, *Shulchan Aruch*)** One must stop forbidden *melacha* even in the middle of a task **(*Mishna Berura*)**	Small *melacha* necessary for Yom Tov is permitted **(*Shulchan Aruch*)**	It is permitted to work for hire if one is destitute **(*Mishna Berura*)**	One must not launder clothing after midday **(*Shulchan Aruch, Mishna Berura*)**	One must not cut hair after midday **(*Shulchan Aruch, Mishna Berura*)**
				Some permit laundering clothing in a washing machine after midday on Erev Pesach **(*Yalkut Yosef*)**; some forbid **(*Piskei Teshuvot*)**, and others are uncertain **(*Shemirat Shabbat K'hilchata*)**	Some forbid shaving oneself at this time even today **(*Piskei Teshvuot*)**, while others permit (although it is preferable to do so earlier) **(*Peninei Halakha*, Rav Mordechai Eliyahu)**
					In cases of need, there are leniencies for cutting hair, especially for a woman before immersion or for modesty **(*Piskei Teshuvot*)**
After ¾ of the daylight hours	It is proper to avoid these activities after ¾ of the daylight hours have elapsed **(Rav Mordechai Eliyahu)**				

Forbidden Permitted Somewhere in-between

29. ערוך השלחן | או"ח תסח:ג

...להסתפר אחר חצות – אסור על ידי ישראל, אבל על ידי אינו יהודי – מותר. ואפילו ליטול צפרנים – אסור אחר חצות. ויש מתירים בנטילת צפרנים אחר חצות כששכח ליטלן קודם חצות, דאין זה מלאכה גמורה לעניין ערב פסח. ויש מי שאוסר להסתפר אפילו על ידי אינו יהודי אחר חצות, משום דגם המסתפר מסייע קצת בהטיית ראשו. ואינו עיקר, דמה בכך?

א Aruch HaShulchan, Orach Chaim 468:3

...Haircutting after midday is forbidden, if done by a Jew. But if done by a gentile, it is permitted. And even cutting nails is forbidden after midday. But some permit cutting nails after midday when one forgot to cut them before midday, as it is not a true *melacha* regarding Erev Pesach. And one opinion forbids getting a haircut even by a gentile after midday, because the one who is having his hair cut helps a little by tilting his head. But this is not correct, for what is there to that?

Today, many activities that in previous times were considered by Chazal complete, skilled *melacha* have now become non-professional activities that everyone can do and are not difficult or time-consuming. Would such activities be permitted now on Erev Pesach afternoon? **Rav Eliezer Melamed** suggests that shaving oneself and nail clipping, as well as ironing clothing and shining shoes, are indeed permitted in our times after midday on Erev Pesach.

30. פניני הלכה | פסח יג:ב

אף שאסור להסתפר אחר חצות היום, להתגלח במכונה אישית מותר, מפני שזו מלאכת הדיוט. וכן מותר לגהץ בגדים ולצחצח נעליים ולגזוז ציפורניים לכבוד החג אחר חצות היום. ויש מהדרים להתגלח ולגזוז ציפורניים לפני חצות.

פ Peninei Halakha, Pesach 13:2

Although it is forbidden to take a haircut after midday, shaving with a personal shaver is permitted, since this is considered a non-professional labor. Likewise, it is permitted to iron clothing, shine shoes, and cut one's nails in honor of the holiday after midday. Some are strict to shave and cut nails before midday.

Rav Mordechai Eliyahu and other Sephardic *poskim* also permit shaving after midday, although he writes that it is preferable to shave before midday.[41]

The ***Piskei Teshuvot*** does not allow shaving, but he lists other terms which would allow a person to have a haircut after midday, such as asking a gentile. With regard to bathing and shining shoes, he writes that if one forgot to do so before midday, he may do so after.

31. פסקי תשובות | או"ח תסח:ג–ד

ג. ...ולענין להסתפר על ידי עכו"ם לאחר חצות הסכימו הרבה אחרונים להקל, אבל על ידי ישראל אסור אפילו בחינם. ומכל מקום מותר להסתפר בשכר אצל ישראל עני, שאין לו מה לאכול כפי הצורך בליל החג וביום טוב של פסח,

פ Piskei Teshuvot, Orach Chaim 468:3–4

3. ...Regarding having one's hair cut by a gentile after midday, many *Acharonim* agree to be lenient. However, [having it done] by a Jew is forbidden, even for free. Nonetheless, it is permitted to have hair cut by a needy Jew, who does not have enough to eat on the night and Yom Tov of Pesach.

---

41. *Peninei Halakha, Pesach* 13:2. See also *Kitzur Shulchan Aruch, Darchei Halacha* 113:5 (Rav Mordechai Eliyahu); *Yalkut Yosef*, O.C. 468:7. For more on nail clipping, see *Mishna Berura*, 468:5; *Shulchan Aruch*, O.C. 532.

ואם אינו מוצא נכרי או ישראל עני ושעריו גדולות מותר לו להסתפר על ידי עצמו.

ולאשה לצורך ליל טבילה או צניעות מותר לה להסתפר אפילו אחר חצות.

ד. ...ונטילת צפרניים. אם שכח ליטול אותו קודם חצות יש להקל אפילו על ידי עצמו או על ידי אחר בחינם. וכמו כן לצחצח מנעליו ולהתרחץ לכתחילה יש לעשותם קודם חצות, ואם שכח לעשותם קודם חצות או מאפס פנאי, יוכל לצחצח מנעליו במשחה ולהבריקם ולרחוץ גופו בסבון אף אחרי חצות.

And if one cannot find a gentile or needy Jew and his hair is long, it is permitted for him to cut his own hair.

Regarding a woman, as necessitated by the night of her immersion or for modesty, she may have her hair cut even after midday.

4. ...Regarding cutting nails, if someone forgot to cut [nails] before midday, one may be lenient even [to cut] by oneself or by another for free. Similarly, regarding polishing one's shoes and washing oneself, one should do these before midday. And if the person forgot to do them before midday or [was unable] due to [having] no time, one may shine his shoes with polish and to make them bright, as well as to wash his body with soap, even after midday.[42]

A similar dispute arises concerning washing laundry after midday. According to the *Piskei Teshuvot* and some other contemporary *poskim*,[43] washing laundry in a washing machine is forbidden and is still considered complete, professional *melacha*. On the other hand, the ***Shemirat Shabbat K'hilchata*** suggests that perhaps today, simply placing clothes in the machine and pressing a button does not constitute this type of *melacha* and might be permitted.

32. שמירת שבת כהלכתה | פרק מב, הערה קלט

Shemirat Shabbat K'hilchata, Ch. 42, n. 139

ויש לעיין בהא דמלאכה גמורה, האם יש היתר בערב פסח אחר חצות להכניס את הכביסה לתוך מכונת כביסה, ואין לו לעשות כל דבר אלא רק ללחוץ על כפתורי ההפעלה... או דילמא אזלינן בתר מחשבתו, והכביסה מתכבסת על ידי מלאכה גמורה; ומותר לגהץ בערב פסח אחר חצות בגדי חג, חזון עובדיה בשם שו"ת בית דוד.

Analysis is required regarding the concept of a complete *melacha*: is it permitted on Erev Pesach after midday to place laundry into a washing machine, where one does nothing other than press the activation buttons?... Or perhaps we follow the person's intent, and since the laundry is washed through a full-fledged *melacha*, it would be prohibited. However, it is permitted to iron Yom Tov clothing on Erev Pesach after midday, as cited in *Chazon Ovadia* in the name of Responsa *Beit David*.

Some *poskim*, such as **Rav Yitzchak Yosef**,[44] rule in practice that one may wash clothes in a washing machine in the afternoon. Even those who rule strictly rule that once the machine has been activated before midday, it may continue running afterward, and using a dryer is also permitted.[45]

42. The *Piskei Teshuvot* recommends bathing with soap before midday due to concern for *memachek*, smoothing (see volume 20, *shiur* 2). However, common practice is to use a bar of soap on Erev Pesach and *Chol HaMo'ed* since it is a non-professional activity needed for the festival.

43. This includes *Piskei Teshuvot* 468:6; *Oholei Halacha*, p. 185, citing Rav Yaakov Ariel, and *Mikraei Kodesh* 2:3.

44. *Yalkut Yosef*, Pesach, vol. 2, p. 731.

45. *Chazon Ovadia*, Pesach, p. 194; *Piskei Teshuvot* 468:6.

Recitations Related to *Korban Pesach*

We have seen in the previous subsections that although we do not offer the *korban Pesach* today, there are still important halachic ramifications to the fact that it was offered on the 14th of Nisan, with respect to performing *melacha.* Is there any other manner to mark or commemorate the day with respect to the *korban Pesach*?

There is a general principle that when a person recites the verses that relate to the offerings, this is considered a form of presenting the offerings themselves. This concept is cited by the **Gemara (*Masechet Megilla*)**.[46]

ח Masechet Megilla 31b

...Avraham **said before** [Hashem]**: Master of the Universe,** It **works out well that when the Temple is standing,** offerings can be brought, but **when the Temple will no** longer **be standing, what will become of them?** Hashem **said to** [**Avraham**]**: I have already established for them the order of offerings,** i.e., the verses of the Torah pertaining to the halachot of the offerings. **Whenever they read those** portions, **I will deem it as if they sacrificed an offering before Me...**

33. מסכת מגילה לא:

...אמר לפניו: רבונו של עולם, תינח בזמן שבית המקדש קיים, בזמן שאין בית המקדש קיים מה תהא עליהם? – אמר לו: כבר תקנתי להם סדר קרבנות, כל זמן שקוראין בהן מעלה אני עליהן כאילו מקריבין לפני קרבן...

The role of recitations as replacements for offerings has other applications in our prayer practices as well, and, in one view cited in the Gemara (*Berachot* 26b), it functions as the major model for our daily prayers today. In fact, specifically regarding Erev Pesach, this appears to be the reason that *Tehillim* 100 (*Mizmor L'toda*) is omitted by Ashkenazim from its regular place in *Pesukei D'zimra* of *Shacharit.*[47]

Consequently, the ***Shulchan Aruch HaRav*** emphasizes the importance of reciting the passages about the *korban Pesach* during the time when the *Pesach* would have been offered as well as praying for the chance to perform the full rite.

א Shulchan Aruch HaRav, Piskei HaSiddur, Seder Korban Pesach

"We will pay our lips as [sacrificial] bulls" (*Hoshe'a* 14:3). The *Amida* of *Mincha* is in place of the daily offering (*Tamid*) of the afternoon, and when the *Beit HaMikdash* was standing, the *Pesach* was offered after the afternoon daily offering. **Thus, it is fitting to be involved with the order of the *korban Pesach***

34. שולחן ערוך הרב | פסקי הסידור, סדר קרבן פסח

ונשלמה פרים שפתינו ותפלת מנחה היא במקום תמיד של בין הערבים ובזמן שבית המקדש היה קיים היה הפסח נשחט אחר תמיד של בין הערבים **כן ראוי לעסוק בסדר קרבן פסח**

46. Compare *Masechet Yoma* 86b. Both passages in the Gemara speak of sacrifices as means of atonement, but more generally speaking, the Gemara's assertion should also apply to sacrifices which are not specifically meant to bring about atonement.

47. See volume 9, *shiur* 7, sources 26–29. Some understand that the chapter of *Tehillim* 100 takes the place of a *korban toda* (thanks offering), which consists of *chametz* loaves and was therefore not offered on Erev Pesach; thus, the chapter is also omitted from its regular place in the prayers (Rema, O.C. 429:2 and *Machatzit HaShekel*, O.C. 429:7). Sephardim, by contrast do recite it, as they maintain that the regular order of the prayer service is always recited (other than *Tachanun* and *Lamnatze'ach*) regardless of any logical reason why it would be omitted.

after the *Mincha* prayer, and he should say, "He brings the *Pesach* offering, etc."[48]

This is the matter very briefly. And a person must be very reverent and attentive regarding the word of Hashem to read it at its time, so that his recitation should ascend in place of its offering. He should also be upset about the destruction of the *Beit HaMikdash* and supplicate before Hashem, Creator of the world, that He may build it speedily in our days, amen.

אחר תפלת המנחה ויאמר זה: קרבן פסח מביא כו'.

זהו הענין בקיצור גדול. וצריך האדם הירא וחרד על דבר ה' לקרות אותו בזמנו שתעלה קריאתו במקום הקרבתו וידאג על חורבן הבית ויתחנן לפני ה' בורא עולם שיבנה אותו במהרה בימינו אמן.

Accordingly, some have the custom to recite the verses pertaining to the offering of the *korban Pesach* before or after *Mincha* on Erev Pesach.[49]

---

48. For the complete text of the *Seder Korban Pesach*, see www.sefaria.org.il/Seder_HaYom%2C_Order_of_Recital_of_Korban_Pesach.1?lang=he.

49. *Mishna Berura* 471:22; *Peninei Halakha, Pesach* 8:13; and *Mikraei Kodesh* (Rav Moshe Harari), *Leil HaSeder* 2:34. See also *Mikraei Kodesh*, ibid., n. 98, that Rav Avraham Yitzchak HaKohen Kook and Rav Yosef Chaim Zonnenfeld both had the practice to recite the *Seder Korban Pesach* at the Kotel on Erev Pesach afternoon, and that Rav Avigdor Nebenzahl noted that many in Jerusalem do so today as well.

Eating on Erev Pesach Afternoon

To optimize the experience of the evening meals at the beginning of every Shabbat and Yom Tov, Chazal restricted a person's eating in the late hours of every Erev Shabbat and Erev Yom Tov.[50] However, in the case of Erev Pesach, this restriction is even more stringent, as recorded in the **Mishna** (***Masechet Pesachim***).

35. משנה | פסחים י:א

ערבי פסחים סמוך למנחה לא יאכל אדם עד שתחשך ואפילו עני שבישראל לא יאכל עד שיסב.

ח Mishna, Pesachim 10:1

On **the eve of Pesach, adjacent to *mincha*** time,[51] **a person** may **not eat until dark. Even the poorest of Jews** should **not eat until he reclines** and eats of the Passover feast on the night of Pesach.

In his commentary, in line with a later statement by Rav Huna, **Rashi** explains that the heightened stringency of Erev Pesach stems from the once-a-year mitzva of eating matza on the first night of Pesach. **Rashbam** and other commentators also accept this interpretation.

36. רש"י | פסחים צט:

לא יאכל – כדי שיאכל מצה של מצוה לתיאבון משום הידור מצוה.

ר Rashi, Pesachim 99b

May not eat – So that he will eat the commanded matza with an appetite, as an enhancement of the mitzva.

Other commentators, including the **Ran,** understand that Chazal forbade eating on Erev Pesach so that a person will not eat the matza as an *achila gasa* (gluttonous overconsumption).

37. חידושי הר"ן | פסחים צט:

ערבי פסחים סמוך למנחה לא יאכל אדם עד שתחשך, פירש"י... דסמוך למנחה קטנה תנן ומשום מצה כי היכי דלא ליתיה למיכליה

ר Chidushei HaRan, Pesachim 99b

"On the eve of Pesach, adjacent to *mincha* time, a person may not eat until dark." Rashi explains[52]... that the Mishna refers to the time adjacent to *mincha ketana*.[53] Accordingly, it is in consideration of the matza, so that one will not come to eat it

50. See volume 16, *shiur* 1, sources 39–48.
51. See the Ran in source 37 below and n. 52–53 that this refers to the time adjacent to *mincha ketana*, i.e., the beginning of the tenth hour of the halachic day (*sha'ot zemaniyot*).
52. This explanation that *mincha* refers to *mincha ketana* is not mentioned in Rashi in the Mishna or Gemara here. However, it is mentioned in the Rashbam here. In any case, it is based on the apparent conclusion of the Gemara later (107b) that *mincha* refers to *mincha ketana*.
53. *Mincha ketana* ("small *mincha*") is the term for the beginning of the late afternoon, the time at which on most days, parts of the afternoon daily offering were offered on the altar in the *Beit HaMikdash* (the slaughter took place an hour before that; see *Pesachim* 58a). It refers to the middle of the tenth daylight hour. According to the commentaries here, the term "adjacent" refers to a half hour before, meaning that the prohibition against eating takes effect at the beginning of the tenth daylight hour, as stated explicitly in the *Shulchan Aruch* below (source 42).

as an *achila gasa*,[54] meaning that he would be able to swallow it only with some difficulty. In such a case, one does not fulfill his [mitzva] obligation, as it is not called eating.

אכילה גסה, כלומר שלא יוכל לבלוע אותה אלא בקושי וכהאי גוונא לא יצא ידי חובתו דלא מקריא אכילה.

Unlike the view of Rashi cited above in source 36, the Ran understands that this is not merely a measure meant to **enhance or optimize** the mitzva of eating matza. Rather, the concern is that if a person eats in the afternoon, it may become impossible to fulfill the mitzva of eating matza altogether. If the concern is merely about eating the matza with greater appetite, it might not be so strictly forbidden to eat. But if the concern is that eating in the late afternoon will make it impossible to fulfill the mitzva of eating matza altogether, then the ban on eating would be treated with greater stringency.

The **Rosh** also writes that the concern is that a person will be too full to eat the matza properly. Accordingly, he suggests that the ban on eating depends on each person's own eating habits and body, such that it might be necessary for some people to cease eating even earlier in the day.

ו Rosh, Pesachim 10:19

38. רא"ש | פסחים י':יט

"A person may not eat adjacent to *mincha* time," etc. We conclude that the Mishna states [one may not eat] adjacent to *mincha ketana* because one might eat the matza as an *achila gasa*. But before then, it is permitted. And all of this is according to each individual. For we say that Rav Sheshet would fast the entire Erev Pesach, because he was delicate, and if he would eat something during the day, he would be unable to eat at night. And we also say in the *Yerushalmi* on this chapter that Rabbi Yehuda HaNasi would eat neither *chametz* nor matza… and the Gemara concludes that Rabbi Yehuda HaNasi was delicate, and if he would eat during the day, he would not eat at night.

לא יאכל סמוך למנחה וכו'. אסיקנא סמוך למנחה קטנה תנן ומשום דילמא אכיל מצה אכילה גסה אבל קודם לכן מותר והכל לפי מה שהוא אדם דהא אמרינן רב ששת הוה יתיב בתעניתא כולי מעלי יומא דפסחא משום דאיסתניס הוה ואי הוה טעים מידי בימּמא באורתא לה הוי מצי אכיל ואמרינן נמי בירושלמי דהך פירקין רבי לא אכל חמץ ולא מצה... ומסיק דרבי איסתניס הוה ואי הוה אכיל בימּמא לא הוה אכיל בליליא.

In any case, as stated by the Mishna, a person must not eat in the late afternoon on Erev Pesach. But the Mishna does not explain which foods are included in this ban. Accordingly, the **Gemara (*Masechet Pesachim*)** clarifies the parameters of the prohibition and notes that some foods are permitted to eat during this time.

ח Masechet Pesachim 107b

39. מסכת פסחים קז:

Rabbi Asi said: It is true that is prohibited to eat a proper meal from *mincha* time onward, **however, one** may **dip** and eat **types of refreshments,** e.g., fruit or meat that do not constitute a full meal and will not fill one's stomach. Similarly, the Gemara relates that **Rabbi Yitzchak** would **dip** and eat **vegetables.**

אמר ר' אסי: אבל מטביל הוא במיני תרגימא. רבי יצחק מטביל בירקי.

---

54. This interpretation comes from the language of the Gemara itself (107b, discussing whether *mincha* refers to *mincha gedola* or *mincha ketana*). However, Rashi and Rashbam would understand the reference to *achila gasa* here as simply meaning that one no longer has an appetite for the matza. See also Tosafot, *Pesachim* 107b, s.v. *dilma*.

Thus, it is permitted to eat certain kinds of foods even in the late afternoon on Erev Pesach. Accordingly, as explained by **Tosafot,** the Mishna's ruling forbidding foods that were permitted until that time on Erev Pesach applies specifically to *matza ashira.*[55]

Tosafot, Pesachim 99b

A person may not eat – . . . And should you ask, what is it that a person may not eat? If it is matza, even before [the late afternoon], it is also forbidden, as we say in the *Yerushalmi* [cited above]. . . And if it is refreshments, the Gemara states, "however, one may dip and eat varieties of refreshments." Thus, one might say that this is dealing with *matza ashira,* for the *Yerushalmi* forbids only matza which is fit for fulfilling one's obligation, if one eats it before its time. But in the case of *matza ashira,* it is permitted; and Rabbeinu Tam practiced accordingly.

40. תוספות | פסחים צט:

לא יאכל אדם – ...ואם תאמר ומה לא יאכל? אי מצה אפילו קודם נמי אסור כדאמרינן בירושלמי... ואי במיני תרגימא הא אמר בגמרא (ד' קז:) אבל מטבל הוא במיני תרגימא. ויש לומר דאיירי במצה עשירה דלא אסר בירושלמי אלא במצה הראויה לצאת בה חובתו ואוכלה קודם זמנה אבל מצה עשירה שריא וכן היה נוהג רבינו תם.

As Tosafot note, even in the late afternoon on Erev Pesach, it is forbidden only to eat filling foods, but the Gemara permits "*minei targima* (refreshments, or delicacies)." What is meant by the ambiguous term "refreshments?" This is subject to some debate. According to the **Rashbam,** the term includes foods such as fruit and meat.[56] However, in the view of **Tosafot** and the **Rosh,**[57] "refreshments" seems to refer to grains.[58]

Tosafot, Pesachim 107b

Varieties of refreshments – Rashbam explains that this is fruit or meat, without bread. But this does not seem correct, for we say in the *Tosefta (Berachot),* "If they brought before him refreshments, he should recite *borei minei mezonot.*" And [the *beracha* of] *borei minei mezonot* is recited only upon the five grains. . .[59]

41. תוספות | פסחים קז:

מיני תרגימא – פי' רשב"ם פירות ובשר בלא לחם ולא נהירא דאמרינן בתוספתא דכיצד מברכין הביאו לפניו מיני תרגימא מברך בורא מיני מזונות ואין מברכין בורא מיני מזונות אלא על חמשת מינים...

Later *poskim,* including the ***Shulchan Aruch,*** agree with the Rashbam that one may eat modest quantities of fruits and vegetables on Erev Pesach but not foods made out of grain.

55. See above on *matza ashira,* sources 13–17.

56. This is the interpretation followed in the translation above. Rashbam also explains that Rabbi Yitzchak would eat these foods specifically on Erev Pesach in order to increase his appetite for the matza.

57. *Pesachim* 10:19.

58. As it is forbidden to eat *chametz* at this time of day, this discussion necessarily involves foods whose doughs or batters are mixed and baked in under 18 minutes and/or products made of "flour" made from baked and ground matza. This may indicate that according to Tosafot, foods made of matza flour, such as Pesach rolls, may be eaten even on Erev Pesach, when matza itself may not be eaten. (However, as we will see below, many do not accept this position as halacha.)

59. It should be noted that Tosafot does mention one approach from the Gemara (*Yoma* 78b) that refreshments does indeed mean fruit. The Rosh, on the other hand, seems to conclude definitively that refreshments refers to grains.

42. שולחן ערוך | או"ח תעא:א

אסור לאכול פת משעה עשירית ולמעלה, כדי שיאכל מצה לתיאבון, אבל אוכל מעט פירות או ירקות, אבל לא ימלא כריסו מהם, (ואם הוא איסטניס שאפילו אוכל מעט מזיק באכילתו הכל אסור).

א Shulchan Aruch, Orach Chaim 471:1

It is forbidden to eat *pat* [grain][60] from the [beginning of the] tenth hour and on so that he will eat matza with an appetite. But he may eat a bit of fruit or vegetables, so long as he does not fill his stomach from them. (And if he is so delicate that even a little food disturbs his eating [later], then everything is forbidden).[61]

On the basis of the Rashbam and other *Rishonim*, the ***Mishna Berura*** adds that meat and the like are also included in the permitted category of "refreshments."

43. משנה ברורה | או"ח תעא:ג

מעט פירות – והוא הדין בשר ודגים וביצים וכהאי גוונא אבל מחמשת המינים שמבושל במי פירות אסור דסעיד.

א Mishna Berura, Orach Chaim 471:3

A bit of fruit – The same is true of meat, fish, eggs, and the like. But [food made] from the five grains that is cooked with fruit juice [and categorized as *matza ashira*] is forbidden, as it satiates.

Although the precise time when this restriction begins is not always listed among the standard halachic times publicized for Erev Pesach,[62] one must nonetheless determine the correct cutoff for that year (often between approximately 3:30 pm and 4:30 pm) and cease eating by that time, aside from small quantities of the exceptions noted above.[63]

---

60. See *Mishna Berura* (471:3), who explains that "*pat*" (lit. bread) refers to any of the five grains baked or cooked, even with fruit juice.

61. This term is used for both bread which is fit for Pesach, i.e., matza, and bread which is *chametz*. As indicated in *Orach Chaim* 471:2, the *Shulchan Aruch* uses the term *pat* here to refer to *matza ashira*.

62. See, e.g., www.star-k.org/articles/wp-content/uploads/usa-zmanim-chart.pdf, https://oukosher.org/passover, and www.myzmanim.com, that do not mention it. However, on the Yeshiva site, it is mentioned (www.yeshiva.co/calendar/timesday?day=1&month=4&year=2026).

63. Practically speaking, *chametz*, matza, and egg/fruit juice matza (for Ashkenazim) are already forbidden in most cases. But cakes or cookies made of matza meal would need to be avoided after this time (according to those opinions that permit them earlier in the day; see source 11 above) and cooked matza dishes, such as matza *kreplach*, would need to be avoided. See *Mishna Berura* (471:2) that one must stop eating even if one began before the time of the prohibition.

Erev Pesach that Falls on Shabbat

Occasionally, Erev Pesach falls on Shabbat, and Pesach begins immediately afterward. The many halachot governing the cessation of *chametz*, preparing for the Seder, and fulfilling the mitzvot of Shabbat create some unique challenges and solutions.[64] Although all of the halachot of this unusual circumstance are too numerous to detail here, we will briefly address some of the issues related to the topics discussed in this *shiur*.[65]

Fast of the Firstborn

When Erev Pesach coincides with Shabbat, the fast of the firstborn cannot be observed on Shabbat, the 14th of Nisan, in accordance with the general rule that it is forbidden to fast on Shabbat. Accordingly, the ***Shulchan Aruch*** writes that some hold that the fast should be observed on Thursday preceding Pesach; but others hold that the fast is cancelled altogether. The prevalent practice is that the fast is observed on Thursday.[66]

44. שולחן ערוך | או"ח תע:ב

אם חל ערב פסח בשבת, יש אומרים שמתענים הבכורות ביום ה', ויש אומרים שאינם מתענים כלל.

הגה: אבל יש לנהוג כסברא הראשונה.

א Shulchan Aruch, Orach Chaim 470:2

If Erev Pesach coincides with Shabbat, some say that the firstborn fast on Thursday, and some say that they do not fast at all.

Rema: It is correct to act in accordance with the first position.

Removing *Chametz* and Disavowing *Chametz* on Shabbat

The ***Shulchan Aruch*** writes that the primary removal of *chametz* should be done before Shabbat. Although *chametz* does not actually become forbidden on Erev Shabbat (which is the 13th of Nisan), so as to adhere to one's normal routine from other years, a person should burn the *chametz* before midday. But one should recite the *bitul* (disavowal of) *chametz*, the statement through which a person declares all his *chametz* cancelled and ownerless, on Erev Pesach even though it is also Shabbat.

64. See *Masechet Pesachim* 66a for an anecdote regarding forgetting the halachot of Erev Pesach on Shabbat with respect to offering the *korban Pesach*.

65. Regarding *bedikat* (search of) *chametz* and *bi'ur* (disposal of) *chametz* when Erev Pesach coincides with Shabbat, see *Shulchan Aruch* (o.c. 444:1) and *Mishna Berura* (444:9).

66. See also *Peninei Halakha, Pesach* 13:4.

45. שולחן ערוך | או"ח תמד:ב

טוב לבער בערב שבת קודם חצות, כדי שלא יבואו לטעות בשאר שנים לבער אחר חצות. (וביום השבת, יבטלנו.)

א Shulchan Aruch, Orach Chaim 444:2

It is proper to destroy [the *chametz*] on Erev Shabbat before midday, so that people will not come to errantly destroy after midday in other years. (And on Shabbat, he should disavow it [see 444:4]).

Shabbat Meals on Erev Pesach

Of all the unique details of Erev Pesach coinciding with Shabbat, it is likely that none is better known and more challenging than establishing one's Shabbat meals with a suitable bread for *lechem mishneh* (two loaves). On the one hand, by the night before Pesach, people will have already stowed away "*chametz* dishes" and taken out Pesach dishes. When Pesach begins at the end of Shabbat, for those who will be home on Pesach, it is virtually impossible to arrange things otherwise. Accordingly, eating *chametz* bread and contending with crumbs is inconvenient and hazardous because of the possibility that *chametz* will not be properly removed before Pesach begins.[67] After all, recall that, in this case, the *bedikat chametz* is done already on Thursday night.[68]

On the other hand, it is forbidden to eat matza on the day of Erev Pesach; and some people have the custom to refrain from eating matza as much as one month before, as noted previously (sources 8–9). Accordingly, no one may eat matza on Shabbat day; and many would not eat matza even the night before.[69]

Even if someone prefers to use *chametz*, this becomes forbidden on Erev Pesach at the beginning of the fifth daylight hour. Thus, if a person recites *Shacharit* earlier than usual and eats the second Shabbat meal earlier in the day, *chametz* provides a manageable solution. Regarding whatever crumbs and pieces of *chametz* remain when the time comes to remove the *chametz*, these must be removed in a way which is permitted on Shabbat.

According to some *poskim*, such as **Rav Moshe Feinstein**,[70] one may also use *matza ashira* on Erev Pesach in place of bread, at least before the time that *chametz* is prohibited.

Even if one can work out one of these solutions for the first two Shabbat meal, as stated in the ***Shulchan Aruch,*** the third meal presents different challenges that must also be addressed.

46. שולחן ערוך | או"ח תמד:א

...ומבערים הכל לפני השבת, ומשיירין מזון שתי סעודות לצורך השבת, דסעודה שלישית זמנה אחר המנחה ואז אינו יכול לעשותה לא במצה ולא בחמץ אלא במצה עשירה, וצריך לעשותה קודם שעה עשירית.

א Shulchan Aruch, Orach Chaim 444:1

...We discard all [the *chametz*] before Shabbat, and we leave food for two meals for the needs of Shabbat. [This is not so] for the third meal, as its time is after *mincha*, when one cannot make [the meal] with either matza or *chametz*, but only with *matza ashira*, and one must make [the meal] before the [beginning of the] tenth daylight hour.

67. Compare *Shulchan Aruch*, O.C. 444:4.
68. *Shulchan Aruch*, O.C. 444:1.
69. See *Magen Avraham* 471; Responsa *Igrot Moshe*, O.C. 1:155.
70. Responsa *Igrot Moshe*, O.C. 1:155.

הגה: במדינות אלו שאין נוהגין לאכול מצה עשירה... יקיים סעודה שלישית במיני פירות או בשר ודגים...

Rema: In these lands, where we are not accustomed to eat *matza ashira*… he should fulfill the third meal with varieties of fruit or meat and fish…

According to the *Shulchan Aruch*, one may use *matza ashira* for *seuda shelishit* since *matza ashira* is permitted for consumption on Pesach as well. However, the **Rema** here notes, as discussed previously (source 16), that Ashkenazim do not generally use *matza ashira* on Pesach and therefore would not use it at *seuda shelishit* either.

The ***Mishna Berura*** (444:15) offers another suggestion to split the morning meal into two, eating bread for both, and the second part of the meal can also fulfill *seuda shelishit*.[71] The ***Aruch HaShulchan*** explores additional options for *seuda shelishit* in more detail, including using cooked matza and not eating *seuda shelishit* at all.

47. ערוך השולחן | או"ח תמד:ה-ו

ה. וכתב רבינו הרמ"א ובמדינות אלו שאין נוהגין לאכול מצה עשירה... יקיים סעודה שלישית במיני פירות או בבשר ודגים עד כאן לשונו. ונראה **שאין הכוונה** דגם בערב פסח אין לאכול מצה עשירה לפי המנהג דאין שום טעם בזה אלא הכוונה כיון שאין מנהגינו לאכול בפסח מצה עשירה ממילא דאין מכינין אצלינו מצה עשירה ולהכין רק על סעודה שלישית אין דרך בני אדם להטריח על מאכל קטן כזה.

והנה גם אצלינו יכולין לעשות סעודה שלישית במצה מבושלת והרבה נוהגין אצלינו כן והקדים מיני פירות לבשר ודגים... בערב פסח פירות עדיפי כדי שלא ישבע

א Aruch HaShulchan, Orach Chaim 444:5–6

5. Our master, the Rema, writes, "In these lands, where we are not accustomed to eat *matza ashira*… he should fulfill the third meal with varieties of fruit or meat and fish." It seems that he **does not mean** that even on Erev Pesach, one may not eat *matza ashira* according to the custom, because there is no reason for that. Rather, the meaning is that since it is not our custom to eat *matza ashira* on Pesach, consequently we do not prepare *matza ashira* [and thus, we do not have it in the home]. And regarding preparing [it] exclusively for the third meal [on Erev Pesach, but not using it on Pesach itself] – it is not the way people behave, to trouble themselves [so much] for a small eating such as this.[72]

Even for us, it is possible to make the third meal with cooked matza [before the tenth daylight hour], and many in our vicinity have this practice. And [the Rema] mentioned varieties of fruit before meat and fish… [because] on Erev Pesach, fruit is better, so that one will not become full,

71. Although the practical halacha is normally that *seuda shelishit* must be eaten in the afternoon (*Shulchan Aruch*, O.C. 291:2), this approach relies on the minority opinion that it may be fulfilled in the morning due to the special circumstances of Erev Pesach on Shabbat.

72. Some *poskim* argue that according to the *Aruch HaShulchan*, *matza ashira* (or "egg" matza) should be permitted for use at *seuda shelishit* or at any other time until the tenth hour since in his opinion, it was not prepared in Ashkenazic lands only because it was not practical to do so in very small quantities. But today, when it is commercially prepared for Sephardim or for Ashkenazic children or the elderly, it would be permitted to use by everyone. In addition, even if one does not accept this position, the *Noda B'yehuda* holds that one may consume *matza ashira* at least until midday. This is the position taken by Rav Hershel Schachter (https://halachipedia.com/images/f/f8/YIW_Pesach.pdf and https://halachipedia.com/index.php?title=Erev_Pesach_That_Falls_out_on_Shabbat), Rav Shlomo Wahrman (*Orot HaPesach* 20, available at https://hebrewbooks.org/pdfpager.aspx?req=51478&st=&pgnum=140), and Rav Eliezer Silver (as cited by Rav Wahrman and https://rabbinicalalliance.org/wp-content/uploads/2025/03/סדר-ערב-פסח-שחל-להיות-בשבת-מהגאון-רבי-אליעזר-סילבר-זצל-עם-זמני-היום-לשנת-תשפה.pdf).

and he will eat the matza with an appetite. And it could be that it is for this reason that he did not also mention cooked matza, because it is very filling, as is known from feeling. Some say to split the morning meal to two, because some say that one fulfills [the mitzva] in this way.

6. The *Zohar* records that Rabbi Shimon bar Yochai would delve into Torah in place of the third meal. It must be understood: could it be that Rabbi Shimon bar Yochai was unable to fulfill the mitzva of the third meal in one of the explained ways? Thus, it appears clear in my humble opinion that all this is superfluous, for on this Shabbat, it is certain that we have not been commanded at all regarding three meals, since it is impossible. This is just like Yom Kippur which coincides with Shabbat. The same is true for Shabbat which is Erev Pesach regarding the third meal…

ויאכל מצה לתיאבון ואולי מפני זה לא הזכיר גם מצה מבושלת מפני שהיא משביע הרבה כידוע בחוש ויש אומרים להפסיק סעודת שחרית לשנים דיש אומרים דיוצא בזה [מג"א].

ו. ובזוהר כתב שרבי שמעון בר יוחאי היה עוסק בתורה במקום סעודה שלישית [שם סק"ב] ויש להבין אטו רבי שמעון בר יוחאי לא היה יכול לקיים סעודה שלישית באיזה מהדברים שנתבארו ונראה לעניות דעתי ברור דכל זה הוא מילתא יתירתא שהרי בשבת זו בעל כרחך לא נצטוינו כלל על ג' סעודות כיון שאי אפשר מידי דהוה ליום הכיפורים שחל בשבת והוא הדין שבת ערב פסח לעניין סעודה שלישית...

In accordance with the ruling of the *Shulchan Aruch*, most synagogues schedule the Shabbat morning services to be early enough to allow people to eat *chametz* at the second Shabbat meal, before *chametz* becomes forbidden at the beginning of the fifth daylight hour.

Rav Yosef Zvi Rimon in his *sefer* on the halachot of Erev Pesach on Shabbat summarizes the most commonly practiced approaches today.

Erev Pesach SheChal B'Shabbat: Halacha Mimekora, pp. 11–12

The obligation to eat bread: … One should adopt one of the following two solutions (the second is more recommended in private homes, but both options are acceptable):

1. Eat *matza ashira* and recite the *beracha* of *hamotzi* on it (even if one eats only a *k'zayit* or *k'beitza*; according to Rav Ovadia Yosef, the *beracha* is *hamotzi* only if one eats the amount of four eggs from the matza). According to Ashkenazic custom, *matza ashira* is eaten only until the end of the fourth hour (i.e., the latest time to eat *chametz*). Therefore, *matza ashira* may be eaten only for the first two meals (provided one finishes before the latest time for eating *chametz*). Ideally, it is proper that the *matza ashira* does not touch the Pesach utensils.

2. Eat bread that is *chametz*. It is proper to leave over only a small amount of bread of the type that does not crumble, such as pita and the like… One should eat the bread… remove the disposable tablecloth, wash one's clothes well, and then bring out the Pesach utensils and foods…

48. ערב פסח שחל בשבת | הלכה ממקורה, עמ' 11–12

חובת אכילת לחם: ...יש לנקוט באחד משני הפתרונות (הדרך השנייה מומלצת יותר בבתים פרטיים, אך שתי הדרכים אשפריות):

א. לאכול מצה עשירה ולברך עליה המוציא (אף שאוכל כזית או כביצה, ולדעת הרב עובדיה יוסף ברכתה המוציא רק אם אוכל שיעור ארבע ביצים מהמצה). למנהג האשכנזים אוכלים מצה עשירה רק עד סוף השעה הרביעית (סוף זמן אכילת החמץ). ולכן ניתן לאכול מצה עשירה רק בשתי הסעודות הראשונות (ובתנאי שמסיימים אותה לפני סוף זמן אכילת חמץ). לכתחילה רצוי להיזהר שהמצה עשירה לא תיגע בכלי הפסח.

ב. לאכול לחם חמץ. רצוי להשאיר רק מעט לחם, ינער היטב את בגדיו מסוג שאינו מתפורר, כגון פיתה וכדומה... יאכל את הלחם... יסיר את המפה החד פעמית, ינער היטב את בגדיו ואחר כך יגיש את כלי הפסח והמאכלים...

סעודה שלישית: ...ויש לנקוט באחד משלשה פתרונות:

א. מי שאוכל מצה עשירה גם לאחר שעה הרביעית יכול לאכול סעודה שלישית בזמנה (חצי שעה אחרי חצות) ולאכול בה מצה עשירה. ויש להיזהר להתחיל את הסעודה לפני השעה העשירית... אולם רוב האשכנזים מחמירים בכך ולא אוכלים מצה עשירה אחרי השעה הרביעית.

ב. ניתן לקיים סעודה שלישית בזמנה באכילת בשר, דגים, או פירות. ניתן גם לאכול קניידלאך... ויש המקילים גם במצה בראייט...

ג. יש הנוהגים להוסיף על פתרון ב׳ את פיצול סעודת הבוקר: לברך ברכת המזון, לעשות הפסקה קלה, ליטול ידיים ולברך שוב המוציא על לחם או על מצה עשירה (כמובן לפני סוף זמן אכילת חמץ).

Seuda shelishit: ...One should adopt one of the following three solutions:

1. One who eats *matza ashira* even after the fourth hour may eat *seuda shelishit* at the normal time (later than a half-hour after *chatzot*) and eat *matza ashira*. One should be careful to begin the meal before the tenth hour... But most Ashkenazim are strict and do not eat *matza ashira* after the fourth hour.

2. *Seuda shelishit* may be held at the normal time with meat, fish, or fruit. One may also eat *kneidlach* [before the tenth hour]... and some also allow eating matza brei...

3. Some have the practice of adding to the second solution by dividing the morning meal into two: Recite *Birkat HaMazon*, make a small intercession, wash hands and recite *hamotzi* again on bread or *matza ashira* (of course before the latest time of eating *chametz*).

FURTHER IYUN

For further *iyun* on the mitzva of *sippur yetziat mitzrayim* (telling the story of the Exodus) at the Seder for women, see page 203.

Removing Ma'aserot

Among the many agricultural mitzvot observed in Eretz Yisrael is the obligation to separate tithes (*ma'aserot*) from domestically grown produce.[73] Once the tithes have been separated from that produce which is subject to this mitzva, the remaining produce may be eaten. ***Ma'aser rishon*** (the first tithe), which is given to a *Levi*, is separated in the first six years of every Sabbatical cycle. In the first, second, fourth, and fifth years of the cycle, ***ma'aser sheini*** (the second tithe) is also separated. This is eaten in the consecrated parts of Jerusalem, or redeemed for money which will be used to buy food in the same sections of Jerusalem. This second *ma'aser* is replaced in the third and sixth years by ***ma'aser ani*** (the tithe for the poor).

A person does not necessarily deliver the *ma'aser* to its intended recipient, or bring it to Jerusalem, immediately. Thus, from time to time, a large quantity of *ma'aser* might accumulate in the home. Accordingly, in regular intervals, the Torah requires a person to remove the *ma'aserot* from his or her possession. This is indicated in the Torah by the verses which make up the ***viduy ma'aser*** (declaration of the tithes).

49. דברים | כו:יב–טו

יב. כִּי תְכַלֶּה לַעְשֵׂר אֶת כָּל מַעְשַׂר תְּבוּאָתְךָ בַּשָּׁנָה הַשְּׁלִישִׁת שְׁנַת הַמַּעֲשֵׂר, וְנָתַתָּה לַלֵּוִי לַגֵּר לַיָּתוֹם וְלָאַלְמָנָה וְאָכְלוּ בִשְׁעָרֶיךָ וְשָׂבֵעוּ:

יג. וְאָמַרְתָּ לִפְנֵי ה' אֱ-לֹהֶיךָ **בִּעַרְתִּי הַקֹּדֶשׁ מִן הַבַּיִת** וְגַם נְתַתִּיו לַלֵּוִי וְלַגֵּר לַיָּתוֹם וְלָאַלְמָנָה כְּכָל מִצְוָתְךָ אֲשֶׁר צִוִּיתָנִי, לֹא עָבַרְתִּי מִמִּצְוֹתֶיךָ וְלֹא שָׁכָחְתִּי:

יד. לֹא אָכַלְתִּי בְאֹנִי מִמֶּנּוּ וְלֹא בִעַרְתִּי מִמֶּנּוּ בְּטָמֵא וְלֹא נָתַתִּי מִמֶּנּוּ לְמֵת, שָׁמַעְתִּי בְּקוֹל ה' אֱ-לֹהָי עָשִׂיתִי כְּכֹל אֲשֶׁר צִוִּיתָנִי:

טו. הַשְׁקִיפָה מִמְּעוֹן קָדְשְׁךָ מִן הַשָּׁמַיִם וּבָרֵךְ אֶת עַמְּךָ אֶת יִשְׂרָאֵל וְאֵת הָאֲדָמָה אֲשֶׁר נָתַתָּה לָנוּ, כַּאֲשֶׁר נִשְׁבַּעְתָּ לַאֲבֹתֵינוּ אֶרֶץ זָבַת חָלָב וּדְבָשׁ:

ת Devarim 26:12–15

12. When you have finished tithing all the tithes of your produce in the third year, the year of the tithe, you shall give [them] to the Levite, the stranger, the orphan, and the widow, so that they can eat to satiety in your cities.

13. Then you shall say before the Lord, your God, "**I have removed the holy [portion] from the house,** and I have also given it to the Levite, the stranger, the orphan, and the widow, according to all Your commandment that You commanded me; I have not transgressed Your commandments, nor have I forgotten [them].

14. I did not eat any of it [second tithe] while in my mourning, nor did I remove any of it while in a state of impurity; neither did I use any of it for the dead. I obeyed the Lord, my God; I did according to all that You commanded me.

15. Look down from Your holy dwelling, from the heavens, and bless Your people Israel, and the ground which You have given to us, as You swore to our forefathers a land flowing with milk and honey.

The **Rambam** describes the terms under which the declaration of the tithes is recited and notes that it is usually recited on Pesach.

---

73. Regarding many aspects of the mitzva to separate tithes, see volume 6, *shiur* 8.

Rambam, Hilchot Ma'aser Sheini and Neta Revai 11:5–7

5. This declaration may be made in any language, as it states: "You shall declare before God your Lord," i.e., in any language in which you declare. Each person should make this declaration individually. If many desire to recite it together, they may.

6. The proper way of performing the mitzva is to recite the declaration in the Temple, as implied by the phrase: "before God." Nevertheless, if he made the declaration in any other place, he fulfilled his obligation.

7. A person may not make this declaration until he has disposed of all the agricultural presents in his possession. For in the declaration he states: "I have removed all the sacred substances from the house." On the day before the final day of the Pesach festival, one must remove [the last of the presents] and on the following day, the declaration is made.[74]

50. רמב"ם | הל' מעשר שני ונטע רבעי יא:ה–ז

ה. וידוי זה נאמר בכל לשון שנאמר ואמרת לפני ה' א-להיך בכל לשון שאתה אומר, וכל אחד ואחד אומרו בפני עצמו, ואם רצו רבים להתודות כאחד מתודין.

ו. ומצותו במקדש שנאמר לפני ה' ואם התודה בכל מקום יצא.

ז. אינו מתודה עד שלא ישאר אצלו אחת מן המתנות, שכן הוא אומר בוידוי בערתי הקדש מן הבית, וערב יום טוב האחרון היה הביעור ולמחר מתודין.

However, according to **Rav Avraham Yitzchak HaKohen Kook**, the declaration of the *ma'aserot* is not formally recited today.

Responsa Mishpat Kohen 56

Regarding the mitzva of the declaration (of the *ma'aserot*) in this time, although the Rambam and Ra'avad dispute whether the declaration of the *ma'aser* is observed other than before the *Mikdash*; according to the Rambam it is observed, even where it is not before the *Mikdash*: Nonetheless, it is difficult that it should be observed in this time for a number of reasons.

This is not a question according to the Rambam, for all the *terumot* and *ma'aserot* apply only *miderabanan* at this time, when most of the Jewish People are not in [their land]. But even according to those who hold that the obligation of *terumot* and *ma'aserot* in this time is observed *mide'oraita*, nonetheless, since we do not give the *teruma* to the *Kohen* in a state of purity, how can one say, "I have done according to all that You commanded me"? [Concerning this,] Chazal said, "I celebrated and gladdened [others] with it," and [if one hasn't given them to their recipients], where is its gladdening now, as in our multitude of sins, it is not eaten.

51. שו"ת משפט כהן | נו

על דבר חיוב הודוי בזמן הזה אף על גב דאיפליגו הרמב"ם והראב"ד, (פי"א מהל' מע"ש ונטע רבעי) אם וידוי מעשר נוהג שלא בפני הבית, ולדעת הרמב"ם הוא נוהג אפילו שלא בפני הבית, מכל מקום קשה שיהיה נוהג בזמן הזה מכמה טעמים.

לא מבעי לדעת הרמב"ם, דכל תרומות ומעשרות הם מדרבנן בזמן הזה, שאין רוב יושבים עליה, אלא אפילו לדסברי דמן התורה נוהג חיוב תרומות ומעשרות בזמן הזה, מכל מקום כיון שאין נותנים תרומה לכהן בטהרתה איך יאמר עשיתי ככל אשר צויתני, שפירשו חז"ל שמחתי ושימחתי בו, ואיה שמחתה כעת בעונותינו הרבים כיון שאינה נאכלת.

74. See below, source 51, that according to some opinions, the tithes must already be removed on Erev Pesach.

Also, how is it possible to say "I have not removed any of it while in a state of impurity"? This implies that one has removed or eaten in a state of purity; but we, in our multitude of sins do not eat [*terumot* and *ma'aserot*] in a state of purity. Therefore, even if one gave the tithe to a Levi, how could one say the declaration in this time?... Moreover, we say in our Mishna that if one has separated in a state of impurity, he cannot recite the declaration, while separating in this time is certainly in a state of impurity. [Thus,] it is impossible to fulfill this at this time, until the righteous teacher [i.e., *Mashiach*] will come.

גם איך יתכן לומר לא ביערתי ממנו בטמא, משמע הא בטהור ביער ואכל, ואנו הרי בעונותינו הרבים אין לנו אכילה בטהרה, ולפיכך אפי' נתן המעשר ללוי איך יוכל להתודות בזמן הזה... ועוד דאמרינן במשנתנו הא אם הפרישו בטומאה אינו יכול להתודות, וההפרשה בזמן הזה ודאי בטומאה היא, ואי אפשר לקיים זה בזמן הזה עד יבוא מורה צדק.

Rav Eliezer Melamed summarizes the process of removing the tithes in Eretz Yisrael today.

Peninei Halakha, Kashrut I, 7:12–13

12. The tithing cycle consists of two sets of three years. Every year, we separate *terumot*[75] and *ma'aser rishon*. However, *ma'aser sheini* and *ma'aser ani* alternate. In the first and second years, we separate *ma'aser sheini*, and in the third year, *ma'aser ani*. And likewise in the second set: in the fourth and fifth years *ma'aser sheini*, and in the sixth year, *ma'aser ani*. In the seventh year, the fruit is ownerless, and correspondingly, no *terumot* and *ma'aserot* are separated from them.

At the end of each cycle of three years, there is a mitzva to complete the separation of *terumot* and *ma'aserot* and to distribute them, and this is the mitzva of *bi'ur ma'aserot* (removing the tithes), as the verse states, "At the end of three years, you shall take out all the tithe of your crop in that year and place it in your gates" (*Devarim* 14:28). This means, by the terminal time of the removal, there is an obligation to complete the separation of *terumot* and *ma'aserot* from the produce of the prior three years; and to give the *terumot* and *challa* [separated dough] to the *Kohen*, the *ma'aser rishon* to the *Levi*, the *ma'aser ani* to the needy, and to bring the produce of *ma'aser sheini* and *neta reva'i* (fourth-year fruits)[76] to Jerusalem and to eat it in a state of purity.

52. פניני הלכה | כשרות א, ז:יב–יג

יב. מחזור המעשרות מורכב משתי סדרות של שלוש שנים. בכל השנים מפרישים תרומות ו'מעשר ראשון', אולם 'מעשר שני' ו'מעשר עני' מתחלפים. בשנה הראשונה והשנייה מפרישים 'מעשר שני', ובשלישית 'מעשר עני'. וכן בסדרה השנייה: בשנה הרביעית והחמישית 'מעשר שני', ובשישית 'מעשר עני'. בשנה השביעית הפירות הפקר וממילא אין מפרישים מהם תרומות ומעשרות.

לאחר כל מחזור של שלוש שנים מצווה לסיים את הפרשת התרומות והמעשרות ולחלקם, וזוהי מצוות 'ביעור מעשרות', שנאמר (דברים יד, כח): "מִקְצֵה שָׁלֹשׁ שָׁנִים תּוֹצִיא אֶת כָּל מַעְשַׂר תְּבוּאָתְךָ בַּשָּׁנָה הַהִוא וְהִנַּחְתָּ בִּשְׁעָרֶיךָ". כלומר, עד זמן הביעור חובה לסיים את הפרשת התרומות והמעשרות מפירות שלוש השנים שעברו, ולתת את התרומות והחלה לכהן, את ה'מעשר-ראשון' ללוי, ואת ה'מעשר-עני' לעני, ואת פירות ה'מעשר-שני' ו'נטע-רבעי' להעלות לירושלים ולאכול בטהרה.

---

75. In principle, *terumot* are separated for the *kohanim*. However, these may be eaten only in a state of absolute ritual purity (*tahara*) and it is a serious offense for non-*kohanim* to eat them, or for *kohanim* to eat them when not pure. Therefore, *terumot* today are wrapped and respectfully discarded, instead of being given to *kohanim*.

76. Produce of the fourth year of a sapling's growth, from which time it is no longer forbidden as *orla* and is treated like *ma'aser sheini*.

If someone has not gotten to bring them to Jerusalem by the time of the removal, he must remove them from his domain by burning or in some other way which destroys them....

The time for the removal is at the conclusion of the holiday of Pesach, after the conclusion of the three years. That means, Pesach of the fourth year, and Pesach of the seventh year...

The mitzva of removal is specifically effective for *ma'aser sheini* and *neta reva'i* (fourth-year fruit), which one was obligated to bring up to Jerusalem... Regarding the *terumot* and *ma'aserot* for the Levi and the needy, there are additional mitzvot which determine earlier times for their delivery.

N. 8

According to Torah law, the time for removal is at the conclusion of Pesach, when it is still possible to eat fruit of *ma'aser sheini*. However, since it is functionally impossible to destroy [the produce] on Yom Tov, because burning these things is forbidden on Yom Tov, the Sages moved forward the time for removal to Erev Yom Tov. According to Rashi, the Rash, Tosafot, and the *Yere'im*, the text of the Mishna states that the removal is on Erev Pesach. But according to the Rambam, Meiri, *Semag*, *Shulchan Aruch*, and Vilna Gaon, it is Erev Yom Tov of the last day of Pesach. According to all opinions, the *viduy* was said at the time of *mincha* of the last day of Yom Tov, for they would leave from the removal the fruits of *ma'aser sheini* which they were planning to eat before the end of Pesach, so that they would actually finish removing the *ma'aser sheini* only just before the conclusion of Yom Tov and would be able to recite the declaration.

13. ...In our times, *vidui ma'asrot* is not recited, because the *Beit HaMikdash* has been destroyed and we are unable to eat the fruits of *ma'aser sheni* in purity in Jerusalem in accordance with the Torah's command. Some have the custom to make a commemoration of the mitzva by reading from the Torah the entire section in which the verses of the confession appear.

מי שלא הספיק להעלותם לירושלים והגיע זמן הביעור, צריך לבערם מרשותו בשריפה או בדרך אחרת שמאבדת אותם מהעולם...

זמן הביעור הוא בסיום חג הפסח שלאחר סיום שלוש השנים. כלומר בפסח של שנה רביעית ובפסח של שנה שביעית...

מצוות הביעור הועילה במיוחד ל'מעשר שני' ו'נטע רבעי', שאותם היה צריך להעלות לירושלים... לגבי התרומות והמעשר ללוי ולעני, ישנן מצוות נוספות שקובעות זמנים מוקדמים יותר לנתינתם (להלן הלכה יד).

הע' 8

מהתורה זמן הביעור בסיום חג הפסח, שעד אז עוד אפשר לאכול מפירות מעשר שני, אולם כיוון שאי אפשר לבער בפועל בחג, כי שריפתם אסורה ביו"ט, לפיכך הקדימו חכמים את זמן הביעור לערב חג. לרש"י, ר"ש, תוס' ויראים, הגרסה במשנה שהביעור בערב יו"ט ראשון של פסח. ולרמב"ם (מעשר שני יא, ז), מאירי, סמ"ג, שו"ע (יו"ד שלא, קמד), וגר"א, ערב יו"ט אחרון של פסח. ולכל הדעות הווידוי היה נאמר במנחה של חג אחרון, כי היו משיירים מהביעור את פירות המעשר-שני שיאכלו עד סיום חג הפסח, כך שרק לקראת סוף החג סיימו באמת לבער את המעשר שני ויכלו להתוודות.

יג. ...בזמן הזה, אין אומרים 'וידוי מעשרות', מפני שבית המקדש חרב ואיננו יכולים לאכול פירות 'מעשר שני' בטהרה בירושלים כמצוות התורה. ויש נוהגים לעשות זכר למצווה, וקוראים מהתורה את כל הפרשיה שפסוקי הווידוי נזכרים בה.

Summary of the Halachot of Erev Pesach

Fast of the Firstborn

1. ***Masechet Soferim*** – The firstborns have a custom to fast on Erev Pesach.
2. ***Shulchan Aruch*** – Some say that firstborn women also fast.
3. **Rema** – This is not the standard practice.
4. **Rema** – A parent should fast in place of a firstborn minor.
5. ***Mishna Berura, Be'erot Yitzchak*** – If a firstborn attends another's celebratory *siyum* upon completing a tractate of Gemara, order of Mishna, or another *seudat mitzva,* it is not necessary to complete the fast.

Matza on Erev Pesach

1. ***Yerushalmi,* Rambam** – It is forbidden to eat matza on Erev Pesach.
2. **Rema** – Regarding children too young to understand the Exodus, it is permitted to feed them matza all day.
3. ***Peninei Halakha*** – Some have the custom to refrain from eating matza as early as Rosh Chodesh Nisan or even Purim.
4. **Rema** – Food that is made from the crumbs of proper matza may not be eaten on Erev Pesach.
5. ***Peninei Halakha*** – If products are baked from matza which has been ground up so finely that it is no longer identifiable, it is possible that these may be eaten on Erev Pesach.
6. ***Aruch HaShulchan*** – If matza is cooked after it has been baked, this may be eaten on Erev Pesach.

- *Matza Ashira*

7. ***Devarim*** – Matza is defined as "poor bread."
8. **Gemara (*Masechet Pesachim*)** – If flour is kneaded with something other than water, this does not constitute true matza but rather "*matza ashira* (rich bread)."
9. ***Tur***
   a. Fruit juice does not cause leavening.
   b. **Rashi** – It is still forbidden to knead even in fruit juice alone.

c. **Rif** – It is permitted to knead even with water and fruit juice, from the first night and on.
d. **Ri** – Fruit juice alone does not cause leavening at all, and it is permitted to knead with it from the first night and on.
e. ***Behag*** – It must be incinerated immediately.
f. **Ritz Giat, Rosh** – If one baked it immediately, it may be eaten.
g. **Rashi** – It is uncertain if the liquid of an egg causes leavening.
h. **Rabbeinu Tam, Rosh** – The liquid of an egg is permitted.

10. ***Shulchan Aruch*** – Matza made from fruit juice and other liquids may be eaten on Pesach, but it is not fit for the mitzva of matza.
11. **Rema** – We do not use it on Pesach, except for those whose health requires it.
12. ***Shulchan Aruch*, Rema** – Although it is forbidden to eat proper matza on Erev Pesach, this category does not include *matza ashira*.
13. **Rabbeinu Tam, *Aruch HaShulchan*** – *Matza ashira* may be eaten on Erev Pesach.
14. **Rav Moshe Feinstein** – According to Ashkenazic custom, from the moment that *chametz* becomes forbidden on Erev Pesach, *matza ashira* should not be eaten by healthy people.
15. **Rav Mordechai Eliyahu** – Today, much of the commercially produced "*matza ashira*" is actually proper *chametz*.
16. **Rav Ovadia Yosef** – Even today, *matza ashira* is permitted according to the *Shulchan Aruch*.

- **Baking Matza on Erev Pesach**

17. ***Shulchan Aruch*** – It is customary to bake matza for the *Seder* only in the afternoon of Erev Pesach.
18. ***Mishna Berura, Peninei Halakha*** – This is merely a custom, and even if matza is baked earlier, it may be used for the *Seder*.

The Holiday of Erev Pesach

1. ***Vayikra*** – Erev Pesach, when the *korban Pesach* is offered, is a holiday in its own right.
2. **Gemara (*Masechet Pesachim*), Rambam** – *Melacha* is forbidden after midday on Erev Pesach.
3. ***Shulchan Aruch*** – It is permitted to perform some small labors for the needs of Yom Tov.

4. ***Mishna Berura***
   a. Someone may work for hire if he needs the pay for food.
   b. One may perform those light labors which are permitted on *Chol HaMo'ed* and are necessary for the festival.
   c. A person must stop performing forbidden labor at midday, even if someone is in the middle of a task.
5. **Rav Mordechai Eliyahu** – It is proper to be stringent regarding even light labor and buying and selling in the last quarter of the daylight hours.

Personal Grooming

1. ***Shulchan Aruch, Mishna Berura*** – Cutting hair and laundering clothing must be done before midday on Erev Pesach.
2. ***Aruch HaShulchan, Piskei Teshuvot*** – It is permitted to have a gentile cut one's hair after midday on Erev Pesach, and one may cut nails at this time if it was not done earlier.
3. ***Peninei Halakha,* Rav Mordechai Eliyahu** – It is also permitted to shave oneself at this time (although it is preferable to do so earlier).
4. ***Piskei Teshuvot***
   a. It is forbidden to shave oneself after midday.
   b. It is permitted to pay a needy Jew to cut one's hair after midday.
   c. If there is no gentile or needy Jew available, and someone's hair is long, he may cut it himself.
   d. A woman may have her hair cut even after midday if she needs to do so to prepare for immersion, or for modesty.
   e. Although it is preferable to do it earlier, it is permitted to polish shoes after midday.
   f. It is forbidden to launder clothing in a washing machine after midday.
5. ***Shemirat Shabbat K'hilchata*** – It might be permitted to launder clothing by pressing the buttons on a washing machine, even after midday on Erev Pesach.
6. ***Yalkut Yosef*** – It is permitted to launder clothing in a washing machine after midday on Erev Pesach.

Recitations Related to *Korban Pesach*

1. **Rema** – Ashkenazim omit *Mizmor L'toda* in *Shacharit* on Erev Pesach and throughout Pesach.

2. ***Shulchan Aruch HaRav, Peninei Halakha*** – Some have the custom to recite the verses pertaining to the *korban Pesach* on the afternoon of Erev Pesach. One should also pray for the restoration of the *Beit HaMikdash* and the chance to once again offer the *korban Pesach.*

Eating on Erev Pesach Afternoon

1. **Mishna (*Masechet Pesachim*)** – One must not eat from the beginning of the tenth daylight hour on Erev Pesach.
   a. **Rashi, Rashbam** – This is so that the person will have an appetite for the matza of the *Seder* night.
   b. **Ran** – This measure is meant to prevent a person from eating the matza on a stuffed stomach.
   c. **Rosh** – Regarding someone who typically remains full for a longer time after eating, it may be appropriate to stop eating even earlier in the day, so that it is possible to eat the matza normally.
2. **Gemara (*Masechet Pesachim*)** – Types of "refreshments" and vegetables may be eaten even in the late afternoon.
   a. **Tosafot** – Thus, only *matza ashira* becomes forbidden at the beginning of the tenth hour.
   b. **Rashbam** – It is permitted to eat fruits and meat in the late afternoon.
   c. **Tosafot** – It is permitted to eat grain products and fruit in the late afternoon.
3. ***Shulchan Aruch*** – It is permitted to eat modest quantities of fruits and vegetables in the late afternoon on Erev Pesach.
4. ***Mishna Berura*** – Meat and the like are also permitted.

When Erev Pesach Coincides with Shabbat

1. ***Shulchan Aruch*** – The fast of the firstborn is observed on Thursday (12 Nisan).
2. ***Shulchan Aruch***
   a. We discard all [the *chametz*] before Shabbat, except for that which is needed for the first two meals of Shabbat.
   b. The third meal is eaten in the afternoon, but before the tenth hour, with *matza ashira.*
3. **Rema** – Because we are not accustomed to eat *matza ashira,* one should eat fruit or meat, etc., for the third meal.

4. ***Aruch HaShulchan***
   a. Even according to the Rema, it would be permitted to eat *matza ashira* for the third meal.
   b. It is permitted to use cooked matza for the third meal, but this is not recommended because it is very filling.
   c. Fruit (or meat) is better.
   d. One may learn Torah in place of eating the third meal on this Shabbat.
5. ***Shulchan Aruch*** – *Chametz* should be burnt at the regular hour, before midday, on Erev Shabbat. (And any remaining *chametz* should be disavowed on Shabbat itself.)
6. **Rav Yosef Zvi Rimon**
   a. **Eating Bread** – One may do either of the following:
      i. Eat *matza ashira* and recite *hamotzi*. Ashkenazim should finish by the end of the fourth hour.
      ii. Eat bread that does not crumble, such as pita.
   b. ***Seuda Shelishit*** – One may do any of the following:
      i. Those who eat *matza ashira* until the tenth hour may use it.
      ii. Eat meat, fish, fruit, or *kneidlach* (before the tenth hour).
      iii. Some add to the second solution by dividing the morning meal into two.

Removing Ma'aserot

1. **Rambam** – The *viduy ma'aserot* (declaration of the tithes) may be recited in any place, after one has disposed of all the tithes and *terumot* in his possession. The *ma'aserot* must be removed by the sixth day of Pesach.
2. **Rav Avraham Yitzchak HaKohen Kook** – The declaration of the tithes is not formally recited today, because we cannot claim to have performed all the details correctly.
3. ***Peninei Halakha*** – All the tithes (*terumot* and *ma'aserot*) are removed at the time of end of Pesach of the fourth and seventh years of each *Shemita* (Sabbatical) cycle. Some say that the time for removal is Erev Pesach, but many say that it is before the last day of Yom Tov. The declaration is recited before the end of the last day of Yom Tov.

Further Iyun

Women's Obligation in the Mitzva of Sippur Yetziat Mitzrayim

Rav Maor Azar (Participant, Manhigut Toranit)

The Importance of the Question

Among the many halachic components of the Seder night, one question lies at the halachic core of the Seder: Are women obligated in the mitzva of *sippur yetziat mitzrayim*? This is not merely a theoretical inquiry. It directly affects the conduct of the Seder itself – most notably, whether a woman may lead the reading of the Haggada and discharge others through her recitation.

The underlying principle is well established:[1] "*Kol she'eino mechuyav b'davar, eino motzi et harabim yedei chovatan*" – one who is not obligated in a mitzva cannot discharge others who are obligated. If women are obligated at the same level as men, they may recite the Haggada and enable others to fulfill their obligation. If their obligation is weaker, or entirely rabbinic, while men's is biblical, the matter becomes more complex. We must therefore examine the basis of the obligation itself.

The General Rule: Time-Bound Positive Mitzvot

The **Mishna** in ***Masechet Kiddushin***[2] states: "All positive commandments that are time-bound – men are obligated and women are exempt." The **Gemara**[3] derives this principle from the mitzva of *tefillin*. Just as women are exempt from *tefillin*, which does not apply at night or on Shabbat, so too, by default, women are exempt from other positive mitzvot dependent on a defined timeframe.

At first glance, *sippur yetziat mitzrayim* appears to fit squarely into this category. It is performed specifically on the night of the fifteenth of Nisan. Why should women not be exempt? However, the **Rambam** cautions in his commentary to the Mishna that the term "all" is not literal. The rule expresses the majority, not an absolute. Numerous exceptions exist, either through explicit verses, special derivations, or distinct conceptual frameworks.

The task, therefore, is not to apply the rule mechanically, but to determine whether *sippur yetziat mitzrayim* falls within its parameters or within one of its exceptions.

Models for Exception to the General Rule

If women are generally exempt from positive time-bound mitzvot, how do exceptions emerge?

1. *Rosh Hashana* 29a.
2. 1:7.
3. 35b.

The *sugyot* reveal that the rule of *mitzvat asei shehazeman gerama* is not always automatic. Rather, women's obligation may arise through distinct halachic mechanisms.

A. Explicit Inclusion

At times, the Torah itself includes women in a time-bound commandment. The clearest example is *Hakhel*: "Gather the people – the men, the women, and the children".[4] Although *Hakhel* occurs only once every seven years, women are explicitly obligated. In such cases, the default exemption is overridden by direct textual inclusion. However, no verse explicitly obligates women in *sippur yetziat mitzrayim*.

B. Special Derivation

In other cases, women are obligated through a specific halachic linkage that overrides the time-bound character of the mitzva. For example:

- **Matza**: "Whoever is included in the prohibition of *chametz* is included in the obligation of matza."[5] Since women are prohibited from *chametz*, they are obligated in matza.
- ***Kiddush***: Similarly, the linkage of "*zachor*" and "*shamor*"[6] teaches that whoever is bound by the prohibition of *melacha* is likewise bound by the positive command of sanctifying Shabbat.

These derivations demonstrate that the time-bound rule yields when a deeper structural relationship between mitzvot is revealed. We must ask: does *sippur yetziat mitzrayim* possess such a derivation?

C. When the Time-Limitation Is Only Technical

There exists a third type of case: mitzvot that appear time-bound, yet whose limitation is not intrinsic to the mitzva itself, but stems from external or practical circumstances. In such cases, the mitzva is not essentially tied to a calendar date. Rather, the "time" reflects when the relevant conditions are present. Several examples illustrate this category:

1. *Bikkurim*

The **Mishna**[7] teaches that *bikkurim* are brought only until Chanuka. At first glance, this seems to be a classic time-bound mitzva. Yet the same Mishna states that women bring *bikkurim*.

The ***Turei Even*** (cited by R. Akiva Eiger) explains that the Chanuka deadline is not a fixed calendrical boundary. Rather, after Chanuka, fruit is no longer found in the fields. If produce were available later, the mitzva would continue. The limitation is thus agricultural, not time-bound in essence. Therefore, it is not considered a true *mitzvat asei shehazeman gerama*, and women remain obligated.

2. *Hakbalat Pnei Rabo*

The **Gemara**[8] derives from the story of the Shunamite woman that one is obligated to greet one's teacher on the festival. If the obligation is tied specifically to the festivals, it would appear to be time-bound. Yet the ***Pnei Yehoshua*** explains that ideally one should greet one's teacher regularly. The only reason it is highlighted on the festivals is because people are not working then,

---

4. *Devarim* 31:12.
5. *Pesachim* 43b.
6. *Berachot* 20b.
7. *Bikkurim*, ch. 1.
8. *Rosh Hashana* 16b.

making the visit more feasible. The festival is not the essential definition of the mitzva, but the practical opportunity for its fulfillment. Thus, women are not exempt because the time is not intrinsic to the command.

3. *Birkat Ha'Ilanot*

Although *Birkat Ha'Ilanot* is recited in the month of Nisan, many *poskim*[9] rule that women are subject to the mitzva in the same manner as men since the operative condition is the blossoming of trees, not the month itself. This is evident from the fact that in the Southern Hemisphere (Argentina, Australia, South Africa), the blessing is recited in Elul, when spring occurs there.[10] The calendar date is incidental; the natural phenomenon defines the mitzva.

4. *Birkat HaLevana*

Although *Birkat HaLevana* can only be recited during specific days of the lunar cycle, the **Gemara**[11] states that "our women recite it as well." The **Meiri** testifies that in his community, women indeed did so. In other words, if we understand the Gemara to mean that women were obligated in this mitzva,[12] the phenomenon of the moon's renewal would be the criteria, rather than the specific time of the month.

D. *"Af Hein Hayu B'oto HaNeis"*

The fourth pathway for obligating women in time-bound mitzvot is the well-known principle of "*af hein hayu b'oto haneis*" – women too participated in the miracle. This reasoning appears in the Gemara (in the name of Rabbi Yehoshua ben Levi) to obligate women in several time-bound rabbinic mitzvot: *Ner Chanuka,*[13] *arba kosot,*[14] and Megillat Esther.[15]

The *Rishonim* raise an immediate difficulty: if *af hein hayu* suffices to obligate women in time-bound mitzvot, why was a special derivation necessary to obligate women in eating matza? After all, the Exodus from Egypt, commemorated by matza, was certainly a miracle in which women participated.

Tosafot[16] answer that the principle of *af hein hayu* generates only a rabbinic obligation. In all of its explicit appearances in the Gemara, it applies to rabbinic mitzvot. Since matza is a biblical obligation, a separate derivation was required to obligate women on a Torah level. Accordingly, even if *af hein hayu* were applied to *sippur yetziat mitzrayim*, Tosafot would understand women's obligation as rabbinic.

Rabbeinu Yosef Ish Yerushalayim adopts a broader understanding. He suggests that the reason a special derivation was necessary in the case of matza is not because *af hein hayu* is limited to rabbinic force, but because there existed a competing *gezeira shava* linking matza to sukka through the phrase "*chamisha asar.*" Since women are exempt from sukka, that linkage could have

9. See *Chazon Ovadia*, Pesach, p. 11.
10. See sources quoted in *Piskei Teshuvot* 226:2.
11. *Sanhedrin* 42a.
12. It should be noted that this is not the understanding of most commentaries, who explain that women are not obligated in the mitzva, but would be allowed to recite the *beracha* according to the Gemara if they wish. The accepted practice today is for women not to recite *Birkat HaLevana* at all, as was explained in *Tzurba M'Rabanan*, volume 23, *shiur* 1.
13. *Shabbat* 23a.
14. *Pesachim* 108b.
15. *Megilla* 4a.
16. *Megilla* 4a.

exempted them from matza as well. A special derivation was therefore needed to override that comparison. However, absent such a competing source, *af hein hayu* itself could ground even a biblical obligation. Tosafot's more limited approach appears to represent the dominant position among the *Rishonim*.

Applied to *sippur yetziat mitzrayim*, the practical consequence is significant: According to Tosafot, women would be obligated only on a rabbinic level; according to Rabbeinu Yosef, their obligation could extend to the biblical level.

The Ruling of the *Shulchan Aruch* and Rema

The ***Shulchan Aruch***[17] rules succinctly: "Women are obligated in the four cups and in all the mitzvot of that night." The ***Mishna Berura*** clarifies that this includes matza, *maror*, and the recitation of the Haggada – i.e., *sippur yetziat mitzrayim*.

The **Rema**[18] adds a practical directive: the Haggada should be recited in a language understood by the women and children, or explained to them. He cites the practice of Rabbeinu Yosef of London, who would read the Haggada in the vernacular so that the women could fully comprehend it. The *Mishna Berura* emphasizes that this concern reflects a real obligation: Women are not passive participants, but fully included in the mitzvot of the night.

However, neither the *Shulchan Aruch* nor the Rema specifies whether the obligation is biblical or rabbinic. The practical inclusion is clear; the conceptual level remains subject to the earlier debate.

The Challenge of the *Minchat Chinuch*

The ***Sefer HaChinuch***[19] writes succinctly that the mitzva of *sippur yetziat mitzrayim* applies to men and women alike.

The ***Minchat Chinuch*** reacts with surprise. How can women be obligated in a *mitzvat asei shehazeman gerama* without an explicit derivation? He notes that the **Rambam**,[20] in enumerating time-bound mitzvot in which women are obligated, includes *kiddush*, matza, *korban Pesach*, *simcha*, and *Hakhel*, and yet does not list *sippur yetziat mitzrayim*. If *sippur yetziat mitzrayim* were biblically obligatory for women, why would the Rambam not list it? The omission is striking. The *Minchat Chinuch* therefore proceeds to examine, and reject, possible explanations.

1. "*Af Hein Hayu B'oto HaNeis*"

Perhaps women are obligated because they too were part of the miracle.

The *Minchat Chinuch* dismisses this as insufficient to explain a biblical obligation. If Tosafot are correct that *af hein hayu* generates only a rabbinic obligation, then at most women would be rabbinically obligated, not biblically, as the *Chinuch* appears to imply (he omits mention of the opinion of Rabbeinu Yosef Ish Yerushalayim).

2. Comparison to *Kiddush*

The **Rambam**[21] compares the obligation of *sippur yetziat mitzrayim* to "*zachor et yom haShabbat*." Perhaps, then, just as women are biblically obligated in *kiddush* through the linkage of "*zachor*" and "*shamor*," so too, they are obligated in *sippur*.

---

17. O.C. 472.
18. O.C. 473.
19. Mitzva 21.
20. *Hilchot Avoda Zara*, ch. 12.
21. *Hilchot Chametz Umatza* 7:1.

The *Minchat Chinuch* rejects this argument. The Rambam does not invoke a formal *gezeira shava*, nor does any classical source establish such a linkage. The comparison appears explanatory rather than derivational. Without a clear source, the *Chinuch*'s ruling cannot rest on this analogy.

3. "*Ishto Sho'alto*"

Chazal structure the Seder around dialogue: if a child is absent, one's wife asks; if alone, one asks himself. Perhaps the wife's role in questioning indicates her independent obligation.

The *Minchat Chinuch* rejects this as well. The obligation lies in telling; the questioning serves as a structural mechanism to generate narrative response. The wife is required to ask only when no sons are present and the fact that she may ask does not establish that she is independently obligated in the mitzva.

4. Dependency on Matza

A further possibility is that *sippur yetziat mitzrayim* is not inherently time-bound, but dependent upon the presence of matza and *maror* – "when matza and *maror* are placed before you." Since women are obligated in matza, perhaps they are likewise obligated in *sippur*.

The *Minchat Chinuch* forcefully rejects this. The Torah defines the mitzva as occurring on the night of the fifteenth of Nisan. The contextual linkage to matza does not alter its temporal nature. It remains a positive time-bound commandment.

The *Minchat Chinuch* concludes with a striking observation: accepting the *Chinuch*'s position without a clear derivation may generate practical leniency. If women are considered biblically obligated, they could discharge men's obligation in *sippur yetziat mitzrayim*. Yet if their obligation is in fact only rabbinic, this would be problematic.

Resolving the *Sefer HaChinuch*'s View

In order to defend the *Sefer HaChinuch*, who appears to obligate women in *sippur yetziat mitzrayim* on a biblical level, two possible explanations may be offered. Each, however, is subject to significant reservations.

1. Mitzvot Instituted Before *Matan Torah*

The ***Kli Chemda*** proposes a bold distinction. The exemption of women from positive time-bound mitzvot is derived from the mitzva of *tefillin*. According to the *Kli Chemda*, this exemption applies only to mitzvot given from Sinai onward. However, commandments that originated prior to *Matan Torah*, such as the obligation to recount the Exodus, which was already commanded in Egypt, were never subject to that exemption. Women, therefore, retained their original obligation.

Nonetheless, this explanation is difficult to sustain. The Gemara in *Masechet Kiddushin* derives the exemption of women from time-bound mitzvot from the verse "*v'haya lecha l'ot al yadcha*," which appears in *Parashat Bo*, which was stated before *Matan Torah*. If the verse establishing the exemption itself predates Sinai, it is difficult to argue that pre-Sinai mitzvot are categorically excluded from the rule. Moreover, *sippur yetziat mitzrayim* is itself commanded in that same pre-Sinai context. It is therefore difficult to maintain that the exemption applies to other mitzvot taught in *Parashat Bo* but not to *sippur* itself.

2. A Midrashic Source and the Comparison to *Kiddush*

As noted earlier, the *Minchat Chinuch* rejects the possibility that the Rambam's comparison between *sippur* and *kiddush* can generate a biblical obligation for women, due to the absence of an explicit Talmudic source linking the two. The ***Yad Eitan***, however, suggests that the Rambam may have drawn this comparison from a Midrash in ***Shemot Rabba*** (end of *Parshat Bo*), which explicitly juxtaposes "*zachor et yom haShabbat*" with "*zachor et hayom hazeh asher yetzatem miMitzrayim.*" If so, the Rambam may have understood that just as women are biblically obligated in *kiddush* through the linkage of "*zachor*" and "*shamor*," so too they are obligated in *sippur*.

Two significant reservations arise regarding this explanation. First, *Shemot Rabba* is a relatively late Midrash, perhaps roughly contemporaneous with the Rambam. It is unclear whether the Rambam had access to this Midrash in its present form. It is equally plausible that the Midrash reflects the Rambam's idea rather than serving as its source.

Second, as the ***Yad Peshuta*** observes, when the Rambam cites Chazal in his *Sefer HaMitzvot*, which was written in Arabic, he typically quotes their language in Hebrew or Aramaic. In this instance, however, he formulates the comparison independently in Arabic. This suggests that the parallel may represent his conceptual formulation rather than reliance on a specific Midrashic source. Accordingly, while the Midrash provides support for the analogy, it does not conclusively establish a derivational basis for obligating women.

An Additional Explanation: A Torah-Technical Limitation

Earlier (section 3), we discussed mitzvot that appear time-bound but are, in truth, only technically limited by circumstance rather than intrinsically defined by time. The *Minchat Chinuch* rejects the argument that since Chazal state that *sippur yetziat mitzrayim* is fulfilled only "when matza and *maror* are placed before you," and since women are obligated in matza, this linkage could extend the biblical obligation of *sippur* to them. In his view, the temporal definition of the mitzva cannot be overridden by such dependency.

However, one might suggest a more nuanced formulation. Perhaps mitzvot that are not directly time-defined, but instead are dependent upon another mitzva which is itself time-bound, are not classified as classic *mitzvot asei shehazeman gerama*. In such cases, the "time" functions through the dependent mitzva rather than as an independent defining feature.

To illustrate, consider the mitzva of *Sefirat Ha'Omer*. The Torah states:

> You shall count for yourselves from the morrow of the Sabbath, from the day you bring the *Omer* offering – seven complete weeks shall there be.

One may ask: Is *Sefira* defined by a specific calendar date ("*mimacharat haShabbat*"), or is it defined by the bringing of the *Omer* offering – which itself is time-bound?

The **Rambam**[22] rules that women and slaves are exempt from *Sefira* because it is a time-bound mitzva. By contrast, the **Ramban**[23] lists *Sefirat Ha'Omer* among mitzvot that are not classified as *hazman gerama*. It would appear that they disagree on this very point: Does a Torah-mandated temporal framework automatically render a mitzva time-bound? Or can a mitzva whose timing is derivative – dependent upon another act – be viewed as only technically limited, and therefore not subject to the general exemption?[24]

22. *Hilchot Temidin U'Musafin.*
23. *Chiddushim* to *Kiddushin,* on the Mishna cited earlier.
24. For further discussion of the nature of *Sefirat Ha'Omer,* see the essay to *shiur* 5.

Applying this model to *sippur yetziat mitzrayim,* one could argue that the mitzva is not defined by the calendar date per se, but by the presence of matza and *maror*. The temporal setting would then be derivative rather than intrinsic. This reading gains support from Chazal's statement: "Whoever did not say these three things on Pesach has not fulfilled his obligation: Pesach, matza, and *maror*." The *poskim* clarify that one has not failed to fulfill the mitzva entirely, but rather has not fulfilled the mitzva in its most proper form. Nevertheless, the statement reflects a tight interdependence between *sippur* and the ritual mitzvot of the night. Indeed, **Tosafot**[25] state explicitly that *sippur yetziat mitzrayim* is dependent upon the eating of matza.

Similarly, the **Ramban**, in his *Hasagot* to the *Sefer HaMitzvot*,[26] writes that *Birkat HaTorah* should not be counted together with the Torah reading as one mitzva, just as *mikra bikkurim* (reciting the passage in *Devarim* 26 when bringing *bikkurim*) is not counted together with bringing *bikkurim*, and *sippur yetziat mitzrayim* is not counted together with eating the *korban Pesach*. This formulation indicates that *sippur* is conceptually bound to the *korban Pesach*, a mitzva in which women are unquestionably obligated (as the Rambam rules in *Hilchot Avoda Zara*).

At first glance, therefore, one might argue that *sippur* is not an independent time-bound mitzva, but a mitzva tethered to other ritual acts of the night.

However, despite its appeal, this explanation cannot ultimately resolve the position of the *Sefer HaChinuch*. In his treatment of *Sefirat Ha'Omer* (Mitzva 306), the *Chinuch* explicitly adopts the Rambam's view that women are exempt because it is a time-bound mitzva. This indicates that the *Chinuch* does not accept the broader thesis that dependency upon another mitzva removes the classification of *zeman gerama*. If so, the same reasoning cannot be invoked to defend his ruling regarding *sippur yetziat mitzrayim*.

Conclusion

Several points emerge with clarity from our analysis. Women are unquestionably obligated in the mitzva of *sippur yetziat mitzrayim* on the night of the Seder, as ruled explicitly by the *Shulchan Aruch* and the Rema. Therefore, they must understand the content of the Haggada in order to fulfill the mitzva properly.

With respect to the level of that obligation, however, the matter is subject to dispute. According to Tosafot, the obligation rests upon the principle of "*af hein hayu b'oto haneis*" and is therefore rabbinic in nature. According to Rabbeinu Yosef Ish Yerushalayim, and seemingly according to the *Sefer HaChinuch*, the obligation may be biblical. It is possible that Ramban and Tosafot could be read in that direction as well, though they do not state this explicitly.

In light of this uncertainty, and in consideration of the *Minchat Chinuch*'s concern that one who is not obligated at the same level cannot discharge another's obligation, a practical distinction emerges.

While women are full participants in the mitzva of *sippur* and should be active and engaged in the telling, it is preferable *lechatchila* that one who seeks to discharge others' obligation through his recitation be someone whose biblical obligation is undisputed according to all views.

Accordingly, if one individual reads on behalf

25. *Megilla* 19b, s.v. *Rabbi Yehuda Omer*.
26. *Shichechat Asein* 15.

of others with the intention of fulfilling their obligation, it is proper that it be a man, who is biblically obligated according to all opinions. In this way, the mitzva is fulfilled in accordance with all views.[27]

27. See also *Shulchan Aruch HaRav* 472:25; *Pri Megadim, Eishel Avraham* 479:2; and *Halichot Bat Yisrael* 23:26.

Further Iyun

The Mitzva of Destroying Chametz (Tashbitu): A Positive Act or Passive Avoidance?

Rav Meir Ben David (Participant, Manhigut Toranit)

As is well known, the Torah commands us to eliminate *chametz* before the holiday of Pesach:

> For seven days you shall eat matzot, but on the first day you shall eliminate ("*tashbitu*") leaven from your houses...[1]

In this essay, we will address the following question: how should the mitzva of *tashbitu* ("you shall eliminate") be understood? Is it a mitzva of active performance (*kum aseh*), requiring a person to physically destroy *chametz*, or is it a mitzva of passive avoidance (*shev ve'al ta'aseh*), whose requirement is simply that no *chametz* remain in one's possession? In other words, if a person has no *chametz* at all, has he merely avoided violating the commandment, or has he actually fulfilled the mitzva?

This situation can be compared to other mitzvot. A person who owns no four-cornered garment does not violate the mitzva of *tzitzit*, yet he also has not fulfilled it. Perhaps the same applies to *chametz*: if one never possessed *chametz*, he has not performed the mitzva of *tashbitu*.

At first glance, the wording of the verse suggests an active obligation to eliminate *chametz*. However, there is room to consider another possibility. We find a similar dual formulation regarding Shabbat. On the one hand, the Torah states: "You shall not perform any labor".[2] Yet elsewhere it states: "Six days you shall perform your work, and on the seventh day you shall rest (*tishbot*)".[3] In its simple sense, the command to "rest" on Shabbat does not require a specific action, but rather the absence of action. The mitzva is fulfilled through refraining from work. Perhaps the commandment of *tashbitu* should be understood in a similar way.

Practical Implications of This Question

This conceptual question has several practical ramifications:

1. One Who Has No *Chametz*

If the mitzva requires an **active act of destruction**, perhaps one should obtain *chametz* in order to destroy it and thereby fulfill the mitzva, just as one would acquire a four-cornered garment in order to fulfill the mitzva of *tzitzit*. If, however, the mitzva is fulfilled simply by ensuring that no

---

1. *Shemot* 12:15.
2. *Shemot* 20:10.
3. *Shemot* 23:12.

chametz remains in one's possession, there would be no reason to do so.

2. The Requirement of Intent

Halacha generally rules that mitzvot require intent.[4]

If the mitzva of *tashbitu* is an active commandment, someone who destroyed *chametz* without intent would not fulfill the mitzva. But if the mitzva consists of a passive state – having no *chametz* in one's possession – intent may not be necessary.

3. "Stealing" a Mitzva

Halacha states that someone who "steals" a mitzva from another person must pay compensation of ten gold coins.[5] If destroying *chametz* is an active mitzva, someone who destroys another person's *chametz* might be considered to have deprived him of the opportunity to perform the mitzva. If, however, the mitzva is passive, no such loss has occurred, as the owner has still fulfilled the requirement that no *chametz* remain in his possession.[6]

4. A Mitzva Accomplished Through a Transgression

Suppose someone eliminates *chametz* by eating it on Pesach. Has he fulfilled the mitzva of *tashbitu*?

Tosafot[7] explain that *mitzva haba'a ba'aveira* applies only when the mitzva is fulfilled through the very act of the transgression, as in the case of a stolen lulav. Accordingly, if the mitzva of destroying *chametz* is a *kum aseh*, eliminating *chametz* by eating it on Pesach would constitute a *mitzva haba'a ba'aveira*, since the mitzva would be fulfilled through the prohibited act. If, however, the mitzva is *shev ve'al ta'aseh*, the mitzva is realized through the resulting state that no *chametz* remains, and it would therefore not be considered a *mitzva haba'a ba'aveira*.

5. Women's Obligation

Women are generally exempt from positive commandments that are time-bound, but they remain obligated in prohibitions. If *tashbitu* is an active positive commandment limited to a particular time, women may be exempt. If it is understood as a passive obligation to ensure that no *chametz* remains, women might be obligated.

6. The Time of the Mitzva

The ***Minchat Chinuch*** suggests that if the mitzva requires an active act of destruction, its time begins only when the prohibition of *chametz* takes effect, which is midday on the fourteenth of Nisan. However, if the mitzva is passive, it could theoretically be fulfilled even long beforehand, since the requirement is simply that no *chametz* remain in one's possession.

How Is the Mitzva of *Tashbitu* Fulfilled?

To understand the different approaches to the question at hand, we must first examine the dispute among the *Rishonim* regarding how the

---

4. *Shulchan Aruch*, O.C. 60:4 and *Mishna Berura* 60:8.
5. *Shulchan Aruch, Choshen Mishpat* 382:1.
6. This practical ramification is mentioned in the *Minchat Chinuch* (mitzva 9, section 1). However, according to the *Taz* (*Yoreh De'ah* 28:8), there would be no practical difference, since he maintains that the rule requiring someone who "steals" a mitzva to pay compensation applies only when the one who took the mitzva actually performs the mitzva himself. If he merely prevents the other person from performing the mitzva, he is not required to pay.
7. *Sukka* 30a.

mitzva of *tashbitu* is fulfilled in practice. The **Gemara** in ***Masechet Pesachim***[8] discusses a case in which a house is presumed not to have been checked for *chametz*, yet women, slaves, or minors testify that they performed the search. Their testimony is accepted. The Gemara explains that this is because *bedikat chametz* is only rabbinic, since on the biblical level mere nullification of the *chametz* suffices.

Rashi[9] explains that the mitzva of *tashbitu* is fulfilled through nullification in one's heart (i.e., intent). This is supported by the wording of the verse itself, which states "*tashbitu*" ("eliminate") rather than "*teva'aru*" ("burn"). The Gemara's statement that "nullification alone suffices" likewise indicates that the biblical requirement can be fulfilled without any physical act.

However, **Tosafot**[10] raise two major objections to Rashi's interpretation. First, later in the Gemara, Rabbi Akiva derives from the verse "On the first day you shall eliminate leaven from your houses" that the obligation of elimination already applies on the fourteenth of Nisan, before the festival begins. Since it is forbidden to kindle fire on Yom Tov, the implication is that the *chametz* must be destroyed beforehand through burning. This suggests that the mitzva of *tashbitu* requires active destruction.

Second, the Gemara teaches that the prohibition of *chametz* begins from midday on the fourteenth of Nisan, thus, the mitzva of *tashbitu* begins only at that time. However, at that time, simple renunciation of ownership is no longer effective. If so, the mitzva cannot be fulfilled merely through mental nullification. Tosafot therefore conclude that the mitzva of *tashbitu* is fulfilled through physical elimination, such as burning the *chametz*.[11]

The **Ramban**[12] offers an intermediate position. In his view, the mitzva of *tashbitu* can be fulfilled either through nullification or through physical destruction, and both represent legitimate forms of eliminating the *chametz*.

The Analysis of the *Minchat Chinuch*

The ***Minchat Chinuch*** discusses at length whether the mitzva of *tashbitu* is a case of *kum aseh* (an active commandment) or *shev ve'al ta'aseh* (a passive obligation). He suggests that this question depends on the dispute between Rashi and Tosafot, as discussed above.

According to the *Minchat Chinuch*, Rashi maintains that the mitzva of *tashbitu* is essentially a case *of shev ve'al ta'aseh*. The obligation is simply that no *chametz* remain in one's possession. For this reason, it is possible to fulfill the mitzva even before the time of prohibition by nullifying the *chametz* mentally, thereby ensuring that it no longer belongs to him.[13] Tosafot, however, understand the mitzva differently. In their view, *tashbitu* is a *kum aseh* that requires an active act of destruction. Accordingly, the mitzva can be fulfilled only once the prohibition of *chametz*

---

8. 4b.
9. s.v. *b'bitul.*
10. s.v. *umide'oraita.*
11. Tosafot explain the Gemara's statement that "nullification alone suffices" differently: before the time when *chametz* becomes prohibited, a person can avoid the obligation of destruction by declaring the *chametz* ownerless. Once the prohibition has begun, however, only active elimination is effective.
12. s.v. *v'chen.*
13. According to the *Minchat Chinuch*, this is also the position of the Rambam, since the Rambam also recognizes nullification as a valid way of fulfilling the biblical obligation.

has taken effect, and therefore, it must be carried out through actual elimination, such as burning.

A Difficulty with the *Minchat Chinuch*'s Approach

Later authorities raise a difficulty with this interpretation. According to the *Minchat Chinuch*, Rashi's view implies that the mitzva of *tashbitu* is fulfilled simply through mental nullification. However, this seems difficult in light of a passage in the **Gemara**[14] discussing the source of the prohibition of *chametz* beginning at midday on the fourteenth of Nisan.

The Gemara asks: what is the source for the prohibition of *chametz* from midday on the fourteenth? After all, the Torah states: "For seven days leaven shall not be found in your houses," which appears to imply that the prohibition begins only with the festival itself. The Gemara resolves this by citing two verses: "For seven days leaven shall not be found in your houses" and "On the first day you shall eliminate leaven from your houses." Abaye explains that these two verses together teach that the obligation of elimination already applies on the fourteenth of Nisan. **Rashi**[15] comments that if the Torah commands elimination on the first day, there must necessarily be at least some moment within the seven days when *chametz* would otherwise remain present, creating a tension between the two verses.

In other words, Rashi understands that there is a tension between the two verses as follows. According to the first verse, the prohibition of *bal yeira'eh ubal yimatzei* applies during every moment of the seven days. But the second verse commands us to eliminate the *chametz* on the first day. If the *chametz* is only destroyed then, there must necessarily have been some moment during the seven days when *chametz* was present, meaning the command that "no leaven shall be found for seven days" could not have been fulfilled perfectly.

According to this reading, one must conclude that the mitzva of destroying *chametz* is a *kum aseh* (an active commandment). For if it were a *shev ve'al ta'aseh* (a passive obligation), the Gemara's difficulty would disappear. The first verse ("for seven days no leaven shall be found") could simply be understood as a prohibition, while the second verse ("on the first day you shall eliminate") would be a positive commandment. Since the mitzva would then be fulfilled passively, by simply ensuring that no *chametz* remains, there would be no moment during the seven days when the prohibition is violated.

But if that were the case, the Gemara would not have raised the problem in the first place. This therefore contradicts the *Minchat Chinuch*'s explanation that Rashi understands the mitzva as *shev ve'al ta'aseh*.

A Possible Resolution: The Approach of the *Chatam Sofer*

The ***Chatam Sofer***[16] offers a different explanation of Rashi than the *Minchat Chinuch* that resolves the difficulty mentioned above. According to the *Chatam Sofer*, Rashi understands the mitzva of *tashbitu* as a single obligation that unfolds in two stages. The first is the practical stage – the stage of the person's action. The second is the stage of fulfillment, when the mitzva is considered fully realized. The practical stage begins at

14. *Pesachim* 4b.

15. s.v. *uketiv*. See, however, Tosafot for an alternative explanation.

16. *Pesachim* 4b s.v. *ha*.

the start of the fourteenth of Nisan, when the person must begin addressing the *chametz*. The stage of fulfillment, however, occurs at midday, when the prohibition of *chametz* takes effect and the requirement that no *chametz* remain becomes operative.

According to this explanation, it is entirely possible to fulfill the mitzva through mental nullification (*bitul*), since the act performed earlier can lead to the state required when the time of the prohibition arrives. Tosafot, however, do not accept this two-stage structure. In their view, there are not two stages to the mitzva. Rather, once there is an obligation that the *chametz* be eliminated, there is immediately an obligation to perform the act of elimination itself.

The Ran appears to understand the dispute between Rashi and Tosafot in a similar manner. His comments suggest that the disagreement is not limited to the laws of *chametz*, but reflects a more general question about whether the Torah obligates a person to take preparatory actions necessary for the fulfillment of a mitzva. The **Ran**[17] discusses a case of a couple who quarrelled on Friday. In his anger, the husband swore that he would not be in the city on Shabbat. Later, after tempers cooled, he wished to annul the oath. However, the halachic rule is that an oath can be annulled only once it has taken effect. Since the oath concerns Shabbat, it would seem that it cannot be annulled beforehand. If so, the husband would have to leave the city before Shabbat in order not to violate his oath. The Ran writes that this question depends on the dispute between Rashi and Tosafot in our discussion regarding whether the mitzva of eliminating *chametz* can be fulfilled through mental nullification or requires physical destruction.

The Ran formulates an important principle: according to Rashi, when the fulfillment of a mitzva requires taking an additional step, that step itself becomes obligatory. Therefore, in this case the husband is obligated to leave the city before Shabbat in order to avoid violating his oath, and consequently the oath may be annulled already on Friday. According to Tosafot, however, a person is not obligated to take such an additional step. Doing so is merely optional. Therefore, the husband would not be required to leave the city before Shabbat, and since the oath has not yet taken effect, it cannot be annulled beforehand.

Practical Rulings of Later Authorities

Some commentaries and later authorities draw practical conclusions from this conceptual debate regarding the nature of the mitzva of *tashbitu*. The ***Sefer HaChinuch***[18] writes concerning this mitzva that it applies "in every place and at all times, to men and women." In light of one of the practical implications noted above, this would seem to indicate that he understands the mitzva as a case of *shev ve'al ta'aseh*. Since women are included in the obligation, it appears that the mitzva is not being treated as a classic positive time-bound commandment requiring an active performance. By contrast, the ***Avnei Nezer***[19] argues at length in support of the position of Tosafot, namely, that the mitzva requires active elimination.

The ***Minchat Chinuch*** also raises a difficulty with Tosafot's approach. In practice, we burn the *chametz* at the beginning of the sixth hour, before midday. If, according to Tosafot, the mitzva of

17. Responsa of the Ran 51.
18. *Parshat Bo, Mitzva* 9.
19. O.C. 318:3.

tashbitu begins only once the prohibition takes effect, it would seem that we are destroying the *chametz* **before the time of the mitzva**, and thus failing to fulfill the biblical commandment. How, then, could the Sages effectively cancel a Torah mitzva merely as a safeguard lest people err in calculating the time?

He answers that while the Sages cannot uproot a fully obligatory positive commandment such as lulav or matza for the sake of a safeguard, they may do so in the case of a mitzva that is not inherently obligatory in every circumstance, such as *tashbitu* or *tzitzit*. Just as one who has no four-cornered garment is not obligated in *tzitzit*, so too, one who has no *chametz* is not obligated in *tashbitu*. In such cases, the Sages may require conduct that effectively prevents the opportunity for the mitzva from arising. Accordingly, the practical outcome is that, according to **Tosafot,** there is no real possibility today of fulfilling the mitzva of *tashbitu* in its ideal biblical form.

Conclusion

The mitzva of *tashbitu* raises a fundamental question: does the Torah require an active act of destruction, or is the mitzva fulfilled by the state in which no *chametz* remains in one's possession? The *Minchat Chinuch* proposed that this issue underlies the dispute between Rashi and Tosafot: Rashi would understand the mitzva as *shev ve'al ta'aseh*, while Tosafot would view it as *kum aseh*. However, later authorities challenged this reading of Rashi. The *Chatam Sofer* explained Rashi differently, suggesting that the mitzva unfolds in two stages: a practical stage beginning at the start of the fourteenth of Nisan, and a stage of fulfillment at midday, when the prohibition of *chametz* takes effect. The Ran may be understood along similar lines, insofar as he too recognizes that halacha can obligate a person to take preparatory steps before the actual time of fulfillment. The *Sefer HaChinuch* appears to support the understanding of *tashbitu* as *shev ve'al ta'aseh*, since he includes women in the obligation, while the *Avnei Nezer* argues in favor of Tosafot's view that the mitzva requires active elimination.

Thus, the conceptual question remains a genuine subject of debate. But in any event, the discussion highlights the complexity of the mitzva of *tashbitu*: it is not merely a technical requirement to get rid of *chametz*, but a fundamental halachic question about whether the Torah commands an act of destruction or demands the resulting state of a *chametz*-free domain.

ERETZ HEMDAH
Institute for Advanced Jewish Studies
Jerusalem

קליפורניה, ארה"ב California, U.S.A.

ניסן, ה'תשנ"ז

נ. זמן "תענית בכורות" למי שטס לארץ-ישראל.

שאלה

אדם היוצא מסן פרנציסקו ביום א' בבוקר, בתאריך יג בניסן, הוא אמור לנחות בישראל ביום ב' בשעות הצהרים, בערב פסח, יד בניסן. מתי עליו להתחיל את הצום ומתי הצום מסתיים לגביו, בהנחה שלא יוכל להשתתף בסעודת "סיום" תוך כדי הטיסה?

תשובה

הצום חל על האדם בעלות השחר של יום י"ד בניסן בכל מקום בעולם[1] שבו הוא נמצא. אם יבוא ממזרח למערב, יארכו לו שעות היום, ואם יבוא ממערב למזרח, יתקצרו לו שעות היום, ועל כן צריך לברר עם קברניט האוירון את מסלול הטיסה - באיזה איזור יהיה המטוס בסוף הלילה ולבדוק אז בלוח-הזמנים של אותו המקום את השעה המדויקת של עלות השחר, ואז יתחיל עבורו הצום.

במקרה זה, כאשר הטיסה היא לארץ-ישראל, הרי יש בה גם שמחה של מצוה הפוטרת את האדם מצום זה של תענית בכורות, וחלות שמחה היא ברגע שהוא נוחת בארץ. לכן יוכל לאכול במטוס כל עוד לא עלה השחר של יום שני, י"ד בניסן, יצום בשארית הטיסה ויוכל לאכול עם הגעתו ארצה ביום שני בשעות הצהריים[2].

---

[1] רבי עובדיה ספורנו (ויקרא כג, ג ד"ה שבת הוא לה'). שו"ת "שואל ומשיב" (כרך ד חלק שני, תשובה קכד).
[2] סברת הרב נחום אליעזר רבינוביץ.

5

Halachot of Mourning Customs of Sefirat Ha'Omer

הלכות מנהגי אבילות של ספירת העומר

Origin of Mourning Customs During Sefirat Ha'Omer

When are Mourning Customs Observed?

Weddings

Shaving and Haircuts

Reciting the Beracha of Shehecheyanu

Dancing and Listening to Music

Lag B'Omer

For quick reference, some long website URLs have been shortened.
For the complete list of referenced websites visit www.tzurbaolami.com.

ת	**Tanach**
ח	**Talmud (Chazal)**
ר	***Rishonim***
א	***Acharonim***
פ	**Contemporary Halachic Sources**

Origin of Mourning Customs During Sefirat Ha'Omer

The time between Pesach and Shavuot is the period of *Sefirat Ha'Omer*, the counting of "the *Omer*."[1] The rising count begins on the day of the communal "*Omer*" offering, a *mincha* (grain-based "meal" offering) offering, which is brought on the second day of Pesach. This communal offering consists of flour made from the new crop of barley measuring an *omer*,[2] and the Torah commands us to count forty-nine consecutive days from the day of the *Omer*, culminating in the Yom Tov of Shavuot, the day celebrating the giving of the Torah.[3]

The halachot relating to the counting were discussed in detail in volume 6. Bridging the festival of our exodus from Egypt with the festival of the giving of the Torah, these days have been described by some as a type of "*Chol HaMo'ed*" between Pesach and Shavuot, and by nature, they should be days of celebration.[4] However, following the death of Rabbi Akiva's students, this became a period of national mourning, accompanied by certain mourning practices. The Gemara in ***Masechet Yevamot*** describes the events of that time.

1. מסכת יבמות סב:

רבי עקיבא אומר: למד תורה בילדותו – ילמוד תורה בזקנותו. היו לו תלמידים בילדותו – יהיו לו תלמידים בזקנותו, שנאמר: "בַּבֹּקֶר זְרַע אֶת זַרְעֶךָ וגו'" (קהלת יא, ו). אמרו: שנים עשר אלף זוגים תלמידים היו לו לרבי עקיבא מִגְּבַת עד אַנְטִיפְּרָס, וכולן מתו בפרק אחד, מפני שלא נהגו כבוד זה לזה.

ח Masechet Yevamot 62b

Rabbi Akiva says that the verse should be understood as follows: If one **studied Torah in his youth he should study** more **Torah in his old age;** if **he had students in his youth he should have** additional **students in his old age, as it is stated: "In the morning sow your seed,** and in the evening, do not withhold your hand, for you know not which will succeed, this one or that one, or whether both of them will be equally good" (*Kohelet* 11:6). **They said** by way of example that **Rabbi Akiva had twelve thousand pairs of students** in an area of land that stretched **from Gevat to Antipatris** in Judea, **and they all died in one period** of time, **because they did not treat each other with respect.**

---

1. As we explain, the word *Omer* can be used in referenced to one of three things. (1) Primarily, *omer* is a volume measurement equivalent to the *issaron* (mentioned in *Bamidbar* 28). (2) An offering brought of an *omer*'s measure of barley flour is thus also called the *Omer.* (3) Finally, the count initiated on the day of the *Omer* offering is called the *Sefirat Ha'Omer*, and this period is thus informally called "the Omer." Here, we will attempt to distinguish between these three by using italics for the first two meanings of *omer*, the measure in lower case and the offering in upper case. With reference to the period of the calendar, it will appear here in upper case and without italics.
2. A volume of equivalent to between 2.49 liters and 4.32 liters.
3. *Vayikra* 23:9–16.
4. See Ramban, *Vayikra* 23:36 and Rabbeinu Bechayei, *Vayikra* 23:16.

And the world was desolate of Torah **until Rabbi Akiva came to our Rabbis in the South and taught** his Torah **to them.** This second group of disciples consisted of **Rabbi Meir, Rabbi Yehuda, Rabbi Yosei, Rabbi Shimon, and Rabbi Elazar ben Shamua. And these are the very ones** who **upheld** the study of **Torah at that time.** Although Rabbi Akiva's earlier students did not survive, his later disciples were able to transmit the Torah to future generations.

With regard to the twelve thousand pairs of Rabbi Akiva's students, the Gemara adds: It is **taught** that **all of them died** in the period **from Pesach until Shavuot. Rav Chama bar Abba said, and some say** it was **Rabbi Chiyya bar Avin: They all died a bad death.** The Gemara inquires: **What is it** that is called a bad death? **Rav Nachman said: Diphtheria** [*askara*].[5]

והיה העולם שמם, עד שבא רבי עקיבא אצל רבותינו שבדרום, ושְׁנָאָהּ להם: רבי מאיר, ור' יהודה, ור' יוסי, ורבי שמעון, ורבי אלעזר בן שמוע, והם הם העמידו תורה אותה שעה.

תנא: כולם מתו מפסח ועד עצרת. אמר רב חמא בר אבא, ואיתימא ר' חייא בר אבין: כולם מתו מיתה רעה. מאי היא? אמר רב נחמן: אסכרה.

The Gemara does not state explicitly that one should observe mourning practices during the period of *Sefirat Ha'Omer*. Nevertheless, the **Geonim** already mention the custom not to hold weddings.

ו Responsa of the Geonim, Sha'arei Teshuva, Siman 278

2. תשובות הגאונים | שערי תשובה, סימן רעח

And regarding your question why we do not perform betrothal or marriage between Pesach and Shavuot, and whether it is because of a prohibition or not: You should know that it is not due to any prohibition, but rather because of a custom of mourning. For the Sages said: Rabbi Akiva had twelve thousand pairs of students, and they all died between Pesach and Shavuot because they did not treat each other with respect. And it was taught further that they all died a strange death of diphtheria. **From that time onward, the early generations were accustomed during these days not to hold weddings.**

ןשאלתם למה אין מקדשי' ואין כונסין בין פסח לעצרת אם מחמת איסור או לאו. הוו יודעי' שלא משום איסור הוא אלא משום מנהג אבלות, שכך אמרו חכמים שנים עשר אלפים זוגים תלמידים היו לו לר' עקיבא וכלם מתו בין פסח לעצרת על שלא נהגו זה בזה, ותני עלה וכלם מתו מיתה משונה באסכרה, **ומאותה שעה ואילך נהגו ראשונים בימים אלו שלא לכנוס בהן.**

5. The disease called *askara* refers to diphtheria, as translated here – a contagious throat disease. It causes swelling of the mucous membrane in the throat and creates a sensation of choking. The disease was common among children and was highly deadly before modern medicine, often resulting in death by suffocation. In Second Temple times, some fasted on Wednesdays to prevent *askara* in infants. In classical sources and commentaries, the disease is described as beginning in the intestines and rising to the throat, likely reflecting the symptoms in children, including vomiting and abdominal pain (see Background notes to the Koren Talmud, *Shabbat* 33a).

When are Mourning Customs Observed?

As we will see in more detail in the coming sections, the primary customs of mourning during *Sefirat Ha'Omer* mentioned by the *Rishonim* are refraining from weddings and haircuts or shaving, and later sources add additional restrictions such as dancing, music, and possibly reciting *Shehecheyanu*. Before analyzing each of the practices in detail, let us first examine when exactly during the period of the *Sefira* these customs of mourning should be observed.

It would stand to reason that our mourning should correspond to the days that Rabbi Akiva's students died. However, the Gemara simply states that they died "from Pesach until *Atzeret* (Shavuot)" and does not specify whether they died only during certain days of that period or during the entire time. The Geonim and *Rishonim* offer a few approaches to this issue.

Approach 1: They Died from Pesach to Shavuot

This would seem to be the simple understanding of the Gemara and the Geonim above (source 2).

Approach 2: They Died from Pesach until Lag B'Omer

This approach is mentioned in the **Meiri**.

3. מאירי | יבמות סב:

...וקבלה ביד הגאונים שביום ל"ג בעומר פסקה המיתה, וכן נוהגים מתוך כך שלא לישא אשה מפסח עד אותו זמן.

ר Meiri, Yevamot 62b

...The Geonim had a tradition that on Lag B'Omer the [students] stopped dying. Indeed, our custom as a result is not to marry a woman from Pesach until that time.

The ***Sefer HaManhig*** explains that although the text in our Gemara states that they died from Pesach until "*Atzeret*," there is another tradition that states they died until "*peros Atzeret*," which is understood to mean fifteen days prior, i.e., Lag B'Omer.

4. ספר המנהיג | הל' אירוסין ונישואין קו

...מנהג בצרפת ופרובינצ' לכנוס מל"ג לעומר ואילך. ושמעתי בשם רבי' ר' זרחיה מגירונדא שמצא כתוב בספר ישן הבא מספרד, שמתו מפסח ועד פרוס העצרת, ומאי פורסא פלגא כדתנן שואלין

ר Sefer HaManhig, Hilchot Eirusin V'nisuin 106

...The custom in France and Provence is to hold weddings from Lag B'Omer and onward. And I heard in the name of Rabbeinu Zerachia of Gerona that he found written in an old book that came from Spain that they died from Pesach until "*peros Atzeret*." And what is *peros*? Half. [And half the preparation time for a holiday is fifteen days] as we learn: One asks about

בהלכו' הפסח קודם לפסח ל' יום ופלגא חמשה עשר יום קודם העצרת וזהו ל"ג לעומר.

the laws of Pesach thirty days before Pesach (*Pesachim* 6a), and half of that is fifteen days before Shavuot, which is Lag B'Omer.[6]

Approach 3: They Died over All but 16 Days of *Sefira*

The sixteen days were those that are days of joy, meaning Yom Tov, Shabbat, and Rosh Chodesh. This approach is mentioned by **Rav Yosef Ibn Shueb**.

5. בית יוסף | או"ח תצג

...שמה שאמרו ל"ג לעומר אינו כמו שנוהגים, אלא שלשים ושלשה יום כשתסיר שבעת ימי הפסח ושבע שבתות ושני ימים של ראש חודש שהם ששה עשר ימים שאין אבלות נוהג בהם, נשארו מן הארבעים ותשעה יום שלשים ושלשה יום.

ר Beit Yosef, Orach Chaim 493

...What they said about Lag B'Omer is not as people commonly practice. Rather, the thirty-three days [are calculated as follows]: If you deduct the seven days of Pesach, the seven days of Shabbat, and the two days of Rosh Chodesh, which together total sixteen days during which mourning practices do not apply, then out of the forty-nine days, thirty-three days of mourning remain.

According to this approach, thirty-three days of mourning are observed, but not necessarily on the days that the students died. Rather, many observe the period of mourning beginning from Rosh Chodesh Iyar. The ***Bi'ur Halacha*** summarizes the second and third customs regarding this question, which are more widely observed.[7]

6. ביאור הלכה | או"ח תצג:ג

...דיש בזה שלש שיטות, ונבאר שתיים מהן שנקטום הפוסקים לדינא.

וזהו שיטה אחת, **דתלמידי רבי עקיבא מתו שלושים וארבעה יום, וראייה ממדרש שמתו מפסח עד פרוס עצרת, והוא ט"ו יום קודם עצרת**, וכשתסיר ט"ו יום מארבעים ותשעה נשארו ל"ד יום שלמים שמתו, אלא דמקצת היום ככולו, ומשום הכי **מסתפרין ביום שלושים וארבעה בבוקר**, והוא הדין לישא אישה מותר מכאן ואילך.

א Bi'ur Halacha, Orach Chaim 493:3

...There are three approaches [as to when the mourning during *Sefira* is observed], and we will explain two that the *poskim* adopted.

1. The first approach is that **Rabbi Akiva's students died over thirty-four days, and proof can be brought from the Midrash that they died from Pesach until *"peros Atzeret,"* which is fifteen days before Shavuot**. Subtracting those fifteen days from forty-nine leaves thirty-four full days on which they died, though [observing] part of the [final] day is treated as if [one observed] the whole thing.[8] Therefore, **haircuts are permitted on the thirty-fourth day in the morning**. Similarly, marrying a woman is permitted from this point onward.

---

6. We will see later that there are two versions of this custom: One is that the restrictions continue until the morning of the thirty-fourth of the Omer, including Lag B'Omer (*Shulchan Aruch*), and the second is that the restrictions are over on the morning of Lag B'Omer (Rema).

7. We cite the chronologically later *Bi'ur Halacha* out of order here, because his synopsis of the issue will greatly aid our understanding of the varied customs cited in the *Shulchan Aruch*, Rema, and other sources.

8. This principle is often applied within the laws of *aveilut* (mourning). According to this, when someone observes even just a small part of the final day of mourning, it is not necessary to complete the full day of mourning. According to most opinions,

וזה דעת המחבר בסעיף א וסעיף ב. אכן לדעת הרמ"א שם בסעיף ב משמע, דסבירא ליה דפסקו מלמות ביום ל"ג, וכמו שכתב הגר"א שם, ומקצת היום ככולו. ולפי שיטה זו, המנהג שאין מסתפרין מפסח **עד יום שלושים ושלושה בבוקר**, ומשם והלאה עד עצרת – מותר.

This is the position of the *Mechaber* [i.e., the *Shulchan Aruch*] in *se'if* 1 and *se'if* 2.

But it seems from the Rema in *se'if* 2 that he holds they stopped dying on the thirty-third day, as the Gra writes there, and a portion of the day is considered like the whole thing. According to this approach, the custom is not to cut hair from Pesach[9] **until the morning of the thirty-third day**, after which it is permitted until Shavuot.[10]

שיטה שנייה, הוא מה שאומרים בשם התוספות, דתלמידי רבי עקיבא **מתו ל"ג ימים שלמים, דהיינו – ביום שאין אומרים תחנון לא מתו.** אם כן כשתוציא שבעת ימי הפסח – דהיינו מיום שני של פסח – ועוד שישה שבתות, ושני ימים ראש חודש אייר, ויום אחד ראש חודש סיוון שלא מתו, אם כן הרי נשארו ל"ג שלמין שמתו, ולפי זה מתו עד עצרת.

2. The second approach is that stated in the name of Tosafot, that Rabbi Akiva's students **died for thirty-three full days, meaning that on the days when Tachanun is not recited, they did not die**. Therefore, when the seven days of illness are deducted, starting from the second day of Pesach, and the following six Shabbats, plus two days of Rosh Chodesh Iyar and one day of Rosh Chodesh Sivan on which no deaths occurred, thirty-three full days remain on which deaths occurred. According to this, they died until Shavuot.

ולנגד אלו ה-ל"ג ימים קבלו ישראל על עצמם קצת אבלות ל"ג ימים (אלא שיום אחד מהן יש להקל במקצת יום, דהוא ככולו, ובחרו ביום ל"ג בעומר, ואולי מאיזה טעם. פרי מגדים) לעניין ספירה ונשואין. דהיינו: **לנכות מ-מ"ט יום של העומר ט"ז ימים הראשונים, דהיינו – מיום שני של פסח עד יום שני של ראש חודש אייר יש ט"ז ימים, שאותן ימים מקילין בהן**, ונשארו ל"ג שלימין עד עצרת, ומתאבלין בהן.

Corresponding to these thirty-three days, the Jewish People adopted some mourning practices for thirty-three days [but not necessarily on those same days]. (But on one of these days, one can be lenient for part of the day, as [mourning for part of the day] is considered a full day, and they selected the thirty-third day of the Omer, possibly for a specific reason.) [The mourning practices are] regarding haircuts and weddings. This means: **subtract from the forty-nine days [of *Sefirat ha'omer*] the first sixteen days, i.e., from the second day of Pesach to the second day of Rosh Chodesh Iyar there are sixteen days, and those days one is lenient** [not to observe the mourning customs], leaving thirty-three days until Shavuot during which mourning is observed.

Thus, the two primary customs are as follows:

1. Some observe the semi-mourning customs from the beginning of the *Sefira* period until Lag B'Omer, with some continuing until the morning of the thirty-fourth, and others stopping on the morning of the thirty-third. This commemorates the students dying on these days.
2. Others observe the customs beginning from Rosh Chodesh Iyar until Shavuot, which commemorates the thirty-three days of their deaths, but not necessarily on the actual days they occurred.[11]

---

it is not sufficient to mourn at night, but one must also observe mourning restrictions during the daytime.

9. During Pesach, weddings are not held in any case and haircuts are also not allowed (see *Shulchan Aruch*, O.C. 531:2 and 546:1; see also *Tzurba M'Rabanan*, volume 23, *shiur* 7).

10. It would seem that this approach maintains that the students until "*peros Atzeret*" means that they died for thirty-three days, not thirty-four.

11. There are different versions of this custom: some observe the restrictions from Rosh Chodesh Iyar (30th of Nisan) until the 4th of Sivan, the first of the three days of preparation before Shavuot (*sheloshet yemei hagbala*), and others observe them

On the topic of haircuts during *Sefirat Ha'Omer*, the **Rema** writes that each community should follow a unified practice and not be split between individuals following different practices.

7. רמ"א | או"ח תצג:ג

...ולא ינהגו בעיר אחת מקצת מנהג זה ומקצת מנהג זה, משום "לא תתגודדו" (דברים יד, א), וכל שכן שאין לנהוג היתר בשתיהן.

א Rema, Orach Chaim 493:3

...Within one city,[12] it should not be observed that some people follow one custom and the others follow the other custom, because of "*Lo titgodedu* (Do not fractionalize)" (*Devarim* 14:1). And certainly it is unacceptable to follow the leniencies of both.

However, in many places, there is no uniform practice. In these circumstances, the ***Mishna Berura*** writes that one may choose which custom one wishes to follow. Nevertheless, where there is a specific custom, one should follow that custom.

8. משנה ברורה | או"ח תצג:יז

היתר בשתיהן – ...יכול לתפוס איזה מנהג שירצה, ואין לו לחוש שמא מנהג המקום ההוא אינו כן, דכיוון שהוא רק מנהג בעלמא אין להחמיר בספיקא. אבל אם ידוע לו מנהג המקום – אין לו לשנות, בין להקל ובין להחמיר.

א Mishna Berura, Orach Chaim 493:17

The leniency in both approaches – ...One may follow whichever custom one desires without concern that the local custom is different, as because it is merely a custom, there is no need to be stringent in a case of doubt. However, if one knows the local custom, he should not deviate, whether to be lenient or stringent.

Today, many *poskim* rule that it is permitted for individuals in the same community to adopt differing periods of mourning during *Sefirat Ha'Omer*, since people come from a wide variety of backgrounds with different customs, and this does not usually create any controversy.[13]

---

from the 2nd of Iyar until Erev Shavuot (see *Mishna Berura* 493:14–15).

12. The first part of the Rema's ruling not cited here is brought below in source 15.

13. See Responsa *Igrot Moshe*, O.C. 1:59 and *Piskei Teshuvot* 493:12. Rav Moshe also permits switching customs in other years, though Rav Aharon Kotler is reported to have disagreed, unless one performs *hatarat nedarim* (annulment of vows).

Weddings

We have already seen that one of the primary observances of the semi-mourning during *Sefirat Ha'Omer* is that weddings are not held. This custom is codified by the ***Shulchan Aruch.***

א Shulchan Aruch, Orach Chaim 493:1

It is customary not to marry a woman between Pesach and Shavuot until the thirty-third day of the *Sefirat Ha'Omer* because Rabbi Akiva's students died during this time. However, it is perfectly acceptable to betroth.[14] And even regarding *nisu'in,* if one did go ahead and marry [his wife], he is not punished.

Rema: But from the thirty-third day of the Omer onward, everything is permitted.[15]

9. שלחן ערוך | או"ח תצג:א

נוהגים שלא לישא אישה בין פסח לעצרת עד שלושים ושלושה לעומר, מפני שבאותו זמן מתו תלמידי רבי עקיבא, אבל לארס ולקדש – שפיר דמי. ונישואין נמי, מי שקפץ וְכָנַס – אין עונשין אותו.

הגה: מיהו משלושים ושלושה בעומר ואילך – הכל שרי.

In some matters, the halacha gives special dispensation to people who have not yet had children, so that they may fulfill the mitzva (of having children) as soon as possible. However, the ***Mishna Berura*** notes even regarding those who have not yet had children, the accepted custom is that they do not marry during this time.

א Mishna Berura, Orach Chaim 493:1

Not to marry a woman – There is no difference between marriage of a mitzva, such as someone who has no children, and someone who does have [children], as the custom in our communities is not to differentiate. Remarrying one's divorced spouse is permitted, as it is not as great a celebration.

10. משנה ברורה | או"ח תצג:א

שלא לישא אישה – ואין חילוק בין נישואין של מצווה, כגון שאין לו בנים, או יש לו, כי כן פשט המנהג במדינתנו, שלא לחלק. ולהחזיר גרושה – שרי, שאינו כל כך שמחה.

---

14. Note that the halacha relates to two distinct processes through which a couple proceeds to married life. Through the first act, called *eirusin* or *kiddushin* ("betrothal"), a woman becomes a man's wife insofar as she may not become married to another, and an intimate relationship with another man would be classified as adultery. However, even after betrothal, a married man and woman are not permitted to live together until the additional act of *nisu'in* ("marriage"), through which a man assumes full responsibility for his wife's needs and takes her into his home. Although today both of these ceremonies are performed together in a Jewish wedding, during the periods of the Mishna and Gemara, these stages were separated by many months. (It should be noted that today's "becoming engaged," i.e., the commitment to become married, does not create a halachic status of marriage at all. Nonetheless, in informal language, in today's spoken Hebrew, this engagement is called *eirusin.*) Accordingly, the *Shulchan Aruch* distinguishes between these two ceremonies. Because the couple begins to live together only after the second ceremony, and it is thus a greater celebration, it is only *nisu'in* (the second stage) which is to be avoided during the days of mourning. However, since today both the acts are done within a unified wedding ceremony, even *kiddushin* is not performed during the days of morning. See *Mishna Berura* 493:3.

15. The Rema's mention of the thirty-third day is consistent with his opinion discussed earlier that if observing mourning restrictions from the beginning of *Sefira,* one may end them on the morning of Lag B'Omer. According to the *Shulchan Aruch,* the restrictions would terminate on the morning of the thirty-fourth.

According to those who follow the first custom mentioned above, weddings may not be held from Pesach until either the morning of Lag B'Omer (Ashkenazim) or the morning of the thirty-fourth of the Omer (Sephardim). **Rav Ovadia Yosef** writes that if Sephardim in Israel come to the rabbinate to plan a wedding for Lag B'Omer, the rabbinate should inform them that the Sephardic custom is to wait until the thirty-fourth day of the Omer.

11. חזון עובדיה | יום טוב, הל' ספירת העומר וימי הספירה ל

וראוי להורות לכל רושמי הנישואין של הרבנות בארץ ישראל, שאם באים לפניהם מהספרדים ועדות המזרח להירשם לנישואין לפניהם, ויבקשו לישא בל"ג לעומר, יעירו תשומת ליבם שאין מנהג הספרדים כן, אלא מנהגם כמו שכתב מרן הבית יוסף בשם הרשב"ץ, **שאין לערוך נישואין לפני ל"ד לעומר**, כדין תספורת שאין להתיר התספורת אלא ביום ל"ד בבוקר, מדין "מקצת היום – ככולו".

Chazon Ovadia, Yom Tov, Hilchot Sefirat Ha'Omer Viymei HaSefira 30

It is proper to instruct all registrars of marriages in the rabbinate in Israel that if Sephardim and Edot HaMizrach couples come to register for marriage and wish to marry on Lag B'Omer, they should be reminded that this is not the custom for Sephardim; their practice follows what the *Beit Yosef* writes in the name of the Rashbatz, **that marriages should not be conducted before the thirty-fourth day of the Omer**, much like the law regarding a haircut; a haircut may be permitted only as of the morning of the thirty-fourth day, based on the law that part of the day counts as the whole [day].

Is a person allowed to attend a wedding during the time period when one is observing the mourning restrictions of *Sefirat Ha'Omer*? For example, regarding someone who observes the customs of mourning from Pesach, is it permitted at the end of Nisan to attend a wedding for one who observes the restrictions only beginning on Rosh Chodesh Iyar? **Rav Yosef Shalom Eliashiv** rules that this is permitted.

12. אשרי האיש | חלק ג, סה:ל

בחור בישיבה שמתחתן בימי הספירה ומנהגו לימי האבילות שונה ממנהג בני הישיבה **מותר לבני הישיבה להשתתף בשמחתו לצורך שמחת חתן וכלה אף כשאצלם נוהגים איסור** שזו שמחת מצוה.

ולאו דוקא חברים מהישיבה אלא כל אחד שנוהג שלא לעשות חתונות אחרי ל"ג בעומר והוא הוזמן לחתונה של אלו הנוהגין לעשות נשואין מותר לו להשתתף בסעודה ולרקוד ולשמוע תזמורת וכו' כיון שהחתן עושה הכל בהיתר

Ashrei Ha'Ish, Vol. 3, 65:30

Concerning a yeshiva student who marries during the period of *Sefirat Ha'Omer* whose custom regarding the mourning practices differs from that of the yeshiva, **it is permitted for the** [other] **yeshiva students to participate in his wedding for the sake of rejoicing with the bride and groom, even if, according to their own custom, they observe a ban** [on weddings at that time]. This is because it constitutes a mitzva celebration.

Moreover, this is not limited specifically to friends from the yeshiva. Rather, regarding anyone who follows the practice of refraining from weddings after Lag B'Omer who is invited to the wedding of those who customarily permit marriage during this period, is permitted to attend the festive meal, to dance, and to listen to live music, and the like. Since the groom is conducting the wedding entirely in accordance with his permitted [custom],

מוטל על כל אחד מצוה לשמח חתן וכלה.

the mitzva of rejoicing with the bride and groom applies to all.[16,17]

16. Rav Moshe Feinstein appears to agree (Responsa *Igrot Moshe,* O.C. 1:159). See, however, *Halichot Shlomo* (11:19) who accepts this idea only if one observes the basic thirty-three days and is stringent not to attend weddings on the other additional days as well – on those days, he may be lenient to attend a wedding.

17. See Responsa *Chatam Sofer* (O.C. 142) and *Bein Pesach L'shavuot* (8:14) that one may also change one's custom from year to year in places where there is no widespread local custom.

Shaving and Haircuts

Another standard practice of mourning during the period of *Sefirat Ha'Omer* involves refraining from taking a haircut or shaving. The custom is already mentioned in the 14th century by the ***Tur***.

13. טור | או"ח תצג

ויש מקומות שנהגו שלא להסתפר ויש מסתפרים מל"ג בעומר ואילך שאומרים שאז פסקו מלמות.

ר Tur, Orach Chaim 493

Some places have the custom not to take haircuts. And some take haircuts from Lag B'Omer and onward, as they say that [Rabbi Akiva's students] stopped dying at that time.

The ***Shulchan Aruch*** and the **Rema** codify this custom as well, but the Rema notes that haircuts are nonetheless permitted for the principal celebrants of a *brit mila*, or on Erev Shabbat before Lag B'Omer which falls on Sunday.

14. שולחן ערוך | או"ח תצג:ב

נוהגים שלא להסתפר עד שלושים ושלושה לעומר, שאומרים שאז פסקו מלמות. **ואין להסתפר עד יום שלושים וארבעה בבוקר**, אלא אם כן חל יום ל"ג ערב שבת, שאז מסתפרין בו מפני כבוד השבת.

הגה: ובמדינות אלו אין נוהגין כדבריו, אלא **מסתפרין ביום שלושים ושלושה**, ומרבים בו קצת שמחה, ואין אומרים בו תחנון. ואין להסתפר עד ל"ג בעצמו ולא מבערב. מיהו אם חל ביום ראשון – נוהגין להסתפר ביום שישי לכבוד שבת. ומי שהוא בעל ברית או מל בנו – מותר להסתפר בספירה לכבוד המילה.

א Shulchan Aruch, Orach Chaim 493:2

It is customary not to take a haircut until the thirty-third day of the Omer, as they say that that is when the deaths ceased. **One cannot have his hair cut until the morning of the thirty-fourth day**, unless the thirty-third day falls on Erev Shabbat, in which case people may have their hair cut due to the honor of Shabbat.

Rema: In these regions, the custom is not in accordance with his words. Rather, **we take haircuts on the thirty-third day** and add a little joy, and we do not say *Tachanun* on that day. Haircuts should not be taken until Lag B'Omer itself, but not from the eve. But if it falls on Sunday, then it is customary to take a haircut on Friday in honor of Shabbat. One who is celebrating a *brit* [i.e., the *mohel* or *sandek*], or one who is circumcising his son, may take a haircut during *Sefirat Ha'Omer* in honor of the circumcision.

Here, the *Shulchan Aruch* adopts the first custom of observing mourning from Pesach. He rules, as we saw above concerning weddings, that haircuts are not permitted until the morning of the thirty-fourth day of the Omer. The Rema is also consistent here with his approach above, according to which haircuts are permitted on Lag B'Omer itself, but only from the morning (*Mishna Berura*).

However, as we have mentioned, some have the alternative practice to observe their period of mourning beginning on Rosh Chodesh Iyar. The **Rema** mentions this practice in the next *se'if.*

15. שלחן ערוך | או"ח תצג:ג

יש נוהגים להסתפר בראש חדש אייר, וטעות הוא בידם.

הגה: מיהו בהרבה מקומות נוהגים להסתפר עד ראש חדש אייר, ואותן לא יספרו מל"ג בעומר ואילך, אף על פי שמותר להסתפר בל"ג בעומר בעצמו. ואותן מקומות שנוהגין להסתפר מל"ג בעומר ואילך, לא יסתפרו כלל אחר פסח עד ל"ג בעומר.

א Shulchan Aruch, Orach Chaim 493:3

There are those who have the practice to take a haircut on Rosh Chodesh Iyar, but they are mistaken.

Rema: However, in many places the practice is to take haircuts until Rosh Chodesh Iyar, and such people should not take haircuts from Lag B'Omer and onward – even though taking a haircut on Lag B'Omer itself is permitted. And in those places where the practice is to take haircuts from Lag B'Omer and onward, they should not take haircuts at all after Pesach until Lag B'Omer.

According to this custom, as explained by the Rema, one may take a haircut until Rosh Chodesh Iyar, as well as on Lag B'Omer itself, but one must then refrain until the very end of *Sefira.*

According to an additional custom mentioned in the name of the **Arizal,** one should not take a haircut throughout the entire *Sefira* period, from Pesach until Shavuot for kabbalistic reasons unrelated to the mourning for Rabbi Akiva's students.[18]

Shaving is also included in the restrictions of haircuts, since it, too, involves cutting hair of one's face.[19] However, more recent *Acharonim* have raised the question of whether it is permitted to shave during *Sefira* for someone who shaves daily or weekly throughout the rest of the year. This was not discussed by earlier authorities, when it was not practical for people to shave regularly in accordance with the halacha.[20]

Many *poskim*, such as **Rav Shlomo Zalman Auerbach**, do not allow shaving during *Sefira* even if one normally shaves every day.[21] By contrast, it is recorded that **Rav Yosef Dov Soloveitchik** ruled that one may shave during *Sefira* if one normally shaves daily.

16. נפש הרב | עמ' קצא

רבינו הסביר שמנהג האבלות מי"ז בתמוז ואילך הוא בבחינת אבלות של י"ב חודש [וכמו כן בימי הספירה]... ועל פי הבנה זו היה סבור **שמותר להתגלח בימי הספירה – לאלו המתגלחים בכל יום**, וכן מי"ז בתמוז עד ראש חודש אב. שמאחר שדין זמנים אלו

Nefesh HaRav, p. 191

Our teacher explained that the custom of mourning from the 17th of Tammuz onward is considered like the mourning of twelve months [and similarly during *Sefira*]... Based on this understanding, he thought **that shaving during *Sefira* would be permitted for those who shave daily**, and likewise from the 17th of Tammuz until Rosh Chodesh Av. Since the status of these periods

---

18. See *Sha'arei Teshuva* (493:4) and *Piskei Teshuvot* (493:15). Most understand the stringency as relating to haircuts alone, though some are strict concerning weddings as well.
19. Although shaving in the modern sense was not widespread in earlier times, contemporary *poskim* assume that the custom to refrain from haircuts includes shaving as well, except for the possible exceptions discussed below.
20. See *Tzurba M'Rabanan*, volume 1, *shiur* 6 for a detailed discussion of the halachic issues involved in shaving with a razor, which was the only way to shave in earlier times, and shaving with a shaver today.
21. *Shalmei Mo'ed*, p. 406. See also *Kaf HaChaim* (551:66) with regard to the Three Weeks (see the next volume), where he rules that even those who cut their hair biweekly should not do so during the Three Weeks. He would presumably say the same during *Sefira*. (See also *Kaf HaChaim* 493:19, who is lenient during *Sefira* in cases where one must fix one's beard to enter an official's court for business purposes). However, as we will see concerning the Three Weeks, it is permitted to trim one's mustache if the hair interferes with eating (*Mishna Berura* 551:80).

שוה לאבלות של י"ב חודש, ובי"ב חודש כבר נהגו העולם כדעת הפוסקים הסוברים, דהנוהג להתגלח בכל יום, וממתין קצת מלהתגלח – דזה כבר מיקרי שיעור גערה.

is equivalent to the mourning during the twelve months [after a parent dies], and in the twelve months of mourning, the common practice follows the authorities who rule that for one who normally shaves every day, delaying somewhat from shaving is already considered the measure of *ge'ara* (reproof)."[22]

Rav Aharon Lichtenstein[23] is quoted as allowing one to shave for Shabbat if one normally shaves every week for Shabbat, since it is a mitzva to honor Shabbat, and it overrides the custom not to shave. Even *poskim* who rule stringently on this question may allow shaving in cases of potential financial loss. For instance, **Rav Moshe Feinstein** allows shaving during *Sefira* if one may lose his job if he arrives for work unshaven during *Sefira*.

17. שו"ת אגרות משה | או"ח ד:קב

Responsa Igrot Moshe, Orach Chaim 4:102

הנה אם אחד עוסק באיזה מסחר למלאכה שאם לא יסתפר את זקנו בימי הספירה ובימים שבין י"ז בתמוז לט' באב יהיה לו הפסד ממון אז מותר כי לא נהגו במקום הפסד.

Now if someone is involved in a commercial business for his job such that if he does not trim his beard during *Sefira* or during the days between the 17th of Tammuz and Tisha B'Av he would incur a monetary loss, then it is permitted, for the custom was not practiced in cases of financial loss.[24]

Women and Cutting Hair During *Sefira*

Does the custom to refrain from haircuts apply to women as well? Recent Sephardic *poskim*, such as **Rav Ovadia Yosef** and **Rav Ben Zion Abba Shaul**, write that the custom was not adopted by women.

18. חזון עובדיה | יום טוב, הל' ספירת העומר וימי הספירה לו

Chazon Ovadia, Yom Tov, Hilchot Sefirat Ha'Omer Viymei HaSefira 36

ואין הנשים בכלל איסור זה.

Women are not included in this prohibition [of haircuts].

19. שו"ת אור לציון | ג:יז:ג

Responsa Ohr L'tzion 3:17:3

נשים מותרות להסתפר בימי העומר.

Women are permitted to take haircuts during the Omer.

However, according to Ashkenazic *poskim*, women customarily do not take haircuts during the Omer

22. When mourning for a parent, which extends in certain respects throughout the entire year from the time of passing, one may take a haircut or shave only after others have rebuked him for his hair looking unkempt, and only after thirty days have passed. See volume 3, *shiur* 5, sources 33–38.
23. See Responsa *Mibashan Ashiv*, cited in *Oholei Halacha, Moadim*, vol. 2, p. 40, and Responsa *Ner Ezra* vol. 2, p. 155, cited in *Peninei Halakha, Zemanim* 3:7, n. 9. Rav Ovadia Yosef holds similarly in *Chazon Ovadia, Yom Tov*, p. 262, but only in cases of great need.
24. See Responsa *Igrot Moshe*, O.C. 5:24:9 and C.M. 1:93 for further discussion as to what qualifies as a potential loss in this context.

except in cases of a mitzva or necessity. This is explained by **Rav Moshe Feinstein**.

20. שו"ת אגרות משה | יו"ד ב:קלז

ובדבר תספורת לאשה בימי הספירה, הנה אף שהיה מסתבר להתיר מאחר שגם באבלות אחר שבעה תוך שלשים מתירין הרבה ראשונים וכן המחבר... אבל מכל מקום נראה הדין שראוי להחמיר אם אינו נחוץ כל כך.

Responsa Igrot Moshe, Yoreh Deah 2:137

Regarding haircuts for women during *Sefira*: although it might seem permissible since, regarding mourning after *shiva*, but within the *shloshim* period, many *Rishonim*, as well as Rav Yosef Karo, permit… nevertheless, it seems that the halacha is that it is still proper to be stringent if it is not so pressing.

Rav Natan Gestetner writes that married Ashkenazic women may cut their hair in principle, though in practice, the custom is to refrain from doing so except for specific cases of need.

21. שו"ת להורות נתן | ב:לב

ולדינא נראה **דאשה נשואה ודאי רשאית להתגלח בימי הספירה**, וכן נראה בקטנה ובוגרת מהטעמים שכתבנו, ואף בנערה... וכל זה מעיקר הדין, ומכל מקום כמדומה **שכבר נהגו הבתולות שלא להסתפר בימי הספירה**, ואף אם נימא שאין זה מעיקר המנהג המבואר בשו"ע, מכל מקום הוה ליה כדברים המותרים ונוהגין בו איסור שאין להתירו, והנח להם לישראל וכו'. ומכל מקום במקום צורך כגון לרפואה או אירוסין וכן לאשה נשואה הצריכה לטבול או ששערותיה מבצבצין החוצה יש להתיר בלי פקפוק.

Responsa L'horot Natan 2:32

According to the halacha, it would seem **that a married woman is certainly permitted to have a haircut during the days of *sefira***, and this also applies to girls and young women for the reasons already stated… But this is all according to the letter of the law. Nonetheless, **the custom seems to have developed that unmarried women refrain from haircuts during the days of *Sefira*.** Even if we say that this is not included in the primary custom described in the *Shulchan Aruch*, nevertheless, it is considered like matters that are permissible but people treat it as forbidden, which one should not permit, and leave the Jewish People [to maintain their custom], etc. Nevertheless, in cases of necessity, such as for medical reasons, engagements, or for a married woman who must immerse or whose hair is sticking out, it may be permitted without doubt.

The ***Piskei Teshuvot*** writes that it is permitted to pluck eyebrows and eyelashes, etc., which is not considered a "haircut" and is readily permitted.

22. פסקי תשובות | או"ח תצג:ז

ואיסור זה הוא בין לאיש ובין לאשה, וכן בקטנים אף שלא הגיעו לחינוך, אמנם כשיש צורך מיוחד יש להתיר לנשים ונערות להסתפר, ולצורך מצוה כגון לצורך ליל טבילה או צניעות ששערותיה יוצאים חוץ לכיסוי הראש מותר אף לכתחילה.

מריטת שער הגבות או הריסים מותרת אף שנעשית ליפוי, כיון שאינה בכלל תספורת...

Piskei Teshuvot, Orach Chaim 493:7

This prohibition [against haircuts] applies to men, women, and children, even those who have not yet reached the age of education. However, in cases of special need, women and girls may take haircuts. For a mitzva, such as for immersion or modesty, when her hair sticks out from a head covering, it is readily permitted.

Plucking eyebrows or eyelashes is allowed even for beautification, as that is not considered a haircut…

Reciting the Beracha of Shehecheyanu

As explored elsewhere, the *beracha* of *Shehecheyanu* is a unique expression of a person's gratitude for living to see a milestone or celebrating some noteworthy personal good news.[25] Is it appropriate to recite this *beracha* amidst the mourning of *Sefirat Ha'Omer*? Unlike weddings and haircuts, the *Rishonim* and early *Acharonim* do not mention that a person must avoid reciting the *beracha* of *Shehecheyanu* as part of the mourning customs observed during *Sefirat Ha'Omer*. Later *poskim* wonder why the earlier sources do not address the question directly; does this mean that there is no objection to reciting *Shehecheyanu* in this time?

The ***Mishna Berura*** writes that although it is not appropriate to increase one's joy excessively during this period, one may recite *Shehecheyanu* when the need arises.

23. משנה ברורה | או"ח תצג:ב

מפני שבאותו זמן וכו' – רוצה לומר, ואין ראוי להרבות בשמחה. ומכל מקום, אם נזדמן לו איזה עניין שצריך לברך עליו "שהחיינו" – יברך.

א Mishna Berura, Orach Chaim 493:2

Since during this time, etc. – Meaning that it is not appropriate to increase joy excessively. Nonetheless, if a situation arises that requires a *Shehecheyanu* blessing, one may recite it.

Rav Avigdor Nebenzahl explains that one may recite *Shehecheyanu* even *lechatchila*.[26] He notes, however, that some Ashkenazim are more stringent due to the tragic events that occurred during this period in Ashkenazic communities in Europe, long after the deaths of Rabbi Akiva's students.

24. ביצחק יקרא | למשנה ברורה תצג:ב

נזדמן – אדוננו מורנו ורבנו זכרונו לברכה לחיי העולם הבא התיר לא רק ב"הזדמן", אלא אפילו לכתחילה. ויש שנהגו להחמיר בזה. וכנראה בארץ אשכנז נהגו להחמיר יותר משאר מקומות, מפני גזירות הצלבנים שהיו בין פסח לעצרת.

פ B'Yitzchak Yikarei to Mishna Berura 493:2

Arises – Our teacher and master [Rav Shlomo Zalman Auerbach] allowed not only "if the opportunity arises," but even from the outset.[27] Some have the custom to be stringent. Apparently, in Ashkenaz, people were more stringent than in other places due to the Crusader attacks that occurred between Pesach and Shavuot.[28]

---

25. See volume 15, *shiur* 4.
26. According to this, it is entirely permitted to purchase and wear new clothes during *sefira*, even for those who customarily recite *Shehecheyanu* upon wearing them for the first time (see volume 15, *shiur* 4 for a discussion of this issue). This is the approach of most Ashkenazic *poskim* (see *Oholei Halacha, Moadim*, vol. 2, p. 41). On the other hand, others hold that it is best to first wear new clothing during *Sefira* on Shabbat (*Ashrei Ha'Ish*, 65:12).
27. Rav Shlomo Zalman Auerbach presumably understood the wording of the *Mishna Berura* "if the opportunity arises" as not being limited to this, and even the *Mishna Berura* would agree that one can plan to recite *Shehecheyanu* during *Sefirat Ha'Omer*. Other *poskim*, such as Rav Chaim Kanievsky (*Bein Pesach L'shavuot*), are quoted as agreeing to this as well.
28. The Crusader attacks occurred during the First Crusade in the year 1096. Following the Pope's call for a crusade against the "infidel Muslims" in the Holy Land, mobs of zealous peasants carried out attacks on Jewish communities in Germany,

Among Sephardic *poskim*, **Rav Ovadia Yosef** rules that there is neither a prohibition nor a binding custom to refrain from reciting *Shehecheyanu* during *Sefirat Ha'Omer*. Moreover, one who was strict because he thought this was forbidden need not perform *hatarat nedarim* (annulment of vows), which is often required when abolishing a personal stringency or custom.

25. שו"ת יחווה דעת | א:כד

...אבל ימי הספירה אינם נחשבים לימי פורענות לעם ישראל, ואדרבה – כתב הרמב"ן, שקדושת ימי הספירה כימי חול המועד... לפיכך נראה, **שאף מי שנהג להחמיר שלא לברך "שהחיינו" בימי הספירה על פרי חדש, בחושבו שכן צריך להיות על פי הדין – יוכל לבטל מנהגו אף בלי התרה**, הואיל והוא מנהג בטעות, שאינו צריך התרה לבטלו. וגדולה מזו נראה לומר, שאפילו אם היה יודע שמעיקר ההלכה מותר לברך "שהחיינו" בימי הספירה, אלא שרצה להחמיר על עצמו להימנע מזה – יכול לבטל מנהגו בלי התרה, מפני שאין בזה משום גדר וסייג, אלא רק מילתא יתרה בעלמא.

Responsa Yechaveh Da'at 1:24

...However, the days of *Sefira* are not considered days of calamity for Israel; on the contrary, the Ramban writes that the sanctity of the *Sefira* days is like that of *Chol HaMo'ed*... Therefore, it would seem **that even someone who was stringent not to recite *Shehecheyanu* on a new fruit during the Omer, thinking that this is the halacha [that it is forbidden], may annul their custom even without *hatarat* [*nedarim*]** (annulment of vows), since it is a mistaken custom, regarding which *hatara* is not needed to annul it. Moreover, it would seem that [one can say] an even greater [leniency, as follows]. Even if someone knew that, in principle, it is permitted to recite *Shehecheyanu* during the Omer, but he voluntarily adopted the stringency to refrain, he may annul his custom without annulment, since it is not a formal preventative measure, but merely an additional personal practice.

Nevertheless, Rav Ovadia recommends a practice of "*midat chassidut*" regarding wearing new garments, refraining from wearing them during *Sefira* unless there is a need.

26. שם

...אך בנוגע לעניין לבישת בגד חדש בימי הספירה – טוב לחוש ממידת חסידות למה שכתב הגאון רבי יוסף יוזפא בספר יוסף אומץ (סימן תתמה), שמיום ראש חודש אייר ואילך נוהגים להחמיר שלא ללבוש בגד חדש... ולכן **כשיש צורך – יש להדר ללבוש הבגד החדש בשבת שבתוך ימי הספירה, ויברך עליו "שהחיינו"** (שהרי אף בשבת שבימי בין-המצרים לפני ראש חודש אב יש מתירים לברך "שהחיינו" על בגד חדש). וכן

Ibid.

...Regarding wearing a new garment during the Omer, it is good to take into consideration as "*middat chassidut*" that which Rav Yosef Yozpa writes in *Yosef Ometz*, that from Rosh Chodesh Iyar onward, the custom is to be stringent and not wear a new garment... Therefore, **when there is a need, one should be careful to wear a new garment during the Omer on Shabbat, and** [in this way, he should] **recite *Shehecheyanu***. (After all, even during Shabbat of the Three Weeks before Rosh Chodesh Av, it is permitted to recite *Shehecheyanu* on a new garment.[29]) Likewise,

---

particularly along the Rhine. Ashkenazic communities suffered greatly – Jews were forced to convert or die, and some communities were completely destroyed, including Shpira (Speyer), Worms, and Mainz, which had been spiritual centers for European Jewry for 200 or more years. These destructions took place in the months of Iyar–Sivan of that year. Some of the *kinot* recited on Tisha B'Av (such as "*Mi Yitein Rosh Mayim*," *Kinah* 25) and the prayer "*Av HaRachamim*," recited on Shabbat by Ashkenazim before *Musaf*, were composed as a result of these events.

29. The rules of reciting *Shehecheyanu* during the Three Weeks are somewhat more stringent and will be discussed further in the next volume.

במקום שמחת בר מצווה או ברית מילה בימי הספירה, יש להקל בזה בפשיטות.

on occasions such as a bar mitzva or a *brit mila* during the Omer, it is certainly proper to be lenient.

In contrast, according to the ***Ohr L'tzion,*** there is no custom whatsoever to avoid reciting *Shehecheyanu* during *Sefira.*

27. שו"ת אור לציון | ג:יז:ב

שאלה: האם מותר לברך ברכת "שהחיינו" על בגד חדש או פרי חדש בימי העומר?

תשובה: מותר לקנות או לתפור בגדים חדשים בימי העומר ולברך עליהם ברכת "שהחיינו". וכן אפשר לברך ברכת "שהחיינו" על פרי חדש, ואף בימות החול.

הערות

ולא נאסרו בימי העומר **אלא** נישואין ותספורת בלבד.

Responsa Ohr L'tzion 3:17:2

Question: Is it permitted to recite the *beracha* of *Shehecheyanu* on a new garment or new fruit during the Omer?

Answer: It is permitted to purchase or sew new garments during the Omer and to recite *Shehecheyanu* on them. Likewise, it is permitted to recite *Shehecheyanu* on a new fruit, even on weekdays.

Notes

During the Omer, **only** weddings and haircuts are forbidden.

Dancing and Listening to Music

Although most of the earlier sources that we have seen do not explicitly address dancing during *Sefirat Ha'Omer*, many *Acharonim* understand that the custom to refrain from weddings also precludes dancing, as noted by ***Mishna Berura***.

28. משנה ברורה | או"ח תצג:ג

...מותר לעשות שידוכין ולעשות סעודה אבל לעשות ריקודין ומחולות נהגו איסור וכל שכן בשאר ריקודין ומחולות של רשות בודאי יש ליזהר.

א Mishna Berura, Orach Chaim 493:3

...It is permitted to resolve a *shidduch* (settle a marital engagement) and to make a [celebratory] meal for it. However, it has become customary to prohibit dancing [*rikkudin*] and dancing circles [*mecholot*][30], and all the more so one should certainly be careful to avoid other dancing unrelated to a mitzva.

If dancing is prohibited during the mourning period of *Sefirat Ha'Omer*, does this prohibition also apply to playing or listening to music?

Many *poskim* rule that just as dancing is prohibited, so too one should refrain from playing or listening to musical instruments during the Omer. This extension is stated explicitly by the ***Aruch HaShulchan***.

29. ערוך השלחן | או"ח תצג:ב

...אבל לארס ולקדש – שפיר דמי. וכן אצלנו לעשות שידוכים ולכתוב תנאים – מותר, שמא יקדמנו אחר. ומותר לעשות סעודה, אך לא בריקודין ומחולות. וכל שכן שאסור לזמר בכלי זמר.

א Aruch HaShulchan, Orach Chaim 493:2

...But it is perfectly acceptable to betroth. Likewise, in our practice, it is permitted to settle an engagement and write an engagement contract (*tena'im*),[31] lest someone else precede him. It is permitted to make a meal, but not with dancing. All the more so, it is forbidden to play musical instruments.

Most contemporary *poskim* assume that recorded music has the same halachic status as live instrumental music.[32] For example, **Rav Moshe Feinstein** explains that although the Rema is generally lenient regarding

---

30. In the language of the *poskim*, "dances" [*rikkud*] usually refers to an individual dancing alone, while "dancing circles" [*mechol*] refers to dancing in a circle with others.
31. In previous generations, it was common for the respective sides to sign an engagement contract, in which each family commits to assuring that the wedding will take place and assumes financial responsibility for damages resulting from a cancelled engagement. (Typically, after the document is signed, the mothers of the bride and groom jointly break a dish.) In some communities, particularly in Eretz Yisrael, it is still common to sign such a document. In other communities, such a document is no longer in use. In some communities, particularly outside Eretz Yisrael, the document is not signed upon the engagement, but to preserve the old practice, the document is signed at the beginning of the wedding (by which time, the document is more ceremonial than functional).
32. See, however, n. 38 below, that some maintain that the custom does not apply to recorded music which one hears privately.

listening to music during the rest of the year,[33] during *Sefirat Ha'Omer*, one should be stringent and follow the approach of the *Shulchan Aruch*, which, in his opinion, includes recorded music as well.

30. שו"ת אגרות משה | יו"ד ב:קלז

ובדבר שמיעת כלי שיר בימי הספירה יש לאסור גם בבית כשהוא בעצמו דהא ברבים – שהוא לשמחה יתרה – מסתבר שאף לרמ"א, שמקל למי שאינו רגיל כשאינו בבית המשתה, נראה שיאסור בקיבוץ רבים, שהוא לכוונת שמחה יתרה גם בכל השנה. אם כן המנהג שנתווסף בימי הספירה הוא אף ליחיד שאינו רגיל בהם.

Responsa Igrot Moshe, Yoreh De'ah 2:137

Regarding listening to musical instruments during the Omer, even when alone at home, it is forbidden. Since in public settings [music] is [generally played] for additional joy, it follows logically that even according to the Rema (O.C. 560:3), who is lenient regarding someone unaccustomed [to music] [allowing such a person to listen] when not at a festive gathering, it is prohibited in a public setting all year round because it constitutes excessive joy.[34] Therefore, the custom during the Omer applies even to an individual who is not accustomed to it [listening to music].

In *Chazon Ovadia*, **Rav Ovadia Yosef** also rules that one should refrain from listening to live and recorded music during *Sefirat Ha'Omer*. At the same time, he delineates several important exceptions, particularly regarding vocal singing without instruments.

31. חזון עובדיה | יום טוב, הל' ספירת העומר וימי הספירה לג

הנוהגים להקל בכל ימות השנה לשמוע שירי קודש המלווים בכלי נגינה, דרך הרדיו והרשם-הקול, נכון שיחמירו בימי הספירה שלא לשמוע בהם שירים המלווים עם כלי נגינה. ומכל מקום שירה בפה כשהיא דרך הודאה לה' יתברך, בלי כלי נגינה, מותרת אף בימים אלה, ומכל שכן שמותר להשמיע נעימה בתפילה, או בשעה שעוסק בתורה, וכל שכן בשבתות שבתוך ימי הספירה או שבתוך ימי בין-המצרים, ואין להחמיר בזה כלל.

Chazon Ovadia, Yom Tov, Hilchot Sefirat Ha'Omer Viymei HaSefira 33

Even regarding those who are lenient throughout the year to listen to religious songs accompanied by instruments via radio or recordings should be stringent during the Omer and avoid listening to [recorded] songs accompanied by instruments. However, vocal singing, when it is an expression of gratitude to Hashem, without music instruments, is permitted even during these days. Likewise, it is certainly permitted to sing a melody during prayer or while engaged in Torah study. This is all the more so, on the days of Shabbat during the Omer or during the Three Weeks, and it is not at all necessary to be stringent.

---

33. The Rema is lenient to allow music in many cases during the rest of the year, while the *Shulchan Aruch* is more stringent. The subject of listening to music throughout the year, following the destruction of the *Beit HaMikdash*, including Rav Moshe's position, will be discussed in detail in *shiur* 7.

34. See *shiur* 7, where it is explained that the *Shulchan Aruch* forbids listening to music all year round even when not drinking wine (*mishteh*), while the Rema is more lenient for those who do not listen constantly (see there as well for the practical rulings of *poskim* on this issue). Rav Moshe argues that even the Rema would forbid listening to music in festive gatherings during the rest of the year, and he would forbid in all situations during *Sefira*.

Is it permitted to play or listen to music at a *simcha* or *seudat mitzva* (mitzva meal), such as *sheva berachot*, *brit mila*, or bar mitzva? Some *poskim*, such as **Rav Dov Lior**, take a stringent position and prohibit music even in these contexts.[35]

32. שו"ת דבר חברון | או"ח א:תקכה

שאילה: האם מותר לערוך שמחת בת מצווה בימי ספירת העומר...?

תשובה: בספירת העומר יש להימנע משמיעת מוזיקה ומריקודים, גם בסעודת מצווה (כולל סעודת מלוה מלכה או בקבלת שבת מוקדמת), וכל שכן בריקודים ומחולות של חולין... לפיכך **מותר לחוג את שמחת בת המצווה, אף בימי ספירת העומר**... **אך ללא ליווי של כלי נגינה.**

Responsa Devar Chevron 1:525

Question: Is it permitted to hold a bat mitzva celebration during *Sefirat Ha'Omer*...?

Answer: During *Sefirat Ha'Omer*, it is correct to refrain from listening to music and from dancing, even at a *seudat mitzva* (including a *melaveh malka* meal or an early *Kabbalat Shabbat*). All the more so is this true regarding ordinary, non-mitzva dancing... Therefore, **it is permitted to celebrate a bat mitzva even during *Sefirat Ha'Omer*... but without accompaniment of musical instruments**.

By contrast, many *poskim* rule that it is permitted to play musical instruments at a celebration that is defined as a *seudat mitzva*. This position is attributed, among others, to **Rav Yosef Shalom Eliashiv**.

33. אשרי האיש | או"ח ג:סה:כא

לעשות ריקודים ומחולות בסעודת שידוכין נהגו איסור. אך בשמחה שהיא של מצוה כאירוסין מותר ריקודין ומחולות. ויש הנוהגים לזמר בכלי שיר אף בסעודת שבע ברכות... ואלו הנוהגים כן מותר להם לשיר בכלי שיר גם בימי הספירה וכגון כשהחתונה היתה בל"ג בעומר.

Ashrei Ha'Ish, Orach Chaim 3:65:21

It is customary to prohibit dancing at an engagement feast [*seudat shidduchin*].[36] But at a celebration that is a mitzva, such as *erusin*,[37] dancing is permitted. There are those who have the practice to sing with musical instruments even at a *sheva berachot* meal... and for those who follow this practice, it is permitted to sing with musical instruments even during the days of *sefira*, such as when the wedding took place on Lag B'Omer.[38]

Sephardic *poskim* also permit music in such situations.

---

35. Others who rule stringently about this issue include Responsa *Minchat Yitzchak* 1:111, *Moadim Uzemanim* 8:338; and *Hilchot Chagim* (of Rav Mordechai Eliyahu) 20:46.
36. It was often customary to hold a formal meal to celebrate an engagement and to agree on the financial commitments of each side for the wedding (see n. 34). This is still done today in some places. In others, a "*vort*" or other celebration may not include a full meal, but just refreshments. The halacha would be the same for both.
37. This refers to a halachic betrothal, as discussed above in source 9, which is considered to constitute a mitzva. See also n. 14 above.
38. In the next halacha, Rav Eliashiv rules that a band may play at a bar mitzva only if that is considered the accepted local custom. However, he does allow a band for a *siyum* on completing a tractate of Talmud, even if that is not the accepted custom. Some arrange for a *siyum* during the bar mitzva celebration held during *Sefirat Ha'Omer* in order to permit having a band play according to all opinions.

Chazon Ovadia, Yom Tov, Hilchot Sefirat Ha'Omer Viymei HaSefira 33

34. חזון עובדיה | יום טוב, הל' ספירת העומר וימי הספירה לג

ובשמחת מצוה כגון מילה, או פדיון הבן, או סיום מסכתא, או בר מצווה (שמלו לו י"ג שנה בימים אלה), מותר לשמוע שירי קודש המלווים בכלי נגינה, **שכל שהיא שמחת מצוה יש להקל בדבר**. ולכן מותר להשתתף בתהלוכה ללוות הכנסת ספר תורה בימי הספירה, עם כלי זמר.

For a mitzva celebration, such as a *brit mila*, *pidyon haben*, completing a tractate, or a bar mitzva (whose thirteenth birthday is during this period), it is permitted to listen to religious songs accompanied by instruments; **one may be lenient in this matter for any mitzva celebration**. Therefore, one may participate in the [dedication and] procession of a Torah scroll, with musical accompaniment, during the Omer.

With the proliferation of recorded music, listening to music as a casual activity has become a common and routine part of daily life, and it appears that it does not signify joy in the sense described by the *poskim* cited above. In addition, a wide range of a cappella music is now readily available. This raises the question: does the custom to refrain from music during *Sefirat Ha'Omer* apply to every type of music, and in every situation?

From the sources cited above, it would appear that no distinction was made between different types of music, and that the custom to refrain from playing or listening to music applies broadly. **Rav Shmuel Wosner** writes this explicitly.[39] However, some contemporary *poskim* suggest that it is possible the custom does not apply to all forms of music, or not in every circumstance.[40] These *poskim* suggest that the determining factor is whether the music generates joy that leads to dancing. For example, **Rav Yaakov Ariel**, cited in *Oholei Halacha*, permits listening to soft, classical, or inspirational Jewish music that does not have a fast tempo and is not intended to evoke joy or dancing.[41]

Oholei Halacha, Moadim Vol. 2, p. 36

35. אהלי הלכה | מועדים חלק ב, עמ' 36

המוזיקה האסורה היא מוזיקה עליזה, אך מוזיקה שקטה שאינה מעוררת לשמחה ולריקוד – מותרת בשמיעה.

The music that is prohibited is lively music. However, it is permitted to listen to quiet music that does not arouse joy and dancing.

39. *Kovetz Mibeit Levi*, Nisan 5766, p. 77.

40. It should also be noted that a minority of *poskim*, such as Rav Yosef Dov Soloveitchik (cited by Rav Aharon Lichtenstein, as noted by Rav Chaim Jachter, *Gray Matter*, vol. 3, p. 5) and Rav Mordechai Willig (cited by Rav Aryeh Lebowitz at www.yutorah.org/lectures/735746), take the position that one may always listen to recorded music privately, as music itself is not forbidden any more on *Sefira* than the rest of the year. Rather, only activities leading to extensive joy should be avoided. Today, listening to music for most people does not fall into that category. In addition, see Responsa *Chelkat Yaakov* (O.C. 64) who contends that recorded music is not included within the ban to listen to music year-round (to be discussed in more detail in *shiur* 7). Perhaps he would say the same with respect to music during *Sefira*.

41. Rav Eliezer Melamed and Rav Yosef Zvi Rimon mention similar approaches, despite some differences between them, and write that one who wishes to rely on it may do so (*Peninei Halakha, Zemanim* 3:10; *Yemei Nisan V'Iyyar*, p. 124). For further discussion of this approach, see Rav Judah Kerbel, "Subjective Experience in Halakhah: Music During Sefirah as a Case Study," https://thelehrhaus.com/holidays/sefirat-ha-omer/subjective-experience-in-halakhah-music-during-sefirah-as-case-study. See also Rav Moshe Bleich, "Music During Sefirah and the Three Weeks," *Tradition*, Spring 2008, available at https://traditiononline.org/music-during-sefirah-and-the-three-weeks, and Rav Shmuel David, "Hearing Music from the Radio or a Recording During the Days of the Three Weeks," *Techumin* 13 (Hebrew), available at www.etzion.org.il/he/holidays/three-weeks/שמיעת-שירים-מרדיו-או-מקלטת-בימי-בין-המצרים.

Rav Shlomo Zalman Auerbach is cited as taking a similar position, though he limits this leniency to cases in which there is a reason for it.

36. הליכות שלמה | מועדים חלק א, יא:יד

יש להמנע בימים אלה מכל שירה המעוררת לריקוד ומחול, אבל שירה המרוממת את האדם אך אינה מביאתו לריקוד ומחול, מותרת.

הערה 54

ומכל מקום הוסיף רבינו דאין לנהוג היתר בזה בשופי, דסוף סוף נהגו במיעוט שמחה בימים אלו, ורק כשקיימת סיבה לכך יש להתיר.

Halichot Shlomo, Moadim Vol. 1, 11:14

During these days, one should refrain from any singing that leads to dancing. However, singing that uplifts a person but does not lead to dancing is permitted.

Note 54

In any case, our teacher added that this leniency should not be applied casually, since, after all, the accepted practice during these days is to observe a reduced level of joy. Only when there is a valid reason should it be permitted.

Poskim also disagree about the status of a cappella music. Some *poskim*, such as the *Chazon Ovadia* mentioned above, maintain that since it consists solely of vocal sounds, it retains the status of regular singing and is therefore permitted. Others, however, such as **Rav Yisroel Belsky,** contend that a cappella music is comparable to instrumental music, since it is produced in a manner intended to enhance and imitate instrumental sound.

37. שולחן הלוי | יג:ו

שאלה: לאחרונה יצאו קלטות שנשמעים בהן שירה בלא לווי כלי שיר האם מותר להאזין לקלטות אלו בימי הספירה...?

תשובה: מעיקר הדין אין לשמוע מוזיקה במשך כל ימות השנה משום זכר לחורבן ואף שבמשך השנה מקילים בהלכה זו אבל בימי אבלות כספירת העומר ובשלושת השבועות מחמירים בזה כעיקר הדין...

אין להתיר שמיעת מוזיקה ללא כלים רק בשירה הנשמעת כנגינה. כל המטרה של ההמנעות משמיעת מוזיקה בספירת העומר היא למנוע מן האדם לחוש את ההרגשה של המוזיקה, ומוזיקה זו תכליתה לתת לשומע הרגשה של מוזיקה בלי מוזיקה...

Shulchan HaLevi 13:6

Question: Recently, recordings have been released that contain singing without instrumental accompaniment. Is it permitted to listen to such recordings during the days of *Sefirat Ha'Omer*?

Answer: According to the fundamental halacha, one should refrain from listening to music throughout the entire year as a remembrance of the destruction [of the Temple]. Although during the year we are lenient with respect to this halacha, during periods of mourning – such as *Sefirat Ha'Omer* and the Three Weeks – we are stringent in accordance with the primary halacha...

One should not permit listening to music without instruments when the singing itself is produced in a manner that resembles instrumental music [i.e., a cappella designed to imitate instruments]. The entire purpose of refraining from listening to music during *Sefirat Ha'Omer* is to prevent a person from experiencing the emotional sensation of music, and this type of music is specifically intended to provide the listener with the experience of music without actual instruments...

The prohibition is not the act of hearing music itself, but rather the injunction of "Do not rejoice, O Israel" (*Hoshea* 9:1). Anything that falls within the category of exultation like the nations is included in the prohibition that the Jewish People have accepted upon themselves...

והאיסור הוא לא עצם שמיעת המוזיקה אלא אל תשמח ישראל וכל שהוא בגדר גיל כעמים הרי הוא בכלל האיסור שכלל ישראל קבלו על עצמם...

Even according to stringent opinions, many *poskim* distinguish between music intended for enjoyment and music heard incidentally or for a functional purpose. For example, **Rav Shmuel Kamenetsky** and others permit listening to music for the purpose of maintaining alertness or concentration, rather than to experience joy.

Kovetz Halachot, Sefirat Ha'Omer 9:14

38. קובץ הלכות | ספירת העומר ט:יד

A driver is permitted to listen to music to ensure he does not doze off.

וכן נהג מכונית מותר לו לשמוע נגינה כדי לשמור שלא ירדם.

Rav Nissim Karelitz writes that young children are not included in the custom of refraining from music during *Sefira*. Therefore, a kindergarten teacher, or someone in a similar role, may play music for the children to engage them during this time of year.

Chut Shani, Shabbat, Vol. 4, p. 379

39. חוט שני | שבת חלק ד, עמ' שעט

A kindergarten teacher who plays music in the classroom during the days of *Sefirat Ha'Omer* cannot be forbidden [from playing music], because the children have not yet reached an age of *chinuch* [formal education]. And [the teacher] herself does not derive joy from it, but she is merely performing her work [to engage the children].

גננת שמנגנת בגן בימי ספירת העומר אי אפשר לאסור דהקטנים לא הגיעו לחינוך והיא עצמה אין לה בזה שמחה אלא שעושה מלאכתה.

Rav Karelitz assumes that the teacher may play or listen to music because she is not doing so for her own enjoyment, but rather to perform her work. The same principle applies when one is present in a place where others are listening to music, such as a store, waiting room, or bus. As Rav Kamenetsky writes, it is permitted to remain in such a place, because one is not there to enjoy the music, but for an entirely different purpose.

Kovetz Halachot 9:17–19

40. קובץ הלכות | ט:יז-יט

17. It is permitted to remain in a waiting room where music is being played.

18. Similarly, one need not refrain from entering a store where music is being played during days when listening to music is customarily prohibited.

יז. מותר לשהות בחדר המתנה שמשמיעים שם נגינה.

יח. בדומה לזה אין צריך להמנע כלל מליכנס לחנות שמשמיעים בתוכו נגינה בימים שנוהג בהם איסור.

יט. מותר להשתתף באירועים שיש שם דרך אגב נגינה [עם כלי שיר] באופן שאין זה עיקר האירוע.

19. It is permitted to participate in events in which music [including instrumental music] is present incidentally, provided that the music is not the main purpose of the event.

In summary, many *poskim* prohibit dancing and instrumental music during *Sefirat Ha'Omer* as an extension of the mourning customs. However, distinctions are drawn regarding the nature of the music and the context in which it is heard. In some cases, such as music at a *seudat mitzva* or certain forms of a cappella music, there is genuine halachic disagreement, while in others, such as functional or incidental music, the permissibility is widely accepted, though its practical application may vary.

Lag B'Omer

Background of the Day

Lag B'Omer is one of several minor festivals on the Jewish calendar, whose observance and/or significance does not originate from the Torah, and whose exact nature is subject to some dispute. As we saw above in sources 3–4, some authorities understood that Rabbi Akiva's students stopped dying on this day.

However, the ***Pri Chadash*** challenges this explanation. He argues that the joy of the day cannot be attributed merely to the cessation of the deaths, since all 24,000 students ultimately perished and none remained. Rather, he suggests that the rejoicing relates to the new students whom Rabbi Akiva later taught – Rabbi Meir, Rabbi Yehuda, Rabbi Yosei, Rabbi Shimon bar Yochai, and Rabbi Elazar ben Shamua – who did not die like their predecessors.

41. פרי חדש | או"ח תצג:ב

ומה שכתב ומרבים בו קצת שמחה כו'. תימא דעכשיו נהגו בזה להרבות בשמחה ושלא לומר תחנון ואף על פי כן אינן מסתפרין אלא עד ל"ד ויראה תרתי דסתרן, ולפיכך מי שנהג עצמו להסתפר בל"ג אין מוחין בידו.

ומיהו יש לדקדק בשמחה זו למה, ואי משום שפסקו מלמות, מה בכך, הרי לא נשארו אחד מהם וכולם מתו ומה טיבה של שמחה זו, **ואפשר שהשמחה היא על אותם תלמידים שהוסיף אחר כך רבי עקיבא שלא מתו כאלו.**

א Pri Chadash, Orach Chaim 493:2

And regarding what [the Rema] writes [in source 14 above], "and we add a little joy, etc.," this is difficult, for nowadays the practice is to increase celebration on that day and to omit *Tachanun*. And yet we still refrain from haircuts until the 34th, and this appears contradictory. Therefore, we do not object to someone who has the practice to take a haircut on the 33rd.

However, this celebration itself needs explanation; why [do we celebrate]? If it is because they stopped dying, what of it? After all, not a single one of them remained; they all died. What, then, is the basis for rejoicing? **It may be that the joy is for the students whom Rabbi Akiva later added, who did not die like the earlier ones.**

Another approach links the joy of Lag B'Omer to Rabbi Shimon bar Yochai. In one of his many books, the **Chida** identifies Lag B'Omer as the day of Rabbi Shimon's passing.

42. מורה באצבע | אות רכג

יום ל"ג לעומר ירבה שמחה לכבוד רשב"י זכותו יגן עלינו **כי הוא יומא דהלולא דיליה.** ונודע שרצונו הוא שישמחו ביום זה כידוע ממעשה מורנו הרב אברהם הלוי זלה"ה

א Moreh B'etzba #223

On the day of Lag B'Omer, one should increase joy in honor of Rabbi Shimon bar Yochai, may his merit protect us, **for this day is his *hilula*** [the anniversary of his passing]. It is well known that it was his desire that this day be celebrated with joy, as is evident from the account involving Rav Avraham HaLevi[42]

42. Rav Avraham HaLevi was a prominent kabbalist of the sixteenth century and a disciple of the Arizal. He is cited in kabbalistic

ומעשים אחרים אֲשֶׁר שָׁמַעְנוּ וַנֵּדָעֵם מפום רבנן קדישי.

ויש מי שנהג לעשות לימוד בליל ל"ג לעומר בי עשרה ללמוד שבחי רשב"י המפוזרים בזהר ואדרא זוטא והוא מנהג יפה.

and from other traditions that we have heard and learned from the mouths of holy sages.

There are those who follow the custom of assembling on the night of Lag B'Omer with a quorum of ten to study the praises of Rabbi Shimon bar Yochai, as scattered throughout the *Zohar* and the *Idra Zuta*,[43] and this is a commendable custom.

However, the Chida himself elsewhere writes differently. He explains that in his own opinion, this day marks not Rabbi Shimon bar Yochai's day of passing, but rather the beginning of his studies and those of the other students of Rabbi Akiva who survived.

43. במראית העין | ליקוטים ז:ח

מה שכתבתי בברכי יוסף שיש שכתבו שפטירת רבי שמעון בר יוחאי היתה בל"ג בעומר, כן כתב בפרי עץ חיים, אך כבר נודע שבנוסחאות כתבי האר"י היה ערבוב וטעויות סופר... ובשער הכוונות... **וכתב של"ג בעומר הוא יום שמחת רשב"י, ולא בא בפיו לומר שהוא פטירת רשב"י**. ואפשר שהכונה כמו שכתבתי בטוב עין, שביום ל"ג בעומר התחיל רבי עקיבא ללמד לרבי שמעון בר יוחאי וחבריו.

B'marit Ha'Ayin, Likutim 7:8

What I wrote in the *Birkei Yosef* that some write that Rabbi Shimon bar Yochai passed away on Lag B'Omer, that is what the *Pri Eitz Chaim* writes.[44] But it is already known that in the text of the writings of the Arizal there was confusion and scribal errors… In the *Sha'ar HaKavanot*… **he writes that Lag B'Omer is the day of Rabbi Shimon bar Yochai's "joy," and he does not say explicitly that it is the day of his passing**. Perhaps the intent is what I wrote in the *Tov Ayin*, that on Lag B'Omer Rabbi Akiva began teaching Rabbi Shimon and his colleagues.

44. טוב עין | יח:פז

מה שעושים שמחה בל"ג בעומר, אפשר שרבי עקיבא היה כלל גדול בתורה ולמדה לכ"ד אלף וכו' ומתו וכו' והיה העולם שמם וכו' **ויום ל"ג לעומר התחיל לשנות לרשב"י ור' מאיר** וכו', ויאור להם שתחזור התורה.

Tov Ayin 18:87

It is possible that the reason for celebrating on Lag B'Omer is that Rabbi Akiva was a great leader of Torah, and he taught it to 24,000 students who died, leaving the world desolate, etc. **On Lag B'Omer, he began teaching Rabbi Shimon bar Yochai and Rabbi Meir**, etc., and he illuminated for them so that the Torah would return.

The ***Aruch HaShulchan*** mentions that the day is known as the celebration of Rabbi Shimon bar Yochai. The celebration may be the commemoration of his passing, but it may also refer to another important

---

literature as having been admonished for expressing mourning on Lag B'Omer, when, according to tradition, Rabbi Shimon bar Yochai desired that the day be observed with joy. This episode is often invoked as a source for the custom to rejoice on Lag B'Omer rather than treat it as a day of sorrow.

43. *Idra Zuta* (lit. the Lesser Assembly) is a section of the *Zohar* (*Zohar* III, *Ha'azinu* 287b–296b) that records the final teachings of Rabbi Shimon bar Yochai on the day of his passing (cited in part below in source 46). It describes how he revealed profound mystical secrets to a select group of disciples before his death, and it is closely associated with the concept of Lag B'Omer as the *yoma d'hilula* (the celebratory anniversary) of Rabbi Shimon bar Yochai. The term *hilula* is typically used in reference to the day of someone's passing, but we shall later see that it may also refer to the celebration of another significant milestone.

44. The Chida in the *Birkei Yosef* (493:1) mentions both of the approaches concerning the significance of Lag B'Omer.

moment in Rabbi Shimon's life. It was then that he and his son exited the cave in which they hid from Roman officials for many years.

45. ערוך השולחן | או"ח תצג:ז

...מפני שמחזיקין היום הזה לקצת יום טוב וגם במנחה שלפניו ורגילין לקרותו הלולא דרשב"י ובארץ ישראל מרבין בתפלה ובהדלקת נרות על קברו הקדוש ואומרים שנסתלק ביום זה **וגם יצא מהמערה ביום זה**.

א Aruch HaShulchan, Orach Chaim 493:7

...Because we treat this day as a minor festival, and [*Tachanun* is omitted] also at *Mincha* of the previous day, and it is called the celebration of Rabbi Shimon bar Yochai. In Eretz Yisrael, special prayers are added and candles are lit at his holy grave, and they say that he passed away **and also exited the cave on this day**.[45]

Customs of Lag B'Omer

The understandings we have seen for the significance of Lag B'Omer are reflected in a range of widespread customs, particularly in Eretz Yisrael. As noted by the *Aruch HaShulchan* above, there is a longstanding practice to visit Meron, the assumed burial place of Rabbi Shimon bar Yochai and his son Rabbi Elazar. In recent years, this has become much more popular, with hundreds of thousands flocking there each year. Some also have their sons' first haircuts there.[46]

At Meron, throughout Eretz Yisrael, and even abroad, in many communities, people light bonfires, although this is not mentioned by the Gemara or the early *poskim*. What is the meaning of this practice? One explanation for this custom is rooted in a passage in the ***Zohar*** that describes the fire and light that surrounded Rabbi Shimon bar Yochai shortly before his passing.

46. זוהר | חלק ג, פרשת האזינו, עמ' רצו:

...כל ההוא יומא, לא אפסיק אשא מן ביתא, ולא הוה מאן דמטי לגביה, **דלא יכילו דנהורא ואשא הוה בסוחרניה**. כל ההוא יומא נפילנא על ארעא, וגעינא.

בתר דאזיל אשא, חמינא לבוצינא קדישא קדש הקדשים, דאסתלק מן עלמא, אתעטף שכיב על ימיניה, ואנפוי חייכין...

ח Zohar, Vol. 3, Parshat Ha'azinu, p. 296b

...Throughout that entire day, the fire did not depart from the house, and no one was able to approach him, **for they could not endure the light and the fire that surrounded him**. All that day I [Rabbi Abba, the speaker in this passage] lay upon the ground and wept.

After the fire departed, I saw the holy luminary, the holy of holies [Rabbi Shimon], who had departed from the world. He lay wrapped [in his garment], resting on his right side, and his face was smiling...

Building on this idea, the ***Bnei Yisaschar*** explains that the custom of lighting candles and bonfires on Lag B'Omer reflects not only the light present at the time of Rabbi Shimon bar Yochai's passing, but

45. For further discussion of the historical background of Lag B'Omer and its connection to Rabbi Shimon bar Yochai and Meron, see https://seforimblog.com/2011/05/printing-mistake-and-mysterious-origins.

46. See *Sha'ar HaKavanot* and www.dirshu.co.il/חלאקה-למה-דווקא-בלג-בעומר-ולמה-דווקא who mention this custom.

the broader spiritual light that began to shine through the Torah and the *Zohar*, which continues to illuminate the Jewish People.

47. בני ישׂשכר | מאמרי חודש אייר, מאמר ג, ל"ג בעומר

...ובזה תבין **מנהג ישראל תורה הוא להדליק נרות ומאורות ביום זה, לכבוד האור כי טוב שמתחיל להתנוצץ ביום זה היקר ל"ג בעומר** טו"ב ימים קודם מתן תורה, ולכבוד נשמת מאור התורה בוצינא קדישא אשר נתגלה ביום הזה, וביום הזה עלה לשמי מרומים והוא יומא דהילולא דיליה לאורו נסע ונלך, לכבוד ספרו הקדוש זהר המאיר ומבהיק מסוף העולם ועד סופו... והוא מאיר לנו בגלותינו עד כי יבא משיח צדקנו...

א Bnei Yisaschar, Ma'amarei Chodesh Iyar, Ma'amar 3, Lag B'Omer

...From this, you can understand **that the Torah custom of Israel is to light candles and lights on this day, in honor of the "light that it is good," which begins to shine on this precious day of Lag B'Omer**, seventeen days before the giving of the Torah; and in honor of the soul of the luminary of the Torah, "the holy lamp," which was revealed on this day.[47] And on this very day, he ascended to the heavens, and it is considered his day of celebration, and in his light we journey. This is also in honor of his holy book, the *Zohar*, which shines and radiates from one end of the world to the other... and continues to illuminate us in our exile until the coming of our righteous Mashiach...

Listening to Music on Lag B'Omer

Is it permitted to listen to or play music on Lag B'Omer? This question depends in part on the underlying basis for the day's festive character and on the differing approaches to the mourning customs of *Sefirat Ha'Omer*. We learned previously that according to the Rema, haircuts are permitted during the day of Lag B'Omer.[48] If so, music would presumably be permitted as well. But according to the *Shulchan Aruch*, haircuts and weddings are permitted only from the morning of the thirty-fourth day of the Omer. If so, one could surmise that music, too, is permitted only after Lag B'Omer. Furthermore, even according to the Rema, haircuts are permitted only beginning on the morning of Lag B'Omer, not at night. If so, playing and listening to music should certainly be forbidden on the night of Lag B'Omer. This appears to be the ruling of the ***Oholei Halacha***.

48. אהלי הלכה | מועדים חלק ב, עמ' 42

...ולכן יש לנהוג מנהגי האבלות עד יום ל"ד בעומר, וכן מנהג יוצאי **ספרד**... למנהג זה, **הזמן**

Oholei Halacha, Moadim, Vol. 2, p. 42

...Therefore, the customs of mourning should be observed until the morning of the thirty-fourth, and this is the **Sephardic** custom... According to this custom, **the time**

47. According to the *Bnei Yissaschar*, Rabbi Shimon bar Yochai was born on the same day as his death. Note that, as he presents it, the number seventeen is significant because seventeen is the numerical value of the word *tov* (good).

48. As discussed earlier in the *shiur*, for those who begin observing the mourning customs of the Omer in Nisan, they cease on Lag B'Omer morning, while those who begin in Iyar take a reprieve on Lag B'Omer but then continue until Sivan.

at which taking a haircut, shaving, and listening to music is permitted is on the morning of the thirty-fourth.

According to the Rema, the students of Rabbi Akiva died on the first thirty-three days of *Sefirat Ha'Omer*. Since part of the day is considered the entire day, the customs of mourning should be observed until the morning of the thirty-third day, and this is the **Ashkenazic** custom. According to this custom, **one may take a haircut, shave, and listen to music on the morning of Lag B'Omer**.

שמותר בו להסתפר, להתגלח ולשמוע מוזיקה הוא יום ל"ד בבוקר.

לדעת הרמ"א, תלמידי רבי עקיבא מתו בשלושים ושלושה הימים הראשונים של ספירת העומר, ומכיוון ש"מקצת היום ככולו" יש לנהוג מנהגי אבלות עד יום ל"ג בעומר בבוקר, וכן מנהג **יוצאי אשכנז**. לפי מנהג זה **אפשר להסתפר, להתגלח ולשמוע מוזיקה כבר ביום ל"ג בעומר בבוקר.**

Nevertheless, many have the custom to permit listening to music on the night of Lag B'Omer. **Rav Eliezer Melamed** defends this custom and explains that when done in honor of Rabbi Shimon bar Yochai, this is entirely permitted.[49]

Peninei Halakha, Zemanim 3:3–4

1. The Sefardi Practice

According to the Shulchan Aruch (O.C. 493:1–2), the customs of mourning begin on the first day of the Omer and last until the morning of the thirty-fourth… Actually, one is permitted to sing, play music, and dance on Lag B'Omer, in honor of the anniversary of R. Shimon bar Yochai's death. However, the other customs of mourning remain binding. Thus, according to this practice, one is forbidden to get married or take a haircut on Lag B'Omer, and when the day ends, it is forbidden to play music or dance on the night of the thirty-fourth…

2. The Ashkenazi Practice

On the day of Lag B'Omer itself, one may get married and take a haircut. There is a dispute, however, regarding the night. Some say that these actions are permissible at night, as well, because the entire day of Lag B'Omer is joyous. Others maintain that… [it is permissible] only after the morning of the thirty-third has arrived… **According to all customs, it is permissible to celebrate with music and dancing on the night of Lag B'Omer.**

49. פניני הלכה | זמנים ג:ג–ד[50]

ג. מנהגי יוצאי ספרד

לדעת בעל השלחן ערוך (או"ח תצג, א–ב), מנהגי האבלות מתחילים מהיום הראשון של ספירת העומר ועד לבוקר ל"ד בעומר... ואמנם ביום ל"ג בעומר מותר לשיר, לנגן ולרקוד, לכבוד הילולת רבי שמעון בר יוחאי, אולם שאר מנהגי האבלות נשארים בתוקפם, ואסור לפי מנהג זה לישא אשה ולהסתפר בל"ג בעומר. ומשנסתיים ל"ג בעומר אסור בליל ל"ד לנגן ולרקוד...

ד. מנהגי יוצאי אשכנז

וביום ל"ג בעומר עצמו, מותר לשאת אשה ולהסתפר. אלא שנחלקו המנהגים בדין ליל ל"ג בעומר: יש אומרים שגם בליל ל"ג מותר לשאת אשה ולהסתפר, מפני שכל יום ל"ג בעומר הוא יום של שמחה. ויש אומרים... רק לאחר שהגיע בוקר ל"ג... **ולכל המנהגים מותר לקיים בליל ל"ג שמחה של ריקודים ונגינה.**

---

49. There are also a number of other possible approaches to explain this custom. One is based on the *Mishna Berura*, who writes that some permit taking a haircut on the night of Lag B'Omer, and they would certainly permit music, which is not even mentioned among the mourning customs discussed by earlier sources. However, the *Mishna Berura* notes that it is not widely accepted to take a haircut at night, and this is still true today. There may also be leniency on the basis of the *Chazon Ovadia* (Yom Tov, p. 254), who writes that in cases of need, one may take a haircut on the night of the thirty-fourth, since some *Rishonim* maintain that the principle of *miktzat hayom k'kulo* applies at night. Perhaps since listening to music is a later custom, one can be more lenient about it even *lechatchila*.

50. The Hebrew text here is lifted from *Peninei Halakha* (5775 edition). The English translation is reproduced from https://ph.yhb.org.il/en/05-03-03/ and https://ph.yhb.org.il/en/05-03-04.

The ***Yalkut Yosef*** also writes that this is permitted (even for Sephardim).

50. ילקוט יוסף | קיצור שולחן ערוך, או"ח תצג:ח

בליל ל"ג לעומר ולמחרתו נוהגים להקל לשמוע שירים מכלי נגינה, וכל שכן מטייפ, לכבוד ההילולא של התנא רשב"י עליו השלום.

Yalkut Yosef, Kitzur Shulchan Aruch, Orach Chaim 493:8

On Lag B'Omer night and the following day, it is customary to be lenient and listen to live music, and certainly recorded music, in honor of the *yahrtzeit* of Rabbi Shimon bar Yochai.

FURTHER IYUN

For further *iyun* on the nature of the mitzva of *Sefirat Ha'Omer*, see page 255.

Summary of the Halachot of Mourning Customs of Sefirat Ha'Omer

Origin of Mourning Customs During Sefirat Ha'Omer

1. ***Masechet Yevamot*** – Rabbi Akiva's 24,000 students died during the period between Pesach and Shavuot.
2. **Geonim** – It is customary not to hold weddings between Pesach and Shavuot in mourning for the death of Rabbi Akiva's students.

When Are Mourning Customs Observed?

1. **There are three traditions regarding when Rabbi Akiva's students died.**
   a. During the entire period between Pesach and Shavuot
   b. **Meiri, *Sefer HaManhig*** – From Pesach until Lag B'Omer
   c. **Rav Yosef Ibn Shueb** – During the entire period except for the sixteen days of joy, such as Shabbat and Rosh Chodesh
2. ***Bi'ur Halacha***
   a. According to approach b., haircuts become permitted either on the thirty-third (Rema) or thirty-fourth (*Shulchan Aruch*) day of *Sefirat ha'omer*.
   b. According to approach (c), haircuts are permitted until Rosh Chodesh Iyar, but then they are forbidden.
3. **Rema** – Each locale should follow a unified practice and not be split between individuals following different practices.
4. ***Mishna Berura*** – One may choose which custom one wishes to follow, unless one knows the local custom is different.

Weddings

1. ***Shulchan Aruch*** – One should not marry during the mourning period of the Omer, though betrothal is permitted.
2. **Rema** – Weddings are permitted from Lag B'Omer onward.
3. ***Mishna Berura*** – Even one who does not yet have children may not get married during this time.

4. ***Chazon Ovadia*** – Sephardic practice follows the view that weddings are permitted only from the morning of the thirty-fourth day; rabbinic authorities should ensure public awareness of this practice.
5. ***Ashrei Ha'Ish*** – One may attend and participate fully in a wedding that follows a different valid custom, including dancing and music, because rejoicing with a bride and groom constitutes a mitzva celebration.

Shaving and Haircuts

1. ***Tur, Shulchan Aruch*** – Some places have the custom not to take haircuts during *Sefirat Ha'Omer*, until Lag B'Omer.
2. **Rema** – Haircuts are permitted from the morning of Lag B'Omer, as well as on Friday if Lag B'Omer falls on Sunday. Those celebrating a *brit* may take a haircut as well.
3. **Rema** – Some refrain from having their hair cut only from Rosh Chodesh Iyar and on, except for the day of Lag B'Omer.
4. **Arizal** – Haircuts should not be taken during the entire period of *Sefira.*
5. **Rav Shlomo Zalman Auerbach** – Shaving is not allowed during *sefira,* even if one normally shaves daily.
6. ***Nefesh HaRav*** – One who shaves daily may shave during *Sefira.*
7. **Rav Aharon Lichtenstein** – Shaving for Shabbat is permitted if one normally shaves weekly for Shabbat.
8. ***Igrot Moshe*** – One may shave if one may otherwise lose his job or incur potential financial loss.

- **Women and Cutting Hair During *Sefira***

1. ***Chazon Ovadia, Ohr L'tzion*** – According to Sephardic custom, women are not included in the custom to refrain from haircuts.
2. ***Igrot Moshe*** – According to Ashkenazic custom, women do not take haircuts except in cases of a mitzva or necessity.
3. ***L'horot Natan*** – Married Ashkenazic women may cut their hair in principle, though in practice, the custom is to refrain from doing so except for specific cases of need, such as medical reasons, engagements, or a married woman whose hair sticks out from her hair covering.
4. ***Piskei Teshuvot*** – It is permitted to pluck eyebrows and eyelashes, etc., as this is not included in the category of "haircut."

Reciting the Beracha of Shehecheyanu

1. ***Mishna Berura*** – Although one should avoid excessive joy during the Omer, it is permitted to recite the *beracha* of *Shehecheyanu* when the situation arises.
2. **Rav Avigdor Nebenzahl** – Rav Shlomo Zalman Auerbach permitted reciting *Shehecheyanu* even *lechatchila*; but some are stringent due to the massacres of the Crusades.
3. ***Yechaveh Da'at***
   a. There is no prohibition or binding custom against reciting *Shehecheyanu* during the Omer, and one who refrained from reciting *Shehecheyanu* due to error or personal stringency may abandon the practice without *hatarat nedarim*.
   b. As a pious practice, it is good to refrain as "*middat chassidut*" and to first wear new clothes only on Shabbat.
4. ***Ohr L'Tzion*** – There is no restriction whatsoever on reciting *Shehecheyanu* during the Omer; only weddings and haircuts are restricted.

Dancing and Listening to Music

1. ***Mishna Berura*** – The accepted custom is to prohibit dancing during the Omer.
2. ***Aruch HaShulchan*** – Just as dancing is prohibited, it is certainly forbidden to play musical instruments during the Omer.
3. ***Igrot Moshe*** – It is forbidden to listen to instrumental music even when alone, as music constitutes excessive joy during the Omer. Even one who is lenient to listen to music all year round should be strict during this period.
4. ***Chazon Ovadia*** – One should refrain from listening to instrumental music during the Omer; vocal singing without instruments, especially in prayer or Torah study, is permitted, and there is no stringency on Shabbat.
5. ***Devar Chevron*** – It is proper to refrain from music and dancing even at a *seudat mitzva* during the Omer.
6. ***Ashrei Ha'Ish, Chazon Ovadia*** – Music and dancing are permitted at a *seudat mitzva*, such as *sheva berachot* or *brit mila*, for those who follow this practice, including during the Omer.
7. **Rav Shmuel Wosner** – All music is prohibited during *sefira*, regardless of whether it is fast or slow.

8. ***Oholei Halacha*** – Quiet, non-joyful music that does not lead to dancing may be permitted.
9. ***Halichot Shlomo*** – Singing that uplifts but does not lead to dancing may be permitted, though this leniency should be applied sparingly and only when there is a reason.
10. ***Chazon Ovadia*** – A cappella music is considered vocal music and permitted during *Sefira*.
11. ***Shulchan HaLevi*** – A cappella music designed to imitate instrumental music is prohibited, as it provides the emotional experience of music.
12. ***Kovetz Halachot*** – Functional listening, such as to prevent drowsiness while driving, is permitted.
13. ***Chut Shani*** – Young children are not included in the custom of refraining from music; therefore, a teacher may play music for educational purposes without deriving personal joy.
14. ***Kovetz Halachot*** – One may remain in places where music is played incidentally, such as stores, waiting rooms, or public transportation, when the music is not the purpose of being there.

Lag B'Omer

- **Background of the Day**

1. **Rema** – We add a little joy to the day because Rabbi Akiva's students stopped dying.
2. ***Pri Chadash*** – The joy of Lag B'Omer is due to Rabbi Akiva's later students, who survived and restored Torah after the deaths of the earlier students.
3. ***Moreh B'Etzba*** – Lag B'Omer is celebrated as the "*hilula*" of Rabbi Shimon bar Yochai and should be observed with joy, Torah study, and praise.
4. ***B'marit Ha'Ayin*** – It may be that Lag B'Omer is not meant to mark Rabbi Shimon bar Yochai's passing, as the *Pri Etz Chaim* says it is the day of his "joy."
5. ***Tov Ayin*** – Lag B'Omer celebrates the renewal of Torah after devastation, as Rabbi Akiva began teaching Rabbi Shimon bar Yochai and other surviving students.
6. ***Aruch HaShulchan*** – Lag B'Omer is treated as a minor festival associated with Rabbi Shimon bar Yochai's passing and his emergence from the cave.

- **Customs of Lag B'Omer**

1. Candles and bonfires are lit in Meron and elsewhere in honor of Rabbi Shimon bar Yochai.
2. ***Zohar*** – A great fire surrounded Rabbi Shimon bar Yochai on the day of his passing.
3. ***Bnei Yissaschar*** – The bonfires symbolize the spiritual light and hidden Torah revealed by Rabbi Shimon bar Yochai, especially through the *Zohar*.

- **Listening to Music on Lag B'Omer**

1. ***Oholei Halacha***
   a. **Sephardim** – Music is permitted on the morning of the thirty-fourth day of the Omer.
   b. **Ashkenazim** – Music is permitted on the morning of the thirty-third day of the Omer.
2. ***Peninei Halakha, Yalkut Yosef*** – According to all customs, music is permitted on the night of Lag B'Omer when in honor of Rabbi Shimon bar Yochai.

Further Iyun

The Nature of the Mitzva of Sefirat Ha'Omer

Rav Eitan Yanai (Participant, Manhigut Toranit)

A Simple Count or a Defining Act?

Few mitzvot appear as simple as *Sefirat Ha'Omer*. Each evening, a brief formula is recited, and within seconds, the obligation seems fulfilled. Yet beneath this minimal act lies one of the most conceptually rich and structurally unique mitzvot in the Torah. What exactly are we counting? Is the mitzva merely a countdown to Shavuot? Why must the Torah command us to count days that would pass in any event? And more fundamentally: what is the *avodat Hashem* embedded in the very act of counting?

These are not philosophical curiosities. They lie at the heart of the mitzva's halachic structure. The rulings of the Ramban, *Ba'al HaMaor*, Tosafot, *Shulchan Aruch*, and *Magen Avraham* reveal that *Sefira* does not fit neatly into the framework of other verbal mitzvot. It generates unusual definitions, unresolved doubts, and distinct halachic parameters. To understand these details, we must first clarify the conceptual core of the mitzva.

The Nature of the Timeframe: Date or Offering?

A striking insight emerges from the **Ramban**,[1] who classifies *Sefirat Ha'Omer* as a *mitzvat aseh she'ein hazeman gerama* – a non-time-bound mitzva (and therefore one in which women would be obligated). At first glance, this seems puzzling. After all, the mitzva applies only during a fixed period of the year. How can it not be considered time-dependent?

The answer lies in the Torah's formulation: "You shall count for yourselves… from the day you bring the *Omer* offering." The Torah does not anchor the mitzva in a calendar date alone, but in an event – the bringing of the *Korban Ha'Omer*. In his commentary to the Torah, the Ramban emphasizes that the defining starting point of the count is the day of the offering. The phrase "*mimacharat haShabbat*" serves a separate exegetical function; the primary anchor is not the day, but the sacrificial act.

Rav Yechezkel Abramsky[2] explains that according to this approach, the mitzva is not inherently tied to a calendar framework, but to a halachic event. The count flows from the *korban Ha'Omer* itself. Even though that offering occurs at a fixed time of year, the mitzva is structurally linked to the act, not to the date.

In contrast, the **Rif** and the ***Tur*** imply a different understanding. For them, the count begins "from the day after the first day of Pesach." The

1. Ramban, *Kiddushin* 33a.
2. *Divrei Yechezkel, siman* 4.

reference to the *Omer* serves only as a temporal marker. The mitzva is thus defined within a fixed calendar period between Pesach and Shavuot.

This disagreement is not technical. It reflects two fundamentally different conceptions: Is *Sefira* an extension of the *Korban Ha'Omer*? Or is it a structured period within the Jewish calendar? This distinction will prove central to many of the mitzva's unique halachic features.

Why Is the Mitzva Called *Sefirat Ha'Omer*?

The debate above sheds light on the very name of the mitzva. According to the Ramban's model, the designation is straightforward. The *Omer* offering is the defining point of departure. We count **from** the *Omer*; the entire process unfolds as an extension of that sacrificial act. The days derive their identity from their relationship to it.

However, if the count is anchored primarily in a fixed calendar period, as implied by the Rif and the Tur, the terminology requires explanation. Why name the mitzva after the *Omer* if the offering merely serves as a chronological reference?

One possible explanation is that, even within this model, the term "*Omer*" describes not only the offering itself but the agricultural season it inaugurates – the opening of the barley harvest. The period between Pesach and Shavuot thus forms a defined agricultural-historical unit, and the count unfolds within that framework. We are not merely counting toward Shavuot; we are counting **within** the days of the *Omer*.

This distinction also clarifies the classic debate regarding the formula *la'omer* versus *ba'omer*. If the *Omer* is the point of origin, *la'omer* reflects counting in relation to that initiating act. If, however, the *Omer* denotes a defined season, *ba'omer* ("within the *Omer*") expresses counting inside an established temporal unit.[3] Thus, what appears to be a minor linguistic variation reflects the deeper conceptual divide: is the *Omer* the source from which the count begins, or the framework within which the count takes place?

If the Date Is Fixed, Why Count at All?

A deeper question now emerges. Today, Shavuot falls on a fixed calendar date. Even in Temple times, once the *Omer* was offered, the fiftieth day would inevitably arrive. If so, what is the purpose of commanding us to count? Time advances regardless of our awareness.

To answer this, we must examine the meaning of counting in the Torah more broadly. Beyond *Sefirat Ha'Omer*, the Torah commands counting in two other contexts: the seven clean days of a *zava* and the cycles leading to *Yovel*. In neither case is counting a passive wait for time to pass. In the case of the *zava*, each day requires active verification; the count reflects ongoing attentiveness. In the *Yovel* cycle, *beit din* does not merely allow years to pass – it formally tracks and defines each stage within the larger structure of *Shemita* and *Yovel*. Counting, then, is not a technical mechanism for tracking days. It is an act of conscious positioning. The Torah transforms the passage of time into a structured process that demands awareness and participation.

Applied to *Sefirat Ha'Omer*, this suggests that the mitzva is not simply a bridge between Pesach and Shavuot. Rather, it requires the individual to situate himself daily within a developing trajectory. Each day counted is not merely one day closer to Shavuot; it is one day further into an unfolding process.

3. See *Taz*, O.C. 489:3.

Why Count the Days That Passed?

The ***Sefer HaChinuch***[4] famously asks: if the purpose of *Sefira* is anticipation of *Matan Torah*, why do we count the days that have already passed rather than the days that remain until Shavuot? A person awaiting a long-anticipated event naturally counts down: "only ten days left." Yet the Torah instructs us to count upward. According to the conceptual framework developed above, the answer becomes clear. The mitzva is not merely anticipation of a future climax. It is recognition that each day already traversed carries independent value. *Sefira* is not a countdown; it is a cumulative process. Each day counted affirms: this day has been incorporated into the journey. The mitzva trains us to mark progression, not merely expectation.

Under this model, the act of counting is not the creation of a new calendrical reality but a form of conscious tracking – an awareness of one's present location within a developing spiritual structure. The emphasis lies not in what will arrive on day fifty, but in the disciplined recognition of where one stands today. This conception now allows us to revisit several of the mitzva's distinctive halachot.

Halachic Implications: The Mitzva as Conscious Tracking

1. Can One Fulfill the Mitzva Through *Shomei'a K'oneh*?

The ***Magen Avraham***[5] questions whether the principle of *shomeia k'oneh*, hearing is equivalent to reciting, applies to *Sefira*. In most verbal mitzvot, such as *kiddush* or *Keriat Shema*, the essence of the mitzva lies in articulated speech. If another recites on one's behalf, and one listens with intent, the halachic act of speech is fulfilled.

However, if the core of *Sefira* is not the formal recitation, but the awareness of the number of days that have passed, the spoken formula becomes secondary. The essence is knowledge, not articulation. Under this understanding, one might argue that *shomei'a k'oneh* is insufficient. Hearing another declare the count does not necessarily generate the internal act of conscious positioning that defines the mitzva.

2. Does One Need to Understand the Words?

The *Magen Avraham* further rules that one who counts in Hebrew without understanding the meaning of the words does not fulfill the mitzva. At first glance, this is surprising. In other mitzvot of speech, one may discharge the obligation even without full comprehension of the Hebrew text. Here, however, if the mitzva consists in knowing which day one occupies within the process, understanding is indispensable. If one declares "Today is fifteen days" but does not grasp what that statement signifies, the essential act of counting has not occurred. The verbalization alone is insufficient. Understanding, therefore, is not an added ideal; it is intrinsic to the mitzva's fulfillment.

3. Why Not Count Two Possible Days in the Diaspora?

The ***Ba'al HaMa'or*** asks: in the Diaspora, where two days of Yom Tov are observed due to historical doubt, why do we not count with uncertainty at the outset – for example, "today is three or four days"?

---

4. Mitzva 306.
5. 489:2.

If counting were merely technical enumeration, one might have expected such a formulation in cases of doubt. Yet, if *Sefira* requires clear knowledge of one's position within the process, a doubtful declaration undermines the very act. To state two possible numbers is to admit that one does not know which day it is. The conscious tracking collapses. Thus, the halachic resistance to counting in doubt reflects the conceptual nature of the mitzva itself.[6]

A Different Model: *Sefira* as Defining the Days Themselves

Until now, we have presented *Sefira* as an act of conscious tracking – a structured awareness of one's progression between Pesach and Shavuot. However, according to the **Ramban** and ***Ba'al HaMa'or***, the mitzva may operate in a fundamentally different way. In their view, *Sefira* is not primarily about awareness. Rather, it is an act that confers identity upon time itself. Each day that is counted becomes a defined unit – "the first day of the Omer," "the second day of the Omer," and so forth. The counting does not merely record reality; it assigns halachic status to it. The days are not passively traversed; they are designated.

Under this model, *Sefira* functions as a process of progressive sanctification. The forty-nine days form a structured unit culminating in Shavuot. Just as the counting of *Shemita* cycles leads to *Yovel*, here too, the count constructs the framework within which the fiftieth day emerges. This conception explains several distinctive halachot.

Halachic Implications: Applying a New Identity to Time

1. Counting Weeks Only at Their Completion

The ***Ba'al HaMa'or*** maintains that weeks must be counted only upon their completion – at the end of each full seven-day unit. If the mitzva merely required daily awareness of progression, there would be no inherent need to wait for the completion of a full week before mentioning it. One could describe the accumulating total at any point.

However, if *Sefira* confers halachic identity upon units of time, then a "week" exists only once seven complete days have passed. Only then can one designate that unit as a "*shavua la'omer.*" The week is not a running awareness but a defined temporal entity. While our practice follows the view that weeks are mentioned each day, this alternative understanding highlights a fundamentally different logic.

2. Can One Count Before Nightfall?

A related dispute concerns whether one may count before the new day has fully entered. **Tosafot**[7] and certain interpretations of the ***Shulchan Aruch***[8] allow, under limited circumstances, counting slightly before nightfall. If *Sefira* is primarily conscious positioning within an unfolding process, one could argue that awareness of the impending transition suffices, at least *bedi'eved*. However, if counting assigns identity to the day itself, the logic changes entirely. One cannot designate a day that has not yet arrived. Halachic identity cannot precede halachic reality. The permissibility or impossibility of early

6. A similar idea can be found in *Sha'arei Yosher* 1:5.
7. *Menachot* 66a, s.v. *zeicher l'mikdash*.
8. O.C. 499:3, according to the interpretation of the *Levush* and *Eliya Rabba*.

counting thus reflects deeper assumptions about the nature of the act.

Sefira and the Seven Clean Days

The **Ramban** draws a sharp distinction between *Sefirat Ha'Omer* and the counting of seven clean days by a *zava*. The latter involves monitoring the passage of time within a purification process. It does not create a new status in the days themselves. Accordingly, the Ramban explains that no blessing is recited over counting the seven clean days. Since the counting serves only as verification – ensuring the completion of a condition – it lacks the character of an independent act worthy of *beracha*. By contrast, *Sefirat Ha'Omer*, in his understanding, actively defines the days and culminates in the sanctity of Shavuot. It is constructive, not merely procedural.

Tosafot,[9] however, maintain that even *Sefira* is fundamentally a form of tracking, similar in nature to the *zava*'s count. They explain the difference in blessing on practical grounds: the *zava*'s count may be interrupted and invalidated, rendering it uncertain, whereas the *Omer* count proceeds with certainty. Once again, the halachic discussion reflects the deeper conceptual divide: is *Sefira* creative designation, or conscious progression?

Conclusion: Two Visions of *Sefira*

We have seen that the *Rishonim* articulate two fundamentally different conceptions of *Sefirat Ha'Omer*. According to the Ramban and *Ba'al HaMa'or*, the count is tethered to the *Korban Ha'Omer* and functions as an act that defines and designates time. Each day counted acquires identity as a day of the Omer, and through the cumulative count the structure leading to Shavuot is formed. The mitzva is creative: it applies halachic definition to successive units of time.

According to the **Rif**, ***Tur***, and **Tosafot**, the mitzva unfolds within a fixed calendar period. Its essence lies not in defining time but in consciously traversing it. The act of counting expresses awareness – a disciplined recognition of one's present position within the progression from Pesach to Shavuot.

This distinction explains the unusual halachic contours of the mitzva: the debate over *shomei'a k'oneh*, the requirement of comprehension, the rejection of counting in doubt, the timing of counting weeks, and even the comparison to the *zava*'s count. What might appear as scattered technical rulings instead reflect coherent conceptual systems. *Sefirat Ha'Omer* thus emerges as far more than a transition between festivals. It shapes our relationship to time itself. Either we actively designate and structure the days, conferring identity upon them, or we consciously inhabit them, marking each stage of advancement.

In both models, the Torah refuses to allow time to pass unnoticed. The forty-nine days between redemption and revelation are not an empty corridor but a defined process, whether constructed through halachic designation or through sustained awareness. Through the mitzva of counting, the passage of time becomes *avodat Hashem*.

9. *Ketubot* 72a, s.v. *vesafra la*.

6

Halachot of Shavuot

הלכות שבועות

Tosefet Yom Tov on Shavuot

Tikun Leil Shavuot

Eating Dairy Foods

Decorating the Synagogue

Megillat Rut

Machshava

For quick reference, some long website URLs have been shortened.
For the complete list of referenced websites visit www.tzurbaolami.com.

ת	**Tanach**
ח	**Talmud (Chazal)**
ר	***Rishonim***
א	***Acharonim***
פ	**Contemporary Halachic Sources**

In the previous *shiur*, we discussed the customs of mourning during *Sefirat Ha'Omer*. In this *shiur*, we move on to discuss the laws and customs of Shavuot, the festival that marks the completion and culmination of *Sefirat Ha'Omer*.

The halachot of Yom Tov, discussed in volume 23 (*shiurim* 2–4), apply to Shavuot just as they do to the other festivals. However, unlike the other festivals, the Torah does not prescribe any mitzvot that are unique to Shavuot. Shavuot is described by the Torah as the festival of weeks (referring to the weeks of the *Omer*), the harvest festival, and the day of *bikkurim* (first fruits). According to Chazal, it also commemorates *Matan Torah*, the giving of the Torah at Har Sinai – an event that has come to define much of the spiritual character of the day, as we will see in this *shiur*. Yet this central theme is not expressed through a distinct mitzva; rather, the day celebrates the Torah itself, without being anchored to a specific mitzva.

Nevertheless, there are some customs that are unique to Shavuot, and these practices raise important halachic questions. We will begin by discussing the conclusion of *Sefirat Ha'Omer* and its relationship to the onset of Shavuot, particularly in light of the mitzva of *tosefet Yom Tov* (adding time to Yom Tov).

Tosefet Yom Tov on Shavuot

According to the **Gemara** in ***Masechet Rosh Hashana***, there is a biblical obligation to add on to the beginning and end of Shabbat and Yom Tov.[1] This is accepted as halacha by most *Rishonim* (although according to the Rambam, only the obligation to start fasting on Erev Yom Kippur is accepted). In addition, even according to the Rambam, one may *daven Ma'ariv* before nightfall on Erev Shabbat. *Kiddush* also may be recited before nightfall.[2]

However, the ***Masat Binyamin*** quotes **Rav Shlomo MiLublin,** who writes that Shavuot is different. Since the Torah says that the seven weeks of the Omer must be *temimot* (whole), one should not recite *kiddush* before nightfall.

1. שו"ת משאת בנימין | חידושי דינים, או"ח ד

מצאתי כתוב בשם מורי מורינו הרב רבי שלמה השני: בליל ראשון של חג השבועות ממתינין עם הקידוש עד הלילה ממש, שאם יקדש קודם הלילה יחסר מעט מיום מ"ט לספירה, וכתיב שבע שבתות תמימות תהיינה.

א Responsa Masat Binyamin, Chidushei Dinim, Orach Chaim 4

I found written in the name of my teacher, the second Rav Shlomo [MiLublin]: On the first night of Shavuot, we wait until actual nighttime for *kiddush*, as if one were to recite *kiddush* before nighttime, a little of the forty-ninth day of the counting would be missing, and it is written, "They shall be seven whole weeks."[3]

1. See *Tzurba M'Rabanan*, English edition, volume 16, *shiur* 4, where all of the issues mentioned here concerning *tosefet yom tov* are discussed in more detail.
2. See volume 17, *shiur* 1.
3. *Vayikra* 23:15.

The same quote from Rav Shlomo MiLublin can also be found in the ***Shenei Luchot HaBerit* (*Shelah*)**. He clarifies that in contrast to *kiddush*, the custom prevalent in his time, to *daven Ma'ariv* early even on Shavuot, is not problematic, as *davening Ma'ariv* before nightfall does not necessarily signify the end of the day. Moreover, reciting *kiddush* at the end of *Ma'ariv* in *shul* before nightfall is also not problematic, as this practice is only for the benefit of guests who stay in the *shul* premises.

2. שני לוחות הברית (של"ה) | שבועות, נר מצוה

וקבלתי ממורי מורינו הגאון הרב שלמה ז"ל מלובלין, שקיבל איש מפי איש עד מפי הגאון רבינו יעקב פולק ז"ל, שלא לעשות קידוש ולאכול בליל ראשון של חג שבועות עד צאת הכוכבים...

ואל תשיבני ממה שמתפללין אז התפלה מבעוד יום. דזה אינו כלום, דהא רבי יאשיה צלי של מוצאי שבת בשבת, כדאיתא בברכות (כז:), אף על גב דעדיין ממש שבת גמור הוא. **ואל תקשה מקידוש השליח ציבור בבית הכנסת.** דזה אינו אלא בשביל אורחים, ולא מחזי כלום כמחסר משבע התמימות, מה שאין כן אילו היה כל יחיד מקדש לעצמו.

א Shenei Luchot HaBerit (Shelah), Shavuot, Ner Mitzva

I received [a tradition] from my teacher, Rav Shlomo MiLublin, who received [this tradition] from a chain of people going back to HaGaon Rav Yaakov Polak that one should not recite *kiddush* and eat on the first night of Shavuot until *tzeit hakochavim*…

Do not challenge me based on that which we recite the *tefilla* then, while it is still day. As this is not at all [problematic], as Rabbi Yoshaya would *daven* [*Ma'ariv*] of *Motza'ei Shabbat* on Shabbat, as is stated in *Berachot* (27b), although it was still absolutely Shabbat. **And do not raise a difficulty from the *kiddush* of the *shali'ach tzibbur* in the synagogue**, as this is only for guests, and does not at all appear as if one is taking away from the seven whole [weeks]. This would not be the case were each individual to recite *kiddush* for himself [before night].

The ***Turei Zahav* (*Taz*)** disagrees with Rav Shlomo MiLublin and the Shelah and writes that we should also delay *Ma'ariv* until nightfall.[4]

3. טורי זהב (ט"ז) | או"ח תצד, הקדמה

מאחרין להתחיל ערבית בכניסת שבועות כדי שיהיו ימי הספירה תמימות.

א Turei Zahav (Taz), Orach Chaim 494, Introduction

We delay starting [*Tefilat*] *Arvit* at the start of Shavuot, so that the days of the counting [of the *Omer*] should be whole.

These *Acharonim*, who all agree that at least *kiddush* should not be recited before nightfall, distinguish between Shavuot and other Yamim Tovim, when *kiddush* may be recited early. This stringency is also quoted by the ***Magen Avraham*** (O.C. 494). However, this distinction between Shavuot and other Yamim Tovim does not appear in the words of Chazal or the *Rishonim*.[5] The ***Korban Netanel*** observes that the

4. According to this view, it appears that simply being passive and refraining from *melacha* is sufficient to fulfill the mitzva of *Tosefet Yom Tov*, although this does not impinge on the requirement to count seven whole weeks. This question is discussed further in volume 16, *shiur* 4.
5. The Gemara (*Menachot* 66a) derives a different halacha based on the requirement to count seven whole weeks – one must count in the night and not wait until the daytime.

Rosh permits reciting *kiddush* before night at the start of any Yom Tov, clearly implying that this applies on Shavuot as well. He therefore rejects the stringency of the *Acharonim*.

4. קרבן נתנאל על הרא"ש | פסחים י:ב

אף על גב דבשבתות וימים טובים יכול להוסיף מחול על הקודש ולאכול קודם שתחשך – מכאן ראיה דלא כמגן אברהם בסימן תצ"ד דבליל שבועות אין מקדשין על היין עד צאת הכוכבים דכתיב תמימות תהיינה.

א Korban Netanel on the Rosh, Pesachim 10:2

Although on Shabbatot and Yamim Tovim, one may add from the mundane to the sacred and eat before it gets dark – From here [i.e., these words of the Rosh][6] there is a proof against the *Magen Avraham*, [who writes] in *siman* 494 that we do not recite *kiddush* over wine until *tzeit hakochavim*, as it is written, "They shall be whole."

Rav Yaakov Emden also writes that this stringency has little basis, and that on the contrary, one who starts Yom Tov early is to be praised for his enthusiasm.

5. סידור בית יעקב | אורח ב' ליום טוב של עצרת ד

יש אומרים שמאחרים להתפלל עד שחשכה, והוא דקדוק קלוש מחודש מהאחרונים, **ומי שמקדים להתפלל בשיעור שמוסיפים מחול על קודש הרי זה זריז ונשכר בקיום מצוה ומתקיים זה וזה בידו,** כי מכל מקום בעוד שמתפללים כבר הוא לילה.

ועיקר הקפידא למאן דחייש לה הוא שלא לאכול קודם הלילה.

א Siddur Beit Yaakov, Orei'ach 2 L'yom Tov Shel Atzeret 4

Some say that we delay *davening* [*Ma'ariv* on Shavuot] until dark. But this is a weak and novel inference of the *Acharonim*, and **one who *davens* early during the time that we add from the mundane to the sacred is enthusiastic and gains fulfilment of a mitzva, fulfilling both this [mitzva to add on to Yom Tov] and that [mitzva of counting seven full weeks]**, as in any event, when one *davens* it is already considered night.[7]

For one who is concerned about this stringency [not to start Shavuot early], the main thing to be particular about is not to eat before night.

However, the ***Mishna Berura*** (494:1) rules in accordance with the *Taz*, that one should not even start *Ma'ariv* before night. The ***Aruch HaShulchan*** (494:3) writes only that one should not recite *kiddush* before night.

Rav Ovadia Yosef writes that where possible, it is proper to wait until night before reciting *kiddush*. But in parts of the world where sunset is late, such that delaying will result in distress for families, or will make it difficult to observe the custom of *Tikun Leil Shavuot*, one may be lenient and eat earlier.

---

6. The Rosh here is saying that one may not eat before nightfall only on the night of the Seder, but every other Shabbat and Yom Tov night (including Shavuot) would be permitted.
7. In other words, *davening Ma'ariv* only starts Yom Tov early by creating the halachic status of night to some extent. To the same extent, since it is considered night, the final day and week of the *Omer* are also considered complete.

6. שו"ת יחוה דעת | ו:ל

במקומות אלו **שאפשר לחוש לדברי האחרונים ולהמתין מלקדש עד לאחר צאת הכוכבים נכון לעשות כן. אבל בארצות אירופה וכדומה שהשקיעה מתאחרת מאד בימי הקיץ,** ובני הבית מצטערים לשבת ולהמתין עד הלילה, וגם זה גורם הפרעה לסדר לימוד הלילה בספר קריאי מועד כפי שנוהגים על פי הזוהר והאר"י ז"ל, וכמו שכתב בספר יוסף אומץ, **יש להקל להם לקדש ולסעוד מבעוד יום.** ואם אפשר טוב שימתינו עד תחלת השקיעה, באופן שהשמש נכסית מעינינו, ואז יקדשו ויסעדו. וטוב שיאכלו כזית בצאת הכוכבים.

Responsa Yechaveh Da'at 6:30

In these places, **where it is possible to be concerned for the comments of the *Acharonim*, and to delay reciting *kiddush* until after *tzeit hakochavim*, it is proper to do so. But in Europe and similar places, where sunset gets very late in the summer,** and waiting until night to sit [for the meal] causes distress to the members of the household, and this also causes disruption to the order of nighttime study from the book *Keri'ei Mo'ed*, as is practiced in accordance with the *Zohar* and [the teachings of] the Arizal, as is written in the book *Yosef Ometz*, **one may rule leniently for them to recite *kiddush* and to eat the meal while it is still day.** If possible, it is preferable that they wait until sunset, such that the sun is hidden from our eyes, and then recite *kiddush* and eat. It is [also] preferable that they eat a *k'zayit* after *tzeit hakochavim*.[8]

Tosefet Yom Tov for Women on Shavuot

Rav Natan Gestetner was asked whether women may start Shavuot early. Since women are not obligated in the mitzva of *Sefirat Ha'Omer* at all, they certainly have no obligation to count seven whole weeks. Nevertheless, Rav Gestetner writes that Shavuot can only start after seven whole weeks, and this applies to women as well.

7. שו"ת להורות נתן | ז:לא

מכיון שיום חג השבועות מתחיל רק בכלות מ"ט ימי הספירה בשלימות, דהא תמימות כתיב, ממילא **אף נשים שאינן חייבות במצות ספירת העומר, מכל מקום גם אצלן אין חג השבועות מתחיל עד כלות מ"ט ימים תמימים, וממילא גם הן אין להן לקדש קודם הלילה,** דהא קודם הלילה אכתי לא חל מצוות חג השבועות. והנשים פטורות רק ממצות הספירה, אבל גם חג השבועות שלהן תליא בכלות שבע שבתות תמימות דוקא.

Responsa L'horot Natan 7:31

Since the day of the festival of Shavuot only starts at the end of the forty-nine days in their entirety, as [the word] "whole" is written, it follows that **even for women, who are not obligated in the mitzva of *Sefirat Ha'Omer*, the festival of Shavuot does not start until the end of forty-nine whole days. It follows that they also should not recite *kiddush* before night**, as the mitzva of the festival of Shavuot does not take effect before night. Women are only exempt from the mitzva of *Sefirat Ha'Omer*, but their festival of Shavuot is also dependent only on the end of seven whole weeks.

The ***Piskei Teshuvot*** adds that women should also not light candles before night, as the *beracha* of *Shehecheyanu* that they usually recite when lighting candles also signifies the start of Yom Tov.

---

8. The reason is that according to some *poskim*, the mitzva to eat meals on Shabbat and Yom Tov cannot be fulfilled during the time of *tosefet Shabbat*. See *Magen Avraham*, O.C. 267:1.

8. פסקי תשובות | או"ח תצד:ב

...גם לענין הדלקת הנרות, אפילו לנשים אלו שמדליקות בכל יום טוב מבעוד יום, מכל מקום בליל שבועות ידליקו אחר צאת הכוכבים, כי כיון שנהגו הנשים לברך שהחיינו בשעת הדלקת הנרות, הרי הן מקבלות קדושת עיצומו של יום, וכקידוש הוא.

Piskei Teshuvot, Orach Chaim 494:2

...Also regarding candle-lighting, even those women who light while it is still day every day [of Yom Tov] should nevertheless light after nightfall on the night of Shavuot, as since women are accustomed to recite the *beracha of Shehecheyanu* at the time of candle-lighting, they accept the sanctity of the day on themselves, and this is equivalent to *kiddush*.

Other *poskim*, such as **Rav Moshe Sternbuch**,[9] disagree, maintaining that women who always light candles on Yom Tov at the same time as for Shabbat should do so for Shavuot as well, as this was not mentioned as one of the stringencies. This is indeed the prevalent custom in many places.

A related issue involves whether women should recite the *beracha* of *Shehecheyanu* when lighting candles for any Yom Tov. The Gemara implies that ideally this *beracha* should be recited over a cup of wine, during *kiddush*, which would support the practice of not reciting it with candle lighting.[10] Rav Moshe Sternbuch writes that on Shavuot, there is an additional reason to avoid reciting this *beracha* when lighting candles – one should not recite *Shehecheyanu* early, similar to the rule regarding *Ma'ariv* and *kiddush*.

9. מועדים וזמנים | ז:רלג

...ביארנו במקום אחר שאין לברך שהחיינו כבר בהדלקה מכמה טעמים, וכל שכן בשבועות שנוסף טעם שביארנו שאין לברך קודם החג, ועיקר המצוה דהדלקת הנרות ביום טוב היא לפני בין השמשות וכמו שבשבת וכמו שכתבנו במקום אחר...

Moadim U'zmanim 7:233

...We explained elsewhere that one should not recite the *beracha* of *Shehecheyanu* while lighting for several reasons, and certainly on Shavuot, when there is an additional reason, as we explained that one should not recite the *beracha* before the festival. The main mitzva of lighting candles for Yom Tov is before *bein hashemashot*, as is the case with Shabbat, as we wrote elsewhere[11]...

9. *Teshuvot V'hanhagot* 4:111. See also *Halichot Shlomo, Shavuot* 12:2 (citing Rav Shlomo Zalman Auerbach) and Responsa *Binyan Av* 4:5.
10. See *Pesachim* 102b; Responsa *Yechaveh Da'at* 3:34.
11. The *Derisha*, in his introduction to *Yoreh De'ah*, writes in the name of his mother that the custom of some women to delay lighting candles until night on Yom Tov, is mistaken. Although lighting candles from an existing flame is permitted on Yom Tov, one should honor Yom Tov by ensuring that everything is ready before Yom Tov starts.

TIMING OF ACTIVITIES ON THE FIRST EVENING OF SHAVUOT

	Before Nightfall	After Nightfall
Lighting Candles	Preferable, as this is the main time for the mitzva. **(Rav Moshe Sternbuch)**	Preferable, to avoid *Shehecheyanu* at night **(*Piskei Teshuvot*)**
Shehecheyanu		Preferable, as *Shehecheyanu* signifies the start of Yom Tov and the *Omer* should be whole **(Rav Moshe Sternbuch, *Piskei Teshuvot*)**
Davening *Ma'ariv*	Acceptable, as *davening Ma'ariv* does not necessarily signify the end of the day **(*Shelah*)**	Preferable, so that the *Omer* should be whole **(*Taz, Mishna Berura*)**
	Preferable, as this shows enthusiasm **(Rav Yaakov Emden)**	
Reciting *Kiddush*	To be avoided, so that the *Omer* should be whole **(*Masat Binyamin, Shelah, Taz, Magen Avraham, Mishna Berura, Aruch HaShulchan*)**	Preferable if not too difficult, so that the *Omer* should be whole **Rav Ovadia Yosef**
	Acceptable **(*Korban Netanel*, Rav Yaakov Emden)**	

Forbidden Permitted Somewhere in-between

Tikun Leil Shavuot

There is a widespread custom to stay awake the entire night of Shavuot, studying Torah or reciting *Tikun Leil Shavuot*, a collection of verses from Tanach, Mishnayot and sections of the *Zohar*. This custom does not appear in the Gemara or mainstream early sources, and is certainly not obligatory, although it can be a valuable opportunity to increase Torah study.

The primary source for staying awake studying Torah on the night of Shavuot is from the ***Zohar***. The *Zohar* explains that counting the *Omer* is a preparation for spiritual purity, and after counting without missing a day, purification is achieved by studying Torah throughout the night of Shavuot.

10. זהר | פרשת אמור, צז:-צח.

...ומאן דמטי טהור להאי יומא, וחושבנא לא אתאביד מניה, כד מטי להאי ליליא, לבעי ליה למלעי באורייתא, ולאתחברא בה, ולנטרא דכיו עלאה, דמטי עליה בההוא ליליא, ואתדכי...

ועל דא, חסידי קדמאי לא הוו ניימי בהאי ליליא, והוו לעאן באורייתא, ואמרי, ניתי לאחסנא ירותא קדישא, לן, ולבנן, בתרין עלמין. וההוא ליליא כנסת ישראל אתעטרא עלייהו, ואתייא לאזדווגא ביה במלכא, ותרווייהו מתעטרי על רישייהו, דאינון דזכאן להכי.

ח Zohar, Parshat Emor 97b–98a

...One who arrives at this day when pure, [in that] he has not missed [any day of] counting [the *Omer*], when that night arrives, he should immerse himself in Torah, cleave to it, guard the higher purity that he receives on that night, and he will be purified...

For this reason, the early pious individuals would not sleep on this night, but would toil in Torah, and would say: Let us come to inherit a holy inheritance, for ourselves and for our children, in both worlds [this world and the world to come]. On this night, the Congregation of Israel adorns itself, and comes to unite with the King. Both are crowned upon their heads, as they are those who merit this.

The ***Magen Avraham*** cites the *Zohar* but also suggests that the custom to stay awake on the night of Shavuot serves as an atonement for the failure of the Jewish People to wake up early on the day that the Torah was given, as described by the *Midrash* in ***Shir HaShirim Rabba***.

11. שיר השירים רבה | א:ב

"כי ביום השלישי ירד ה' לעיני כל העם." ישנו להם ישראל כל אותו הלילה לפי ששינה של עצרת עריבה והלילה קצרה... בא הקדוש ברוך הוא ומצאן ישנים התחיל מעמיד עליהם בקלאנין הדא הוא דכתיב "ויהי ביום השלישי בהיות הבקר ויהי קולות וברקים" והיה משה מעורר לישראל ומוציאן לאפנתי של מלך מלכי המלכים הדא הוא דכתיב "ויוצא משה את העם לקראת הא-להים."

ח Shir HaShirim Rabba 1:2

"As on the third day, Hashem will descend before the eyes of all the people" (*Shemot* 19:11) – Israel slept that entire night, because the sleep of *Atzeret* [Shavuot] is pleasant and the night is short... The Holy One, blessed be He, came and found them sleeping, and He began to rouse them with thunder. This is [the meaning of] what is written: "It was on the third day, when it was morning, and there was thunder and lightning" (*Shemot* 19:16). Moshe was waking Israel and bringing them out to the audience of the King of kings. This is [the meaning of] what is written: "Moshe brought the people out to meet God" (*Shemot* 19:17).

א Magen Avraham, Orach Chaim 494, Introduction

It is stated in the *Zohar* that the early pious individuals would stay awake the whole night and would study Torah, and now most learners practice this. It is possible to give a simple reason, as [on the night before the Torah was given] the Jewish People slept the whole night and it was necessary for The Holy One, blessed be He to wake them, as is stated in the *Midrash*. Therefore, we must make amends for this.

12. מגן אברהם | או"ח תצד, הקדמה

איתא בזוהר שחסידים הראשונים היו נעורים כל הלילה ועוסקים בתורה וכבר נהגו רוב הלומדים לעשות כן ואפשר לתת טעם על פי פשוטו, לפי שישראל היו ישנים כל הלילה והוצרך הקדוש ברוך הוא להעיר אותם כדאיתא במדרש, לכן אנו צריכים לתקן זה.

As we explained above, the practice of staying awake learning all night on Shavuot is not mandatory. The ***Brisker Rav*** is quoted as expressing surprise as to why many people observe this **custom**, while on the first night of Pesach, they do not fulfill the **obligation** to stay awake to speak about the Exodus from Egypt until one is overcome with sleep.

Uvdot V'hanhagot L'veit Brisk, Vol. 2, p. 79

Now our teacher, Rav Yitzchak Zev Soloveitchik, would express surprise over the fact that people are particular to be awake on the night of the festival of Shavuot, which is a custom, whereas on the night of Pesach, when halacha dictates that one must sit and retell of the Exodus from Egypt until sleep overcomes him, people are not careful about this. In the house of Brisk they were not particular to be awake the entire night on Shavuot.

13. עובדות והנהגות לבית בריסק | חלק ב, עמ' עט

הנה מרן הרב יצחק זאב סולובייצ'יק זצ"ל היה תמה על כך שמדקדקים להיות ערים בליל חג השבועות שהוא מנהג, ואילו בליל פסח שמדינא צריך לישב ולספר ביציאת מצרים כל הלילה עד שתחטפנו שינה אין נזהרים האנשים בכך, ובבית בריסק לא היו מקפידים על המנהג להיות ניעור בכל הלילה בשבועות.

Rav Eliezer Melamed summarizes some of the factors to consider when deciding whether to stay awake to learn throughout the night of Shavuot.

Peninei Halakha, Moadim 13:8

...The kabbalists emphatically insisted that those who stay up all night must dedicate the time to intensive Torah study, and not waste time on frivolous matters (*Ben Ish Chai*, Year 1, Bamidbar §3).

In any case, following this custom is not obligatory. If it is difficult for one to stay up all night studying Torah, he may go to sleep. **Even some great rabbis preferred to sleep on Shavu'ot night. They evaluated the situation and decided that if they remained awake all night, the loss would outweigh the gain**: they would not be able to focus properly on praying in the morning, or they would not be alert enough at night to learn

14. פניני הלכה | מועדים יג:ח

...הזהירו המקובלים מאוד שהנשארים ערים יעסקו בתורה כל הלילה בלא לבטל את זמנם בדברים בטלים (בן איש חי במדבר ג).

מכל מקום אין חובה לקיים מנהג זה, ומי שקשה לו להישאר ער ולעסוק בתורה כל הלילה, רשאי לישון. **ויש מגדולי הרבנים שהעדיפו לישון בליל חג השבועות, כי שיערו בעצמם שאם יישארו ערים כל הלילה**, לא יוכלו לכוון כראוי בתפילת שחרית ומוסף, או שלא יוכלו ללמוד בלילה

בערנות מספקת, או שיאלצו לעסוק בהשלמת שעות שינה עד שהדבר יגרום לביטול תורה, או שלא יוכלו לשמוח כראוי בחג בהיותם עייפים.

אולם הנשארים ערים סוברים, שגם אם הלימוד בלילה אינו איכותי כל כך וקשה לכוון בתפילת שחרית, יש במנהג הקדוש הזה ביטוי לאהבת ה' ואהבת התורה, ואדרבה יש בו מעלה מיוחדת של מסירות נפש לכבוד שמיים ולכבודה של כנסת ישראל. **ונכון לכל אדם לבחור את מנהגו לשם שמיים.**

productively, or they would need to catch up on their sleep later on and learn less Torah, or they would not be able to enjoy the rest of the festival properly on account of exhaustion.

On the other hand, those who do stay up all night feel that even if their Torah study is not of the highest caliber, and it is difficult to focus on the morning prayers, this holy custom gives expression to love of God and love of Torah. It has the special advantage of showing dedication to God's glory. Such dedication enhances the glory of the Jewish people as well. **Each person should choose the practice that will allow him to serve God best.**

Birkot HaShachar for Those Awake All Night

What is the halacha concerning reciting *Birkot HaShachar* for those who stay up all night? Should one recite *Birkot HaShachar* in the morning? On one hand, since the *Birkot HaShachar* were designed to thank Hashem upon awakening, perhaps one should not recite it, since one never went to sleep. On the other hand, according to the opinion of the *Tur* and the Rema, the *berachot* were established based on the way the world works.[12] Therefore, it should make no difference if a person slept at night or not, and he should recite them.

Many of the *poskim* accepted the second approach. However, the ***Sha'arei Teshuva*** cites differing opinions as to whether one who did not sleep should recite *Elokai Neshama* and the final *beracha* of *hama'avir sheina* ("who removes sleep from my eyes"). According to the ***Ateret Zekeinim*** one does not recite those two *berachot,* while **Rav Chaim Vital** in the ***Pri Etz Chaim*** indicates that one would recite those *berachot* as well.

15. שערי תשובה | או"ח מו:יב

ועיין בעטרת זקנים שכתב שהניעור בלילה ולא ישן כל הלילה לא יאמר אלקי נשמה והמעביר שינה, וכתב שהסכים עמו מ"ו הגאון מוהר"ר יושע ז"ל.

אמנם בפרי עץ חיים כתב וז"ל: ...והנה כל הח"י ברכות השחר עד סוף כל ברכות התורה חייב כל אדם לברך בכל יום אפילו שלא נתחייב בהם ביום ההוא, **כגון שלא ישן בלילה כל עיקר או לן בכסותו או באזורו ומצנפתו או לא התיר מנעליו** והטעם כי לא נתקנו אלא על מנהגו של עולם ולא על כל אדם בפרטות ועוד כי כולן יש בהם רמז אל אורות העליונים... עיי"ש.

א Shaarei Teshuva, Orach Chaim 46:12

See the *Ateret Zekeinim* who writes that one who is awake at night and did not sleep the entire night should not recite *Elokai Neshama* or "*hama'avir sheina.*" He also writes that our teacher, HaGaon Rav Yosha agreed with him.

However, in the *Pri Etz Chaim*, the author wrote: ...Every person is required to recite all eighteen morning blessings until the end of the blessings for Torah, even if he was not obligated in them on that day. For example, **if one did not sleep at all during the night, he slept in his clothes or with his belt or his turban, or did not remove his shoes [he must still recite them].** The reason is that the blessings were established for the way of the world and not forevery individual person. Furthermore, they all allude to supernal lights...

12. See volume 9, *shiur* 4, where this was discussed in detail.

It is clear from here that one should recite the blessing of "*hama'avir sheina*" even if he did not sleep at all, as it is included as one of the eighteen blessings. If so, presumably *Elokai Neshama* should also be recited even if one did not sleep at all…

The *Eliya Rabba* cites a précis of the *Ateret Zekeinim*. Therefore, it appears that one should force oneself to sleep a little bit. If not, he should hear the blessings of *Elokai Neshama* and *hama'avir sheina* from someone else, since there is a principle that one who hears the blessing is as if he recited it, especially if he answers *amen* after the blessing.

מבואר מזה דגם המעביר שינה יאמר אע"פ שלא ישן כלל, שהרי הוא בכלל הי"ח ברכות. ואם כן מסתמא גם אלקי נשמה יש לומר אע"פ שלא ישן כלל...

ובאליה רבה הביא דברי העטרת זקנים בקצרה. ולכן נראה שיש להביא את עצמו לידי שינה כל שהיא, ואם לאו יש לשמוע אלקי נשמה וברכות המעביר שינה מאחר והוה ליה 'שומע כעונה', ובפרט שעונה אמן אחריו.

Thus, due to the dispute, the *Sha'arei Teshuva* recommends listening to someone else recite the *beracha* if he does not sleep even a small amount.

The ***Mishna Berura*** cites the opinion that one should not recite the two *berachot* if one did not sleep. Although he notes that some *poskim* question this ruling, he concludes with the *Sha'arei Teshuva*'s recommendation to listen to someone else reciting those *berachot*.[13]

א Mishna Berura, Orach Chaim 46:24

16. משנה ברורה | או"ח מו:כד

Look at the *Eliya Rabba* who writes that the *berachot* of *Elokai Neshama* and "removing sleep" should not be recited if one was awake all night. However, the *Pri Megadim* and *Sha'arei Teshuva* leave his opinion as requiring further examination. The *Sha'arei Teshuva* concludes that one should try to hear these *berachot* from someone else and have in mind to discharge his obligation. If one slept sixty breaths [about half an hour] during the night, everyone agrees he may recite the blessings.

עיין בספר אליה רבה שכתב דברכת אלהי נשמה וברכת המעביר שינה אין לברך אם היה ניעור כל הלילה, ובפמ"ג ובשערי תשובה השאירו דבריו בצריך עיון. ומסיק בשערי תשובה דיראה לשמוע אלו השתי הברכות מאחר ויכוין לצאת. ואם ישן בלילה ששים נישמין לכולי עלמא יש לו לברך אותם.

The ***Piskei Teshuvot*** explains that the reason these *berachot* are different from the others is because they are worded as applying to the specific individual. In other words, these two *berachot* appear to refer subjectively to the person much more than the other *berachot*, even according to the opinion of the Rema.

The *Piskei Teshuvot* also writes that despite the recommendation to avoid reciting these two *berachot* when not sleeping all night, who does recite them certainly has opinions to rely upon.

פ Piskei Teshuvot, Orach Chaim 46:15

17. פסקי תשובות | או"ח מו:טו

Mishna Berura 46:24: The *Eliya Rabba* writes that the *berachot* of *Elokai Neshama* and *hama'avir sheina* should not be recited if one was awake all night. Even according to the Rema that the *Birkot HaShachar* are for the order of the world

מ"ב סקכ"ד: בס' אליה רבה כתב דברכת אלהי נשמה וברכת המעביר שינה אין לברך אם היה ניעור כל הלילה וכו'. ואפילו לשיטת הרמ"א דברכות השחר על מנהגו של עולם

13. The *Mishna Berura* in the halachot of Shavuot (494:1) in fact writes to see his comments quoted in this source.

מברך אפילו הוא עצמו לא נהנה, **נשתנו ברכות אלו שנוסחתם פרטית על עצמו (המעביר שינה מעיני ותנומה מעפעפי, א' נשמה שנתת בי וכו').**

והנה, אם כי לכתחילה בודאי יש לחזור אחר מי שיוציאנו בברכות אלו, וכהכרעת הפמ"ג והשערי תשובה ומשנ"ב ועוד מגדולי הפוסקים, **מכל מקום בדליכא, המברך לעצמו שפיר יש לו על מי לסמוך**, ובצירוף קבלת האר"י ז"ל שגם ברכות אלו מודה בהם להשי"ת שהוא בכלל הנהגת העולם הכללית של התחדשות הבריאה בכל יום תמיד, אע"פ שביום זה לא נתן לעפעפיו תנומה, אמנם נכון מאד שימתין מלברכם עד לאחר עלות השחר.

ואם יוכל להביא עצמו לידי שינה אפילו רק למשך כמחצית שעה, ודאי שפיר עביד שיוכל לברך ברכות אלו לדברי הכל, ואפילו שינתו לאחר הנץ החמה, ואפילו אם שינתו תהיה לאחר התפילה אם משער שקימתו תהיה כשעדיין לפני חצות היום, יעדיף להמתין ולברך בעצמו שני ברכות אלו לאחר שינתו (ובעת תפילתו שמו"ע בברכת מחיה המתים יכוין שאינו רוצה לצאת בזה ברכת אלהי נשמה).

and apply even if one did not personally derive benefit, **these two blessings are different because their wording refers specifically to the person himself ("Who removes sleep from my eyes and slumber from my eyelids," "The soul that you gave me.")**

Even though ideally, one should certainly look for someone else to recite these blessings on his behalf, in accordance with the ruling of the *Pri Megadim, Sha'arei Teshuva, Mishna Berura,* and other *poskim*, **nevertheless, if that is impossible, he should recite the blessings himself and he has opinions to rely upon**. [This is true] especially when we include the Kabbalistic opinion of the Arizal that these blessings give thanks to God for the general way of the world and the constant renewal of creation each day, and even though on this particular day the person did not give slumber to his eyelids. Nevertheless, it is more correct that he should not recite them until after dawn.

If a person is able to sleep, even half an hour, it is certainly preferable to do so, in order that he may recite those blessings according to all opinions. Even if he only sleeps after dawn, and even if that sleep is only after prayer, if he thinks he will wake up before midday, it is preferable to wait and recite those two blessings after he sleeps. (When he recites the *Shemoneh Esrei* prayer, in the blessing of "Who resurrects the dead" he should have in mind that he does not want to fulfill his obligation to recite the blessing of "God, the soul that You gave me" with this blessing.)

The ***Aruch HaShulchan*** agrees that one may recite the *Birkot HaShachar* even if one did not sleep. But in contrast to the opinion of the *Mishna Berura*, the *Aruch HaShulchan* argues that according to the Rema, he should recite even *Elokai Neshama* and *hama'avir sheina*, as these too are considered *berachot* that refer to the way of the world.

18. ערוך השולחן | או"ח מו:יג

לכן נראה לי ברור דלדעת רבינו הרמ"א גם אם לא יישן כל הלילה יאמר ברכת "אלהי נשמה" וברכת "המעביר שנה מעיני". וראיתי מי שכתב דבניעור כל הלילה לא יאמר שני ברכות אלו (אליה רבה סעיף קטן י"ב). ולא נראה לי, דוודאי לפי דעת רבינו הבית יוסף אין לומר.

א Aruch HaShulchan, Orach Chaim 46:13

Therefore, it seems clear to me that according to the opinion of our teacher the Rema, one should recite *Elokai Neshama* and *hama'avir sheina* even if one did not sleep all night. I saw that some write that one who is up all night should not recite these two *berachot* (*Eliya Rabba*). But this does not seem correct to me. Certainly according to our teacher, the *Beit Yosef*, one should not recite them, but according to our teacher the Rema, based upon whose custom everyone recites all of the *berachot,* here too the same is true [that they should be recited]...

אבל לרבינו הרמ"א דעל מנהגו של עולם מברכין, אם כן הכא נמי כן הוא...

The ***Yalkut Yosef*** agrees that one who did not sleep should recite all of the *Birkot HaShachar,* based upon the opinion of the Rema.

Yalkut Yosef, Orach Chaim 46:9

19. ילקוט יוסף | או"ח מו:ט

Therefore, one who is awake all night **recites all the morning blessings** apart from the blessing on washing hands, and "Who created man." For the widespread custom is to recite all the blessings in the morning even if one is not obligated in all of them.

לפיכך הניעור כל הלילה **מברך כל ברכות השחר**, מלבד ברכת 'על נטילת ידים', ו'אשר יצר', שכבר פשט המנהג לברך בשחר כל ברכות השחר אף שלא נתחייב בהם.

Based upon the sources above, it would seem that in practice, *poskim* agree that one who was awake all night long on Shavuot night may recite the *Birkot HaShachar* himself. According to the *Mishna Berura* and *Piskei Teshuvot,* it is preferable to try to hear the two *berachot* of *Elokai Neshama* and *hama'avir sheina* from someone else in order to fulfill the obligation, but many *poskim* hold that these too, one may recite oneself.

Birkot HaTorah for Those Awake All Night

Those who remain awake all night must also confront the question of whether to recite *Birkot HaTorah* in the morning. The *poskim* discuss whether *Birkot HaTorah* is determined based on sleep (in which case they would not recite it) or based on the beginning of a new day (in which case they would). The ***Mishna Berura*** writes that the resolution to this question is uncertain. Therefore, if someone stays awake throughout the night, instead of reciting his own new *beracha* in the morning, he should hear the *beracha* from someone who slept.

א Mishna Berura, Orach Chaim 47:28

20. משנה ברורה | או"ח מז:כח

If one was awake all night, some say that he is not required to recite the *beracha* in the morning, while others say that he is required to recite the *beracha* because Chazal established that this blessing should be recited daily, akin to the other *Birkot HaShachar*. [The rule is] that blessings are omitted when in doubt [*safeik berachot l'hakel*].

However, if possible, he should see to it to hear the *Birkot HaTorah* from another (who has slept overnight). He should tell the other to intend to discharge his [the non-sleeper's] obligation with these blessings, and he [the non-sleeper] should intend to fulfill [his obligation] and should answer *amen*. Thereafter, he should say some verses so that [the blessing] may be considered adjacent to the study...

ואם היה ניעור כל הלילה, יש אומרים דאין צריך לברך בבוקר, ויש אומרים דצריך לברך, כי קבעו חכמים ברכה זו בכל יום דומיא דשאר ברכות השחר, וספק ברכות להקל.

אך אם אפשר לו יִראה לשמוע ברכות התורה מאחר (שישן בלילה). ויאמר לו שיכוין להוציאו בהברכות והוא יכוין לצאת ויענה אמן. ויאמר אחר כך איזה פסוקים כדי שיהא נחשב לו במקום לימוד...

By contrast, the ***Yalkut Yosef*** rules that it is better for one staying up all night to recite the *beracha* himself, and the ***Aruch HaShulchan* (47:23–24)** adopts this position as well.

21. ילקוט יוסף | או"ח מז:ח

הניעור כל הלילה, וכמו שנהגו ישראל קדושים בלילי חג השבועות והושענא רבה, וכן בלילי תיקון כרת, וכיוצא בזה, חייב לברך ברכות התורה בזמן עלות השחר, שכן דעת מרן ורוב הפוסקים, וכן הסכים האר"י ז"ל, ונמשכו אחריו כל גדולי המקובלים. וכן פשט המנהג בכל תפוצות ספרד. וידוע שבמקום מנהג אין אומרים "ספק ברכות להקל". ואין צורך "להדר" ולשמוע ברכות התורה מאדם אחר שישן שנת קבע בלילה. ואדרבה, מצוה בו יותר מבשלוחו.

Yalkut Yosef, Orach Chaim 47:8

If someone is awake the whole night, as has been practiced by the holy Jewish People on the nights of Shavuot and Hoshana Raba, and on nights of *tikkun kareit*,[14] and all the like, a person is obligated to recite *Birkot HaTorah* at dawn. That is the opinion of *Maran* (our master, Rav Yosef Karo) and most of the *poskim*, and so agreed the Arizal; and most of the great Kabbalists followed him. This practice has spread throughout the Sephardic communities, and it is known that where there is a custom, we do not say *safeik berachot l'hakel*. Moreover, there is no need to pursue a stringency and hear the *Birkot HaTorah* from another person who slept substantially overnight. On the contrary, the mitzva is greater when he performs it than when his representative does.

Rav Akiva Eiger suggests an interesting *chiddush* (novelty) that if someone sleeps substantial sleep in the afternoon and thereafter remains awake for the entire night, that person may recite a new *beracha* according to all opinions. According to those who hold that the *beracha* is recited on a daily basis, it would be recited in the morning, and according to the Rosh and others who hold that it must be recited after sleeping during the day, one would still be obligated to recite it the next morning.

22. הגהות רבי עקיבא איגר על מגן אברהם | או"ח מז:יב

...והוא הדין בישן ביום ונעור כל הלילה שלאחריו, דמברך בבוקר בממה נפשך, לרבינו תם צריך לברך דלא נפטר רק מעת לעת, ולרא"ש גם שינת היום הוי היסח הדעת...

על כל פנים בישן ביום וניעור כל הלילה שלאחריו בודאי יש לברך מדין ממה נפשך הנ"ל, ואין צריך לחוש דנפטר באהבת עולם, דלהרבה פוסקים אינו פוטר

Glosses of Rabbi Akiva Eiger to Magen Avraham, Orach Chaim 47:12

...The same is true of someone who sleeps in the day and remains awake the entire following night; he should recite the *beracha* in the morning according to all angles. According to Rabbeinu Tam, he must recite the *beracha* because he is exempted [by the previous time in which he recited the *beracha*] only for twenty-four hours; and according to the Rosh, substantial sleep during the daytime already constitutes an interruption...

In any case, if someone sleeps during the day and remains awake the entire following night, certainly that person should recite the *beracha* according to all angles, as stated. And there is no need to be concerned that perhaps he became exempt with [the recital] of *Ahavat Olam* [in *Ma'ariv*] as many *poskim* hold that this exempts

14. *Tikkun kareit* is a night spent in study, undertaken as part of a course of repentance for a severe sin associated with the spiritual punishment of *kareit*, excision. The concept of such a night is mentioned in the writings of the Arizal, and a specific curriculum is outlined by the Chida.

only that which the person subsequently learns immediately. And for many *poskim*, *Keriat Shema* is not considered "study." So it appears in my humble opinion.

רק מה שלומד מיד, ולהרבה פוסקים קריאת שמע לא הוי לימוד. כן נראה לעניות דעתי.

The ***Mishna Berura*** adopts the position of Rav Akiva Eiger.

א Mishna Berura, Orach Chaim 47:28

23. משנה ברורה | או"ח מז:כח

If he slept a substantial sleep in his bed in the day, and the subsequent night he was awake the whole night, HaGaon Rav Akiva Eiger rules in that case that according to all opinions, he must recite the *Birkot HaTorah* in the morning.

אם היה ישן ביום שינת קבע על מטתו ובלילה שלאחריו היה ניעור כל הלילה, פסק הגאון רעק"א דבזה לכולי עלמא צריך לברך בבוקר ברכות התורה.

The ***Piskei Teshuvot*** cautions that someone who has remained awake throughout the night must interrupt his study at dawn, though he notes that some *poskim* hold this is unnecessary.

פ Piskei Teshuvot, Orach Chaim 47:16

24. פסקי תשובות | או"ח מז:טז

Ideally, someone who has remained awake all night must be careful to interrupt his learning at the moment of dawn, for from this moment onward he is subject to the obligation [to recite] *Birkot HaTorah*. However, he may be lenient until the late reckoning of dawn (seventy-two minutes prior to sunrise).[15] And some write that he may continue to study the matter at hand until he completes it.

ולכתחילה יש למי שניעור כל הלילה ליזהר להפסיק לימודו מיד עם עלות השחר, כי משעה זאת ואילך חלה עליו חובת ברכת התורה, אמנם יוכל להקל עד זמן עלות השחר המאוחר (שהוא 72 דקות לפני נץ החמה), ויש הכותבים שרשאי להמשיך בלימודו עד שגומר הענין.

We will conclude this section by emphasizing the importance of observing the day of Yom Tov in the manner described by Chazal, dedicating half to Hashem through Torah study and *tefilla*, and half to personal enjoyment.[16] One who remains awake throughout the night on Shavuot may find that fatigue significantly diminishes the quality or extent of the daytime Yom Tov experience. Each individual should therefore carefully consider whether the benefit gained from staying awake outweighs the potential loss in fulfilling the day's broader obligations.

15. Concerning the different calculations of dawn, see volume 9, *shiur* 3.
16. Details of this obligation were discussed in volume 23, *shiur* 4. It is clear from the Rambam quoted there that this obligation applies during the day, rather than the night.

Eating Dairy Foods

The widespread custom of eating dairy foods on Shavuot already began many centuries ago in Ashkenazic communities. For example, the ***Kol Bo*** mentions a custom to eat honey and milk on Shavuot, since the Torah is compared to these foods.

Kol Bo, Siman 52

It is customary to eat honey and milk on the festival of Shavuot, as the Torah is compared to honey and milk, as it is written, "Honey and milk under your tongue" (*Shir Hashirim* 4:11).

25. כל בו | סימן נב

נהגו לאכול דבש וחלב בחג שבועות מפני התורה שנמשלה לדבש וחלב כמו שכתוב דבש וחלב תחת לשונך (שיר השירים ד:יא).

The **Rema** offers a different reason for the custom. He suggests that one should first eat dairy and then meat to mirror the two cooked foods taken on the first night of Pesach in memory of the *korban Chagiga* and the *korban Pesach*. This also necessitates using two loaves of bread, one to eat together with the dairy foods and one to eat together with meat, and this commemorates the two loaves of bread brought as an offering in the *Beit HaMikdash* on Shavuot.

Rema, Orach Chaim 494:3

It is customary in all places [in Ashkenaz] to eat dairy foods on the first day of Shavuot. It appears to me that the reason is that this is similar to the two cooked foods that we take on the [first] night of Pesach, in memory of the [*korban*] *Pesach* and in memory of the *Chagiga*. Similarly, we eat dairy foods and then a meat dish. It is necessary to bring two loaves of bread with them on the table, which is in place of the altar, and this acts as a commemoration of the two loaves of bread that were brought on the day of the *bikkurim* [Shavuot].

26. רמ"א | או"ח תצד:ג

ונוהגין בכל מקום לאכול מאכלי חלב ביום ראשון של שבועות. ונראה לי הטעם, שהוא כמו שני תבשילין שלוקחים בליל פסח, זכר לפסח וזכר לחגיגה, כן אוכלים מאכל חלב ואחר כך מאכל בשר וצריכין להביא עמהם שני לחם על השולחן שהוא במקום המזבח, ויש בזה זכרון לשתי הלחם שהיו מקריבין ביום הביכורים.

The ***Mishna Berura*** quotes another reason, that we commemorate the fact that the Jewish People had to eat dairy immediately after the Torah was given, as their utensils were not kosher and they were therefore not able to prepare meat.

Mishna Berura, Orach Chaim 494:12

I heard further, in the name of a certain great person, who gave a sound reason for this. **At the time that they stood at Mount Sinai and accepted the Torah** (as through the Ten Commandments, all parts of the Torah were revealed to them, as Rav Sa'adia Gaon writes, that the entire Torah is included within the Ten Commandments) **and they descended from**

27. משנה ברורה | או"ח תצד:יב

ואני שמעתי עוד בשם גדול אחד שאמר טעם נכון לזה **כי בעת שעמדו על הר סיני וקבלו התורה** (כי בעשרת הדברות נתגלה להם על ידי זה כל חלקי התורה כמו שכתב רב סעדיה גאון שבעשרת הדברות כלולה כל התורה) **וירדו מן**

the mountain to their homes, they initially only found dairy foods [that they were permitted to eat].

ההר לביתם לא מצאו מה לאכול תיכף כי אם מאכלי חלב.

As meat requires extensive preparation: to slaughter with an inspected knife [to ensure that the blade is perfectly smooth] as Hashem commanded, to remove the forbidden fats and the blood, to rinse, salt, and cook in new utensils, as the utensils they had previously, in which they had cooked [non-kosher food] within the previous twenty-four hours, became prohibited to them. Therefore, they chose dairy foods at that time, and we commemorate this.

כי לבשר צריך הכנה רבה: לשחוט בסכין בדוק כאשר צוה ה', ולנקר חוטי החלב והדם, ולהדיח, ולמלוח, ולבשל בכלים חדשים, כי הכלים שהיו להם מקודם שבישלו בהם באותו מעת לעת נאסרו להם על כן בחרו להם לפי שעה מאכלי חלב ואנו עושין זכר לזה.

Although the earlier sources discussing the custom for eating dairy on Shavuot are primarily Ashkenazi, Sephardim have also accepted this custom, as noted by Rav Ovadia Yosef.

Chazon Ovadia, Yom Tov, Hilchot Chag HaShavuot 12

28. חזון עובדיה | יום טוב, הל' חג השבועות יב

It is customary to eat dairy foods on Shavuot… and our custom is to first eat dairy foods, then wipe and rinse one's month as required,[17] and then eat meat foods.

נוהגין לאכול מאכלי חלב בחג השבועות... ומנהגנו לאכול תחלה מאכלי חלב, ואחר קינוח והדחה כמשפט, אוכלים מאכלי בשר.

It should be clear from the sources above that the custom to eat dairy foods on Shavuot was never intended to replace the standard mitzva on all Yamim Tovim to rejoice through eating and drinking. As has been discussed previously,[18] drinking wine is mandated on Yom Tov, and there is also a mitzva to eat meat (although this is not an absolute requirement according to most *poskim*).

Accordingly, **Rav Mordechai Eliyahu** writes that one should not eat only dairy foods, unless one does not enjoy eating meat. However, he does write that one can eat meat at night and dairy in the day.

Ma'amar Mordechai, Mo'adim V'yamim 23:14–15

29. מאמר מרדכי | מועדים וימים כג:יד–טו

14. One is obligated to rejoice on this festival [of Shavuot], and rejoicing is only with meat and wine. Therefore, one should not suffice with dairy foods alone. However, one who does not rejoice over meat dishes is not obligate to eat them.

15. One may eat the meat dishes at night and the dairy foods in the day. They are not both required to be [eaten] in the day specifically.[19]

יד. חייב אדם לשמוח בחג הזה ואין שמחה אלא בבשר ויין, ולכן לא יסתפק אדם במאכלי חלב בלבד. אמנם מי שאינו שמח במאכלי בשר אינו מחויב לאוכלם.

טו. יכול לאכול בלילה את מאכלי הבשר וביום את מאכלי החלב ואין צריך שניהם להיות דווקא ביום.

---

17. See *Shulchan Aruch*, Y.D. 89:2, that one must wipe and rinse out one's mouth in between eating dairy and then meat. See volume 4, *shiur* 2, where these halachot were explained in detail.

18. See volume 23, *shiur* 4.

19. This is different than the Rema, who describes the custom as eating meat immediately after eating dairy. As we saw in volume 23, *shiur* 4, the mitzva to rejoice on Yom Tov applies primarily in the day, so for this reason, it may be preferable to eat meat in the day. For a summary of the different customs concerning this issue, see *Minhag Yisrael Torah* 494 and *Piskei Teshuvot* 494.

Rav Eliezer Melamed writes that the primary purpose of these customs is to enhance the joy of the festival and to honor the Torah, and this perspective should guide one's observance.

Peninei Halakha, Moadim 13:14

...Of utmost importance is the mitzva of *simcha*; all these customs are meant to add joy to the holiday and honor to the Torah.

30. פניני הלכה | מועדים יג:יד

...והעיקר לקיים את מצוות השמחה בחג, שכל המנהגים הללו נועדו להוסיף שמחה בחג וכבוד לתורה.

The ***Magen Avraham*** cautions that one who observes the original custom of the Rema to eat meat immediately after dairy must be careful to adhere to the required precautions, such as eating meat and dairy on separate tablecloths.[20] However, one need not recite *Birkat HaMazon* in between eating dairy and meat.

א Magen Avraham, Orach Chaim 494:6

...The custom of our fathers is Torah, but one must be careful to avoid transgression. See *Yoreh De'ah* 89, that one need not interrupt by [reciting] *Birkat HaMazon* if one does not eat hard cheese,[21] and one should be careful to take another tablecloth [for meat].

31. מגן אברהם | או"ח תצד:ו

...ומנהג אבותינו תורה היא אך יש ליזהר שלא יבא לידי איסור. ועיין ביורה דעה סימן פ"ט דאין צריך להפסיק בברכת המזון אם אינו אוכל גבינה קשה, ויזהר ליקח מפה אחרת.

The ***Mishna Berura*** (494:16) rules in accordance with the *Magen Avraham*. However, the ***Darkei Teshuva*** (Y.D. 89:14) writes that one must recite *Birkat HaMazon* before eating meat, and some are stringent in accordance with this opinion.

---

20. See n. 19.
21. In volume 4, *shiur* 2, it was explained that according to many *poskim*, most modern cheeses do not have the status of hard cheese regarding these halachot.

Decorating the Synagogue

In many communities, it is customary to decorate the synagogue with flowers or other greenery in honor of Shavuot. This custom is first mentioned by the **Maharil**, who explains that this is simply to express joy for the festival.

ר Sefer Maharil (Minhagim), Shavuot 2

It is customary to lay out herbal spices and roses on the floor of the synagogue, for the joy of the festival. When Shavuot falls on Sunday, Mahari Segal[22] directed [the synagogue's management] to lay out the herbs [before] the start of Shabbat.[23]

32. ספר מהרי"ל (מנהגים) | שבועות ב

נוהגין להשטיח רצפת בית הכנסת בבשמים של עשבים ובשושנים לשמחת הרגל. ומתי שחל שבועות ביום ראשון הנהיג מהר"י סג"ל להשטיח העשבים בהכנסת שבת.

The **Rema** specifies that we decorate the synagogue to celebrate the giving of the Torah, and adds that for the same reason we also decorate our houses.

א Rema, Orach Chaim 494:3

It is customary to spread herbs in the synagogue and in the houses on Shavuot, as a remembrance of the joy of the giving of the Torah.

33. רמ"א | או"ח תצד:ג

ונוהגין לשטוח עשבים בשבועות בבית הכנסת והבתים, זכר לשמחת מתן תורה.

The ***Levush*** explains further that when the Torah was given, greenery surrounded Mount Sinai.

א Levush, Orach Chaim 494:1

It is customary to lay out herbs on the Yom Tov of Shavuot in the synagogue and the houses, as a remembrance of the joy of the giving of the Torah. As there were herbs around Mount Sinai, as it is written, "The sheep and cattle should not pasture, etc."

34. לבוש | או"ח תצד:א

ונוהגין לשטוח עשבים ביום טוב דשבועות בבית הכנסת ובבתים זכר לשמחת מתן תורה, שהיו עשבים סביב הר סיני כדכתיב הצאן והבקר אל ירעו וגו'.

The ***Magen Avraham*** adds that it is also customary to place trees in the synagogue and in homes for Shavuot. He suggests that this is to remind people to pray for fruit, as Shavuot is the time of judgment regarding the produce of trees.

22. Sefer Maharil was compiled primarily by a student of the Maharil, known as Zalman of Sankt Goar. The acronym "Maharil" is short for Moreinu HaRav Yaakov Levi, Levi being his title as a *levi* rather than a surname. He is also known as Mahari Segal, Segal being another title commonly given to *levi'im* at the time. Segal stands for *Segan Leviya* (assistant of the Levites) or *Segan L'kehuna* (assistant to the priesthood).

23. The *Magen Avraham* (494:5) suggests that laying out the greenery on Yom Tov may be prohibited due to *muktzeh*, but he appears to conclude that if one planned to lay them out before Yom Tov this would not be an issue. Certainly, however, one should not lay them out on Shabbat in preparation for Yom Tov.

א Magen Avraham, Orach Chaim 494:5

35. מגן אברהם | או"ח תצד:ה

נוהגין להעמיד אילנות בבית הכנסת ובבתים. ונראה לי הטעם שיזכירו שבעצרת נידונין על פירות האילן ויתפללו עליהם.

It is customary to set up trees in the synagogue and in the houses. It appears to me that the reason is so that people will remember that on Shavuot, we are judged regarding the fruit of the tree[24] and pray for them.

However, the ***Chayei Adam*** (Vol. 2–3, 131:13) writes that the **Gra** ended this custom, as he felt that since the gentiles also set up trees in their churches to celebrate their festival,[25] this is a violation of *chukot hagoyim*, following the statutes of the gentiles. In the ***Chochmat Adam***, Rav Danzig[26] explains that although setting up trees is not an obligation according to Christianity, since it is their practice and there is no biblical source for this custom, it must be discontinued.

א Chochmat Adam, Sha'ar Issur V'heter 89:1

36. חכמת אדם | שער איסור והיתר פט:א

...מה שאינו חוק לעבודה זרה אלא להבל ושטות אם כתיב בתורה מותר ואם לא כתיב אף זה אסור, ומטעם זה אסר הגר"א להעמיד אילנות בחג השבועות כמו שכתבו האחרונים כיון שכן נהגו בחג שלהם.

...That which is not mandated for idolatry, but is merely a vain and futile practice, if it is written in the Torah, it is permitted, but if it is not, even this is prohibited. For this reason, the Gra prohibited setting up trees on the festival of Shavuot, like the *Acharonim* write, since [the gentiles] are also accustomed to do so on their festival.

The ***Mishna Berura*** (494:10) also cites the *Chayei Adam* and the Gra, and the same position appears to be taken by the ***Aruch HaShulchan***[27] and **Rav Moshe Feinstein** as well.[28]

As we have seen, the *Chochmat Adam* appears to understand that setting up trees is prohibited because it is a "vain and futile practice." This is based on a ruling of **Tosafot** (*Avoda Zara* 11a) that gentile practices of this nature are prohibited.[29]

However, **Rav Yosef Shaul Nathanson** argues that this is not the case regarding the practice of setting up trees, and since there is a logical reason for decorating the synagogues in this manner, it is not included in the prohibition against *chukot hagoyim*.

א Divrei Shaul, Yosef Da'at, Yoreh De'ah 348:1

37. דברי שאול | יוסף דעת, יו"ד שמח:א

כל דבר שההיקש השכל מחייבו לית ביה משום חקה וזה שכתב הריב"ש דמה שעושין

Any practice that stems from rational thinking does not involve [the prohibition against] *chuka* [*chukot hagoyim*]. This is the meaning of what the Rivash writes, that practices done

24. See Mishna, *Rosh Hashana* 1:2.
25. The Christian festival of Pentecost, itself based on Shavuot.
26. Rav Avraham Danzig was the author of both the *Chayei Adam* and *Chochmat Adam*.
27. O.C. 494:4.
28. Responsa *Igrot Moshe*, Y.D. 4:11:5. These sources indicate that the Gra also ended the custom of decorating the synagogue with any greenery or flowers, and that this should also be followed. See, however, n. 32 below.
29. See volume 1, *shiur* 3, where the laws of *chukot hagoyim* are discussed at length, including these sources.

for "importance" are not considered *chuka*… From what has been stated, it becomes clear that one can uphold the Jewish custom of setting up trees on the festival of Shavuot. HaGaon, our master Rav Eliyahu of Vilna [the Gra] of blessed memory stopped it, and said that it involves the prohibition of *chukat akum*…. But according to what I have written, anything done for the sake of honor is not included among statutes of idolatry.

Accordingly, I instructed [people] to ask the gentiles why they do this practice, and the elder among them stated that it is only for honor and beautification of the house with pleasant trees. If so, it stems from rational thinking, and it does not involve *darkei ha'emori* [prohibited gentile practices]… **In any event, this is sufficient to uphold the custom of Israel to set up trees on the festival of Shavuot…**

משום חשיבות לא מקרי חקה... ומן האמור נגלה מבואר לקיים מנהג של ישראל שמעמידין אילנות בחג השבועות, והגאון מורינו הרב אליהו וילנער ז"ל מנעו, ואמר דיש בו משום חוקת עכו"ם... ולפי מה שכתבתי כל דעושין משום כבוד אם כן אינו בכלל חק לעבודה זרה.

וכן צוויתי לשאול מהגוים על מה הם עושים זאת והישיש בהם הגיד שאינו רק משום כבוד והדור הבית בעצים נאים ואם כן ההיקש השכל מחייבו ואין בו משום דרכי האמורי... **ועל כל פנים בזה די לקיים מנהגן של ישראל שמעמידין אילנות בחג השבועות...**

In truth, the Gra elsewhere (Y.D. 178:7) disputes the entire principle that Rav Nathanson bases his leniency upon, and maintains that gentile practices that have no Torah source are prohibited, even if they do have a logical reason.[30] The ending of the custom of setting up trees in the synagogue on Shavuot is consistent with this ruling of the Gra.[31] However, in many communities, the custom to decorate the synagogue at least with greenery or flowers is still continued today, as even according to the Gra, perhaps the prohibition against gentile practices is limited to trees.[32]

30. This position of the Gra was also quoted in volume 1, *shiur* 3 on *chukot hagoyim*.
31. See *Minchat Asher*, *Vayikra* 43 and Responsa *Yechaveh Da'at* 4:33, who point this out.
32. See *Shalmei Mo'ed*, p. 459, citing Rav Shlomo Zalman Auerbach, and *Yerushalayim B'moadeha*, *Shavuot*, p. 184. See also *Peninei Halakha*, *Moadim* 13:13, who writes that according to most *poskim*, this custom is not problematic.

Megillat Rut

The custom to read *Megillat Rut* on or around Shavuot is at least a thousand years old. ***Masechet Soferim***[33] records a custom to read half of it on the second night of Shavuot (in *chutz la'aretz*) and the other half on *Motza'ei Yom Tov*, or to start reading it from the *Motza'ei Shabbat* before Shavuot.

38. מסכת סופרים | יד:טז

ברות, במוצאי יום טוב הראשון של עצרת עד חציו, ומשלים במוצאי יום טוב האחרון, ויש אומרים בכולן מתחילין במוצאי שבת שלפניהם.

ח Masechet Soferim 14:16

[We read] until halfway through [*Megillat*] *Rut* after the first day of Yom Tov [i.e., on the second night], and complete it after the last day of Yom Tov. Some say that we start [reading] each of the *megillot* from the *Motza'ei Shabbat* before [the Yamim Tovim that they are related to].

Earlier in the same chapter, ***Masechet Soferim*** lists the *berachot* that are recited when reading from *Ketuvim*. Before reading any of the five *megillot*, one recites the *beracha* of *Al Mikra Megilla* ("on the reading of the *megilla*").

39. מסכת סופרים | יד:א

ברות, ובשיר השירים, בקהלת, באיכה, ובמגילת אסתר, צריך לברך, ולומר על מקרא מגילה, ואף על פי שכתובה בכתובים. והקורא בכתובים צריך לומר, ברוך אתה ה' א-להינו מלך העולם אשר קדשנו במצותיו וציונו לקרוא בכתבי הקודש.

ח Masechet Soferim 14:1

On [reading] *Rut, Shir HaShirim, Kohelet, Eicha* and *Megillat Esther*, one must recite the *beracha* "*Al Mikra Megilla*," although they are written in the *Ketuvim*. One who reads from [other *sefarim* in] *Ketuvim* must recite "*Baruch ata Hashem E-loheinu Melech HaOlam, asher kideshanu b'mitzvotav, v'tzivanu likro bekitvei hakodesh*."

The **Abudraham** also mentions the custom to read *Megillat Rut* on Shavuot and suggests a few reasons for it. He explains that this is because many of the events of the *Megilla* occur during the harvest season, when Shavuot also falls. In addition, Rut converted and accepted the Torah, as we did on Shavuot.

40. ספר אבודרהם | תפלות הפסח

...בחג השבועות נהגו לקרות רות מפני שכתוב בו (רות א:כב) בתחלת קציר שעורים והוא זמן הקציר. ועוד טעם אחר לפי שאבותינו לא קבלו את התורה ולא נכנסו לברית אלא במילה וטבילה והרצאת דמים כדאיתא בפרק החולץ (יבמות מו:). ורות גם היא נתגיירה...

ר Abudraham, Tefillot HaPesach

...On the festival of Shavuot, it is customary to read Rut, as it is written in it (*Rut* 1:22) "At the beginning of the barley harvest," which is the time of the harvest. Another reason is that our fathers only accepted the Torah and entered the covenant through circumcision, immersion [in a *mikveh*], and offering blood [of a *korban*], as the Gemara says (*Yevamot* 46b). Rut also converted [through the same process]...

33. *Masechet Soferim* is one of the "Minor Tractates (*Masechtot Ketanot*)." These collections of *baraitot* are not part of the canon of the Gemara, either *Talmud Bavli* or *Talmud Yerushalmi*. However, the Gemara does occasionally cite *baraitot* from them, especially from *Masechet Soferim*.

With respect to reciting a *beracha*, the Abudraham subsequently quotes the obligation to recite a *beracha* when reading from *Ketuvim*, clearly implying that this also applies when reading in shul on Yom Tov.

The **Maharil** writes that the custom is to read *Megillat Rut* on the second day of Yom Tov (in *chutz la'aretz*) and that everyone recites the *beracha*.

41. ספר מהרי"ל (מנהגים) | הלכות שבועות ג

מגילת רות אומרים ביום שני וכל אחד מברך לפניה על מקרא מגילה.

ד Sefer Maharil (Minhagim), Hilchot Shavuot 3

We read *Megillat Rut* on the second day, and everyone[34] recites the *beracha* of "*Al Mikra Megilla*" beforehand.

The **Rema** also quotes the custom to read *Rut* on Shavuot, but in contrast to the above sources, he writes that the custom is not to recite a *beracha*.

42. רמ"א | או"ח תצ:ט

ונוהגין לומר רות בשבועות. והעם נהגו שלא לברך עליהם על מקרא מגילה ולא על מקרא כתובים.

א Rema, Orach Chaim 490:9

It is customary to read Rut on Shavuot.[35] The people have the custom not to recite a *beracha* on [the *megillot*], neither "*Al Mikra Megilla*" nor "*Al Mikra Ketuvim*."

The Rema himself was asked why he wrote that the custom is not to recite a *beracha*, contrary to the ruling of the Maharil. He answers in a responsum that there are four reasons to justify the custom not to recite a *beracha*, the primary reason being that the custom is not to read these *megillot* from a scroll, but from *chumashim*, and it is not appropriate to recite a *beracha* over *chumashim*. He concludes that we should continue not to recite a *beracha*, based on the rule that when in doubt, *berachot* are not recited.

43. שו"ת הרמ"א | סימן לה

...אמת כי כדברי מהרי"ל כתב בעל אבודרה"ם. והם הקדמונים שיסדו המנהגים... וכן דקדקתי במה שכתבתי והעם נהגו שלא לברך כו' ולא כתבתי סתם וכן נוהגין כמו שהוא מדרכי בשאר מקומות, **ופוק חזי מה עמא דבר וכן נראה לי מכמה טעמים.**

א Responsa of the Rema, Siman 35

...It is true that the author of the Abudraham wrote as did the Maharil, and they are the early authorities who established the customs... I was also precise when I wrote, "The people have the custom not to recite a blessing," and I did not write simply, "and such is customary," as is my manner elsewhere.[36] **Go out and see what the people do, and [their practice] appears correct to me for several reasons.**

34. It appears that the original custom was for everyone to read these *megillot* for themselves, rather than for one person to read and the congregation to listen. This is also clear from the Responsa of the Rema, quoted in source 43.

35. The Rema earlier in this comment also mentions the custom to recite *Shir HaShirim* on Shabbat *Chol Hamo'ed* Pesach and *Kohelet* on Shabbat *Chol HaMo'ed* Sukkot.

36. "Such is customary" implies that the common practice is in line with previous rulings. In this case, the practice is not in line with previous rulings, but the Rema nevertheless believes it to be correct.

א' שבמנהגים של מוהר"ר אייזק טירנא שאנו נוהגין בתרייהו לא כתב כלל לברך על שיר השירים ורות וקהלת ובידוע כי אילו היה דעתו לנהוג לברך היה כותבו כמו שכתב לגבי איכה לברך. ויש לחלק בין אלו לקריאת איכה, כי שם החזן קורא להשמיע הציבור והוי כמו קריאת מגילה לכן מברך עליו כמו במגילה.

ועוד, כי אותה קריאה מוזכרת בגמרא סוף תענית דקאמר קורין בקינות והביאו הפוסקים כדאיתא בהגהות מיימוניות, אבל קריאה של מגילות אלו אינן אלא מנהג בעלמא כמו שיתבאר. ולכן נראה מדברי מהר"א טירנא שדינן חלוק מאיכה ומגילה ואין לברך עליהן. וכן נראה מדברי הגהות מיימוניות דקאמר וכן נהג מהר"ם מכלל דשאר אינשי לא נהיגי הכי.

הטעם השני נראה לי שלא לברך, וזה כי... ובמרדכי פרק קמא דמגילה בהג"ה מייתי הגירסא בסגנון אחר וכתב, דאם כתובים בין הכתובים מברך עליהם על מקרא כתובים. ומאחר דאיכא חילוף בגירסות נראה, דאם כתובים בין הכתובים כמו בזמן הזה דאין מגילות אלו כתובים במגילות כמו בימיהם, להוציא נפשם מפלוגתא נראה דאין לברך עלייהו כלל, דהרי אם מברך שלא כדינו אינו מועיל ומברך ברכה לבטלה.

הטעם השלישי כי יש לתמוה על ברכה זו למה, וכי קריאות אלו חיובא לברך עלייהו אשר קדשנו במצותיו וצונו. והיכן מצינו שצוו חכמים על כך, שהרי לא נזכרו קריאות אלו בתלמוד ולא בשום פוסק מפורסם, כי אם בדברי האחרונים ובקצת מדרשות וכמה נתחבטו הראשונים ז"ל אם יש לברך על קריאת הלל בראש חודש...

The first reason is that in *Sefer HaMinhagim* of Rav Isaac Tirna, which we follow, he does not write at all to recite a blessing over *Shir HaShirim, Rut,* or *Kohelet*. It is known that were his view that one should recite a *beracha,* he would have written so, just as he writes regarding *Eicha,* that one should recite a *beracha*. One can distinguish between these [*megillot*] and the reading of *Eicha,* as there the *chazzan* reads aloud so that the congregation can hear, and it is like the reading of the *Megilla* [of Esther]; therefore, one recites a *beracha* over it as over the *Megilla* [of Esther].

Furthermore, that reading is mentioned in the Gemara at the end of *Ta'anit,* where it states that we may read *kinnot*[37] [on Tisha b'av], and the *poskim* cite this, as appears in *Hagahot Maimoniot.*[38] But the reading of these other *megillot* is only a custom, as will be explained. Therefore, it appears from the words of Mahara Tirna that their status differs from that of *Eicha* and the *Megilla* [of Esther], and one should not recite a *beracha* over them. This is also apparent from *Hagahot Maimoniot,* which states that Maharam practiced this [reciting a *beracha*], implying that others do not.

The **second reason** that it appears to me that one should not recite a *beracha* is because... In the Mordechai in the first chapter of *Megilla,* in a gloss, a different version [of *Masechet Soferim*] is brought which states that if [the *megillot*] are written among the *Ketuvim,* one recites over them the *beracha* "*Al Mikra Ketuvim*." Since there is variation in the textual versions, it appears that if these *megillot* are written among the *Ketuvim,* as they are nowadays, as these *megillot* are not written on [individual] scrolls as they were in earlier times, then in order to avoid adjudicating the dispute [as to which version of the *beracha* is correct], one should not recite a *beracha* over them at all. As if one recites a *beracha* incorrectly, it is of no effect and is a *beracha* in vain.

The **third reason** is that one should wonder about the reason for this *beracha*: Are these readings an obligation, such that we should recite a *beracha* [which reads] "*Asher kideshanu b'mitzvotav, v'tzivanu*"? Where do we find that the Sages commanded this? These readings are not mentioned in the Gemara nor in [the writings of] any well-known *posek,* only in later sources and in some *midrashim*. How much did the *Rishonim* struggle over whether to recite a *beracha* over *Hallel* on Rosh Chodesh?...

---

37. Lamentations, the name that Chazal give to *Megillat Eicha*.
38. This halacha primarily tells us that although learning Torah is prohibited on Tisha B'av, reading from books of Tanach with a sad theme, such as *Eicha*, is permitted.

Certainly [this question exists] regarding a custom such as this. Although Rabbeinu Tam wrote that one should recite a *beracha* over *Hallel* on Rosh Chodesh and that one recites a *beracha* over a custom… nevertheless, it appears to me that [our case] is not comparable. *Hallel* is different, as it is a universal custom of all Israel as is mentioned in the Gemara;[39] it is not so regarding this custom…[40]

The fourth and primary reason in my view is that even if we were to say that one should recite a *beracha* over [the *megillot*], and that this is what *Masechet Soferim* means, this is only when they are written properly on parchment in scrolls, as was the manner of earlier *sefarim* written in rolled scrolls like a *sefer Torah*… But one should not recite a blessing over our *chumashim*…

From all this it appears that there is greater reason to be concerned about reciting an unnecessary *beracha* than about failing to recite a *beracha*, as [failure to recite] *berachot* do not prevent [fulfillment of a mitzva].

וכל שכן במנהג כזה. ואף כי רבינו תם ז"ל כתב לברך על הלל דראש חודש ושמברכין על מנהג... מכל מקום נראה לי דלא דמי להתם דשאני הלל שהוא מנהג קבוע בכל ישראל כמוזכר בתלמוד, מה שאין כן במנהג זה...

הטעם הרביעי ועיקר הוא בעיני, דאף אם נאמר דיש לברך עלייהו ושלזה נתכוונו מסכת סופרים היינו דוקא כשהם כתובים כתקנם בקלפים ובמגילות, כמו שהיה דרך הספרים הראשונים כתובים בגלילה כספר תורה... אבל בחומשים שלנו אין לברך עלייהו...

מכל אלה נראה דיותר יש לחוש לברכה שאינה צריכה ממה שיש לחוש שלא לברך, דברכות אינן מעכבות.

Despite the Rema's arguments, the ***Levush*** argues that there is no reason not to recite a *beracha* and adds that one should also recite the *beracha* of *Shehecheyanu*. He also questions whether the custom not to recite a *beracha* was really so widespread, and whether it was simply due to ignorance.

א Levush, Orach Chaim 490:5

We recite the *berachot* of *Al Mikra Megilla* and *Shehecheyanu* over [*Shir HaShirim*], since it comes from time to time [like other mitzvot over which *Shehecheyanu* is recited]. My teacher, Rav Moshe Isserles, writes that the people have the custom not to recite any *beracha* on these *megillot*, meaning *Shir HaShirim* and *Rut*. **But I do not know why they should not recite a *beracha* over them. Furthermore, I wonder how he knew this custom so easily**, as everyone reads quietly and recites a *beracha* quietly, and who told him that they did not all recite a *beracha*? If he heard that some of them did not recite a *beracha*, perhaps they did so out of ignorance, as they did not read the glosses of Mahara Tirna, and those who read them did recite a *beracha*. As it is written explicitly there that we recite a *beracha* on these two *megillot*.

44. לבוש | או"ח תצ:ה

ומברכין עליו על מקרא מגילה ושהחיינו, דהא מזמן לזמן קאתי. וכתב מורי רבי משה איסרלס ז"ל שהעם נהגו שלא לברך כלל על אלו המגילות, רצונו לומר שיר השירים ורות, **ואיני יודע למה לא יברכו עליו. ועוד תמיהני עליו היאך ידע זה המנהג כל כך בפשיטות**, שהרי הכל קורין בלחש ומברכין בלחש ומי הגיד לו שלא ברכו כולם? אם שמע שקצת מהם לא ברכו, שמא מחסרון ידיעה עשו שלא קראו בהגהות מהר"א טירנא, ואותם שקראו בה ברכו, שהרי כתוב שם בפירוש שמברכין על אלו שתי מגילות.

39. It should be noted that although today, reciting *Hallel* on Rosh Chodesh is indeed a universal custom, this was not the case at the time of the Gemara. See *Ta'anit* 28b, where it is clear that Rav was unaware of this custom until he came to Bavel.

40. Although the Rema acknowledges that *Masechet Soferim* states that a *beracha* is recited over reading the *megillot*, he suggests that this refers to an earlier custom to read a *haftara* from *Ketuvim* at *Mincha* on Shabbat, or to one who studies *Ketuvim* before reciting *Birkot HaTorah* (according to one opinion in the Gemara, the regular *Birkot HaTorah* is not recited over *Nevi'im* or *Ketuvim*).

The ***Taz*** writes that one should not recite a *beracha* based on the third reason of the Rema that no *beracha* was ever instituted on these readings. He claims that for this reason, we are not particular to write these *megillot* in scrolls.

45. ט"ז | או"ח תצ:ט

...וכל זה דברי הבאי דבתשובת רמ"א האריך על זה וביאר דבריו שבכאן ושנראה לו שלא לברך על שום מגילה זולת מגילת אסתר מטעם שלא מצינו בדברי התלמוד שתקנו לקרותה שיאמר ע"ז וצונו לקרות... **ואלו היה שייך ברכה עליהם היו נזהרים לכותבם דרך מגילה בקלף כמו במגילת אסתר וזה לא נשמע מעולם...**

א Taz, Orach Chaim 490:6

...All the words [of the *Levush*] are worthless, as the Rema writes about this at length in a responsum and explains his words here, that it appears to him that one should not recite a *beracha* on any *megilla* other than *Megillat Esther*, as we do not find in the words of the Gemara that they instituted to read it, such that we should say over it "*vetzivanu likrot*"... **Were a *beracha* appropriate over [these *megillot*], they would have been particular to write them in the way of a *megilla*, on parchment, as with *Megillat Esther*. We have never heard that this is done...**

The ***Magen Avraham*** (490:9) rules that one should recite a *beracha*. The **Gra** concurs and writes that a *beracha* should be recited even if one does not have a scroll.

46. ביאור הגר"א | או"ח תצ:ט

...וכך כתב ב"ח ולבוש ומנהגים ומטה משה לברך אף שאינם כתובים בגליון וכל שכן כשהם כתובים בגליון כספר תורה וכן מנהג כל הראשונים וכך כתב מגן אברהם.

א Bi'ur HaGra, Orach Chaim 490:9

...The *Bach*, *Levush*, *Minhagim* and *Mateh Moshe* write that one should recite a *beracha* even if they are not written in a scroll,[41] and certainly if they are written in a scroll like a *sefer Torah*. This is the custom of all the *Rishonim*, and the *Magen Avraham* writes accordingly.

Although the Gra maintains that one recites a *beracha* even when reading without a scroll, the *sefer* ***Ma'aseh Rav*** (175) confirms that the Gra holds that the *megilla* should ideally be read from a scroll, and that the *ba'al keriya* should recite the *berachot* of *Al Mikra Megilla* and *Shehecheyanu* before reading.

The ***Mishna Berura*** writes that at least when one does have the *megilla* written in a scroll, reciting a *beracha* should not be protested.

47. משנה ברורה | או"ח תצ:ט

...הנוהג לברך על כל פנים כשכתובין על קלף בודאי אין למחות בידו.

א Mishna Berura, Orach Chaim 490:9

...If one has the practice to recite a *beracha* at least when [the *megillot*] are written on scrolls, one certainly should not object to this.

Today, in places where the *megilla* is not read from a scroll, it is not customary to recite a *beracha*. Where a scroll is used, different customs exist. **Rav Eliezer Melamed** summarizes the different customs. He adds

---

41. The *Acharonim* quoted by the Gra do not write explicitly that a *beracha* may be recited even when the *megilla* is not written in a scroll, but this is implied since it was not usual in their times to have the *megillot* written in scrolls.

that some question the reciting of the *beracha* of *Shehecheyanu*, and suggests that the *ba'al keria* should wear a new item of clothing, so that if necessary, the *beracha* can be made on this.

Peninei Halakha, Mo'adim 2:10

...Many are of the opinion that on account of the uncertainty, it is proper not to recite a *berakha* over the four *megillot* whose reading is not mentioned in the Gemara. This is the current custom of all those who pray with *Nusach Sepharad* (including *Chasidim*), as well as some of those who pray with *Nusach Ashkenaz*.[42]

Others maintain that a *berakha* must be recited before reading a *megilla*. This is the custom of Jerusalemites whose ancestors were students of the Vilna Gaon who helped found the Old Yishuv. It is also the custom of many who are of Lithuanian descent. Those who recite a *berakha* make sure to read from a *megilla* written on parchment.

Of those who recite "*al mikra megilla*" prior to reading the *megillot*, many also recite the *berakha* of *She-hecheyanu*. Many others question this, since *She-hecheyanu* does not appear in this context in *Masekhet Sofrim*, and most of the Acharonim do not mention it.[43] Therefore, for those with a custom to say *She-hecheyanu*, it is proper to wear a new item of clothing, in which case all agree that the *berakha* may be recited.[44]

48. פניני הלכה | מועדים ב:י

...רבים סוברים שמחמת הספק נכון שלא לברך על קריאת ארבע המגילות. וכך נוהגים כיום כל החסידים מתפללי נוסח 'ספרד' וחלק ממתפללי נוסח אשכנז.

ויש אומרים שצריך לברך על קריאתן. וכך נוהגים בני הישוב הישן בירושלים, שנוסד על ידי תלמידי הגאון מווילנא. וכן נוהגים רבים מיוצאי ליטא. והנוהגים לברך מקפידים לקרוא מתוך מגילה שכתובה על קלף.

רבים מהנוהגים לברך על המגילה, מברכים גם 'שהחיינו' על קריאתה. ורבים תמהו עליהם, שכן במסכת סופרים לא אמרו שמברכים 'שהחיינו', ורוב האחרונים לא הזכירו ברכה זו. ונכון שהנוהגים לברך, ילבשו בגד חדש, ויברכו 'שהחיינו' לכל הדעות.

42. It should be noted that many Sephardim read *Rut* at different times than Ashkenazim. Ashkenazim generally read it either before the Torah reading (the historical custom) or before the beginning of the *tefilla* (a later development due to people staying up all night), while Sephardim either read it toward the end of the *tefilla* or at night together with the *Tikun Leil Shavuot*.

43. Presumably, the reasoning of the *Levush* and the Gra is that we recite *Shehecheyanu* on any mitzva that is performed periodically or rarely, and there is no need for this to be repeated regarding each mitzva. However, this only applies if one indeed has not read a *megilla* recently. If, for example, the *ba'al keria* reads the *megilla* in two different *minyanim* on the same day, he should not recite *Shehecheyanu* a second time.

44. It should be pointed out that this solution is not straightforward, as one should not recite an unrelated *beracha* between the *beracha* of *Al Mikra Megilla* and starting to read.

Machshava

The Gemara in ***Masechet Pesachim*** writes that the *Amora'im* disagree as to whether Yom Tov should be devoted entirely either to God or to ourselves, or be divided – half "for Hashem" through Torah, and half "for yourselves" through physical enjoyment.[45] However, when it comes to Shavuot, all agree: we must include at least a portion "for yourselves," since it is the day the Torah was given.

49. מסכת פסחים סח:

אמר רבי אלעזר: הכל מודים בעצרת דבעינן נמי לכם. מאי טעמא? יום שניתנה בו תורה הוא.

ח Masechet Pesachim 68b

Rabbi Elazar said: All agree with regard to *Atzeret*, the holiday of Shavuot, **that we require** that it be **also "for you,"** meaning that it is a mitzva to eat, drink, and rejoice on that day. **What is the reason? It is the day on which the Torah was given,** and one must celebrate the fact that the Torah was given to the Jewish People.

This seems surprising – shouldn't a day marking divine revelation be purely spiritual? **Rav Eliyahu Lopian** beautifully explains that this is precisely the point: the Torah was given not to remove us from the world, but to sanctify our worldly lives.

50. לב אליהו | פרשת אמור

...דלפיכך הכל מודים דבעצרת בעינן נמי לכם... דהא כל עבודתנו להשי"ת ואהבתנו אותו תלויה בזה שעל ידי התורה נוכל לעבדו גם באכילה ושתיה... שעל ידי התורה שקבלנו בהר סיני – יכולים אנו לעשות שיהיה ה"לכם" גם הוא לשם השם! ואדרבה זה כל תכלית בריאת האדם.

פ Lev Eliyahu, Parshat Emor

...Therefore, all agree that with regard to *Atzeret*, we also require "for you"... as all of our service to Hashem and our love for Him is dependent on this, that through the Torah, we can serve Him through eating and drinking as well... As through the Torah that we received on Har Sinai, we are able to transform the "for you" to also be for the sake of Hashem. On the contrary, this is the whole purpose of the creation of Man.

Thus, the joy of Shavuot is not just about Torah study, but about celebrating the Torah's power to uplift our physical reality and make it holy. We eat, rejoice, and live Torah – not only in the Beit Midrash, but at our tables, in our homes, and in our lives.

Through learning how to apply the principles of halacha to daily life, we fulfill the vision of *Matan Torah* – bringing Hashem into every corner of our lives.

---

45 See volume 23, *shiur* 4, sources 2–3, where this was discussed, and the halacha was determined as being in accordance with Rabbi Yehoshua.

Summary of the Halachot of Shavuot

Tosefet Yom Tov on Shavuot

1. ***Masat Binyamin*** – Rav Shlomo MiLublin writes that on Shavuot, one should not recite *kiddush* before nightfall.
2. ***Shelah*** – *Davening Ma'ariv* early even on Shavuot is not problematic, as *davening Ma'ariv* does not necessarily signify the end of the day. Reciting *kiddush* at the end of *Ma'ariv* in *shul* before nightfall is also not problematic.
3. ***Taz, Mishna Berura*** – We should also delay *Ma'ariv* until nightfall.
4. ***Korban Netanel*** – The Rosh permits reciting *kiddush* before night on any Yom Tov, and this includes Shavuot.
5. **Rav Yaakov Emden** – The stringency to delay *kiddush* has little basis, and one who starts Yom Tov early is to be praised for his enthusiasm.
6. **Rav Ovadia Yosef** – Where possible, it is proper to wait until night before reciting *kiddush*. If delaying will result in distress for families, or will make it difficult to observe *Tikun Leil Shavuot*, one may eat earlier.

- ***Tosefet Yom Tov* for Women on Shavuot**

1. **Rav Natan Gestetner** – Shavuot can only start after seven whole weeks, and this applies to women as well.
2. ***Piskei Teshuvot*** – Women should also not light candles before night, as the *beracha* of *Shehecheyanu* also signifies the start of Yom Tov.
3. **Rav Moshe Sternbuch** – On Shavuot, there is an additional reason to avoid reciting *Shehecheyanu* when lighting candles – reciting *Shehecheyanu* begins Yom Tov before night, and one should not delay lighting candles until night.

Tikun Leil Shavuot

1. ***Zohar*** – After counting the *Omer* without missing a day, purification is achieved by studying Torah throughout the night of Shavuot.
2. ***Magen Avraham*** – We also stay awake on the night of Shavuot as an atonement for the failure of the Jewish People to wake up early on the day that the Torah was given.
3. ***Brisker Rav*** – It is surprising that people observe this custom, whereas they do not fulfill the obligation to stay awake to speak about the Exodus from Egypt on the first night of Pesach.

- ***Birkot HaShachar* for Those Awake All Night**

1. ***Acharonim*** – The widespread custom is to recite all the *berachot* in the morning, even if one is not obligated in them.
2. ***Sha'arei Teshuva*** – Cites differing opinions as to whether one should also recite the *berachot* of *Elokai Neshama* and *hama'avir sheina,* and recommends hearing someone else recite them.
3. ***Mishna Berura*** – It is preferable to hear these two *berachot* from someone else, since there is a dispute as to whether he can recite them.
4. ***Piskei Teshuvot*** – These two *berachot* are different since they focus on the experience of the person himself. But one who does recite them himself has opinions upon whom to rely.
5. ***Aruch HaShulchan, Yalkut Yosef*** – Even these two *berachot* should be recited by one who does not sleep based upon the overall approach of the Rema that all of the *berachot* relate to the order of the world.

- ***Birkot HaTorah* for Those Awake All Night**

1. ***Mishna Berura*** – Whether a person must recite a new *beracha* the following morning is subject to a dispute, and therefore it is best for the person to hear the *beracha* from another.
2. ***Yalkut Yosef, Aruch HaShulchan*** – A person may recite a *beracha* and there is no need to hear the *beracha* from another.
3. **Rav Akiva Eiger** – If a person sleeps a substantial sleep during the day and then remains awake the whole subsequent night, he is required to recite the *beracha* according to all opinions.
4. ***Piskei Teshuvot*** – Some hold one must stop learning at dawn to recite *Birkot HaTorah* while others hold one may continue.

Eating Dairy Foods

1. ***Kol Bo*** – It is customary to eat honey and milk on Shavuot, since the Torah is compared to these foods.
2. **Rema** – The custom is to eat dairy and then to eat meat, to mirror the two cooked foods taken on the first night of Pesach in memory of the *korban Chagiga* and the *korban Pesach.* The two loaves of bread necessary to eat together with dairy and meat foods also commemorate the two loaves of bread brought in the *Beit HaMikdash* on Shavuot.
3. ***Mishna Berura*** – We also commemorate the fact that the Jewish People had to eat dairy immediately after the Torah was given, as their utensils were not kosher and they were not able to prepare meat.

4. ***Chazon Ovadia*** – Sephardim also customarily eat dairy on Shavuot.
5. **Rav Mordechai Eliyahu** – One should not eat only dairy foods, unless one does not enjoy eating meat. One can eat meat at night and dairy in the day.
6. ***Peninei Halakha*** – One's primary focus should be to increase joy and to honor the Torah.
7. ***Magen Avraham*** – One who eats meat immediately after dairy must be careful to adhere to the required precautions, such as using separate tablecloths. However, one need not recite *Birkat HaMazon* in between eating dairy and meat.
8. ***Darkei Teshuva*** – One must recite *Birkat HaMazon* before eating meat,

Decorating the Synagogue

1. **Maharil** – It is customary to decorate the synagogue with greenery because of the joy of the festival.
2. **Rema** – We decorate the synagogue and our house to express joy for the giving of the Torah.
3. ***Levush*** – The custom also commemorates the greenery that surrounded Mount Sinai.
4. ***Magen Avraham*** – It is also customary to place trees in the synagogue and in the home. This reminds people to pray for fruit, as Hashem judges us regarding the produce of trees on Shavuot.
5. ***Chayei Adam, Mishna Berura, Aruch HaShulchan,* Rav Moshe Feinstein** – The Gra ended this custom, since the gentiles also set up trees in their churches to celebrate their festival. Since it is a Christian practice and it has no biblical source, it must be discontinued.
6. **Rav Yosef Shaul Nathanson** – Since there is a logical reason for decorating the synagogues with trees, it is not included in the prohibition against *chukot hagoyim*.
7. In many communities, the custom to decorate the synagogue at least with greenery or flowers is still continued today.

Megillat Rut

1. ***Masechet Soferim*** – It is customary to read half of *Megillat Rut* on the second night of Shavuot (in *chutz la'aretz*) and the other half on *Motza'ei Yom Tov*, or to start reading it from the *Motza'ei Shabbat* before Shavuot.
2. ***Masechet Soferim*** – Before reading any of the five *megillot*, one recites the *beracha* of *Al Mikra Megilla*.

3. **Abudraham** – It is customary to read *Megillat Rut* on Shavuot, because many of the events of the *Megilla* occur during the harvest season, when Shavuot also falls. Rut also converted and accepted the Torah, as we did on Shavuot.
4. **Maharil** – The custom is to read *Megillat Rut* on the second day of Yom Tov (in *chutz la'aretz*). Everyone recites the *beracha*.
5. **Rema** – The custom is not to recite a *beracha*. There are four reasons for this, but the primary reason is that it is not appropriate to recite a *beracha* over *chumashim*. We should uphold the custom not to recite a *beracha*, since there is a doubt.
6. ***Levush*** – There is no reason not to recite a *beracha*, and one should also recite the *beracha* of *Shehecheyanu*.
7. ***Taz*** – One should not recite a *beracha*, as no *beracha* was ever instituted on these readings. For this reason, we are not particular to write the *megillot* in scrolls.
8. **Gra** – A *beracha* should be recited even if one does not have a scroll, but ideally the *megilla* should be read from a scroll.
9. ***Mishna Berura*** – At least when one does have the *megilla* written in a scroll, reciting a *beracha* should not be protested.
10. ***Peninei Halakha*** – Some question the reciting of the *beracha* of *Shehecheyanu*. The *ba'al keria* should wear a new item of clothing, so that if necessary, the *beracha* can be made on this.

7

Halachot of Zeicher L'churban

הלכות זכר לחורבן

Introduction

Leaving One's Home Unfinished

Leaving Out One Dish and One Item of Jewelry

Ashes on the Head of a Bridegroom and Breaking a Cup

Music

Nighttime Prayer and Tikun Chatzot

Machshava

For quick reference, some long website URLs have been shortened.
For the complete list of referenced websites visit www.tzurbaolami.com.

ת	**Tanach**
ח	**Talmud (Chazal)**
ר	***Rishonim***
א	***Acharonim***
פ	**Contemporary Halachic Sources**

Introduction

One of the recurring themes throughout the Torah, Tanach, the teachings of Chazal, and our *tefillot* is the centrality of yearning and striving to build the *Beit HaMikdash*, serving Hashem there, and mourning its destruction. This theme is particularly appropriate to consider during the days between Shavuot – discussed in the previous *shiur*, when the Jewish People would ascend to the *Beit HaMikdash* – and the Three Weeks, which are devoted to mourning its destruction and will be discussed in the opening *shiurim* of the next volume.

The **Gemara (*Masechet Bava Batra*)** relates that after the destruction of the Second *Beit HaMikdash*, many people were so deeply pained by the loss that they sought to express their mourning in excessive ways. Rabbi Yehoshua responded by demonstrating that while mourning is essential, it must be balanced in a manner that allows for continued, functional religious life.

1. מסכת בבא בתרא ס:

תנו רבנן: כשחרב הבית בשניה, רבו פרושין בישראל שלא לאכול בשר ושלא לשתות יין. נטפל להן רבי יהושע, אמר להן: בני, מפני מה אי אתם אוכלין בשר ואין אתם שותין יין? אמרו לו: נאכל בשר שממנו מקריבין על גבי מזבח, ועכשיו בטל? נשתה יין שמנסכין על גבי המזבח, ועכשיו בטל?

אמר להם: אם כן, לחם לא נאכל, שכבר בטלו מנחות! אפשר בפירות. פירות לא נאכל, שכבר בטלו בכורים! אפשר בפירות אחרים. מים לא נשתה, שכבר בטל ניסוך המים! שתקו.

אמר להן: בני, בואו ואומר לכם: שלא להתאבל כל עיקר אי אפשר – שכבר נגזרה גזרה, ולהתאבל יותר מדאי אי אפשר – שאין גוזרין גזירה על הצבור אלא אם כן רוב צבור יכולין לעמוד בה, דכתיב: במארה אתם נארים ואותי אתם קובעים הגוי כולו.

ח Masechet Bava Batra 60b

The Sages taught in a *baraita* (*Tosefta, Sota* 15:11): **When the *Beit HaMikdash* was destroyed a second** time, there was **an increase** in the number of **ascetics among** the **Jews,** whose practice was **to not eat meat and to not drink wine. Rabbi Yehoshua joined them** to discuss their practice. **He said to them: My children, for what** reason do **you not eat meat and** do **you not drink wine? They said to him: Shall we eat meat, from which** offerings **are sacrificed upon** the **altar, and now** the altar **has ceased** to exist? **Shall we drink wine, which is poured** as a libation **upon the altar, and now** the altar **has ceased** to exist?

Rabbi Yehoshua **said to them: If so, we will not eat bread** either, **since** the **meal-offerings** that were offered upon the altar **have ceased.** They replied: You are correct. It is **possible** to subsist **with produce.** He said to them: **We will not eat produce** either, **since** the bringing of **the first fruits have ceased.** They replied: You are correct. We will no longer eat the produce of the seven species from which the first fruits were brought, as it is **possible** to subsist **with other produce.** He said to them: If so, **we will not drink water, since the water libation has ceased. They were silent,** as they realized that they could not survive without water.

Rabbi Yehoshua **said to them: My children, come, and I will tell you** how we should act. **To not mourn at all** is **impossible, as** the **decree was already issued** and the *Beit HaMikdash* has been destroyed. **But to mourn excessively** as you are doing is also **impossible, as** the Sages **do not issue a decree upon the public unless a majority of the public is able to abide by it, as it is written: "You are cursed with the curse, yet you rob Me, even this whole nation"** (*Malachi* 3:9), indicating that the prophet rebukes the people for neglecting observances only if they were accepted by the whole nation.

אלא כך אמרו חכמים: סד אדם את ביתו בסיד, ומשייר בו דבר מועט. וכמה? אמר רב יוסף: אמה על אמה. אמר רב חסדא: כנגד הפתח.

עושה אדם כל צרכי סעודה, ומשייר דבר מועט. מאי היא? אמר רב פפא: כסא דהרסנא.

עושה אשה כל תכשיטיה, ומשיירת דבר מועט. מאי היא? אמר רב: בת צדעא, שנאמר: אם אשכחך ירושלים תשכח ימיני תדבק לשוני לחכי וגו'.

מאי על ראש שמחתי? אמר רב יצחק: זה אפר מקלה שבראש חתנים. אמר ליה רב פפא לאביי: היכא מנח להי? במקום תפילין, שנאמר: לשום לאבלי ציון לתת להם פאר תחת אפר.

Rabbi Yehoshua continues: **Rather, this** is what **the Sages said: A person** may **plaster his house with lime, but** he must **leave** over **a small amount in it** without plaster to remember the desolation. The Gemara interjects: **How much** is a small amount? **Rav Yosef said:** One ***amah*** **by** one ***amah*****. Rav Chisda said:** This should be **opposite the entrance,** so that it is visible to all.

Rabbi Yehoshua continues: The Sages said that **a person** may **prepare all** that he **needs for a meal, but** he must **leave** out **a small item** to remember the desolation. The Gemara interjects: **What** is **this** small item? **Rav Pappa said:** Something akin to **small, fried fish.**

Rabbi Yehoshua continues: The Sages said that **a woman** may **engage** in **all** of **her cosmetic treatments, but** she must **leave** out **a small matter** to remember the desolation. The Gemara interjects: **What** is **this** small matter? **Rav said:** She does not remove hair from the place on the ***Beit HaMikdash*** from which women would remove hair. The source for all these practices is a verse, **as it is stated: "If I forget you, Jerusalem, let my right hand forget its cunning. Let my tongue cleave to the roof of my mouth,** if I do not remember you; if I do not set Jerusalem above my highest joy" (*Tehillim* 137:5–6).

The Gemara asks: **What** is the meaning of: **Above my highest** [***rosh***] **joy? Rav Yitzchak says: This** is referring to the **burnt ashes** that are customarily placed **on the head** [***rosh***] **of bridegrooms** at the time of their wedding celebrations, to remember the desolation. **Rav Pappa said to Abaye: Where are they placed?** Abaye replied: **On** the **place** where ***tefillin*** are placed, **as it is stated: "To appoint to them that mourn in Zion, to give to them a turban in place of ashes"** (*Yeshayahu* 61:3). Since *tefillin* are referred to as a turban (see *Yechezkel* 24:17), it may be inferred from this verse that the ashes were placed in the same place as the *tefillin*.

Rav Eliezer Melamed summarizes the main idea of the Gemara that we must balance commemorating the *Beit HaMikdash* together with normal life.

2. פניני הלכה | העם והארץ ט:א

...החיים חייבים להימשך, ואין להסכים שהאבל הנורא על חורבן בית המקדש ישרה דיכאון שהעם לא יוכל לעמוד בו. אולם בכל עת שאדם נמצא בשמחה מיוחדת, עליו לזכור את חורבן בית המקדש, שכל זמן שבית המקדש חרב, השמחה אינה יכולה להיות שלימה.

Peninei Halakha, Ha'Am Veha'aretz 9:1

...Life must go on, and one cannot allow overpowering mourning for the destruction of the *Beit HaMikdash* to cause depression that the people cannot bear. However, at any time when a person experiences special joy, he must remember the destruction of the *Beit HaMikdash*. For as long as the *Beit HaMikdash* lies in ruin, the joy cannot be complete.

We will now explain the details of each halacha.

Leaving One's Home Unfinished

We saw above in source 1 that one who plasters his home is required to leave a square *amah* unplastered opposite the entrance.

3. מסכת בבא בתרא ס:

...אלא כך אמרו חכמים: סד אדם את ביתו בסיד, ומשייר בו דבר מועט. וכמה? אמר רב יוסף: אמה על אמה. אמר רב חסדא: כנגד הפתח.

ח Masechet Bava Batra 60b

...Rabbi Yehoshua continues: **Rather, this** is what **the Sages said: A person** may **plaster his house with lime, but** he must **leave** over **a small amount in it** without plaster to remember the desolation. The Gemara interjects: **How much** is a small amount? **Rav Yosef said:** One ***amah*** **by** one ***amah*****. Rav Chisda said:** This should be **opposite the entrance,** so that it is visible to all.

The **Gemara** earlier also quotes a *baraita* that prohibits plastering, tiling and painting one's house. In this passage, however, no allowance is given if one leaves over a small amount without plaster.

4. שם

אין מסיידין ואין מכיירין ואין מפייחין בזמן הזה...

ח Ibid.

One may not plaster, one may not tile, and one may not paint [***mefayyechin***] images **in the present,** as a sign of mourning for the destruction of the *Beit HaMikdash*...

Rishonim disagree as to how to understand the discrepancy between the passages. The **Rambam** appears to resolve the contradiction by understanding the second passage cited above to mean that one may never build one's home in an ornate fashion, similar to the style of kings, even if one leaves one *amah* by one *amah* unplastered.

5. רמב"ם | הל' תעניות ה:יב

משחרב בית המקדש תקנו חכמים שהיו באותו הדור שאין בונין לעולם בנין מסוייד ומכוייר כבנין המלכים, אלא טח ביתו בטיט וסד בסיד ומשייר מקום אמה על אמה כנגד הפתח בלא סיד.

ר Rambam, Hilchot Ta'aniyot 5:12

After the *Beit HaMikdash* was destroyed, the Sages of that generation decreed that one may never build a building [whose walls are] plastered and tiled in the style of the palaces of kings. Rather, one should cover [the walls of] one's home with mortar and plaster with lime, and he must leave an unplastered area of one *amah* by one *amah* opposite the entrance.

According to the Rambam, plastering and tiling is prohibited entirely only when done in the style of kings. But if one plasters in an ordinary fashion, then one may leave an *amah* by an *amah* unplastered, based on the first passage cited above.

The ***Beit Yosef*** discusses what the Rambam includes within his prohibition of building in the style of kings and suggests two possibilities, the second of which is more stringent than the first:

1. Plastering the walls and then decorating them with ornate designs is prohibited. Plastering alone (provided one leaves a square *amah*) or painting ornate designs without plastering is permitted.
2. The standard practice of covering with mortar and then plastering with lime is permitted (provided one leaves a square *amah*). Using lime alone for everything is considered the style of kings and is prohibited.

6. בית יוסף | או"ח תקס

ואפשר דאין מכיירין ואין מפייחין הם פיתוחים וציורים ואין מסיידין אינו מיני ציור אלא כמשמעו **והכי קאמר אין מסיידין ועל הסיוד יכייר ויפייח** דאילו כיור ופיוח בלא סיוד לא תואר לו ולא הדר הלכך לא מיתסר.

ואפשר עוד לומר שדרך העולם כשרוצים לסוד בתיהם טחים בטיט תחלה ואחר כך סדים בסיד אבל **המלכים אין טחים בטיט תחלה אלא הכל סיד וקתני דאין מסיידין בענין זה** שהוא דרך גדולה ומעלה ובסיוד וכיור כזה אין שום תקנה ואפילו על ידי שיור אמה.

ו Beit Yosef, Orach Chaim 560

It is possible that "One may not tile" and "One may not paint" refer to engravings and drawings; whereas "One may not plaster" is not a type of decoration but rather literal. [**Thus, the *baraita***] **means that one may not plaster and** [**then**] **engrave and draw on the plaster**, whereas engraving and drawing without plaster have neither form nor beauty, and therefore are not prohibited.

It is also possible to say that the common practice when people wish to plaster their houses is first to cover with mortar and afterwards to plaster with lime; but **kings do not coat with clay first, rather** [**they use**] **lime for everything.** [**The *baraita***] **teaches that one may not plaster in this manne**r, as this is the way of grandeur and nobility. There is no solution that permits plastering and decorating of this kind, not even by leaving a [square] *amah*.

In contrast to the understanding of the Rambam and the *Beit Yosef*, in his work ***Darkei Moshe***, the Rema writes that according to the ***Tur***, all forms of plastering and decoration are permitted if one leaves a square *amah* unplastered, and he writes that the custom is in accordance with this view.

7. דרכי משה | או"ח תקס

ומיהו המנהג כדברי הטור דעל ידי שיור אמה על אמה נוהגין היתר בכל.

א Darkei Moshe, Orach Chaim 560:1

However, the custom is in accordance with the comments of the *Tur*, i.e., our practice is to permit everything by leaving an *amah* by an *amah* [unplastered].

According to this approach, the two *baraitot* cited by the Gemara indeed conflict with each other, and the halacha follows the more lenient one that leaving an *amah* by an *amah* unplastered is always permitted. The ***Shulchan Aruch*** (O.C. 560:1) uses similar language to the Rambam when codifying this halacha. The ***Magen Avraham*** (560:1) and the ***Mishna Berura*** (560:1) quote the second explanation of the *Beit Yosef*, but they also conclude that the custom is to rule leniently, in accordance with the *Tur* and the Rema.[1]

1. Sephardim also rule this way (see *Kaf HaChaim* 560:3).

The Placement of the Square *Amah*

We have already seen above in source 3 that the unplastered square *amah* must be opposite the entrance. The ***Mishna Berura*** confirms that this is indeed the meaning of the Hebrew word *k'neged*, although he observes that some people instead leave the unplastered area above the entrance. Although this practice is not consistent with the Gemara, he explains that this area may be visible more often.

8. משנה ברורה | או"ח תקס:ג

כנגד הפתח – היינו נוכח הפתח כדי שיראה מיד שיכנס בפתח. ויש שמניחים פנוי למעלה מן הפתח בגובה, ואינו נראה לנכנס, ואפשר כדי שיתראה תמיד לפני בעל הבית היושב בפנים שעל רוב הוא יושב אצל הקיר אשר נוכח פתח הבית.

א Mishna Berura, Orach Chaim 560:3

Opposite [*k'neged*] the entrance – This means opposite the entrance, [and the purpose of this is] so that it will be seen immediately when one enters. But some leave [an] unplastered [area] above the entrance, and it is not visible to one who enters. It is possible [that the purpose of doing so is] so that it will be seen constantly by the homeowner who sits inside, as most of the time he sits next to the wall which faces the entrance of the house.

The ***Sha'arei Teshuva*** cites a dispute as to whether one is obligated to leave a square *amah* unplastered in every room of a house,[2] or whether it is sufficient to leave one square *amah* unplastered for the entire house. Although Rav Ya'akov Emden ruled leniently in this regard, he nevertheless left a small area unplastered in an additional room.

9. שערי תשובה | או"ח תקס:א

אלא טח ביתו כו' – **ועיין באליה רבה שכתב** דלפי מה שכתב בסימן א' בשם לקוטי מהרי"ל דבית נקרא חדר, **אפשר דהכא צריך להניח לכל חדר וחדר** עיין שם.

אך בשאילת יעב"ץ סימן קס"ט כתב: "באמה על אמה פעם אחת סגי לכל חדרי הבית אף על פי שיש לו חדרים רבים... ומכל מקום כשהוספתי לעצמי חדר נאה לשם מצות סוכה הנחתי כנגד הפתח איזה טפחים בלתי מסויד בסיד לבן כדרך שעושים לכתלים על גבי הסיד שְׁטַחִין אותו בו... והקלתי בו עוד שלא להקפיד על מדת אמה, דחומרא סגי."

א Sha'arei Teshuva, Orach Chaim 560:1

Rather, one should cover [the walls of] one's home – See *Eliya Rabba*, who writes that according to that which he writes in the name of *Likutei Maharil*, that a house [*bayit*] means a room, **it is possible that here one must leave [an unplastered square *amah*] in each room.**

However, in *She'eilat Ya'avetz*, [Rav Ya'akov Emden] writes: "One square *amah* is sufficient for all the rooms of the house, even if the house has many rooms... Nevertheless, when I added a fine room for myself for the sake of the mitzva of *sukka*, I left a number of *tefachim* opposite the entrance without the white lime-plaster that is usually applied over the lime coating on the walls... I was lenient further, not to insist on the exact measure of an *amah*, as [since this is a mere] stringency, [any amount] is sufficient."

2. This would be similar to the requirement to fix a *mezuza* in each room of a house. Although the commandment in the Torah is to write on the doorpost of the house [*bayit*], the Hebrew word *bayit* in the Torah is understood to mean a room.

The accepted practice today is to leave just one square *amah* unplastered for the entire house. **Rav Mordechai Eliyahu** rules accordingly.

10. סידור קול אליהו לתשעה באב | הל' זכר לחורבן ג

Siddur Kol Eliyahu L'tisha B'av, Hilchot Zeicher L'churban 3

אין חיוב להשאיר אמה על אמה אלא רק בחדר אחד בכל הדירה – בחדר הכניסה.

There is an obligation only to leave a square *amah* [unplastered] in one room in the entire apartment – the entrance room.

The **Dirshu edition** of the *Mishna Berura* cites this as also being the position of **Rav Yaakov Yisrael Kanievsky** and **Rav Yosef Shalom Eliashiv**. In a situation where the entrance room is a hallway leading to the living room of a house, they both rule that one should leave the unplastered square *amah* in the living room rather than in the hallway.

11. משנה ברורה בהוצאת "דרשו" | או"ח תקס:ג, הערה 6

Dirshu Edition of the Mishna Berura, Orach Chaim 560:3, n. 6

ובבית שנכנסים בתחילה לפרוזדור צר וממנו לחדר הרחב, הורה הגאון רבי יעקב ישראל קנייבסקי (ארחות רבינו ב', עמ' קמ"ז) שיעשו את האמה על אמה בקיר שכנגד הכניסה לחדר הרחב ולא בקיר שכנגד הפתח. אכן, דעת הגאון רבי יוסף שלום אלישיב (תורת המועדים סעיף קטן ג) שבזמנינו שעיקר השימוש הוא בסלון, יש לעשות את האמה על אמה בסלון.

In a house where one first enters a narrow corridor and this leads to a larger room, HaGaon Rav Yaakov Yisrael Kanievsky ruled that one should leave the [unplastered] square *amah* on the wall opposite the entrance to the large room and not on the wall opposite the entrance [to the house]. Indeed, the view of Rav Yosef Shalom Eliashiv is that in our times, when the main use [of the house] is in the living room, one should leave the [unplastered] square *amah* in the living room.

The ***Magen Avraham*** infers from the language of the Rambam (quoted above in source 5) and *Shulchan Aruch* that the obligation applies only to a private home. One need not leave an unplastered area when building a *shul*.

12. מגן אברהם | או"ח תקס:ב

א Magen Avraham, Orach Chaim 560:2

ביתו בטיט – משמע דבית הכנסת שרי בכל ענין, וכן המנהג.

[One should cover the walls of] one's home with mortar – This implies that [fully plastering] a *shul* is permitted in all situations, and this is the custom.

The ***Piskei Teshuvot*** writes that the obligation to leave a square *amah* unplastered applies everywhere, although some cite Rav Akiva Yosef Shlesinger as ruling that in Jerusalem one need not do so, as the desolation is visible there.

13. פסקי תשובות | או"ח תקס:א

ודע, כי אין חילוק בין ארץ-ישראל לחוץ לארץ לעניין 'זכר לחורבן', וגם בירושלים תיבנה ותיכונן נוהגים להשאיר אמה על אמה בלתי מסויד. ויש המביאים בשם הגאון רבי עקיבא יוסף שלעזינגר זצ"ל (בעל "לב העברי"), שבעיר הקודש ירושלים תיבנה ותיכונן אין חיוב לעשות זכר לחורבן כיון שרואים החורבן בעיניים.

Piskei Teshuvot, Orach Chaim 560:1

Know that there is no distinction between Eretz Yisrael and the Diaspora regarding remembering the desolation, and even in Jerusalem, may it be built and established, the custom is to leave an unplastered square *amah*. Some cite HaGaon Rav Akiva Yosef Shlesinger [as ruling] that in the holy city of Jerusalem, there is no obligation to make a memorial to the desolation, since one sees the desolation clearly [there].

Coloring or Covering the Square *Amah*

So far, we have learned the basic halacha concerning the square *amah*. The *Rishonim* also discuss whether one may color this area black or cover it. The ***Aguda*** writes that one should leave the square *amah* without any color, or a simple thin black color.

14. אגודה | תענית ד:כב

יניח בלא ציור סיד או מראה שחור דק בלא תיקון כלל.

Aguda, Ta'anit 4:22

One should leave [the square *amah*] without any coloring with lime, or a thin black color without any decoration.

The ***Levush*** argues that one should not even color the square *amah* black, as this improves the look of the building.

15. לבוש | או"ח תקס:א

ונראה לי מה שנוהגים עכשיו הבונים בתים ומסיידים אותו שמסיידין ומכיירין אותו כולו, ואחר כך משחירין אמה על אמה בשיחור כנגד הפתח, דלא יפה הם עושין, כי אדרבה השיחור זה אינו מגנה את הבנין, אבל מייפהו ומשמח הלב כשאר ציורים הנאים, וחז"ל אמרו משייר בו אמה על אמה, כלומר שמניחו כך מקולקל ובלי מתוקן כדי לגנות הבנין ולשבר לבו, שמתוך כך יזכור החורבן ובשברון לב ולא שייפהו ויזכור מתוך שמחת לב.

Levush, Orach Chaim 560:1

It seems to me that the current practice of those who build houses and plaster them, that they plaster or tile the entire house, and afterwards blacken a square *amah* opposite the entrance, is not proper. As on the contrary, this blackening does not make the building look untidy, but rather it enhances it and gladdens the heart like other pleasing designs. Chazal said that one leaves a square *amah*, meaning that one leaves it in its poor and undecorated state, in order to make the building untidy and to break one's heart, as through this one will remember the desolation with a broken heart, not beautify it and remember through a gladdened heart.

The Chafetz Chaim, in the ***Mishna Berura*** and ***Sha'ar HaTziun,*** cites the ***Chayei Adam*** who writes that coloring the square *amah* black is not permitted even if one writes "*zeicher l'churban*" (remembrance of the desolation) on the blackened area. However, the Chafetz Chaim writes that one should not protest against those who do this.

16. משנה ברורה | או"ח תקס:ג

ואותו השיור יהיה בלא סיד, ודלא כאותן העושין אמה שחור דזהו גם כן ציור. ויש מקומות שעושין שחור וכותבין על זה זכר לחורבן. ואותן התולין בגדי רקמה סביב כל הכתלים ישיירו גם כן אמה על אמה.

א Mishna Berura, Orach Chaim 560:3

That unplastered space should be left without lime, unlike those who make a black square *amah*, as that too is a decoration. In some places, they blacken an area and write on it "*zeicher l'churban*." Those who hang embroidered cloths around all the walls must also leave a square *amah* [uncovered].

17. שער הציון | או"ח תקס:ח

אף דחיי אדם מחמיר גם בזה, מכל מקום נראה דאין למחות ביד המקילין, אחרי שהאליה רבה הביא בשם האגודה סמך להמקילין שעושין שחור המקום ההוא.

א Sha'ar HaTziun, Orach Chaim 560:8

Although the *Chayei Adam* rules stringently even regarding this [practice of writing "*zeicher l'churban*" on a blackened area], it appears that one should not protest against those who act leniently, since the *Eliya Rabba* quotes the *Aguda* in support of those who are lenient to blacken that area.

Rav Moshe Feinstein permits blackening the square *amah* even without writing "*zeicher l'churban*," despite acknowledging that many *Acharonim* are stringent in this regard. He contends that contrary to the position of the *Levush*, the purpose of leaving the square *amah* unplastered is simply to remember the desolation, and provided that this is achieved, there is no need for the house to look untidy.

18. שו"ת אגרות משה | או"ח ג:פו

בעירב בו תבן מותר גם לר' יהודה... אם כן מסתבר שיהיה מותר אף כשעשה כל הבית בסיד ורק את האמה שכנגד הפתח עשה בסיד שמעורב בו חול ותבן...

ומאחר שזה מותר אף שהוא רק חסרון קטן משמע להו **דאין הטעם משום שמגרע היופי של הבית, אלא שהוא להיכר שיבינו שבשביל הזכר לחורבן נעשה זה. ולכן אף במשחירין על ידי צבע נמי** כיון שהשחרות הוא סימן לאבלות כדאיתא בבבא קמא דף נ"ט אליעזר זעירא הוה מסאני אוכמי שפרש"י מנהג אבלים, וכן בתוספות...

פ Responsa Igrot Moshe, Orach Chaim 3:86

If one mixed straw into it, it is permitted even according to Rabbi Yehuda[3]... Accordingly, it seems reasonable that this should be permitted even if one plasters the entire house with lime and only plasters the square *amah* opposite the entrance with lime mixed with sand or straw...

Since this is permitted even though it is only a small deficiency, this implies that **the reason [for the obligation to leave a square *amah* unplastered] is not in order to detract from the beauty of the house, but rather as a reminder, so that people will understand that this was done in remembrance of the desolation. Therefore, even if one blackens it with paint**, since blackness is a sign of mourning, as stated in *Bava Kama* (59b) regarding Eliezer Ze'eira who wore black shoes. Rashi explains that it was a custom of mourners, and Tosafot [write] similarly...

---

3. The Gemara quotes a *baraita* in which the *tanna kamma* explicitly permits plastering one's house if one mixes sand or straw into the plaster (Rabbi Yehuda prohibits using plaster mixed with sand, but permits using plaster mixed with straw). Although the Rambam and *Shulchan Aruch* do not codify this leniency, the *Beit Yosef* (o.c. 560) explains that this is implicit in the prohibition being specifically against plastering with lime. The Ritva (source 23 below) also assumes this is correct, and the *Mishna Berura* (560:2) brings this approach as "*yesh mekilin*" (some are lenient). See, however, *Nishmat Adam* 137:1, who infers that the Rif understands that other *baraitot* quoted by the Gemara dispute this leniency, and that the halacha is in accordance with these *baraitot*.

There is no mention that this is because black garments are inferior and less beautiful than white ones… We see that blackness is a sign of mourning, not because it is not attractive.

Therefore, the *amah* that they require one to leave unplastered is not in order to make the house untidy, nor to make this area alone untidy, but rather so that it not be so white. Therefore, it suffices if the *amah* is plastered with lime mixed with sand or straw, which dulls the whiteness, even though the house and the *amah* remain attractive… Even though this beautifies the house further, it is nevertheless a remembrance of the desolation, especially since the blackening is done entirely for this purpose.

Furthermore, **in this matter one may be lenient, as it is merely rabbinic**… Although this is not the view of our teachers, the *Levush*, the *Shelah*, the *Magen Avraham*, the *Ateret Zekeinim* and the *Pri Megadim*.

ולא הוזכר שהוא מחמת שבגדים שחורים הם גרועים ואינם יפים כלבנים... אלמא דהשחרות הוא סימן לאבלות לא מצד שאינם נאים.

לכן גם האמה שהצריכו להשאיר אינו בשביל שיגנה את הבית ואף לא לגנות רק מקום זה לבד אלא שלא יהיה לבן כל כך, שלכן סגי כשיסוד האמה בסיד המעורב בחול ותבן שמכהה לבנונו אף שעדיין הבית וגם האמה הם נאים... ואף שמיפה יותר הבנין דעל כל פנים הוא זכר לחורבן ובפרט כשכל השחרות הוא בשביל זה.

ובאשר שבדבר זה יש להקל משום דהוא רק מדרבנן... אף שהוא דלא כרבותינו הלבוש והשל"ה והמגן אברהם והעטרת זקנים והפרי מגדים.

However, **Rav Mordechai Eliyahu** writes that one should not color the unplastered square *amah* black.

Siddur Kol Eliyahu L'tisha B'av, Hilchot Zeicher L'churban 4

19. סידור קול אליהו לתשעה באב | הל' זכר לחורבן ד

Whether one colors the walls or covers them with wallpaper, one must leave a square *amah*. One may not color the square *amah*, not even with black paint.

יש לשייר אמה על אמה בין אם צבעו את הקירות או ציפו אותם בטפט. ואין לצבוע את מקום ה"אמה על אמה" אפילו לא בצבע שחור.

The **Dirshu Edition of the *Mishna Berura*** cites the *Nimukei Orach Chaim* who writes that covering the square *amah* with a picture of the Kotel is certainly prohibited. However, Rav Chaim Kanievsky is cited as permitting partially covering the square *amah* with such a picture.

Dirshu Edition of the Mishna Berura, Orach Chaim 560:3, n. 7

20. משנה ברורה בהוצאת "דרשו" | או"ח תקס:ג, הערה 7

The *Nimukei Orach Chaim* writes that drawing a picture of the Western Wall on this space is certainly prohibited, as on the contrary, this appears like an additional decoration for the house. However, the view of the Gaon, Rav Chaim Kanievsky, is that hanging a picture of the Kotel on this space in a manner such that part of the square *amah* is still visible outside of the picture is permitted.

ולעשות על מקום זה צורה של הכותל המערבי, כתב הנימוקי אורח חיים שודאי שאסור, שאדרבה זה נראה כעוד ציור נוי לבית. אכן, לתלות על אותו מקום תמונה של הכותל ובאופן שעדיין נראה חלק מהאמה על אמה מחוץ לתמונה, דעת גאון רבי חיים קנייבסקי שמותר.

Buying or Renting a Fully Decorated House

The *baraita* quoted in source 1 continues by stating that one who purchases a property that is already fully plastered need not remove any plaster.

ח Masechet Bava Batra 60b

21. מסכת בבא בתרא ס:

If one **purchased a courtyard** that was **plastered, tiled,** or **painted** with images, **this** courtyard **may remain as it is**. If **it** then **fell, he may not return and build it** in its previous form.

לקח חצר מסוידת, מכוירת, מפויחת – הרי זו בחזקתה; נפלה – אינו חוזר ובונה אותה.

Tosafot explain that leaving the plaster is permitted as we can assume that the house was plastered before the *Beit HaMikdash* was destroyed.

ו Tosafot, Bava Batra 60b

22. תוספות | בבא בתרא ס:

If it fell, he may not return and build it – ...If one purchased a courtyard that was plastered, the courtyard may remain as it is... as we can assume that it was done in a permitted manner, when the *Beit HaMikdash* stood... [But] even if it was certainly built in a permitted manner, if it fell, building it and plastering it is prohibited.

נפלה אינו חוזר ובונה אותה – ...וכשלקח חצר המסוידת הרי זו בחזקתה... יש לנו לתלות שבהיתר עשה בזמן שבית המקדש קיים... דאפילו ודאי נבנה בהיתר כי נפלה אסור לבנותה ולסייד.

The **Ritva**, quoting Tosafot of Évreux, adds that even if the house was certainly plastered after the *Beit HaMikdash* was destroyed, one can assume that it was plastered in a permitted manner, by adding sand to the lime.[4]

ו Ritva, Bava Batra 60b

23. ריטב"א | בבא בתרא ס:

...Tosafot of Évreux explain... that we can assume that it was built in a permitted manner, even if we know for certain that a Jew plastered it after the destruction [of the *Beit HaMikdash*], as we can say that he may have mixed a small amount of sand into the plaster.

...ובתוספות של איברא פירשו... שתולין שנבנה בהיתר ואפילו ידענו ודאי שעשאה ישראל לאחר החורבן דאמרינן שמא עירב בו חול קצת.

Rav Achai of Shabcha writes that if gentiles decorated a house, irrespective of when and how, a Jew may use it without making any changes.

4. See n. 3 above.

24. שאילתות דרב אחאי | יתרו, שאילתא נז

דאעשייה קא קפיד קרא והרי עשאום אחרים שרי לאישתמושי בהון ישראל ולא חייש לחשדא כדתניא לקח חצר מפוייחת מצויירת הרי זו בחזקתה.

ו She'iltot Derav Achai, Yitro, Sheilta 57

The Torah is particular about making [graven images of the heavenly bodies], as if others made them, a Jew is permitted to use them and we are not concerned about suspicion [that the Jew may have made them].[5] This is similar to that which we have learned in a *baraita* [regarding the prohibition against plastering a house], if one purchased a courtyard that was tiled or painted with images, this courtyard may remain as it is.

The **Rambam** also writes that the prohibition against plastering a house does not obligate one who purchases a house to peel off the plaster.

25. רמב"ם | הל' תעניות ה:יב

והלוקח חצר מסויידת ומכויירת הרי זו בחזקתה ואין מחייבים אותו לקלף הכתלים.

ו Rambam, Hilchot Ta'aniyot 5:12

If one purchased a courtyard that was plastered or tiled, it may remain as it is; he is not obligated to scrape [the plaster from] the walls.

The ***Shulchan Aruch*** (O.C. 560:1) writes similarly. However, the ***Magen Avraham*** explains in accordance with Tosafot, and therefore concludes that if one knows that the building was built in a prohibited manner, one must scrape a square *amah* area from the wall.[6]

26. מגן אברהם | או"ח תקס:ד

והלוקח חצר – דתלינן שנעשה קודם החורבן או שנעשה ביד עכו"ם ולקחה ישראל ממנו, אבל אם יודע שנעשה באיסור חייב לקלפו.

א Magen Avraham, Orach Chaim 560:4

If one purchased a courtyard [he is not obligated to scrape the plaster from the walls] – As we assume that [the plastering] was done before the destruction [of the *Beit HaMikdash*], or by a gentile and the Jew purchased it from him. But if one knows that it was done in a prohibited manner, one is obligated to scrape it.

Rav Mordechai Eliyahu rules similarly and adds that even one who rents such an apartment is obligated to scrape a square *amah* of plaster from the wall.

---

5. This topic was discussed at length in volume 1, *shiur* 2. Here the *She'iltot* appears to permit using even three-dimensional images made by gentiles in all circumstances, a view that is more lenient than any of those quoted in the aforementioned *shiur.*

6. See *Chazon Ovadia, Arba Ta'aniyot, Hilchot Zeicher L'churban Beit HaMikdash,* 1, and *Nechemat Tzion* 21:9 (written by Rav Benzion Mutzafi), which both quote the *Shulchan Aruch* without the interpretation of the *Magen Avraham.* It is possible that they understood the intent of the *Shulchan Aruch* to be that one is never obligated to scrape plaster off the wall, even if it was built by a Jew. Indeed, Rav Mutzafi raises this possibility in the footnotes, though he notes that many *Acharonim* do not accept this.

27. סידור קול אליהו לתשעה באב | הל' זכר לחורבן ג

מי שקנה או שכר מיהודי דירה מסוידת, שאין בה אמה על אמה... חייב לקלוף את הקיר.

Siddur Kol Eliyahu L'tisha B'av, Hilchot Zeicher L'churban

One who purchased or rented a plastered apartment from a Jew, that does not have an [unplastered] square *amah*... is obligated to scrape [the plaster from] the wall.

Rav Moshe Feinstein argues that a tenant is never obligated to scrape plaster from the wall. Moreover, even one who purchases a property in order to sell (or rent) is not obligated to leave an unplastered square *amah* since he does not live in it himself.

28. שו"ת אגרות משה | או"ח ג:פו

...ומה שחידש כבוד תורתו הרמה **שהבונה בית למוכרו... אינו מחוייב להשאיר האמה...** ואף מה שמשמע מדברי כבוד תורתו הרמה שאף כשאין נכרים שם שודאי יקנה רק ישראל נמי היה מותר שכן הביא מספר מגדל השן, נמי הוא דבר המסתבר... דכיון דבלשון האיסור בתרי ברייתות נאמר ביתו... שלשון ביתו משמע ביתו שדר בו כמו לשון ביתך שדרשינן במזוזה שהוא דוקא הבית שדר בו... וכיון שלשון ביתו נאמר בהאיסור הוא דוקא בית הדר בו אסרו.

וגם הקלו בזה יותר שלא אסרו אף הדר בו אם לא בנאו בעצמו אלא לקח בית בנוי כמו שלא אסרו על הלוקח מעכו"ם, וממילא נמצא **שהבונה למכור אף לישראל פטור מלהשאיר האמה בין המוכר הבונה בין הלוקח הדר בו ובין השוכר** כדכתב כבוד תורתו הרמה, ומה שבמגן אברהם איתא שחייב לקלוף הוא בקנה בית מישראל שבנה בעצמו לדירתו שנאסר שבזה מצריך את הלוקח לקלוף...

Responsa Igrot Moshe, Orach Chaim 3:86

...That which the honorable [questioner] has innovated in his lofty Torah [writings], **that one who builds a house in order to sell it... is not obligated to leave the [unplastered square] *amah***... and that which is implied from his lofty Torah [writings], that even when there are no gentiles present, such that certainly only a Jew would buy it, this would also be permitted, as he cites from the *sefer Migdal HaShein*, this too is reasonable... Since the language used in two *baraitot* for the prohibition is "his house" ...[and] the term "his house" implies the house in which he dwells, similar to the term "your house" that [appears in the Torah] regarding *mezuza*, which we explain refers specifically to the house in which one dwells... Since the term "his house" is used regarding the prohibition, [this implies that] they only prohibited [plastering the entire house] in the house in which he himself resides.

They were also more lenient in this regard, that even for one who dwells in the house, they did not prohibit [plastering the entire house] if he did not build it himself, but rather purchased a completed house, just as they did not prohibit one who purchased [a house] from a gentile [from plastering the entire house]. Consequently, it follows that **if one builds in order to sell, even to a Jew, the seller who built it and the buyer or tenant who reside in it are both exempt from leaving the square *amah* [unplastered]**, as he has written in his lofty Torah [writings]. That which appears in the *Magen Avraham*, that one is obligated to scrape [the plaster], is in a case where he bought a house from a Jew who built it himself for his own dwelling when [plastering the entire house] was prohibited. In such a case, even the buyer is required to scrape...

והשוכר מסתבר לעניות דעתי דאף בשכר בית שבנאו המשכיר לדור בו בעצמו שנעשה באיסור נמי אין לחייבו כדהביא כבוד תורתו הרמה מספר מגדל השן...

Regarding the tenant, in my humble opinion it seems that even if he rented a house which the landlord built for his own residence, such that the plastering carried out was prohibited, he is nevertheless not obligated to [scrape the plaster off], as he cites from the *sefer Migdal HaShein*...

The ***Piskei Teshuvot*** also writes that when an apartment is rented, there is no obligation to scrape off existing plaster, although he writes that if one is re-plastering, he must leave a square *amah*. In addition, a tenant must not scrape off plaster without the consent of the landlord, although it is proper to attempt to obtain consent.

29. פסקי תשובות | או"ח תקס:ג

...הנכנס לגור בבית בשכירות חודשית, אם השוכר מסייד את הבית או אם המשכיר מסייד את הבית לצורך השוכר, חייב להשאיר אמה על אמה בלתי מסויד. אבל אם אינו מסייד מחדש, **אין על השוכר חיוב לקלף את הסיד אמה על אמה, אף שהמשכיר יהודי ומצד הדין חייב. ואם רוצה לקלף, אסור לעשות זאת ללא נטילת רשות מהמשכיר**, אבל נכון יעשה אם ייטול רשות ויקלף אמה על אמה, ואף יפייס את המשכיר במעות אם אינו מתרצה בלא זה.

הקונה דירה בדמי מפתח, מסתבר שהחיוב מוטל על הקונה לעשות זכר לחורבן.

Piskei Teshuvot, Orach Chaim 560:3

...[Regarding] one who moves into a house on a monthly rental, if the tenant plasters the house, or if the landlord plasters the house for the tenant's sake, he is obligated to leave one square *amah* unplastered. But if one is not re-plastering, **the tenant has no obligation to scrape off a square *amah* of plaster, even though the landlord is a Jew and is, in principle, obligated. If he wishes to scrape, this is prohibited without permission from the landlord.** However, it is proper that he obtain permission and scrape one square *amah*, and even appease the landlord with money if he does not agree otherwise.

[Regarding] one who purchases [protected tenancy rights in] an apartment on a key-money arrangement,[7] it appears that the buyer is obligated to make a remembrance of the desolation.

Rav Menashe Klein takes issue with the leniencies accepted by Rav Moshe Feinstein.[8] He writes that one who builds a house is certainly obligated to leave a square *amah* unplastered, irrespective of whether he lives in it, or sells or rents to a Jew.

---

7. This refers to a payment made by tenants to a landlord or the previous tenants in exchange for lifelong protected tenancy rights, securing a nominal monthly rent.
8. Rav Shalom Yechezkel Shraga Rubin, the third Cheshinover Rebbe, asked both Rav Moshe Feinstein and Rav Menashe Klein regarding the leniencies found in the *sefer Migdal HaShein* (written by Rav Shmuel Nachum Gesenbauer, a 19th century Polish rav) regarding leaving the square *amah* unplastered. While Rav Moshe Feinstein broadly accepted these leniencies (as we saw above in source 28), Rav Menashe Klein rejected them outright. However, there is no indication that Rav Moshe Feinstein and Rav Menashe Klein saw each other's responsa on this matter.

30. שו"ת משנה הלכות | ה:עא

...דבריו תמוהים מאד... דהרי הבונה בית ומוכרו או משכירו לישראל ממה נפשך חייב בזכר אם מצד הבונה שהוא גברא בר חיובא ואם מצד הלוקח או שוכר שהוא גם כן בר חיובא ומהיכא תיתי יפטרו אחד מהם מזכר זה דהנה נראה מדברי הגמרא והפוסקים דהחיוב לעשות זכר הוא על הבית כשנבנה על ידי ישראל **וכל שנבנה על ידי ישראל מחויב לעשות זכר ואין נפקא מינה בין עושה לעצמו או למכור...**

גם במשכיר בית נראה פשוט דחייב לעשות זכר... ופירשו התוספות הרי זו בחזקתה דיש לתלות שבהיתר עשה בזמן שבית המקדש קיים... מבואר מדברי הריטב"א ז"ל דהרי היא בחזקתה משום דאמרינן דישראל בנאו באופן של צד ההיתר היינו שעירב בו חול או תבן אבל בלאו הכי לעולם אמרינן דהוא בחזקת איסור...

Responsa Mishneh Halachot 5:71

...The words of [the *Migdal HaShein*] are very puzzling... As one who builds a house and sells it, or rents it to a Jew, is obligated to make a remembrance [of the desolation] whichever way one looks at it, whether on account of the builder, who is obligated, or on account of the buyer or tenant, who is also obligated. Why should either of them be exempt from this remembrance? As it appears from the words of the Gemara and the *poskim* that the obligation to make a remembrance takes effect on the house when it is built by a Jew. **Whenever it is built by a Jew, one is obligated to make a remembrance, with no distinction between whether he built it for himself or to sell...**

Also, regarding one who rents out a house, it seems obvious that he is obligated to make a remembrance... Tosafot explain the expression "this [courtyard] may remain as it is" that we can assume that it was done in a permitted manner, when the *Beit HaMikdash* stood... It is [also] clear from the words of the Ritva that it may remain as it is because we assume that the Jew built it in a permitted manner, i.e., by mixing in sand or straw. But without this, we would always say that [retaining the plaster] is presumed to be prohibited...

Contemporary Practice

Even when none of the leniencies quoted above apply, in practice, many people are lax regarding this halacha and do not leave a square *amah* unplastered. The ***Mishna Berura*** struggles to find any justification for this practice.

31. משנה ברורה | או"ח תקס:ב

...ויש מקילין על ידי חול דסבירא להו דהיכא דעירב חול שוב לא מיקרי בשם סיד. **והנה בזמנינו לא נהגו לשייר**, ואפשר משום דסומכין על היש מקילין, ועל כל פנים תמוה, שהרי מלבנין הבתים בסיד לבד! **ואפשר דדוקא במיני סיד הנקרא גופ"ש שהוא לבן ביותר אסור, מה שאין כן סיד שלנו, אך כל זה דוחק, וצריך עיון על מה נוהגין היתר.** והיכא שהוא טח בטיט לבד לכולי עלמא אין צריך לשייר כלל.

א Mishna Berura, Orach Chaim 560:1

...Some are lenient through [mixing] sand, as when one mixes sand [into the plaster] it is no longer considered lime.[9] **Now in our times the practice is not to leave [a square *amah* unplastered]**, and it is possible that this is because we rely on this lenient view. But in any event, [this practice] is astonishing, as we whiten the houses with lime alone! **It is possible that only types of lime known as "*gopsh*," which are exceedingly white, are prohibited, not our lime. But all of this is tenuous, and further thought is required regarding a basis for the lenient practice.** If one covers [the walls] with mortar alone, according to all views one need not leave any area uncovered whatsoever.

9. See n. 3 above. This comment of the *Mishna Berura* is almost an exact quote of the *Nishmat Adam* cited there.

The ***Piskei Teshuvot*** also concludes that there is no valid justification for the lenient practice, and one should certainly leave a square *amah* unplastered.

32. פסקי תשובות | או"ח תקס:א

...ובאחרונים מובא עוד טעמים ללמד זכות על אלו שאינן מקפידים על מנהג זה, אבל אינם שייכים בזמננו, ולכן ודאי יש להקפיד על הלכה זו ולשייר אמה על אמה זכר לחורבן על פי כל כללי ההלכה... וכשם שנהגו כל גדולי הדורות להניח בביתם אמה על אמה בלתי מסויד.

Piskei Teshuvot, Orach Chaim 560:1

...Other reasons to justify that which people are not particular regarding this practice are brought in the *Acharonim*, but they are not relevant in our times. Therefore, one should be particular regarding this halacha and one should leave a square *amah* [unplastered] as a remembrance to the desolation, according to all the halachic guidelines... Just as all the great authorities of the generations followed the practice of leaving an unplastered square *amah* in their homes.

Nevertheless, based on what we have learned, one may be lenient many times in the Diaspora, where the homes are usually built by gentiles, and no obligation is therefore incurred when a Jew rents or purchases the home either. In Israel, this justification is not usually relevant. If one rents a home, one may perhaps rely on the approach of Rav Feinstein, but if one purchases a home, even that leniency would not apply.

Those who are lenient because sand is mixed into the lime may, perhaps, still be lenient in Israel, where often the lime used is not pure lime, but includes sand or other materials. Although the *Mishna Berura* does not appear to recommend relying on this, the ***Aruch HaShulchan*** does indeed write that this forms the basis for the contemporary lenient practice and may be relied on *lechatchila*.[10]

33. ערוך השלחן | או"ח תקס:ד

ולפי זה יש לנו ללמד זכות על רוב ישראל שאין נזהרין עתה בדין זה לשייר אמה על אמה כשסדין בסיד כותלי הבית לפי שידוע שעתה מערבין בהסיד הרבה חול כמעט מחצה על מחצה ואם כן מדין גמור אין צריך שיור כלל.

ואף על פי שהרי"ף והרא"ש וכן הרמב"ם והטור והשולחן ערוך לא הביאו רק הברייתא האחרונה לא חששו להאריך אבל גם בדבריהם יש לומר כן דבעירוב חול אין צריך שיור וראיה ברורה לזה שהרי הר"ן והנמוקי יוסף הם מפרשי הרי"ף ואי סלקא דעתך שאינו כן דעת הרי"ף איך לא הזכירו זה אלא וודאי כדברינו.

(וגם בבית יוסף הזכיר כעין זה והב"ח חלק עליו עיין שם ותמיהני למה

א Aruch HaShulchan, Orach Chaim 560:4

According to this, we are able to find merit for the majority of Jews nowadays, who are not careful [to observe] this halacha of leaving a square amah when plastering the walls of the house. As it is known that nowadays, much sand is mixed with the lime, almost half and half. Accordingly, based on genuine halacha, one need not leave any [area unplastered] at all.

Although the Rif and the Rosh, as well as the Rambam, the *Tur* and the *Shulchan Aruch*, quote only the latter *baraita* [that does not mention this leniency, this is simply because] they did not deem it necessary to elaborate. Even according to their view, one can apply the same [leniency], that when sand is mixed in, no [area] need be left [unplastered]. There is a clear proof to this, as the Ran and the *Nimukei Yosef* are commentators on the Rif, and if it were to enter your mind that this was not the view of the Rif, how could they not mention this at all? Rather, it is certainly as we have written.

(The *Beit Yosef* also mentions something similar, but see the *Bach* who disagrees with him. I am astonished as to why [the *Beit Yosef*]

10. Rav Ovadia Yosef also mentions this as a reason to be lenient (*Chazon Ovadia, Arba Ta'aniyot, Zeicher L'churban* 1), and he may rely on this alone to permit *lechatchila* (see https://halachayomit.co.il/he/default.aspx?HalachaID=428).

does not mention this at all in the *Shulchan Aruch*, and this requires investigation.)

לא הזכיר זה כלל בשולחן ערוך וצריך עיון).

Rav Eliezer Melamed suggests potential leniency even in Israel for another reason, that most Jewish contractors who construct houses build them in order to sell. Therefore, according to Rav Feinstein, neither the Jewish seller nor the Jewish purchaser would be obligated to leave the wall unplastered. However, he himself rules that it is proper to follow the stricter opinion.[11]

Peninei Halakha, Ha'Am V'ha'aretz 9:3

Some say that the obligation to leave a [square] *amah* without plaster applies to one who builds his own house, but a contractor who builds houses in order to sell them, even if he intends to sell them to Jews, has no mitzva to leave a square *amah* without plaster, since these houses are not intended for his personal use. Consequently, the purchasers are also exempt from scraping [the plaster] of that [square] *amah*. Only from then on, if the resident wishes to repaint the house, he is obligated to leave the [square] *amah* opposite the entrance without paint (*Igrot Moshe*, O.C. 3:86). However, if the apartment was purchased from the contractor before its completion, even according to this view one must leave in it an *amah* unplastered, and if the workers plastered it, the buyer must scrape it off.

Others say that in any case, if the contractor is Jewish there is an obligation to leave an *amah* by an *amah* without plaster, and if he plastered it, the buyer must scrape it off. This also appears to be the correct practice. Even if the first resident did not do so, anyone who purchases the apartment subsequently will be required to scrape that [square] *amah*, as since the first homeowner was Jewish, the apartment became obligated in leaving a [square] *amah* as a remembrance of the destruction (this is implied by the *Magen Avraham* 560:4 and many other *poskim*, and it is stated explicitly in the *Mor U'ketzia* 560).

34. פניני הלכה | העם והארץ ט:ג

יש אומרים שהחובה להשאיר אמה ללא סיד היא על מי שבונה את ביתו, אבל קבלן שבונה בתים כדי למוכרם, אפילו אם הוא מתכוון למוכרם ליהודים, אין עליו מצווה להשאיר אמה על אמה ללא סיד, הואיל ובתים אלו לא נועדו לשימושו האישי. וממילא גם הקונים פטורים מלשייף את מקומה של אותה אמה. ורק מכאן ואילך, אם ירצה הדייר לצבוע את ביתו, חובה עליו להשאיר את האמה שמול הפתח ללא צבע (אגרות משה, או"ח ג:פו). אמנם אם הדירה נקנתה מהקבלן עוד לפני סיומה, גם לשיטה זו צריך להשאיר בה אמה לא מסוידת, ואם הפועלים סיידו אותה, על הקונה לשייפה.

ויש אומרים, שבכל אופן אם הקבלן הוא יהודי ישנה חובה לשייר אמה על אמה ללא סיד, ואם סייד אותה על הקונה לשייפה. וכן נראה שנכון לנהוג למעשה. וגם אם הדייר הראשון לא עשה כן, כל מי שיקנה לאחר מכן את הדירה, יצטרך לשייף את אותה האמה, שהואיל ובעל הבית הראשון היה יהודי, הדירה התחייבה בשיור אמה זכר לחורבן (כך משמע ממגן אברהם ד ועוד פוסקים רבים, וכך כתב במפורש במור וקציעה תקס).

---

11. See also Responsa *Ohr L'tzion* (3:30:1), who maintains that if one's spouse does not want the area exposed, then one may paint a spot measuring an *amah* by an *amah* in a different color than the rest of the wall instead. However, Rav Yisroel Belsky is quoted as ruling that this should not be done *lechatchila* (*Piskei Halacha* vol. 1, p. 114, cited in *Halachically Speaking*, https://thehalacha.com/wp-content/uploads/Vol7Zecher.pdf). Rav Nachum Rabinovitch also writes that one may allow the lenient custom not to leave any area unplastered to continue simply so as not to portray earlier generations in a negative light [*shelo l'hotzi la'az al harishonim*] (Responsa *Siach Nachum* 38). For further discussion of this topic, see https://halachipedia.com/index.php?title=Zecher_LeChurban#Leaving_one's_home_unfinished; www.torahmusings.com/2021/10/a-renter-having-a-zecher-lchurban; and www.toraland.org.il//מאמרים/אמונה-והלכה/אקטואליה-בהלכה/שיור-אמה-על-אמה-בבתים-חדשים.

Leaving Out One Dish and One Item of Jewelry

The **Gemara (*Masechet Bava Batra*)**, quoted above in source 1, mentions a number of other halachot enacted in commemoration of the *Beit HaMikdash*. One requires a person to leave out a small item from a meal, while the second is that a woman must also refrain from one standard cosmetic treatment.

35. מסכת בבא בתרא ס:

...עושה אדם כל צרכי סעודה, ומשייר דבר מועט. מאי היא? אמר רב פפא: כסא דהרסנא.

עושה אשה כל תכשיטיה, ומשיירת דבר מועט. מאי היא? אמר רב: בת צדעא, שנאמר: אם אשכחך ירושלים תשכח ימיני תדבק לשוני לחכי וגו'.

ח Masechet Bava Batra 60b

. . .Rabbi Yehoshua continues: The Sages said that **a person** may **prepare all** that he **needs for a meal, but** he must **leave** out **a small item** to remember the desolation. The Gemara interjects: **What** is **this** small item? **Rav Pappa said:** Something akin to **small, fried fish.**

Rabbi Yehoshua continues: The Sages said that **a woman** may **engage** in **all** of **her cosmetic treatments, but** she must **leave** out **a small matter** to remember the desolation. The Gemara interjects: **What** is **this** small matter? **Rav said:** She does not remove hair from the place on the **temple** from which women would remove hair. The source for these practices is a verse, **as it is stated: "If I forget you, Jerusalem, let my right hand forget its cunning. Let my tongue cleave to the roof of my mouth,** if I do not remember you; if I do not set Jerusalem above my highest joy" (*Tehillim* 137:5–6).

The ***Shulchan Aruch*** codifies this halacha.

36. שולחן ערוך | או"ח תקס:ב

וכן התקינו שהעורך שלחן לעשות סעודה לאורחים, מחסר ממנו מעט ומניח מקום פנוי בלא קערה מן הקערות הראויות לתת שם.

וכשהאשה עושה תכשיטי הכסף והזהב, משיירה מין ממיני התכשיט שנוהגת בהם, כדי שלא יהיה תכשיט שלם.

א Shulchan Aruch, Orach Chaim 560:2

Similarly, they instituted that one who sets a table in order to prepare a meal for guests should leave out a small [item] and leave an empty space without any of the bowls that would be appropriate to place there.

When a woman prepares silver and gold jewelry, she must leave out one type of jewelry that she is used to, so that there should not be a complete set of jewelry.

The ***Mishna Berura*** clarifies further and cites Rav Yaakov Emden who writes that one should not leave out anything from Shabbat and Yom Tov meals.

א Mishna Berura, Orach Chaim 560:5–8

5. **To prepare a meal for guests** – Even a *seudat mitzva* such as a circumcision or wedding [celebration], and certainly for other meals. **See *Mor U'ketzi'a*** (Rav Yaakov Emden's commentary on the *Shulchan Aruch*)**, which states that for Shabbat or Yom Tov meals, nothing should be lacking.**[12]

6. **Should leave out a small [item]** – Meaning that one should not serve all the dishes that are appropriate for the meal but should withhold a small item. Even [leaving out something as minor as] a dish of fried fish is sufficient.

7. **And leave an empty space** – As otherwise, the lack would not be noticeable. But if one leaves a place empty, people will notice that another dish ought to have been there, but it was withheld…

8. **That she is used to** – This means that if she has many types of jewelry, she should not wear them all at once, but each time leave one out, to remember the destruction. Women who adorn themselves fully, as well as [violating] this halacha, also cause many [other] harms, from the nations who are jealous of them.

37. משנה ברורה | או"ח תקס:ה-ח

ה. **לעשות סעודה לאורחים** – אפילו סעודת מצוה כמילה וחתונה וכל שכן שאר סעודות, **ועיין במור וקציעה דבסעודת שבת ויום טוב לא יחסר שום דבר.**

ו. **מחסר ממנו מעט** – כלומר שאין נותן כל תבשילים הראויים לסעודה אלא מחסר מעט אפילו כסא דהרסנא די בזה.

ז. **ומניח מקום פנוי** – דאי לאו הכי, לא יהיה ניכר החסרון אבל כשיניח פנוי ירגישו שהיה ראוי עוד תבשיל אלא שנחסר...

ח. **שנוהגת בהם** – היינו אם יש לה הרבה מיני תכשיטין לא תשים כולם עליה בבת אחת רק בכל פעם תשייר אחת לזכור החורבן. ונשים המתקשטות במילוי גורמין לבד זה רעות רבות מאומות העולם המתקנאים בהם.

Rav Shmuel Wosner infers from the language of the *Shulchan Aruch* that one need only leave out a dish from a large meal, to which guests are invited.

Responsa Shevet HaLevi 10:85

I will say in broad terms that it has been accepted from long ago that [regarding the obligation to leave out an item of food] large meals are spoken of, i.e., a celebratory meal or a large *se'udat mitzva*, where common practice is to provide as many types of food as possible… But **with regard to an [ordinary] weekday meal, which is defined by Chazal and the *Shulchan Aruch* as a regular small meal, or even a regular Shabbat or Yom Tov meal, we have not heard [such a requirement].** Therefore, the Rambam[13] writes of a meal for guests, i.e., a meal for many, for honor and rejoicing.

38. שו"ת שבט הלוי | י:פה

ואומר באופן כללי, הנה מה שמקובל מאז כי עיקר המדובר בסעודות גדולות סעודת שמחה או סעודת מצוה גדולה שדרך העולם להרבות במינים של מאכלים כל מה דאפשר... אבל **סעודת חול דהיינו לפי הגדרת חז"ל ושולחן ערוך סעודה קטנה רגילה או אפילו סעודת שבת ויום טוב רגילה, לא שמענו**, ועל כן נקט הרמב"ם סעודה לאורחים דהוא סעודה לרבים, לכבוד ולשמחה.

The *Acharonim* note that it is common to be lax in the observance of these halachot, but it is not immediately clear why this would be the case. For instance, the ***Chayei Adam*** writes that the reason for this laxity requires thought.

---

12. He explains that this is because public displays of mourning are prohibited on Shabbat and Yom Tov.

13. *Hilchot Ta'aniyot* 5:13. The language of the *Shulchan Aruch* above in source 36 is based on this halacha of the Rambam.

39. חיי אדם | קלז:ב

וצריך עיון שכל זה אין נוהגין כלל.

א Chayei Adam 137:2

It requires thought as to why none of this is practiced at all.

The ***Bi'ur Halacha* (560:2)** also quotes this difficulty raised by the *Chayei Adam* and does not offer a resolution. However, the ***Kaf HaChaim*** suggests that today, since our meals do not follow a fixed menu, there is no value to leaving out one dish from a meal since this would not be recognizable.

40. כף החיים | או"ח תקס:יח

...ואפשר לתת טעם לזה לבד שבזמניהם היה סדר לתבשילין שמביאים לפני האורחים ועל כן כשמחסר תבשיל אחד הראוי להביא בסעודה ניכר שהוא זכר לחרבן **אבל בזמנינו שלא יש סדר אלא כל אחד מביא כפי יכולתו אם כן כשמחסר אינו ניכר שהוא זכר לחרבן אלא אומרים זהו יכולתו של בעל הבית ועל כן לא נהגו בזה.**

ומכל מקום נראה דעל כל פנים יניח מקום פנוי בלתי קערה כדי שיהיה היכר קצת ויכוין עליו שהוא זכר לחורבן.

א Kaf HaChaim, Orach Chaim 560:1

...It is possible to give a reason for [the failure to leave out one dish] alone. As in their times, there was an established order to the cooked dishes that were brought before the guests, and therefore, when one left out one dish that was fitting to bring at a meal, it was recognizable that this was in remembrance of the destruction. But **in our times, where there is no fixed order, and rather each person serves according to his ability, then when one leaves out [a dish] it is not recognizable as being in remembrance of the desolation, but rather people would say, "This is the [limit of] the host's ability." Therefore, this practice was not observed.**[14]

Nevertheless, it would seem that at the very least one should leave an empty space without a dish, so that there be some sign, and he should have in mind that it is in remembrance of the destruction.[15]

---

14. See, however, *Peninei Halakha, Ha'Am V'ha'aretz* 9:8, who writes that although these halachot are not usually practiced, since the *Acharonim* do mention them, one should try to fulfill them. Thus, one who chooses a menu for a large meal with guests should consider which foods he would like and then leave one out. Likewise, a woman who makes use of many cosmetics at once should leave one out.
15. See also *Aruch HaShulchan* (560:6) for another defense of the common practice that today it is difficult to know where the empty space should be placed and how everyone would readily identify this as being in commemoration of the *churban*.

Ashes on the Head of a Bridegroom and Breaking a Cup

There are other practices related to the destruction of the *Beit HaMikdash* mentioned in the Gemara that relate to weddings. The **Gemara (*Masechet Bava Batra*)**, quoted above in source 1, provides a source from Tanach for the custom to place ashes on the head of a bridegroom, in the place where one usually lays *tefillin*, to remember the destruction.

41. מסכת בבא בתרא ס:

מאי על ראש שמחתי? אמר רב יצחק: זה אפר מקלה שבראש חתנים. אמר ליה רב פפא לאביי: היכא מנח לה? במקום תפילין, שנאמר: לשום לאבלי ציון לתת להם פאר תחת אפר.

ח Masechet Bava Batra 60b

The Gemara asks: **What** is the meaning of: **Above my highest** [*rosh*] **joy? Rav Yitzchak says: This** is referring to the **burnt ashes** that are customarily placed **on the head** [*rosh*] **of bridegrooms** at the time of their wedding celebrations, to remember the desolation. **Rav Pappa said to Abaye: Where are they placed?** Abaye replied: **On** the **place** where ***tefillin*** are placed, **as it is stated: "To appoint to them that mourn in Zion, to give to them an** object of **splendor** [*pe'er*] **in place of ashes"** (*Yeshayahu* 61:3). Since *tefillin* are referred to as an object splendor (see *Yechezkel* 24:17), it may be inferred from this verse that the ashes were placed in the same place as the *tefillin*.

The ***Sefer HaMichtam*** cites an alternative practice of placing a black cloth on the heads of the bride and groom and breaking a cup. He explains that this practice developed in places where people did not usually lay *tefillin*. The ashes normally used for a groom are designed to replace the *tefillin* that is placed there. But if *tefillin* is not normally worn, there was concern that if ashes are placed, the prophecy in *Yeshayahu* that the ashes will be replaced by an object of splendor will also not be fulfilled.

42. ספר המכתם | תענית ל.

ויש מקומות שלא נהגו לתת אפר בראש חתנים, אלא פורסין על ראש החתן והכלה מפה שחורה זכר לזה. וכן מנהג שבירת הכוס הוא בשביל זה, כמעשה דראש פרק אין עומדין (ברכות לא.) דתבר כסא דזוגיתא קמיהו. וכן נהגו בעיר נרבונה.

ו Sefer HaMichtam, Ta'anit 30a

There are places where they do not customarily place ashes on the bridegroom's head; rather, they spread a black cloth over the heads of the bride and groom in remembrance of [**the desolation**]. **Likewise, the custom of breaking the cup is for the same reason**, similar to the case at the beginning of chapter *Ein Omdin* (*Berachot* 31a), where [Rav Ashi] broke a glass cup in front of [the students, to limit their joy].[16] This is also the practice in the city of Narbonne.

16. The Gemara there relates that Rav Ashi observed his students acting a bit too frivolous at his son's wedding, so he broke an expensive glass cup to temper their mood. See Tosafot, who write that this is the source for the custom to break a glass cup at weddings. Tosafot appear to understand the purpose as ensuring that the joy at weddings does not exceed reasonable

ושמענו כי לכך נמנעו הראשונים מלתת האפר בראש החתנים, מפני שאין העם מוחזקים כלל בהנחת תפלין, ולא יהיה אפר תחת פאר, יחושו שמא לא יהיה גם כן פאר תחת אפר, ולכך קבעו הנדון אחר במקום.

We have heard that the earlier authorities refrained from placing the ashes on the heads of bridegrooms because the people were not at all used to laying *tefillin*, and the ashes would not be in place of an object of "splendor" [i.e., *tefillin*], people may be concerned that similarly there will be no object of splendor in place of the ashes [i.e., our mourning for the desolation will not be replaced by joy in the future]. Therefore, they established an alternative practice in the same place.

The ***Beit Yosef*** (O.C. 560) quotes this custom in the name of the ***Kol Bo***. However, the **Rema** reports that in his city, the custom was to place ashes on the head of the bridegroom, together with breaking an earthenware cup used for the *beracha* on *eirusin*.

43. דרכי משה | או"ח תקס:ב

ובעירנו נהגו בשתיהן נותנין אפר על ראש החתן וגם החתן משבר הכוס שמברכין עליו ברכת האירוסין, ולכן נהגו לברך ברכת האירוסין על כוס של חרס.

א Darkei Moshe, Orach Chaim 560:2

In our city, both are practiced. We place ashes on the head of the bridegroom, and the bridegroom also breaks the cup over which the *beracha* on *eirusin* is recited. Therefore, it is customary to recite the *beracha* on *eirusin* over an earthenware cup.[17]

The ***Shulchan Aruch*** also codifies the custom of placing ashes on the head of the bridegroom.

44. שולחן ערוך | או"ח תקס:ב

...וכשהחתן נושא אשה, לוקח אפר מקלה ונותן בראשו במקום הנחת תפילין.

הגה: ויש מקומות שנהגו לשבר כוס בשעת חופה, או לשום מפה שחורה או שאר דברי אבילות בראש החתן.

א Shulchan Aruch, Orach Chaim 560:2

...When a bridegroom marries a woman, he takes burnt ashes and places them on his head in the place where *tefillin* are laid.

Rema: In some places it is customary to break a cup at the time of the *chuppa* or to place a black cloth or other items of mourning on the head of the bridegroom.

However, in some communities, the custom cited by the *Sefer HaMichtam* persisted. The ***Aruch HaShulchan*** writes that where he lived, these alternative customs replaced placing ashes on the head of the bridegroom.

45. ערוך השולחן | או"ח תקס:ו

ואצלינו המנהג במקום אפר מקלה לשבר הכוס בשעת החופה או לשום מפה שחורה או שאר דברי אבלות בראש החתן.

א Aruch HaShulchan, Orach Chaim 560:6

In our place, instead of [placing] burnt ashes [on the head of the bridegroom], the custom is to break the glass at the time of the wedding, or to place a black cloth or other item of mourning on the head of the bridegroom.

---

limits, but they do not specifically identify the custom as a "*zeicher l'churban.*" By contrast, the *Sefer HaMichtam* here and the Meiri (*Ta'anit* 30b) explicitly mention that the cup is broken as a *zeicher l'churban*, as does the Rema cited below.

17. This is because earthenware cups can be broken, unlike metal cups, and are inexpensive, unlike the glasses of their times.

The ***Piskei Teshuvot*** writes that today, the custom of placing ashes on the bridegroom's head has again become widespread.

Piskei Teshuvot, Orach Chaim 560:8

Regarding placing ashes on the bridegroom's head, the custom to be particular about this has already become widespread, although some have the practice of removing the ashes immediately afterwards. It is a proper custom for the one who places the ashes on the bridegroom's head to recite the verse, "If I forget you, Jerusalem, let my right hand forget its skill… If I do not set Jerusalem above my highest joy," and the bridegroom repeats it after him.

46. פסקי תשובות | או"ח תקס:ח

ובענין להניח אפר בראש החתן כבר נתפשט המנהג להקפיד על כך, אם כי יש הנוהגים שמיד מסלקים את האפר, ומנהג נכון הוא שהמניח האפר בראש החתן יאמר הפסוק "אם אשכחך ירושלים תשכח ימיני וכו' אם לא אעלה את ירושלים על ראש שמחתי" והחתן אומר אחריו.

It appears, however, that this is not necessarily the case in Sephardic communities. The ***Kaf HaChaim*** writes that in his time it was not customary to place ashes on the head of the bridegroom.

א Kaf HaChaim, Orach Chaim 560:21

He takes burnt ashes, etc. – Now it is not customary to observe any of these practices, except to break the cup at the time of the *chuppa* after the *beracha* over *kiddushin* and *sheva berachot*.

47. כף החיים | או"ח תקס:כא

לוקח אפר מקלה וכו' – ועכשיו לא נהגו לעשות שום גם אחד מאלו אלא לשבר את הכוס בשעת חופה אחר ברכת קידושין ושבע ברכות.

Rav Ben Zion Abba Shaul expresses surprise at this practice and writes that one should certainly observe the custom instituted by Chazal to place ashes on the head of the bridegroom.

Responsa Ohr L'tzion 3:30, n. 2

This matter is astonishing: How can the institution of the Sages mentioned in the Gemara, to place burnt ashes [on the head of the bridegroom] under the *chuppa*, be replaced by something not mentioned in the Gemara as an institution of the Sages in remembrance of the desolation?… **Therefore, one should not refrain from placing burnt ashes on the head of the bridegroom.** One should take paper and burn it a little, and place some of the ashes on the head of the bridegroom in the place where *tefillin* are laid. In order to fulfill the institution of the Sages, it is sufficient [to leave the ashes there] for one moment, and afterwards one may remove it.

48. שו"ת אור לציון | ג:ל, הערה ב

והדבר תמוה. כיצד יפטור את תקנת חכמים המוזכרת בתלמוד ליתן אפר מקלה תחת החופה על ידי דבר שלא מוזכר בתלמוד שהוא תקנת חכמים זכר לחרבן... **ועל כן למעשה אין להמנע מליתן אפר מקלה על ראש החתן.** ויקחו נייר וישרפוהו מעט, ויתנו מהאפר על ראש החתן במקום הנחת תפילין. ודי ברגע אחד כדי לקיים תקנת חכמים, ואחר כך יכולים להסירו.

On the other hand, **Rav Ovadia Yosef** writes that there is no need for Sephardim to restore this custom.[18]

18. *Chazon Ovadia, Arba Ta'aniyot, Hilchot Zeicher L'churban Beit HaMikdash*, n. 2.

Regarding the custom of breaking a cup, the ***Mishna Berura*** explains that since this achieves the purpose of directing attention to the desolation, this does not violate the prohibition against destructive acts. For the same reason, it is customary to break a plate at an engagement.

א Mishna Berura, Orach Chaim 560:9

To break a cup at the time of the *chuppa* – This is also the reason for breaking a vessel at the time of the writing of the *tenai'im* [the engagement contract]. It appears [correct] to break a whole cup under the *chuppa*, and this does not [violate] *bal tashchit* [the prohibition against destructive acts], since one does this in order to hint at an ethical principle, so that people should pay attention.

49. משנה ברורה | או"ח תקס:ט

לשבר כוס בשעת חופה – וזו היא גם כן הטעם של שבירת כלי בשעת כתיבת התנאים. ויראה לשבור תחת החופה כוס שלם, ואין בו משום בל תשחית, כיון שעושין כן לרמז מוסר למען יתנו לב.

The ***Piskei Teshuvot*** observes that the widespread contemporary practice is to break a plate at an engagement and a glass at a wedding, and he offers one explanation for the symbolic distinction between them.

Piskei Teshuvot, Orach Chaim 560:9

...Many reasons have been given as to why, at the *tena'im*, we break an earthenware plate, while under the *chuppa* we break a glass. The simple reason is that at the *tena'im*, the breaking is in order to startle and to remind people that the joy is not complete in this time, and for this purpose a simple earthenware dish suffices. At the wedding, however, the reason for the breaking is so as not to increase joy excessively, and to include a little sadness, as our joy is not complete in this time. Therefore, a glass is taken, and indeed it should be a somewhat valuable cup so as to sadden the celebrants.[19]

50. פסקי תשובות | או"ח תקס:ט

...והרבה טעמים נאמרו מדוע שוברים בתנאים צלחת של חרס ותחת החופה כוס זכוכית, ובפשטות, הטעם, כי בתנאים השבירה היא כדי להבהיל ולזכור שאין השמחה במלואה בזמן הזה, ודי לזה בקדירת חרס פשוטה. מה שאין כן בחתונה – טעם השבירה כדי לא להרבות בשמחה יתירה ולהכניס עצבות קצת כי אין שמחתנו שלימה בזמן הזה, ולפיכך לוקחים כוס זכוכית, ואכן צריך שתהיה הכוס יקרה קצת כדי להעציב את בעלי השמחה.

Rav Avigdor Nebenzahl objects to the practice of making the broken pieces into a memento.

B'Yitzchak Yikarei to Mishna Berura 560:9

It is not proper to make a picture or the like from the broken pieces as a memento, as the purpose of the broken pieces is to cause loss, not decoration.

51. ביצחק יקרא | למשנה ברורה תקס:ט

אין ראוי לעשות מהשברים תמונה וכו' למזכרת, כי השברים מיועדים להפסד ולא לנוי.

---

19. It should be noted that contemporary practice follows the *Sha'arei Teshuva* (560:2), citing *Even HaShoham*, that specifically a glass cup should be broken. This differs from the *Darkei Moshe* cited above (source 43), who writes that an earthenware cup was broken in his time. See also *Yalkut Yosef* (*Sova Semachot*, vol. 1, 11:3), who writes that although ideally a glass cup is broken, an earthenware cup, or any other type of expensive cup, may also be used if necessary, based on the comment of the *Darkei Moshe*.

RABBI AVIGDOR HALEVI NEBENZAHL (B. 1935)

Rav Avidgor Yechezkel HaLevi Nebenzahl was born in 1935 to Yitzchak (who would become the Comptroller of the State of Israel in 1961) and Hilda (née Hollander) Nebenzahl. In his youth, he learned in Yeshivat Chorev, and thereafter in Kol Torah (where he became a close disciple of Rav Shlomo Zalman Auerbach), Ponevezh, and Mir.

He served in the IDF as a combat medic in the rabbinic corps for tending to casualties and burial, as well as in reserve duty during the Yom Kippur War and the First Lebanon War (1982). In later years, he also volunteered with Zaka.

Between 1973 and 2008, Rav Nebenzahl served as the Chief Rabbi of the Old City of Jerusalem. In parallel, he taught in several yeshivot, including Yeshivat Hakotel and Yeshivat Netiv Aryeh. His writings include responsa; reconstructions of the weekly discourses that he gave on the *parsha*; *Yerushalayim B'Mo'adeha*, collections of writings and rulings related to the major holidays; and the *B'Yitzchak Yikarei* edition of the *Mishna Berura* with his notes.

Once the glass is broken under the *chuppa* and the remembrance of the desolation is concluded, it is customary to shout "*Mazel tov!*" as the celebrations now begin. However, **Rav Yitzchak Yosef** writes that one should wait a few moments, so that it is clear that this blessing is not connected to the breaking of the cup.

52. ילקוט יוסף | שובע שמחות חלק א', יא:ב

מנהג שבירת הכוס בגמר השבע ברכות שתחת החופה, נועד לשם עגמת נפש על חרבן בית מקדשינו, ולהעלות את ירושלים על ראש שמחתינו. ולכן אין להכריז "מזל טוב" מיד בעת שבירת הכוס, אבל ימתינו איזה רגעים אחר שבירת הכוס, ורק כאשר סיימו את מעמד החופה, אומרים לחתן ולכלה "מזל טוב", באופן שלא ייראה שאמירת מזל טוב קשורה לשבירת הכוס.

Yalkut Yosef, Sova Semachot Vol. 1, 11:2

The custom of breaking the cup at the conclusion of the *sheva berachot* under the *chuppa* is intended as an expression of grief over the destruction of our *Beit Mikdash*, and to place Jerusalem above our highest joy. Therefore, one should not call out "*Mazel tov*" immediately at the moment of the breaking of the cup. Rather, people should wait a few moments after breaking the cup, and only once the *chuppa* ceremony has concluded should they say "*Mazel tov*" to the bride and groom, so that it not appear as though the "*Mazel tov*" greeting is connected to the breaking of the cup.[20]

20. This source assumes that the cup is broken at the conclusion of the *chuppa*, following the recitation of *sheva berachot*. This is the approach of the Rema (E.H. 65:3) and other *poskim*. However, some maintain that the cup should be broken after the betrothal is performed, before the *ketuba* is read (e.g., *Siddur Derech HaChaim*; see also *HaNisuin K'hilchatam* 12:69 for further sources). This subject will be discussed further in a future *Tzurba M'Rabanan* volume on *Even Ha'Ezer*.

Music

Among the enactments instituted by Chazal to commemorate the *churban* is one limiting the singing and playing of music, an enactment that carries particular significance today. Unlike other expressions of *zeicher l'churban*, which arise only on limited occasions, music accompanies daily life and is listened to regularly by many people. The **Mishna** and **Gemara (*Masechet Sota*)** state that once the Sanhedrin ceased to function,[21] song was no longer permitted during feasts where wine is served. This is derived from verses in *Yeshayahu*.

53. מסכת סוטה מח.

משנה: משבטלה סנהדרין – בטל השיר מבית המשתאות, שנאמר (ישעיהו כד, ט): "בַּשִּׁיר לֹא יִשְׁתּוּ יָיִן" וגו'...

גמרא: וממאי דמשבטלה סנהדרי כתיב? אמר רב הונא בריה דרב יהושע, דאמר קרא (איכה ה, יד): "זְקֵנִים מִשַּׁעַר שָׁבָתוּ בַּחוּרִים מִנְּגִינָתָם"!

אמר רב: אודנא דשמעא זמרא תעקר. אמר רבא: זמרא בביתא חורבא בסיפא, שנאמר (צפניה ב, יד): "קוֹל יְשׁוֹרֵר בַּחַלּוֹן חֹרֶב בַּסַּף כִּי אַרְזָה עֵרָה".

ח Masechet Sota 48a

MISHNA: From the time **when the Sanhedrin ceased, song was** also **nullified from the places of feasts,**[22] i.e., it was no longer permitted to sing at a feast where wine was served, **as it is stated: "With song they shall not drink wine"** (*Yeshayahu* 24:9)...

GEMARA: From where is it derived **that** the verse: "With song they shall not drink wine" **is written** about the period **from** the time **when the Sanhedrin was nullified? Rav Huna, son of Rav Yehoshua, said:** From **that** which **the verse states: "The Elders have ceased from the gate, the young men from their music"** (*Eicha* 5:14). This indicates that the dissolution of the Sanhedrin, who are the Elders from the gate, is linked to the end of the young men singing.[23]

Rav said: The **ear that hears song should be uprooted,** as it is prohibited to listen to music after the destruction of the Temple.[24] **Rava said:** If there is **song in a house** there will be **destruction on the threshold, as it is stated: "Voices shall sing in the windows; desolation shall be in the doorposts; for its cedar work shall be uncovered"** (*Tzefania* 2:14). The word "uncovered" [*era*] could be read to mean: Its city [*ira*].[25]

---

21. See *Rosh Hashana* 31b and Rashi there, that the Sanhedrin ceased to function in the time of Rabbi Yehuda HaNasi, which was after the destruction of the *Beit HaMikdash*. See, however, *Meromei Sadeh* to this Mishna, which suggests that the time referred to here is when the Sanhedrin was exiled from the Temple Mount, which took place forty years before the destruction of the *Beit HaMikdash*.
22. Although we have translated the Hebrew word משתה as "feast," the root שתה means drinking, and the word משתה refers to a feast in which the drinking of wine is a significant element.
23. The Meiri, citing the *Yerushalmi* (*Sota* 9:12), explains that as long as the Sanhedrin functioned, its authority instilled a sense of fear that restrained people from incorporating coarse, debased, or morally degrading speech into their songs [*divrei nevala*]. Once the Sanhedrin ceased to function, this restraint was lost, giving rise to concern that songs not directed toward the praise of Hashem would devolve into such content.
24. Although the Mishna and Gemara above linked not listening to music to the Sanhedrin, many other sources assume that it is also related to the *churban*, as will be evident from the continuation of the *shiur*.
25. The Gemara goes on to explain this to mean that that even a house interlaced with cedars that are as strong as a city, it will become unstable [*mitroe'a*] if song is heard there.

Elsewhere, the **Gemara (*Masechet Gittin*)** derives from an additional verse that song is prohibited even without any musical instruments.

Masechet Gittin 7a

54. מסכת גיטין ז.

שלחו ליה למר עוקבא: זמרא מנא לן דאסיר? שרטט וכתב להו: אל תשמח ישראל אל גיל בעמים.

ולישלח להו מהכא: בשיר לא ישתו יין ימר שכר לשותיו! אי מההוא, הוה אמינא הני מילי זמרא דמנא, אבל דפומא שרי, קמשמע לן.

They sent the following question **to Mar Ukva: From where do we** derive that **music is forbidden** in the present, following the destruction of the Temple? **He scored** parchment[26] **and wrote to them: "Rejoice not, O Israel, to exultation, like the peoples"** (*Hoshea* 9:1).

The Gemara asks: **Let him send them** a response **from here: "With song they shall not drink wine; strong drink is bitter to them who drink it,"** indicating that song is no longer allowed. The Gemara answers: **If** he had answered **by** citing **that** verse, **I would say** that **this matter** applies only to **instrumental music,** in accordance with the previous verse: "The joy of drums ceases, the noise of them who rejoice ends, the joy of the harp ceases" (*Yeshayahu* 24:8); **however, vocal** song is **permitted.** Therefore, Mar Ukva **teaches us** that all types of song are forbidden.

Rashi explains that like the Mishna and Gemara in *Masechet Sota*, this passage in *Masechet Gittin* also refers to song during feasts where wine is served.

Rashi, Masechet Gittin 7a

55. רש"י | גיטין ז.

זמרא – לשורר בבית המשתאות.

Song – To sing in places of feasts [where wine is served].

Tosafot concur with Rashi but add that it is proper to avoid any singing that brings excessive enjoyment, unless this is for the purposes of a mitzva, such as at a wedding.

Tosafot, Masechet Gittin 7a

56. תוספות | גיטין ז.

זמרא מנא לן דאסור – פירש בקונטרס לשורר בבית המשתאות וכן משמע... וראוי להחמיר בכיוצא דההוא בירושלמי דהוה קאים ודמיך בזמרא שמתענג ביותר ושיר של מצוה שרי כגון בשעת חופה שעושין לשמח חתן וכלה.

From where do we derive that music is forbidden – Rashi explains [that this refers to] singing in places of feasts [where wine is served], and this is also implied [by the Gemara here and in *Masechet Sota*]... But it is proper to be stringent regarding cases similar to that in the *Yerushalmi*,[27] where [the Exilarch] would arise and lie down while music [was played, and Mar Ukva told him that this was not appropriate], as this is excessive enjoyment. Songs for [the sake of] a mitzva, such as to bring joy to a bride and groom at the time of the *chuppa*, are permitted.

---

26. Earlier, the Gemara explains that one must score the page [*sirtut*] whenever one writes three or four words or more from Tanach. The related halachot are complicated and beyond the scope of this *shiur*.

27. *Megilla* 3:2.

According to Rashi and Tosafot, singing both with and without instruments is forbidden during feasts with wine, while singing in other contexts would be permitted. According to Tosafot, even singing without instruments should be avoided when this brings excessive enjoyment.

The **Rambam** implies that whereas vocal song is only prohibited in places where wine is served, playing musical instruments is prohibited in all places.[28] Nevertheless, he notes that the custom is to permit singing praises of Hashem and thanksgiving songs, even while drinking wine.

57. רמב"ם | הל' תעניות ה:יד

וכן גזרו שלא לנגן בכלי שיר כולם. וכל מיני זמר, וכל משמיעי קול של שיר אסור לשמוח בהן ואסור לשמען מפני החורבן, ואפילו שירה בפה על היין אסורה שנאמר (ישעיהו כד, ט): "בַּשִּׁיר לֹא יִשְׁתּוּ יָיִן". וכבר נהגו כל ישראל לומר דברי תשבחות או שיר של הודאות לאל וכיוצא בהן על היין.

Rambam, Hilchot Ta'aniyot 5:14

Similarly, they decreed that one should not play any musical instrument.[29] Celebrating with all types of song and all producers of musical sound is prohibited, and hearing them is prohibited, because of the desolation. Even vocal song is prohibited over wine, as is stated (*Yeshayahu* 24:9): "Do not drink wine with song." It has, [however,] become the accepted custom among the entire Jewish People to recite words of praise, songs of thanksgiving to God and the like, over wine.[30]

However, in a responsum, the **Rambam** appears to rule more stringently and prohibits even vocal singing in all places.

58. שו"ת הרמב"ם | סימן רכד

שעצם הזמר והניגונים כלם אסורים, אפילו אין אומרים עליהם מלים כלל, לאומרם זה לשונם: אודנא דשמעא זמרא תעקר. וכבר באר התלמוד שאין הבדל בין שמיעת הזמר או ניגון על מיתרים או השמעת הנעימות בלא מלים, אלא כל מה שמביא לידי שמחת הנפש והתרגשותה, אסור, כמו שאמרו, וסמכו דבריהם אל איסור הנביא, אל תשמח ישראל אל גיל כעמים.

וטעם זה ברור מאד, לפי שכוח תאוה זה צריך לכובשו ולמונעו ולמשוך ברסנו, ולא שיפעל ויחיה מתו...

Responsa of the Rambam, Siman 224

The actual song and melodies are all prohibited, even if no words are sung at all, as they said, "The ear that hears music should be uprooted." The Gemara already explained that there is no difference between hearing song and melody on stringed instruments or playing tunes without words; rather, anything that brings a person to joy or excitement is prohibited, as they said, and they based their words on the prophet's prohibition: "Rejoice not, O Israel, to exultation, like the peoples."

The reason for this is very clear, as one must conquer, prevent and restrain this power of desire, not allow it to act and be resurrected...

---

28. See *Yad Peshuta* who explains that this distinction is based on the different words used by Chazal. Song (שיר) can mean vocal singing alone, and this is prohibited specifically while drinking wine. Music (זמר) is prohibited everywhere – this term always implies musical instruments and not vocal singing alone, and is prohibited everywhere.
29. We have followed the text of the Rambam appearing in Rav Kapach's edition and other accurate editions of the Rambam, based on all of the early manuscripts. Although the word כולם does not appear in most printed versions of the Rambam, this makes it difficult to understand the precise meaning.
30. Since the decree against song over wine was not accepted by the people in relation to songs of praise and thanksgiving to Hashem, the decree became null and void in this respect (*Yad Peshuta*, see *Hilchot Mamrim* 2:6).

שאין הבדל בין הדיבורים העבריים לדיבורים הערביים, ואין זה אסור או מותר אלא לפי העניין הכלול באותם הדיבורים. ואליבא דאמת אסור לשמוע דבר טפשות, אפילו נאמר שלא בשירה, ואם מנגנים אותו על כלים, יש כאן שלשה איסורים, איסור שמיעת דבר טפשות ונבלות הפה איסור שמיעת שירה, רוצה לומר זמרא בפומא, ואיסור שמיעת מיתרים. ואם זה במקום שתיית יין, יש איסור רביעי, והוא אומרו יתעלה והיה כנור ונבל תוף וחליל ויין משתיהם. ואם המזמרת אשה, יש שם איסור חמישי, לאומרם ז"ל קול באשה ערוה, ומכל שכן אם היא מזמרת.

There is no difference between Hebrew lyrics and Arabic lyrics; the matter is only prohibited or permitted because of the content of the words. In truth, hearing foolish talk is prohibited even if it is not sung; if it is played with instruments, three prohibitions are [violated]: the prohibition against hearing foolishness and vulgar speech, the prohibition of hearing song, meaning vocal music, and the prohibition against hearing instrumental music. If this is accompanied by drinking wine, there is a fourth prohibition, as it says: "The harp, the lute, the drum, and the flute, and wine at their feasts…" (*Yeshayahu* 5:12). If the singer is a woman, there is a fifth prohibition, as Chazal say: "The voice of a woman is *erva* [a prohibited source of sensuality]," and certainly if she is singing.

The ***Yad Peshuta*** explains that here the Rambam speaks of songs with content that can lead a person's thoughts astray. Singing or listening to these songs is always prohibited, irrespective of remembering the desolation.

According to the printed version of Tosafot (quoted above in source 56), strictly speaking, listening to song or music is prohibited only during feasts with wine. However, the ***Tur*** cites Tosafot as ruling that listening to song or music on a regular basis is prohibited even outside the context of a feast.[31]

59. טור | או"ח תקס

Tur, Orach Chaim 560

והתוספות מפרשים דאפילו בלא משתה נמי, ודוקא למי שרגיל בכך כההיא דאיתא בירושלמי, "ריש גלותא הוה קאים ודמיך בזמרא," פירוש: בשכבו ובקומו היו מזמרין לפניו.

Tosafot explain that [song or music is prohibited] even without a feast, but only for one who regularly listens, like the case in the *Yerushalmi*, "The Exilarch would arise and lie down while music [was played]," meaning that they would play music before him when he lay down and when he arose.

The ***Orchot Chaim*** adopts a particularly stringent position, ruling that the use of musical instruments is prohibited in all circumstances, even for praises of Hashem. He understands this prohibition as biblical in nature.

60. אורחות חיים | הל' תשעה באב יד

Orchot Chaim, Hilchot Tisha B'av 14

וזמרא דמנא לעולם אסור בכל מקום ואפילו על ידי שבחות של הקדוש ברוך הוא ואסורן מן התורה דכתיב אל תשמח ישראל אלא גיל כעמים וכו' ודברי קבלה כדברי תורה דמי.

Instrumental music is always forbidden in all situations, even for praises of Hashem, and the prohibition is biblical, as it is stated: "Rejoice not, O Israel, to exultation, like the peoples, etc." Matters of *kabbala* [i.e., *Nevi'im* and *Ketuvim*] are like matters of the Torah.

---

31. See, however, Responsa *Igrot Moshe* (O.C. 1:166) who writes that the printed version of Tosafot should also be understood in accordance with the *Tur*, as both listening to music together with wine and listening to music on a regular basis are considered excessive enjoyment.

The ***Shulchan Aruch*** rules in accordance with the Rambam (in *Hilchot Ta'aniyot*). The **Rema** also cites the view of Tosafot as quoted by the *Tur*, that the prohibition applies only to listening to song or music regularly, or during a feast where wine is served.

61. שולחן ערוך | או"ח תקס:ג

וכן גזרו שלא לנגן בכלי שיר וכל מיני זמר וכל משמיעי קול של שיר לשמוח בהם. (**הגה:** ויש אומרים דוקא מי שרגיל בהם, כגון המלכים שעומדים ושוכבים בכלי שיר או בבית המשתה.) ואסור לשומעם מפני החורבן; ואפילו שיר בפה על היין, אסורה שנאמר: "בשיר לא ישתו יין".

וכבר נהגו כל ישראל לומר דברי תשבחות או שיר של הודאות וזכרון חסדי הקדוש ברוך הוא, על היין.

הגה: וכן לצורך מצוה, כגון, בבית חתן וכלה, הכל שרי.

א Shulchan Aruch, Orach Chaim 560:3

Similarly, they decreed that one should not play musical instruments. Celebrating with all types of song and all producers of musical sound [is prohibited]. (**Rema:** Some say that this [prohibition applies] only for one who listens to them regularly, like the kings who arise and lie down to the sound of musical instruments, or in the place of a feast [where wine is served][32]), and hearing them is prohibited, because of the desolation. Even vocal song is prohibited over wine, as is stated: "Do not drink wine with song."

It has, [however,] become the accepted custom among the entire Jewish People to recite words of praise, songs of thanksgiving, and remembrance of the benevolence of Hashem, over wine.

Rema: Similarly, for mitzva purposes, such as in the home of a bride and groom [during the week after marriage], this is all permitted.

According to the *Shulchan Aruch*, playing or listening to instrumental music is generally prohibited due to the *churban*. Vocal singing over wine is likewise prohibited, while vocal songs of praise to Hashem are permitted even over wine. Instrumental music is permitted only in the context of a *seudat mitzva*.

According to the Rema, the prohibition is more limited. Music is prohibited only when listened to on a regular basis or in the context of a feast accompanied by wine, where the enjoyment is heightened.[33]

Rav Moshe Feinstein rules that even for Ashkenazim, who generally follow the Rema, listening to instrumental music is prohibited in all settings, including through the radio, in accordance with the Rambam and the *Shulchan Aruch*. He argues that even Rashi and Tosafot, upon whom the Rema bases his lenient ruling, may ultimately agree with the Rambam. Therefore, one should rule stringently.

Rav Moshe further adds that even those who generally rely on lenient opinions should act stringently during the period of *sefirat ha'omer*.[34]

---

32. The Rema here means to say that the prohibition of music is limited to either when it is played regularly, like the kings, or when played at a feast with wine (aside from a *seudat mitzva*). In the second case, the Rema agrees with the *Shulchan Aruch* that even singing without musical instruments is prohibited (see *Mishna Berura* 12). However, see *Sha'ar HaTziun* 23 that perhaps a meal with food and wine is not defined as a *mishteh*, and is not included within the prohibition.
33. The *Bach* takes an even more stringent position that vocal music is always prohibited, based on the continuation of the passage in *Sota* 48a, which discusses singing while working (see *Magen Avraham* and *Mishna Berura* 560:13, who also cite it).
34. The subject of listening to music during *sefirat ha'omer* was discussed at length in *shiur* 5 and relates closely to the material here. It may be worthwhile to review the discussion there again after studying this section.

62. שו"ת אגרות משה | או"ח א:קסו

...ובזמרא דמנא אסור בכל מקום שכן סובר הרמב"ם והמחבר, ולמה שבארתי אפשר שגם רש"י ותוספות לא פליגי לכן אף שהרמ"א והדברי חמודות סברי שפליגי ומתירין שלא בבית משתה ואינו רגיל יש להחמיר אף שהוא איסור דרבנן...

ועל ידי הרדיו אם נשמע זמרא דפומא מותר ואם בכלי זמר אסור. ובימי ספירה יש לאסור בזמרא דמנא אף להמתירין.

Responsa Igrot Moshe, Orach Chaim 1:166

...**Instrumental music is prohibited everywhere**, as this is the view of the Rambam and the *Shulchan Aruch*, and according to that which I have explained, it is possible that even Rashi and Tosafot do not dispute this.[35] Therefore, although the Rema and the *Divrei Chamudot* understand that they dispute this and permit music other than in a feast [where wine is served] or on a regular basis, one should act stringently although this is a rabbinic prohibition...

Listening to vocal music on the radio is permitted, but instrumental music is prohibited. During *sefirat ha'omer*, one should prohibit instrumental music even for those who [otherwise] act leniently.

These rulings raise a major question today, when music is a very significant part of our lives and found ubiquitously in the modern world. According to the *Shulchan Aruch*, which is usually followed by Sephardim, it would seem that one should not even listen to Jewish music except for at a festive celebration, such as a wedding. Although the Rema is more lenient, according to Rav Moshe, even Ashkenazim should abide by this stringent ruling. Even according to the Rema, listening to music is problematic when done on a constant basis, which is often the case today for many people. Does the halacha, in fact, require refraining from listening to music?

Some *poskim*, such as **Rav Eliezer Waldenberg** and **Rav Ben Zion Abba Shaul,** assume that listening to music would be permitted at least according to the Rema, since he forbids only when listening similar to the manner of the kings.[36] However, according to the *Shulchan Aruch*, it might still be forbidden.

Rav Ovadia Yosef argues that there is a basis for leniency even for those who follow the opinion of the *Shulchan Aruch*. He infers that the Meiri permits all forms of music when they are used for praising Hashem. Since many *Rishonim* limit the prohibition of music to festive meals accompanied by wine, Rav Ovadia contends that it is possible to combine these lenient views to permit listening to appropriate Jewish music.

Rav Ovadia further cites an additional factor for leniency regarding recorded music, based on **Rav Yaakov Breisch** in *Chelkat Yaakov*. Rav Breisch argues that recorded music, such as radio broadcasts, was not included in the original rabbinic decree, as this form of listening did not exist at the time. Since the listener neither sees the musicians nor hears them directly, this form of music constitutes a new category.

Rav Ovadia concludes that all would agree that even live music is permitted at a wedding meal, or any *se'udat mitzva*.

---

35. Earlier in the responsum, he explains that the Rambam understood the Gemara in a novel way, and Rashi and Tosafot do not explicitly contradict this interpretation.

36. See Responsa *Tzitz Eliezer* (15:33) and *Ohr L'tzion* (3:30:3). Although, as mentioned above, many today do listen to music on a regular basis, one could argue that the Rema, based on Tosafot, refers to fixing a set time every day specifically for listening to music. Most people today who listen to music do so while also engaging in other tasks and do not set a time for listening to music alone. Alternatively, it may refer to listening or playing for a large part of the day or non-stop for the entire day, which is often not the case (see *Peninei Halakha, Ha'Am V'ha'aretz* 9:11).

Responsa Yechaveh Da'at 1:45

However, the Meiri (*Gittin* 7a) writes: "Listening to and enjoying all forms of music for the purpose of revelry and not for praising Hashem, but rather in a frivolous manner and for pleasure with food and drink is prohibited, whether the music is produced by musical instruments or by vocal song. However, anything that contains praise and glory of Hashem, such as *piyutim* [liturgical poems] or psalms, is permitted..." **From his words, it is clear that even with musical instruments, any music produced for praise and glory of Hashem, not in a lewd or frivolous way, is permitted...** Therefore, one who acts leniently in accordance with the Meiri has a basis to rely upon...

Furthermore, see **Responsa *Chelkat Yaakov* who writes** that there is a strong reason to permit [listening to music on the radio], since at the time they decreed to prohibit music, the radio did not exist, so the decree did not apply to it. Although all forms of music, even those that were introduced afterward, are included in the decree of Chazal, nonetheless, **with radio, where the musicians are not seen by the listeners[37] and the sound is heard from a distance, it is considered a new category and not included in the decree...**

It appears that according to all views, at a wedding meal, which is a *se'udat mitzva*, and there is a mitzva to make the bride and groom happy, it is permissible *lechatchila* to sing *piyutim*, songs, and praises to Hashem, accompanied with musical instruments... It also appears that the same applies to any mitzva celebration, such as a *brit mila*, *pidyon haben*, or the completion of a *masechet* [of Gemara]... Similarly, on *Chol HaMo'ed* it is permissible to play and rejoice with musical instruments... The same applies that it is permissible to play with musical instruments on Purim, which is a day of feasting and rejoicing...

In summary: Those who act leniently to listen to songs, praises, and thanksgiving to Hashem, from the radio or recordings, provided that they are not in a frivolous or revelrous manner, have a basis to rely upon, even though they are accompanied by musical instruments. Leave the Jews [to their own devices], and one who acts stringently will be blessed...

63. שו"ת יחוה דעת | א:מה

אולם מדברי המאירי (גיטין ז.) שכתב: כל מיני זמר העשויים לשמחת הוללות ושלא לכוין בהם לשבח השם יתברך, אלא דרך קלות ראש ותענוג במיני מאכל ומשתה, אסור לשומעו ולהשתעשע בו, בין כשנעשה הזמר בכלי שיר, בין בשירה על פה, ומכל מקום כל שיש בו שבח ותהלה להשם יתברך, כגון פיוטים ומזמורים, מותר... **מוכח שאף בכלי נגינה כל שנעשה דרך שבח ותהלה להשם יתברך, שלא בדרך פריצות וקלות ראש מותר...** ולכן המיקל כדברי המאירי יש לו על מה שיסמוך...

ועוד עיין **בשו"ת חלקת יעקב (סב:ב), שכתב** שיש סברא גדולה להתיר, שהואיל ובשעה שגזרו לאסור הזמר לא היה הרדיו בעולם, ולא חלה עליו הגזרה, ואף על פי שכל מיני זמר אפילו אלו שנתחדשו אחר כך נכללים בגזרת חז"ל, מכל מקום **ברדיו שאין המנגנים נראים לשומעים, והקול נשמע ממרחקים, נחשב כפנים חדשות ואינו בכלל הגזרה...**

ונראה שלכל הדעות בסעודת חתן וכלה שהיא סעודת מצוה, ומצוה לשמח חתן וכלה, מותר לכתחילה לומר פיוטים שירים ותשבחות להשם יתברך בכלי נגינה... ונראה עוד שהוא הדין לכל שמחת מצוה כגון ברית מילה או פדיון הבן או סיום מסכתא... וכן בחול המועד מותר לנגן ולשמוח בכלי שיר... והוא הדין שמותר לנגן בכלי שיר ביום פורים שהוא יום משתה ושמחה...

בסיכום: המקילים לשמוע מהרדיו או מהרשם קול שירות ותשבחות והודאות להשם יתברך, כל שאינם דרך קלות ראש והוללות, יש להם על מה שיסמוכו, ואף על פי שהם מלווים בכלי נגינה, והנח להם לישראל. והמחמיר תבוא עליו ברכה...

---

37. Based on this reasoning, this leniency would not apply to music broadcast on television or to music watched on platforms with video, such as YouTube.

שיש לצרף טעמו של החלקת יעקב הנ"ל שברדיו וכן ברשם קול יש מקום להקל יותר משאר כלי שיר שרואים אותם ושומעים מהם... שיש כעין ספק ספיקא, שמא הלכה כרוב הפוסקים שלא נאסר לשמוע כלי שיר אלא על היין, ואם תמצא לומר כדעת הרמב"ם... שמא ברדיו וברשם קול שאינם נראים לעין יש להקל כששומעם שלא על היין.

As one can combine [for leniency] the aforementioned reason of the *Chelkat Ya'akov*, that with the radio and a recording, there is room to be more lenient than with other musical instruments that one sees and hears… as there is a *safeik sefeika* (double doubt) of sorts: perhaps the halacha follows the majority of *poskim* [who rule] that listening to musical instruments is only prohibited together with wine, and even if one follows the view of the Rambam… perhaps with radio and recording, where [the music] is not seen, there is room to be lenient when one listens to them without wine.

The ***Piskei Teshuvot*** presents an additional contemporary basis for leniency applicable to both Ashkenazim and Sephardim. He notes that due to the emotional and psychological challenges of modern life, many contemporary *poskim* have justified listening to music for those who feel a genuine need.[38]

In addition, the *Piskei Teshuvot* explains that music that strengthens a person emotionally or draws them closer to Hashem is also included in this leniency. Nevertheless, he concludes that this approach is fundamentally a justification rather than an ideal, and that those who are able to refrain from listening to instrumental music are encouraged to do so.

64. פסקי תשובות | או"ח תקס:יא-יב

יא. ...ובזמננו נתפשט בין ההמונים לשמוע נגינה ושירה מכלים שונים, וכבר כתבו גדולי הפוסקים ללמד זכות על זה עקב חולשת הדורות והעצבים הרופפים, ושמיעת הניגונים מחזק הנפש, ובפרט לאנשים שטבעם נוטה לעצבות ומרה שחורה, שהרי היא להם בגדר רפואה ממש, ואיסור חז"ל הוא כשהכוונה לשם תענוג גרידא ולא לשם רפואה.

וכן שמיעת שירה המביאה לידי דביקות בה' יתברך וגורמת התעוררות הלב לעבודת ה' וליראת שמים בכלל ההיתר...

Piskei Teshuvot, Orach Chaim 560:11–12

11. **…In our times, it has become widespread among the masses to listen to music and song played on various instruments. The great *poskim* have already written to defend the grounds for leniency about this due to the weakness of the generations and the fragility of the nerves.** Listening to melodies strengthens the spirit,[39] especially for people whose nature inclines toward sadness and melancholy. For them, it is considered an actual form of healing, and the prohibition of Chazal applies when the intention is solely for pleasure and not for therapeutic purposes.

Similarly, listening to songs that bring a person to cleave to Hashem and that arouse the heart toward service of Hashem and fear of Heaven is included in the leniency…[40]

---

38. Another challenge to many contemporary Jewish music songs beyond the scope of this *shiur* arises based on the Gemara (*Sanhedrin* 101a), which strongly criticizes using *pesukim* for music. This passage is cited by the *Mishna Berura* and other *poskim*. Many contemporary *poskim* defend the common practice for a variety of reasons. See, e.g., Responsa *Igrot Moshe* (Y.D. 2:142); Responsa *Yabia Omer* (vol. 3, O.C. 15); *Piskei Teshuvot* (560:14); and Rav Chaim Jachter, *Gray Matter*, vol. 3, pp. 7–12, available online at www.sefaria.org.il/Gray_Matter_III.

39. See Responsa *Chelkat Ya'akov* (1:62), Responsa *Shevet Halevi* (6:69; 8:127) and Responsa *Mishneh Halachot* (6:106), who all suggest this line of reasoning that considering the fact that we live in challenging times and depression is fairly common in our community, one may listen to music to help raise his spirits.

40. This approach is suggested by the Responsa *Shevet HaLevi* (6:69).

However, all of the above is only [an ex post facto] justification. Therefore, Torah scholars and those who are scrupulous in mitzva observance should refrain from listening to instrumental music (unless it is needed for therapeutic purposes, as mentioned above). But vocal singing for the sake of joy in serving Hashem, or for devotion and arousal, or during study to stimulate thought and the like, is of no concern at all, and all the *gedolei hador* (great sages of the generations) practiced this…

אמנם כל הנ"ל הוא לימוד זכות, ולכן לתלמידי חכמים ואנשי מעשה המדקדקים במצוות, יש להימנע משמיעת ניגונים מכלי זמר (אלא אם כן צריך לכך לצורך רפואה וכנ"ל), אולם שירה בפה לצורך שמחה בעבודת ה', או דביקות והתעוררות, או בשעת הלימוד לעורר המחשבה וכדומה, אין חשש כלל, וכל גדולי הדורות נהגו בכך...

12. **Likewise, for the sake of a mitzva, such as at a wedding, everything is permitted.** Similarly, other mitzva celebrations, such as a *brit mila, pidyon haben*, bar mitzva, the seven days of feasting [after a wedding], *Chol Hamo'ed* and Purim, are all included in this leniency. Likewise, at *seudot mitzva* such as a *siyum* (completion of Torah study), the welcoming of a *sefer Torah*, and the like, there is no prohibition against instrumental music.

יב. **וכן לצורך מצוה כגון בבית חתן וכלה הכל שרי.** וכן בשאר שמחות של מצווה כברית מילה ופדיון הבן, בר מצוה, ושבעת ימי המשתה, חול המועד ופורים, הכל בכלל ההיתר. וכן בסעודות מצוה כסיומים והכנסת ספר תורה וכיוצא בזה אין איסור נגינה בכלי זמר.

Regarding gatherings held for fundraising and charity drives, it is uncertain whether they are considered "for the sake of a mitzva." It is preferable to act stringently, but one should not protest against those who act leniently.

ויש להסתפק בהתאספויות שעושין לצורך התרמה ומגביות לצרכי צדקה אם הם בכלל "צורך מצוה", וטוב להחמיר, אבל אין למחות ביד המקילים.

According to the approach that listening to songs that raise our spiritual sensitivities and connect us to God, one could argue that much of contemporary Jewish music is included in this category. Moreover, although this source still recommends being stringent for those who are able, others would allow in our generation *lechatchila* based on this reason and the others mentioned.[41]

41. See Responsa *Tzitz Eliezer*, loc cit. and Rav Yosef Zvi Rimon, "*Yemei Iyyar*," p. 125. It is worth noting that although we have seen that many contemporary *poskim* rule leniently with regard to listening to music, we saw in *shiur* 5 that during *sefirat ha'omer* (as well as the Three Weeks), many *poskim* rule strictly. The reason is that although there are multiple reasons why it may be necessary to be more lenient the rest of the year, but during sad portions of the Jewish calendar, it is appropriate to rule more strictly. For further discussion of the subject of music all year round, see Rav Aharon Kahn, "Music in Halachic Perspective," *Journal of Halacha and Contemporary Society*, Fall 1987, available online at www.yutorah.org/lectures/lecture.cfm/735711, and Rav Chaim Jachter, *Gray Matter*, vol. 3, pp. 1–6, available online at www.sefaria.org.il/Gray_Matter_III.

WHEN IS LISTENING TO MUSIC PERMITTED?

	With Wine	Without Wine
Musical Instruments	Prohibited even for mitzva purposes **(*Orchot Chaim*)**	Prohibited **(Rambam, *Shulchan Aruch*, Rav Moshe Feinstein)**
	Prohibited except for mitzva purposes **(Rav Ovadia Yosef)**	Prohibited on a regular basis **(*Tur*, Rema)**
		Permitted **(Rashi, Tosafot)**
Radio/ Recorded Music	Prohibited even for mitzva purposes **(*Orchot Chaim*)**	Prohibited **(Rav Moshe Feinstein)**
	Prohibited except for mitzva purposes **(Rav Ovadia Yosef)**	Permitted, although one who is stringent will be blessed **(Rav Ovadia Yosef)**
Vocal Song	Prohibited even for mitzva purposes **(*Orchot Chaim*)**	Permitted
	Prohibited except for mitzva purposes **(Rav Ovadia Yosef)**	

Forbidden Permitted Somewhere in-between

The Custom in Jerusalem

Some communities in Jerusalem have the custom, known as "*minhag Yerushalayim*," to be stringent regarding playing musical instruments even at weddings. The *sefer* ***Sha'arei Yerushalayim***[42] describes how this custom originally developed in Eretz Yisrael.

42. This *sefer*, written by Rav Moshe Reisher (1840–1880), compiles *midrashim* relating to Eretz Yisrael and describes the geography and customs of the country in the 19th century.

65. שערי ירושלים | שער ט, מנהגי הארץ

בכל ארץ ישראל אין מי שיודע לנגן בנבל וכנור, ואיזהו אנשים שבאו מחוץ לארץ לשם והיו מנגנים על החתונות אך לא האריכו ימים שמה, וזה כשתי שנים בא יודע נגן בכנור לעיר הקודש צפת ועשה שם אותו כשני חדשים וקראו אותו על החתונות, ואחר כך הלך לחוץ לארץ וחזר והביא אתו עמו כנור חדש קטן וכנור הגדול הנקרא (באס) וחליל הנקרא (קלארנעט) ולאחר שתי שבועות נפטר לבית עולמו **אז ראו בחוש שאסור לזמר בכנור בעת החרבן כמאמר רז"ל...**

בארץ ישראל יש חבורות משמחים חתן וכלה ויש להם תוף וכשיש חתונה בין עשיר ובין עני הולכים לשם ומכין בתוף ומרננים בפיהם בכל כחם, ורוקדים במחול בכל מיני שמחה עד אור הבוקר והם האשכנזים.

א Sha'arei Yerushalayim, Sha'ar 9, Minhagei Ha'Aretz

In all of Eretz Yisrael, there [was] no one who knew how to play the lyre or harp. There were some people who came from *chutz la'aretz* who would play at weddings, but they did not live long there. About two years ago, someone skilled at playing the harp came to the holy city of Tzfat and remained there for about two months, and they would call him to play at weddings. Afterwards, he went to *chutz la'aretz* and returned, and he brought with him a new small harp, and a large harp called bass, and a flute called clarinet. But after two weeks he passed away to the next world. **Then people saw clearly that playing the harp is prohibited during the time of the destruction, as Chazal said[43]...**

In Eretz Yisrael, there are groups who bring joy to the bridegroom and bride. They have a drum, and whenever there is a wedding, whether [from the] wealthy or the poor, they go there and beat the drum and sing with their mouths with all their strength, and they dance in circles with every kind of joy until the light of morning. This [is the practice of] the Ashkenazim.

Rav Yosef Chaim Zonnenfeld quotes Rav Yehoshua Leib Diskin, who rules that this custom should at least be observed in Jerusalem, where the desolation is most felt.

66. שו"ת שלמת חיים | עניינים שונים קב

נסתפקתי בענין למחות בכלי זמר בשמחת חתן וכלה, האם יש לומר דדוקא בימיו ז"ל שייך למחות אבל אחר כך שאני, ומשום דעיקר הדבר מוקשה להרבה משום קול באשה (מאחר דאין כלי זמר הוצרכו הנשים לזמר אצל הכלה)...

ל Responsa Salmat Chaim, Inyanim Shonim 102

[**Question:**] I was unsure whether to protest against musical instruments at the celebration of a bride and groom. Is it possible to say that it is only relevant to protest at the time [that the decree was made], but after this it is different? Since the principle decree is difficult for many [to observe] due to [violation of the prohibition against hearing] the voice of a woman (as since there are no musical instruments, women needed to sing around the bride)...

43. Although as we have seen, *Rishonim* permit music at a wedding, this leniency does not appear in the words of Chazal.

תשובה: כבר כתבתי שהגאון בעל אמרי בינה גזר על זה, **ושמעתי ממרנא הגאון דבריסק זצללה"ה שאמר בוודאי בירושלים ראוי על כל פנים**... והרי חורבן בית המקדש לעינינו.

Answer: I already wrote that the Gaon, the author of the *Imrei Bina* decreed against this, and **I heard my master, the Gaon of Brisk [Rav Yehoshua Leib Diskin], saying that at least in Jerusalem, it is proper [to observe this custom]**... Behold, the desolation of the *Beit HaMikdash* is before our eyes.[44]

Rav Ben Zion Abba Shaul writes that the Sephardic communities of Jerusalem did not accept this practice.

67. שו"ת אור לציון | ג:ל, הערה ג

והנה בעיר הקודש ירושלים היתה מקובלת תקנה לפני יותר ממאה שנה באיסור חמור מגדולי ירושלים ועוד גדולים שלא לנגן בחתונות בכלי שיר אלא בתוף בלבד, ואומרים שהיא בעקבות מגיפה שפרצה בירושלים. **אולם נראה שבני ספרד אין צריכים לחוש לזה כלל, שלא קיבלו כן אלא בני אשכנז, אבל לא בני ספרד**, ורשאים הם לנגן בכלי שיר בשמחת נישואין בכל מקום בעיר הקודש ירושלים.

Responsa Ohr L'tzion 3:30, n. 3

Now in the holy city of Jerusalem, an enactment was accepted more than a hundred years ago, of a strict prohibition made by the great authorities of Jerusalem and others, not to play musical instruments other than a drum at weddings.[45] It is said that this was because of an epidemic that erupted in Jerusalem. **However, it appears that Sephardim need not be concerned about this at all, as only the Ashkenazim accepted this, not the Sephardim.** They are permitted to play musical instruments at wedding celebrations in any part of the holy city of Jerusalem.

Today, many Ashkenazic communities in Jerusalem also do not observe this custom. **Rav Dov Lior** writes that each custom is valid, as long as some remembrance of the desolation (such as placing ashes on the head of the bridegroom) is observed.

68. הרב דב ליאור, אתר ישיבה

יש קהילות שנוהגים שלא לנגן בכלי נגינה בחתונות בירושלים, ומי שנוהג כך אינו תימהוני ויש מקום לחומרא זו. אולם גם מי שלא נוהג כך עושה זכר לחורבן.

Rav Dov Lior, Yeshiva Website[46]

Some communities have the custom of not playing musical instruments at weddings in Jerusalem. One who observes this is not an eccentric, and there is room for this stringency. However, one who does not observe this also customarily makes a remembrance of the desolation.

44. This consideration would seem to apply mainly in the Old City of Jerusalem, and some *poskim* maintain this in practice. But many others assume the enactment was intended to apply in all parts of modern Jerusalem as well. See Dirshu Edition of the *Mishna Berura*, 560, n. 35, for further sources.

45. See, however, *Piskei Teshuvot*, O.C. 560:13, who understands that any single musical instrument is permitted, and only playing two or more instruments is prohibited. See also Dirshu Edition of the *Mishna Berura*, 560, n. 35 for further sources. According to this approach, playing a keyboard or guitar at weddings in Jerusalem would be permitted.

46. See www.yeshiva.org.il/ask/61841.

Nighttime Prayer and Tikkun Chatzot

A final example of practices associated with the *churban* is the recitation of special prayers. The **Gemara (*Masechet Berachot*)** relates that the night is divided into three "watches" of equal duration. During each of these watches, Hashem declares His regret for our sins causing the destruction of the *Beit HaMikdash*.

ח Masechet Berachot 3a

Rav Yitzchak bar Shmuel said in the name of Rav: The night consists of three watches, and over each and every watch the Holy One, Blessed be He sits and roars like a lion, and says: "Woe to Me, that due to their sins I destroyed My house, burned My Temple and exiled them among the nations of the world."

69. מסכת ברכות ג.

אמר רב יצחק בר שמואל משמיה דרב: שלש משמרות הוי הלילה, ועל כל משמר ומשמר יושב הקדוש ברוך הוא ושואג כארי ואומר: אוי לבנים שבעונותיהם החרבתי את ביתי ושרפתי את היכלי והגליתים לבין אומות העולם.

Accordingly, the **Rosh** writes that at these times, it is proper for a person to mourn over the desolation and to pray to Hashem.

ר Rosh, Berachot 1:2

It is proper for every God-fearing person to be distressed and worried at that time, and to pour out supplication over the desolation of the *Beit HaMikdash*, as it says (*Eicha* 2:19), "Arise, cry out at night, at the head of watches."

70. רא"ש | ברכות א:ב

וראוי לכל ירא שמים שיהא מצר ודואג באותה שעה ולשפוך תחנונים על חורבן בית המקדש כמו שנאמר קומי רוני בלילה לראש אשמורות.

The ***Shulchan Aruch*** codifies this recommendation and understands that "the head of watches" means at the end of each watch.

א Shulchan Aruch, Orach Chaim 1:2–3

2. One who arises to beseech his Creator should aim for the hours during which the watches change, i.e., a third into the night, the end of two thirds of the night, and the end of the night. As the prayer that one prays at these hours regarding the desolation and the exile is favorable.

3. It is proper for every God-fearing person to be distressed and worried over the desolation of the *Beit HaMikdash*.

71. שולחן ערוך | או"ח א:ב–ג

ב. המשכים להתחנן לפני בוראו יכוין לשעות שמשתנות המשמרות, שהן בשליש הלילה ולסוף שני שלישי הלילה ולסוף הלילה, שהתפלה שיתפלל באותן השעות על החורבן ועל הגלות, רצויה.

ג. ראוי לכל ירא שמים שיהא מיצר ודואג על חורבן בית המקדש.

The **Mishna Berura** notes that the Kabbalists instead write that rising at midnight to *daven* is preferable, for one who is able to do so. The customary order of prayers for those who observe this custom is known as *tikkun chatzot*.

72. משנה ברורה | או"ח א:ט-י

ט. **ראוי לכל וכו' – והמקובלים האריכו מאוד בגודל מעלת קימת חצות** כי רבה היא, וכבר נדפס בסידורים סדר ההנהגה על פי כתבי האר"י ז"ל... והעת להתאונן על החורבן נכון יותר שיהיה קודם חצות מעט, ומחצות ואילך יעסוק בתורה, ובסוף הלילה יבקש צרכיו...

חבורה שנתחברו יחד לומר תיקון חצות בצבור אין למנעם, ואדרבה, "ברב עם הדרת מלך". ומי שאינו יכול להשכים קודם אור הבוקר מחמת שהוא חלש בטבעו, או שהוא יודע בעצמו שאם יקום באשמורת יישן בעת התפלה, מוטב לישן כל הצורך.

י. **שיהא מיצר** – אבל התורה והתפלה יהיה בשמחה.

א Mishna Berura, Orach Chaim 1:9–10

9. **It is proper for every, etc. – But the Kabbalists wrote at great length about the immense virtue of rising at midnight**, as it is great. The order of conduct according to the writings of the Arizal has already been printed in the siddurim… The proper time to lament the desolation is a little before midnight. From midnight onward one should engage in Torah study, and at the end of the night one should request one's [personal] needs…

One should not prevent a group from gathering together to recite *tikkun chatzot* publicly, and on the contrary, "The King's glory is in a multitude of people." [*Mishlei* 14:28]. One who cannot rise before dawn because he is weak by nature, or because he knows that if he rises in the night, he will fall asleep during prayer [in the morning], it is better for him to sleep as much as needed.

10. **To be distressed [over the destruction]** – But Torah study and prayer should be with joy.

Rav Ovadia Yosef writes that reciting *tikkun chatzot* takes precedence over reciting *selichot* during the period preceding Rosh Hashana and Yom Kippur.

73. שו"ת יחוה דעת | ג:מד

תלמידי חכמים שעוסקים בתורה עד שעה מאוחרת בלילה, ואי אפשר להם להשכים קום, ישתדלו לומר סליחות בצבור אחר חצות לילה, וכן ישתדלו מאוד לומר תיקון חצות, כי מעלת אמירת תיקון חצות חשובה יותר מאמירת סליחות עם הצבור.

Responsa Yechaveh Da'at 3:44

Torah scholars who engage in Torah study until late at night and are unable to arise early in the morning should try to recite *selichot* after midnight. Similarly, they should try very hard to recite *tikkun chatzot*, as the virtue of reciting *tikkun chatzot* is greater than reciting *selichot* together with the congregation.

However, it should be noted that while reciting *selichot* is an accepted practice of the majority of God-fearing Jews, only a small minority recite *tikkun chatzot*, especially in Ashkenazic communities.[47] Some

---

47. See *Piskei Teshuvot* for a summary of sources extolling the virtues of reciting *tikkun chatzot*, which is based on the writings of the Arizal. He notes there as well that one who wishes to recite *tikkun chatzot* on occasion, such as once a month or during the Nine Days, is also praiseworthy. Moreover, one may fulfill the custom to some extent by reciting even a portion of it, or even just a few *pesukim*. The text of *tikkun chatzot* can be found at https://he.wikisource.org/wiki/תיקון_חצות and elsewhere online.

have pointed out that in this responsum, Rav Ovadia Yosef is likely referring to those who usually observe the custom to recite *tikkun chatzot*.[48]

The ***Mishna Berura*** also cites the **Shelah**, who mentions the custom of reciting *Tehillim* 137 ("*Al Naharot Bavel*") before *Birkat HaMazon* in commemoration of the *churban*. He also mentions the custom to recite "*Shir HaMa'alot*" (*Tehillim* 126) on more festive days, specifically those on which *Tachanun* is not recited.

74. משנה ברורה | או"ח א:יא

חורבן בית המקדש – כתב "שני לוחות הברית", שבכל סעודה יאמר "על נהרות בבל", ובשבת וכן בימים שאין אומרים בהם תחנון יאמר "שיר המעלות בשוב ה'" וגו'. והעיקר שידע מה קאמר, ואחר כונת הלב הן הדברים.

א Mishna Berura, Orach Chaim 1:11

The desolation of the *Beit HaMikdash* – The *Shnei Luchot HaBerit* [*Shelah*] writes that at every meal one should recite "By the rivers of Babylon" [*Tehillim* 137]. But on Shabbat, as well as on days when *Tachanun* is not said, one should recite "A song of ascents [*Shir HaMa'alot*]: When Hashem returned the captivity of Zion…" [*Tehillim* 126].[49] The fundamental principle is that one should understand what one says, as it is the intent of the heart that matters.

FURTHER IYUN

For further *iyun* on tearing one's garment when seeing cities formerly inhabited by Jews that are not currently under Israeli control, see page 344.

48. See www.yeshiva.org.il/ask/124068.
49. Interestingly, today, many individuals recite "*Shir HaMa'alot*" on Shabbat and Yom Tov, but there are fewer who recite "*Al Naharot Bavel*" on other days. Perhaps this is an appropriate custom to consider accepting ("*bli neder*") to help incorporate the idea of commemorating the *churban* into one's daily life.

Machshava

We have learned in this *shiur* that although mourning for the *Beit HaMikdash* is usually associated with the Three Weeks, the Nine Days, and Tisha B'av (to be discussed further in volume 25), the halacha reminds us of the *Beit HaMikdash*'s absence throughout the year. These *zeicher l'churban* practices are intended to keep us aware that our lives are not complete without the return of the *Beit HaMikdash*.

Rav Aharon Kotler observes that in our time, much of this sense of loss has faded, and he highlights both what is lacking in our experience of *aveilut* and what is missing from our world without the *Beit HaMikdash*.

75. משנת רבי אהרן | חלק ג, עמ' מז

והנה העיקר הוא הצער בלב והרגשת האבילות על החורבן והגלות... והנה אצלנו חסר כמעט לגמרי העיקר הנ"ל... אחד מהסיבות... מיעוט העיון כדי לעורר הרגשת הלב, כי נחוץ עיון לעורר ההרגשה...

כל העובר על עם ישראל קשור עם החורבן וכל המתרחש הוא תולדה ממנו. אך החורבן נוגע גם למדרגתו הרוחנית של עם ישראל כולו ולמדרגתו של כל יחיד ויחיד. כבוד שמים היה מורגש ונראה בעליל, ויסודות האמונה היו נראים בעליל לכל באי העולם בביהמ"ק, והיתה השפעה גדולה בענין תורה ודעת ד' והיה בנקל לבוא במדרגות דקדושה...

Mishnat Rabbi Aharon, Vol. 3, p. 47

Now the primary [aspect of mourning for the *Beit HaMikdash*] is the pain in one's heart and the feeling of mourning over the destruction and the exile... yet for us, this is almost entirely lacking... One of the reasons for this... is the lack of contemplation necessary to awaken the heart, for reflection is required in order to arouse feeling...

Everything that occurs to the Jewish People is bound up with the *churban*, and all that transpires is a consequence of it. However, the *churban* also affected the spiritual level of the Jewish People as a whole, as well as that of every individual. The glory of Heaven was tangibly perceived, and the foundations of faith were clearly evident to all who came to the *Beit HaMikdash*. There was a powerful influence of Torah and knowledge of Hashem, and it was far easier to ascend to levels of holiness...

Rav Kotler teaches that genuine mourning requires reflection. By contemplating the clarity of *emuna*, the palpable presence of Hashem, and the spiritual heights that were once readily accessible, we can begin to sense what is missing today and awaken a deeper feeling of loss.

Rav Reuven Leichter builds upon this idea, extending it even further. Beyond recognizing what we have lost, he suggests that we are mourning something even more fundamental: the world Hashem intended, which never fully came to be.

76. Rav Reuven Leichter, "Mourn What Might Have Been"[50]

Aveilus isn't just about personal tragedy — it's about Hashem's plan that fell through. We're not mourning our own personal loss; we're mourning the destruction of the world Hashem wanted. So even though we never experienced that world, we can mourn it. We grieve not because we lost something we once had, but because the world Hashem wanted, the world we were meant to have, was shattered.

50 The complete article is available at https://mishpacha.com/mourn-what-might-have-been.

Hashem wanted a world where His presence was manifest. The Beis Hamikdash was a physical place that called for *avodas Hashem* and the recognition of Hashem's sovereignty. When we had the Beis Hamikdash, the whole world was fundamentally different. That world is gone. Our world calls for many things, but definitely not *avodas Hashem*. It incites the worst *aveiros*, preaches greed, infidelity, and godlessness. Hashem's plan didn't endure; the world He wanted was destroyed…

No tragedy was as calamitous as the Churban, when Hashem's plan for the entire world was incinerated in the flames that consumed the Beis Hamikdash.

Although Rav Kotler and Rav Leichter were primarily addressing the mourning of Tisha B'av, their insights are relevant for the *zeicher l'churban* practices observed throughout the year as well. Rav Kotler teaches us to reflect on what was lost, while Rav Leichter teaches us to consider what could have been. Through both, we come to recognize not only the absence of the *Beit HaMikdash*, but the diminished spiritual reality in which we live.

Each time we observe or consider these practices, we are given an opportunity to reflect, to internalize this loss, and to renew our awareness of what is missing. Through this, we strengthen our connection to the *Beit HaMikdash* and our hope for its rebuilding, speedily in our days.

Summary of the Halachot of Zeicher L'churban

Introduction

1. **Gemara (*Masechet Bava Batra*)** – After the destruction of the Second *Beit HaMikdash*, many wished to mourn excessively. Rabbi Yehoshua demonstrated that a balanced approach is required.
2. ***Peninei Halakha*** – Excessive mourning causes depression and is not productive. However, when a person experiences special joy, he must remember the *Beit HaMikdash* and the joy cannot be complete.

Leaving One's Home Unfinished

1. **Gemara (*Masechet Bava Batra*)** – One who plasters his home must leave a square *amah* unplastered, opposite the entrance. A *baraita* prohibits plastering, tiling and painting one's house.
2. **Rambam, *Shulchan Aruch*** – One may never build one's home in an ornate fashion, in the style of kings.
3. ***Beit Yosef***
   a. **Possibility 1** – Plastering and then decorating ornately is prohibited. Plastering alone, or painting ornate designs without plastering, are permitted.
   b. **Possibility 2** – The standard practice of covering with mortar and then plastering with lime is permitted. Using lime alone for everything is the style of kings and is prohibited.
4. **Rema** – According to the *Tur*, all plastering and decoration is permitted if one leaves a square *amah* unplastered. The custom is in accordance with this view.

- **The Placement of the Square *Amah***

1. ***Mishna Berura*** – Although the unplastered square *amah* must be opposite the entrance, some people instead leave the area above the entrance unplastered. This area may be visible more often.
2. ***Sha'arei Teshuva*** – Some require leaving a square *amah* unplastered in every room of the house. Rav Ya'akov Emden ruled leniently but nevertheless left a small area unplastered in an additional room.

3. **Rav Mordechai Eliyahu** – One need only leave the square *amah* unplastered in the entrance room.
4. **Dirshu Edition of the *Mishna Berura*** – Rav Yaakov Yisrael Kanievsky and Rav Yosef Shalom Eliashiv rule that one should leave the unplastered square *amah* in the living room rather than in the hallway that leads into it.
5. ***Magen Avraham*** – The Rambam and *Shulchan Aruch* imply that the obligation applies only to a private home, not to a *shul*.
6. ***Piskei Teshuvot*** – Some cite Rav Akiva Yosef Shlesinger as ruling that in Jerusalem, one need not leave the square *amah* as the desolation is visible there.

• Coloring or Covering the Square *Amah*

1. ***Aguda*** – One should leave the square *amah* without any color, or a simple thin black color.
2. ***Levush*, Rav Mordechai Eliyahu** – One should not color the square *amah* black, as this improves the look.
3. ***Sha'ar HaTziun*** – The *Chayei Adam* writes that coloring the square *amah* black is not permitted even if one writes "*zeicher l'churban*" there. However, one should not protest against those who do this.
4. **Rav Moshe Feinstein** – Blackening the square *amah* is permitted, as its purpose is simply to remember the desolation, not for the house to look untidy.
5. **Dirshu Edition of the *Mishna Berura*** – The *Nimukei Orach Chaim* writes that covering the square *amah* with a picture of the Kotel is certainly prohibited. However, Rav Chaim Kanievsky permits partially covering the square *amah* with such a picture.

• Buying or Renting a Fully Decorated House

1. **Gemara (*Masechet Bava Batra*)** – One who purchases a property that is already fully plastered need not remove any plaster.
2. **Tosafot** – The reason is that we can assume that the house was plastered before the *Beit HaMikdash* was destroyed.
3. **Ritva** – Even if the house was plastered after the *Beit HaMikdash* was destroyed, one can assume it was plastered in a permitted manner, by adding sand to the lime.
4. **Rav Achai of Shabcha** – If gentiles decorated a house, a Jew may use it without making any changes.
5. **Rambam, *Shulchan Aruch*** – One who purchases a house need not peel off the plaster.

6. ***Magen Avraham*** – If one knows that the building was built in a prohibited manner, he must scrape a square *amah* area from the wall.
7. **Rav Mordechai Eliyahu** – Even one who rents such an apartment is obligated to scrape a square *amah* of plaster from the wall.
8. **Rav Moshe Feinstein** – A tenant is never obligated to scrape plaster from the wall. One who purchases a property in order to sell (or rent) is also not obligated to leave an unplastered square *amah*.
9. ***Piskei Teshuvot*** – If a tenant is re-plastering, he must leave a square *amah*. A tenant must not scrape off plaster without the consent of the landlord, although it is proper to attempt to obtain consent.
10. **Rav Menashe Klein** – One who builds a house is certainly obligated to leave a square *amah* unplastered, even if he sells it or rents it to a Jew.

- **Contemporary Practice**

1. ***Mishna Berura*** – Many are lax regarding this halacha, but justification for this is tenuous.
2. ***Piskei Teshuvot*** – There is no valid justification for the lenient practice, and one should certainly leave a square *amah* unplastered.
3. ***Aruch HaShulchan*** – Since nowadays, sand is mixed with the lime, one need not leave any area unplastered.
4. ***Peninei Halakha*** – According to Rav Moshe Feinstein, when a house is built in order to sell, neither the seller nor the purchaser is obligated to leave a square *amah* unplastered. However, it is proper to follow the stricter opinion.

Leaving Out One Dish and One Item of Jewelry

1. **Gemara (*Masechet Bava Batra*), *Shulchan Aruch*** – One must leave out a small item from a meal. A woman must refrain from one standard cosmetic treatment.
2. ***Mishna Berura*** – Rav Yaakov Emden writes that one should not leave out anything from Shabbat and Yom Tov meals.
3. **Rav Shmuel Wosner** – One need only leave out a dish from a large meal to which guests are invited.
4. ***Chayei Adam, Bi'ur Halacha*** – It is puzzling that none of this is observed today.
5. ***Kaf HaChaim*** – Today, since our meals do not follow a fixed menu, there is no value to leaving out one dish from a meal, since this would not be recognizable.

Ashes on the Head of a Bridegroom and Breaking a Cup

1. **Gemara (*Masechet Bava Batra*), *Shulchan Aruch*** – The custom to place ashes on the head of a bridegroom, in the place where one usually lays *tefillin*, has a source from Tanach.
2. ***Sefer HaMichtam, Kol Bo*** – There is an alternative practice of placing a black cloth on the heads of the bride and groom and breaking a cup. This practice developed in places where people did not usually lay *tefillin*.
3. **Rema** – In his city, the custom was both to place ashes on the head of the bridegroom and to break the cup used for the *beracha* on *eirusin*.
4. ***Aruch HaShulchan*** – Where he lived, the alternative customs replaced placing ashes on the head of the bridegroom.
5. ***Piskei Teshuvot*** – The custom of placing ashes on the bridegroom's head has again become widespread.
6. ***Kaf HaChaim*** – It is not customary to place ashes on the head of the bridegroom.
7. **Rav Ben Zion Abba Shaul** – One should certainly observe the custom instituted by Chazal to place ashes on the head of the bridegroom.
8. **Rav Ovadia Yosef** – There is no need for Sephardim to restore this custom.
9. ***Mishna Berura*** – Since breaking a cup directs attention to the desolation, this does not violate the prohibition against destructive acts. Similarly, it is customary to break a plate at an engagement.
10. **Rav Avigdor Nebenzahl** – It is not proper to make a memento from the broken pieces.
11. **Rav Yitzchak Yosef** – One should wait a few moments before shouting "*Mazel tov!*"

Music

1. **Mishna, Gemara (*Masechet Sota*)** – Once the Sanhedrin ceased to function, song was no longer permitted during feasts where wine is served.
2. **Gemara (*Masechet Gittin*)** – Song is prohibited even without musical instruments.
3. **Rashi, Tosafot** – The Gemara in *Masechet Gittin* also refers to song during feasts where wine is served.
4. **Tosafot** – It is proper to avoid any singing that brings excessive enjoyment, unless this is for the purposes of a mitzva, such as at a wedding.

5. **Rambam, *Shulchan Aruch*** – Playing musical instruments is prohibited. Even vocal song is prohibited where wine is served, but the custom is to permit singing praises of Hashem and thanksgiving songs.
6. **Responsa of the Rambam** – Even vocal singing is prohibited in all places.
   a. ***Yad Peshuta*** – This refers to songs with content that can lead a person's thoughts astray.
7. ***Orchot Chaim*** – The use of musical instruments is prohibited even for praises of Hashem.
8. ***Tur*, Rema** – According to Tosafot, listening to songs or music on a regular basis is prohibited, even outside of a feast.
9. **Rav Moshe Feinstein** – Listening to musical instruments is always prohibited, even on the radio. Even those who rely on the lenient views should act stringently during *Sefirat Ha'Omer*.
10. **Rav Ovadia Yosef** – The Meiri permits everything for the praises of Hashem, and one may rely on this where wine is not being served, especially with non-live music. All agree that even live music is permitted at a wedding meal, or any *se'udat mitzva*.
11. ***Piskei Teshuvot*** – Modern *poskim* permit listening to music for those who need to spiritually, but those who can manage without should refrain.

- **The Custom in Jerusalem**

1. ***Sha'arei Yerushalayim*** – Historically, in all of Eretz Yisrael no one who knew how to play musical instruments. Musicians arrived from *chutz la'aretz* and would play at weddings, but they passed away swiftly, so people decided not to continue this practice.
2. **Rav Yosef Chaim Zonnenfeld** – Rav Yehoshua Leib Diskin rules that musical instruments should at least be avoided at weddings in Jerusalem.
3. **Rav Ben Zion Abba Shaul** – The Sephardic communities of Jerusalem did not accept this practice.
4. **Rav Dov Lior** – Both customs exist (also for Ashkenazim) and are valid.

Nighttime Prayer and Tikkun Chatzot

1. **Gemara (*Masechet Berachot*)** – Hashem declares His regret for our sins causing the destruction of the *Beit HaMikdash* at each of the three watches of the night.
2. **Rosh, *Shulchan Aruch*** – At the end of each watch, it is proper for a person to mourn over the desolation and to pray.

3. ***Mishna Berura*** – The Kabbalists instead write that rising at midnight to recite *tikkun chatzot* is preferable, for one who is able to do so.
4. **Rav Ovadia Yosef** – *Tikkun chatzot* takes precedence over reciting *selichot* during the period preceding Rosh Hashana and Yom Kippur.
5. ***Mishna Berura*** – The *Shelah* mentions the custom of reciting *Al Naharot Bavel* before *Birkat HaMazon* in commemoration of the *churban*, or *Shir HaMa'alot* when *Tachanun* is not recited.

Further Iyun

Tearing One's Garments Zeicher L'churban: The Halachic Definition of "Churban" in the Context of Arei Yehuda

Rav Avichai Goodman (Graduate, Manhigut Toranit)

The halachic framework of *zeicher l'churban* includes a number of practices that preserve awareness of the destruction of the *Beit HaMikdash*, some of which we studied in detail in the accompanying *shiur*. Among these is the obligation of *keria* – tearing one's garment – upon encountering certain manifestations of the *churban*. Chazal established that one must perform *keria* upon seeing the site of the *Beit HaMikdash* and upon seeing Jerusalem in its destroyed state.[1]

In addition, the Gemara records a parallel obligation when one encounters *arei Yehuda b'churbanan*, the cities of Yehuda in their destroyed condition.[2] This additional category raises a fundamental question: how is *churban* defined in this context? Is the determining factor the physical devastation of the city and the absence of Jewish habitation, or does the halachic status of *churban* reflect a broader reality, such as the presence or absence of Jewish sovereignty? Clarifying this question is essential both for determining the practical scope of the obligation and for understanding the halachic conception of national destruction.

I. The Talmudic Source

The primary source appears in ***Masechet Moed Katan***,[3] where a *baraita* states:

הרואה ערי יהודה בחורבנן אומר: "ערי קדשך היו מדבר," וקורע.

One who sees the cities of Yehuda in their destruction recites the verse "Your holy cities have become a wilderness"[4] and performs *keria*.

The Gemara derives this obligation from the narrative in *Yirmiyahu*,[5] which describes individuals arriving in the Yehuda region from Shechem, Shilo, and Shomron following the destruction of the First Temple. Upon reaching Mitzpah, they tore their garments.

This passage establishes that the obligation of *keria* extends beyond the site of the *Mikdash* itself and applies as well to cities whose halachic status reflect the broader condition of national *churban*. Furthermore, the Gemara explains that this is one of those cases where the *keria* is considered severe and may not be mended.

II. The Interpretation of the *Beit Yosef*

The ***Beit Yosef***[6] addresses the nature of this

1. *Mo'ed Katan* 26a; *Shulchan Aruch*, o.c. 561:1–2.
2. Ibid.
3. 26a.
4. *Yeshayahu* 64:9.
5. Ch. 41.
6. o.c. 561.

obligation and presents two possible interpretations of the term *churban*.

The first interpretation understands *churban* in its straightforward sense: physical destruction and desolation. According to this approach, *keria* would be required only upon seeing a city whose physical infrastructure has been destroyed and whose Jewish communal life has ceased.

The *Beit Yosef*, however, introduces a second interpretation, based on the Ramban's discussion in *Torat Ha'Adam*, which defines *churban* in political rather than purely physical terms. According to this formulation, a city may be halachically classified as being in a state of *churban* even where Jewish residents remain and communal life continues, if the city is no longer under Jewish rule.

The *Beit Yosef* concludes unequivocally: "וכך עיקר".

This ruling establishes that the determining criterion of *churban*, for purposes of this halacha, is the absence of Jewish sovereignty.

III. The Position of the *Bach* and the Proof from *Yirmiyahu*

The ***Bach***[7] affirms this conclusion and clarifies its basis. He notes that the Gemara's proof from the episode in Mitzpah cannot be understood as referring to physical destruction, since the verse itself indicates that Jews continued to reside in the city at that time. Rather, the obligation of *keria* arose because Jewish political authority had been displaced and the city was under Babylonian rule.

This interpretation resolves an apparent difficulty in the biblical narrative. **Rashi** and **Radak**, in their commentary to *Yirmiyahu*, explain that the *keria* described in the verse was performed in response to the destruction of the *Mikdash* itself. However, the **Maharsha**[8] observes that *keria* for the *Mikdash* is required only upon reaching a vantage point from which the site of the *Mikdash* is visible. Since the individuals described in *Yirmiyahu* tore their garments upon reaching Mitzpah – before arriving at such a location – the *keria* must instead reflect the halachic status of the city itself.

The *Bach*'s analysis thus reinforces the conclusion that *churban*, in this halachic context, is defined by the loss of Jewish governance rather than by physical destruction alone.

IV. Acceptance Among the *Acharonim*

This interpretation of the *Beit Yosef*'s ruling is widely accepted among the *Acharonim*. The *Magen Avraham*,[9] *Taz*,[10] *Eliya Rabba*,[11] *Chayei Adam*,[12] *Mishna Berura*,[13] and *Kaf HaChaim*[14] all cite the *Beit Yosef*'s conclusion without qualification.[15]

According to this consensus, the defining element of *churban* is the absence of Jewish

---

7. O.C. 561.
8. *Mo'ed Katan* 26a, *Chiddushei Aggadot*, s.v. *arei*.
9. 561:1.
10. 561:1.
11. 561:1.
12. 135:6.
13. 561:2.
14. 561:4.
15. See Responsa *Yaskil Avdi* (vol. 1, O.C. 25:4); Responsa *Igrot Moshe* (O.C. 4:70:11); Responsa *Minchat Shomo* (1:73:10); *Kitzur Shulchan Aruch* Toledano (396:1); *Kitzur Shulchan Aruch Mekor Chaim* (51:5); Rav Ovadia Yosef in many places (for example, *Chazon Ovadia, Ta'aniyot*); *Sefer Meshiv Milchama* (ch. 4); annotations of Rav Mazuz, *Ish Matzliach* (subsection 1) on the aforementioned *Mishna Berura*; and Rav Devlitzky (*Zichron Betzalel*, p. 143).

sovereignty. The presence or absence of Jewish residents, while relevant in other halachic contexts, does not independently determine the halachic status of a city for purposes of this obligation.

This formulation reflects a conception of *churban* that encompasses not only the destruction of physical structures, but also the dissolution of Jewish political authority. Conversely, area under Jewish control that are inhabited primarily by gentiles would not be subject to the obligation of *keria.*

V. Alternative Interpretations

Some later authorities offer a more expansive reading of the *Beit Yosef*'s formulation. According to these *poskim*, the *Beit Yosef* does not redefine *churban* exclusively in political terms, but rather establishes that the loss of sovereignty is sufficient to constitute *churban*, even in the absence of physical destruction.

This interpretation appears in the writings of *Mishnat Ya'avetz*[16] and Rav Eliyahu Bakshi-Doron,[17] and may also be inferred from a responsum in the *Minchat Yitzchak.*[18]

According to this approach, both the loss of sovereignty and the absence of Jewish settlement may independently contribute to the halachic classification of *churban*. While sovereignty remains a central factor, the absence of Jewish communal life or other similar lackings may likewise bear halachic significance.

These differing interpretations reflect two distinct models: one in which sovereignty alone defines *churban*, and another in which both political authority and Jewish habitation form part of the halachic definition.

VI. Contemporary Applications

These principles have practical implications in evaluating modern circumstances in which Jewish sovereignty over particular regions has changed.

For example, in the context of the evacuation of Jewish communities from Gush Katif, **Rav Zalman Nechemia Goldberg** ruled that soldiers present at the time of evacuation were obligated to perform *keria*, on the grounds that Jewish settlement and governance were being removed. Similarly, **Rav Mordechai Eliyahu**[19] addressed the question of whether *keria* would be required upon subsequently encountering cities that had formerly been under Israeli control.

These rulings illustrate the continued application of the halachic criteria established by the *Beit Yosef* and subsequent authorities, and demonstrate how the halachic definition of *churban* provides a framework for evaluating contemporary realities.

VII. The Broader Halachic Framework

The centrality of sovereignty within the halachic definition of *churban* finds resonance in other areas of halachic thought. The **Rambam**, in his description of the messianic era (*Hilchot Melachim* 11–12), characterizes that period in terms of the restoration of Jewish political autonomy. Likewise, in *Hilchot Ta'aniyot*,[20] he writes that the fast days commemorating the destruction are destined to be nullified in a future era of national restoration.

---

16. O.C. 48.
17. Responsa *Binyan Av* 4:30.
18. 10:10.
19. *Kol Tzofayich*, Matot–Masei 5759.
20. 5:19.

While these sources address distinct halachic categories, they reflect a consistent recognition of sovereignty as a defining feature of national destruction and its reversal. Within this broader framework, the halachic conception of *churban* encompasses not only physical devastation, but also the condition of political displacement.

Conclusion

The obligation to perform *keria* upon seeing *arei Yehuda b'churbanan* depends upon the halachic definition of *churban* itself. The ruling of the *Beit Yosef*, as affirmed by the *Bach* and widely accepted by subsequent authorities, establishes that *churban* is defined not solely by physical destruction, but by the absence of Jewish sovereignty.

Alternative interpretations further expand this framework, recognizing additional relevance in the presence or absence of Jewish communal life.

These discussions demonstrate that the halachic conception of *churban* reflects a multifaceted reality, encompassing physical, demographic, and political dimensions. The halachic framework developed by Chazal and elaborated by later authorities continues to provide the basis for evaluating both historical and contemporary situations in which these criteria apply.

Made in the USA
Monee, IL
21 September 2026

63491705R00195